THE
PLOW
THE
HAMMER
AND THE
KNOUT

THE PLOW THE HAMMER AND THE KNOUT

An Economic History of Eighteenth-Century Russia

Arcadius Kahan

With the editorial assistance of
Richard Hellie

The University of Chicago Press
Chicago and London

ARCADIUS KAHAN was born in Vilno, Poland, in 1920. At the time of his death in 1982 he was professor in the Department of Economics, the Department of History, and the College at the University of Chicago, fellow at the Russian Research Center of Harvard University, and visiting professor at both the London School of Economics and Hebrew University in Jerusalem. He was the author of many influential journal articles and coauthor, with Blair Ruble, of *Industrial Labor in the U.S.S.R.*

RICHARD HELLIE is professor of Russian history at the University of Chicago. He is the author of *Enserfment and Military Change in Muscovy*, which was awarded the American Historical Association's Herbert Baxter Adams Prize, and *Slavery in Russia, 1450–1725*, both published by the University of Chicago Press.

The University of Chicago Press, Chicago 60637
The University of Chicago Press, Ltd., London
© 1985 by The University of Chicago
All rights reserved. Published 1985
Printed in the United States of America
94 93 92 91 90 89 88 87 86 85 54321

Library of Congress Cataloging in Publication Data

Kahan, Arcadius.
    The plow, the hammer, and the knout.

    Bibliography: p.
    Includes index.
    1. Soviet Union—Economic conditions—To 1861.
2. Soviet Union—Social conditions—To 1801. I. Hellie,
Richard. II. Title.
HC334.K25 1985   330.947   84-16338
ISBN 0-226-42253-4

For Vivian and Miriam

CONTENTS

FOREWORD

Roger W. Weiss

When Arcadius Kahan came to the University of Chicago in 1955, he had completed his studies toward the doctorate in economics at Rutgers University. He was brought to the university as a research associate to collaborate with D. Gale Johnson at the beginning of Johnson's research into Soviet agriculture, and over the next years a steady output of studies, some by him alone and others jointly with Johnson, securely established his reputation as a leading scholar of the Soviet economy. By 1962 he had joined the College faculty and the departments of economics and history and had published the first of fifteen papers that were to define and explore the themes of this book. These were the outgrowth of his teaching at Chicago and of periods in London, Jerusalem, Helsinki, Washington, Austin, and Paris and of his participation in many scholarly conferences. These published studies of the aftermath of Peter the Great's policies, of plagues and natural calamities, of Russian trade with Britain during the industrial revolution, on the problems of serfdom and the role of the gentry, laid out the structure of the book and were supported by his exhaustive gathering of statistics in libraries and archives, particularly in London, Amsterdam, and Helsinki. More than fifteen years passed from the first essay to the completion of the book manuscript.

If Kahan had lived, he would have carried the economic history of Russia through the nineteenth century and up to the Revolution. A massive collection of economic and social statistics was undertaken and a number of articles, a long essay on capital formation, and a monograph surveying the whole subject were published; these segments would have been reworked into a whole as mature and comprehensive as this book on the eighteenth century; they will appear shortly in a volume of papers on the nineteenth century. He thus came very close to completing the study of Russia's economic history over the entire period from 1700 to the present. We are fortunate that publication will make most of this work accessible.

Kahan was thirty-one years old when he began his studies toward the Ph.D., newly arrived with his family from Germany, a newcomer to the language and institutions of America, separated by a period of eleven years from his earlier university training in the faculty of law at the Stefan Batory University, in Vilna, by the tragic events of World War II and by his attempt to participate in the reconstruction of Poland after the war. During this period he was a prisoner in the Vorkuta labor camp on the Arctic Circle, a fugitive in Minsk, and in 1944 a member of the Polish army that advanced across Poland into Germany. He returned to Poland as a leader in the Socialist Bund and edited the Yiddish-language *Yugnt-Veker* in Lodz. In 1947 he was a delegate from Poland to the first world conference of the Bund in Brussels. When the Polish government forced the Bundists to join the Jewish Communists, Kahan and the other leaders, faced with the annihilation of their movement, escaped to Germany. His insights into autocracy and the efficiency of totalitarian regimes surely were deepened in the decade of his struggles with the Soviets, a tragic adventure whose detail he never discussed. Characteristically, he avoided any reference to his own painful experiences, although he freely recalled the heroism and suffering of his friends.

In the circumstances of his youth, in prewar Vilna, it is not likely that he could have entertained the thought of a career as a scholar. Even though he attended the university and demonstrated a passion for learning, the rising Polish nationalism and anti-Semitism eliminated opportunities for scholarship except outside Poland or within the Jewish community. His early association with the YIVO Institute for Jewish Research, of which his father was one of the founders, in its prewar location in Vilna, brought him in close contact with leading scholars, but he was brought equally in contact with the Bund's activities, in which his father also played a leading and distinguished role. Thus it was not obvious to his family and friends that he would turn from his own activist career to a life of scholarship when he settled in the

United States. Except for his participation in the councils of the University of Chicago, he totally immersed himself in research and teaching, as if born again. Yet his skill in listening, in participating in the common work of administration and policy-making, in counseling his colleagues in their anxieties continued to draw on his deep and experienced fund of compassion and dedication to others. In his mature years he pursued the questions that had challenged his father's generation: the social question of the Jews in Eastern Europe in the period from 1850 to 1939. His collected papers on the social and economic history of the Eastern European Jews will be published shortly and are an important statement on the problems of poverty, emigration, adaptation to industrialization, and the secular movements of assimilation, socialism, and the varieties of cultural and religious renewal in the Jewish community.

Kahan, according to D. Gale Johnson, "had more interests and concerns than there was time to pursue. At any one time, he had three or four different types of work and papers underway." Despite these many concerns and a crowded schedule, he brought to completion his studies in the three areas of his research, Soviet economic performance, the economic history of Russia, and the social and economic history of Eastern European Jews in the last century. The present book, Kahan's remarks about "provisional essays" or studies notwithstanding, reflects a comprehensive and mature judgment based on a gathering of data that will stand for many years as the most complete available. In the other areas we are left with the form and much of the structure, but not all of the detail that he intended to add.

With this legacy of scholarship, a remarkable achievement in a short career, we are also left a legacy of love for work and for the gift of life. The deep springs of his moral values, his courage, modesty, and optimism, the selflessness when others turned to him with their problems and his intense pleasure in friendship, will be remembered by all who knew him. His readers will see the qualities of his wisdom, his search for the long view in which friend and foe, landlord and serf, Jew and Pole, bureaucrat and worker, are bound together in the complex structures of a changing society. His readers will see the analysis of eighteenth-century agriculture through the eyes of one who has understood the problems of Soviet backwardness; they will see the analysis of the possibilities of Petrine leadership and transformation presented with an understanding of the inertia of the rest of society; and they will see the universal traits of autocracy persisting through three centuries.

At the time of Arcadius Kahan's sudden death in February 1982, the manuscript of this book had been completed and accepted for publication by the University of Chicago Press. After submitting the manuscript, Kahan continued work on some of its parts, adding to the chapters on agriculture and the political order, and adding the short introductory statements. He would have added to the work as he uncovered more data and expanded his introduction. But unlike a number of works published posthumously, this book was not left in fragments to be reconstructed or completed from sketches of missing parts. The present study represents Kahan's mature and completed thought, however much he himself referred to it as essays "toward an economic history of Russia in the eighteenth century" or spoke of his conclusions as "provisional." What remained at his death was to edit the text to create a uniformity of Russian transliteration and citation and to ensure that the articulation of the chapters and their parts fully carried out his intentions.

Fortunately Professor Richard Hellie, an authority on Russian social history and on the institutions of slavery and serfdom in the periods before those addressed by this book, and a former student and colleague of Arcadius Kahan, offered to undertake the responsibility of editing the manuscript. No one could have been better situated to assure the integrity of the project and to supply authoritative judgment on the text. Professor Hellie has helped to realize a book that is in language, order, and detail true to the original manuscript. All students of Russian social and economic history are greatly in his debt.

PREFACE

At the time of his untimely and unexpected death on February 26, 1982, Arcadius Kahan had completed the essays that make up this book.

In preparing these essays for publication, I made every attempt to leave the original text as it was. I did, however, attempt to perform such ordinary editorial functions as removing repetition and standardizing the treatment of words and terms. I also removed unspecific statements about the limitations of the data used in the work and moved some of the commentary in the notes into the text. I was unable to find sources for the tables where they are missing and did not verify or add to the note apparatus.

In the introductory chapter I added a few paragraphs on the seventeenth-century background and some facts about the eighteenth century that should help the reader place the work in context. I also wrote the conclusion and, with the assistance of Mikhail Khodarkovsky and Edward Reisman, compiled the bibliography.

Mikhail Khodarkovsky helped proofread the text and David Galenson read through the text to assure that I did not distort the author's economic analysis. Roger Weiss rendered similar invaluable services.

Most of this editing work was done during the tenure of a grant from the Translations Program of the National Endowment for the Humanities, an independent federal agency. I am deeply indebted to the Endowment for its support.

Richard Hellie

INTRODUCTION
Russia in the Eighteenth Century

Few Western Europeans outside the trading community would have known anything of Russia's economic life at the beginning of the eighteenth century. Otherwise well-educated Western Europeans knew primarily that Russia was vast in territory, had a culturally varied population that was subjected to "despotic" political rule, and that it represented in their view a civilization both distinct from the general European one as well as from the Asiatic ones they claimed to understand, a hybrid grown at the boundaries of Europe and Asia. Western Europeans assumed that Russians were unenlightened by the prevailing standards of Western Europe, that they were ignorant of the achievements of political thought, of science and philosophy, and that the state of the arts in Russia, including the industrial arts, was very primitive indeed. Russia in the eyes of Europe represented a large territory, sparsely populated, with a low level of urbanization, technologically backward, and relatively poor.

Few Western Europeans were aware of the fact that, at the beginning of the century, Russia was already emerging from what twentieth-century writers would term a "traditional society." Western Europeans were also not aware of the fact that this process, which manifested itself in institutional changes and a steep rise in demand for Western technology, would continue for at least a quarter of a century under the guidance of the ruthless driving spirit of Peter the Great. It is better, with hindsight, to see the Petrine period as an intensification of trends already present before Peter, however, than to pretend that all of the Petrine developments were totally new in every respect.

Peter's death did not bring an end to the Petrine policies. The post-Petrine period, ca. 1725–62, was a consolidation of Russia's move to Western technology, changing organizational structures, and growing international specialization. This was also the time when internal tolls on domestic trade were abolished.

The reign of Catherine the Great began a third period in which a new direction of institutional change was taken. The central government relaxed its control over enterprise and gave small-scale enterprises a chance to compete with the formerly favored large-scale ones. The benefits of the abolition of internal tolls on domestic trade began to be sensed.

To sum up: the eighteenth century, from an economic and social perspective, can be divided into three periods: from 1700 to 1725, the Petrine period, a period of rapid institutional change and economic growth; 1725–62, a period of consolidation and continuity after the one of extreme effort; and the third period, after 1762, a period of growth and "liberalization."

Social Structure

Russia's social classes at the beginning of the century were distinct; each had a different place in the legal and political hierarchy and a different economic function. There was little movement between them. The aristocracy, the heirs of the Muscovite upper service class stationed in the capital, and the gentry, the heirs of the Muscovite middle service class stationed in the provinces, were at the top. They sought power and competed with one another for status and prestige. They were distinct from other classes particularly because of their right to own agricultural land and the serfs tilling that land. During the course of the eighteenth century they were gradually fused by the government into a single class of the nobility. At the beginning of the century they still held to traditional Russian values, but, with the passage of time, they became even more competitive in conspicuous consumption.

The merchant classes, virtually excluded from entry into the gentry, pursued profit while simultaneously performing service to the state and acting under regulation, license, and subsidy. They accepted their inferior status and adapted to the system of monopoly privileges granted by the state, protec-

1

tion in domestic commerce from competition with foreigners. Income and status differentiation continued within the merchant class, and a particular group became distinct as it entered the early phase of industrial entrepreneurship under the protection of the state. Domestic entrepreneurs were recruited from among the merchant class, although some noblemen and even peasant-serfs were engaged in entrepreneurial activities.

The urban artisans in Russia, lacking the legal autonomy characteristic of this class in Western and Central Europe, constituted the lower stratum of the urban tax-paying population. Rural craftsmen were legally indistinguishable from the bulk of the rural agricultural population.

During the Muscovite period the peasantry had been enserfed. Between the middle of the fifteenth century and 1592 the peasants were gradually bound to the land, from which they could not legally move. Then their persons were abased, as they were gradually equated juridically with the numerous group of slaves and increasingly bound to the persons of their lords. During the eighteenth century this process continued until, by the end of the century, there was relatively little de facto difference between Russian serfs and the slaves in many other parts of the world. The lowest ranks of Russian society suffered a continuous extension of enserfment as increasing numbers of free and dependent peasants were enserfed over the century. With low productivity, peasant agriculture yielded a small potential for taxation and rent. The measures extending serfdom can be seen as motivated by the need to secure increased taxes for the government and to augment the income of the serf-owning nobility. In spite of the law, vast stretches of uncultivated arable land induced peasants to escape to the frontier as a means to escape enserfment.

Civil disorders were relatively frequent in early modern Russia. The Muscovite period had witnessed major uprisings involving both the urban and rural populations. The first major conflict was the Time of Troubles, an event sparked by the extinction of the seven-century-old Riurikid dynasty in 1598 which was fed first by massive internal discord and then by intervention by the Poles and Swedes. Uprisings in Moscow and a dozen other towns in 1648 forced Tsar Aleksei Mikhailovich to cashier his ruling group of oligarchs and also caused the convocation of an Assembly of the Land (a proto-parliamentary institution) that participated in and approved the compilation of a law code that was to remain Russia's major code until 1830, the *Ulozhenie* of 1649. There were other urban uprisings throughout the second half of the seventeenth century. The major rural uprising was led by cossacks, first by Vasilii Us and then by

Stenka Razin in 1667–71. This tradition of disorders continued into the eighteenth century, which in its first decade witnessed a major uprising in Astrakhan' and then a large-scale frontier peasant revolt led by Kondratii Bulavin. The rest of the century witnessed few frightening urban disturbances, but the peasant rebellion led by Emel'ian Pugachëv in 1773–74 terrified the ruling elements more than any other event in the century.

Industry

In industrial production, cottage industry was widespread, but capital and skills were in short supply for large-scale enterprises. Initially the latter were brought from abroad by state initiative and adapted to Russian institutions. The opening of Russia to foreign capital, organizational structures, and technology was greatly accelerated by Peter the Great, a towering figure whose extreme demands on the economy exceeded those of any other ruler prior to the twentieth century. During the remainder of the eighteenth century Russia developed a solid base in the metallurgical and textile industries.

The Government and Its Activities

In no other European country has government played as prominent a role in so many aspects of life as was the case in early modern Russia. Although the government could not pretend to, and did not try to, control everything, its power and authority unquestionably were immense. This was a major element of the Muscovite heritage.

There were two major rulers in the eighteenth century, Peter the Great (1682–1725) and Catherine the Great (1762–96). They were important not only because of their long reigns but because they managed to impose their forceful personalities on their eras. Three of the other rulers (Anna, 1730–42; Elizabeth, 1742–62; and Paul, 1796–1801) would have been standard fare in almost any country, neither very strong in their own right nor ciphers. The remaining rulers properly could be termed ciphers, both for the length of their terms and the force of their personalities.

No ruler ran Russia by himself, and nearly all reigns were a combination of autocratic and oligarchic rule. One of the features which distinguished some reigns from others was the extent to which the autocrat managed to manipulate the oligarchs, or the extent to which the oligarchs managed to employ the image and legitimacy of the autocrat for their own purposes. Regardless of where the balance lay, the autocrat and oligarchs relied on a rather lean, but effective, bureaucracy to effect their commands. Efficient bureaucracy had been a hallmark of Muscovy, a heritage that was certainly compromised in the eighteenth century.

The Petrine Era

The strengthening of absolutist power, the subordination of widening areas of social activity to centralized command, and the militarization of government decision-making and organization that is discernible in the Table of Ranks enabled Peter the Great to mobilize more resources and to drive the society and economy at a previously unprecedented pace toward his goal of the "Europeanization" of Russia.

Some of the reforms enacted by the Petrine government had a lasting effect. The whole gentry class was more closely tied to the interests of the state and to state service. Moreover, its position advanced relative to the heirs of the old aristocracy with whom it shared power in the military and in the civilian bureaucracy. Western European manners and rudiments of education became the terms on which membership in the new elite rested. The nobility (gentry and aristocracy), suffering from the population losses and deteriorated economic conditions brought on by Peter's prolonged and exhausting wars, were compensated with the extension of a harsher enserfment of formerly free and "unattached" sections of the population. An opportunity was afforded by the first count of the taxable population (known as the *reviziia*) and was seized upon: ambiguous and "unattached" potential taxpayers were reduced to the status of serfs once they were identified by interested members of the gentry and included in the census. The nobility were thus provided with additional resources of labor and income as a consequence of Peter's need for revenues and his need to reward the nobility for their loyalty. This reduced the labor force available for voluntary hire, with the consequence that the industrial sector was obliged to rely on serf rather than free labor. The scarcity of labor, which had appeared originally in agriculture, was shifted to industry by Peter's enserfment policies.

Industry

During the Petrine period the principal achievement in industry was the establishment of large-scale enterprises in the armaments industry for the manufacture of cannon, small arms, and munitions. This industry was linked to expanded iron production, aided by government support, in remote areas where iron ore, charcoal, and water power were plentiful. Russia became not only self-sufficient in iron, but later became a major exporter of much of its production. The iron industry, the first to be organized with borrowed technology, became a model for other large-scale industries, private and governmental. In iron production, the local cottage industry based on supplies of bog iron was suppressed. In other industries, small-scale production continued even where large-scale production was encouraged. Government support for large enterprises was, however, a mixed blessing. While, on the one hand, the government provided subsidies, sometimes monopoly privileges, often foreign specialists, and most important, serfs for labor-intensive operations, nevertheless the system of licensing, rigid insistence on quality standards, and forced delivery contracts to the government often hampered industrial production.

The construction of St. Petersburg was a genuine monument to its instigator in terms of the scale of resources committed and the amount of central direction exercised. It was the most spectacular of the Petrine investments in the early part of the century. The impact of this investment endured throughout the century in terms of the symbolic and cultural influence of Westernization on the entire country and in terms of the redirection of economic activity toward foreign trade.

Commerce

The acquired direct access to the Baltic and, later in the century, to the Black Sea, provided an additional stimulus to foreign trade. It was principally the rising demand for Western goods on the part of the upper classes and the government, however, as well as the increasing demand in the West for Russian forest products, agricultural raw materials, and especially linen and iron, that was responsible for the growth of Russia's foreign trade. Although foreign ships carried the bulk of Russian goods, and foreign merchants financed most of the trade, Russian merchants were instrumental in collecting the increasing volume of goods for export and in distributing the imported goods. Under conditions of growing commercialization of agriculture, large regional markets were developing.

Government interference in the area of trade took a number of forms. During the early period government monopolies of the sale of particular goods were conspicuous, and later in the century prohibitions of grain exports remained as a remnant of direct government interference. Protection against foreign competitors was awarded to domestic trade, and customs duties were raised for the protection of Russian merchants and industrialists. Most-favored-nation status was awarded selectively to partners in foreign trade, and a policy to achieve and maintain a favorable trade balance was pursued.

The massive internal investments and expenditures for war made heavy fiscal demands and led to currency debasements and the proliferation of new taxes. One of these, the poll tax on males enacted at the end of the Northern War, was to be the most enduring in Russia's fiscal history. Peter's fiscal operations were hastily improvised and hand-to-mouth; it was not until forty years later that a state budget was instituted on a more or less regular basis.

The Post-Petrine Era

Although Peter's death in 1725 brought to an end a period of strong leadership, it did not mark a discontinuity in the transformation of Russian society that was Peter's chief impact. There was no return to political or diplomatic isolation, no relapse into traditionalism, and no turning away from the economic and cultural ties with Western Europe created by Petrine policy. The new instruments of government, never models of efficiency, remained viable, with minor adjustments, under a succession of rulers who, until 1762, were less than distinguished.

The tasks of the post-Petrine period were recovery from the burdens of war, inflation, heavy taxation, the excessive dependency of industry on governmental subsidies, and the policy of extreme mobilization. The post-Petrine period, while lacking spectacular achievements, was marked by internal stability and a healthy economic expansion, visible in the early 1740s in the large grain exports during Western Europe's famine, in investment in the iron industry, and in foreign trade. Deflationary policies may have dampened economic expansion, but did not end it. Population grew and, with it, internal trade and the regional grain markets.

The growth of regional specialization was supported by the government's abolition of internal tolls in 1753. The effect on domestic prices was not immediately visible, but there is no doubt that a significant irritant to internal trade was removed. Transport was also speeded and new patterns of trade were established. The measure was well received by merchants and the population at large, even allowing for the shift of the tax burden to exports and imports. War expenditures in the 1740s brought earlier deflationary policies to an end and the money supply was expanded to finance fiscal deficits. Increases in taxation brought an increase in the marketing of rural production. In the 1750s, major governmental construction activity was resumed; the Winter Palace and St. Isaac's Cathedral in St. Petersburg were two of the projects vigorously undertaken.

In agriculture, a stable period appears to have succeeded the massive flight of serfs in the 1720s and 1730s, but population growth created new problems with respect to land allotment in the more densely populated regions. By the 1750s the government recognized the need for a land cadastre that would define more adequately government and privately owned land while also helping to create informed policies that would redistribute population toward less densely settled regions. The actual work on the land cadastre, however, was not carried out until the last period, during the reign of Catherine the Great. In the 1750s the recognition of the need for the cadastre indicated the dissatisfaction of the serf-owning nobility, and of the serfs as well, with the status quo. The famous peasant uprising of Pugachëv during 1773–74, a violent jacquerie, confirmed the validity of the nobility's anxiety.

The Era of Catherine the Great and Her Son Paul

The final third of the century saw an extensive reform of the obligations of the different classes. The nobility were relieved from obligations of military and civilian government service to the state and were allowed to devote their efforts to their estates, if they so chose. For the middle ranking nobility, obligatory government service, even as modified by Peter's successors, was a heavy burden. For some of the rich nobles, as for the poor gentry, government service was an important source of additional income and often exceeded private income from their estates, but for the middle nobility government income failed to compensate for the foregone income from their estates and for the large expenditures required of the officeholder. Relief from obligatory service in 1762 resulted in a return of a considerable number of nobles to their estates. They began to extract larger returns from their estates and to acquire new lands in both old and newly settled regions. Their demand for a distribution of the secularized church estates was not met, however, apparently out of respect for tradition by the government. But in meeting most of the demands of the nobility, whose power for increased discipline was felt on their estates, the government stirred up deep resentment in the serf population.

This resentment was more strongly felt on the periphery, where the tradition of serfdom was newer, than in the old settled regions, where the state's police power was stronger and where private ownership of serfs predominated. The suppression of the Pugachëv rebellion by the regular army had a profound effect upon the relationships between the serf-owners, serfs, and government. It drew the serf-owners closer to the government, their only recourse against the wrath of the serfs, and it convinced the serfs that the government would support the existing system and that it was futile to attempt change. It imbued the government with a fear of the spontaneous, fiercely destructive power of popular uprisings, and also made it apprehensive of any liberalizing trend that might lead to expectations that the state would relax its effectiveness in repression. Anything and everything that might weaken the arbitrary power of autocratic rule was viewed as undermining the social order. Yet the previous assumption that serfs would not know what to do with freedom and were by nature lazy and undisciplined was demonstrated to be false. The view that supervision by their masters was necessary for their own welfare was supplanted by a view that serfs were unruly, wicked, destructive, and must be kept in bounds. Yet economic reality dictated a policy of greater flexibility in everyday arrangements. While general policy became guided by a resolve to keep the serfs firmly under control, a policy of greater freedom of economic activity also was implemented. The system of state licensing of industrial enterprise was abolished and freedom of entry was granted to all free citizens. Even serfs could enjoy this freedom under the sponsorship of their owners. The state policy of favoring large-scale enterprises was relaxed, and burghers and serfs began to enter trade and industry, formerly the preserve of merchants and noblemen. The legalization of previously nonlicensed production almost certainly had a stimulating effect on production and increased the demand for hired labor in industry.

At the initiative of the serfs who purchased passports and paid dues to their owners, or at the initiative of owners who entered into contracts directly with employers, serf labor for hire was made available to industry, either as seasonal labor or for longer-term work outside agriculture. Although serfowners, as well as the state, tried their best to syphon off the increased income of the serfs, it is doubtful that they captured all of it. Nonetheless, there is considerable ground for uncertainty whether the real incomes of the serfs increased or declined in the last fifteen years of the eighteenth century. (Resolution of the question is made more difficult because of the high rate of inflation in the period.)

Serf-owners attempted to maximize the income from their estates by shifting from a money rent to labor dues. This was accompanied by an increase in the arable area of the demesne and the production of more grain for the market. Their attempts were often thwarted by the existing system of open fields and the difficulty of raising the productivity of the serf labor force. Moreover, the expansion of land cultivation into new, high-yielding areas with greater variability in precipitation also increased the amplitude of grain yields from year to year. This in turn had an impact upon consumption, price fluctuations, and the incomes of agricultural producers. Thus the weather asserted itself more strongly as a destabiliz-

ing factor in Russian agriculture toward the end of the century.

Last but not least, the territorial expansion of Russia at the expense of Poland and through the conquest of the Crimean Khanate added not only territory but also population to the Russian Empire. This renewed the concern of the government with population problems, migration, and colonization schemes, all of which stemmed from the strong belief that, ultimately, the size of its population determines the political and military potential of a state. The expansion was also an occasion for land distribution, enserfment, and massive serf-grants by the government to the members of the elite. This strengthened existing institutions. Although the involvement in European politics resulted in the growth of the empire, the costs of the wars and maintenance of the largest army in Europe were formidable and became a serious strain upon government finances.

New government taxes imposed burdens on the peasantry after the 1760s, but inflation in the 1770s and 80s reduced the actual burden. The remaining years of the century continued the cycles of increased taxation nullified by continued inflation. Whether as the effect of a greater burden of taxation or as a response to market opportunities, the share of agricultural production reaching markets seems to have risen, and industrial as well as agricultural output grew.

In spite of growth in output and participation in the market sector, Russia lagged behind Western and Central European countries, where skills, education, and agricultural and industrial technology grew more rapidly. While in the West new forms of voluntary associations and new types of social organization grew up, in Russia the existing modes of organization, headed by the state, persisted. Although Russia made significant strides in the eighteenth century, particularly in the development of its physical resources, by the end of the century it was still very much behind the West in social organization, at a juncture in history when further economic development depended increasingly upon the development of new forms of social organization.

The chapters in this book are unified by a common theme and a delineated time period and deal with some social and economic aspects of eighteenth-century Russian economic history. They are offered in lieu of a comprehensive economic history of Russian society and reflect my interest in the transition from a preindustrial to a capitalist-type social order. The title was not chosen for the vividness of its symbols, but because the symbols embody important characteristics of Russian society under conditions of serfdom. The plow stands for the incessant toil of the Russian serfs, the hammer for the new elements of nonagricultural labor, and the knout for the power wielded either by the serf-owners or by the Russian state—most of the time by both. These three set the rhythm for the life and activities of the majority of the population. The knout determined where, how fast, and how deep the plow turned over the soil, how hard the plowman had to grip his implement. The knout directed the hand of the smith, often determining whether the piece of iron on the anvil would take the form of a gun barrel or a sickle. Moreover, the knout sometimes was swinging, hitting, and pounding out of habit, for no good reason except inertia. More important, it shielded Russian society from the impact of new ideas, as the pain of the flesh deadened the longings and sensitivity of the spirit.

The three symbols were imbedded in the fabric of society. Simultaneously, each of them had its own sphere, its own momentum. More important, they were set in motion by the hands and minds of humans acting both out of habit and by intent, within the limits set by their natural and social environment. The following essays are devoted to the autonomous and cooperative actions of the members of that society. Eighteenth-century Russian society should not be judged in light of our social and economic relations. We can only perceive its members and try to explain their lives by using analytical tools and appropriate methodology. I have tried to keep frivolous imagination at bay, but the extent to which an author can build a bridge to a distant culture without some measure of arbitrariness is a matter to be judged by intelligent readers only.

1
THE RECORD OF POPULATION GROWTH

The changes in the size, composition, and distribution of the population of Russia during the eighteenth century were a result of a number of complex, intricately interrelated factors: the natural growth-rate, wars, famines, epidemics, and governmental policies. The changing population profile inevitably initiated or affected other historical, economic, and cultural processes.

In estimating the changes in the size and distribution of the population, one has to rely upon the data collected by the Russian government during five consecutive population counts, called *revizii,*[1] and upon the works of historical demographers.[2]

The main obstacles to the presentation of estimates for the whole of the eighteenth century are the lack of population data for the first twenty years[3] and the likelihood that the first population census taken in Russia during the period of our investigation, in 1719, was the least complete of all. Another obstacle is that the population censuses of the eighteenth century registered and reported only the number of males, and primarily the taxpaying males, the "male souls" (*dushi muzhskogo pola*). The lack of data for the size of the female population[4] forces one to utilize the data for the male population as a proxy for the total population. Whenever references are made specifically to the *total* population, an equal distribution of the sexes is assumed.

The population changes for eighteenth-century Russia can be represented by the official population figures for the period 1719–95, encompassing five censuses (or population counts) within different state boundaries (see table 1.1).

Simple inspection of table 1.1 indicates that the population of Russia grew during the period 1719–95. This growth was both through natural population increase and as a result of boundary changes. About 35 percent of the total increase may be traced to the acquisition of new territories. However, using a comparable territory basis, one sees that the population of Russia grew quite unevenly during the periods between the various population counts (table 1.2).

Certain general demographic characteristics of the Russian population in the eighteenth century are apparent. First of all, it suffered from a very high rate of child mortality. Without exception, all population data point to a mortality rate approaching .5 during the first months and years of life. In many instances, the mortality of the newborn was even higher. Thus we are dealing with a high-birth and high-mortality society in which people married at an early age, usually during their twenties, had many children, and buried many of them. The high marriage-rate was not only supported by the economic demands of the peasant agrarian society but also was encouraged by the institution of serfdom in order to broaden the base for rent payments to the landlords and taxes to the government. With birth rates up to the 50s per thousand and death rates up to the 40s per thousand, the net natural population increment in some periods reached about 1 percent per annum.

It is hoped that the subsequent discussion of the factors affecting the rate of population growth will provide some explanation of this phenomenon, or at least offer some plausible reasons for the fluctuations that characterized it.[5]

Impediments to Population Growth

The Impact of Wars

The eighteenth century in Russia, as in most of the rest of Europe, was a bellicose period. Wars were frequent and long. Times of peace were relatively brief. The wars waged by Russia may be divided into two categories: those of major importance that taxed the resources of the country, and those of lesser and only peripheral significance (see table 1.3).

Also of national importance because of its demographic impact was the peasant uprising of 1773–75 under the leadership of Emel'ian Pugachëv.

During the eighteenth century the standing army was expanded in Russia from about 200,000 to about 450,000 men.[6] To sustain an army of such size,

Table 1.1   The Size of the Male Population of Russia, 1719–95, according to the Population Counts (*Revizii*)

	1719	1744	1762	1782	1795	1719–95
Total male population	7,791,063	9,105,017	11,580,043	14,209,733	18,617,650	10,826,587
Total civilian population	7,572,512	8,934,781	10,942,812	13,691,312	18,168,574	10,596,062
Civilian population in the territory of first population count	6,345,131	7,399,546	8,436,779	10,474,399	11,352,774	5,007,643
Population in territories acquired during period preceding population count	—	—	—	640,567	3,202,396	3,842,963
Total increase of population on territory of first population count by census periods	—	1,054,415	1,037,233	2,037,620	878,375	5,007,643
Total increase between periods of civilian population, exclusive of acquisitions	—	1,362,269	2,008,031	2,107,933	1,274,866	6,753,099
Total increase between periods, exclusive of acquisitions	—	1,313,954	2,475,026	1,989,123	1,205,521	6,983,624

Note: The differences, very slight indeed, between the above table and the one published by V. M. Kubuzan (*Narodonaselenie Rossii*, pp. 159–65) can be explained as follows: two printing errors were corrected, one for the Irkutsk district during the first reviziia (47,453 instead of 27,453); the second for the Kostroma district for the third reviziia (865,744 instead of 365,744). They do not affect the totals and are clearly printing errors. The first difference pertains to Siberia during the first reviziia. Kubuzan estimates the indigenous, local (non-Russian) population as being 71,744 on the basis of a tax collection figure of 50,242,50 rubles. This estimate first appeared in an article by V. M. Kubuzan and S. M. Troitskii ("Dvizhenie naseleniia," p. 144, n. 1). Since he assumes a tax rate of 70 kopeks per male, the accurate figure would be 50,242.50 rubles divided by .70 ruble = 71,775 males. Because the authors did not report any other basis or source for their calculations, I felt free to correct what I consider to be an arithmetic error. This error affects the population estimate for Siberia and the total was therefore corrected. The other corrections for the first revizii are based upon a later article by V. M. Kabuzan ("Krest'ianskaia kolonizatsiia") and pertain to the territory of Novorossiia region. He claims these figures supersede the previously published data. The corrections in the data and tables are the following:
1st reviziia: Siberia population + 31 (241,115 instead of 241,084)
    Novorossiia + 2,106 (39,771 instead of 37,665)
    Total territory of the first reviziia + 31 (6,345,132 instead of 6,345,101)
        Total (except armed forces) + 2,137 (752,513 instead of 7,570,376)
        Total (including armed forces) + 2,137 (7,791,064 instead of 7,788,927)
2d reviziia: Novorossiia + 16,415 (61,656 instead of 45,241)
        Total (except armed forces) + 16,415 (8,949,566 instead of 8,933,151)
        Total (including armed forces) + 16,415 (9,119,802 instead of 9,103,387)
3d reviziia: Novorossiia − 37,649 (138,852 instead of 175,501)
        Total (except armed forces) − 37,649 (10,942,812 instead of 10,980,461)
        Total (including armed forces) − 37,649 (11,580,043 instead of 11,617,692)

Table 1.2   Average Yearly Rates of Population Growth between Population Counts in the Territory of the First Reviziia

Period	Rate of Growth
1719–44	.66
1744–62	.94
1762–82	1.02
1782–95	.61

Source: Table 1.1

Table 1.3   Wars Conducted by Russia during the Eighteenth Century

Nationally Important	Peripherally Important
1700–21—with Sweden	1711 —with Turkey
1735–39—with Turkey	1716–17—with Khiva
1756–62—with Prussia	1722–35—with Persia
1768–74—with Turkey	1733–35—with Poland
1787–91—with Turkey	1741–43—with Sweden
	1768–72—with Poland
	1788–90—with Sweden
	1792 and 1794—with Poland
	1795–96—with Persia
	1798–1800—with France

Source: Kabuzan, *Narodonaselenie*, p. 16.

large numbers of men had to be drafted.[7] The death rate was high, both through direct war losses on the battlefield and through sickness.

Table 1.4 estimates the direct war losses suffered by the Russian armed forces during the eighteenth century. It distributes the totals of dead and wounded among the various wars fought and attempts to separate battlefield losses from disease losses in the field during the various military campaigns. In the absence of direct data on mortality in the Russian army and navy during the peaceful periods of the eighteenth century, we can perhaps use as a guide the data that are available for the first half of the nineteenth century.[8] Table 1.5 presents mortality estimates based on the assumption that the mortality rate unrelated to military operations was 40 per thousand in the armed forces.

A document from Rumiantsev's army (probably stationed in the south of the country) provides an illustration of the health status of those in the army.

Table 1.4 War Losses of the Armed Forces in Russia, 1700–1799 (in Thousands)

Wars	Battlefield Losses			Died of Wounds	Total Dead	Died of Diseases	Death Toll
	Killed	Wounded	Total Casualties				
Northern War	35	85	120	10	45	54	99
Russian-Swedish (except Northern)	6	14	20	2	8	17	25
Russian-Turkish	59	141	200	17	76	139	215
Russian-Polish	9	21	30	2	11	26	37
Russian-Persian including Caucasus and Central Asia	15	35	50	4	19	131	150
Seven Years War	18	42	60	5	23	97	120
Suvorov's Expedition to Italy and Switzerland	4	10	14	1	5	2	7
Total foreign wars	146	348	494	41	187	486	653
Pugachëv uprising	20	20	40	2	22	4	26
Total	166	368	534	43	209	470	679

Source: Urlanis, *Voiny*, pp. 54–58, 261–70, 340.

Note: Relation between numbers of killed and wounded assumed to be 1:2.4, following Urlanis's procedure (except for the Pugachëv uprising). Deaths from lethal wounds are assumed to be 12 percent of the total wounded. Number of "Died of Diseases" is arrived at by treating it as residual after the dead on the battlefield are subtracted from the total death toll. The estimate for the Pugachëv uprising includes the losses of Pugachëv's forces.

Table 1.5 Mortality in the Armed Forces in Russia during the Eighteenth Century, War Losses Excluded (in Thousands)

Years	Assumed Strength of Armed Forces	Number of Years Included	Mortality
1720–44	200	15	120
1744–63	300	12	144
1763–82	468	14	262
1783–95	482	7	135
1796–99	482	4	77
Total, 1720–99			738

Source: Kabuzan, *Narodonaselenie*, p. 163.

Note: The mortality rate was assumed to be 4 percent per year. The estimate of the strength of the armed forces was derived from the following estimates and data: 1719—219,000; 1744—170,000; 1762—418,000; 1782—518,000; 1795—449,000.

For a particular week during the year 1768 the document reported a total of 4.29 percent of the army personnel as "sick." Of those, 4.42 percent were soldiers in the line-regiments and 3.54 percent were in auxiliary formations (*nestroevye*). For noncommissioned officers, the percentage was 2.63 percent. The figure was higher for senior and staff officers, for whom sick leave might have been a form of temporary leave not necessarily caused by illness.[9]

It can be assumed that the level of medical care in the armed forces was inadequate to cure the illnesses of the enlisted men even by the prevailing medical standards of the times. By the end of the century, the medical corps of the army consisted of 233 senior physicians, 253 junior physicians, and 410 paramedical personnel (known in Russian as *feldshera*), and this at a time when the number of the military exceeded 400,000.[10]

The number of medical personnel per regiment toward the end of the century was established as two or three, depending upon the type of regiment; the number coincided only roughly with the different sizes of regiments.

The first body of representative and massive data pertaining to the "normal" mortality in the armed forces falls outside our period. The earliest available published reports on hospitalization of members of the lower ranks and the mortality rates of the hospitalized for a "normal" year (a year of peace) are from 1802.[11] We would expect the mortality for 1802 to be below the level of the eighteenth century. According to the reports for 1802, about one-half of the lower ranks of the armed forces were hospitalized during the year. These data cover the hospitalization of a total of 164,536 persons, of whom 157,898 recovered and 6,638 died. The mortality rate of the hospitalized amounted to 4.03 percent. If we assume that in any given "normal" year about half of the armed forces were hospitalized, the mortality rate was about 2 percent per year. This mortality rate appears to be nearly three times the average mortality rate of males in the 20–45 age bracket compiled for the Orthodox population of the Russian Empire by C. Th. Hermann.[12] Therefore, on the basis of documentary evidence for a normal year, one may conclude that military service was a constant drain upon the population resources of Russia because mortality rates were higher in the military service than outside it.

Table 1.6   Losses Due to Military Service Inclusive of Wars (in Thousands)

Years	War Losses	Military Service	Total	Yearly Average
1720–44	217	120	337	13.48
1744–62	128	144	272	15.11
1763–82	120	262	382	19.1
1783–95	108	135	243	18.69
Total	573	661	1,234	

Table 1.7   The Military Draft in Russia, 1701–1799

Ruler	Years	Total Number	Yearly Average
Peter the Great	1701–24	365,262	15,219
Catherine I & Peter II	1726–29	80,918	20,230
Anna	1730–40	279,871	27,987
Elizabeth	1741–61	431,251	20,536
Catherine II*	1762–96	1,088,861 (1,040,047)	32,025 (30,590)
Paul I	1797–99	163,917	54,639
Total	1701–99	2,410,080 (2,361,266)	24,344 (23,851)

Note: Not all of the male population was subject to draft in eighteenth-century Russia. The figures in parentheses represent an attempt to deduct from the gross figures of the draft the numbers of draftees who were not sent to the armed forces but were included in the military draft. The total of the military draft in the armed forces proper—2,361,266—is very close to the estimate made by Major General Rusanov in his reports of May 30, 1802 (Urlanis, *Voiny*, p. 341). Rusanov's original estimate for 1701–99 was 2,271,571. When his figures are adjusted for the underestimation during 1701–18 of 61,855 draftees, his estimate increases to 2,333,426, which is very close to the one presented in the table.

Indirect evidence on the mortality rate in the armed forces points to harsh treatment of draftees even prior to their induction. Although the *General'noe Uchrezhdenie* of 1766 forbade the earlier practice of putting draftees in chains and keeping them in prison before marching them to their army units (at which point they became entitled to a food ration), the high mortality rate continued.[13] Field Marshall Rumiantsev reported the following on April 15, 1774: "Suffering from exhaustion on their way to the field army, due to the long marches during the worst time of the year, they [the recruits] were brought here in a state of extreme weakness, and a large part of them died without even experiencing the direct hardships of military life."[14]

In order to synchronize the data of the war losses with estimates of mortality in the army (tables 1.4 and 1.5) and to put them into the available framework of the census data for the male population, a rough, highly tentative distribution of military service losses by intercensus periods is offered in table 1.6.

In the absence of mortality tables for the male population in eighteenth-century Russia, we cannot do more than state a general impression: the treatment of soldiers and the shamefully poor conditions within the armed forces contributed substantially to a high mortality rate.

In table 1.7 estimated figures for the military draft are grouped by reigns, and yearly averages are derived.[15] The figures are more meaningful, of course, when compared with the data on the population that provided the draftees. The absence of continuous population data makes the presentation of a continuous series impossible. The percentages of draftees out of the total population can only be approximated.

From an approximation of the average number of males subject to draft during the reigns of the various rulers, and on the assumption that 40 percent of them were of draft age, the percentages of yearly military draft can be derived (see table 1.8).

If we accept the total of military recruitment in the Russian armed forces as being approximately 2.3 million men, and accept the estimates of 1.5 million casualties (about .7 million attributed to wars and .8 million to mortality in the armed forces), the residual figure of about .8 million has to be explained. Available evidence points to an approximate figure of about 200,000 deserters, including both draftees and soldiers on duty. The remaining number, 600,000, retired from the armed forces, either upon completion of service or at an earlier date for other reasons.[16]

For the period covered by the population censuses, 1720–95, the draft data indicate a total of 1,908,169 draftees. If we accept the total of 1,234,000 casualties, the residual figure could be about 674,000. That residual can be distributed between about 174,000 deserters and 500,000 retired soldiers.

Considering the heavy casualties in the armed forces, it is not hard to appreciate both the general unwillingness of the peasant-serfs to serve in the army and their willingness to run the risk of severe punishment for desertion rather than almost certainly die in service.[17]

Since the draft age covered the years between 16 and 45, and no stipulated age for retirement was prescribed, for most soldiers recruited forcibly from among the taxpaying population, predominantly serfs, death and incapacitation were the "liberating" causes for the termination of their military careers. Therefore, in addition to direct casualties, the military draft also led to a loss of potential population growth, since the majority of the soldiers were unmarried, and the retired ones entered marriage at an advanced age. The impact of the armed services upon population growth was stronger in eighteenth-century Russia than in other countries. Although most European countries in the eighteenth century had standing armies of considerable size, none (with the exception perhaps of Germany) had such a high proportion of its *own* population in the armed forces.

It is thus possible to draw the conclusion that military service and wars resulted in heavy casualties and adversely affected population growth in Russia during the eighteenth century. Moreover, the military draft was a considerable drain upon manpower resources.[18]

Still another institution that had a detrimental impact upon the rate of population growth in Russia during the eighteenth century was the penal system, including forced public works. Although the data are far from precise, we have adequate figures showing high mortality among the labor forcibly recruited to construct St. Petersburg, among the penal institutions required to construct Rogervik or to mine silver in Nerchinsk, and, above all, among the unruly serfs banished by their masters to Siberia, (the masters were rewarded with government certificates for delivering military recruits for the draft). This information suggests that the penal system, forced labor, and banishment to Siberia, institutions that involved tens of thousands of people, impeded population growth.

Famines

For the overwhelming majority in eighteenth-century Russia, the rhythm of life was not determined by wars, the reforms of Peter the Great, or by anything his successors managed to accomplish or fail in, but by the conditions affecting the agricultural cycle of plowing, planting, and harvesting. The sustenance of the vast majority of Russians depended less upon the level of rents, the burden of government taxation, or the profits derived in domestic or foreign trade than upon the vagaries of nature. Of paramount importance was the size of the harvest, or, to be more specific, the ratio of harvested grain to seed planted (the output-seed ratio). The major calamities of the century were not the occasional defeats of the Russian armies or the failures of Russian diplomacy, but the famines that frequented the Russian countryside.

The reason for the damaging influence of droughts and frosts upon the food supply of the Russian population has to be sought in the low output-seed (yield) ratio of grains in Russia even during years of normal weather conditions. With an output-seed ratio of 3.5–4:1 for grains during normal weather conditions and grain reserves of not more than one year's consumption, any single year of adverse weather put rural households in a precarious situation in their food supply. Bad weather conditions, whether they were severe winters, excessive rainfall, or droughts that affected the yields of both spring and winter grains, caused famine if they lasted for two consecutive years. When the exhaustion of grain reserves, following a decline in the available current grain supply, was accompanied by a decline in output and a rise in grain prices, various degrees of privation were inevitable.

During the first half of the eighteenth century, adverse weather (known throughout Europe as "the Little Ice Age," often attributed to a period of low sun-spot activity known as "the Maunder minimum") had a severe impact on the agricultural sector and the population at large. Although the rate of population growth during this period cannot be attributed solely to the conditions of the food supply, its low level of increase relative to the rate in other periods is an indicator of the effects of frequent crop failures. During the second half of the century, bad weather conditions were less frequent and apparently of shorter duration; as a result, the impact of such conditions was less severe and did not lead to widespread famines.[19] The expansion of the planted area, particularly in the blacksoil steppe zone, had the effect of dispersing the population, and, although the steppe zone was susceptible to droughts, the risks of famine were more dispersed and diminished.

Since the frequencies and intensities of natural calamities affecting the food supply varied by periods,[20] it is necessary to investigate their effect upon population growth within the periods for which population data are available. For the first period, 1719–44, we find, by comparison with a similar period during the nineteenth century (1833–50), that a frequency of natural calamities in the neighborhood of every second year can be associated with a lower than average population growth rate.[21] In addition, the population data for Moscow, Iaroslavl', Nizhnii Novgorod, and Vladimir districts reveal a decrease of the population for 1719–44 which might be associated with the 1721–24 and 1732–35 decrease in food availability caused by famines in these regions.[22] For the subsequent period, 1744–62, we find a negligible rate of growth of the population in the Orel and Kursk districts, which could perhaps be traced to the reported severe famine of 1747–50 in Belgorod province, which included those districts.[23] The two districts exhibited a pattern different from that of the neighboring districts within the Central Agricultural region.

The natural calamities of the next period, 1763–82, are by and large not reflected in the population growth data available, except for the district of Khar'kov, which exhibited a relatively low rate of population growth.[24] It is possible that the famines that affected the Khar'kov district intensified the well-documented out-migration from it to the newly opened lands of the neighboring Ekaterinoslav and Kherson districts.

Table 1.8   Assumed Male Population of Draft Age

	N	Yearly Draft (%)
Peter the Great	2,843,000	.54
Catherine I and Peter II	2,843,000	.71
Anne	3,080,000	.91
Elizabeth	3,800,000	.54
Catherine II	4,800,000	.67

For the subsequent period, 1783–95, the natural calamities that affected the food supply are reflected in the population growth pattern of the Riazan' and Orel districts of the Central Agricultural region and the low rate of growth of the Central Industrial region.[25] One should not, however, exaggerate the impact of natural calamities during this period on the Central Industrial region: the colonization of new lands offered opportunities of resettlement, the pull-effect of which might have been as attractive and effective as the push-effect of natural calamities.

Since the impact of adverse weather conditions was primarily concentrated in the southern and south-eastern regions of Russia, the areas that were beginning to be colonized during the second half of the eighteenth century, the full impact of the weather upon the food supply, and indirectly upon population growth, during the eighteenth century was smaller than during the nineteenth century and should not be exaggerated.[26]

Table 1.9 uses contemporary sources to characterize the weather conditions associated with famines or low yields and provides a chronological distribution of the natural calamities that befell Russia during the eighteenth century.

Table 1.10 compares the data on the availability of grain for export in the years of major calamities and examines the impact on price changes for the major grain crops.

The effects of most of the severe weather calamities on both grain exports and prices were discernible and expected. The time lag between the calamity and its effect on exports is due to the period that elapsed between the end of the agricultural year and the time-consuming process of the collection of the marketable grain, as well as of its transportation to the major markets or ports of embarkation. Except for a few cases in which the volume of exports was influenced by the extraordinary demand created by pan-European famines, when short-term price changes were superimposed upon a longer-term price movement in the European grain market, the Russian market seems to respond in the proper direction. Under the conditions of serfdom, the serfs did not receive increased compensation for their marketable production in times of lower yields. The reduction of the marketable output or, in some cases, the debts

incurred as well as the reduction of consumption, outweighed the opportunity to charge higher prices. Thus, as a rule of thumb, one should accept the notion, articulated by the late Professor Witold Kula,[27] that low grain prices can be correlated with high real incomes for the serfs. Weather calamities that led to the decrease of the grain supply in eighteenth-century Russia had the opposite effect: they decreased the real income of the agricultural serf population, affecting adversely the health of this population and perhaps also the rate of its growth.

Natural calamities also affected the serf-owners, or landowners, whether the serfs lived under conditions of rent in kind or money rent (*obrok*), or labor dues (*barshchina*). However, the serf-owners who engaged in grain production for the market at least had an opportunity to benefit from higher grain prices. Three elements limited their freedom to profiteer from natural calamities: first, customary law (and, later in the eighteenth century, written law) required the serf-owners to support indigent serfs during such calamities, and this was coupled with their self-interest in maintaining the serfs; second, their responsibility to the government as collectors of the poll tax required them to advance the tax payment with the hope of collecting it from their serfs in the future; and third, there were prohibitions against exporting grain during periods of high grain prices and diminished domestic grain supplies. During the 1760s, in spite of the conditions of domestic supply and the level of domestic prices, the gentry, in an alliance with the merchants, achieved the right to trade in grain and, except when the government imposed emergency measures (such as permitting duty-free grain importation in 1787), the landowners were able to benefit from higher grain prices and thus to reduce the impact of low yields upon their incomes.

This short survey of the problem of the reduction in the grain supply and of its effect upon the income of the majority of the population indicates the differences between the first half of the century, with poor climactic conditions, and the second half of the century, when potential income was less impaired by weather calamities.

Epidemics

The epidemics that struck many regions of Russia during the eighteenth century were an added scourge on population growth. Although our records may be incomplete because they register only the most violent and damaging outbreaks, they nevertheless provide a general impression of high frequency and severity. The most virulent diseases that assumed epidemic dimensions were the plague (especially bubonic), influenza, and smallpox. Table 1.11, drawn

Table 1.9   Natural Calamities Affecting the Grain Yields in Russia in the Eighteenth Century

Year	Type of Calamity	Location	Degree of Intensity
1704	Cold winter	Moscow and central Russia	Relatively mild; killed the winter crop; grain supplies brought from southern provinces
1709	Severe winter and spring floods	Most of Russia	Severe; coincided also with plague epidemic
1716	Excessive rainfall and floods	Moscow Province	Relatively mild; casualties more from floods than from starvation
1721–24	Excessive rainfalls and cold	Moscow, Smolensk and most of central Russia	Crop failures for four successive years in a large area. Famine conditions, food shortages, high grain prices, human casualties
1729	Extremely cold winter	All of Russia	Interrupted communications, winterkill
1732–36	Early frosts	All of Russia, especially Nizhnii Novgorod province and the Ukraine	Crop failures for successive years in the Upper Volga and the Ukraine; famine conditions
1735	Floods	Northern and central Russia	Severe floods and famine
1739	Very cold winter	All of Russia	Winter crops affected, food shortages
1740	Lack of precipitation in winter; excessive rainfall in the summer	Southern Russia	Winter crops froze; spring crops did not sprout; "very hungry summer."
1747–49	Drought and locusts	All of Russia, especially Belgorod Province and the Ukraine	Famine in Belgorod Province; low yields in many provinces
1757			Low yields
1767	July hailstorm followed by drought		Primarily spring grains suffered
1774	Drought	Left-Bank Ukraine	Crop losses and low yields in adjacent provinces
1780	Drought	Central and southern Russia	Low yields and crop losses
1781	Low yields	Same	Faminelike conditions because of cumulative effect of previous year
1786	Drought	Central and southern Russia	Crop losses leading to high prices for grain and import of grain into St. Petersburg in 1787
1788	Drought	Western and central Russia	

Source: Kahan, "Natural Calamities."

from the descriptive literature of the period, lists the types, location, and effects of such epidemics.

Although, to be sure, this list of epidemics in Russia during the eighteenth century is incomplete, the data point to several tentative conclusions. First, plague was centered ordinarily in southern Russia. Outbreaks were sparked by the intrusion of newcomers, probably with a relatively low immunity to the disease, who acted as carriers to other areas of the country. The "ideal" carriers of the disease were the armed forces, given their mobility and supply transportation methods, which also facilitated the movement of rodents. Given the population density of the armed forces, it was military garrisons, cities, and particularly sea and river ports, that were especially vulnerable to, and the primary targets of, the plague. Attempts to cure the afflicted were by and large futile; no campaign to erase the disease could be under-

taken as long as its origin and its primary carriers were unknown. Consequently, reliance was placed on the age-old practice of cordoning off cities or other territorial units to prevent the spread of the plague to other regions. The more human resources used in those operations, the less the potential casualties. The widely heralded operations of the quarantine services along the border crossings and in the ports, services that by the end of the eighteenth century employed forty-seven physicians and that purported to prevent the plague from being imported from abroad, were probably exaggerated in terms of their effectiveness.[28]

The outbreaks of influenza epidemics in Russia accentuated the relatively high incidence of mortality attributed to respiratory illnesses.

Although smallpox was endemic in Russia and affected people of all strata of the population, its

Table 1.10   The Impact of Natural Calamities

Years	Upon Grain Exports	Upon Grain Prices
1709	Exports of wheat during 1710 about ½ of average for the decade, of rye about ⅕.	
1716	Exports during 1717 and 1718 10 percent and 5 percent of normal years.	
1721–24	Exports negligible, followed by a prohibition of grain exports.	The highest prices during the first half of the century, except for the pan-European famine of 1739–41.
1729	Rye exports maintained at level of previous year for Baltic ports; all other grain exports decline in 1730.	Slowdown of price decline from the high level of the middle 1720s.
1732–36	Precipitous decline of rye exports, beginning with 1732–33, to 20 percent and 10 percent of the previous year; low level of exports during 1735–37, about 25–30 percent of previous years' volume.	Reversal of downward price trend for rye, oats, and barley.
1739–40	Very high level of exports, 1739–41, due to famine in Western and Central Europe and very high grain prices, which led to a rapid depletion of reserves and a ban on grain exports in 1742 and for most of the 1740s.	1740–41, highest level of grain prices during the first half of the eighteenth century due to foreign demand and local scarcities; subsequent prohibition of exports caused price declines.
1747–49	No grain exports from the Russian territories.	Rise of all domestic grain prices.
1757	No rye and wheat exports from the Russian territories through the Baltic ports.	No rise in rye and wheat prices; rise in prices of oats and barley probably as a result of war conditions.
1767	No discernible short-run effects upon exports.	Rise in prices related to growth of export demand.
1774	80 percent decrease in exports from Baltic and White Sea ports during 1776.	Decline in prices from the high levels reached during 1771–73 of the European famine.
1780–81	45 percent decrease of rye exports in 1780 and smaller decreases of wheat exports during 1781 and 1782.	Resumption of increase in grain prices, followed by rise in price level due to inflationary pressures.
1786	No rye exports in 1787 and a drastic decline—75 percent of wheat exports; exports of other grain during 1787 and 1788.	
1788	No wheat and rye exports in 1788 and 1789 from Russian territory through the Baltic ports.	

Note: The effect of the decreases in grain supply, due to the weather calamities, upon the volume of exports was traced by using the data in the tables on Russian grain exports. The effect upon grain prices was traced by examining the series of average yearly prices for grains and grain products for the city of Riga.

strongest effect was upon the indigenous populations of Siberia. Like populations in other parts of the world that had not developed an immunity over a long time-period, they suffered heavy casualties from smallpox. It was, however, the outbreak of smallpox epidemics in St. Petersburg, with their potential impact upon the elite, that frightened the authorities and inspired action. Although the mortality figures might have been exaggerated (they are not supported by the evidence cited in the essay by Krafft),[29] they had the desired effect of introducing smallpox vaccination in Russia after Empress Catherine II set an "illustrious example" by allowing herself to be vaccinated. Although the number vaccinated rose very slowly from about 10,000 annually in the 1780s to less than 60,000 yearly by the end of the century, some positive effect was nevertheless discernible.

The general impression given by the descriptive data is that in the second half of the century the impact of the plague lessened, with the notable exception of the 1770–73 epidemic. With respect to the other two diseases that reached epidemic proportions, influenza and smallpox, the lack of data for the first half of the century prevents any comparison among the various periods within the eighteenth century.

During this period Russia experienced no major outbreaks of typhoid fever, a disease that assumed epidemic dimensions during both the seventeenth and the nineteenth centuries. I do not find any plausible explanation for this phenomenon. Although the "hot fever," mentioned sometimes in the sources, might have included typhoid fever, and although the disease was one of the most frequent killers, it was not cited as an epidemic by contemporaries.

The largely descriptive evidence cited above leads to the conclusion that the epidemics registered during the eighteenth century had a detrimental effect on population growth by striking at the armed forces, a relatively young population, and by thwarting the growth of urban centers.

The destructive force of epidemics was obviously magnified when epidemics coincided with other natural calamities, such as famines or serious livestock diseases. The malnutrition resulting from the latter two causes made the population more vulnerable and less resistant to the spread of disease.

Table 1.11   Descriptive Account of Epidemics in Russia during the Eighteenth Century

Type of Epidemic	Years	Location	General Information
Plague	1709–13	Riga, Reval, Narva Pskov, Novgorod, Ukraine	Brought by Swedish troops from Southern Poland. Decimated Russian troops and urban population in the Baltic region. Relatively mild in Ukraine.
Plague	1718–19	Belgorod, Kiev, and Azov Provinces	Generally mild in view of effective quarantine measures.
Plague	1727–28	Astrakhan', Crimea	Severe in Astrakhan', where about half of the population perished. Affected the Caspian navy.
Plague	1738–39	Ochakov, then all of Ukraine	Outbreak in the Russian army around Ochakov during the war with Turkey. Population losses in the cities of Kursk, Belgorod, Khar'kov, Poltava, and Azov ranged from several hundred to over one thousand per city.
Influenza	1757–58, 1761–62 1767	Most regions of the country	Increased death rates
Smallpox	1768–69	Siberia and Kamchatka	Heavy losses among the indigenous population.
Plague	1770–73	Moldavia, Kiev, and Moscow	Apparently started in the armed forces stationed in Moldavia, with several thousand victims. Population losses in Kiev estimated of up to 14,000 and another 10,000 in other cities of Ukraine. Casualties in Moscow estimated at 60,000, or about ⅓ of the total population.
Smallpox	1772–1776	St. Petersburg	Population losses led to introduction of smallpox vaccination.
Influenza	1781 1798	Most regions of the country	Increased death rates.
Plague	1783–84	Kremenchug, Kherson	Localized and contained due to newly established quarantine measures in the South
Plague	1796	Crimea	Localized and contained.
Plague	1798	Caucasus and Volynia	First major outbreak in the Caucasus, probably brought by troops from Southern Russia.

Source: Kahan, "Natural Calamities."

Thus the ravages of war, famine, and disease had a substantial impact on the Russian population profile during the eighteenth century. They were indeed major impediments to growth. There were times when they stalked the land together—and, joined by Death, they became the Four Horsemen.

Government Policies, Migration, and Colonization

In order to balance the impact of the exogenous factors that tended to depress the rate of population growth, we should consider at least some of the factors that favorably affected the rate of population growth.

Apart from the fact that the rates of population growth differed between periods within the century, and that no consistent tendency of acceleration can be surmised from the data available prior to 1782, a closer inspection reveals that among regions the rates of population growth differed widely. This can be demonstrated by comparing the growth rates of two categories of regions, grouped according to the growth rates for the whole period. One group repre-

sents lower than average areas and the other areas of higher than average population growth. As shown in table 1.12, the difference is apparent: it can be attributed partly to the fact that the first group represents the areas of net out-migration, while the other group represents the areas of higher than average rates of natural population growth as well as considerable in-migration and colonization. The contention that the second group represents not only the areas of in-migration but also a higher rate of natural increase, is based upon the general observation that the land-labor ratio was higher in those areas that were variously described as "the areas of colonization," "the fringes of the empire," or, simply, the frontier areas.

The contention that the land-labor ratio might have been one of the decisive factors in the determination of the differential rate of natural population increase is based on the assumption that, within the peasant household, at the then prevailing rate of income, children were an "investment good,"[30] from which the parents expected a return in the form of a contribution to the labor of the household. It is also assumed that, at the existing level of agricultural

Table 1.12   Population Growth in Various Regions of Russia (Males Only)

Date	Comparable Territory[a]	North and Northwest[b]	Central-Industrial[c]	Central Agricultural[d]	Total "Old Territory"[e]	Areas of Colonization[f]
1st reviziia (1719)	6,345,101	834,484	2,278,535	1,443,349	6,740,183	832,330
2d reviziia (1744)	7,399,546	983,157	2,275,275	1,633,099	7,640,762	1,308,804
Yearly % change	.6	.7	.0	.5	.5	1.8
3d reviziia (1762)	8,436,779	1,040,143	2,540,465	1,819,897	9,014,287	1,928,525
Yearly % change	.7	.3	.6	.6	.9	2.2
4th reviziia (1782)	10,469,767	1,235,293	2,938,056	2,315,110	10,209,797	2,836,327
Yearly % change	1.1	.9	.7	1.2	.6	1.9
5th reviziia (1795)	11,352,774	1,304,398	3,036,913	2,515,612	10,685,352	3,519,486
Yearly % change	.6	.4	.3	.6	.4	1.7
Yearly % increase (1719–95)	—	—	—	—	.58	2.0

Source: Kabuzan, *Izmeneniia.*

[a]Territory of the first population census.
[b]Includes the districts of Arkhangel'sk, Vologda, St. Petersburg, Novgorod, Olonets, and Pskov.
[c]Includes the districts of Moscow, Vladimir, Kaluga, Iaroslavl', Kostroma, Nizhnii Novgorod, and Tver'.
[d]Includes the districts of Riazan', Tambov, Orel, Kursk, and Tula. The adjacent Voronezh district was included in the area of colonization.
[e]Includes the sum of North and Northwest, Central-Industrial, and Central Agricultural
[f]Includes the district of Voronezh and the areas of Novorossiia, Lower Volga, the Urals, and Siberia.

Table 1.13   Assumed and Actual Population Increases in the Areas of Colonization

Year	Actual Rate between Periods (%)	Actual Population	Kabuzan Rates (%)	Assumed Population	1.2% Rate	Assumed Population
1719		832,330		832,330		832,330
1744	1.8	1,308,804	.66	990,897	1.2	1,121,506
1762	2.2	1,928,525	.94	1,164,304	1.2	1,390,095
1782	1.9	2,836,327	1.02	1,420,660	1.2	1,764,614
1795	1.7	3,519,486	.61	1,535,534	1.2	2,060,593

technology, a more favorable land-labor ratio meant a higher output per unit of labor. The empirical evidence about higher land-labor (or land-population) ratios in the areas of the frontier, or colonization, and greater per capita output of grain cereals there than in the areas of out-migration[31] supports the above assumptions and indirectly the contention of a higher rate of population growth.[32]

Among the factors that contributed to the population growth in the regions of in-migration were the government's population policies, the impact of industrial development, and the growing availability of new lands that were gradually opened up for colonization and were brought successively under cultivation.

The existence of migration toward the "areas of colonization"[33] can be surmised even without direct evidence of a population transfer. We could compare the actual rates of population increase in the "areas of colonization" with two assumed rates of population increase. One of the rates is represented by the between-census rates of population growth derived by Kabuzan for the territory of the first census,[34] which constitutes one of the few continuous series in a large part of the Russian territory not affected by subsequent acquisitions. The other rate of 1.2 percent yearly was the one given by I. P. Fal'k for the

Tobol'sk region of Siberia and is based upon local vital statistics for the years 1771–72.[35] (See table 1.13.)

If we reject the Kabuzan rate as too low and assume the 1.2 percent increase as being uniform for the entire period, we can attribute the increases between the periods to the migration shown in table 1.14.

The calculation in table 1.14 gives us roughly 1.1 million male migrants from the "old territories" to the areas of colonization for the period encompassed by the censuses of the eighteenth century. Even if we were to assume that the above figure was overestimated by 25 percent and that the percentage of women involved in migration was only 85 percent of the male population, we would still end up with 1.5 million total migrants. In view of the magnitude of this figure, the data discussed below on the extent of "peasant flight" become intelligible. Other social processes during the eighteenth century are dwarfed in comparison with this massive redistribution of population in Russia.

These factors not only counteracted adverse conditions, thus assuring a higher population growth rate, but brought about a major shift in the locational distribution of the population of Russia during the eighteenth century. In fact, it is legitimate to contend that the eastward migration of the Russian population during this period approximated in its magnitude and characteristics the contemporary migration to the American colonies.

Although the migration of the Russian population eastward and southward did not occur only in the eighteenth century, but started at least in the fifteenth century and indeed continues even now, it was greatly intensified during the eighteenth century and began to affect many aspects of Russian economic, social, and political life.

Within the framework of this study, however, only a limited number of aspects of this problem can be considered. For our purpose, it is sufficient to investigate briefly the nature of the private migration, a process to some extent involving free decisions of migrants to settle in a new location, and to distinguish between agricultural migration and industrial migration. The other aspect of the problem to be considered is government-induced migration, which was important during most periods of Russian history and which resulted from a remarkably consistent set of policies.

Governmental policies during the eighteenth century can be understood only as a blend of traditional political goals and the mercantilist (or pseudophysiocratic, during the reign of Catherine II) political and economic philosophy to which the supreme decision-makers subscribed. Population growth was considered by the mercantilists not only as a means of strengthening the tax base of the state, and thus increasing the state revenue in absolute terms, but also, and primarily, as a source of military (and therefore political) power vis-à-vis the state's foreign adversaries.

The traditional element of Russian policies with which the mercantilist ideas of Peter the Great and his successors so harmoniously blended was the gradual expansion of the Muscovite state (later, the Russian Empire), at the expense of its weaker neighbors. Whether the process was labeled "the ingathering of the Russian lands," "dominance within the Slavic sphere," or plain "Great Russian imperialism" is immaterial for our analysis.[36] What is of interest is the mechanics of this process, which involved not only the use of military force but a concerted effort on the part of Russian society, directed by the government, to incorporate, colonize, and thus integrate the acquired lands into the body politic and the economy of the country. Thus the eastward and southward expansion of the Russian state depended not only upon the strength of Russian armies in military contests with their opponents, but to a very real extent upon the ability to direct and shift at least a part of the population increment to those new areas. The larger the population increment in traditionally Russian areas, the greater was the possibility of generating the stream of migrants necessary to colonize the new lands, to dominate them ethnically, economically, and culturally, thus assuring political stability and the irreversibility of the political expansion.

With the exception of the Russian expansion toward the West, which involved the relatively densely settled areas of Belorussia, right-bank Ukraine, and some parts of the Baltic regions, the main expansionary thrust was toward the sparsely populated areas of the east and south. It was a thrust from the forest area toward the steppes and toward areas with a low-density, nonagricultural native (*autochthon*) population.

The means employed by the government during the eighteenth century to induce population growth and encourage colonization into areas with a relatively high land-labor ratio were the following:

1. Construction of "fortified lines" and military border settlements which protected the civilian settlers from enemy attacks.

2. Inducement of agricultural settlement in the border areas by policies of land distribution to serfowners, tax exemptions, and subsidies to state-owned peasants.

3. Inviting and encouraging immigration from abroad of selected groups.

4. Forced repatriation of former Russian nationals from abroad.

5. Forced transfer of state-owned or penal labor.

6. Incentives for the forced transfer of dependent individuals to areas of high-colonization priority.

7. Forced transfer of women (criminals) into areas where there was a sexual disequilibrium.

The utilization of foreigners in the colonization and population of Russian lands requires some historical explanation. Three elements must be considered: 1. the traditional governmental attitude and policies with respect to the colonization of new lands; 2. the territorial expansion of Russia during the eighteenth century and the need for a change of attitudes toward foreigners; 3. the influence of prevailing theories of population.

With respect to the first element, it could be said that the traditional pattern of colonization of new lands was to build a fortified line (preferably a continuous one) on the border and to man the line with personnel obligated to render military service. Simultaneously, the land behind the lines was populated either with volunteers or those forcibly resettled. Thus, during the sixteenth and seventeenth centuries there was an effort to "populate the defense lines" on both the southern and southeastern frontiers.[37] Agricultural settlements were obviously more permanently successful in providing the regions with a stable population than were military settlements.

In the effort to deal with the various non-Russian ethnic groups, mass resettlements of population into other regions were often used both to break old ties of solidarity and to further the process of Russification. In carrying out its policies of resettlement and the colonization of sparsely populated regions, the Russian government was not adverse to the practice of including non-Russian residents (Swedes, Finns, Balts, Lithuanians, Poles), but tried to relocate them away from the areas bordering on their native countries. Nevertheless, serious reservations existed with regard to foreigners, thanks to the isolationist attitudes of the Russian rulers vis-à-vis Europe. These reservations were expressed by making entrance into Russia difficult (except for the places designated for visiting by foreigners, such as Pskov, Moscow, Arkhangel'sk, and a few other cities), the rarity of Russian merchants trading abroad, and the virtual ban on leaving Russia after once settling there. Consequently colonization by foreigners required an irreversible decision on their part: during the sixteenth and seventeenth centuries, there was almost no possibility of changing one's mind about staying in or leaving Muscovy.[38]

Colonization was also difficult for foreigners because religious freedom was granted only to merchants and foreign specialists, to individuals whose services were in high demand. It was denied to other categories of foreigners, and, given the spirit of the times, this was deterrent to mass migration. In addition, the growth of serf obligations in Russia proper, coupled with a decline in religious tolerance, kept the authorities busy trying to prevent the flight of serfs and religious dissenters abroad. In summation, Russia's historical attitudes toward the importation of foreign colonists did little to encourage mass migration.

The eighteenth century, however, witnessed the entrance of Russia into European politics on a major scale and its direct participation in the shaping of international relations. The decline of Poland as an effective buffer between Western Europe and Russia forced the latter to shape its policies with regard to the other European powers. Two aspects of the new reality had to be faced. One was the fact of Russian territorial expansion at the expense of its neighbors, Sweden, the Ottoman Empire, and Poland, which provided the Russian Empire with some sparsely settled lands and the perceived obligation to populate them. The second aspect was the realization that Russian military power depended to a very large extent upon the size of its armed forces rather than upon its own military technology. Thus it was dependent on its population size rather than on its level of economic and technical development, areas in which the Russian government acknowledged its weakness

relative to the other European powers. One of the solutions appropriate for long-term Russian policy, therefore, was to maintain its relative advantage with respect to the size of the nation's population. Since large tracts of fertile steppe land were available, the idea of inviting or recruiting foreign colonists was no longer rejected.

The realization of the relationship between population size and military-political potential marked Russian statesmanship in the eighteenth and early nineteenth centuries and blended very well with the traditional views of the Western mercantilists. The emphasis on population, rather than on the balance of payments, "beggar my neighbor" policies, and the like, offended neither the physiocrats nor the ascending school of classical political economy. Indeed, there was a rich literature to draw on, going back to the school of "Political Arithmetic" and succeeding economic thinkers and prestigious and influential political tract writers as far back as Sonnenfels. Moreover, Prussia's long-term policies during the seventeenth and eighteenth centuries were a splendid example of what a consistent policy of colonization could accomplish in the process of state-building and military and economic development.[39] It was clear that foreign policy considerations, as well as considerations of internal policies to augment both government revenue and national income, dictated the need for a program of colonization and settlement.

This element of the solution to Russia's population problems had already been reached during the reign of Elizabeth. prior to the outbreak of the Seven Years' War. It resulted in the recruitment of a number of colonists from among the Balkan Slavs resettled in the southern steppes at the border with the Crimean Khanate, which was appropriately named New Serbia. These military border settlements demanded military service in the defense of the border and the organization of two regiments staffed and led by local leadership. In this respect the status of these colonists was similar to that of the free cossacks and the *odnodvortsy* prior to their descent to peasant status.

Elizabeth's order to compile a land cadastre to clarify the land titles of private and government-held land can be seen as a stimulus for colonization or settlement in underdeveloped areas. Such land conceivably could be appropriated by private landowners, who could obtain legal land titles and thus transfer peasants there without risk of losing legal title to their labor force.

It was, however, bureaucratic inertia plus the outbreak of the Seven Years' War in 1756, with its great financial burden and absorption of substantial human and economic resources, that prevented the large-scale projects from getting off the ground. A few years later, however, early in the reign of Catherine II the initiative to expand the empire's population was taken up by the empress herself.[40] Convinced that governmental policies, or inactivity, was responsible for the lack of population growth, Catherine felt the need for a coherent policy with respect to foreign immigration.[41] A high-level administrative apparatus was set up to deal with the practical problems of recruiting settlers, and a colonization and settlement policy was established.[42] The administrative authority was headed by Count Grigorii Orlov, then the favorite of the empress, and both the College of Foreign Affairs and the College of Fiscal Affairs were instructed to lend their support and cooperation to the new chancellery that he headed. The setting up of the Chancellery for the Guardianship of Foreigners was followed by the publication of a manifesto that spelled out the general conditions under which the recruitment of settlers would take place.[43]

The tsarina's manifesto guaranteed foreigners the freedom to cross the borders into Russia upon an announcement of intent to settle and an expression of preference for a place of settlement. Prospective settlers without means to pay for their own transportation to the Russian border were to have transportation arranged and paid for by Russian diplomatic representatives abroad. Upon arrival on Russian soil, settlers were expected to announce their choice of employment, either in trade, crafts, or farming. After receiving an appropriate assignment, settlers were to take an oath of allegiance according to the rituals of their religion and receive free transportation and maintenance until reaching their destination. Freedom of religious worship and construction of churches (but not monasteries) was guaranteed, but, in deference to the sentiments of Orthodox believers, proselytizing was prohibited.[44]

The settlers were entitled to receive sufficient land for farming or for setting up industrial enterprises, as well as funds with which to set themselves up in their respective trades. Prospective industrial entrepreneurs were granted the right to export their products free of tolls for ten years, as well as to obtain, at their own expense, serfs to work in their plants. Farmers were entitled to housing, livestock, implements, and seed purchased with the help of interest-free loans, repayable after ten years in three yearly installments.

Immunity from taxes was granted to prospective settlers in the northwestern border regions and in the capitals, St. Petersburg and Moscow, for five years; in provincial cities for ten years; and in the agricultural colonies for thirty years. After the announced periods, settlers were to pay taxes equal to those paid by Russian citizens of similar status. They were exempted forever, however, from military and civil service (other than local corvee obligations).[45]

Apart from the above, a handful of additional privileges appeared to be especially attractive to some categories of prospective immigrants. One was the provision that settlers in the agricultural colonies had the right to set up an internal local autonomy according to their own customs, a privilege clearly designed to attract certain groups of religious dissenters. Another provision guaranteed duty-free import of settlers' property, plus duty-free import of commodities for sale up to a value of 300 rubles per household. This provision had an appeal to more affluent prospective settlers, who could profit from the importation of a part of their capital. But the novel and most significant break with earlier conditions of immigration into Russia was the provision of the right to return abroad, at the settlers' own expense, upon the payment of a tax on income earned in Russia. The tax rate was set at 20 percent for settlers who had spent up to five years in the country and 10 percent for those who had resided in Russia over five years. To a large extent, the generosity of the Russian government's terms for prospective immigrants and colonists reflected the competition for settlers then occurring among the various governments of Europe. The Russian government, mindful of its earlier bad reputation, had to be at least as generous in its promises as other governments.

The organization of colonist recruitment followed the models and examples of similar attempts by other countries in the eighteenth century. The drive focused on German territories, which provided colonists for Russia's three "competitors" in attracting immigrants, England, Prussia, and the Imperial Government that was recruiting colonists for Hungary. France and Spain had laws prohibiting the outmigration of their subjects, except to their own colonies. Recruitment usually combined governmental and private initiative. This was the case in the Russian drive. The government acted through appointed agents (commissars) to entice prospective candidates to volunteer for colonization. The commissars arranged for their travel and assisted them in the settlements. Private entrepreneurs acted as agents of the government. They were paid under contract for each household recruited. Such entrepreneurs were not notably scrupulous in their recruitment methods, and did not enjoy the highest reputation in Europe.[46] The future colonists recruited by such private entrepreneurs included a substantial contingent of urban plebeians who often bordered on the criminal, but, nevertheless, the majority of prospective colonists were impoverished peasants and rural laborers familiar with agricultural work who were seeking opportunities to obtain farms in distant lands.

It is doubtful whether anyone, either contemporary government official or more recent historian, has

Table 1.14   Assumed Migration Figures between Census Periods at a 1.2% Natural Rate of Population Growth

Years	Migration
1719–44	187,298
1744–62	306,249
1762–82	388,200
1782–95	207,394
Total 1719–95	1,089,141

Table 1.15   Population in the Territories Acquired by Russia, 1773–95

First partition of Poland, 1773	1,226,966
Acquired from Turkey, 1774 and 1789	171,610
Acquired from Turkey, 1791	42,708
Second partition of Poland, 1793	3,745,663
Third partition of Poland, 1795	1,407,402
Total	6,594,349

succeeded in providing exact figures for the size of the voluntary immigration into Russia during the second half of the eighteenth century. Be that as it may, the estimates provided in the work by Pisarevskii give some basis for a comparison of the results of the successive efforts to attract foreign settlers.[47] As might be expected, the data are more exhaustive for the farm settlements than for the scattered immigrants in the cities and towns. Also, as one would expect, the initial effort of the 1760s was the most successful in attracting immigrants. The first partition of Poland in 1773, the conquest of parts of the Black Sea coast, the subsequent incorporation of the Crimea, and the later partitions of Poland took the edge off the population problem. This can be seen in the approximate population estimates of the new territorial acquisitions shown in table 1.15.

In comparison with the population of the acquired territories, the increment resulting from the colonization effort would have been dwarfed. There were, however, two reasons why the policy of trying to attract foreign settlers was continued. First, the population that was acquired in the occupied territories had little or no mobility. Serfdom limited mobility, and thus the new territories, where much of the populace was enserfed, could contribute little to the settlement of the sparsely populated south of Russia (the provinces of Novorossiia and North Caucasus), a project high on the agenda of the Russian authorities. Thus any source of settlers who could be induced to come to settle in the south had to be tapped. The second reason, primarily a political one, involved Russia's Balkan and Mediterranean policies in support of the Slavic and Greek struggle against the Ottoman Empire. In order to live up to its demands made on the Ottomans and its image as the protector of the Greek Orthodox and Slavs, Russia's colonization officials became involved in schemes to save some Greeks from Minorca (where they were oppressed by the Spaniards), Montenegrins (oppressed by the Ottomans), Serbs (discriminated against by the Austrians), and others.

It is fortunate that we have a record of the first period of intensive government recruitment in 1763–66, a comprehensive report submitted by Count Grigorii Orlov to his empress. It included information on the agricultural settlements in the Volga region, primarily within a radius of roughly 100 miles from Saratov, where immigrants recruited directly by governmental officers and by contract-recruiters were being resettled. Table 1.16 clearly shows the results of the activities by major recruiters as well as by state officials.

The available evidence points to the settlement of smaller groups of foreign immigrants in a few other regions as well. For example, 202 families were settled in the St. Petersburg district, 1,742 persons in the Chernigov district, 196 persons in Serepta—all areas which were not designated for mass colonization, but in which government-owned land was available for settlement by smaller groups.[48]

The decade following the first recruitment drive witnessed only a trickle of immigration, most of which appears, retrospectively, as the immigration of households that were recruited earlier but were unable to leave on time. Thus for the entire 1762–72 period, the number of immigrants reported from Western Europe was only 128 families consisting of 574 persons. They were followed by 30 families in 1773.[49] The subsequent years were marked by the massive peasant rebellion of Pugachëv and foreign policy complications, years not auspicious for renewing the recruitment and settlement drive. However, in 1778–79 a "rescue operation" of Christian merchants in the Crimea provided an opportunity to gain foreign settlers for southern Russia. Obviously the national composition of this group of settlers differed radically from those drawn from Western Europe. The data in table 1.17 provide information about the sex distribution, nationality, and broad employment categories of this special group of immigrants. This group was resettled not far from the Crimea, in the Azov province of southern Russia. The large number of nonagricultural settlers among them was directed to the cities of Rostov on the Don, Mariupol, and other urban settlements in the region, where they were set up in crafts and in trade.

The 1780s witnessed a new drive to attract colonists, energized by the governor-general of southern Russia, Prince Potëmkin. For Potëmkin, the settlement of southern Russia was not only a national goal, a political necessity, but a matter of personal pride. In order to accomplish his objective, he used a wide

Table 1.16   Data on Settlement of Foreign Colonists in the Saratov Region by Major Recruitment Agents, 1769

	de Beauregard	le Roy and Pictet	de Boffe	Government	Total
Total number of households	1,523	1,530	434	2,946	6,433
Households capable of farming	1,357	1,347	403	2,747	5,854
Households incapable of farming	166	183	31	199	579
Males in the population	2,820	2,792	863	5,670	12,145
Females in the population	2,470	2,547	723	5,224	10,964
Total population	5,290	5,339	1,586	10,894	23,109
Horses	3,139	3,179	877	6,647	13,842
Oxen	22	153	159	370	704
Cows and calves	1,588	2,427	927	6,610	11,552
Sheep	40	78	58	2,093	2,269
Pigs	65	55	83	816	1,019
Planted (chetvert')	3,738	3,803	820	6,264	14,626
Harvested last year (chetvert')	2,792	4,533	4,489	34,691	46,506
Homes built	901	1,204	269	2,186	4,560
Grain-storage buildings built	390	417	95	1,184	2,086
Stables built	473	628	85	1,458	2,644

Source: Report by Grigorii Orlov, President of the Chancellery, St. Petersburg, February 14, 1769. Reproduced in Pisarevskii, *Iz istorii innostrannoi kolonizatsii.*

variety of means: lobbying with the central state authorities to support his schemes, employing recruiting agents abroad as well as in Russia proper, and, last but not least, trying to persuade the empress of the value and success of his enterprise.[50]

It was during this period (1785) that Catherine published a manifesto inviting colonists to the northern Caucasus (Stavropol province), and Potëmkin invited German immigrants to settle in southern Russia (Ekaterinoslav and Tavria provinces). Potëmkin's agent Trappe recruited 910 volunteers (510 males and 400 females) in Danzig. Of them, 755 (404 males and 351 females) settled as colonists on farms and received ten-year tax exemptions.[51]

Another, even more successful, case of attracting foreign colonists to southern Russia was the movement of Mennonites from Danzig. Settled there for hundreds of years, the Mennonites farmed in the delta of the Vistula River. Known to the local Polish-Kashubian population as the "holiendry," or Dutchmen, they were successful farmers who felt oppressed by the rule of Prussia, which had occupied this territory at the time of the partitions of Poland. The Prussian policy most threatening to their religious beliefs was the requirement of military service, and so they were receptive to Russian promises of land and religious freedom, which, in their case, involved exemption from military service. After they had sent out scouts to the region assigned to them and bargained with the Russian authorities, 1,333 persons (most of them were Mennonites; 90 Lutheran families also joined in the venture) moved in 1788 from the vicinity of Danzig to the banks of the Dnepr River in southern Russia—in spite of Prussian objections and harassment. The land grants given them were substantial. Although they were unable to use

their land to the maximum extent because of a shortage of hired labor, their freedom and relative prosperity became attractive to other foreign Mennonite groups that joined them during the years 1793–96.

The settlement of southern Russia was not exclusively a success story. Potëmkin was not very discriminating in his recruitment drive, either inside Russia or abroad. His attempt to move Swedish peasants from the island of Dago (Oesel) to Berislavl' on the Dnepr River (in Kherson province) had a less than favorable outcome. The casualties during the journey were heavy (86 out of 968 persons), and, although the land grants were lavish (60 desiatinas of land per family of four), the scarcity of water in the region created major difficulties for farming operations.[52]

The most conspicuous failure in the colonization drive was experienced in the attempts to bring groups of Greeks, Corsicans, and Italians from Minorca and some Italian cities. The recruitment of an urban, plebeian element, in spite of the best intentions of the Russian recruitment representative, Count Mocenigo, resulted in a mutiny on one of the ships carrying future colonists (the "Borisphene incident"), and in the colonists' abandonment of the land. With few exceptions, they moved into the towns, where they were employed either as artisans or (in the case of the unskilled) as servants. Although this particular group augmented the population count, it failed to satisfy the effort of the Russian authorities to put more workers on the land.

It would be inaccurate and exaggerated to consider the population policy of the Catherinian period as one of high priority. It must be viewed both within the political context and in terms of the prevailing ideologies of eighteenth-century Russia. For example, although about 31,000 Christians from the Crimean Khanate were resettled in Azov province after the treaty of Küchük-Kainarca (1774), the exile of a much larger number of Crimean Tatars to the Ottoman Empire was "encouraged" following the official annexation of the Crimea. Thus, political, if not strictly religious, considerations prevailed over a policy of population augmentation.[53] In general, however, it would be correct to assume that, for the second half of the eighteenth century, in approaching the population problem, the government gave priority to economic and political considerations rather than to ideological-religious ones. For example, in the policy toward Jews and Old Believers, we see a notable reversal from previous approaches. Jews had been prohibited from settling in Muscovy since the time of Ivan the Terrible. The efforts by the Amsterdam Jewish community to pressure both Peter the Great and Elizabeth to abolish this prohibition were singularly unsuccessful. An intervention on behalf of Minorca Jews to accept them as colonists under the general scheme of settlement of foreigners was also declined. However, when faced with the presence of a large Jewish population in the Polish territories annexed in 1772, Catherine decided not to exile them, but rather to leave them in their own homes.

Another about-face was noticeable with respect to the Old Believers from Poland whose spectacular, forced repatriation had been carried out twice during the first half of the eighteenth century. In the latter part of the century, however, there was a considerable relaxation of official discriminatory activity. The numerous clashes between the Mining College and the Tobol'sk church hierarchy over the Old Believers in the Urals and Western Siberia region reflect the dichotomy of economic interests and the traditional attitudes of the Orthodox church. Although the church usually prevailed during the reign of Elizabeth, under Catherine the Great it was excluded from policy-making. The government, recognizing the economic value of the Old Believers, tried not to provoke this group into the mass self-immolation with which they reacted to discriminatory activities.[54]

Thus it is clear that the immigration policy of the Russian government during the second half of the eighteenth century, at least, was a selective one which served the ends of Russian foreign policy and endeavored to add to the empire people who either could improve Russia's agricultural technology or could become assimilated into its cultural and religious community. Although limited in numbers, the immigration of foreigners constituted a net addition both to the broad stream of government-induced migration to newly opened areas of settlement and to the population of the empire.

Legal Status

The Rural Population

The population data for eighteenth-century Russia that are available can give us insights into the legal status of the various groups.

During the eighteenth century Russia was a hierarchically stratified society in which various groups of the population were legally distinguishable and hierarchically organized, and in which the transfer from one estate to another was regulated by law and legal procedures. At the top of the population pyramid were the aristocracy and gentry, then the clergy, the free men of various orders (raznochintsy) who constituted a part of the bureaucracy, the merchants and burghers, and, at the bottom of the pyramid, the serfs. The Petrine table of ranks provided an avenue for social advancement through government service, by which, at least theoretically, merit and seniority could lead a person into the ranks of the nobility. Although one must be very cautious in translating the language of decrees into social realities, such possibilities for advancement existed, and consequently the number of newcomers into the nobility during the eighteenth century was probably higher than the traditional view would allow for. Nevertheless the nobility guarded its monopoly of power and restricted the entrance into its privileged status by trying its best to keep the number of new entrants as limited as possible. Of course, a serious problem was created for the Russian nobility with the incorporation of the Polish provinces with their more numerous gentry and with the legal introduction of serfdom in the Ukraine, which implied gentry status for the owners of the serfs. As a result, during the latter part of the century, the gentry estate grew over and beyond the natural increase of the Russian nobility.

Apart from the nobility, the nontaxable population included clergymen and non-noble government officials as well as certain non-Russian inhabitants who were tax-exempt because they performed certain specialized services. One of the characteristics of this group was its horizontal mobility, which was due to two factors. First, it was due to the unwillingness on the part of the government to have the clergy expand, a policy which, short of enserfing some of the offspring of the lower clergy, forced its members to seek employment within the bureaucracy.[55] Second, the expansion of the government apparatus, especially during the second half of the century, provided opportunities for free people with some education to enter the ranks of the bureaucracy.

The urban estates were made up of free people with heavy obligations toward the state, taxpayers mostly employed in crafts, trade, and services. They included a whole array of social groups, from un-

Table 1.17   Christian Immigrants from the Crimea (1778–79)

Nationality	Number	Agricultural	Nonagricultural	Males	Females
Greeks	18,400	14,000	4,400		
Armenians	12,606	300	12,303		
Georgians	287				
Walachians	161				
Total	31,454			16,199	15,255

skilled laborers to merchant princes. These estates constituted a heterogeneous group as far as incomes and employment were concerned and grew in membership, particularly during the second half of the century. The acquisition of new but more urbanized territories coupled with an administrative reform (in 1785) that bestowed (or imposed?) urban status upon a relatively large number of administrative centers also contributed in the legal sense to the growth of the urban estates, the merchants and burghers, who were not distinguished by a means test and different rates of taxation.

The serfs were divided into broad legal categories: (1) court serfs, belonging to the court estates, including the estates of the monarch; (2) state serfs, belonging to the state and under the jurisdiction of the state bureaucracy; (3) church serfs, who belonged to bishoprics, cathedrals, and monasteries until 1764, and after the secularization of the church estates came within the jurisdiction of the state under the name of "ekonomicheskie" (during the nineteenth century this group merged with the group known as state-owned peasants); (4) private serfs, belonging to private individuals and under their jurisdiction, who constituted a category that could be referred to either as *instrumentum vocale* or as *baptized property*, usually referred to by their owners in eighteenth-century parlance as "souls" (*dushi*).

Within the serf category of the population, apart from changes in designation and status (secularization of church estates and conversion of their serfs into state serfs), and in spite of the vast and massive distribution of state serfs to private owners, the natural increase of the state-owned serfs exceeded the rate of increase of the private-serf population. Indirect evidence about land-labor ratios and opportunities for upward social mobility suggests the existence of a slight income differential that may have contributed to a higher growth rate of the state serf population.

The short review of the existing categories of the population by legal status has to be supplemented with an explanation of the patterns of mobility, which was more extensive within these legal groups than between or among them. For example, a peasant could be sold or transferred from a private to a government estate or vice versa much more easily

than he could "escape" into another category. An urban dweller could rise from the status of craftsman to that of a merchant, or even a *gost'* (a member of the privileged corporation of the richest merchants), more easily than he could become part of the nobility. It was not impossible for a civil servant, however, to attain a patent of nobility as a result of seniority and merit. It is important to keep these distinctions in mind in looking at the tables in this part of the chapter. Changes in the size of the various groups result both from natural population increases and from voluntary or forced mobility. The reader must keep in mind both the way in which populated court and state estates were distributed among private individuals, a process engaged in by every eighteenth-century ruler from Peter to Paul, and the occasional confiscations of landed estates from members of the aristocracy, both important in explaining, for example, the fluctuations in the number of court peasants.

The data that reflect changes in population on a fixed territory are most significant. They reveal apparent divergent tendencies: the decreasing proportion of private peasants in the total peasant population of the "old Russian territories," and the increasing proportion of private peasants on the boundaries of the empire.

This dichotomy with respect to the proportion of the private-serf population in relation to the total number of serfs in Russia is, in part at least, responsible for a major debate among Russian economic historians. What one sees in data such as those in table 1.18 depends on one's vantage point. Using the data of the Russian territory proper, many historians have assumed that the declining share of the private-serf population is a sufficient indicator of what has been variously described as the immiseration of the private serfs, the intensification of the burden of exploitation, or the beginning of the decline of serfdom as a socioeconomic system and its increasing failure to satisfy the needs of both the serf-owners and the serfs. Here conclusions were based upon a unilinear relationship between income and population growth.

These historians have obviously excluded exogenous demographic effects which are not related to income and other more complex factors that also have

Table 1.18   Male Population Distribution by Legal Status

A. *In the Territory of Russia*

	PEASANTS					Urban	Nontaxable
Reviziia	Court	State	Church	Private	Total	Dwellers	Population
1st (1719)	509,484	1,700,430	813,741	3,528,722	6,552,377	295,799	444,241
2d (1744)	429,283	2,117,149	898,471	4,348,873	7,793,776	355,240	451,938
3d (1762)	524,075	2,780,868	1,061,639	5,611,531	9,978,113	321,582	293,851
4th (1782)	634,993	3,932,878	1,310,276	6,714,331	12,592,478	421,502	672,711
5th (1795)	520,840	4,547,873	1,465,469	9,787,802	16,321,984	771,317	1,075,273

B. *In the Territory of the First Reviziia*

	PEASANTS					Urban	Nontaxable
Reviziia	Court	State	Church	Private	Total	Estates	Population
1st (1719)	509,484	1,227,965	791,798	3,193,085	5,722,332	230,910	391,859
2d (1744)	429,283	1,588,559	898,471	3,781,097	6,697,410	285,475	416,661
3d (1762)	493,307	2,029,585	1,026,930	4,401,599	7,951,421	258,532	226,826
4th (1782)	601,454	2,733,447	1,187,654	5,104,991	9,627,546	309,055	533,166
5th (1795)	494,262	2,953,039	1,304,794	5,617,256	10,369,351	398,122	585,302

Source: Kabuzan, *Izmeneniia*, pp. 59–118.

Note: Armed forces are excluded. For 1st–3d revizii, figures in (A) are exclusive of the Baltic provinces. For the 3d reviziia, data on urban estates and nontaxable population are computed differently than for other revizii.

an impact upon population growth. I would like to argue that, for a population engaged in rural crafts and services, in households increasingly removed from agriculture, the economic benefits of children are probably less than in an agricultural household. And although one would have to prove that by the end of the eighteenth century families had the knowledge and the will to limit their family size, such a possibility is not entirely out of the question. But such observations are actually superfluous since, if we take as our point of departure the data pertaining to the territory of the whole empire, there is an obvious shift in the heavy concentration of private serfdom from the old center to the newly acquired or relatively recently settled peripheries.

If we consider the growth deceleration of the serf population in the central industrial region not as a result but as a cause, we must accept the possibility that per capita income was not decreasing but perhaps remained stable or even rose in the last decades of the century. That the share of nonagricultural services in the per capita income of those regions was increasing has been demonstrated by many scholars, and seems to contradict the notion of declining overall per capita incomes. Thus the hypothesis of a declining curve (*potukhaiushchaia krivaia*) of serfdom has to be reexamined with better evidence than that used by the previous generation of Russian economic historians.

While the censuses of the taxpaying male population (*revizii*) provide the basic data for the size and legal composition of the serf population, we do not

have comparable data for the other rural group—the nobility.[56]

The data available in the secondary sources, such as that in table 1.19, provide only a very general picture of the size of the nobility and its growth during the eighteenth century.

One of the primary characteristics of this population group was its small size relative to the size of the serf population. Even by comparison with the group of the privately-owned serfs, the size of this legal stratum was relatively small, making for a large average size of serf-ownership.[57] Territorially, the population of the nobility was concentrated in the western and central areas of the Russian Empire with negligible residence in the North of Russia and in Siberia, regions which were populated by state-owned peasants. The growth rate of the noble population was relatively modest, especially if one assumes that those economic constraints upon population growth which might have affected the growth rate of the serfs were largely absent for the nobility. The spectacular growth of the nobility during the second half of the eighteenth century was chiefly due to the territorial expansion of the Russian state. The incorporation of the right-bank Ukraine, Belorussia, and Lithuania as a result of the partitions of Poland augmented the ranks of the nobility by the absorption of the numerous Polish nobility and Ukrainian officer-corps, ennobled with the introduction of serfdom into the Ukraine. Thus, the numerical growth of the nobility increased the density of the nobility in the western regions of the country and added elements which were ethnically and culturally foreign to the Russian state but shared with the older Russian nobility an interest in maintaining their common legal and economic privileges.

The Urban Population

The fact that we have no exact data for the urban population during the eighteenth century complicates the task of estimating the population of the Russian cities. Heinrich Storch has reported for the end of the century an urban population of 2,273,000.[58] Accepting his figure, which was presumably based upon the early returns of the fifth *reviziia* (population count) of 1795, or the figure of 2.4 million, one can speculate about the composition of the urban population on basis of available data from the fifth and sixth (1811) *revizii*. We also have the Kabuzan estimate of the 1795 *reviziia* for the urban estates, 771,317 male souls. Doubling this would give us over 1.5 million accounted for out of the estimate of approximately 2.3 million.[59]

There is some basis for assuming that approximately one-third of the armed forces was stationed in the cities.[60] For the end of the century, when the armed forces averaged about 480,000 men, this would amount to about 160,000. About 100,000 members of the nobility resided full-time or part-time in the cities, and they, plus the clergy and rich merchants, had with them at least 100,000 domestics.[61] A conservative estimate for the urban clergy would be about 40,000, and up to 100,000 for the nontaxpaying civil officials and clerks.[62] This raises our estimate for the urban population to 1.9 million. To assume the urban presence of about 80,000 workers in manufactories and 320,000 peasants would appear not out of line with the available circumstantial evidence.[63] The urban peasants were of three categories: some of them received urban rights when villages were converted into urban centers; another group consisted of peasant-serfs who stayed in the cities on the basis of long-term passports and were employed at various jobs (care must be taken to avoid double counting of those working in the manufactories); and the rest were seasonal laborers who repeatedly came to the cities to find employment. This distribution of the urban population is presented in table 1.20.

C. Hermann provided an alternative distribution of the urban population for the first decade of the nineteenth century that differs in some respects from mine. This is shown in table 1.21. Hermann's estimate of the number of the merchant population is about 30,000 less than that provided by the incomplete data of the Soviet historian P. G. Ryndziunskii that pertain to 74 percent of the urban estates for 1800, while the number of burghers is approximately the same.[64] Even in view of the volatility of the officially registered number of merchants,

Table 1.19 Size of Hereditary Male Nobility Population in Russia at Dates of the Revizii

Year	No. of Nobles
1744	37,326
1762	49,777
1783	n.a.
1795[a]	77,199
1795	193,132

Note: Number of nobles is for the territory of the second and third revizii.

[a]Kabuzan, *Narodonaselenie*, p. 154.

Table 1.20 Approximate Social Distribution of the Urban Population in Russia by End of Eighteenth Century

Urban estates	1.5 million	Officials	.10 million
Nobility	.10 million	Domestics	.10 million
Clergy	.04 million	Industrial workers	.08 million
Military	.16 million	Peasants	.32 million
Total			2.40 million

the total of merchants and burghers is only 1,151, compared with Kabuzan's 1,542, unless guild artisans and the like were shifted to the category "others" used by Hermann. The main difference lies in deciphering this category, and in Kabuzan's figure for the urban estates which might have included not only merchants and burghers but also other groups such as the guild artisans.

The distinctions, both legal and social, between the merchant and burgher subgroups in the urban population increased as a result of the fiscal measures of 1775, which levied separate taxes upon them, and also as a result of the "reform of the cities" of 1785. Another factor influential in underscoring the distinction was the inclusion of the Jewish population of the acquired territories into the burgher estate after 1772.

For the eighteenth century, our data on the distribution of burghers and merchants are only fragmentary, even though the fifth *reviziia* of 1795 made the distinction explicit. P. G. Ryndziunskii has provided the most comprehensive data on this problem; beginning in 1800, these data permit the calculation of an approximate distribution of the two groups.[65] Ryndziunskii's data cover 41 gubernii of Russia and a total of 571,024 males, of whom 115,696 (20.26 percent) were classified as merchants belonging to one of the three existing guilds and 453,854 (79.48 percent) were classified as burghers. Inclusion in the two categories depended upon income, employment, and taste for specific services and obligations which each group had to perform for the state or municipalities. One of the interesting features of the distribution between the two groups is geographic. In table 1.22 the percentage of merchants in the total of merchants and burghers is used for illustrative purposes. But even the regional averages, which present a broad

Table 1.21   Distribution of Urban Population by Estates and Social Groups, 1811

Nobility	112.2
Clergy	53.2
Merchants	201.2
Burghers	949.9
Military	176
Service	195.3
Others	1,017.7
Total	2,705.8

Table 1.22   Percent of Merchants among Merchants and Burghers in Population for 1800, by Regions

Region	Merchants (%)
North	15.97
Northwest	32.17
Nonblacksoil	31.04
Blacksoil	33.62
Volga	28.78
Urals	20.91
Baltic	22.07
Ukraine	5.15
Byelorussia	4.03
Siberia	5.77
Average	20.26

Source: Ryndziunskii, *Gorodskoe grazhdanstvo.*

spread, are derived from intraregional data that differ substantially. Perhaps the most striking examples are for the Urals region, where 13.91 percent were merchants in Viatka and 53.21 percent in Orenburg, and in the nonblacksoil region between the two adjacent gubernii of Kostroma (16.16 percent) and Vladimir (46.19 percent).

Table 1.22 also reveals that the average percentage of merchants was reduced because the newly acquired territories had a low percentage of merchants. Excluding the Ukraine and Belorussia, the percentage of merchants increases to 28.32 percent of the total merchants and burghers.

In eighteenth-century Russia the legal classification of "merchant" (*kupets*) did not necessarily mean that an individual was active in commerce. In fact, the majority of merchants, the ones registered in the third guild, were only marginally active in trade. Most of them did not own any trading establishments. Some of them were employed in crafts or in laboring for other merchants. Only the first two merchant guilds represented real traders. Moreover, numerous peasants residing in the cities were actually traders, although they did not belong to any of the merchant guilds. This peculiarity of Russian trade and of the legal groupings has to be kept in mind when comparing the relationship between the shares of merchants to burghers in the "old Russian territories" and the newly acquired ones. The lower percentage of merchants in the total merchant and burgher population in the acquired territories is nei-

ther an indicator of low concentration of commercial capital, nor necessarily, of more advanced development of crafts relative to the Russian regions. It is primarily the heritage of a system that described differently various categories of economic activity, and did this perhaps more correctly in terms of actual employment.

The Nobility

One of the features of the growth of the urban population apart from the territorial expansion of Russia was the growth of the groups outside the traditional "urban estates." The nobility was one of the groups which contributed to the numerical growth of the urban population, especially after they were emancipated from compulsory government service by Peter III in 1762 and began increasingly to take up urban residence. If we exclude the Jews, who were prohibited from residing permanently in the Russian Empire from the time of Ivan the Terrible until 1772, the ranks of the nobility increased in percentage terms more than any other estate or group as a result of territorial expansion. According to the available data, the noble estate was augmented between 1772 and the fourth *reviziia* of 1782 by 24,189 nobles from a part of Belorussia, which raised the number of nobles from 84,066 in the old territories to 108,255 in 1782, an increase of 28.77 percent in a decade.[66]

By 1795 there were already 362,574 nobles, of whom 111.600 were in the old territory (including 4.296 newly acquired in Kurland) and 250,974 from the acquired territories in Poland. This had the effect of raising the percentage of the nobility as a part of the total population drastically, from 0.79 percent in 1782 to 2.22 percent, while in the "old territories" it went only from 0.64 to 0.77 percent.

Such a drastic increase in a population that had, for Russia, a relatively high mobility had a clear effect of augmenting the number of nobles residing in the cities. In addition to their own residence, it also increased the number of domestics who provided service for their lords in the new places of residence.

The growth of the urban population benefited from the increase in the number of people employed in manufactories. Of the two leading industries in which large-scale enterprises developed, iron and textiles, the latter was largely based in urban areas. Moscow, Iaroslavl', and Kazan' were some of the early centers of the linen and woolen industries. The abolition of the licensing system for manufactories under Catherine II provided a boost for entrepreneurship in the textile industry, which used its freedom to move to new geographic areas, to other cities such as Kostroma, Shuia, Kineshma, and many others. Thereby the growth of industrial employment, particularly in industries which primarily used hired labor, augmented the urban population. Consequently, if one is to attempt to estimate the size of the urban population of Russia for an earlier period, the development of employment in the manufactories ought to be of some assistance.

The greatest reservoir of potential urban dwellers in Russia, as everywhere, during this period, was the rural population, the peasant-serfs. Their incessant drive toward the cities, in spite of legal obstacles, in spite of heavy cost, caused by the demand for their employment was the underlying force behind urban growth in the eighteenth century. One has the impression that the larger cities had the greatest attraction for potential and actual migrants. Whether it was due to greater opportunities or to a desire to move further away from the peasants' previous habitats is of no importance. It was also not essential whether those moving realized their dream within one or a few generations; of importance was the fact that a migration from smaller cities to larger ones was taking place and that actual as well as potential urban dwellers were involved in it. This phenomenon warrants a glance at the distribution of Russian cities by size and the identification of the major urban centers in Russia.

At the close of the eighteenth century, Russia possessed only two cities, the capitals of St. Petersburg and Moscow, in the category of population size exceeding 100,000. In fact, the combined population of both capitals was about 400,000 inhabitants, or about one-sixth of the total urban population. There were no cities within the 50,000–100,000 range, while only four cities were within the 30,000–50,000 range. Seven cities fell within the 20,000–30,000 range and there were fourteen in the 10,000–20,000 range. All the others had populations of less than 10,000. Thirty-two of the existing guberniia centers had a population ranging from 4,000 to 17,000. Table 1.23 presents the largest cities in Russia in these categories. Of the twenty-seven largest, three were acquired toward the end of the century (Vilna, Vitebsk, Minsk), five were seaports (St. Petersburg, Astrakhan', Riga, Revel', and Arkhangel'sk), and five were ports on the Volga River. As far as their geographic location is concerned, seven cities were located in the northwestern part of the country, one of the extreme north, two in Siberia, two in the Ukraine, one in the southeast, and thirteen in the interior of Russia. Eight of these major cities were in the blacksoil zones and five in the nonblacksoil zones.

The classification of cities by size fails to reveal much about their functions as centers of commerce, craft, industry, or administration. Therefore it is important to classify the Russian cities into particular

Table 1.23 Size Categories of 27 Russian Cities at Close of Eighteenth Century

Size	Cities
Over 100,000	St. Petersburg, Moscow
30,000–50,000	Vilna, Astrakhan', Kazan', Tula
20,000–30,000	Riga, Saratov, Kiev, Kaluga, Kursk, Orel, Iaroslavl'
10,000–20,000	Revel', Tver', Tambov, Nizhnii-Novgorod, Penza, Tobol'sk, Irkutsk, Smolensk, Simbirsk, Minsk, Arkhangel'sk, Vitebsk, Nezhin, Kostroma

categories. The basic criterion for my proposed classification is the economic characteristics of the city in terms of its dependency upon and interaction with a given hinterland. This participation in an exchange of goods and services determines the chief characteristics of cities. It also influences the size and social composition of the population. If one uses this criterion, the following categories appear to be significant:

(1) The seaports, river ports, and some border cities which specialized in services facilitating trade and the transportation of goods. They were dependent on and interacted mostly with distant markets, although some of them served as an outlet of a regional market also.

(2) The commercial and manufacturing cities which interacted with distant and regional markets.

(3) The commercial cities which interacted with regional and local markets.

(4) The administrative towns; settlements which did not serve primarily as markets and some of which were at best cities *in statu nascendi*.

(5) The capitals, St. Petersburg and Moscow, which combined characteristics of some of the above-mentioned categories.

Although the largest group, both in terms of total numbers and of share in the urban population, was that of cities of the third category, commercial cities which interacted with regional and local markets, some of the cities, notably of the second category, and the capitals represented hybrids in which the commercial element was combined with industrial activity or with high concentrations of administrative activity. In fact, the hybrid nature of some of the cities made their rate of population growth less dependent upon the economy of one particular hinterland than in the case of cities closely tied by commercial relations with their local or regional markets.

My first category embraces Russian cities that were engaged in international commerce, cities whose function was primarily to facilitate the flow of goods between the country and distant markets. These were primarily the port cities or major border points along the land routes leading abroad. They specialized in trade and its ancillary services, not in the production or even the processing of goods. Whatever industry or craft existed in these cities served either the primary specialization or the consumption and service needs of the population employed in trade and shipping.

An interesting feature of these cities toward the end of the eighteenth century is the average size of their populations. A review of eleven port cities (exclusive of St. Petersburg) reveals that their average size was approximately 11,500 inhabitants. Of the eleven ports, only three cities (Astrakhan', Riga, and Revel') exceeded the average, and the rest were below average size. The relative size of the populations of these cities did not reflect the value of trade carried on through the port. What was necessary, apart from capital, was a critical mass of people to engage in transactions, to serve the port facilities, to handle the cargo, but a city's size was not determined by fixed coefficients of the value, or even the tonnage, of freight.

A similar conclusion can be reached by a cursory glance at twelve cities which were fundamentally river ports, most of them along the Volga River route. Their average size was about 9,000 inhabitants, but only three of the twelve (Saratov, Orël, and Nizhnii Novgorod) exceeded the average. The correlation between the size of the city and the volume of freight that originated there was a very weak one. The city's size depended not only upon the sheer volume, but also upon the type of commodity traded and the transactions involved, the nature of the port services, the availability of shipbuilding facilities, the influx of outside labor as a substitute for services rendered by residents.

The cities which served as outlets for foreign trade using land routes also varied in size. The average size of seven selected such cities was 7,600 inhabitants, of which two exceeded the average. Although my choice was not a random one and it did not include all the border cities through which commodity trade was carried on, for this category there is a closer connection between the population size and the value of trade. Thus Irkutsk, representing the China trade through Kiakhta, had a larger population than did Kizliar, representing the Caucasus, or Orenburg and Semipalatinsk, representing the trade with Central Asia and the Kirgiz Steppe.

This incomplete review of the population size of these thirty cities with a total population of approximately 300,000 indicates that their growth did not depend primarily upon their hinterlands, but upon the volume of trade that they were servicing. In the long run their population size depended upon the total activity required to handle the flow of exports and imports. Barring external shocks, such as the interruptions in the China trade or the trade on the

Black Sea, the cities of this category grew gradually during the century at rates less spectacular than those of the volume or value of the goods flow.

The next category of cities was the commercial-industrial, a hybrid because these cities combined two types of activities, the production and the sale of goods. The cities varied in size depending upon their location, the mix of commercial and industrial activities, the branch of industry which they represented, and the time when large-scale industrial production was introduced. Thus the city of Tula was not the same size as Ustiuzhna Zhelezopol'skaia, even through both specialized in ironwares production, because Tula was the major arsenal of Russian small-arms production during the eighteenth century, in addition to the fact that it was the center of a relatively prosperous agricultural guberniia. The same could be noted when comparing the cities of Iaroslavl' and Kineshma, where textiles for the foreign market were produced. But the former in addition was a Volga River port, a guberniia center, and one of the earliest centers of textile manufactories, which were established at the beginning of the century. A third example might be the salt-mining towns of Staraia Rusa and Solikamsk. The latter produced more salt (with the help of serf labor from the surrounding villages), while the populace of Staraia Rusa not only produced salt but also had carried on extensive trade for generations. Thus this category of cities in which commercial, industrial, and mining activities took place did not represent uniformity of size but, once a certain size had been reached, would grow under the impact of demand for industrial goods as well as for their commercial services. Few of these cities were predominantly industrial. Petrozavodsk and Ekaterinburg, at both geographical extremes of the empire, are examples of cities in which industrial interests predominated. Both cases owed their founding to state-owned ironworks and other state enterprises (notably the Ekaterinburg mint, the largest producer of copper coins in the eighteenth century). That the size of such cities was relatively small (less than 5,000 inhabitants) indicates the limited size of industrial enterprises during the eighteenth century.

Commercial cities made up the largest category of Russian cities throughout the century. They possessed strong ties with their hinterlands, carrying on trade both through established permanent stores and warehouses and by means of periodic fairs (iarmarki). The relatively low density of the rural population, the low level of commercial agricultural output, coupled with the limited purchasing power of most agricultural producers and their limited mobility, made the fairs a most important form of trading in eighteenth-century Russia. The bulk of commercial transactions had therefore a typically seasonal pattern, tied to both the agricultural year and to the dates of tax payments by the taxable population. The issue of the overall efficiency of the fair's trade is discussed below in the section on internal trade, and so here I shall only point out that the fairs made the commercial activity of the urban dwellers an activity with clear employment peaks and therefore one that required more manpower than if the same volume of activity were spread more evenly throughout the entire year. This also tied up capital for longer periods, which affected not only the trading population but also the artisans engaged in producing goods to be sold at the fairs. Although the fairs played a crucial role in the economy of most of those cities, one caveat is necessary: the largest and most famous fairs of national or major regional scope, such as the Makar'ev, Irbit, Rostov, Korennaia, and Svenskaia fairs, had very little impact upon the population size of their locations. Of all the cities mentioned, only one, Rostov, had more than 5,000 inhabitants, a size due to factors not necessarily connected with the fair. All the others had populations in the 1,000–2,000 range, which tells us something about the nature of those fairs' locations as convenient points of institutionalized exchange of goods in transit but as insufficient to support employment and incomes during most of the year.

The population size of the commercial cities depended upon the radius of their effective trade with the hinterland, upon the supply of goods by the population of the hinterland and its demand for goods produced by the urban population or imported from other areas. One might add parenthetically that a contributing effect upon the volume of trade of such cities was made by their role as distributors of both salt and alcohol for the rural population, commodities which attracted buyers from the countryside.

The fulfillment of their role as a center of trade with the hinterland would have been impossible for most of the cities without the existence of a class of urban artisans. Regardless of the extent of self-sufficiency that one ascribes to the rural population during this period, to the development of rural crafts, the evidence of purchases of goods produced by urban artisans who specialized in such work for both the rural and urban markets is overwhelming. That most of the work was performed not for specific customers but for the fairs, whether the work was traded directly by the artisan or through a contractor, is also noteworthy. Distinct from the fairs, the number of which was still growing due to population increase and growth of the marketable share of agriculture, there was a discernible expansion in the commercial cities of the number of permanent trading establishments, warehouses, and private dwellings. This ex-

pansion not only kept pace with the growth of population but resulted in the erection of stone and brick buildings in the larger cities. Although wood was the prevailing construction material and all of the cities in this category were predominantly wooden, the increase in stone structures was not only a result of growing affluence of a stratum of urban dwellers but of an increase in the value of urban real estate. No study has been made to determine the value of urban housing in eighteenth-century Russia, although such a study would help greatly to evaluate the resources of the urban sector of the economy, and the role of the commercial cities in particular.[67] This fact underscores how little we actually know about the most widespread and typical category of Russian cities.

The existence of a large number of small administrative centers, having the designation of cities but deprived of actual commercial and industrial activity, is both a reflection of an existing reality and a source of debate among Russian historians who, using this example, argued about the "artificial" nature of early urbanization. Not only the small size, often less than a thousand inhabitants, but also the social composition of these towns or villages designated as cities with their few officials and more agriculturalists, contradicted the shared concept of a city in the economic, social, and cultural sense. That such cities existed was in part due to the inertia of a bureaucratic system or to the uniformity of application of bureaucratic rules. (The inertia consisted in failing to change the designation of a city that declined, the blind uniformity in always designating administrative centers for a certain size of the rural population.) Although the abolition of city status for a particular settlement was not an easy matter from the legal and fiscal point of view, it was probably more inertia than actual difficulty that was at the root of the problem.

From the demographic as well as historical point of view, the capitals of Russia are the most interesting urban centers. Although St. Petersburg through most of the century was *the capital*, nevertheless Moscow maintained its importance not only as the place of coronation of the rulers and the seat of many central government offices, but also as the commercial center of Russia, the largest industrial center, and until the 1780s, the largest city.

The view of Moscow as *the* traditional city of Russia, remindful of large Asiatic cities rather than European ones, is a commonplace in the literature of the West, but one that passes as something meaningful for historians and social scientists. On the other hand, the view that contrasts Moscow with St. Petersburg, with the former being the product of organic, gradual growth and the latter being credited to the genius of Peter the Great, by the will of the state in a modern, planned fashion, is not confined to the West but is strongly embedded in the minds of Russians. This view also explains very little to students of the Russian population.

Important for the eighteenth century is the fact of the rapid growth of the St. Petersburg population. Part of that growth must have replaced urbanization that would have taken place elsewhere, but yet another part must have been a net addition to urbanization thanks to the overall impact of the founding of the new capital city.

Although one of the striking features of both Moscow and St. Petersburg was the size of the city in relation to that of the other Russian cities, this relationship between the capital city and the rest of the urban centers can be found in many more urbanized societies of Western Europe during the same period and in other parts of the world at various points in time. During the nineteenth century Moscow and St. Petersburg were contrasted as the cities of "the merchants" (*kupecheskaia*) and of "the officials" (*chinovnicheskaia*), or in the early twentieth century as the cities of textile production and of metal production; but during the eighteenth century the social composition of both populations was much more similar, as is shown in table 1.24. Both possessed large components of commercially active inhabitants, although Moscow's might have been greater, because of the lower efficiency of the internal trade in which it was the leading center, and St. Petersburg's lesser, because the foreign trade in which it excelled required a lesser commercial population. The stratum of officials and military personnel was larger in St. Petersburg than in Moscow, the working population in large-scale manufactories perhaps somewhat higher in Moscow than in St. Petersburg. The population in the private sector was higher in Moscow, and the influx of peasants was massive in both cities. Although each of the cities had its share of foreigners, perhaps St. Petersburg was a place more amenable to them, not only because of the presence of foreign diplomats, the seat of government, and employment opportunities, but primarily because its society was younger, less settled, and less traditionally segregated.

During the first half of the century Moscow was still the cultural center of Russia, but primacy passed to St. Petersburg in the second half because of the court, the press, the publishing of books, the schools, and the theaters. Western ideas penetrated into St. Petersburg earlier and more easily than into Moscow. The feature typical of St. Petersburg, that of an unusually high percentage of males in the population, was the result of the in-migration of peasants and domestics as well as the presence of the military. The data for Moscow for the first half of the century show a predominance of women in the population

Table 1.24   The Social Composition of Moscow and St. Petersburg Populations

	Moscow		St. Petersburg
	1730s	1788–95	1801
Merchants		11,900	14,310
Burghers	23,707		12,676
Artisans		9,100	10,738
Clergy	5,456	3,600	520
Military	15,348	7,000	39,058
Nobles		8,600	13,171
Raznochintsy[a]	32,475		
Officials	7,233	17,600	35,002
Domestics	35,959	61,300	26,104
Peasants	18,310	53,700	50,454
Foreigners	—	2,200	—
Raskol'niki[b]	304	—	—
Others	—	—	—
Total	138,792	175,000	202,033
Males	65,313	114,000	148,591
Females	73,479	61,000	53,552

Sources: Akademiia nauk SSSR, *Istoriia Moskvy*, 2:307. Data of the synod, pertaining to Russian Orthodox population, Kopanev, *Naselenie Peterburga*, pp. 17, 25.

[a]Civil servants
[b]Old Believers, religious dissidents

(probably the consequence of numerous draft levies of males for the army), but by the end of the century the imbalance between the sexes was similar to that observed in St. Petersburg, no doubt due to an increased number of peasants.

The data for both Moscow and St. Petersburg indicate unmistakably that the growth of the population which took place in both cities can be accounted for primarily by in-migration rather than by the rate of natural increase. The demographic data as well as the data of the changes in the social composition of the population, bear witness, no matter how imperfectly, to vigorous development, of which the processes of migration and urbanization (so much clearer in the case of the capitals than in many other cities) were an integral part. This image, in contrast to the notion of a stagnant, immobile, strictly controlled, regulated, and stratified society that moved only when ordered or forced by its government, is perhaps the leading message that is conveyed by a study of Russian population in general, and of the urban population in particular. The scope for spontaneity, for individual action, was, to be sure, limited in eighteenth-century Russia. Nevertheless, there was movement, and not only in directions prescribed by the state, but often in opposition to and in conflict with the state. The behavior of the urban population provides ample evidence to support the view of social dynamics accompanying economic activity.

The Demographic Profile

In rounding out a demographic profile of eighteenth-century Russia, we must of necessity extrapolate from the data available to us. This section will examine the patterns of births and mortality and the age distribution of the population. I shall use as case studies several aspects of the population question for which more extensive data are available.

Although the data on primary population counts are relatively extensive, we must rely on contemporary materials that can enhance our understanding of such demographic variables as birth and death rates, marriages, and family formation. The available materials do not pretend to be representative, and in fact they are not typical for the total population. Nevertheless, they provide a glimpse into the unknown realm of Russian population.

The most relevant published studies were authored by two members of the St. Petersburg Academy, W. L. Krafft and C. Th. Hermann, both of whom were engaged in what was commonly called "political arithmetic."

Krafft's publication pertains to births, marriages, and deaths in St. Petersburg during the years 1764–96, while Hermann's essays deal with the population changes of the Russian Orthodox faith in 34 bishoprics of Russia.[68] The population data on St. Petersburg, based upon the police records of that city, are clearly not representative of Russia as a whole for at least two reasons: the peculiar sex composition of the population, with two-thirds of it male, and the unusually large share of foreigners in the St. Petersburg population. The official data in table 1.25 are illustrative.

The population estimates for St. Petersburg given in accounts by contemporaries are grossly inaccurate. Some population counts took place in the summer, when seasonal labor was present and when many merchants and traders were away on business. Little actually was known about the total population of St. Petersburg. An estimate by the bishopric of St. Petersburg of the population (presumably Russian Orthodox) prior to the establishment of the bishopric in 1742 included 52,319 inhabitants. Of these, 33,494 were males and 18,825 were females.[69] The estimate presumably pertains to the 1730s.

A population count of 1750 reported a total of 74,283 adult residents, including 4,046 foreigners.

Table 1.25   Population Composition of St Petersburg

Year	Males	Females	Total	Foreigners
1784	126,827	65,619	192,446	27,299
1789	148,520	69,428	217,948	31,587
1792	143,935	67,700	211,635	32,559

Table 1.26   St. Petersburg Population, 1789

	Males	Females	Total
Military (army and guards)	30,635	5,792	36,427
Navy	10,160	3,717	13,877
Schools	3,265	2,056	5,321
Imperial stables	2,096	910	3,006
Civil servants, clergymen, burghers, peasants, servants	102,312	54,956	157,268
Others	52	1,997	2,049
Total registered	148,520	69,428	217,948

Source: Georgi, *Versuch*, pp. 135–37.

This figure was considered unreliable, and led Krafft to attempt to estimate the population size of St. Petersburg for the 1760s and 1770s.[70] Much more credence, however, apparently was given to the population counts of the 1780s. The 1784 (fourth) population *reviziia* reported 192,446 residents of both sexes of whom 126,827 were males and 65,619 were females.

The police report of 1789 gives the interesting distribution by various groups shown in table 1.26.

Krafft's data for St. Petersburg presented in table 1.27 strongly imply that the population growth of the city was predominantly a result of in-migration, rather than of a net increase in the number of native inhabitants.

The rate of child mortality reported in the St. Petersburg data also differs from the evidence presented for the population at large. The number of male children surviving the ages 0–5 in St. Petersburg was given as 756 per 1,000 for the years 1781–85 and 762 for 1791–96, whereas the figure given by Hermann for Russian Orthodox male children for all Russia who survived the ages 0–5 was less than 555 out of 1,000. Many explanations of the differences might be offered, ranging from faulty recording for St. Petersburg to differences in the social composition of the population or even the presence of a large colony of foreigners. Regardless of the reason, there can be no doubt that the rate of child mortality in St. Petersburg was among the lowest in the country.

The range of causes of mortality in the St. Petersburg population was very broad indeed, but modern scholars are at the mercy of eighteenth-century diagnoses. Table 1.28 shows the deaths attributed to various diseases or causes for the years 1764–80, 1781–85, 1786–90, and 1791–96.

Although infant and child mortality had the greatest impact on the demographic profile, mortality was high among other age groups as well. Hermann provided two tables for Russian Orthodox males for all of Russia which apply chiefly to the beginning of the nineteenth century but are also nearly representative for the second half of the eighteenth century. In table 1.29, the first column of survivors by age (at five-year intervals) is based upon 1798, 1799,

Table 1.27   Annual Averages for the St. Petersburg Population within Selected Periods

	Mar-riages	Births			Deaths			Net Increase		
		Male	Female	Total	Male	Female	Total	Male	Female	Total
1764–70	1,351	2,592	2,530	5,122	3,036	1,641	4,677	−444	889	445
1771–75	1,221	2,639	2,476	5,115	3,244	1,677	4,921	−605	799	194
1776–80	1,305	2,898	2,740	5,638	2,752	1,559	4,311	146	1,181	1,327
1781–85	1,368	3,004	2,885	5,889	3,474	1,688	5,162	−470	1,197	727
1786–90	1,391	3,272	3,041	6,313	5,598	1,782	7,380	−2,326	1,259	−1,067
1791–96	1,490	3,558	3,346	6,904	3,589	1,915	5,504	−31	1,431	1,400

Source: Krafft, *Mémoires*, 4 (1798): 258.

and 1801–5 data (denoted as Hermann I), the second column concerns the period 1804–14 (denoted as Hermann II). The figures in Hermann II for Russian Orthodox males can be compared with Swedish and French data for the same period. The survival tables that put Russian male mortality in a comparative perspective with both Sweden and France indicate not only the extent of child mortality but also the mortality during the ages of labor-force participation and military service. A different set of relevant data, in table 1.30, from the Hermann II table provides additional insight, particularly into the problem of the geographic distribution of male mortality.

It is clear from the geographical distribution shown in this table that infant and child mortality was much higher in areas of relatively recent settlement. For example, mortality rates for children and youngsters up to 15 years of age were considerably higher in the eastern and southern provinces of Russia (indicated by the boundaries of the Russian Orthodox bishoprics) than in the northern, western, and central regions of Russia (with the exception of Vologda, Moscow, Iaroslavl', and Nizhnii Novgorod provinces). A similar phenomenon has been documented for the American frontier in the nineteenth century.

The growth rate of the total population of the more recently settled lands in Russia during the eighteenth century, however, cannot be explained entirely by the migration data. It should therefore be assumed that the birth rate in those areas was higher than the average for the country in order both to sustain the high mortality rates and to provide a substantial number of survivors. The ranking of survivors by province (bishopric) for the older ages (60 and above) differed to some extent from the ranking obtained for the infant and child survivors. As in the first case, the eastern and southern provinces were prominent among those areas with a low number of survivors, but the newly acquired Belorussian, western bishoprics (Mohilev, Minsk, and the bordering Smolensk) also joined the list. Most intriguing, however, was the case of the St. Petersburg bishopric, an area with very low child mortality, which turned out to have the lowest survival rate at age 60. Whether the cases

of Smolensk, Belorussia, Moscow, and St. Petersburg can be explained primarily by the effects of the Napoleonic wars is still open to debate. Contemporary accounts tended to explain the low male-survival rates of St. Petersburg, which are also apparent from the earlier data by Krafft, as a result of the unhealthy climatic conditions of the city.

The high incidence of death among the various age groups of the adult population in Russia explains at least in part the relatively high percentage of second marriages. Economic and social considerations would also help to explain the high incidence of marriages between widows and single men, but it appears that the factor of the high death rate makes the second marriages even more intelligible. The net effect of the observed mortality rates is that fewer males were single and that the average male married younger. The data that Krafft assembled for St. Petersburg appear to support this hypothesis. Krafft classified the marriages in St. Petersburg by the former civil status of the marriage partners and distinguished the following four categories:

1. first marriage for both partners;
2. marriage between widowers and previously unmarried females;
3. marriage between widows and bachelors;
4. marriage between widows and widowers.

The yearly data quoted by Krafft are summarized in table 1.31.

First marriages tended to increase in their share of the total as the century progressed, from 66.9 percent during the years 1764–80 to 76 percent during the period 1791–96. The high rate of second marriages is also striking. One has to deal gingerly with St. Petersburg data. For example, there was a clear effect of the presence of the court and probably of the guard regiments upon the number of marriages. During the years 1767 and 1775, when the court absented itself from St. Petersburg, the number of marriages declined by about one-quarter. Although we do not have corroborating evidence for such a high rate of second marriages from other localities in the country, it stands to reason that the high number of second marriages would not have been limited to the capital.

Table 1.28 Major Causes of Death of St. Petersburg Population (per 1,000 Deaths)

Diseases	Russians 1764–80			Foreigners 1764–80			Russians 1781–85			Russians 1786–90			Russians 1791–96		
	Males	Females	Total	Males	Females	Total	Males	Females	Total	Males	Females	Total	Males	Females	Total
Pleurisy	264.4	385.2	308.1	23.09	11.95	17.84	211.1	344.9	255.2	125.7	284.8	164.1	207.5	314.2	244.9
"Hot Fever"	286.25	132.6	230.7	223.80	137.45	183.10	398.5	165.1	321.6	437.7	188.7	377.7	330.0	174.5	275.4
Tuberculosis	156.1	148.3	153.3	115.45	111.55	113.62	162.8	169.2	164.9	118.9	181.0	133.0	158.1	171.3	162.7
Convulsions	43.1	62.1	50.0	204.26	199.20	201.88	32.1	56.1	40.0	19.4	44.7	25.5	19.3	34.2	24.5
Old age	29.3	60.6	40.6	14.21	33.86	23.47	31.1	85.1	48.9	25.4	105.9	44	40.2	107.2	63.7
Dysentery	51.6	18.4	39.6	14.24	21.91	17.84	51.5	12.5	38.6	136.9	25.1	109.9	89.3	22.9	66.0
Smallpox	29.2	54.4	38.3	42.63	75.70	58.22	29.7	63.9	40.9	10.1	32.3	15.5	26.7	48.1	34.2
Scurvy	13.6	2.5	9.6	0	5.97	2.87	8.1	3.6	5.4	52.5	15.0	43.4	33.8	11.3	25.9
Childbirth	—	22.0	7.9	—	33.86	15.96	—	24.5	6.6	—	29.0	7.0	—	25.1	8.8

Source: Krafft, *Mémoires.*

Table 1.29 Survivors by Age Cohorts in Russia in 1798–1805 (Hermann I) and 1804–14 (Hermann II) Compared With Contemporary Swedish and French Data (per 1,000 Births)

Age	Hermann I	Hermann II	Sweden	France
5	554.70	550	532	584
10	497.87	499	480	552
15	469.01	474	457	530
20	440.07	446.3	431.4	503.3
25	410.05	416.8	412.8	476.4
30	377.08	383.7	386.8	439.2
35	347.91	353.4	357.2	405.1
40	311.70	315.9	330.2	371.0
45	278.63	280.8	298.2	336.0
50	238.57	238.8	266.2	299.0
55	206.29	203.8	230.7	259.2
60	161.39	160.0	195.0	215.5
65	125.94			
70	83.69			

Sources: German, *Statisticheskie issledovaniia*, 1 (1819); Hermann, *Mémoires*, vol. 1 (1832), part 1: 121–47, part 2: 205–19; vol. 2 (1834), part 3.

To put Hermann's survival data for 1798–1805 in a historical perspective, they are compared in table 1.32 with two sets of eighteenth-century data for St. Petersburg which do not differ substantially, when presenting child mortality, from the Hermann data of 1804–14 for St. Petersburg and the data for European Russia from the census of 1896–97.

The data seem to suggest that the mortality rate among foreigners residing in St. Petersburg was higher than among the local Russian population. For all periods covered in table 1.32, Russia is portrayed as a high-mortality society. This confirms the impression that for a period of about one hundred years very little progress was made in diminishing infant and child mortality. Most of the extension of life expectancy was gained by the higher rates of survival (or decline in mortality) of young adults.

The population data pertaining to the bishopric (*eparchiia*) of Nizhnii Novgorod for the period 1728–40 presented in table 1.33 are the only published data based upon the registers of the parishes for the Russian Orthodox population. Although potentially this source can serve as a check upon the data of the *revizii* and the calculations by Krafft and Hermann, there are a number of reasons why it is actually only of limited significance for the study of population changes in eighteenth-century Russia. It provides supporting evidence about the impact of the famine years of 1734–35 upon population growth, showing mortality exceeding births during those years and a corresponding negative population growth. The sharp decreases in the rates of population increase for 1733 and 1737, although they may reflect local conditions, nevertheless support a contention about low rates of population growth in many areas of Russia during the decade of the 1730s.

Table 1.30 Mortality Tables for Russian Orthodox Males, 1804–14, in Various Bishoprics (per 1,000 Births)

	Age											
	5	10	15	20	25	30	35	40	45	50	55	60
St. Petersburg	306	334	357	410.6	488.4	577.3	650.6	731.3	788.8	838.2	870.9	901.4
Moscow	473	523	554	583	613.7	645.4	675.1	708.3	741.4	777.2	811.2	846.9
Arkhangel'sk	447.4	—	522	548.6	583.2	620.7	655.2	693.6	727.0	764.5	798.2	839.2
Vologda	475.7	—	550	569	589.7	611.9	635.6	664.6	694.6	730.9	768.9	817.1
Novgorod	380.2	—	437	460.8	488.3	541.3	572.5	611.5	648.3	694.3	735.3	790.1
Tver'	381.7	—	455	477.8	506.5	538.8	570.5	608.7	646.3	690.9	731.1	784.1
Iaroslavl'	534.6	—	583	610.5	628.7	648.5	668.9	693.5	720.0	750.4	783.1	825.8
Kostroma	305.2	349.7	374.4	399.2	427.3	460.6	491.8	528.6	566.4	616.8	663.3	723.8
Vladimir	329.3	372.1	393.1	413.8	437.8	465.8	492.8	527.8	565.0	612.0	658.3	722.5
Nizhnii-Novgorod	616.5	647.7	660.9	675.2	691.0	709	723.4	744.2	765.6	791.1	817.3	850.4
Riazan'	291.8	354.6	388.3	420.5	455.2	492.8	525.2	567.4	607.9	653.5	691.1	746.1
Tula	327.7	—	419	451.1	486.2	523.7	559.4	599.7	638.7	683.9	723.4	775.7
Kaluga	281.7	334.3	363.9	396.3	432.9	469.3	506.1	551.8	596.3	649.6	698.3	758.8
Orel	455.3	—	535	562.4	593.2	624.7	652.6	686.9	719.7	757.7	792.3	834.8
Tambov	342.8	—	428	456.4	486.7	521.3	552.0	591.5	626.6	674.3	711.8	767.8
Penza	391.1	—	477	508.4	538.2	572.9	597.9	633.1	664.6	707.8	740.5	788.0
Kazan'	428.1	—	506	532.6	561.6	591.9	618.7	654.4	685.8	724.4	754.9	800.7
Orenburg	520.3	—	584	608.2	632.9	662.6	690.6	720.6	745.0	778.0	800.8	837.4
Viatka	540.9	594.6	614.4	635.8	660.7	687.4	714.0	745.2	774.2	807.6	837.2	876.4
Perm'	596	631.2	648.0	667.6	692.4	719.2	742.1	765.1	788.1	813.9	839.8	872.4
Pskov	247.1	292.3	315.9	347.1	391.1	445.3	500.1	564.7	626.1	693.1	749.1	807.3
Smolensk	378.5	—	484	521.7	563.3	607.0	650.7	694.2	737.9	783.1	825.3	873.0
Mogilev	346.4	—	439	474.3	514.0	562.3	604.3	654.0	703.0	758.8	801.3	848.2
Minsk	261.7	328.2	359.2	395.4	441.4	497.4	549.4	611.4	674.6	744.6	801.1	857.8
Volyn'	446	—	538	565.8	592.1	623.5	651.5	695.1	739.1	795.3	836.8	885.8
Podol'e	507.3	—	592	619.6	641.2	670.0	690.7	726.4	759.6	805.8	836.6	879.1
Kiev	533	593.8	619	645	667.2	694.9	717.0	749.9	781.4	822.4	852.9	890.4
Poltava	500.9	—	597	626.7	653.0	681.2	707.6	742.0	774.0	815.6	848.8	890.4
Chernigov	485.8	—	577	605.2	630.9	661.3	692.5	732.4	766.8	813.2	851.2	895.2
Kursk	413.8	—	504	534.6	565.8	598.2	628.6	664.2	700.6	749.3	789.7	834.9
Khar'kov	497.1	—	589	619.2	647.9	677.5	705.8	740.0	772.5	812.1	847.3	887.0
Ekaterinoslav	501.1	—	576	608.8	638.4	676.2	708.0	756.0	789.6	835.3	858.1	892.7
Voronezh	475.7	—	550	577.8	604.6	634.4	660.6	693.6	725.1	763.7	794.8	835.9
Astrakhan'	320.4	—	402	444.4	500.5	565.5	619.5	687.8	736.8	791.3	825.7	870.5
Tobol'sk	604.8	640.5	655.9	673.9	695.4	717.5	737.8	760.5	781.9	806.4	829.6	857.9
Irkutsk	537.5	—	590	607	628	655	681.5	713.0	743.5	777.2	805.7	843.7
Total Russia	450	501	526	553.7	583.2	616.3	646.6	684.1	719.2	761.2	796.2	840.0
Sweden	468	520	543	562.6	587.2	613.2	642.8	669.8	701.8	733.8	769.3	805.0
France	416	448	470	496.7	527.6	560.8	594.9	629.0	664.0	701.0	740.8	784.5

Source: Hermann, *Mémoires* 1 (1832), pt. 1: 121–47, pt. 2: 205–19.

Table 1.31   Categories of Marriages by Civil Status of the Marriage Partners, St. Petersburg

Year	Category I	Category II	Category III	Category IV	Total
1764–80	14,080	1,783	3,187	1,989	21,039
1781	898	77	157	75	1,207
82	1,008	116	160	80	1,364
83	1,057	113	157	84	1,411
84	1,019	100	172	96	1,387
85	1,057	112	195	107	1,471
Total	5,039	518	841	442	6,840
1786	1,072	102	235	99	1,508
87	1,037	123	169	87	1,416
88	958	86	170	105	1,319
89	929	98	172	107	1,306
1790	1,013	104	188	101	1,406
Total	5,009	513	934	499	6,955
1791	1,258	124	219	126	1,727
92	1,200	116	185	86	1,587
93	1,119	95	181	83	1,478
94	1,071	119	163	77	1,430
95	962	101	133	78	1,274
96	1,101	128	138	78	1,445
Total	6,711	683	1,019	528	8,941
Grand Total	30,839	3,497	5,981	3,458	43,775

Source: Krafft, *Mémoires*, 8: 18.

Table 1.32   Comparison between Survival Data for Various Age-Groups

Age	St. Petersburg 1764–80	St. Petersburg Foreigners 1764–80	Russia— Males 1798–1805	Russia— Males 1896–97
5	667.72	517.30	554.70	556.09
10	646.29	484.43	497.87	531.29
15	632.22	456.75	469.01	507.27
20	603.53	429.07	440.05	493.47
25	503.57	391.01	410.05	476.29
30	424.67	356.41	377.08	458.51
35	331.86	314.89	347.91	439.55
40	271.87	273.37	311.70	418.26
45	210.38	192.06	278.63	392.61
50	159.87	150.54	238.57	361.74
55	118.43	115.94	206.29	324.88
60	86.81	88.26	161.39	281.83
65	59.04	55.39	125.94	231.95
70	38.98	24.25	83.69	173.47
75	22.00	13.87	55.95	117.43
80	11.57	5.20	30.63	70.22

Sources: St. Petersburg—Krafft; 1798–1805—Hermann; 1896–97, Novosel'skii, "Smertnost'."

Table 1.33   Vital Statistics by Sex in the Bishopric of Nizhnii Novgorod, 1730–40.

Year	Births		Deaths		Natural Increase	
	Males	Females	Males	Females	Males	Females
1730	13,791	7,062	7,060	4,164	6,731	2,898
1731	13,434	6,071	6,693	3,703	6,741	2,368
1732	12,473	5,366	6,384	3,939	6,089	1,427
1733	10,123	3,989	8,205	3,846	1,918	143
1734	9,194	3,712	10,199	4,589	−1,005	−877
1735	8,997	3,358	9,773	3,377	−776	−19
1736	10,907	4,167	7,477	3,382	3,430	785
1737	10,404	6,195	9,218	5,945	1,186	250
1738	11,763	6,823	5,538	3,669	6,225	3,154
1739	11,212	6,010	5,203	3,752	6,009	2,258
1740	10,177	5,874	6,282	4,347	3,895	1,527
Total	122,475	58,627	82,032	44,713	40,443	13,914

Source: "Russkoe geograficheskoe obshchestvo," *Sbornik* 3 (1858): 636–57.

distribution of births is 67.6 percent for males and 32.4 percent for females. If this was reality, it was a strange reality indeed.[71] Although the sex distribution of deaths for the same period is already marginally more realistic, 64.7 percent for males and 35.3 percent for females, it cannot correct the absurd sex distribution of the natural increase, 74.4 percent male and 25.6 percent female.

The reporting bias affecting the female population, regardless of whether its origin was with the family or with the parish, persisted for a very long time and affected the data throughout the eighteenth century and into the beginning of the nineteenth. It tended to distort the data on fertility, rates of natural increase,

In an interesting way the defects of the Nizhnii Novgorod data, which make them less usable for general analysis, help us to understand some of the pitfalls of the parish registers as a source for historical or demographic studies. There are two basic flaws in the data pertaining to the Russian Orthodox parish population reported to the synod. One is the under-reporting of female births, a flaw that can be illustrated by the fact that for the period 1730 the sex and the survival pattern. It is also probably responsible for the difficulty in ascertaining the birth rates for the closing years of the century for which summary data have been reported for the entire Orthodox population of Russia.

The other bias of the Nizhnii Novgorod data, a distortion that tended to persist in the reports, concerns the reported mortality by age. Although the tables for Nizhnii Novgorod are more detailed than the data by Hermann, who reported deaths by five-year age intervals, to the extent that they pretend to report the deaths for each year during the ages 1 to 100, they are less trustworthy and exhibit a definite bias toward five-year and decennial intervals. Thus in many instances the number of deaths at age 20 exceeds the sum of deaths for ages 16–19, or at 30 exceeds the sum of deaths for 26–29 and 31–34. It is clear that the age of death was not checked against the birth records and reflected the tendency of the populace to age-heap in five- and ten-year intervals. As a result of these distortions, there is a much lower rate of infant mortality in the Nizhnii Novgorod data than in the data for the end of the century, a discrepancy that seems implausible on the basis of circumstantial evidence. On the other hand, there is an inner consistency with respect to years of unusually high total mortality, when the data point to a relative decrease of infant mortality.

The Nizhnii Novgorod data are a precious source that can yield positive results. Having established the undeniable fact of their bias in reporting female birth rates, let us assume that they reflect more accurately the changes of the male population. Assuming that the overwhelming majority of the male population was Russian Orthodox, I shall also assume that the data of the first *reviziia* are nearly identical with the number of Russian Orthodox males, and that there was a total population of approximately 270,000.[72]

Under those assumptions, the average birth rate for the years 1730–40 for males was 4.12 percent and the average death rate was 2.76 percent, a rate of increase of 1.36 percent. The range for birth rates during this short period was between 3.33 and 5.11 percent; the range for death rates from 1.93 to 3.78 percent; and the rate of natural increase from -0.37 to +2.50 percent. These figures point to a demographic pattern typical of a population under stress, with characteristic wide fluctuations of its birth pattern, population losses, and compensating responses. Given our knowledge of the overall population loss in the Nizhnii Novgorod guberniia for 1719–44, we must assume that the 1730–40 data reflect similar or even more severe fluctuations during the 1720s. Even if my assumptions are later proved to be off the mark, at the moment they appear to support impressionistic notions about this period gained from data on natural calamities, wars, and other exogenous effects upon the population.

The availability of population data increases rapidly with the closing years of the eighteenth century thanks to numerous studies of various districts (*gubernii*) and administrative changes such as the organization of ministries and centralization of reporting to the Ministry of the Interior. Although the quality of the data remained rather poor, it is incumbent upon the student of Russian society to come to grips with the volume of often contradictory information in order to assess the demographic processes and to investigate any clues they may provide on what happened earlier in the century.

The data pertaining to the Russian Orthodox population for the years 1796–1800, which were used by Hermann, suffer from some of the same shortcomings discussed earlier. They do not reflect fully the population data on females, and they appear also to bias upward the size of the natural population increase, probably because of mortality underreporting. The *reviziia* data indicate for all of Russia a population increase of about 14 percent between 1795 and 1811 and about 16 or 17 percent for the areas inhabited exclusively or predominantly by Russian Orthodox; and yet the reported increase for the Russian Orthodox population is almost 25 percent. It is likely that, after the relatively hungry years of the second half of the 1780s, the relatively prosperous second half of the 1790s witnessed an upsurge in population growth which lasted until approximately 1805, when it was checked by wars and other calamities. For the last years of the century, the movement of population growth and the reported number of marriages coincide with changes in the size of grain exports.

Although contemporary observers of Russian society and economy such as H. Storch and Ch. Th. Hermann hinted that the rate of yearly marriages as a percentage of the total population was declining by the turn of the century in comparison with earlier periods, changes in the number of marriages ordinarily appear to be an indicator of substantial sensitivity for short-term changes of income. My calculations show that the percentage of yearly marriages according to the data for the Russian Orthodox population increased from 0.9 percent of the population in the middle of the 1790s to 0.95 in 1801. The reported data cannot be accepted uncritically, for one cannot assume that under conditions of serfdom the peasants had absolute freedom to decide such matters as marriage solely on the basis of their own desires and that the heavy hand of the serf-owner or his steward interfered only in other aspects of their private lives. On the other hand, there is no doubt that important economic factors affected the demography of the

Russian population, and if we can find out their biases and be certain that they do not change often, the otherwise defective data have a logic and consistency of their own.

The evidence available is sufficient to conclude that population during the last years of the century grew on a rising curve. This trend had a major impact on the overall trend toward growth that characterized the development of Russian society and the Russian economy during the second half of the eighteenth century.

The Size of the Household in the Eighteenth Century: A Cursory View

Demographers, historians, and sociologists can claim some knowledge of the size and characteristics of Russian families and households of the nineteenth and twentieth centuries. No such claims can be made about the eighteenth century.[73]

I shall treat only the size of the Russian nuclear family in the eighteenth century. It was typically created by marriage and was two-generational. Its members were related by specific kinship ties and they exercised control over its labor resources. I shall consider as a household a social unit that included all present members sharing one budget and also exercising control over resources beyond the labor of its members. (This is one of the reasons for concentrating on the rural population of the agricultural peasants [krest'iane] and omitting from the discussion the households of agricultural workers [dvorovye].) As a rule, the size of the household exceeded the size of the family as defined above. To the extent that the family was defined in terms of definite kinship relationships, the household could include kinsmen at the same or different generational levels who had already formed their own family units, as well as persons unrelated to any member of the families which composed the household.

The size of the Russian nuclear family exceeded four persons, but by a relatively small margin. The eighteenth century censuses of the male civilian population provide the yearly growth rates of population and indirectly the evidence on the approximate size of the nuclear family, as shown in table 1.34. The lack of a clear trend of secular growth suggests the relative stability of the existing pattern. Inclusion of estimated effects of changes in the size of the armed forces and of out-migration from this territory probably would smooth out the differences between the intercensus periods.

The above pattern of the size of the younger age cohorts in relation to the older ones is supported by fragmentary evidence pertaining to various popula-

Table 1.34   Average Yearly Rates of Growth of the Male Population in Territory of First Population Census, 1715–95

Period	Average Yearly Rate (%)	Size of Nuclear Family
1719–44	.66	4.3
1744–62	.94	4.36
1762–82	1.02	4.44
1782–95	.61	4.18

Source: Kabuzan, *Narodonaselenie*, pp. 164–65.

tion groups during different periods of the eighteenth century in Russia.[74]

After ascertaining the evidence on the average size of the nuclear family, one still faces the problem of family formation and growth pattern, the solution to which can be found in examining the conditions of the rural, or agricultural, families.

The formation of a new family was a joint decision by the members of the "old family" to enter into negotiations with another party. (That some members of the old family did not possess a "vote" equal to the one exercised by the father of the family is relatively unimportant within the framework of our discussion.) The process was subject to a number of social constraints. One of them was the availability of partners, or of "suitable" partners, within a particular age bracket and permissible under church and customary law. "Suitable" partners were defined in terms of belonging to similar social substrata within the villages. The scarcity of such partners on the estate tended to increase the costs of marriage when the future spouse had to be obtained from another estate. A second constraint was the availability of both a dowry and the "bride payment," the amounts of which did not necessarily coincide. A third constraint was the interference and pressure by the estate owner or estate administration. As a rule, estate owners encouraged early marriages of their serfs; the owners had an obvious interest in having populated estates in an environment of low population density in which the number of serfs determined the value of an estate. Many estate owners imposed special taxes upon unmarried serfs above a certain age. Some estate owners even went to the extreme of forcing marriages upon reluctant serfs in a most arbitrary fashion by pairing serfs according to lists in their administrative offices. In most cases, apparently, the pairing of serfs was more of a threat than a fact of life, but nevertheless it was a threat that conditioned the decisions regarding family formation. A fourth constraint was interference by the village commune, an institution that usually was reluctant to enter the sphere of family decisions, but which sometimes acted either in specific cases to forestall actions by the estate administration, or in order to form families of persons who would otherwise become charges of the commune.

For males first marriages took place usually within the 20 to 25 year old age group, and for females within the 17- to 22-year-old-age group. Marriages at younger ages were reported. Primary documentary sources reveal numerous cases of wives from five to ten years older than their husbands. There are several explanations of this phenomenon, but one is the observed tendency to marry off a minor male to an older woman to gain the benefit of her labor for a family which had a particularly unfavorable age composition for its members.

Once a new family was formed, its subsequent numerical growth became a random phenomenon. Even assuming the practice of no form of birth control, one cannot ignore the impact on fertility of long absence from home for seasonal work, periods of famine, or even long periods of breast-feeding. The available data indicate that the result was fewer than the maximum possible births. Since the age data for surviving children do not indicate any regularity of spacing of births (intergenesic intervals), and since I have assumed that there were no birth control measures, the randomness of surviving children can be attributed to some extent to the impact of child mortality.

Although size was a random phenomenon for individual families, changes in the structure and profile of all families over time were predictable. The most important characteristic of the growth pattern of the family was, first, the growth of the number of consumers, followed by the growth of the number of producers within the family. Although children within an agricultural setting contributed some labor to farm or household work, it was only when they were old enough to switch from auxiliary tasks to the basic farm work that their contribution to the income of the family began to exceed the costs of consumption by them. Accordingly, for the family in the process of its growth, the balance between consumption- and production-needs became the overriding consideration, and the age structure as well as the size and sex composition of the family became the critical variables in this process. A disequilibrium between consumption and production is assumed to exist whenever the structure of the family shows an excessive number of consumers relative to the number of producers. This disequilibrium cannot be resolved by the family itself. It requires the existence of a separate or joint household to find a satisfactory solution.

For data on the size of the household, one has to rely upon the land cadastre of 1678, which, among the sources published by Ia. E. Vodarskii, covered the largest population.[75] From these sources two cat-

Table 1.35   Average Size of Peasant and Landless Peasant Serf Households in 1678

(Males per Household)		
Province	Peasant	Landless Peasant
Moscow	3.91	3.00
Novgorod	4.10	3.11
Arkhangel'sk	3.39	—
Smolensk	4.53	2.99
Belgorod	5.09	4.12
Voronezh	4.50	3.17
Nizhnii-Novgorod	3.96	3.25
Kazan'	3.91	—
All provinces	3.96	3.18

Source: Vodarskii, "Chislennost' naseleniia," pp. 228–29.

Table 1.36   Average Size of Peasant and Landless Peasant Serf Households in 1678 for 89 Uezdy of Russia

	Lay Estates	Ecclesiastic Estates	All Estates
Peasants	4.19	3.70	4.06
Landless Peasants	3.17	2.74	3.08
Total	3.86	3.46	3.76

Source: Ia. E. Vodarskii, "Krest'ianie i sel'skie bobyli," pp. 58–59.

egories of the population were selected, the peasants (krest'iane) and landless peasants (bobyli) of lay and ecclesiastical estates. Table 1.35 presents the approximate data for those categories by their geographic distribution (according to 1727 administrative districts), and table 1.36 is based upon a more limited population of 89 uezdy, mostly of the central regions of Russia distributed by institutional affiliation.

The average size of the male population in the households classified by the geographic-administrative regional distribution was 3.96 for peasants, within a range of 3.39 to 5.09. For landless peasants, the average was 3.18 within a range of 2.99 to 4.12 males per household. (These averages were compiled from complete and incomplete data representing 403,219 households of peasants and 144,546 households of landless peasants that had, respectively, populations of 1,596,845 and 459,731 males.)

The average size of the male population per household of 89 uezdy classified by categories of ownership between lay and ecclesiastical estates was 3.76, with 4.06 for peasants and 3.08 for landless peasants. Within each category the difference among lay and ecclesiastical estates was significant. For peasants it was 4.19 for lay estates and 3.70 for ecclesiastical estates, for landless peasants, 3.86 and 3.46, respectively. (These averages were compiled from data representing 356,658 households of lay estates and 121,955 households of ecclesiastical estates with a combined population of 1,800,046 males.)

The most obvious things to be seen in the Vodarskii data are the regional differentials in the average sizes

Table 1.37   Size of Peasant Households (Males per Household) in Labor Services and Money Rent Estates

	Labor Service Estates				Money Rent Estates		
Years	Households	Males	Males per Household	Years	Households	Males	Males per Household
1680–1712	1,453	5,303	3.65	1682–1705	53	183	3.45
1712–25	280	1,578	5.64	1715–24	703	3,506	4.99

Source: Tikhonov, *Pomeshchich'i krest'iane*, tables 47–49.

of the households, the difference in the average size between the peasants' and the landless peasants' households, and the differences in size between the households on lay estates and ecclesiastical estates. Of these differences, the third appears to be primarily a function of the first two. The available evidence of the late seventeenth and early eighteenth centuries indicates a strong correlation between the size of the rural households and the availability of land in serf-tenure on the estate, as well as between the size of the household and total arable land on the estates. This information is valuable in determining one of the sources of the differential between geographic regions, which is apparent for the late seventeenth century and becomes even more crucial for the subsequent periods.[76] The differential between the household sizes of peasants and landless peasants would also suggest differentials in the endowments of farmland between the two categories.[77]

With respect to the regional geographic differences in the average sizes of households, "geography" is a shorthand description of a number of factors including availability of farmland, yield differentials, and perhaps also money rent versus labor services. A comparison between the Vodarskii data for particular *uezdy* with the data on average household size of the Sheremetev estates for 1799–1800 covering a serf population of 95,591 males reveals a strong rank order correlation between the various geographic regions, similar average size of households, and differences due to location that are both related to land-labor ratios as well as forms of rent payment.[78]

Using data for the same periods and the same regions, Iu. A. Tikhonov found differences in the size of households attributable to the forms of rent payment, whether labor or money rent. To the extent that the household paying money rent had more discretion and fewer constraints imposed upon it in arranging its labor resources, it was perhaps more flexible in varying the household size. One of the possibilities was to have a smaller household combined with a higher degree of new household formation. Some of Tikhonov's data are presented in table 1.37.

The formation of a new rural household depended upon a number of significant conditions: (1) the kinship relations among the members of the original household, including the number of competing inheritors; (2) the relationship of the total number of producers or members of working age to consumers within the household, adjusted for the size of the landholding of the original household; (3) the availability of suitable land on the estate and its existing distribution, which may or may not have required land repartition in order to supply the needs of a newly formed household; (4) availability of some savings or capital to set up a farm for the new household; and (5) the existence of a tax structure that would either retard or encourage the formation of new households.

The conditions of formation of new households fail to explain the initial, subsequent, or "optimal size" of the households. For this it is necessary to glance at the more general problems of Russian agriculture. During the eighteenth century Russian agriculture was characterized by a low output/seed ratio. This necessitated the use of extensive land resources in order to support the existing population, which in turn required much labor input per unit of agricultural output. Under the existing conditions a household required relatively abundant land and a labor force commensurate with its land requirements. For each economic region there existed a certain minimum or threshold requirement of arable land and a certain empirically derived volume of labor inputs into the land that would make a household a viable unit. Such a unit was the *tiaglo*. The *tiaglo* was simultaneously a land unit and a labor team. The amount of land depended upon local conditions, such as the quality of the land, necessary to support a household of average size and to support labor for its own needs and for the demesne. The labor unit was usually represented by two able-bodied adult workers. In addition, the *tiaglo* also represented a unit of account for rent payments and for apportioning of tax payments.

Although the *tiaglo* as a unit set the minimum land and labor requirements for a viable agricultural household, households of different sizes could, if not constrained by external conditions, represent various multiples of a *tiaglo*. One of the most frequently observed differences in size of households among different regions can be attributed to variations in the land-labor ratio. Scarcity of arable land limited the labor requirements and was conducive to smaller households.[79] Nonagricultural work and perhaps out-migration were the outlets for the population that could not be supported when land resources were scarce. In areas with relatively abundant land resources, labor was the relatively scarce factor and households tended to be larger and multigenerational. Households in such areas tried to keep as much of their labor resources as possible to take advantage of abundant land and resisted the pressure for new household formation. We can see in household behavior an attempt to recoup from the younger generation the past costs to the adult generation of consumption by the young and a recognition of certain indivisibilities of productive factors and the advantage of unified management of farm operations. The differences in household size reveal the mechanism by which the household adjusted to its basic economic environment, the land-labor ratios of the different regions.

In periods when population was increasing, the household could absorb additional numbers by bringing into cultivation new arable land that was at its disposal and had previously been used as forest or pasture. The household might also, on rare occasions, rent or purchase land.[80] However, beyond a certain point the households could not resolve the problem by themselves. They could postpone it further with outside help of either the estate or the village commune. The estate administration could apportion additional land, when available, to the village, acquire through purchase adjacent land, resettle some households on more sparsely populated lands that it owned in other regions, or permit individuals and households to engage in nonagricultural employment.

The interference of the village commune was usually sought for the purpose of land repartition. When population growth within individual households varied, some growing more numerous, others declining, land repartition was a measure that could relieve the problems of many households at least temporarily. Such repartition was not opposed by the estate owners, who as a rule preferred viable taxpaying households to advanced income differentiation within their villages, so long as the number of *tiagla* as rent-paying units was not decreased. Repartition involved a bargaining process within the village commune in which the interests of various households, both as production and consumption units, had to be balanced and reconciled.[81] The procedure of repartition was tortuous and involved going into the minutiae of the resources of each household. It was complicated by the customary differences in "user rights" to various types of land—past investments made by the household in improving lands. For example, the "right" of a household to an orchard or hemp field was much "stronger" than to a grain field or a meadow. Land repartition within the commune was adopted as a corrective device to forestall more drastic changes in the size and composition of the households. The hypothesis that repartitions served merely to execute a principle of economic egalitarianism has to be rejected for lack of positive evidence. The redistribution of land was always accompanied by a redistribution of tax and rent burdens.

After the estate and the village commune had exhausted their corrective devices, the task of adjustment of the household's size was thrown back where it had originated, to the household. Even the very fragmentary data dispersed over tens of volumes of primary sources, the published records of bishoprics, estates, and court proceedings, indicate changes in the sizes of households during the last third of the eighteenth century that differ from the sizes reported for the first half of the century. The changes were not only statistically, but also socially, significant.

One of the most vivid examples of the adjustment of household size to external conditions was its adjustment to the volume of taxation. Thus the average size of households grew during Peter the Great's Northern War, prior to the institution of the poll tax. At that time there was clearly an increase in household size, perhaps largely through the postponement of new-household formation, in order to diminish the impact of rising taxes levied upon the households.[82]

In using the data on the size and composition of the serf agricultural households it was tacitly assumed that the household could not hire labor and could not purchase land, that it could not vary its factor proportions, under conditions of stable technology to meet the demands of output maximization that a nonserf agricultural household performed. The available data, however, indicate that the agricultural household could adjust to such long-range endogenous changes as population pressure, and to variations in land-labor ratios. In addition the data indicate the impact of such exogenous forces as different forms of rent payments and government taxation upon the agricultural households, as well as indicating the response of the households. We are confronted with a social mechanism by the use of which, within the broader institutional setting, the household was capable of varying its size, balancing its productive capacity with its consumption, and even making limited investments. This social mechanism provided a major link between the demographic behavior of the rural household and the realities of Russian agriculture of the eighteenth century.

Some additional insight into the structure of the Russian household can be gained by a comparison of the rural household with some urban households. Although research into the structure and composition of urban households has barely been undertaken, a glance at some of the available materials both cross-sectionally and over time for a small population is instructive. The object of the inquiry into household size was the group of Moscow merchants who constituted during most of the eighteenth century a corporation dating from much earlier times known as the "Merchants' Hundred" (Gostinaia sotnia), in which some degree of generational continuity can be established and for which some data are available for most of the century.[83]

These households were not representative of the mass of the urban population, for the Gostinaia sotnia was a privileged group representing the commercial and industrial elite of Moscow. Some of the characteristics of this group were shared by other groups within the urban population of Russia. The characteristics are primarily those of the males, for the census was interested primarily in them. The data represent the changes in approximately twenty-year intervals, except for a thirteen-year interval between the fourth and fifth census. Two additional caveats are necessary. First, the precipitous decline from the third to the fourth census was to a large extent caused by the plague epidemic in Moscow of 1771, which clearly reinforced the long-term trend of decline of this group stemming from economic conditions and the withdrawal of government privileges and protection. Second, the changes in the size of the households and their size distribution was in large part brought about by the fecundity of a few households,[84] or by those who maintained legally common households to avoid the payment of higher taxes.

As expected on the basis of economic theory and historical experience in other countries, the size of the urban household tended to be smaller than that of the rural one. Table 1.38 shows the average sizes of households, measured in males per household, of the Gostinaia sotnia.

The data suggest for the Gostinaia sotnia a long-term average of about two males per household, subject to

Table 1.38   Number of Males per Household of the Gostinaia Sotnia

1st reviziia	2.01
2d reviziia	2.50
3d reviziia	2.03
4th reviziia	1.79
5th reviziia	1.92

Note: Only households with male members were included. This led to the exclusion of one-third of all households for the fifth census.

Table 1.39   Percentage Distribution of Households by Number of Generations Represented

Generations	1st Reviziia	2d Reviziia	4th Reviziia
1	44.5	46.4	62.5
2	47.9	49.1	37.5
3	7.6	4.5	—

Table 1.40   Percentage Distribution of Households and Population

No. of Males	Gostinaia Sotnia (1761)		Kadashev Settlement (1766–67)	
	Households	Population	Households	Population
1	48.4	23.9	49.5	25.7
2	26.8	26.4	27.9	28.9
3	9.3	13.7	12.0	18.7
4	7.2	14.2	4.8	10.0
5	5.2	12.7	2.9	7.5
6	3.1	9.1	2.4	7.5
7	—	—	.5	1.7

fluctuation caused by social mobility or natural calamity.

Considering the secular decline of this group, both numerically and economically, one would expect a decline in the share of multigenerational households. The data in table 1.39 appear to confirm this hypothesis, although the impact of the plague of 1771 clearly had a contributory effect.

To put the data of the Gostinaia sotnia in a somewhat broader perspective, I have employed the household data for the population of the Kadashev settlement, a micro-region in Moscow with a predominantly merchant population, collected in 1766–67. The latter data have an advantage in that they identify households by membership in one of the three guilds, which are assumed to be a proxy for income or wealth differences. The percentage distribution of households by size of the male population in table 1.40 does not differ substantially from that of the Gostinaia sotnia for the third reviziia, and the average size of the household's 1.93 members is only slightly below the average of 2.03 for the Gostinaia sotnia.

The differences are more revealing in table 1.41 where the average household size and generational distribution of the Kadashev settlement households are analyzed by their membership in the various guilds.

The distribution very clearly indicates the dependency of the size of the households and their distribution by number of generations per household upon the membership in the different guilds. To the extent that membership in any particular guild depended upon the assessment of income and taxes to be paid

Table 1.41   Distribution of Generations and Average Household Size of Kadashev Settlement by Membership in Merchant Guilds

	1 Generation	2 Generations	3 Generations	Size of Household
1st guild	45.2	51.6	3.3	2.64
2d guild	61.1	35.2	3.7	1.94
3d guild	65.2	34.8	—	1.58
Total Average	60.1	37.5	2.4	

by the members, I have assumed membership in the guilds as a proxy for broad income categories. In this particular case we find the size of the household to be positively correlated with income. The wealthier members of the first guild had larger households, the members of the guilds with lesser incomes had smaller households. This result was not obtained by procedures as rigorous as one would like; the various groups could not be not standardized by age, for example, even though age may have been highly correlated with guild membership. Regardless, I assume that these calculations are correct because they correspond to other circumstantial evidence.

This brief excursion into the area of urban household size and generational structure has provided results of a general nature that point to the basic differences between rural and urban households, and the impact of government taxation policy on their relative size and structure. Rural households included on average between three and four male members. Moscow urban households were relatively smaller, about two male members as the long-term average. The frequency of multigenerational households was greater among the rural population than among the urban one. Although the differences in the average size of households within the urban population may be attributable in part to discernible income differentials, our data on the rural population do not permit pointing out direct income differentials, and the existing differences, therefore, have been attributed to the endowment in land resources.

The impact of particular taxation policies upon the process of new household formation in the rural areas has been noted for at least one period during the century. With respect to the urban population, at least the data for the third *reviziia* of the Kadashev settlement in Moscow point to a difference between the fiscal definition of a household and the definition based upon the actual residence pattern. Since the actual residence pattern suggests about 10 percent more households for the same population than the number of households that were defined for tax purposes, there is reason to believe that the existing taxation system did not stimulate the formation of new households.

The Population of the Ekaterinburg State Ironworks and Mint

It is perhaps a paradox, or just an accident, that the best published demographic data pertaining to any population group in Russian society at the end of the eighteenth century are available for one of the smallest distinct population groups, the workers and employees of the state ironworks in the Urals.[85] From data that include 16,816 persons, the figures covering 8,467 individuals have been selected for analysis and discussion.

This collection of data describing the household members of a highly skilled group employed in two ironworks, a copperworks, a steel factory, and the Ekaterinburg mint is interesting not only for its intrinsic value but primarily for its significance in comparison with other, more general data and the way in which it supplements information from other sources.

A brief outline of some of the characteristics of this group will enable me to compare it with the observed characteristics of larger populations. (For the data, see tables 1.42–44.) The group had a relatively high child-mortality rate. Whether the high mortality rate was due to the living conditions of the frontier cannot be ascertained. It is, however, congruent with the general tendency observed for the larger population (members of Russian Orthodox parishes), where high child-mortality rates are seen in the eastern areas of Russia, which are tantamount to the "frontier." The group also exhibited high birth rates. The reported birth rate of the group is considerably higher than the birth rates for the St. Petersburg population. The reasons for this higher birth rate may range from higher levels of income to less mobility during the year for the population of workers compared with a peasant population or a younger average age of the total population.

The group shows a difference in the survival pattern of males and females. The mortality of both female children and females during the prime childbearing age was also higher than among males. For the age groups of those over 40, the mortality of males was higher than that of females. This last

Table 1.42   1802 Distribution of Deaths by Age of the Ekaterinburg Mining and Metallurgical Labor-Force Population, and Mortality by Age

Age	Males	Females	Total	% of Males	% of Females	% of Total
Below 1 year	93	86	179	41.3	43.4	42.3
1–5 years	38	39	77	16.9	19.7	18.2
5–10	4	6	10	1.8	3.0	2.4
10–15	6	3	9	2.7	1.5	2.1
15–20	7	8	15	3.1	4.0	3.5
20–30	9	8	17	4.0	4.0	4.0
30–40	14	15	29	6.2	7.6	6.9
40–50	12	8	20	5.3	4.0	4.7
50–60	13	6	19	5.8	3.0	4.5
60–70	17	13	30	7.6	6.6	7.1
70–80	9	3	12	4.0	1.5	2.8
above 80	3	3	6	1.3	1.5	1.4
Total	225	198	423			

Note: The total deaths of 423 represents the mortality out of a total population of 16,816, which consisted of 8,720 sales and 8,096 females.

Table 1.43   1802 Distribution of Births by Reported Age Groups of Mothers

	Ekaterinburg Ironworks	Nizhne Isetsk Steel Factory	Kamensk Pig-Ironworks	Miass Copperworks	Ekaterinburg Mint	Total
Total Births	72	36	66	131	143	448
Age of Mothers						
15–20	17	1	12	9	50	89
20–30	36	27	36	59	61	219
30–40	14	6	15	50	17	102
40–50	5	2	3	13	15	38

Table 1.44   1802 Distribution of Marriages by Age Groups

Total married	30	26	36	36	56	184
Below 20	18	12	8	26	33	97
Males	10	5	4	13	14	46
Females	8	7	4	13	19	51
20–40	12	14	24	8	21	79
Males	5	8	12	4	13	42
Females	7	6	12	4	8	37
Above 40			4	2	2	8
Males			2	1	1	4
Females			2	1	1	4

phenomenon may have been due to the effects of labor upon the males.

The group distinguished itself by relatively early marriages. More than half of the individuals in the state ironworks were married at age 20 or younger. Among females, early marriages were more pronounced than among men, for whom the marrying-age interval of 20 to 30 years came a close second to the below 20 category. It is possible that with the skilled workers dependent upon apprenticeship and salary, some of the deterrents to early marriage operating in the peasant milieu (late distribution of family wealth, lack of an available parcel of land, lack of accumulated savings for a separate farm) were

absent. The acquisition of skills was arranged not only in the work place, but often within the family itself in which it was transferred from generation to generation. Young workers were less restrained in the formation of new families, and at the Ekaterinburg mint, for example, there was probably a higher correlation between the workers' skill, income, and early marriage. This is suggested by the ratio of houses to the number of males above 20 years of age.

The group provides some information, lacking in other published data collections, on ages of mothers at the birth of their children. The data indicate that the largest number of children were born to mothers in the 20-to-30-year-old age group, followed by the

15-to-20-year-old age group, with a decline among the 30-to-40-year-old age group.

The data on this particular group of industrial workers and their families not only tend to support some of the conclusions reached on the basis of the analysis of more general population data with regard to child mortality and birth rate, but supplement our information with useful data on family formation and age of childbearing. They also alert us to the important relationship between income and some of the demographic characteristics of this group. Even if one were to employ rough estimates of wage differentials within this group, economic variables would emerge in the differences of such social indicators as size of household, number of dependents per worker, or relative congestion per dwelling unit.

The view of the Russian population of the eighteenth century I have been able to piece together is at best an uneven one. I have been able to gather clues on how population trends fitted into the economic and political history of the day, how population became a crucial instrument of national policy, and how natural forces conspired with those harnessed and unleashed by man.

2
AGRICULTURE

The Land Area

Apart from human labor, the most important input in agricultural production is land. Consequently the land resources, their size and quality, are significant determinants of agricultural production. Estimates of the size and distribution of the land resources are available for a few dates during the eighteenth century for European Russia and are presented in table 2.1. The data reveal the changes which took place during this period. Table 2.1 indicates the limitations of the usable land resources in Russia, the low share of plowland, the relative availability of usable hay lands in the form of meadows and pastures, the relatively high density of the forestry resources, and the fact that more than 20 percent of the land was not usable at all. The data in the table suggest also that the area of plowland grew by incorporation of land at the expense of Russia's neighbors, by forest clearing, and by the conversion of meadows and pastures into plowland.

A comparison of the growth of the plowland area with the growth of the Russian peasant population for the period 1726–96 yields insight into the change in the availability of land per capita of the rural population. We know that under the three-field system about one-third of the plowland area was kept fallow each year, and thus the upper bound of the actually planted area must have been two-thirds of the land suitable for cultivation. The maximum of the actually planted area was in the vicinity of 21,320,000 hectares (19,512,000 desiatinas) in 1696; 27,900,000 hectares (25,512,000 desiatinas) in 1725; 35,910,000 hectares (32,870,000 desiatinas) in 1763; and 54,240,000 hectares (49,648,000 desiatinas) in 1796.

On a per male "soul" calculation, the maximum planted area actually decreased from 3.50 desiatinas in 1725 to 3.19 desiatinas in 1763 and 3.04 desiatinas in 1796, while the actually planted area probably increased during this period. If we assume even only 3 males per household, or about 1.5 ablebodied males in the 18–60 age group, 6 desiatinas of planted area

would far exceed the work capacity of a single male worker. Therefore one must assume that a portion of the available plowland was not utilized even at the end of the eighteenth century. The Soviet historian N. L. Rubinshtein argued that by the end of the century in the nonblacksoil (podzol) zone about 2 desiatinas and in the blacksoil (chernozëm) zone 3 desiatinas of plowland were the prevailing areas of land worked per "soul," which would have amounted to an average of 2.3 to 2.4 desiatinas per "soul."[1] There was no scarcity of land in general or even within particular regions. Land scarcity could occur on a particular estate and persist only under conditions of an immobility of resources, an untenable assumption.

In addition to the size of the land resources used in agricultural production, the quality of that land is obviously important in determining the total yield of crops. The overall land quality was low by comparison with other regions of Europe. However, during the eighteenth century the fertility of the land in Russia did not deteriorate. Bringing under cultivation an increasing part of the blacksoil zone, a region of relatively higher than average soil fertility, increased the average quality of the land overall. On the other hand, the lands in the blacksoil zone were more susceptible to droughts, and thus to greater fluctuations in the level of yields, than were the old lands of the nonblacksoil zone.

The combination of a relative abundance of agricultural land and the relatively low quality of that land created problems for Russian agriculture. The relative abundance of land did not force an intensification of agricultural production when new lands could be brought under cultivation at reasonable cost, but the new lands tended to increase the amplitude between yearly yields that under the prevailing conditions of low yields exposed the producers to uncertainty and imposed high costs of maintaining a grain reserve. The relative abundance of land had an additional effect, that of keeping the economic price of labor relatively high. However, the institution of

Table 2.1   Size and Distribution of Land Resources in Eighteenth-Century Russia (in 1,000 Hectares)

Year	Total	Plowland	%	Meadows	%	Forest	%
1696	405,091	31,976	7.89	67,068	16.56	213,416	52.68
1725	418,219	41,848	10.01	66,296	15.85	213,958	51.16
1763	423,128	53,865	12.73	63,308	14.96	205,890	48.66
1796	485,465	81,359	16.76	76,650	15.79	217,322	44.76

Source: Tsvetkov, *Izmenenie lesistosti*, pp. 110–14.

serfdom prevented by noneconomic means the real price of labor from manifesting itself and inhibited technological improvements which might have lowered its economic price.

The Agricultural Cycle and Natural Calamities

For the overwhelming majority of the inhabitants of eighteenth-century Russia, the rhythm of life was determined not by the wars or reforms of Peter the Great, nor by anything his successors managed to accomplish or failed to do, but by the conditions of the agricultural cycle of plowing, planting, and harvesting the Russian fields. The sustenance of the vast majority of Russians depended less upon the level of rents, the burden of government taxation, or profits derived in domestic or foreign trade than upon the work of nature. Of paramount importance was the size of the harvest, the ratio of harvested grain to the seed planted (the output-seed ratio). The major calamities of the century were not necessarily the occasional defeats of the Russian armies or the failures of Russian diplomacy, but the famines that frequented the Russian countryside.

The reason for the harmful influence of droughts and frosts upon the Russian food supply lay in the low output-seed ratio of grains even during years of normal weather conditions. With an output-seed ratio of 3.0–3.5:1 for grains during normal weather conditions and grain reserves of not more than one year's consumption, any single year of adverse weather put rural households in a precarious situation as far as food supply was concerned. Repetitive bad weather conditions, severe winters, excessive rainfall, or droughts that affected the yields of both spring and winter grains produced a famine if they lasted for two consecutive years. The exhaustion of grain reserves followed the decline of the available current grain supply. This was accompanied by a decline of commercial output, a rise in grain prices, and privation of various degrees.

The first half of the eighteenth century was abundantly endowed with adverse weather, the impact of which was seriously felt by the agricultural sector and the population at large. The low population growth during this period cannot be attributed solely to the conditions of the food supply, but it is an additional indicator of the effects of the frequent failures of the grain yields during this period. According to V. M. Kabuzan, the yearly growth rate of the population in the territory of the first population census was 0.66 percent during the 1719–44 period.[2] Prior to the census, however, three severe famines occurred during the years 1704–16. Strong evidence supports an assumption that during the Petrine period, years that were part of the last third of the Maunder Minimum throughout Europe, the population increased at an even lower rate than during the period between the first and second censuses. Consequently the rate of population growth for the first half of the eighteenth century was probably even less than 0.66 percent.

During the second half of the century bad weather conditions that influenced yields were less frequent and apparently of shorter duration. Their effect was less severe and did not lead to famines covering most of the territory of Russia. The growth of the planted area, particularly in the blacksoil steppe zone, had the effect of dispersing the population. Although the steppe zone was susceptible to droughts, there was more of a compensating substitution effect between the nonblacksoil and the blacksoil zones which resulted in spreading and diminishing the risks of famine.

Referring back to the previous chapter, the descriptive table 1.9 uses contemporary sources to characterize the weather conditions associated with famines or low yields and provides a chronological distribution of the natural calamities during the eighteenth century. Table 1.10 examines the impact the calamities had, first on the availability of grain for export, and then upon the changes in price for the most important grain crops.

Most of the severe weather calamities had discernible and expectable effects upon grain exports and prices. A time lag between the actual calamity and its effect on exports was due to differences between the agricultural year and the period of trading and navigation; it was accentuated by the time-consuming process of collecting the marketable grain and transporting it to the major markets and ports of embarkation. Except for a few instances when the volume of exports was influenced by extraordinary demand created by pan-European famine, or when short-term price changes were superimposed upon a longer-term price movement in the European grain market, the Russian market seems to have responded in the proper direction. There can be no doubt that, under the conditions of serfdom, the peasants did not receive the compensation of increased prices for their marketable production in cases of lower yields. The reduction of marketable output, the incurring of debts, and the reduction of consumption outweighed the opportunities to charge higher prices. As a rule, Witold Kula's notion that low grain prices were correlated with high real incomes for serfs is supported by eighteenth-century Russian reality. Meteorological calamities leading to a decrease of the grain supply had the opposite effect: the real income of the serf population declined, the agriculturalists' health was adversely affected, and their rate of population growth declined.

Natural calamities that affected the size of the grain crop also affected the serf-owners. Whether under conditions of rent in kind, money rent, or labor dues, the diminished real incomes of the serfs affected their owners. Those engaged as grain producers for the market, however, had an opportunity to benefit from higher grain prices. Three factors limited their freedom to profit from meteorological disasters: (1) the customary law (and after 1734, the state law) that required serf-owners to support their indigent serfs after such calamities, which was coupled with their own self-interest in maintaining their wealth (embodied in the serfs); (2) their responsibility to the government as collectors of the poll tax, which meant advancing tax payments that were due regardless of the success or failure of harvests, with the hope of collecting the tax from the serfs at some point in the future; (3) the prohibitions against exporting grain during periods of high grain prices and diminished domestic grain supplies. The last limitation was removed in the 1760s when the landowning gentry were given the freedom to trade in grain regardless of the conditions of domestic supply or the level of domestic prices. This was achieved in an alliance with the merchants. Later on, the government tried to impose emergency measures (such as the decree of 1787 allowing duty-free importation of grain), but in general the land owners benefited from higher grain prices and were able to reduce the impact of low yields upon their incomes.

This short survey of the problem of the reduction of the grain supply and its effect on the income of the majority of the population indicates the difference between the first half of the century, when calamities were more frequent and consequences more severe, and the second half of the century, when the potential growth of incomes was less interrupted by natural weather disasters.

The Agricultural Routine

One of the most vivid descriptions of the activities of the agricultural labor force was provided by Vasilii Levshin, a Tula landowner and member of the Free Economic Society. It conveys the routine of agricultural labor in its seasonal sequence and is arranged by calendar months.[3] Although the timing of the various activities is determined to a major extent by the geographical position of the Tula guberniia in the central region of Russia, both the sequence and variety were typical for most of the agricultural regions of the country and are worth reproducing in full.

January. Continuation of grain threshing and hemp processing. Transportation of hay from meadows. Transportation of grain for sale. Hiring out for day labor in the city. At home the remaining men are making ropes and weaving bast sandals (*lapti*), while the women are spinning and taking care of the sheep, which are giving birth to their young ones.

February. Continuation of the previous activities. The ones who are leaving for work outside the villages are getting their passports and by the end of February are leaving for work. Preparation of a reserve of flour for the time of the thaw (when the snow melts and the roads are impassable) and for the summer.

March. Besides the above-mentioned activities, men are repairing their carts and agricultural implements for the coming field-work season. Repair of roofs, cleaning off the snow, and spreading straw on the floors of the farm buildings, inspecting the beehives and cleaning the hives by the end of March. Women are weaving their cloth and linen and continue to do it throughout April. They take care of the hens laying eggs and keep the hens on the nests.

April. Repair of wattle fences. Threshing of grain for spring seed. Plowing the soil for spring grains begins. By the end of the month, planting of wheat, peas, and early oats. The women and children take the cattle out to feed on pasture. They continue weaving and caring for the poultry and the newborns. Dyeing of the yarn, planting of cabbage plants, and row plantings of the seeds of garden vegetables.

May. Planting of oats, hemp, flax, millet, and part of the barley. Plowing of the gardens. Women take care of the poultry, are finishing their weaving, and begin to bleach their linen. Collecting of birch leaves for dyeing. Pasturing on the meadows being prohibited, they move the cattle to the fallow land strip. In the garden various kinds of vegetables are planted and the cabbage is replanted.

June. Planting of buckwheat and the rest of the barley. Transportation of manure to the fallow-field strips, and by the middle of the month, plowing up all of them. By the end of the month, planting of turnips and preparation for hay cutting. Women finish the bleaching of linen. Shearing of sheep, weeding of the spring grains and from the 24th, collection of dyeing-herbs. The agriculturalists look after the beehives. Men and women gathering and preparing bast and bark.

July. Beginning of hay mowing, gathering of the hay. From the middle of the month, second plowing and harrowing of the fallow strip. Women begin to harvest rye and weed the flax. Beehiving is continuing. The hungry cattle begin to rest after being moved to the harvested meadows.

August. Threshing of grain for seed, planting of winter grain. Harvesting of barley and wheat, cutting of oats and buckwheat, and gathering of the grains from the fields. Gathering of mushrooms and nuts. The cattle move to the rye fields. Second shearing of sheep.

September. Taking out the honey. Finishing the gathering of harvested grains from the fields. In some places, finishing the planting to winter grains. Women collecting the hemp, men threshing it and putting it into water. Threshing of grains begins. New construction and finishing of construction as well as repair of roofs begun earlier. Youngsters gather firewood in nearby small woods. Harvesting of flax and putting it in prepared places for retting. Digging up of turnips. The cattle enjoy having all the fields to themselves.

October. Taking the hemp out of the water, drying and processing it. In some places, plowing of the harvested rye fields for the next spring grains and spring wheat. Spreading manure on the field. Repair and rebuilding of dwellings continues, as well as gathering of firewood. The carders are carding the wool and the women begin the spinning. The village tailors leave to find work. Preparation of the beehives for the winter. Hunters are hunting hares and grouse.

November. The main threshing. Beginning of transportation of firewood prepared for the winter and summer. Completion of hemp processing. Women begin spinning hemp and continue throughout the entire winter. They put the pigs on feeding, and with the arrival of strong frosts, or the beginning of winter, they slaughter the geese and ducks from the fields for sale. Major hunting of rabbits. Discontinue the pasturing of cattle in the fields. Repair the sleighs.

December. Threshing. Finish transporting firewood. Send out grain caravans. Leaving for the steppe for harvested grain and to trade in various goods. The ones who left for outside work return home. Slaughtering of the fattened pigs, sometimes of the fowl that were not slaughtered toward the end of November.

The superfluous workers leave the household for the city for day labor. Trap-hunting of wolves and hares, partridges and grouse. In the evenings, the men are weaving bast sandals and making ropes and other home implements.

Yields

Russian agriculture during the eighteenth century was marked by low yields, the low output-seed ratio of grain and legumes. Neither individuals nor institutions collected that information, and the absence of such data is a serious gap in our knowledge that cannot be bridged either by the use of nineteenth-century data collected and reported by the governors of the various *gubernii* or by the impressionistic data provided by eighteenth-century travelers and authors. The first attempt to collect systematically the data for particular regions of central Russia was undertaken by the Soviet historian Elena I. Indova, known for her work on the court peasants.[4]

As tentative as Indova's data are, they are worthy of being reproduced and discussed. Undoubtedly they will be corrected by future historians, but now they represent the best approximation of the output-seed ratios in eighteenth-century European Russia.

The general significance of data on the output-seed ratio lies in their providing a general characteristic of crop agriculture prevailing in a particular region. A low output-seed ratio indicates that obtaining a desired volume of grain required not only a relatively high volume of seed but also a larger crop area than would be required were the ratio higher. Much of the labor in crop production is expended on plowing, harrowing, weeding, and harvesting a particular crop area, and labor requirements are higher when yields are low. Crop production at low output-seed ratios requires additional land and more labor to increase the planted area. Apart from the larger farms and more labor, a low output-seed ratio requires also the maintenance of more workstock to perform the extensive farming operations. This in turn creates a larger demand for fodder and competition between arable land and meadows for the production of that fodder.

There is also a consumption aspect to low output-seed ratios. A low ratio, which is tantamount to low yields given the constraints on land and labor, is often translated into a precarious food supply for the population. A low ratio does not permit a rapid adjustment to changing market conditions because it is difficult and costly to increase the level of output even when prices increase. It is possible that this sluggishness in responding to the price signals of the market was at the root of the large price amplitudes in the eighteenth-century Russian grain economy. Thus

Table 2.2   Output/Seed Ratios for the Major Grains in Central Russia, by Decades

Grain	1710s	1720s	1730s	1740s	1750s	1760s	1770s	1780s	1790s
Rye	2.9	3.55	3.2	4.25	3.7	4.65	4.2	3.3	3.1
Wheat	3.9	3.7	3.9	3.6	3.3	3.8	4.3	3.2	3.0
Oats	2.7	4.1	3.3	3.8	3.5	4.45	4.8	3.35	3.6
Barley	3.9	4.5	4.0	3.7	4.3	4.7	4.2	3.5	3.1

Source: Indova, "Urozhai," pp. 146–51.

the low output-seed ratio contributed to a low level of marketability of grain and a difficulty in increasing the marketable share of the output and also made difficult the prevention of the consequences of natural calamities upon the food consumption of the population and thereby contributed to the disastrous impact of famine on the rate of population growth.

To the extent possible, Indova's data will be examined in conjunction with the data on population growth from the censuses and the fragmentary price data for grains.

In its most general form Indova's compilation of output-seed ratios for the four major grain crops is presented by decades in table 2.4. (There are no data for the first decade of the eighteenth century. The rye and oats data provided by Indova for the decades of the 1720s, 1740s, 1760s, 1780s, and 1790s were slightly modified: the regional data were adjusted by using as weights the number of peasants in each region, following the census data published by Kabuzan.

The output-seed ratios for the chief grains, rye and oats, largely agree with the information available on famines and weather calamities affecting grain yields. The notable exception is the decade of the 1790s, for which no major famines were recorded. Otherwise, the famines of the 1720s, 1730s, and 1780s explain the relatively low ratios of those decades.

An interesting and more complex case is presented by the ratios of wheat. According to Indova's data, these ratios exceeded the ones for rye only from the 1710s through the 1730s and during the 1770s. During the other decades they were below those for rye. The agricultural expansion of the eighteenth century occurred in two regions which were relatively well suited for wheat cultivation, the blacksoil and Volga regions, and therefore one would assume that the output-seed ratio of wheat would have increased, rather than decreased, relative to rye over the span of the century. The data, however, suggest that the opposite was happening. An explanatory factor for this phenomenon is the likelihood that the Russian agricultural producers expanding into the new regions were planting rye alongside wheat, because rye was the habitual consumption crop. Consequently the greater natural fertility of those regions affected both the rye and the wheat output-seed ratios. It is

also possible that, while in the regions of older settlement the wheat crop was grown on better land and may have received relatively more fertilizer than did the rye or oat crops, the planting of wheat in the new regions relatively further away from the wheat market centers and therefore commanding less of a price premium took place in the general fields with less care and attention. Moreover, the year-to-year variability of the weather conditions in the steppe regions of the blacksoil zone and the Volga region may have affected more strongly the wheat crop, while the chief support of the rye crop remained the more balanced weather conditions of the nonblacksoil zone.

Table 2.3 clearly indicates, not the advantage of wheat over rye in terms of output-seed ratios, but the advantage of the blacksoil zone over the central nonblacksoil zone for both rye and wheat. This advantage, when coupled with the availability of extensive land resources in both the central blacksoil zone and the Volga region, helps to explain why the agricultural population during the period 1720–95 increased in the former by over 90 percent, by more than 100 percent in the latter, but in the central nonblacksoil zone by only one-third. The output-seed ratios, although an imperfect indicator of the yields for the various grain crops, when viewed on a regional basis nevertheless help explain the growth patterns of the Russian population by regions. They explain the higher than average rate of population growth, for the century, during the period between the third and fourth *revizii* (1762–82) as well as the below average rate of population growth between the fourth and fifth *revizii* (1782–95).

There is one phenomenon that the output-seed ratios do not explain: the exhaustion of the soil, which according to some Soviet historians (including Indova) occurred during the last quarter of the century. The low ratio during the 1780s was clearly due to adverse weather conditions, and thus only the 1790s might have experienced an exhaustion of the soil. The fact that the lowering of output-seed ratios during the 1790s occurred in the central blacksoil zone and in the Volga region rather than in the central nonblacksoil zone calls for additional explanation rather than for acceptance of a soil-exhaustion thesis.

Table 2.3   Rye and Wheat Output/Seed Ratios by Major Regions

Rye	1710s	1720s	1730s	1740s	1750s	1760s	1770s	1780s	1790s
Central nonblacksoil	2.7	3.2	3.5	3.8	3.2	3.3	3.7	3.0	3.0
Central blacksoil	4.0	4.3	3.2	4.7	4.6	6.8	4.8	3.6	3.2
Volga	3.0	3.3	3.7	5.1	4.0	4.4	4.8	3.6	3.1
Wheat									
Central nonblacksoil	3.2	4.9	3.0	3.5	2.7	3.4	3.7	2.5	3.0
Central blacksoil	4.5	4.1	5.5	4.3	4.1	5.1	5.7	4.0	3.0
Volga	—	3.0	3.7	—	3.6	3.2	4.9	3.3	3.1

Source: Indova, "Urozhai," pp. 146–51.

Market Formation

Agricultural Products

The formation of markets in eighteenth-century Russia was a process that depended upon the purchasing power of consumers and upon the extent of production destined for sale rather than for consumption by the producers. It thus depended upon the exchange of goods produced by various social groups, often located at a considerable distance from one another, and their ability to benefit from this reciprocal demand. The exchange occurred predominantly in local meeting places—markets or fairs—in which producers and consumers, but more often middlemen and consumers, conducted their business.

The existence of numerous markets and fairs in eighteenth-century Russia is sufficient evidence that a substantial volume of goods was produced for the market. The contemporary authority on Russian trade, M. M. Chulkov, estimated the total number of fairs in Russia for the 1770s as 1,637. That figure is undoubtedly an underestimate, and there were probably a total of about 2,200 fairs in that period. The number of fairs grew in Russia during the eighteenth century, but less rapidly than the population.

It is not the formation of markets in the sense of loci of general exchange that is of particular interest here. Rather, it is the market in the sense of the institution of exchange of a particular commodity, its scope, and other characteristics which is the issue. It is the market as the territory within which the price differential is low or can be attributed to differences in the cost of transportation that is the object of investigation.

There is no doubt that the market for some imported commodities was unified in Russia, especially for high-priced commodities for which no readily available substitutes, domestically produced, existed. For a number of industrial commodities, such as iron, produced in only a few regions of the country, the market was also quite well unified, or at least regionally delineated. Of particular interest, however, is the formation of a market in agricultural commodities, some of which had to be transported over a long distance at very considerable cost. Formation of mar-

kets was even more significant for such commodities as grains, which were produced literally everywhere.

A presumption arises: grain markets were primarily local, they consisted of relatively small areas producing a grain surplus that could be transported cheaply to urban-type settlements, to alcohol distilleries, or to any party in the vicinity demanding grain. On the basis of such a presumption, one must assume that the production of marketable grain, demanded locally or within a short radius, grew only very slowly, and certainly no faster than the nonagricultural population of that micro-region.

We know that this was not the case all over Russia in the seventeenth and eighteenth centuries. There were large population centers that could not be supplied by the immediately adjacent regions. There were grain suppliers for the standing army. Last, but hardly least, there was relatively rapid growth of quantities of marketable grain in areas in which no increase in local demand was occurring. The existence of much more extensive markets, connected by uniform price movements, had to exist to explain all of these phenomena.

There were already major regional markets for grain in the seventeenth century. They were capable of supplying the city of Moscow, exports to Arkhangel'sk and Sweden, and the demands of Siberian settlements and fur hunters. It was during the eighteenth century, however, that both the expansion and the integration of local markets into major regional markets took place. The available data permit tracing some of the patterns of market formation and the changes that occurred.[5]

The oldest and most extensive mega-region for marketed rye was the territory along the Volga River and its major tributaries. The Volga was the major artery of Russian domestic trade for bulk commodities such as grain and it was the main route connecting the local markets of this vast region. The new agricultural lands were settled and opened up for commercial traffic along the Volga during the eighteenth century. Although this mega-region included subregions of different densities, its boundaries can be clearly delineated. Two basic characteristics of the mega-region can be noted. First, the lowest prices prevailed in the more sparsely settled regions of the southeastern part, or middle Volga region, while higher prices prevailed in the northwestern, more populated, areas. This points to the impact of transportation costs up the Volga. Second, price correlations were the highest (variance was the least) approximately at the midpoint of the region along the extended river route. This was a result both of the higher density of population and urban settlements, the smaller distances between the observable locations, and the relatively minor differences of the impact of local supply sources on the one hand and the extremities of the mega-region on the other. At both extremities of this Volga mega-region, the correlations of prices were much lower. This suggests fluctuations in the local supply situation at the southeastern end and perhaps fluctuations in both supply and demand situations in the extreme northwest.

Another distinct market region can be observed in the first half of the eighteenth century, the Northern Dvina River basin, north of the Volga region. This region reached, in the west, the settlements on the Karelian border and, in the east, via the northern Urals, the area of northwest Siberia. Arkhangel'sk was its port outlet. This region had a much more limited supply capacity than did the Volga region, and probably a higher degree of grain marketability. The price level was high, reaching that of the northwestern extremity of the Volga mega-region. That in part reflected the foreign demand for Russian grain. The price differentials prevailing in the northern region were strongly affected by the transportation costs from the supply areas to the ones which were clearly grain-consuming ones.

The Baltic grain region presents a complicated case. This was an area of relatively high yields and there was a strong local supply. It was also affected by the Volga mega-region and the eastern Belorussian region, which was outside the Russian national boundaries throughout the first half of the eighteenth century but was strongly linked economically to the Baltic provinces and exported its marketable grain via those provinces. The presence of the ports of Riga, Revel', and Pernau, even more than the relative proximity of St. Petersburg, imposed a uniformity of responses to price stimuli as well as price fluctuations which were often independent of the changes in marketable grain supply. The impact of the world market made the Baltic-provinces grain market a price taker for most of the first half of the eighteenth century, but also increased the price correlations (decreased the price variance) within the Baltic provinces.

The other mega-region formed during the first half of the eighteenth century extended southward from the southern part of Moscow province and encompassed many of the blacksoil areas from Tula, Kaluga, and Riazan' through Voronezh and Orël all the way to Kiev. During the first half of the eighteenth-century Russia had no outlet to the Black Sea via the Dnepr River, and the commercial grain from this mega-region in part flowed northward toward the Baltic or was distributed along this broad belt among the extremities of the region. The price data for this region indicate the existence of a nuclear subregion of higher density and greater price uniformity for southern Moscow province and the adjacent Tula, Riazan', and parts of Orël district than there was for the other territories within this expanding mega-region.

The abolition of internal tolls, territorial expansion, population growth, increasing urbanization, the growth of total as well as marketable agricultural production during the second half of the eighteenth century introduced significant changes in the shape and structure of the grain market. These transformations took the form of boundary changes among the previously existing regional markets as well as in the integration of new areas which tended to form new regional markets.

Starting with the giant Volga region, one can follow its expansion westward toward a link with the Baltic areas; this involved both the supply of St. Petersburg as well as an outlet to foreign markets. The link with the Baltic areas assumed increased significance in view of the integration of the Belorussian and Lithuanian provinces, some of which formerly used East Prussia as the outlet for grain exports. Extending itself westward, the Volga region toward the end of the century contracted in its southern and eastern parts by losing the territory of the Lower Volga.

This loss was symptomatic, for it signaled the emergence of a new mega-region extending from the southern Urals across the Lower Volga to reach the lower Dnepr basin, including the Black Sea areas. The formation of this new regional market was precipitated by the opportunity to export grain via the Black Sea ports and was supported by the spread of crop production in southern Russia. The force of this new regional market integration process was most strongly felt on the middle Volga, where the choice of the direction in which to make grain shipments, either via the Volga to the Baltic or toward the south to the Black Sea, became a reality.

The second change in the configuration of the Volga mega-region occurred under the impact of the northward expansion of the central blacksoil region. Not only was the Moscow region largely overtaken by the flow of grain from the southern region, but so was the Vladimir nonblacksoil area. The latter, previously one of the mainstays of the Volga region, was detached from its previous supply line and was incorporated in the expanding blacksoil region.

This region also expanded northward and northwestward toward northern Belorussia and Smolensk. It was partly seeking an outlet to the Baltic ports, chiefly because the Black Sea trade in grains was developing slowly and was affected by wars. For those reasons the Ural-Black Sea region and the blacksoil region failed to become one region in the eighteenth century; in the case of the market for rye, that happened only in the nineteenth century.

The grain market in the second half of the eighteenth century witnessed a decrease of the price differentials both within the regions and among the regions, by comparison with the first half of the century. This tendency was noted by Koval'chenko and Milov, although they considered the preservation of the distribution of price differentials as a rather stable characteristic of the grain markets. Their ratio of extreme price quotations for rye declined from 4.77 to 4.0 between the periods of 1744–53 and 1809–19, and some price differentials within the Volga region declined by over 20 percent in the same period. They still found, however, a preserved "hierarchy" of price levels in most of the areas of the blacksoil region.[6] The blacksoil region, which was formed later than the Volga region, was slow in exhibiting the decline of price differentials and was therefore prone to "preserve the hierarchy of price levels."

The narrowing of price differentials was a consequence of the expansion of the grain market and the absorption of a multitude of previously separated local markets. The slowness of the process of the narrowing of the price differentials was due to the specific conditions prevailing in Russian agriculture and trade. Market formation can be attributed to the general expansion of the economy, the growth of the urban population, the foreign trade in grains, and the beginnings of specialization in agriculture. Moreover, serf-owners were increasingly participating in the marketing of their estates' crops, which coincided with the expansion into the blacksoil areas and the rise of grain prices. Holding back the process, on the other hand, were the very slow rate of transportation improvements, the fact that the urban share of the total population was small, the slow rise in the domestic and foreign demand for marketable grain, and the poorly developed apparatus for collecting the marketable surplus.

The role of the state in this process remains to be noted. As with other areas of governmental interference in the economy of eighteenth-century Russia, there were credit and debit entries. On the credit side were the construction of a few canals, improvement of some waterways, and the distribution of state purchases of grain for the armed forces, which tended to minimize price differentials (and perhaps save the government some expense in transporting the grain). On the debit side of the ledger were the internal tolls (until 1754), the prohibition of grain exports during periods of high prices, and the inability to set up sufficient reserves to cope with the impact of famines. The government's introduction of free trade in grains in the 1760s removed a serious obstacle and uncertainty in the grain market and contributed to the more rapid development of the grain market.

Grain Consumption by the Armed Forces

Grain consumption by the armed forces ought to be the easiest to quantify in view of the remarkable stability of the prescribed consumption norms. Major variations in the grain consumption by the armed forces should have occurred either when the size of the armed forces was drastically increased or during wartime, when, according to military statutes, normal rations were augmented by special field rations. The size of the armed forces is known for particular dates during the eighteenth century, and thus it should be possible to arrive at a general order of magnitude of grain consumption by this category of users. There are a number of specific reasons why there may be as much as a 15-to-20-percent error in estimating military grain consumption. For one, there is a lack of specific data for the navy. Moreover, officers and petty officers received more than one ration per person. The number of rations depended upon rank and was computed as a multiple of what the basic soldier got. For example, a sergeant received 3 rations and a general field marshall 200 rations.[7]

The basic grain ration per rank-and-file member of the armed forces was 3 chetverti of rye flour and 15 chetveriki (a chetverik was one-eighth of a chetvert') of groats. The battle ration (portsiia) given during a military campaign was an additional 2 pounds of bread per day and one and a half garnets of groats per month. The combat ration also included a pound of meat per day, 2 charki (glasses) of alcohol, and one garnet of beer.[8]

The horses of the armed forces, both in the line of combat and as motive power in noncavalry regiments, consumed a considerable volume of oats. This was calculated as 6 chetverti per year per horse in the years 1712–40, and 8 chetverti in later years. Table 2.4 presents an estimation of the armed force's grain consumption in selected years of the eighteenth century.

The data in table 2.4 indicate that the consumption of food grain rose from about 600,000 chetverti during the Petrine period to over 800,000 chetverti by the middle of the century and more than a million chetverti by the end of the century. A conservative estimate would be a doubling of the food-grain consumption of the armed forces during the eighteenth

Table 2.4   Estimates of Grain Consumption by the Armed Forces

Year	No. in Armed Forces	Flour (in chetvert')	Groats (in chetvert')	No. of Horses	Oats (in chetvert')
1712	174,757	524,271	32,767	77,980	467,880
1720	173,844	521,532	32,596	76,247	457,482
1731	204,086	612,258	38,266	63,745	382,470
1740	246,690	740,070	46,254	76,165	456,990
1746	262,900	788,700	49,294	—	—
1750	320,329	960,987	60,062	81,851	630,808
1774	274,557	823,671	51,479	—	—
1795	495,663	1,486,989	92,937	—	—
1796	368,924	1,106,775	69,173	70,096	533,816
1798	322,783	968,349	60,522	57,828	462,624
1799	407,700	1,223,100	76,444	—	—

Note: For the size of the armed forces and number of horses, see Zhuravskii, *Statisticheskoe obozrenie*, pp. 7, 12, 41, 42, 57, 72, 103, 136, 145.

century. On the subject of feed grains, the figures on the consumption of oats reflect a stability in the number of horses throughout most of the period, and the increase in the oats ration after 1740 was balanced (except for war years, when the data are less accurate anyway) by a decrease in the army's horse population.

The fact that the armed forces were a source of steady and gradually rising demand for grains clearly affected the operation of the grain market. During the Northern War, when the entire Russian economy was subordinated to the object of winning the war and makeshift arrangements were devised and changed to deal with crisis situations, the food and feed requirements of the armed forces were met by using supply contractors for the army and collectors of the extraordinary food tax in kind. Since much of what was done for the war effort were emergency measures, there is little in the documents indicating the costs of feeding the Petrine armies or the exact procedures that were followed to insure an adequate food and feed supply. A 1711–12 outline of the maintenance costs of the various branches of the armed forces excluded food and forage, perhaps because of the persistence of the old service landholding (*pomest'e*) system for the natural supply of the army, in which every landholding cavalryman brought his own supplies.

It was only in 1720, after the new military regulations were announced, that an estimate of food and forage costs was published (1,243,353 rubles) and was included in the new poll tax designed to pay for the total upkeep of the armed forces. In 1720 the food and forage rations per soldier and per horse were established as shown in table 2.5.

The total projected food and forage volume and costs for 1720 are shown in table 2.6. The discrepancy between the estimated costs and the computed ones can be explained either in terms of the zonal prices for the purchase of food and forage (see table 2.7) or by

Table 2.5   Food and Forage Rations, 1720

Ration per Soldier	Quantity	Price per Unit	Total Cost (in Rubles)
Flour	3 chetverti	1.50 rubles p. chetvert'	4.50
Groats	1.5 chetverik	2.00 rubles p. chetvert'	.375
Salt	24 pounds	.25 rubles p. pood	.15
Meat			.72
Total			5.745

Ration per Horse	Quantity	Price per Unit (in Rubles)	Total Cost (in Rubles)
Oats	6 chetvert'	.50 p. chetvert'	3.00
Hay	90 poods	.03 per pood	2.70
Total			5.70

Source: Zhuravskii, *Statisticheskoe obozrenie*, p. 20.

Table 2.6   Food and Forage Volume and Costs, 1720

	Volume	Costs (in rubles)
Flour (chetvert')	503,394	755,091
Groats (chetvert')	31,461	62,924
Oats (chetvert')	457,482	220,881
Hay (poods)	6,862,230	198,792
Salt (poods)	100,678	22,029
Total		1,259,717

Source: Zhuravskii, *Statisticheskoe obozrenie*, p. 20.

the fact that food and forage in the Baltic provinces and in some areas of the Ukraine were collected in kind.

The establishment of zonal prices for food and forage reflects price differentials in markets of various regions and clearly indicates the relative costs as well as the development of regional grain markets in Russia. In fact, the prices shown in table 2.7 tend to confirm what one would expect in the regional markets: low prices in the fertile but sparsely inhabited areas of the south, southeast, and east, and higher prices in the central and western parts of the country,

Table 2.7   Zonal Prices for Food and Forage, 1720

	Price per Unit (in Rubles)			
Zone	Flour	Groats	Oats	Hay
St. Petersburg	2.00	2.00	1.00	.06
Novgorod, Pskov	2.00	2.00	1.20	.03
Tver', Torzhok, Zhetsk,				
Uglich	1.50	2.00	.60	.02
Kiev, Azov	.60	2.00	.40	.01
Smolensk	1.20	1.50	.60	.02
Kazan'	.60	1.00	.25	.01

Source: Zhuravskii, *Statisticheskoe obozrenie*, p. 24.

where there was a higher population density and greater opportunity for marketing the grain surplus.

To the extent that the armed forces relied primarily during peacetime for their food and forage either upon the services of contractors (*podriadchiki*) or upon the purchases by officials of the supply commissariat of the War College, they basically relied upon the market. The zonal or average prices served as a ceiling for their transactions. The vagaries of the grain market and its price fluctuations clearly affected governmental policies, especially in times of famines and extraordinarily high prices. The famine of 1724, for example, forced the government to return to a policy of food requisitioning from the taxpaying population at prices which were below the market price. The decree (*plakat*) of 1724 established the following prices (in lieu of taxes) for requisitioned grains and fodder: flour, groats, and oats, 1.50, 2.00, and 0.50 rubles per *chetvert'*, respectively, and hay, 3 kopeks per pood. The decree shifted the burden of higher prices from the government to the taxpayers. This extraordinary tax was so burdensome that, after the death of Peter, the requisitions were abolished by a decree of the new rulers on October 11, 1725.[9]

The Seven Years' War involved very substantial expenditures, budget deficits, payment of high prices for food and forage, and the overcoming of temporary supply shortages. During the war the issue of the buildup and maintenance of substantial food and fodder reserves for the armed forces was raised. To accomplish this task within a relatively short period, the government deliberated about the level of price ceilings and settled for the same level as the 1731 prices for flour and groats (1.20 and 1.50 rubles per *chetvert'*, respectively), but raised the price for oats from .50 to .75 rubles per *chetvert'*. Following the general rise in prices, the next price revision was effected in 1786. The yearly price of a food ration for a soldier in a field army was increased to 4.02 rubles, but the government tried to keep the price of the rations for soldiers in provincial garrisons at the previous level.

The Russian government responded to price fluctuations in the grain market in two ways: it adjusted to the market and it tried to secure food and fodder supplies outside the market through taxation in kind. The prevalence of the first policy indicates that for most of the century supplying the army with its basic grain requirements presented no major difficulties of an economic or organizational nature. The scattering of the markets for grain purchases for the armed forces over many areas of the country created outlets for marketable grain that might otherwise not have existed and thus stimulated the commercial output of grains.

In 1789, primarily because of a war with the Ottoman Empire, a grain tax in kind was levied in the blacksoil and southern regions of the Russian Empire. (The tax per male was 2 *chetveriki* of flour and 1.5 garnets of groats.) Payment for the grain, calculated at prevailing market prices, was applied against tax arrears or toward future taxes. This tax could be viewed as a supply rather than a fiscal measure, but the grain tax in kind survived the conclusion of the Russo-Turkish War in 1794 and, in conjunction with the increase in the poll tax, became a semipermanent adjustment to the tax in most of the Russian provinces.[10] In view of the declining value of the ruble and the rise in grain prices, the government fixed the purchase price under the tax arrangement.

The government expected that the tax in kind in 1796 would yield a total of 1,572,615 *chetverti* of flour and 126,412 *chetverti* of groats, a major part of the expected requirements of 2,404,600 *chetverti* of flour and 236,166 *chetverti* of groats. The government also expected major savings in the face of its alternative, paying the market price. However, the tax in kind proved clearly unpopular and was abolished by a decree of December 18, 1797.[11]

Through such actions the government's reaction to rising grain prices constituted a search for budgetary solutions by circumventing the market in securing food and forage supplies for the armed forces. They did not exhaust the government's responses to the behavior of the grain market. The problem of food and forage prices was also raised during a major review of the military organization, when changes were introduced in the size and composition of the armed forces.

The statutory Petrine prices of 1720, listed in table 2.7, were set during a period of high food prices. Debating and deciding the further fate of the Russian armed forces in 1731, the authorities came up with the idea of lowering the ceiling prices for grains. The idea was joyfully accepted and decreed: the 1720 price for flour was reduced 20 percent (from 1.50 to 1.20 rubles per *chetvert'*), the price for groats was reduced 25 percent (from 2 to 1.50 rubles per *chetvert'*), and the price of oats for the field army was reduced by 10 percent (from .50 to .45 ruble per *chetvert'*).[12] This measure had the effect of lowering the cost per soldier's ration (the cost of flour and groats) to 3.88125 rubles and introduced savings that enabled the government to increase the size of the armed forces without increasing budget expenditures.

One issue remains to be clarified with respect to the grain consumption by the armed forces, the matter of supply in two areas of Russia's territory, Siberia and the Baltic provinces. The supply of grain to the garrisons located in Siberia was in part achieved by the obligatory deliveries of grain by the state serfs, and in part by the transportation of grain from European Russia. The very substantial transportation costs raised the price of soldiers' rations in Siberia. Thus in 1766 the accepted calculation of the costs per soldier's ration in European Russia was 3.88 rubles maximum, the allowance for Siberia per ration was 6.75 rubles. The Baltic provinces (and to some extent, provinces of the Ukraine) differed to the extent that throughout most of the century the supply of grains to the armed forces was guaranteed by local taxes in kind. Either the relative ease of gathering the taxes in a grain-exporting region, the relatively higher prices for grains in the Baltic provinces, or bureaucratic routine kept this system going for a long time. Grain was delivered to a few major storage places (*magaziny*), the largest of which were those in Riga and Pernau. The data for the yearly inventories of those storage places preserved from the years 1730–75 provide an interesting insight into the long-term stability of the amounts stored and of the decline of stocks as a result of the Seven Years' War.

The consumption of grain by the armed forces exhibited a secular rise over the century. In most years the demand by the armed services did not have a disturbing impact on the grain market. The armed forces' consumption constituted only a part of the demand by the Russian government for grain. The calculations presented in this section have not included the grain allowances for the navy. (The admiralty demanded for 1796 311,798 *chetverti* of flour and 47,067 *chetverti* of groats for naval and supporting personnel.) Grain allowances for civil servants, for various categories of other government employees, grain subsidies to technical specialists, ration supplements to salaries in various geographic areas and on many occasions all added to the government's grain bill. These amounts, however, tended to fluctuate more than did the consumption by the armed services, and did not exceed it. Estimating total government demand for marketable grain is both risky and complicated. My calculations assume that the consumption by the armed services represented a fixed proportion of the total government demand.

Grain for Alcohol Distilling

One of the major users of commercial grain in eighteenth-century Russia was the alcohol distilling industry. The total conversion of grain into alcohol during the century can be estimated to have reached up to 1,200,000 *chetverti* of grain annually, but not all of it can be classified as commercial grain in the strict sense of the term.

First, the grain converted into alcohol for the home consumption of the nobility must be excluded, at least the volume that was legally permitted and tax exempt. The use of grain for alcohol distilling in the households of the gentry and nobility has been determined by the alcohol norms per household scaled according to the ranks of the noblemen. The range was from 30 pails of alcohol for home consumption per year for a holder of the fourteenth rank to 1,000 pails for a holder of the first rank. This volume of alcohol did not appear, at least officially, in the market and was distilled from grain that, for the most part, did not originate in the market. For this one should exclude a volume of grain of about 100,000 *chetverti*.

Second, the state-owned distilleries used primarily or exclusively grain produced by the state serfs on the state domains. It was supplied directly to the distilleries, avoided the market, and involved a total of up to 150,000 *chetverti* of grain. According to the 1753 estimates of the Revenues (*Kamer*) College, the productive capacity of state-owned distilleries was 500,416 pails of alcohol. Of this, according to the Soviet historian N. I. Pavlenko, the actual output was within the range of 65 to 70 percent of capacity.[13] If the volume of actual production depended upon the availability of raw materials, in the middle of the century about 140,000 *chetverti* of grain which was used in the state production of alcohol cannot be included in the category of grain actually marketed.

Still another volume of grain was supplied by the noble estate owners to their own commercial distilleries out of their own production. It was at least as large as the amount they consumed at home and the state's production combined. This quantity of grain is not included in the grain supplied to the commercial distilleries because the gentry plants were an integral part of the estates and thus the grain supplied by the estates themselves constituted an intrafirm transfer. This volume of grain can be estimated at between 350,000 and 450,000 *chetverti* per year, depending upon the period and the territorial coverage.

The rest of the 1,200,000 *chetverti* of grain converted annually into alcohol, about 400,000 to 500,000 *chetverti*, was obtained in the market.[14]

Prior to 1754 most of the grain for alcohol distilling purchased in the market was obtained by merchant distillers. After 1754, when alcohol distilling became a monopoly of the gentry and nobility, the gentry entrepreneurs substituted, at least in part, for the previous purchases of the merchant distillers in turning toward the market for a part of their grain supply.

A very large proportion of the total alcohol consumption was accounted for by the two capital cities and the garrison towns in which the armed forces were stationed. Toward the end of the century, however, most of the alcohol production was supplied by the gubernii of Penza, Riazan', Tambov, and Kaluga, located in the northern tier of the blacksoil region. These four provinces produced 1,657,000 pails of alcohol out of the total of 3,348,278 pails produced in seventeen provinces of Russia. (These figures do not include the Baltic provinces and the Ukraine, both major alcohol-producing regions. Two Ukrainian provinces, Chernigov and Kiev, accounted in the same year for 1,184,000 pails of alcohol.)[15] The four Russian provinces were areas of high levels of both grain output and commercial grain production. The estates of the nobility and the lands of the peasants in those regions could supply grain for alcohol distilling either directly or through the market. Given the distance of some provinces, such as Penza, from major population centers, one may conclude that the shipping of alcohol outside the region was considerably cheaper than was the shipping of grain.

The supply of grain for alcohol distilling has been tacitly assumed as stationary, at least during the second half of the century, in spite of the rising population. The major causative factor was technological improvement in alcohol distilling, which increased the volume of alcohol obtained from a unit of grain. Around the middle of the century a *chetvert'* of grain yielded 2.25 to 2.5 pails of alcohol, and by the end of the century the yield rose to 4.5 to 5 pails. Consequently the utilization of grain by the industry remained almost unchanged in spite of the doubling of alcohol production during the second half of the century on the same territory.

In summary, the total utilization of grain for legitimate alcohol distilling exceeded a million *chetverti*, but the actual volume of grain purchased for this purpose in the market was within the range of 400,000 to 500,000 *chetverti*. The rest flowed through nonmarket channels. To the extent that alcohol distilling yielded monopoly profits to the nobility, tax revenues to the state, profits to grain merchants, and incomes to grain producers, the government did not consider it an inferior alternative to foreign trade in grains. It had a stimulating effect upon grain production, provided employment in production, transportation, and distribution, and thereby broadened the scope of the market in the Russian economy.

The Production and Availability of Grain in Russia

Some of the global figures or estimates for the economic performance of agriculture during the eighteenth century are not available. They must somehow be pieced together and estimated if we are to form, albeit roughly, some basic parameters to deal with central economic problems. There is no other problem which can compete for significance and centrality with the one of the production and availability of grain. All of the few attempts to apply methods of "political arithmetic" to estimate the wealth and income of Russia, by eighteenth-century statesmen or modern scholars, have started with an estimate of the size of the grain crop. Instead of citing the few and usually unreliable estimates of contemporaries, I have adopted a different procedure.

The objective is to estimate approximately the per capita gross and net production of grain for the bulk of the rural population in as much of the territory within the boundaries of Russia as is feasible. For this purpose a region was chosen for which relatively reasonable data are available for planted areas, yields of grains, and size of the rural population. The last were primarily peasants. The data for members of the nobility were not available for certain districts, and for the sake of uniformity the nobility was therefore excluded from the population estimates.

My working region included three subregions, the nonblacksoil zone, the blacksoil zone, and the Volga region. It included eight *gubernii* of the nonblacksoil zone (Moscow, Iaroslavl', Kostroma, Kaluga, Tver', Smolensk, Pskov, and Novgorod), seven of the blacksoil (Tula, Riazan', Orël, Kursk, Tambov, Penza, and Voronezh), and three of the Volga region (Nizhnii Novgorod, Simbirsk, and Saratov). The chosen provinces encompass areas of old settlement going back in time to the early history of Russia, areas of settlement from the times of Muscovy's expansion during the sixteenth and seventeenth centuries, and some areas which grew rapidly in population and agricultural production during the eighteenth century. For each of the *gubernii* within the subregions, normal years (in terms of weather conditions) were chosen, as far as was possible, and data for plantings, in volume of seed and harvesting yields for five grains (rye, oats, wheat, barley, and buckwheat), were obtained for the decade of the 1790s.[16] Those five grains represented about 87.7 percent of the total estimated volume of seeds and about 88.6 percent of the estimated harvested volume of crops.

The seed and yield data were then converted to a uniform measure. (The grain measure used in the eighteenth century was one of volume, not of weight. For example, a *chetvert'* of rye was approximately 130 kgs, a *chetvert'* of oats was only about 100 kgs.) It was

Table 2.8   Gross and Net per Capita Grain Output (in Kgs)

	Rye		Oats		Wheat		Barley		Buckwheat		5 Grains	
	Gross	Net	Gross	Net	Gross	Net	Gross	Net	Gross	Net	Gross	Net
Nonblack-soil	212	120	148	90	17	10	39	23	8	5	424	248
Blacksoil	394	244	154	111	24	13	12	8	123	91	707	467
Volga	192	116	125	96	67	44	18	12	38	25	440	293
Average:	260	173	147	100	28	17	24	15	62	45	521	350

then possible with the aid of regionally differentiated seeding norms to estimate not only the gross and net (gross harvested minus seed) output of grains, but also the planted areas under grains. One of the tests of the reasonableness of the obtained results for the planting areas was the approximate equality of the winter and spring grains, one of the marks of a three-field system in which little fertilizer was used and the crop rotation (including the fallow land) was supposed to take care of the restoration of the soil fertility.[17]

Another test of reasonableness of the obtained results on the estimated planted area was conducted by calculating the area of planting per agricultural worker. The approximate number of male peasants employed in agriculture was estimated for the different subregions from the available numbers of the male peasant population.[18] The division of the planted area by the estimated number of employed provided results which appear to be consonant with what is available in the descriptive literature.

The last step of the procedure was to calculate the per capita output and availability of the five grains for the rural population. This was not an attempt to estimate the level of actual food grain consumption, since even the net output figure included grain for industrial and commercial purposes such as alcohol distillery, urban and army consumption, grain exports, and feed for farm animals. It was an exercise in estimating a volume of per capita availability of grains within which decisions about allocation for various purposes could be made. It was a way of arriving at some quantitative estimates of agricultural activity with an emphasis on output, with the additional benefit of gaining understanding with respect to labor and productivity.

The major result of the inquiry into the output of five grains on a territory inhabited by over 14,500,000 people of both sexes points to a per capita annual gross output in excess of 520 kgs and about 350 kgs net output. Table 2.8 summarizes the results and provides the distribution of the various grains in total gross and net output for the major subregions. Given the prevailing level of marketings, the industrial uses of grain, and the utilization of feed grains, the available volume of grain appears to have been sufficient to provide even for the prevailing extensive grain component of the population's food intake.

Commercial Grain Production

The commercial output of grain in Russia during the eighteenth century cannot be estimated with any degree of accuracy. Although data are available for a number of estates, they tend to reflect the economy of estates of a particular size or location, not to help estimate the commercial output of major regions or of the country as a whole. For example, it is not known whether shifts from labor dues to money rent, or vice versa, changed materially the volume of commercial grain output. One might argue that an increase of grain production on land tilled by the serfs within their allotment, when compared with the previous production of the estate on the same land, yielded a higher potential or actual production, which would be marketed in order to pay the money rent. In many areas of Russia, however, an increase in grain production by the serfs helped to increase their home consumption, while the money for rent and taxes was earned in nonagricultural labor services. Moreover, our knowledge is fragmentary in the absence of representative data for serf farms and estates, or for particular important grain producing regions.

The only way to arrive at an approximate estimate of commercial grain production is to enumerate and estimate the use of grain outside the producers' households. There were five major categories of grain consumption in eighteenth-century Russia: (1) by the urban population; (2) by the armed forces; (3) for alcohol distilling; (4) exports abroad; and (5) shipments within Russia for consumption in grain-deficit areas.

These categories together account for the bulk of grains consumed outside the producers' households and therefore can be viewed as an approximation of the commercial output of the most important branch of Russian agriculture. To the extent possible, each of the components of the commercial grain production by use will be discussed and the evidence collated in order to arrive at a comprehensive view.

Table 2.9   Urban Population Estimates for Census Years (in 1,000s)

Year	Population
1721	1,240
1744	1,260
1762	1,520
1783	2,080
1795	3,040

Table 2.10   Estimated Grain Consumption of the Urban Population

Decade	Grain Consumption (1,000 chetverti)
1720s	2,480
1740s	2,520
1760s	3,040
1780s	4,160
1790s (2d half)	6,080

Urban Grain Consumption

The absence of general censuses accounting for the actual population in the Russian cities makes the estimation of the urban inhabitants a risky and questionable task. The Russian population *reviziia*, which included the taxpaying population, not only left out such groups as the nobility and clergy, but often registered the taxpayers at their place of origin rather than actual habitat. For the Russian total there are only estimates of the male members of the urban estates, who constituted a minority of the actual urban population. It is only for the capital cities (St. Petersburg and Moscow) that we have some population estimates referring to the distribution of the legal estates of the population.

To generalize from the St. Petersburg and Moscow data about the composition of the total urban population would be wrong. The urban estates were only 12 percent of the entire Moscow population in 1788–94 and only 18.7 percent for St. Petersburg in 1801. The capitals attracted large numbers of noblemen and gentry and their retinues of domestic servants, peasants engaged in industry, crafts, and other services. Moreover, there were large contingents of government officials as well as military garrisons. Thus the population composition of the capitals differed very much from that of the smaller cities, which accounted for the bulk of the urban population.

To obtain an approximation of the actual urban population, it was assumed that the nonurban estate population was equal to the urban estate population, which itself was calculated as double the size of its male component. The estimates of the approximate urban population are presented in table 2.9. These estimates contain an element of error,[19] but they can be used to estimate the volume of grain consumed by the urban population.

Assuming a consumption norm of 2 *chetverti* per inhabitant (including the feed consumed by urban livestock), one arrives at the grain consumption totals for the urban population presented in table 2.10.

If these assumptions and calculation are correct, the estimated grain consumption of the urban population appears to be the largest component of the commercial grain output. Certainly it is larger than the figures presented above on the armed forces'

consumption of grain and the use of grain in alcohol production combined.

The peasants directly provided more of the grain for urban consumption than they did for alcohol distilling or for supplies delivered under contract to the military. Unquestionably the large seignorial estates provided the larger part of the grain consumed in urban areas, but serfs participating in local fairs and small urban markets not only marketed industrial crops, livestock products, and products of their cottage industries, but they also sold some grain.

Russia's Grain Exports

The topic of grain exports is presented in greater detail in chapter 4, and will only be summarized here. Table 2.11 presents the available quantitative data on the export of Russian grain from Arkhangel'sk, the Baltic Sea ports, and the Black Sea ports (for the last, only during the last two decades of the eighteenth century).

In comparison with the proportions of the commercial grain production used by the distilleries and by the military, grain exports were in third in terms of sheer volume. In value terms, the share of exports rises in comparison with the other components of the marketed output. Moreover, beginning in the 1770s the increasing share of wheat in the total volume of grain exported raised the value of the exports more than the volume alone indicates. Rye continued to provide the bulk of the military consumption, and alcohol distilling continued to use the cheaper grains.

The share of grains in the overall export trade of Russia, or even in agricultural exports, during the eighteenth century was much more modest than at the later periods in Russian history. In 1769, the share of grain in total exports was 16.8 percent and it was 26.6 percent of agricultural exports. In 1793–95, the share of grains in total exports amounted to 6.66 percent, and to 11.14 percent of agricultural exports.[20] During the second half of the century grain exports constituted a small share of all exports and were not increasing relative to the exports of industrial crops or processed and manufactured goods.

Domestic Deficit-Area Grain Consumption

An estimation of the commercial grain output in Russia would not be complete without including the

Table 2.11   Yearly Average Grain Exports by Decades (in chetvert')

	Wheat	Rye	Oats	Barley	Other
1711–20	94,388	88,024	4,879	1,485	—
1721–30	12,939	12,518	4	295	122
1731–40	121,261	103,798	5,190	12,147	126
1741–50	51,306	43,895	4,983	2,428	—
1751–60	36,965	34,600	452	1,663	210
1761–70	204,896	165,142	25,487	7,394	6,324
1771–80	499,670	360,150	100,463	23,825	12,716
1781–90	405,833	272,479	75,065	20,257	27,522
1791–99	337,282	172,982	187,165	49,754	12,022

Table 2.12   Estimated Yearly Commercial Grain Consumption (in 1,000 Chetvert')

Decade	Urban Use	Military Use	Alcohol Distill.	Foreign Trade	Inter-region Trade	Total
1760s	3,000	1,200	800	200	1,100	6,300
1770s	3,200	1,300	900	500	1,200	7,100
1780s	4,400	1,500	1,000	400	1,300	8,600
1790s	6,100	1,700	1,200	350	1,400	10,750

interregional and intravillage grain trades. Considerable shipments of grain were supplied to Siberia and to the European North of Russia on a regular basis to feed the population. Presumably part of that has been accounted for already in the urban grain supply. Moreover, grain was exchanged for livestock products with the nomads of the eastern steppes within the boundaries of the Russian Empire. When there were local crop failures and famines grain was moved from surplus areas to those affected by drought and other natural calamities. Regrettably, regional grain balances indicative of the magnitudes involved are lacking.

I have assumed, therefore, a very low figure, about 1,100,000 to 1,400,000 *chetverti* of grain, enough to supply about 500,000 to 700,000 people. This is a volume insufficient to meet the requirements caused by a major calamity, but rather one which only supplemented the diets of grain deficit regions. (As noted in chapter 1, there were few major famines in the eighteenth century, a time when lords kept reserves for their serfs and when specialization was not yet intense in Russian agriculture.)

Conclusions

Minimum, rather than maximum, figures have been presented for each of the five major components of the Russian commercial grain output in the eighteenth century. These lower bounds are summarized for the second half of the century in table 2.12.

The growth of the commercial grain output in Russia estimated in table 2.12 acquires meaning only when compared with other indicators. The most significant ones are the change in population size, the share of commercial grain in the total grain output, and the share of grain marketings in the marketings

of agricultural products in general. Assuming that the total net grain output was about 3 *chetverti* of grain per capita, one may calculate a gross grain output (in terms of rye) of 104.4 million, 127.8 million, and 167.4 million *chetverti* for the 1760s, 1780s, and 1790s, respectively. The net output would have been 69.6 million, 85.2 million, and 111.6 million *chetverti* for the same decades. The share of the commercial grain output of the total net grain production is confined to the 9-to-10 percent range, with a slight increase over time. A similar stability can be observed when the marketed grain output is related to the population size, as represented by the peasant population. However, when the volume of estimated commercial grain is divided by the size of the nonagricultural population, the numbers grow over time—something one would expect in an economy in which growth of the market was occurring.

Agricultural and Nonagricultural Pursuits of the Serfs

Agriculture was the chief area of employment of the serfs in Russia, but it was not the only one, nor was it the exclusive source of serf income. Groups of the serf population were permanently employed in commerce, the crafts, the extractive and manufacturing industries, and the services. An even larger number of serfs combined employment in agriculture with part-time employment in the other sectors of the economy. Both forms of rent payment, money rent as well as labor services on the lord's demesne, permitted serfs, in principle, to engage in auxiliary, nonagricultural activities from which they could derive income. The money-rent (*obrok*) type of arrangement left to the serfs themselves the decisions about the allocation of time and effort between their farms and off-farm work. Serfs obliged to render labor services on the demesne were also permitted to allocate their residual time between their own farms and other pursuits. (The relative freedom to allocate time and effort between agricultural work and other pursuits, auxiliary or substituting for agriculture, did not imply that the serf-owners abdicated their right to control the activities of their serfs. Given the requirement that serfs carry internal passports when they moved about Russia, permission to engage in any lawful economic activity off the farm required the approval of the serf's owner. Such permission was granted in exchange for a fee, a share in the profits, or some other advantage that the owner might derive.)

Opportunities to engage in nonagricultural pursuits varied according to region, the demand for labor in agricultural vs. nonagricultural employment, and upon the need of the serf household to augment its income from off-farm employment. Given the favorable land/labor ratios in the blacksoil zone, and the prevalence of labor services there, agricultural employment left little room for competing activities. In the nonblacksoil zone the share of nonagricultural employment was relatively high in view of the less favorable conditions for agriculture, the higher degree of urbanization, and wider use of money rent.

There are a number of criteria by which the nonagricultural activities of the serfs could be classified. A central criterion was the compatibility of a particular type of employment with agricultural work, and the degree to which types of employment provided an income substitute for the agricultural labor of a household. If we use this criterion, different crafts and trade provide a range, starting with arrangements requiring the serf to be away from his household and farm for an extended period of the year and ending with arrangements in which the agricultural work and the craft or trade could fit together without conflict. Some trades forced the serf either to give up agricultural work or to hire help (or a substitute for labor services due the landlord), while other trades were of a shorter, perhaps seasonal period during the year and did not conflict with the peak demands for agricultural work.

Another criterion for classifying various crafts and trades is the distinction between those requiring migration far away from places of residence and those types of activities which could be pursued on the spot or in the vicinity. In addition to these criteria of time constraints or spatial mobility requirements, another distinction can be made between services or crafts the products of which were designed for local consumption and those which produced for distant markets. Finally, one might distinguish between motivations to earn income: those instances in which agriculture

proved insufficient to assure the serfs' subsistence, and those cases where earning money was necessary because of the lack of markets to dispose of any agricultural surplus.

One area of the Russian serfs' craft production, the spinning of flax and hemp and the weaving of linen, absorbed more labor than any other craft activity. For unknown reasons, these activities have not been included in the standard treatments of serfs or rural crafts by any writers except G. S. Isaev, who devoted a part of his book on the early history of the textile industry in Russia to this problem. Perhaps because of their prevalence, possibly because of the preponderance of female labor involved, spinning and weaving have hardly been noted as special crafts. Regardless, they were activities which provided a major share of the clothing needs of the Russian population, and "narrow Russian linen" was a standard item of Russian export.

The Soviet historian Isaev tried to estimate the volume of labor involved in the village output of linen and came up with the staggering figure of approximately 960,000 serfs working in that craft in the wintertime during the 1760s. His calculations were based upon the following assumptions: out of the noncommercial output of flax and hemp fiber which remained in the villages and was used in the production of textiles, a total of 650,000 poods of yarn were spun. Assuming that during the winter months a spinner produced about 1 pood of yarn, the required labor would be in the neighborhood of 650,000 persons. Out of the total yarn about 140,000,000 arshins of narrow linen were produced. The weaving machine of the type prevailing in the villages produced during the winter up to 900 arshins of narrow linen, and thus about 155,000 weaving machines were required to produce this total. A weaving machine was serviced by two people, which brought the total number of full-time winter weavers to 310,000. Consequently the spinning and weaving of linen absorbed about 960,000 workers during the winter season.[21]

To the extent that spinning was done exclusively by women, and weaving was done predominantly during the winter months, textile labor did not interfere with agricultural work. Conflicts tended to arise, however, when weaving became a full-time male occupation. Other occupations in the production of clothing, such as the production of sheepskins or tailoring, also had a pronounced seasonal character with employment confined to the winter months.

The construction trades were another large arena of auxiliary serf employment. It is impossible to estimate the labor inputs in this line of activity. One can only describe the array of trades and focus on the requirements of the time involvement during the year to determine compatibility with agricultural work.[22] At one end of the spectrum were the sawmill workers (*pil'shchiki*), who were engaged in cutting logs for ship timber and for urban housing construction. For them the work year started in early September and lasted until early July. This permitted only very limited agricultural work, chiefly hay bailing, and not the gathering of the grain harvest. The trades of brickmaking and stone masonry were also time-consuming. They kept laborers away from agriculture during the summer months, but did not provide employment during the winter months. In comparison with the sawmill workers, the brickmakers and stonemasons derived less income from their nonagricultural work and may have been forced to seek other types of employment during the winter. Large numbers of serfs worked as carpenters (*plotniki*). Their employment pattern was marked by two peaks, in the spring and in the autumn. They could help in the gathering of the harvest, provided their employment was not too distant from their farm.

The involvement of serfs on a mass scale in both water and overland transportation services is well known. (The problems and scope of labor participation of serfs in water transportation is discussed in chapter 6.) Transportation services for lords and corvée-type transportation for the state were considered among the special burdens of serf existence, but transporting goods to markets on a contractual basis, especially during the winter, was a welcome addition to serf income and helped many serf households in the year-round maintenance of their workstock.

The relative serf earnings in various trades were in part determined by the costs of skill acquisition for skilled trades (e.g., years of apprenticeship combined sometimes with payments for learning the trade) and by the relative scarcity of labor during the particular seasons of both semiskilled and skilled labor. Labor, in general, was relatively more expensive during the summer months and nonagricultural producers encountered difficulties in hiring unskilled and semiskilled labor at the times of peak demand for labor in agriculture. In the winter months, however, labor was available and wages were considerably lower. Therefore wages and earnings in different trades varied, depending in part on the time pattern of labor use during the high- and low-wage seasons.

Although employment in both the household and the village economy, as well as in the extra-village labor market, represented the main areas of nonagricultural economic activity of the serfs, commerce was another branch of their activity. The phenomenon of "trading serfs" is described in chapter 5. Serf commercial activity involved trading in the commercial output of both the village and the estate

and required not only time and skills but also capital. Most important is the fact that serfs competed with the urban merchants and traders and thus required the protection of their lords to legalize their involvement in commerce.

This leads to the problem of the owners' attitudes toward their serfs' employment in crafts and trade. One of the early surviving instructions of estate management, by V. N. Tatishchev, offers as a general proposition the advantage of having serfs endowed with literacy and skill training, both for the estate owner and for the serfs.[23] In practice, the serf-owners went beyond generalities and provided tangible encouragement to their serfs who learned trades and engaged in nonagricultural pursuits. On some estates the encouragement took the form of exemptions from army draft, or options to buy substitutes, with the owners thereby protecting their own households. Incentives also took the form of rent exemptions for the duration of apprenticeship into a particular trade, and often the assurance that the possessors of skills would receive passports for leave even at times of pressure of agricultural work on the estate.[24] The majority serf-owner opinion and attitude, certainly within the nonblacksoil zone, favored nonagricultural employment of serfs, but there also existed a minority negative opinion among the serf-owners, who, for a variety of reasons ranging from personal circumstances to physiocratic beliefs, bemoaned the spread of crafts and trade among the serfs and held them responsible for the problems of agriculture.

Those who favored nonagricultural serf employment had two models of the estate economy. Each was compatible with an increase of nonagricultural activity. One model was that of the estate as a "closed economy." According to this model, the estate was supposed to become as self-sufficient as possible, to reduce the purchase of inputs, and thus retain as much cash revenue as possible from the sale of its final products. The maximization of net revenue, achieved through a reduction of expenditures, was the objective of this model. The presence of crafts and skills, utilized on the estate by both the demesne and the serfs, was an important means to save on money expenditures for goods and services. An extension of the same attitude was visible in the tendency for the estate owner to insert himself between the serfs and the commodity markets by requiring that his serfs give him the option of purchasing any agricultural surplus. V. N. Tatishchev's instruction required that serfs offer their marketable surplus to the estate owner, and then to their fellow serfs on the estate, before taking it off the estate to market. Tatishchev stipulated that the internal transactions should be conducted according to the market price minus transportation costs, and thus no obvious exploitation was involved—except for the required preference for intraestate transactions and control over the economic activities of the serfs.

By the middle of the eighteenth century the sentiment in favor of a "closed estate economy" was giving way to a preference for a greater involvement and more intensive interaction with the market. Whatever could be saved by the substitution of domestically produced inputs or services was dwarfed by the opportunities for income gains from interaction in the labor and commodity markets. Thus the estate operating within an open economy became the second model. The logic of operating within an open economy led to incentives for nonagricultural labor, to the organization of estate enterprises for the processing of agricultural raw materials using the labor force of the estate, and to measures designed to involve serfs in such activities as the grain trade, either in partnership with the serf-owner or on their own account. (The title of section 33 of Prince Shcherbatov's instruction to his stewards reads: "On Forcing the Peasants to Trade in Grain.") Interaction with the market becomes visible also when one reads serf-owners' suggestions on the use of wage labor at the market wage for nonagricultural tasks, or recommendations that current market prices be used in determining the value of payments in kind. The application of such measures brought the estate accounts closer to evaluating the real costs and profits of the agricultural serf estate.

This discussion on the utilization of serf labor in nonagricultural activities without alienating the serfs from their agricultural pursuits suggests that the system of serfdom possessed a flexibility to employ more labor resources than the production requirements of agriculture dictated. The serfs who had such auxiliary sources of income were less dependent upon the vagaries of the weather and could meet their obligations to their lords and the state more easily. In numerous instances they were able to augment their household consumption and in some instances derived means to invest in their farms. The owners, still exercising control over their serfs, derived additional benefits from the expanded labor activities of their serfs.

The Status of the Dependent Population

One of the features of the social scene in eighteenth-century Russia was the change in the status of a part of the dependent population. The first decades of the century witnessed a leveling of various categories of dependent people whose status was previously differentiated. There was a merging of such strata and groups as the landless peasants (bobyli), household slaves (dvorovye liudi), and also the formerly free settlers (odnodvortsy) into the large stratum of serfs. The only remaining meaningful distinction in the serf world was between state- and church-owned serfs on the one hand and privately owned serfs on the other.

This process, which involved enserfment for some, harsher or less harsh dependency for others, was also accompanied by a shift in the status of some serfs from ownership by the state to private ownership. Historians have variously described the change in ownership from state to private as payments or rewards for outstanding services rendered by members of the nobility, who received grants of "souls" as signs of special favor by the ruler; as a squandering of public property; and as a source of enrichment not only for individuals but also for the entire stratum of the Russian nobility.

Focusing upon the transfer of serfs from the state into private property, the following discussion will center upon two issues: 1) the enrichment of the beneficiaries of the distributions of serfs; 2) the effect of such actions upon those serfs whose status was changed.

A reasonable estimate of the size of the population affected by the giveaway of state peasants to private owners in the eighteenth century would be about 1.8 to 1.9 million people of both sexes, or .9 to .95 million male "souls," to use the conventional term applied to serfs in the period. The estimate is derived by using Semevskii's estimates of approximately 850,000 distributed during the reign of Catherine II, about 600,000 distributed by Paul I, and the rest distributed by Russian rulers prior to 1762.[25]

The estimated numbers of state peasants turned into private serfs must be considered in the context of changes in the size of the dependent population, whose total number was increasing not only as a result of natural increase, but also due to the incorporation of new territories and their population into the empire. The numbers represent the net changes in the distribution of state peasants to members of the nobility rather than the gross figures for gifts of serfs. The tsars' redistributions of heirless estates or of estates confiscated by imperial order are not included in the figures because such acts did not change the total ownership by the nobility nor did they alter the status of the serfs affected. Those grants have to be viewed as wealth redistribution between particular groups, families, or individuals within the Russian nobility. In most cases they were caused by group or factional rivalries within the aristocracy for positions of power in the government and access to the court. They did not represent any accretion of wealth or income for the total nobility. In the first half of the eighteenth century, redistributions of confiscated or heirless populated estates were more numerous than outright grants of state peasants to private owners.

This situation changed radically during the reign of Catherine II, when the acquisition of new lands by the Russian Empire provided a major source of populated estates that could be disposed of. Peter the Great's acquisition of Ingermanland province, or even of the Baltic provinces, was very small by comparison with the vast areas acquired from Poland in the successive steps that led to the dismantling of the Polish-Lithuanian state. Catherine II did not have to upset the status quo of land ownership and serf ownership of the core provinces of Russia when, as a result of the partitions of Poland, hundreds of thousands of Polish crown peasants in Belorussia, the right-bank Ukraine, and Lithuania became available for private grants.

The nobility during the eighteenth century was the most vocal group in Russian society in demanding a larger share of the national income or national wealth. In the first decades of the century the nobility became aware of its role in the transformation of Russia under Peter the Great and of its role in the military and government apparatus. It demanded and was granted the equalization of service estates (*pomest'ia*) and inherited patrimonial estates (*votchiny*). This assured a higher degree of legal property rights to service estates than before. The nobility was also vocal in its opposition to the principle of primogeniture in the inheritance of estates, which was introduced by Peter, and then rescinded by his successors. Additional grants of populated estates were received by the groups of Russian nobles that associated themselves with the Petrine reforms.

Following the Petrine period, the Russian nobility insisted upon the maintenance of a legal monopoly of serf ownership by the nobility. They also demanded a decrease of mobility into the ranks of the Russian gentry. After 1725 the ranks of the nobility swelled as a result of population increase, but the number of serfs on their estates increased less rapidly. After a generation, around the middle of the century, the nobility began to demand new lands and more serfs. A number of governmental responses followed the nobility's demands for increased incomes. One was the 1762 decree by Peter III liberalizing the nobility's obligation to render military and civil service so that more time could be devoted to the management of the private estates.

Another response was the "general surveying" (*general'noe mezhevanie*), which took decades to complete. It resulted in the expansion of private landholdings, primarily at the expense of state landholding. In addition, sales of lands on the fringes of the empire were held. Leases on the common lands of the various non-Russian minorities were

facilitated. All of these measures provided additional land for the resettlement of serfs, for the expansion of the arable and plowlands that enabled Russian agriculture to respond to the growing foreign and domestic demand for agricultural products during the second half of the eighteenth century.

It is impossible to calculate the precise effects of these opportunities upon the incomes of the nobles. Indirect evidence, however, such as the rapid increase of planted areas during the 1780s and 1790s, data on regional population shifts, and documentary evidence on the growth of agricultural exports, all point in the same direction—the expansion of private estates.

Two features appear clearly in a regional analysis of the expansion of agriculture in the second half of the eighteenth century. One is the continuation of expansion eastward and southward in which the private estates assumed the role of the *spiritus movens;* the second is the enserfment of the peasants in the Ukraine, completed by 1783, which bound to the person of the estate owners (many of them recruited among the Russian nobility) the population of a region that was experiencing a shift from extensive pastoral livestock production to sedentary crop production. The grants of populated estates to members of the nobility assume their proper proportions and significance against this complex background of various responses to the demands of the nobility.

The time pattern of granting populated estates was not uniform during the whole period. Many of the grants were related to political events or to ceremonial aspects of political events. Many were facilitated by the expansion of boundaries. A typical occasion for grants was the coronation of a new ruler. Succession to the throne in eighteenth-century Russia was anything but orderly; the military, and especially the guard regiments, played the role of kingmaker. It is not surprising that the "irregular" successions to the throne by Elizabeth and Catherine II were accompanied by grants of estates to the ones who brought them to power. The years 1742 and 1762 showed higher than average grants of populated estates and were dwarfed only by the nearly 100,000 male "souls" distributed by Paul during his coronation on April 5, 1797. (Although Paul was a legitimate heir, his assumption of the throne was strongly opposed by powerful interests at court and was followed by radical personnel changes in the government. Paul passionately hated his mother, Catherine II, and tried to remove every vestige of her memory from his presence.)

The many grants bestowed upon victorious military leaders in recognition of significant battles or victorious wars were politically determined and timed. The victors in the wars against the Ottomans,

Table 2.13   Population of Estates Distributed Among Favorites by Catherine II

Name	No. of Males
Chernyshev, Zakhar	5,131
Orlov, Grigorii (and brothers)	24,000
Vasilchikov, Alexander	2,927
Potëmkin, Grigorii	21,866
Zavadovskii, Petr	10,837
Zorich, Semen	12,821
Rimskii-Korsakov, Ivan	4,875
Ermolov, Alexander	6,000
Dmitr'ev-Mamonov, Alexander	2,250
Zubov, Platon	13,669
Total	104,376

Table 2.14   Population of Estates Granted by Catherine II

Years	No. of Males
1762–72	78,762
1773–94	205,412[a]
1795–96	135,689
Total	419,863

[a]144,699 of these were in Belorussia.

such as Rumiantsev, Suvorov, Kutuzov, and Nassau-Siegen, were given grants following the peace treaties. Other military men who led the suppression of the Pugachëv rebellion, such as Bibikov, Golitsyn, and Michelson, received their grants upon the completion of the pacification of the countryside. Grants to civilian members of the bureaucracy operating in the areas of foreign policy, such as Panin, Repnin, Tutolmin, Bulgakov, and Igelström, were made at the conclusion of difficult diplomatic missions.

Uncertain in their timing were the grants extended by the rulers to their favorites and lovers. The grants made by Catherine II to her lovers either in appreciation of their service or as severance pay were the most conspicuous. The total grants by Catherine II to her lovers included 101,376 male serfs distributed to the ten individuals listed in table 2.13. They were about one-quarter of the population of all recorded grants and did not fit into the general time pattern of the other grants. (Aleksandr Lanskoi was the only one among Catherine's favorites who received only land, 24,250 *desiatiny*, no peasants.)

An attempt to estimate the time pattern of the distribution of populated estates was made by the Russian historian V. Semevskii, as presented in table 2.14. He clearly tried to link the periods to the dates of major territorial expansion, and thereby suggested a location pattern for those estates. Semevskii's dates are those of the partitions of Poland.

Semevskii's data on the number of males on the populated estates turned over to private owners make possible an estimate of the value of the grants and their wealth effect based on the approximate

Table 2.15   Hypothetical Value of the Serf-Population Distributed by Catherine II to Private Owners (in 1,000 Rubles)

Decade	No. of Male Serfs	Value of All Serfs
1760s	79,000	7,110
1770s	105,000	15,750
1780s	100,000	30,000
1790s	136,000	48,960

Table 2.16   Estimated Loss of Yearly Revenue from Distribution of State Peasants in Each Decade during Catherine II's Reign

Decade	Annual Government Revenue Lost (in Rubles)
1760s	79,000
1770s	178,500
1780s	270,000
1790s	408,000

market prices for serfs per decade. Table 2.15 presents an approximate distribution of wealth in serfs by decades.

It is also possible to estimate on the basis of the Semevskii data the approximate loss of governmental revenue previously collected as rent from the state serfs who were turned over to private owners. My estimates are presented in table 2.16.

A review of the above estimates suggests a number of conclusions. From the perspective of the enrichment of the noble stratum of society, the increment of wealth and income was substantial but did not introduce any major changes in the attitudes or behavior of its beneficiaries. A major reason was the high concentration of the grants in the hands of a relatively small number of recipients. By remunerating a number of upper-level bureaucrats and military figures in such a fashion, the government succeeded in maintaining for perhaps another generation the high degree of concentration of serf ownership. That hardly contributed to an increase in the efficiency of Russian agriculture. The granting of land and peasants decreased somewhat the government's revenue, but it did not cause the government's deficits. A different policy would not have closed the gap between budget incomes and expenditures.

If one subscribes to the view that enserfment by private owners is a more reprehensible status than ownership by the state, the transfer of state-owned peasants to noble owners was a socially negative phenomenon. However, before arriving at such a judgment, one should analyze some of the effects of the transfer of ownership upon the population of those estates. That aspect of the granting of populated estates to members of the Russian nobility is not as clear as is the matter of the enrichment of the grantees.

First, one must distinguish between the grants in the traditional Russian areas and the grants on the periphery. The government's consistent refusal to grant the estates previously owned by the church and monasteries to the nobility limited the area of grants on the old Russian territory. Government policy also made impossible the creation of large private estates in Siberia. It was also impractical to organize private estates on the lands of the former "tax-paying peasants" (*chernye krest'iane*) in the European Russian North.

Thus, for all practical purposes, the concentrations of state peasants in the middle Volga region settled by ethnic minorities (the Mordva, Chuvash, Tatars, and others) were the logical targets for distribution within the old territories of the Russian state. In those territories, particularly during the second half of the eighteenth century, the freedom of action by the private landowners in attempting to increase income from their estates was still quite limited. The proximity to abundant land resources in the Volga, Ural, and southeast regions, the frequency of peasant flights, the alternative opportunities to earn income from nonagricultural pursuits, the prevalence of money rent among the state peasants, the influence of the commune on state-owned estates—all were factors limiting the "exploitative instincts" of the private landowners. Regardless of such restraints, the growth in demand for agricultural products enabled at least some of the new serf-owners, such as Rumiantsev, Zorich, Suvorov, and one of the Orlov brothers, to reorganize their estates on the basis of demesne and labor rent (*barshchina*) exacted from their serfs. Such cases were not numerous, however. In few of them were there grants of contiguous estates, and the setting up of an efficient estate administration to exact labor rent often required more time and energy than the old courtiers and government officials were ready to devote to the task.

In the newly acquired territories of Belorussia, the Ukraine, and Lithuania, where the bulk of Catherine II's and Paul's grants were located, the Russian state "legally acquired" the ownership of the crown lands as well as the lands which the Polish government had confiscated from the Jesuits. Without going into a detailed description of the administrative structure of the Polish crown lands, one can note that the system was one of long-term tenancy by members of the nobility who used the labor of the state serfs or kept them on money rent. In the case of the Polish crown lands, as in the case of the Russian private estates, the central issue was whether the estate had demesne using serf or hired labor, or largely derived its rent in kind or in money. The Polish estates in Belorussia and Lithuania were more closely and directly connected with the market than were estates in the Russian provinces. Even in the Polish-held part of the Ukraine, the market share of agricultural output of estates was larger than in the Russian-held Ukraine.

The transfer of the crown-land estates into the hands of private landowners was often accompanied by the removal of the tenant, or by a change in his function from that of a tenant to that of an administrator or steward, at best. This shift from tenant to absentee-landlord supervision was tantamount in a number of cases to diminishing, rather than increasing, the peasants' burden and the degree of bureaucratic control over them.

Serfdom

During the eighteenth century serfdom was the most important social institution in Russia. Its impact was not only decisive in determining and shaping the processes of social production, the distribution of income, and the distribution of power in society, but also determined the private lives of the majority of the population and dominated the area of social relations of individuals as well as the various forms of organized social action. The institution of serfdom grew and developed during the sixteenth and seventeenth centuries, but the eighteenth century witnessed its most elaborate forms. Eighteenth-century serfdom can be considered the "classic" form. It was the high point in the growth of this institution, the time when it exerted the greatest impact on various other social institutions.

The institution, or system, of serfdom concerns the relationship between the serf-owners and their "baptized property," the serfs. The serf-owners, whether individuals or institutions (such as the church and state), usually combined the ownership of humans with the ownership of another factor of production, the land. The landholdings, organized in the form of estates and populated by serfs, were the property of the lords and were divided between a demesne for the direct use of the lord and landholdings assigned to the serfs in exchange for rent payments. The main feature of this social arrangement was the immobility of the serfs, who became nominally *glebae ascripti* on the estate of the lord. That immobility became increasingly compromised by the freedom of the serf-owner–landowner to dispose of his serf and his land according to the laws regulating seignorial property.

The institution of serfdom was legally defined and circumscribed by the norms of public and private law in Russia. According to the prevailing legal norms, a serf was simultaneously the property of his lord and a subject of the state sovereign, and owed services to both. As a Christian, he was also subject to the laws of the church. His status as a subject of the state provided the serf with nominal protection of his life, of which he could not be deprived except by a court decree. As a Christian, he was considered to be in the possession of a soul and expected to be concerned about his salvation. Consequently the behavior of the serf was expected to conform to the laws of the state and the church, as well as to the commands of his lord. As the property of his lord, he could not initiate any legal proceedings against his lord except for cases of treason and manslaughter. He was not considered liable for any private debts and could not own any immovable property except that which was acquired with the consent of his lord and kept at his lord's discretion. The serf was, however, liable for any criminal act committed, as well as responsible for insubordination to his lord, and punishable for both. Nearly all of the slave-like features of Russian serfdom were borrowed from the native institution of slavery in the course of resolving seventeenth-century trouble cases.[26]

The serf's relationships with his lord and fellow serfs were defined not only by the law but also by the arbitrary power of the lord and by custom. Traditions and customs affecting the lord-serf relationship were mostly defined in terms of mutual obligations and, therefore, in the eighteenth century mitigated the arbitrary decisions of the serf-owners. The customary role of, and sometimes the power delegated by, the serf-owner to the village commune gave it a central place in regulating the relations between serf households.

In historical terms, the eighteenth century witnessed an expansion of the rights of the serf-owners in the area of jurisdiction over their serfs. Except in some pathological cases of serf-owner cruelty which involved repeated serf deaths, the government did not intervene on behalf of the serfs but provided the owners with both protection and support in any known case of serf transgression and insubordination. As a rule, the government did not intervene in the serf-lord relationship as long as the authority of the owner was not threatened.

Comprehension of the mechanics of the serf system's social relations and its economic dynamics requires cognizance of its environmental characteristics. A chief such characteristic was the relative abundance of land. Not only was new land being brought under cultivation and forestland converted into plowland, but throughout the eighteenth century some of the available plowland was left uncultivated in the system of crop rotation. Russian agricultural production was based upon an extensive use of land resources. An accompanying characteristic was the low output-seed ratio in grain production, which suggests minimal use of land improvements and a general reliance on primitive technology. It also tends

to confirm the evidence from the nineteenth century that the Russian peasants practiced downward genetic selection by selling or paying rent with the best grains, eating the next best grains, and sowing the worst. Another characteristic, which indicates the dependence of Russian agriculture upon the vagaries of climatic conditions, was the presence of wide fluctuations in agricultural yields and the frequency of famines, which, when repeated at short intervals or during successive years, affected both the food supply and population growth.

The most significant characteristic of the social environment of serfdom was the high ratio of serfs to serf-owners. The approximate number of male serfs per owner was 277 in 1744, 228 in 1762, 230 in 1783, and 222 in 1795.[27] Apart from the distribution of serf holdings, the high average number of serfs determined both the income level of the owners and the magnitude of the share of the product being alienated from the serfs.

The social and economic characteristics of serfdom can be studied from two vantage points. One is the individual estate, in which case a study at the micro-level of production relations to delineate the areas of decision making would be in order. Another approach, the one adopted here, would be to study serfdom at the macro-level, to concentrate on its more general characteristics and view it as a vector of many units' activities. For the second approach, three areas have been chosen for more detailed scrutiny: (1) the impact of the institution of serfdom upon serf-household formation; (2) the extent and nature of the command over the labor of the serfs; (3) the impact of serfdom upon income distribution and the distribution of power in Russian society.

The topic of the impact of serfdom upon household formation has some implications for the problems of population growth. The serf-owners were interested in the growth of the serf population, for serfs represented their largest asset. The evidence overwhelmingly points to an encouragement of early marriages among the seignorial serfs. Owners prominently displayed a concern about the increase of their "baptized property" in the instructions to their estate stewards and in their private papers. Written accounts of their behavior tell the same story. The system of redemption payments for marrying outside the estate, the system of fines for remaining single, the orders of wholesale marriages for particular age cohorts, and even the wholesale marriages arranged by the village communes to avoid their lords' interference in the private choices of individual serfs all bear witness to the active interference and persistent attitude favoring early marriages within the serf population. Less evidence has survived on state- and church-owned serfs, but there can be no doubt that some degree of pressure or encouragement was applied by the estate stewards and administrators to stimulate early household formation within this group of serfs as well.

The creation of new households, the basic rent-paying, labor-service-rendering, and tax-paying units, was vital to the income maximization of the serf-owners. Consequently interference to correct the labor deficiency of some households, or the creation of new households from existing large ones, was a constant concern of the serf-owners. The decision-making capacity of the heads of households to counteract the interference of the serf-owners was limited and often ineffective. Land for newly formed households was provided by the owner directly, or by the village commune through repartition, rather than through inheritance and division of the landholdings of serf households, and thus the ability of the household to retain labor by its own decision was seriously impaired.

The evidence reveals numerous attempts on the part of serf households to retain labor at least to the point where the retained labor would have repaid the costs of the older generation's contribution to the consumption of the younger generation. The attempts to marry off adolescent males to somewhat older females and thereby to gain the labor of the females for a longer time period is perhaps an extreme, but nevertheless interesting, illustration of that practice.

The tendency of serf-owners to accelerate the process of household formation had a number of interesting consequences. First, it kept the age at marriage relatively low, 20 to 22 for males, and somewhat lower for females. This influenced the fertility of women in marriage and increased the birth rate, if we assume the absence of contraceptive practices. Second, it lowered the propensity to save within the serf households because of the diminished significance of inheritances to be passed on to the younger generation. Third, it conformed to the preference of the serf-owners for relative income equality in the serf milieu, a preference for "middle"-income serf households that produced sufficiently for their subsistence and for regular rent and tax payment or effective labor services. The serf-owners, as a rule, preferred middle-income serf households to income-differentiated ones. The presence of rich serfs, in the zero-sum view of the serf-owners, was tantamount to the presence of poor serfs as well, a situation which called for income redistribution in rent payments or labor services and created unnecessary tensions within the village commune. Under the conditions of serfdom, income equality for the serfs was an idea common, not among serfs, but rather among serf-owners. Their decisions and actions kept income differentiation among the serfs within bounds.

The command of the serf-owners over the labor of their serfs was the most important area as far as the economic function of the serf system was concerned. This command was justified by a number of considerations. According to the prevailing state ideology, the command was originally justified by the special services provided by the gentry and the nobility to the sovereign and the state. This justification was accepted and internalized by some of the serfs, who therefore expected a release from their bondage when the nobility was freed from obligatory military service in 1762; apparently the serfs assumed the existence of a *quid-pro-quo* arrangement between the state and the gentry in which they were mere objects. The serf-owning gentry rationalized their command over the labor of the serfs as congruent with their status as owners of both the serfs and the land. Command over the serfs' labor required determination by the gentry of the amount of that labor and the particular form in which it was to be extracted and utilized. The two forms of appropriation of serf labor were either the direct use of labor services on the lord's demesne (*barshchina*) or the appropriation of a part of the serf's product, whether in kind or money (*obrok*). Quite often the serf-owners appropriated to themselves the serfs' labor in a combination of labor services and money rent.

The division (geographic as well as economic) between the regions in which money rent or labor services prevailed became a cliché in the historical work on serfdom in Russia. Geographically, the concentration of money-rent arrangements by seignorial serfs was most pronounced in the central nonblacksoil zone; labor-service arrangements were in the central blacksoil zone. Within those zones, within various provinces (*gubernii*), and even within particular counties there were very substantial variations in the proportions of one or another mode of serf obligations. The presence of counties where labor-service arrangements predominated in the midst of otherwise predominantly money-rent districts, or vice versa, was the rule rather than the exception.

A few interpretations of the choices in favor of one or the other mode of obligation can be offered. One interpretation is based on an assumption of higher average yields in the serf parts of the estates than on the demesne. If one accepts the existence of a yield differential, the problem then becomes one of the size of the differential. Assuming there was a differential, one would expect that in areas where the differential was considerable the serf-owners would tend to distribute among the serfs most of the land of the estates in order to appropriate to themselves a larger part of the product over and above the part needed for the serfs' subsistence. Under conditions of a small differential, the serf-owners were either indifferent to the distribution between the demesne land and serf-occupied land, or preferred to retain a larger proportion of the land within the estate under direct control.

It appears that the grain yield differential between the demesne and the serf-occupied lands was more significant in the nonblacksoil zone, where the application of manure, more careful plowing, and other agricultural techniques accounted for the difference between higher and lower yields. In the blacksoil zone, one of relatively higher soil fertility, the yield differentials were less pronounced given the overall higher yields achievable on both the demesne and serf-occupied land. This observation tends to explain some of the distribution of rent and labor-service regions that coincided with the blacksoil and nonblacksoil zones.

Another explanatory factor of the choice by the serf-owner in opting for one or another form of rent and organizing his estate accordingly was the relation to the market for goods and labor. Proximity to markets worked in two separate ways. In areas of low access to product markets, with high transportation and transaction costs, serf-owners preferred that the serfs bear the costs of marketing their output and pay a money rent. On the other hand, in the vicinity of product markets, or in locations of easier access to cheap transportation, it paid for the estate to produce on the demesne, to use additional serf labor for transportation, and consequently to use most or all of the serf labor directly on the demesne. This explains the prevalence of *barshchina*-type estates in the vicinity of cities, along rivers, and on easy trade routes, even in the nonblacksoil zone.

It was not only the market for goods, or for agricultural products, that played an important role in influencing the decision whether *obrok* or *barshchina* would be the prevailing form of rent payment, but also the market for labor. The demand for labor was relatively high in a number of areas outside agriculture, particularly in transportation and in both large-scale and small-scale manufacturing. The demand for transportation services was concentrated along the main river and canal routes and serviced the large volume of goods using the river traffic as well as the subsidiary flows of commodities feeding into the river routes. The demand for hired labor by industry was concentrated in the central nonblacksoil region around the location of the various textile industries. The employment opportunities in the nonblacksoil zone provided a source of nonagricultural income for the serfs of this region. This was particularly the case for those among the serfs who were liable for money-rent payments, who possessed

freedom of decision-making about the combination of agricultural and nonagricultural work in which they were to engage. To the extent that in a number of cases industrial employment or even seasonal transportation labor paid a higher wage than that attainable in agriculture in this region, it is not surprising that serf-owners were only too happy to share in the money incomes of their serfs, rather than having them till and husband the estate's demesne.

Inflationary pressures became a determining factor in the last quarter of the eighteenth century in shifting estates from money rent to labor services. Such pressure had been felt earlier, but the rate of price inflation accelerated during the 1780s and continued unabated during the rest of the century. A rise in money rent charged the serfs as well as in the rates of government taxation followed the general rise in the price level. However, because of serf resistance to the raising of money rents and the tendency of rents left unchanged for a long period to become "institutionalized," and because there was not only a change in the general price level but also changes in relative prices of different commodities, some serf-owners found it advantageous to shift from *obrok* to *barshchina* and to market the estates' production.

On many estates there was a mixed form of rent payments. Both forms probably coexisted on estates where the serf-owners were indifferent about the origin of their incomes or in instances where they perceived special advantages in the use of both. For example, the existence of a large retinue of household serfs might necessitate a considerable supply of agricultural commodities derived from the serf-owner's demesne to feed the household serfs and simultaneously a high money-income to support his style of life.

In the eighteenth century income maximization of the serf-owners was identical with the maximization of money income. They had a very high preference for money over other forms of income. The maximization of money income and the minimization of money expenditures in the process of production was typical for the estate economy. To the extent that some estate resources had no opportunity costs, or very low opportunity costs, estate owners did not economize on their uses. The opportunity-cost of money, however, was very high relative to other productive resources. The effectiveness of both forms of rent collection (*obrok* and *barshchina*) must be considered in this context. As discussed in the context of environmental conditions, the possibilities of raising either money rents or labor services were limited because of the low productivity of agricultural labor. Prices of agricultural goods were relatively low and the nonagricultural population was too limited to permit a major expansion of marketable output. The limitations on both marketable output and nonagricultural employment allowed serfs who paid their rent in cash to increase their money incomes only very slowly.

Under the *barshchina* system a high number of serfs had to be assigned to specific tasks on the demesne. Their labor was relatively underutilized because of the seasonal peaks in crop production. The system probably resulted in a loss in total output because of the simultaneous demands for labor on the demesne and on the land occupied by the serfs, which the peasants had to farm in order to maintain their own households. This resulted in a situation where even under the *barshchina* system the demesne could not utilize more than a third of the estate's plowland; the other two-thirds was occupied by the serfs. This is partly explained by the fact that under the three-field system, one-third of the plowland was kept in fallow and supported by a large long-term fallow reserve.

The demand for labor in most of the agricultural areas and the relatively low incomes of the serfs put severe limits on the revenue per serf that could be extracted by the serf-owners. The available generalized data for individual provinces (*gubernii*) for the latter part of the century indicate that the *obrok* payments per capita constituted approximately 20 percent of serf income. Included in that income were agricultural production for home consumption and for sale as well as the nonagricultural money incomes of the serfs; excluded was the value added in cottage-type industry when the work was performed in the household. The relatively low share of *obrok* in the total income of the serfs is not surprising in view of the level of governmental taxation and low level of agricultural marketings.

Seignorial *obrok* and governmental taxation were but two components of the total serf obligation. The distribution of the total between the serf-owner and the government was not of major concern for the serfs. That distribution in reality depended upon the power relationship of the two partners. Under Peter the Great the government's share tended to exceed the owners' share. Under his successors, however, the government's share was somewhat curtailed, while the owners' share increased. If the share of rent was approximately 20 percent of the serf's income, the government's share was approximately 12 percent. Toward the end of the century, in view of rising prices, both the government and the serf-owners tried to catch up with the inflationary pressures and to maintain rent and taxes in real terms at previously existing levels.

For the serfs producing a marketable surplus, the rising prices for agricultural products and the lag in the rise of rent and taxes resulted in a temporary rise of their disposable income. For the serfs employed in nonagricultural labor who had to purchase some of their food, no such advantage existed, for wages, as rents and taxes, lagged behind the rise in agricultural prices. Their real disposable income did not increase during this period.

The rent levels paid by the serfs varied not only by geographic area but also by the size of estate. As a rule, rents on the largest estates were somewhat lower than on the middle-sized and small-sized estates. The difference ought not be sought in more "liberal" attitudes of the large-estate owners, or in the degrees of control exercised by absentee landlords and those who administered their estates directly. No rational explanation can be provided by any difference in intensity of the serf-owners' demand for income, if it existed. The most logical explanation lies in the existing differential in land-labor ratios between large estates and smaller estates. As a rule, the land-labor ratio on the larger estates was higher, and therefore more advantageous for the serfs, than on the smaller estates. The compilation of the land cadastre (*general'noe mezhevanie*) in the second half of the eighteenth century resulted in the large landowners' gaining property rights to more land. Moreover, huge grants of uninhabited land in the south and southeast parts of the empire provided an opportunity for the large-estate owners to resettle their serfs from the more densely populated estates in the center to more sparsely populated ones on the periphery and thereby to achieve a relatively high land-labor ratio. The income of the serfs on such estates was higher and the rent-income ratio relatively lower.

It is also possible that the large estates, having accepted one of the forms of rent payment, were slower in reacting or adapting themselves to short-term changes in market conditions or changes in the value of money than were some of the middle-sized estates which probably had more flexibility. The small estates probably lacked the means to effect a meaningful change in factor proportions. Their reaction was typically a response with a short time-horizon, whenever possible, to increase labor services or money rents by the use of the means of direct pressure at their disposal.

The differentiation of the serf-owners by the size of their holdings is suggestive also on the matter of the income distribution of this social class as well as on the distribution of power within the Russian state. The Russian serf-owners were not a homogeneous social class. There was very little continuity and commonality between the Russian aristocracy, which possessed huge numbers of serfs, and the lower gentry, who possessed few serfs.[28]

The data in table 2.17 show the approximate distribution of the serf-owners by the size of their serf-

Table 2.17   Percentage Distribution of Serf-owners and Serfs by
Size of Holding, 1797

Size of Holding	Distribution of Serf-owners	Distribution of Serfs
Less than 100 serfs	83.8	11.1
101–500 serfs	12.1	43.1
501–1000 serfs	2.6	10.5
Over 1000 serfs	1.5	35.3

Source: Kahan, "Costs of Westernization," p. 61.

holdings and estimate the distribution of the seignorial serfs within the same categories. Although the data may be biased in favor of the lower serf-holding groups and underestimate the share of the highest serf-holding group, they conform to the general trends during the eighteenth century.

The high degree of concentration of serf ownership within large holdings by a relatively small number of owners indicates the concentration of wealth and power in the hands of an oligarchy. It does not tell us about the size of particular estates and obscures what would be the results of a micro-analysis of the estate economy. For macro-analysis, however, the distribution presented in table 2.17 is sufficient.

State activities in the economic sphere supported and strengthened the existing distribution of income and wealth. This was true both in the state's fiscal and income redistributive actions and in its behavior as the largest serf-owner in Russia. The results of inquiry into the wealth and income position of the policy-makers of the Russian government and the fact that government subsidies to the members of the serf-holding aristocracy exceeded the subsidies to other subgroups within the nobility should suffice to demonstrate how political power was concentrated and distributed in congruence with the distribution of economic wealth.

Neither the nobility as a class nor the aristocracy as a group was immune to the processes of upward social mobility. None of the existing barriers to entry into those groups operated perfectly. The Petrine Table of Ranks allowed an influx of military and civilian bureaucrats into the ranks of the nobility upon consideration of merit, but also, and more important, upon seniority achieved in government service. Economic advancement and growth of wealth enabled some individual merchants and industrialists to enter the ranks of the nobility. Merchants did so with relatively modest economic means, but industrialists increased the total wealth of the nobility by adding their capital accumulated or accrued in previous nonagricultural economic activities. Upward mobility into the nobility was rapid during the Petrine period, slower during the Elizabethan period, and finally considerably accelerated during the reign of Catherine II. To some extent, this

mobility coincided with the expansion of the institution of serfdom. During the Petrine period the process of the enserfment of various social groups, whose status had been vaguely defined earlier, was intensified. In the Catherinian period serfdom expanded geographically, in 1783 embracing the territory of Ukraine; it was also strengthened by the broadening of the judicial authority of the serf-owners over their serfs. Serfdom was thus still growing during the eighteenth century, drawing within its orbit an increasing share of the total population and expanding territorially.

Serfdom was not only a relationship between lord and peasant, but also the accepted ideology of the Russian state. It was the institution that permeated political relations. Alternatives to seignorial serfdom were popular among the serfs and found expression in various forms ranging from advocacy of state serfdom to the abolition of serfdom. Serf resistance to the authority of the lords was also expressed in a broad spectrum of action, from mild insubordination to largely spontaneous serf revolts. Contemplation of alternatives to serfdom also occurred among some of the nobles under the impact of foreign Enlightenment ideas. Censorship and outright punishment were the weapons used against those few nobles by the state authority. Military expeditions, exile to Siberia, and the knout were used to discourage "rebellious" ideas among the serfs. The entire apparatus of the state's police power was at the disposal of the serf-owners to protect and perpetuate serfdom. Politics and economics in the eighteenth century supported the institution fully.

Differentiation among the Serfs

The adversary relationship between lord and serf in eighteenth-century Russia clearly dominated the social scene. As we have seen, there were enormous distinctions among the serf-holders. It also would be a gross simplification to view the serf milieu as a homogeneous and uniform one. The serf population was differentiated along various lines in addition to the legal differentiation between state- or church-owned peasants and private serfs. The distinction between household serfs and village serfs was meaningful for both life-style and employment, and also from the perspective of the degree of control exercised by the serf-owner over the life and activity of the serf. Within the villages there were still meaningful differences along occupational lines between purely agricultural serfs and those employed in nonagricultural pursuits such as crafts and commerce.

Differences in employment were overshadowed by differences in income and wealth (the latter term refers to movable property) among the village serfs. Higher incomes and possession of above-average quantities of movable property were correlated with size of household and the availability of resources to which labor could be applied. The position of a relatively "rich" peasant was neither a stable state nor one that could be transferred easily from generation to generation through inheritance. That very instability was an indicator of the socioeconomic dynamics prevailing in the Russian serf village.

The existence of some, albeit unstable, income differentiation cannot be denied. It is necessary to provide evidence for some areas in which the conflict of interests between the more and the less affluent surfaced in order to comprehend some of the manifestations of the conflict. Regrettably, adequate documentary evidence about intravillage transactions involving labor hiring, land leasing, and other such transactions is lacking. Consequently, another area has been chosen to illustrate the economic conflicts within the serf village community—tax and rent payments.

Peter the Great's introduction of a poll tax completed the shift of the basis of assessment of taxation in Russia from land to households to individuals. The poll tax, which established uniform rates for large categories of taxpayers, did not disregard entirely the problem of income differentiation. It correctly assumed that there was a positive correlation between the size of the serf household and the levels of income of serf households. Since the tax was levied upon each male serf, larger households paid a proportionally higher volume of taxes. However, this proportionality, which depended on the number of males, was clearly insufficient to equalize the tax burden and to capture the income- or wealth-differential. A struggle ensued within the village community between the more affluent serfs, who self-interestedly insisted on the letter of the law that each "soul" had to pay his share of the tax, and the less affluent serfs, who demanded a distribution of the tax burden based upon the ability to pay by households representing different income levels. The state, primarily interested in the collection of the total assessed tax, stayed aloof from the conflict. Turning the responsibility for the serfs' tax payments and the collection of taxes over to the serf-owners, the government left the issue of distribution of the tax burden to them. The owners had to resolve the conflict within the villages.

In the overwhelming majority of cases the tax burden was differentiated. Only in very rare cases were the serfs held to an observance of the letter of the law requiring each peasant household to pay the tax according to its number of male serfs. The serf-owners had two options in their attempts to modify the execution of the law. One was to prescribe a distribution of the burden by themselves for their estates. The second was to turn the decision over to the peasant commune, if such existed on the estate. In the first case, the owner had to state clearly what his preference was, in the second he could either clarify his position and instruct the commune to follow a particular set of principles or he could leave it entirely to the commune to resolve the matter within the village. In the latter case, the serf-owner was certainly familiar with the commune's sentiments.

This leads to the issue of the politics of the commune, of who was wielding power there. Circumstantial evidence, in part derived from some landowners' instructions, suggests that landowners preferred the propertied elements to wield influence in the commune. In fact serf-owners had no preference for either a serf population that was sharply differentiated economically or for rule by the rich minority in the commune. The owner's interests were in "middle-income" serfs who could pay the stipulated rent or provide labor demanded for the demesne, serfs who were taxpayers in good standing and who would be pliable executors of orders directed at maximizing the owner's revenues. The enrichment of a minority accompanied by the immiseration of large numbers of the serfs was not in the interests of the estate owners. Consequently the landowners were not in sympathy with a commune leadership that used its influence to increase or sharpen the existing income inequality among the serfs and employed the distribution of the tax burden toward this particular end. Serf-owners who left documentary evidence were quite outspoken on this point. Baron Nikolai Grigor'evich Stroganov, one of the richest serf-owners of Russia, wrote on this subject in the instruction to his estate stewards in 1725:

It happened in the past and still happens at the present time that the wealthier and propertied peasants try to give themselves a break, to burden the poorer ones and their children with equal payments of the poll tax and rents. They base their calculations on the basis of sheer numbers rather than the volume of property they possess. Poor peasants all come in force to provide their labor either for the government's tasks or for the transportation duties, while the richer ones send only one member from their household. Therefore I order you to act as follows: all government taxes ought to be collected according to the commune's distribution of duties. The commune will assess the payments according to the revenues derived from crafts, commerce, land, and from all other activities, and also according to quantity of personal possessions, not according to the number of "souls," so that the poor will not be overburdened. The stewards shall be present at the apportionment of tax payments and rent and record the yearly assessments. The stewards shall follow the true Christian law, they shall not favor anyone and not injure anyone. Any wrongdoing will be subject to penalty.[29]

Baron Stroganov was explicit about the attempts of the well-to-do to shift the tax and rent burdens to the poor and about his own preference that the commune should tax its members according to income. Other serf-owners were perhaps less explicit and designed schemes less obvious, but they nevertheless strove for a more just distribution of the tax burden. The statesman and author Prince M. M. Shcherbatov also preferred that the commune both allocate the taxes and be responsible for their collection. Shcherbatov tried to ease the burden of the poor by assigning reduced payments to children and the elderly members of households. Children of the ages 10–13 paid only 10 kopeks, ages 13–14 paid 15 kopeks, and age 15 paid 40 kopeks, and the elderly and invalids, depending on their earnings, paid one of the rates applicable to the children. The rest was equally distributed among the *tiagla*, apparently on the assumption that the richer peasants held more than one *tiaglo*. Consequently the richer peasants were assessed a higher share of the total tax. Shcherbatov used the commune and the tax assessment power to enforce both work discipline and to promote technical training. He insisted that "fifteen-year-olds who have not assumed a *tiaglo* should pay a penalty of double taxation. The commune shall pay the tax for those who serve an apprenticeship to qualify for a trade."[30]

Spatial Mobility of the Serf Population

Both the descriptive and the analytical literature about serfdom lay heavy stress on the immobility of the serfs as one of the basic features of Russian serfdom. The immobility of serf labor is often contrasted with the mobility of freely hired labor in subsequent periods. Even accounting for lower costs of information and travel in the postemancipation period, the relative immobility of labor under serfdom stands out in stark contrast to the mobility of the free man.

It would be a mistake, however, to assume that under the eighteenth-century serf regime spatial mobility was nonexistent, or that none of the serfs moved from the place of his birth or original habitat. Extant documentary evidence permits the detection of migration movements including such diverse forms as massive flights of fugitive serfs, movement from rural areas to the cities, relocations following

Table 2.18   Registered Mobility of Peasants and Serfs in Flight, 1719–44

Province	Registered Mobility	Serfs in Flight
Moscow	26,547	12,753
Uglich	7,736	6,018
Iur'ev-Pol'skii	1,364	2,297
Vladimir	8,884	7,694
Suzdal'	4,414	5,600
Kostroma	4,719	3,097
Iaroslavl'	2,544	5,984
Periaslavl'-Zalesskii	4,507	6,428
Riazan'	12,775	3,895
Kaluga	18,887	7,974
Tula	13,319	3,017
Total	105,496	64,757

Source: Kubuzan, *Izmeneniia*, pp. 186–89.

military service, exile as part of the penal system, and relocation of serfs by owners to newly acquired lands on the agricultural frontiers.

Regrettably, the published documents are insufficient to delineate and categorize the various types of serf spatial mobility and to explain their origin and causes. It is also doubtful that such sources exist in the archives, for governmental inquiries about population movements directed to local bureaucrats were confined to fugitive serfs rather than to broader issues.

Fragmentary data on fugitive serfs exist for particular localities and various periods. It is difficult to deal with some of it, such as the official claim that the number of fugitives in the period 1722–27 was 200,000.[31] Most of the evidence for other types of spatial mobility is from literary sources.

The Soviet historian and demographer V. M. Kabuzan provided evidence on the mobility of serfs other than through flight and compared those data with the data on flights. His data, presented in table 2.18, estimate that the mobility of 105,496 male serfs was caused by their owners' orders or consent in the years 1719–44 in several provinces of central Russia. At the same places and times the flight of 64,757 male serfs was registered by their owners or the authorities.

Kabuzan's data suggest that the ratio of serfs in flight to those in lawful migration was higher in the provinces from which the relocation of serfs (relative to the population) was lower. The absence of a better safety valve that would allow the release of a part of the serf population from the areas of relatively higher population density left some serfs with no alternative but to become fugitives. In the provinces where legal outmigration occurred at a higher rate, fewer serfs resorted to flight. (Not only serfs participated in flight or "lawful migration," but also members of the urban estates. However, the overwhelming majority of fugitives and migrants were serfs. For example, during the years 1719–44, 12,775 of the 13,280 migrants from Riazan' were peasants and 3,895 of the 4,171 fugitives were peasants. In Tula during the same period, 13,319 of 13,916 migrants were peasants and 3,017 of the 3,153 fugitives were peasants.)

Our knowledge of the origins of migration is fragmentary, but almost nothing is known about the destinations of specific groups of migrants. For example, information about the apprehension of 13,188 fugitive males in Kazan' *guberniia* during the years 1722–27, or about 18,000 fugitives found in Nizhnii Novgorod *guberniia*, does not tell us where the fugitives came from.[32] One can surmise on the basis of more concrete evidence from the seventeenth century that they most likely came from a neighboring province, or from regions along the Volga river route used for transportation and communication. The same uncertainties exist about legal migration.

The relocation of peasants from the Middle Volga region to the southern Urals during the years 1744–62 provides another example of the uncertainties surrounding migratory movements. Documents record that 26,323 males migrated from Kazan' *guberniia* to the southern Urals. Of these, only 5,590 were private serfs. The rest were state peasants of ethnic and religious minorities (*iasachnye inovertsy*). It is not clear, however, why the migration was from Kazan' to the southern Urals instead of to the much closer Lower Volga region, where the government tried during the late 1760s to settle foreign colonists recruited at considerable expense from abroad. Perhaps the Kazan' state peasants and private serfs preferred agriculture in a forest region similar to their habitat, rather than steppe agriculture as practiced in the Lower Volga region. No one knows, however, whether the peasants were even asked about their preference, or who made the migration decisions.

The evidence suggests that there were various causes and types of mobility, legal and illegal, some controlled by the owners of labor, others beyond their control. It also suggests that the Russian system of serfdom, like that in other countries such as Germany and Poland, was compatible with higher rates of spatial mobility than is conventionally assumed.

Historians unanimously assume that serfs fled as a result of inhuman treatment and exploitation, that flight was an act of desperation, a form of social protest. Unquestionably that was true in many cases. On the other hand, it is possible that restrictions on the market for serfs, specifically the prohibition against buying them without land, did not allow landowners to buy as many serfs as they desired to populate their estates. When the mechanisms of population relocation did not work properly, when the serf-owners did not effectively redistribute their serfs, then the serfs had little choice other than to make their own decisions to relocate themselves where more land might be available, even when they did not suffer inhuman treatment but simply suffered from adverse land-labor ratios. Such an interpretation of causation shifts the blame for peasant flight from individuals to the restrictiveness of the system and its inability to grant greater autonomy to individuals.

Fugitive Serfs

Although historians and laymen freely use the term "serfdom," and there is a plethora of descriptions of conditions under the regime of serfdom, very little systematic work has been devoted to the problem of how the system of serfdom was actually enforced. It certainly took more than a legislative decree to bind the serfs to the land or to the person of those who were declared their legal owners. Individual serfs had to be kept in place regardless of their taste for more attractive opportunities that might come their way. Even if serfdom implied collective responsibility of all serfs on any particular estate for the actions of individuals, such responsibility could not always be elicited without force.[33] Given the small number of serf-owners relative to the serf population, the institution of serfdom required an enforcement apparatus that was adequately efficient and effective. Although some serf-owners were economically and politically able to organize their own police forces on their estates, the majority of the owners were unable to do this. In the absence of an outside police force, they were vulnerable and likely to lose their serfs to those owners who possessed political and economic power. During the seventeenth century, and particularly prior to the organization of massive hunts for fugitives following the enactment of the *Ulozhenie* of 1649, the recovery of fugitive serfs was often left to the initiative of the individual serf-owner.[34] By the eighteenth century demands for maximum involvement of governmental institutions in the enforcement of the legal strictures of serfdom were increasingly vocal, especially after Peter the Great forced the serf-owners to participate fully in the seemingly endless Northern War.

To legitimize serfdom, it was sufficient for the government to use the principle of service obligations due the state by the different social strata or estates. If military or civilian governmental service was demanded from the nobility, whether aristocracy or gentry, the general compensation for such service was the ownership title to land and to the serfs inhabiting those lands. As logical as this particular proposition appeared to the majority of seventeenth-century lawmakers or members of the governing elite, the eighteenth-century experience proved it to be an imperfect argument, for the performance by the nobility of its service became in the eyes of the serfs the determinant and primary justification of the serfs' obligations to their masters. When the nobility was freed from its service obligations in 1762, serfdom, at least for some serfs, lost its raison d'etre.

During the eighteenth century, the most wide-spread justification for the government's role in enforcing serfdom was the assumption that unauthorized mobility of the taxpaying population was injurious to the state and, in the case of unauthorized mobility of the serf population, also injurious to their owners. Unauthorized mobility reflected clear motivation, intention, and action against the state and private property; in other words, it constituted a criminal act. The crime was redefined from an object of private law to one of public law. The state became the instrument which had to prevent incursions against the law and to punish the perpetration of crime. Fugitive serfs were put in the same legal category as vagabonds and those who moved around without passports (*beglye, brodiagi, i bespasportnye*). A subsequent step was to equate them with army deserters and criminal fugitives from justice.

Every taxpayer who departed further than 30 *versts* from his place of legal habitation or crossed the county (*uezd*) line without written permission of the authorities, either of owner or local rural administrator, was liable to be legally prosecuted as a fugitive.[35]

The punishment for flight depended upon the legal status of the fugitive, the circumstances of his/her unauthorized mobility, and the discretion of the owner (in the case of seignorial serfs). Somehow severe punishment of fugitive serfs did not prevent recidivism or the participation by others in that risky endeavor.

Given the widespread instances of serf flight, one may safely assume that it was an accompanying phenomenon of the institution of serfdom itself so long as measures of control and supervision were imperfect, so long as both borders and an internal frontier existed. The number of fugitive serfs increased when the plight of the serfs, the degree of exploitation, or the brutality of their owners increased. Serf flights were positively correlated with periods of famine or a worsening of the economic condition of agricultural estates, which resulted in increased exploitation, increased brutality, or arbitrary behavior. It is difficult to compare the brutality or arbitrariness of private-estate owners with that of stewards of state and church estates. Moreover, the available evidence gives no clue as to whether the majority of the fugitive serfs were recruited from the private serfs or the serfs belonging to state and church institutions. Consequently it is difficult to ascertain how ownership factors were related to the treatment of serfs or their flight.

The state apparatus which dealt with the flight of serfs did not make much distinction between the flights of private serfs and state-owned serfs, and the distinction seems not to have been essential in the minds of those responsible for the prevention and forcible return of fugitives. The evenhandedness of the authorities in the matter of different categories of fugitives is illustrated by a case from the Altai region, where 1,905 cases of flight were reported, nearly equally divided between 968 agricultural serfs and 937 workers ascribed to the mines and the ironworks. In another instance involving 714 fugitives apprehended in the same region, 223 were agricultural serfs, 22 were house serfs, 184 were former soldiers, and 179 were criminals of various types.

The continuity in the methods used to hunt down and return fugitive serfs in the seventeenth and eighteenth centuries was striking. It reflected the continuing growth of the state apparatus and its maturation as a tool of political repression. In the second half of the seventeenth century an institution of special investigative officials (*syshchiki*) was implemented by the activity of the census takers (*pistsy*) who registered the population. In the eighteenth century the function of the latter was assumed by the registrars of the regular population counts (*revizii*) conducted to establish the identity of the taxpaying population. Between 1650 and 1750 the *syshchiki* were sent by Moscow and then St. Petersburg to districts in which large numbers of fugitives were reported; during their extraordinary searches for fugitives, military units were employed to deal with the fugitives on a mass scale. Already at the beginning of the seventeenth century, during the reign of Vasilii Shuiskii, local administrators were told to be continuously alert for newcomers, and this became a routine in the attempt to curtail serf flights.

The system of looking for fugitive serfs evolved as follows: until 1650, it was largely a private matter in the hands of the serf-owners who themselves had lost peasants. For roughly the next century, the *syshchiki* sent out by the central authorities assumed that task. In the second half of the eighteenth century the *syshchiki* were abolished and their obligations were assumed by local civil administrators. This was a transition from a paramilitary police process to a civilian police process which the reorganized and regularly paid local administration in the reign of Catherine II was able to handle.

When serfdom was legally introduced into the Ukraine in the 1780s, there was a greater emphasis on the principle of collective responsibility in the villages. The office of the *desiatskii* (decurion, a head of ten households) was established and made responsible for the behavior of those under its control. Moreover, each individual was required to report to the authorities on his neighbor, and on any intention by his neighbor to abandon his residence. The rest of the households of the group of ten were obliged to pay the poll taxes of the entire group. The law required the maintenance of liaison between village officials such as the *desiatskii* and *sotskii* (centurion, head of one hundred households) and the civilian authorities, who could employ the police powers at their disposal or mobilize those of the villages in their attempt to control fugitives.[36] The expanded local bureaucracy and the use of the organization of the serfs themselves made it possible to deal with the problem of fugitive serfs in a more routine manner than previously had been possible with the special investigators and delegated military forces.

The routinization in the dealing with the phenomenon of fugitive serfs in the Russian Empire in the eighteenth century was unable to prevent flights or even substantially diminish their numbers or frequency. This would seem to confirm the thesis that the serfs did not consider serfdom a benevolent, humane institution.

The phenomenon of fugitive serfs created not only sagas but also a special culture under that regime. To be a fugitive serf meant to live dangerously, precariously, on the fringe of organized society. It meant a likely existence of uncertainty because of the danger of having one's identity revealed and then being punished and forcibly returned to one's lawful place of habitation, or the danger of being blackmailed and subjected to exploitation by those who guessed or knew one's real status. Living under a false identity, the inability to communicate freely with relatives and friends, often made the life of the fugitive so unbearable that discovery and its consequences could seem a relief rather than a punishment. A fugitive serf could meet his destiny with a measure of fatalism, resignation, or indifference, but the inducement to escape, or the perseverance to endure the discomforts and sufferings of a fugitive were often fed by and gave rise to chiliastic dreams, if not to a chiliastic philosophy. The phenomenon of peasant flight in this respect was closely related to the various beliefs in pretenders, in the schismatic teachings of the Old Believers and other sectors, and the attempts to set up communal settlements in remote places of the empire that denied any allegiance to political society or political authority.

Some fugitive serfs gained freedom for at least one generation. For some it was a shorter experience of a thoroughly failed attempt. For yet others flight constituted a repetition of attempts which placed them as incorrigibles outside of society. The proximity of the world of the fugitives to the world of common criminals left its imprint not only upon the consciousness of the fugitives but upon the rest of society as well.

Eighteenth-century Russia did not make heroes of its criminals or romanticize them. The "Robin Hood" syndrome probably was not yet invented. Cruelty on both sides of the chasm dividing society was more typical than noble intentions. Another feature of the culture of fugitive serfs must be noted: fugitives could not expect sympathy, refuge, or safety in the general serf milieu. It was not the efficiency of the fugitive-serf hunters or the police forces, military or otherwise, which raised the probability of fugitives' being caught or made their existence in flight precarious, but the lack of support by the other serfs. The high reward for revealing and arresting a fugitive, five rubles, a sum approximately double the yearly tax and rent paid by a serf, was a powerful incentive during most of the century for cooperation with the authorities. Still, attributing cooperation with the authorities primarily to the monetary reward is a superficial interpretation. It is likely that large numbers of serfs resented fugitives because it was the village commune, the totality of the serfs, who had to pay the taxes for their fugitive brethren in the approximately twenty-year intervals between the *revizii*, the population censuses which certified the absence of fugitives and removed them from the tax rolls. Thanks to the fact of collective fiscal responsibility, the fugitives' tax burden was transferred to the remaining serfs of each village commune. This procedure in many cases motivated the serfs themselves either to prevent flights or to help uncover the fugitives. In any case, it created a hostile attitude toward fugitives. This is not the place to offer additional psychological explanations of such attitudes, but it remains a fact that, had there not been tacit support by the mass of the serfs themselves, had the serfs not participated in the search for fugitives and in their punishment, the struggle of the Russian state and the serf-owners against serf flights would have been doomed to failure.

The frontier attracted fugitives because serfdom could not be enforced easily there. Even when serfdom existed on organized estates in those areas, the economic conditions were much more favorable in view of the lower population density and the low labor/land ratio. Much of the Russian frontier movement east and south was by its nature a colonization movement in which either livestock herding penetrated sparsely populated areas or in which sedentary agriculture encroached upon pasture lands. Simultaneously the colonization movement was characterized by the construction of military settlements which guarded the expanding frontier against the steppe nomads. The arrival of fugitives at the frontier

Table 2.19   Distribution of 2,096 Fugitives Inducted into the Orenburg Cossack Service, 1740

Peasants—court	982
Peasants—church	327
Peasants—private	159
Peasants—total	1,468
Cossack settlements	366
Soldiers settlements	135
Non-Russian Iasak taxpayers	89
Posad members	28
Inhabitants of Lithuania	10

was often welcomed by the local administration entrusted with the construction of military settlements, much to the chagrin of the St. Petersburg bureaucracy concerned with the enforcement of serfdom.

A vivid example of such a situation is provided by a document dated 1740 which reflects the inclusion of fugitives in Orenburg cossack service.[37] It reported 2,096 male fugitives distributed among fourteen towns of the "Orenburg fortified line." Of this total, the 2,065 who were accepted as "cossacks" had 1,567 additional male and 2,343 female family members. They reported as their previous places of residence 121 cities and districts (*uezdy*), plus 5 settlements (*slobody*) and 10 Ukrainian regiments. Geographically, they had come from: the Volga region, unspecified, 410; the Middle and Lower Volga regions, 674; the Upper Volga and the Trans-Volga regions, 142; the Far North, 46; the Oka region, 112; the Volga-Oka mesopotamia region, 212; the Don and Iaik cossacks, 152; and the Ufa region, 71. The previous status of the 2,096 fugitives is shown in table 2.19.

Most of the fugitives were previously state-owned serfs and state servitors. The inclusion of those fugitives in Orenburg cossack service signified from the government's point of view an unauthorized move but was a continuation of government service just the same. The only area of conflict involved the private serfs, who constituted a small minority in this case.

Flight to the frontier was much more threatening in cases where government service was terminated or service by serfs to their lords was not replaced by service to the government. An example of such flights is provided by 42 male state serfs and 778 male private serfs accompanied by 57 and 298 females, respectively, who had fled from Ekaterinoslav and Elizavetgrad to the territory of the Zaporozh'e Sech during the years 1767–74.[38] This escape route was particularly threatening to the government, for the fugitives were accompanied by 2,585 males and 141 females from the local military regiments and military settlers.

Throughout the eighteenth century the Middle and Lower Volga regions were the frontier regions par excellence of the Russian Empire. They possessed a special attraction for fugitive serfs not only because land was available for settlement and employment on the Volga transportation system could be obtained easily without much bureaucratic red tape, but also because, at least during the first half of the century, the military and civil administrations had a very imperfect grip on the movement of people in that region. The constant complaints about the insecurity of life and property, the interruption of traffic due to banditry or river piracy, and the settlement of private accounts among land owners by violent, extra-legal means provided this region with the characteristics of frontier communities in which the enforcement of legal norms to combat serf-flights and vagabondage were almost nonexistent. The Volga region served as an attraction for fugitive serfs and later a way station for fugitives on their way to the Urals and Siberia. Toward the end of the century population pressure on the land increased in the Volga region, which began to contribute its own share of fugitive serfs. For example, the court records for Arzamas *uezd* for the period 1787–1800 reveal the flight of at least 607 ablebodied serfs, including 171 household serfs and 436 agricultural serfs. Of these, 431 were males and 176 females, 43 were solitaries and 564 were married.[39]

One of the major causes and motives for serf flight was the army draft. Although events such as famines, increased exploitation, heightening of hopes, or illusions of change in status were factors which generated increased flight during certain periods, the army draft was a continuous and almost constant contributor to this phenomenon. Although the changing frequency or size of the draft may have altered the rate of flight, the draft itself can be dealt with as a constant. Flights originated in anticipation of the draft and then in the process of the draft procedure; later, both recruits and soldiers deserted from the armed forces. This explains why recruits were transported in chains like criminals under guard to their respective army units. During the century desertions and flights of serfs motivated by the army draft involved hundreds of thousands of individuals.

In this case, as in the cases of other categories of fugitives, opportunities to flee varied with the period and location. The frontier areas were the most exposed, particularly the frontier with Poland during the period prior to the partitions. The groups of fugitives who crossed the borders of Russia included private and state serfs, deserters from the armed forces, military auxiliaries (the case of the Bashkirs comes to mind), and religious dissenters. Such flights abroad were mentioned more prominently in the legislative literature than were domestic flights. For one, they often involved deserters; secondly, as fugitives abroad were outside the jurisdiction and power of the Russian government, their return had to be secured by incentives rather than punishments. Punishments were prominently represented and embedded in the existing legislation, so each incentive had to be decreed *ad novum*. During the period 1737–97 at least thirty-seven governmental decrees were published that mentioned the problems of returning fugitives from abroad. Twelve of them dealt specifically with deserters, three with the Bashkirs, and two with the Old Believers. The rest were more general. Usually they took the form of declarations of amnesty. During the second half of the century amnesties were proclaimed thirteen times.

The incentives were not only promises of amnesty, but also promises of land allotments, tax exemption for as many as six years, or the status of state serf. The land allotments were provided in various parts of the empire. Sometimes they were at sites selected by the government, such as the Altai region during the 1760s, or in regions determined by negotiations between the government and large groups of returning fugitives. For example, sites in Belgorod and Voronezh *gubernii* were selected by fugitives returning from Poland and Moldavia in 1749, when Sidor Tarasovich Zagrabskii negotiated their return with the government of Empress Elizabeth.[40]

Fugitives who returned without the protection of an amnesty and were captured at the frontier were returned to their old residences and owners or sent to Siberia. Moreover, at every opportunity when Russian armies marched through foreign territories where fugitive Russian serfs or deserters had found refuge, the fugitives were repatriated by force even though this constituted a clear violation of international law.

How can one explain the Russian authorities' insistence on repatriating fugitives from abroad, whether by force or by offering incentives? The answer may lie partly in the logic of the belief in population theories to which the Russian government subscribed during the eighteenth century: a larger population is the basis of the state's military and economic potential. That the application of such principles to Russian fugitives abroad might not be congruent with the enormous waste of human resources within the borders of the state did not trouble the ruling elite of Russia.

Historiography

The historical treatment of eighteenth-century Russian agriculture has varied over time. One older generation of historians stressed the legal status and legal differentiation of various groups within the enserfed peasantry and the legal aspects of lord-serf relations. Another school of populist-minded historians stressed the social content of the lord-serf rela-

tions and the impact of environmental conditions on the performance of agriculture. For a long time Soviet historians elaborated and emphasized the legal, social, and economic aspects of the adversary relations between lords and serfs and the dire consequences of that relationship, in which the state clearly aided the lords, for the income of the serfs. According to most Soviet historians, it was the institution of serfdom that was directly responsible for the backward state and all the ills that befell the primary agricultural producers. Only during the last decade or two have Soviet historians begun to pay attention to, and to publish materials about, the economic conditions transcending the institutional framework of Russian agriculture.

Discussions of the economic and social problems of eighteenth-century Russian agriculture have focused on a number of issues that might call attention to hitherto less explored areas of analysis of the agricultural scene and reveal the dynamics of the economic process.

An understanding of the changes that occurred in agriculture cannot be achieved by concentrating exclusively on the relationships between lords and serfs, if only because the market and the state were two other institutions that increasingly affected the agricultural sector. The market's impact began to be felt in Russia already during the second half of the seventeenth century, a century after economic growth had been terminated by political and economic developments and Russia had been cast into a state of isolation and economic stagnation. The restoration of the impact of the external and internal market on the Russian economy coincided with a number of governmental policies, some of which reinforced market tendencies and some of which limited their effect. Examples of the different impacts of an activist state policy were Peter's strengthening of the institution of serfdom, limiting the mobility of labor, and giving active support to trade and industry, or Catherine II's liberalizing policies on the matter of entrepreneurial activity.

During the bellicose first decades of the eighteenth century, when Russia was embroiled in the Northern War and Peter's mobilization policies had the effect of increasing the demand for agricultural products and for fiscal revenues, a time when inflationary pressures were strong, the government assumed that population declined and it strengthened the institution of serfdom. The assumption was based on the fiscal count of 1710, which revealed a sharp decline in the number of serf households, the result of households combining to escape escalating taxes. Moreover, during the first taxpayer ("soul") census of 1721, 964,000 out of a total of 5,296,000 escaped the census.[41]

The simultaneous "opening of a window to Western Europe" and the increasing demand for goods by the Russian nobility, the profound changes in the life style and consumption of the nobility in comparison with that of their forefathers, caused a change in the form of agricultural rent, from payments in kind to money rent. Inflation was controlled after 1725 and the shift to money rent and cash payments of government taxes became widespread. When the government in 1762 finally yielded to the demands of the nobility and freed them from stringent service requirements to devote more time and effort to the management of landed estates, greater attention was paid to the economic aspects of estate management. The estate owners, however, soon faced a changing economic situation. Demand for agricultural products both in the internal and foreign markets began to rise rapidly, and the rising prices for agricultural products implicitly increased the rent for land.

The Russian land owners did not feel that they could return to the abandoned system of collecting rent in kind, and they had no faith in the ability of the serfs to raise their output. They decided instead to increase their demesne on the estate in order to shift to a rent in the form of labor services (*barshchina*). They believed that with proper supervision of the serf labor force on the demesne land, they could obtain a higher portion of the product and could realize additional gain by selling it in the market. Thus commenced the transition from money rent to labor services on a mass scale, particularly in areas with above-average crop yields and relatively easy access to the market. The restructuring of the estates, the expansion of the demesne, the pressure on the serfs to render more labor services, the intensification of the workday under supervision were all pursued by the serf-owners in the expectation of a total revenue that would exceed that derived from money rent paying arrangements.

This pressure upon the estate management system was perceived by many historians not as a means by which Russian agriculture could reach higher levels of output, but primarily as a redistribution of a fixed total income from the serfs to their masters. The creation or expansion of the demesne was viewed by those historians as a decrease in the share of the serfs' landholdings. This overlooks the fact that this was a period when private landowners were appropriating to themselves large tracts of government-owned land, or were acquiring title to such lands for very low prices. By focusing primarily upon the experience of the largest estates, in which the costs of labor supervision were so high that they cancelled out the advantages of the labor-service system over the money rent-paying one, historians have overlooked the broad stratum of middle-sized estate owners who

clearly benefited from the new arrangements, who increased not only output but also their marketable share of the agricultural production, who often achieved their objectives not by diminishing the serfs' landholdings but by expanding both the demesne and the serfs' holdings and thus called into existence additional labor resources of the serfs' households that previously had been underutilized.

Historians have stressed the oppressive nature of the labor services under the assumption that free decision-making by the serf household would have created a more optimal relation between land and labor and would have resulted in a higher overall output. They have overlooked, however, the fact that the estate owners were more responsive to changes in the market demand and that they had both economic as well as noneconomic means to evoke a higher labor input by the serfs. Unlike some other historians, I have failed to find the consequences of a "declining curve of feudalism" or signs of economic deterioration in Russian agriculture during the second half of the eighteenth century.

More apparent are the effects of increased market activity on the serf-owners and the serfs. A gradual income differentiation arose which moved certain members of each group into higher income positions. The institutional framework of serfdom prevented the deterioration of the condition of the less successful. The share of the successful ones rose out of the increment of the total income of the respective groups because of the growth of production and income. This is an example of how an interchangeable use of economic, social, and moral criteria by historians often prevents them from recognizing the true features of a reality they are describing and analyzing.

The crop production branch exhibited some of the stark examples of the impact of the market upon the agricultural economy, as in the growth of such marketable grains as wheat and buckwheat and in the uninterrupted growth of the industrial crops such as hemp, flax, and oil seeds. The market also had an impact on the marketing growth of livestock and livestock products such as tallow, hides, butter, and meat. The agricultural population increasingly was busy with goods obtained from the Russian forests, which provided a substantial component of the serfs' consumption and incomes. The forests provided not only game, honey, berries, and mushrooms, but also pastures for cattle, bast for footwear, firewood, and construction materials, as well as raw material for tools, wagons, and other things.

In the eighteenth century, masts, shipbuilding materials, and wood for fuel used in making processed and industrial goods were taken out of forests in addition to the traditional products such as pitch, tar, and potash. Forest products were utilized as fuel for distilleries, glass manufactories, and, above all, ironmaking. The abundance of forests greatly enhanced Russia's ability to compete in the world iron market. Economic incentives were combined with extra-economic compulsion to enable Russia to allocate serf labor resources to industrial enterprises on either a full- or part-time basis. If one adds the various forms of entrepreneurship in the textile and other industries involving both serfs and estate owners, one realizes the impact of the market on the agricultural sector.

There is a widespread belief in the historical literature that the huge share of nonagricultural employment in the nonblacksoil region was a response to a need to compensate for below-subsistence levels of income derived from agriculture. This is a part of the erroneous belief that agriculture moved southward and eastward because of soil exhaustion in the older regions of Russia. Additionally, many historians believe that the need to pay rent and taxes, and even to survive, drove many serfs paying money rent to seek nonagricultural employment. In my opinion, this view is false. It ignores the fact that the pull of developed market regions and urban centers such as Moscow, St. Petersburg, and Iaroslavl' were a strong attraction for agricultural serfs from a wide region. It ignores the fact that, although the market was less effective in attracting goods because of distance or transportation costs, it was nevertheless effective in attracting labor.

By and large, the attraction of nonagricultural pursuits consisted in the income differential they offered in comparison with the remuneration from agricultural work. This does not deny the existence of serfs who had to augment their small incomes to reach a subsistence level. For most of those employed, however, it was a way to raise incomes above the level attainable in agriculture with the existing set of endowments.

The agricultural sector of the Russian economy was by far the dominant one during the eighteenth century in terms of employment and income. The changes it experienced were primarily induced by market forces. The consequences were a slowly increasing productivity, a more intensive utilization of the factors of production, and the creation of areas of specialization. Local markets were integrated into regional ones, and "mega-markets" appeared for some goods. The market impact was enhanced by development of other branches of the economy such as transportation and industry. The market forces created tensions as they clashed with traditions, customs, habits, and government policies. The three chief claimants on the fruits of economic improvements, the landowners, the peasant-serfs, and the state, competed for their shares and each adjusted to the new conditions. Productive factors increased market mobility and benefited from it.

Increments in production and productivity were small, in part, because of the low levels of skill and education, the low savings ratio, the backward governmental structure, and the ignorant bureaucracy. Politics was slow in catching up with economic change. Both the Russian absolutist government and most of the serfs themselves viewed serfs as animated property, as beasts of burden existing to support the needs of the state. Paying lip service to the role of agriculture, the government found it more congenial to use nonagricultural tools such as the knout to achieve its ends.

3
INDUSTRY

The Development Pattern of Particular Industries

This discussion will commence with a description of the development pattern of particular major branches of industry and conclude with a summary of the common general pattern of industrial development. The peculiarities of each industry, regardless of their importance to the student of economic history, will recede to the background and the general characteristics of an industrialization process will clearly emerge.

In order to establish a logical sequence for the discussion of the particular industries, an appropriate classification of the dominant industries is required. Out of the multitude of criteria according to which the industries can be classified, the choice has been narrowed to three: (1) technology; (2) labor force characteristics; (3) degree of governmental interference.

Given the fact that eighteenth century technology was relatively primitive, that water was the almost exclusive source of motive power for industry, and that physical capital constituted a minor share of the total resources of the industrial firm, classification along the lines of minor differences in the production process, or even by differences in type or origin of raw materials used (whether mineral, agricultural, or something else) possesses little of explanatory value.

The second type of classification, using the distinction between freely hired and serf labor as its main criterion, or the share of value added to the total output (even if it could be established with some degree of accuracy), is certainly more interesting and useful since it involves one of the fundamental problems of eighteenth-century manufactories, the nature of the labor market. Nevertheless classification by type of labor, although it raises one of the fundamental problems of factor supply, leaves the demand side totally outside the classification criteria. Therefore the third type, classification by degree of governmental interference, will be used.

The degree of governmental interference ought to be understood as the intensity of demand on the part of the government for the output of a particular industry, measured by the relative shares of output purchased or otherwise acquired by the government. Since the government's command over the resources of the country was very substantial, its intensity of demand for the products of particular industries was a major determinant in the supply of factors (labor, capital, and land) forthcoming for the various industries. Government policies were of utmost importance in determining not only the degree of monopsony of the different industry branches, but also the degree of monopoly power of the industries.

Therefore the distribution of the industries in question, defined by their end product, will be in terms of degree of government monopsony.

To the first group, where the government purchased the largest share of output, belong the production of precious metals, the production of armaments, and the woolen-cloth industry. To the second group, where governmental purchases were intermediate, belong the copper- and ironworks. To the third, where government purchases were small, belong the remaining branches of the textile industry (in the order of diminishing government interference), the linen, cordage, silk, and cotton-goods industries.

The direct involvement of the government in the production of various goods by and in itself does not necessarily determine the degree of government interference. On the one hand, for example, the government chose to sell a major part of its own iron output abroad, while acquiring relatively substantial quantities of iron for its armed forces from the domestic private producers. On the other hand, the government acquired sailcloth for its navy exclusively from private producers. Thus it is not the direct share in the production by the state that I consider crucial, but rather the state's share in the total demand for the output.

The Production of Precious Metals

The government established an undisputed monopoly of production and consumption throughout the eighteenth century in mining and smelting of precious metals.[1] Gold production in the eighteenth century was never more than one-third of the total value of silver and gold output, and thus the emphasis here will be on silver. Silver was the chief raw material for coinage during the eighteenth century, and production of the precious metal was considered an integral part of the state monopoly of coinage. In addition, the mining of silver in particular regions yielded relatively high profits, which the state preferred not to share with private entrepreneurs.[2] Taking a long-term view, the state was even ready to invest heavily in the production of precious metals.[3]

The demand for silver in Russia was for coinage and for private consumption. At the beginning of the century both the private demand and the government demand for coinage were satisfied by foreign imports.[4] The demand by private individuals for silver goods continued to be met during the rest of the century either by foreign imports of such goods or by the use of domestic coins. It is virtually impossible to estimate the private demand for silver goods. It is possible, however, to establish with some degree of certainty the size of the supply of silver for coinage by converting the total volume of coins minted into the appropriate weights of silver for different periods. This can be estimated as shown in table 3.1.

The increase in the money supply of Russia, which was accelerated at the beginning of the eighteenth century, required an increasing supply of silver.[5] However, the Northern War, which interrupted normal trade relations to some extent, and the need to pay for extra imported military supplies from abroad, both decreased the supply and increased the demand. This prompted the government to seek energetically for domestic sources of silver.

As a result of the search, the first silver-producing region in Nerchinsk (Eastern Siberia) was established and gave its first silver output in 1704–5. The size of

Table 3.1   Silver Coinage in Terms of Pure Silver (in Poods)

Years	Total	Yearly Average
1699–1717	35,549.3	1,871.0
1718–24	6,229.3	889.9
1725–29	6,529.2	1,305.8
1730–40	25,433.3	2,384.3
1741	1,406.9	1,406.9
1742–60	40,911.6	2,272.9
1761	814.0	814.0
1762–96	77,937.9	2,226.8
1797–1800	11,006.3	2,751.6
1699–1800	205,817.8	2,017.8

Table 3.2   Customs Duties Paid in Foreign Currency (Converted to 1,000 Current Rubles)

Year	Customs Duties	Year	Customs Duties	Year	Customs Duties
1730[a]	523	1765	1,207	1791	1,020
1735[b]	639	66	1,210	92	1,049
1740[c]	647	67	531	93	812
42	699	68	467	94	857
43	793	69	406	95	722
44	729	1770	417	96	1,288
1745	744	71	448	97	3,630
46	776	72	973	98	—
47	741	73	919	99	—
48	654	74	911	1800	—
49	750	1775	913		
1750	904	76	718		
51	938	77	763		
52	1,027	78	801		
53	1,006	79	849		
54	945	1780	979		
1755	909	81	820		
56	939	82	953		
57	909	83	1,186		
58	911	84	1,119		
59	952	1785	1,023		
1760	908	86	762		
61	961	87	1,083		
62	1,140	88	925		
63	1,241	89	866		
64	1,200	1790	991		

Source: Lodyzhenskii, *Istoriia russkogo tamozhennogo tarifa*, pp. 96, 144.

[a]Converted from 523,000 Joachimsthalers at 1:1 parity.
[b]Converted from 547,000 Joachimsthalers at 1:1.1674 parity.
[c]Converted from 539,000 Joachimsthalers at 1:1.2 parity.

the output initially was small, and until the 1740s Nerchinsk remained the sole producing region.[6] But even after the addition of the Altai silver production, the total output until the 1760s remained totally inadequate to meet the demands of coinage. The price of silver in Russia was relatively high (the gold-silver ratio was 1:13 at the beginning of the century and 1:14 in the 1740–50s), and consequently one would expect the silver imported into Russia to be substantial.[7]

In its competition for silver even the government had to deviate from the officially decreed silver prices and secretly purchase silver at the market price.[8] It is difficult to establish the volume of old coins offered for sale to the government. The data are scarce and the impressions often conflicting.[9] The volume probably varied, depending upon the secretly allowed price and the free-market price of silver. Regardless, as indicated in table 3.2, one would probably be on the safe side estimating the supply of old coins during the various periods as constituting about 15 percent of the total volume of coinage.[10]

The government exhibited an increasing propensity for coining copper money. This can be explained by an examination of its need to rely upon imports of silver, the recoinage of solid domestic silver coins, and the very limited silver production during the first half of the century.[11] Although the relatively low level of domestic silver production might help to explain the growing reliance upon copper currency for the second half of the century as well, and also the necessity to begin to borrow abroad, it would be a mistake to attribute the issuance of paper money (assignats) initiated in 1767 entirely to the silver scarcity.[12] In fact, as shown in table 3.3, during the second half of the century silver production increased substantially and accounted for approximately one-half of the silver coinage in Russia.[13]

The trends in the production of silver were paralleled by the trends in the production of the second precious metal then produced in Russia, gold. For all practical purposes, gold was a by-product of silver output in all except the Berezovsk mines, where silver was derived as a by-product of the smelting of gold-containing ores.

The demand for gold coinage on the part of the government can be surmised roughly from the volume of the coinage. The price relationship between gold and silver in Russia was such that gold could not remain as a part of the currency in circulation in view of the incentive to export gold coins abroad. Thus for most of the period the coinage of gold ought to be considered as a matter of prestige for the government (or the rulers) rather than as a serious attempt to introduce bimetallism into the monetary system.

The volume of gold coinage is presented in table 3.4. It seems that, whereas during the early part of the eighteenth century the insignificant volume of gold coinage had to be supplied by gold imported from abroad, during the second half of the century the domestic gold output approximately covered the issues of gold coins in Russia. During most of the century the balance of trade was in favor of Russia, and thus the insignificant volume of gold imports may be explained by the relatively lower prices for gold in Russia than abroad. The result was that Russia did not import gold or was unable to stop its export.

The value of the output of precious metals in Russia for a number of selected years during the second half of the eighteenth century can be estimated from official sources, as shown in tables 3.5, 3.6, and 3.7. The development of the precious-metals mining and industry was an import-substitution measure which alleviated the government's demand for precious metals for the purpose of coinage.

It is difficult to estimate either the private or the social costs of this industry in Russia during the eighteenth century. The resources used in precious-

Table 3.3   Output of Silver and Coinage in Russia (in Poods)

Years	Average Yearly Silver Coinage	Year	Domestic Silver Output
1762–71	2,676	1770	1,336
1772–81	2,353	1775	1,497
1782–91	1,894	1785	966
		1790	1,160
1792–96	1,741	1795	1,161
1797–1800	2,752	1799	1,247

Source: Storch, *Supplementband*.

Note: In addition, the customs rendered during 1763–96 a total of 42,418 poods of Joachimsthaler or a yearly average of 1,247.6 poods of silver coins which was used for coinage.

Table 3.4   Gold Coinage in Russia, 1718–1800

Years	In Current Rubles	In Pounds of Pure Gold	Yearly Average
1718–24	706,231	2,458.7	394.1
1725–29	145,558	568.6	113.7
1730–40	176,652	659.2	65.9
1742–60	1,524,142	5,606.1	295.1
1762–96	16,052,338	47,028.3	1,343.7
1797–1800	2,054,597	6,019.3	1,504.8
Total	20,659,518	62,340.2	763.9

Source: Kaufman, *Serebrianyi rubl'*, pp. 151–59. The weight in gold calculated from the Kaufman data.

Table 3.5   Value of Output of Precious Metals (in Current Silver Rubles)

Year	Silver Output	Gold Output	Total Output
1765	604,881	281,642	886,523
1770	1,000,284	448,718	1,449,002
1775	1,120,766	502,632	1,623,398
1780	877,575	375,430	1,253,005
1785	723,303	238,961	962,264
1790	868,589	331,350	1,199,939
1795	868,918	357,178	1,226,096
1800	933,566	420,077	1,353,643

Note: The quantities are based upon tables 3.3 and 3.4, except for 1765, where some missing data were substituted by 1766 reported production figures. The price for silver used was the official government price of 19.5 kopeks per zolotnik, although both the market price and the actual purchase price were at least 10% higher. The gold price was assumed to be 2.925 rubles p. zolotnik, which is equal to the 1:15 parity between silver and gold. I assumed lower-than-market prices in the full knowledge that the market price was 10–20% higher.

metals production were by no means idle, and the major input, labor, had alternative uses. In fact, the conditions of production of precious metals in Russia were such that they made the production costs very high indeed, and the social costs might be valued even more highly.

The regions where precious metals were produced in Russia (northeastern Urals, southwest and eastern Siberia) were located at very great distances from the economic and population centers of the Russian state, in sparsely populated areas. They were also far

Table 3.6   Reported Gold Output by Major Producing Regions (in poods and pounds)

Years	Nerchinsk		Altai		Berezovsk		Total (in poods)		Total (in pounds)
1704–47 (total)	1	4							
1745			–	15					
1745–55 (total)					–	29			
1747–48			3	37					
1748–59	5	12							
1750			4	18					
54					–	15			
55			13	3					
1760			8	31	1	15			
65			21	5	2	33			1,000
66	1	5							
1770	1	18	33	34	4	26	39	38	1,598
75	2	4	38	34	3	32	44	30	1,790
1780	1	9	26	2	6	6	33	17	1,337
85	1	25	15	38	3	28	21	11	851
1790	1	1	20	35	7	20	29	16	1,176
95		21	20	38	10	13	31	32	1,272
1800		38	20	7	15	38	37	16	1,496

Sources: Danilevskii, *Russkoe zoloto*, pp. 32, 51; Karpenko, *Gornaia promyshlennost'*, p. 193.

Note: Slightly different figures were reported by B. F. J. Hermann ("Sur l'exploitation").

apart from one another. The remoteness of the mining centers and the sparseness of population created serious problems of labor supply, food and materials supply, and also transportation problems for the finished output.

The major problem was obtaining an adequate labor supply. A distinction must be noted here, as in other industries, between the skilled and unskilled labor force consisting of former army draftees, and skilled workers who were forcibly attached to the mines and refineries. The offspring of the skilled workers received training either on the job or in the factory and schools, and were attached to their places of work. The unskilled were recruited from penal labor. The largest share of penal laborers (called *katorzhniki*) was in the Nerchinsk silver mines, the most remote source of precious metals and the place that suffered the most severe labor shortages. The conditions of work and the maintenance of the *katorzhniki* were regulated by special decree.[14]

The wages and conditions of work of the skilled labor force were regulated either by the decrees of the Mining College or of the Urals and Siberia Mining Authority.[15] Expecting some increase in labor productivity, the authorities could not direct the various categories of forced skilled labor by coercion alone. For example, during the second half of the century, when grain prices were rising, the mining administration purchased grain at the wholesale price and resold it to the labor force at cost, compensating for what otherwise would have been a decrease in the real wage. The location of the work made it necessary

to provide additional incentives for every free, highly skilled employee. These specialists and administrators encompassed a heterogeneous group of Russian mining technicians, noblemen graduated from the Mining Academy, and foreign specialists.[16] Most characteristic of the labor force employed in the mining and smelting of precious metals, however, was the high number of state-owned peasants attached to the mines and smelters for the performance of unskilled jobs. The numerical relationship between skilled and unskilled workers is shown in table 3.8.

By the end of the century the total industry, including the Altai copper mines and the Ekaterinburg mint, which coined copper money, employed about 16,000 workers at some level of skill and about 115,000 state peasants who, in lieu of paying taxes, were obliged to burn charcoal, to transport the ore, and to perform other auxiliary work of this type for several days a year. In terms of their labor input, therefore, the 115,000 male peasants represented an actual labor input of 6,670 yearly workers.[17]

Technological advancement was relatively slow in the industry in spite of the presence of a number of outstanding technical specialists and innovators such as the Frolovs and Polzunov. Many of their inventions, some of which, although technically feasible, might have been too expensive, remained buried in the archives of the mining authorities. Until the last part of the century there was no clear incentive to economize on labor so long as the labor force could be enlarged by further attachment of groups of state

Table 3.7   Reported Silver Production (in Poods and Pounds)

Year	Nerchinsk		Altai		Total		5-Year Average	
1704		1						
1705	1	23						
06	3	19						
07	5	8					4	0
08	5	26						
09	2	3						
1710	8	4						
11	8	15						
12	11	4	10				10	8
13	11	26						
14	11	31						
1715	2	16						
16	12	4						
17	15	14					9	2
18	10	9						
19	5	6						
1720	4	2						
21	5	33						
22	10	5					6	30
23	7	18						
24	6	10						
1725	3	10						
26	1	16					1	15
27		4						
28		23						
1729	1	22						
30		35						
31							–	13
32								
33								
34		29						
1735	1	15						
36	2	24					3	34
37	4	4						
38	3	20						
39	7	25						
1740	13	17						
41	12	20					13	5
42	9	33						
43	15							
44	14	37						
1745	17	0	44	6	61	6		
1746	19	4					249	12
47	35	3	237	13	343	22		
48	71	6						
49	82	8	309	22	391	30		

peasants and military draftees who could be trained in the appropriate mining skills.

During the second half of the century a trend toward the use of contracted or hired labor to supplement or substitute for the work of serfs became discernible. After 1779 the rates paid to state-owned serfs increased and they were compensated for travel from their villages to the place of work, and consequently it became more convenient and relatively less costly to use hired labor instead.[18] There were a number of reasons why hired labor did not fully replace serf labor. Chief among them were the government's desire to keep the wage bill low and the rise in wages or income from other occupations relative to wages paid by state enterprises. An illustration of the inadequacy of the state wage is presented by the serfs who hired substitutes on a large scale at rates double the state wage. Pressure upon the serfs to increase their labor input at fixed wage rates intensified the serfs' demand for hired substitutes and decreased the supply of labor available for hire by the state enterprises themselves. For example, in the Altai region the early 1780s were the years of peak utilization of hired labor in the transportation of ore. In the 1790s the share of hired labor in ore transportation stabilized, as shown in table 3.9.

The available evidence demonstrates the relative labor scarcity in the areas of precious-metals produc-

Table 3.7, cont.   Reported Silver Production (in Poods and Pounds)

Year	Nerchinsk		Altai		Total		5-Year Average	
1750	81	32	209	30	291	22		
51	39	27	366	35	406	22		
52	51	8	304	26	355	34	370	13
53	100	25	310	27	411	12		
54	51	36	334	19	386	15		
1755	139	17	303	21	442	38		
56	126	16	321	18	447	34		
57	100	2	222	31	322	33	411	32
58	134	34	264	3	398	38		
59	173	7	273	10	446	17		
1760	149	14	264	22	413	36		
61	151	27	333	21	485	8		
62	176	3	405	27	581	30		
63	322	26	499	24	822	10	624	28
64	399	9	421	9	820	18		
1765	298	2	575	34	873	36		
66	314	33	767	14	1,082	7		
67	435	36	779	20	1,215	16	1,075	36
68	343	32	741	23	1,085	15		
69	321	31	809	19	1,122	10		
1770	414	26	1,013	12	1,427	38		
1771	470	7	1,298	20	1,768	27		
72	503	36	1,277	34	1,781	30		
73	523	30	1,181	12	1,705	2	1,689	33
74	619	2	1,146	24	1,765	26		
1775	539	15	1,059	33	1,599	8		
76	398	39	1,027	20	1,426	19		
77	323	22	1,035	26	1,359	8	1,367	21
78	380	39	913	1	1,294	–		
79	349	16	809	12	1,158	28		
1780	458	1	802	31	1,260	32		
81	399	3	546	14	945	17		
82	470	38	400	13	871	11	1,058	10
83	507	38	730	25	1,238	23		
84	457	18	517	27	975	5		
1785	288	36	600	21	889	17		
1786	340	31	771	20	1,112	11		
87	320	9	771	18	1,091	27	1,119	33
88	273	3	868	13	1,141	16		
89	314	6	1,050	10	1,364	16		
1790	213	1	1,054	34	1,267	35		
91	278	2	1,152	25	1,330	27		
92	263	–	1,022	39	1,285	39	1,286	24
93	237	37	1,011	22	1,249	19		
94	256	36	1,042	6	1,299	2		
1795								

tion. Akinfii Demidov paid the serfs, as shown in table 3.10, a premium for work performed above their obligations that was 40 to 60 percent above the wage decreed by the government for obligatory work. A petition of March 9, 1745, by the serfs attached to the Altai mines submitted to state administrator Beyer indicates that when they hired substitutes they usually paid a wage 2.7 times the wage they received for fulfillment of their poll tax requirements.[19] Even assuming that their claims were somewhat exaggerated, or that the wage differential was even larger in such labor-deficit areas, the figure indicates the existence of a substantial differential between the market wage and the wage received for fulfillment of poll tax

requirements, the existence of a lag between prices and wages, and a substantial differential due to differences in productivity between freely hired and serf labor.

Having considered the specific problem of the labor supply for the precious-metals industry, one wonders whether limitations upon the labor supply were the primary reason for the inability to increase output further or, in fact, to prevent its decline during the last decade of the eighteenth century. Although limitations on the labor supply is a plausible explanation, I doubt whether it should be accepted as *the* major explanation.[20] The available level of technology in Russia was insufficient to overcome the relative labor

Table 3.8   Labor Force in the Precious-Metals Industry

Mining Region	1747 Skilled	1747 Unskilled	1756 Skilled	1756 Unskilled	1764 Skilled	1764 Unskilled	1781–83 Skilled	1781–83 Unskilled	1796–98 Skilled	1796–98 Unskilled
Nerchinsk	736	4,286			1,944	8,070	2,664	11,854	8,470	
Altai[a]				10,935		39,810		54,750		63,355
Berezovsk			355	9,171	1,524[b]	18,567			1,539	13,451
Ekaterinburg gold mines							1,890[b]	13,176	2,703	9,207
Ekaterinburg mint							1,169[b]	8,209	853	

[a]The Altai mining region labor-force was also employed at copper mining and smelting; it is impossible to separate the work force according to the end-product.
[b]Out of the 1,524 skilled workers in Berezovsk in 1764, only 1,068 were permanent workers; out of 1,890 in the Ekaterinburg mines in 1781 only 1,504 were permanently employed; out of the 1,169 workers in the Ekaterinburg mint in 1781, 490 had steady employment.

shortages at the wage rates paid by the state enterprises in this industry. Given the rising costs of labor and shrinking profits (as calculated by the producers), and the diminishing state incomes from coinage, the industry became less profitable in real terms. With the monetary price of precious metals (very often set below the market price), the demand for coinage (which absorbed all of the domestic output), and rising costs, the only solution was either a technological breakthrough using the existing sources of ore or the discovery of new sources to which different technological processes could be applied.

The production of precious metals contributed to the development of the monetary system, to the acquisition and development of new skills, to the transfer into nonagricultural activities of a portion of the labor force, and to a degree of import substitution. Listing these economic benefits makes sense, however, only when one takes into account as well the substantial social costs, which included the cost of allocating a large, bound labor-force to the industry.

Shipbuilding

A special place among the state-owned and state-operated industrial enterprises was occupied by the shipbuilding complex in St. Petersburg, the Admiralty. The history of this institution, which deserves a monographic study, cannot be told here, where I

Table 3.9   Payment for Ore Transportation in the Altai State Mining Enterprises (in Rubles)

Year	Payment to Hired Labor	Payment to Serfs
1783	157,891	n.a.
1789	132,971	61,368
1790	82,265	73,795
91	84,816	82,978
92	83,027	71,497
93	69,414	71,618
94	74,445	79,132
95	98,949	83,493
96	79,742	80,232
97	91,425	89,719

Source: Karpenko, *Promyshlennost'*, p. 80.

Table 3.10   Daily Wage Paid to Serfs by Demidov in Altai Mines, Beginning of 1740s

	To Serfs for Poll-Tax	To Serfs above Poll-Tax Requirements
Winter		
Without horse	4 kopeks	6–7 kopeks
With horse	6 kopeks	10 kopeks
Summer		
Without horse	5 kopeks	7 kopeks
With horse	10 kopeks	12 kopeks

Source: Karpenko, *Promyshlennost'*, p. 53.

Table 3.11   Employment in the Admiralty by Occupation

Occupation	1715	1717	1720	1721
Carpenters	1,867	1,483	3,677	3,609
Sawyers	93	124	138	165
Joiners	122	n.a.	126	124
Caulkers	n.a.	242	111	228
Blacksmiths	251	308	351	500
Flax & hemp spinners	275	381	592	448
Sailmakers	135	185	100	246
Total	2,743	2,723	5,095	5,320

Source: Semenova, *Rabochie Peterburga*, p. 63.

shall only make some references to its character and attributes. The Admiralty was the largest industrial complex in eighteenth-century Russia, one that combined the production of various industries. It produced ships exclusively for the navy, not for the merchant marine, and therefore its output and labor force fluctuated widely, depending upon the government's naval construction program. The management and "labor relations" at the Admiralty were not only bureaucratic but also totally military.

The Admiralty was one of the earliest enterprises set up in St. Petersburg and employed a number of outstanding foreign shipbuilders in addition to the experienced Russian labor force earlier employed on the wharves of Voronezh, where the first attempts to build seagoing vessels were made in conjunction with Peter's Azov expedition in 1696. Recruiting its labor force, the Admiralty had to compete with the demands for labor by the construction program of St. Petersburg itself. The skills of carpenters, blacksmiths, and others were in demand for both tasks and made the recruitment of labor difficult. There was competition not only for skilled workers but for the unskilled as well, and especially when the naval construction program occasionally exceeded the statutory number of workers the Admiralty was allowed to employ. Although the statutory level was 5,496 workers, by November 7, 1716, total employment reached a figure of 7,515, which was not the highest number reached during Peter's reign, when naval construction enjoyed a high priority.[21] During the Petrine period even the number of skilled workers employed in the Admiralty fluctuated widely, as shown in table 3.11. The increase in the number of skilled workers serving the Admiralty was made possible by a decrease in the demand for workers in the construction of St. Petersburg.[22]

The means by which the Admiralty's labor force was recruited during the Petrine period depended upon the timing of naval construction and the situation in the labor market. Apart from outright mobilization of skilled workers for short periods, the workers and their families were forcibly resettled from other cities. There were also inducements for them to

resettle voluntarily. For the unskilled labor force, the government both permitted the hiring of substitutes by people mobilized for labor services and accepted the monetary equivalent of a market wage from the mobilized population to hire substitute laborers, provided that a supply of labor for hire existed at that particular moment.

Another source of unskilled labor for the Admiralty was the army and navy recruits sent to the wharves instead of to military units. Beginning in the 1720s, after the Admiralty had achieved its goal of creating a labor force of steady workers, labor replacement was expected from the natural increase of the employed population. The Admiralty also expected that the younger generation would be educated at the state's expense and trained in the various skills by their parents on the wharves and in the shops.

After Peter's death the decline in demand for naval construction left the Admiralty with excess labor capacity. The early 1730s witnessed the beginning of the disintegration of this production complex. The war with the Crimean Khanate in 1737 witnessed a mass transfer of Admiralty workers to wharves on the Dnepr and Don rivers.[23] Although one cannot assume a serious loss of skills as a result of the dispersal or dislocation of the Admiralty personnel, there is no doubt that the productive capacity of the Admiralty shipyards was impaired. This forced the government during the 1740s, particularly during the war with Sweden, to resort again to forced labor mobilization measures.

The experience of the Admiralty during the second half of the century indicates that the problem of the fluctuating size of the labor force was not resolved. Regardless of the inconvenience and delays caused by the need to expand or contract the labor force at each turn in the naval construction program, the skills acquired at the Admiralty were not lost for the economy as a whole.

The character of the Admiralty as a militarized enterprise is seen most vividly in the area of wage determination. Although skill differentiation was clearly reflected in the relative wage levels as well as in the differences between occupations of basic importance for shipbuilding and occupations of secondary or auxiliary importance, the limits for each category were rigidly prescribed. There seems to have been little leeway for job security or a wage response to relative labor scarcity at any given time.

The wages of less-skilled workers and apprentices were inflexible. In addition to a monetary wage, Admiralty workers and their family members were entitled to a food ration. Every Admiralty worker earning less than 40 rubles per year, which included the majority of the labor force, was entitled to a food ration. The food ration was crucial as an income supplement for the lower-paid categories of workers. It also had an equalizing effect upon wages by decreasing the wage differentials. The idea of a food ration was derived from and reflected the idea of military or naval services, and had very little connection with the notion of a wage reflecting the quantity and quality of labor. Both the idea of the food ration as well as its size was transferred from the armed services to state-owned armament industries and enterprises.

Linen Manufacturing

The development of linen manufactories in Russia was due to a large extent to Peter the Great. He expected them to serve the following purposes: (1) to supply the needs of the navy for sailcloth; (2) to provide suitable substitutes for broad linen, hitherto imported from abroad; (3) to increase the demand for domestically produced raw materials, flax and hemp; (4) to provide additional items of exportable goods.

The production of linen was a traditional craft, employing mostly peasants. Most of the production was narrow, coarse linen cloth. Peter the Great, in addition to setting up state-owned linen manufactories and encouraging the establishment of manufactories by private individuals, also tried to reform the rural handicraft output of linen by prescribing on October 31, 1715, new technical standards for linen output and forbidding the production of the narrow cloth.[24] In spite of the harsh punishment prescribed by the decree, the new law was not effective and was abolished in 1718 (only to be reintroduced later with little success).[25]

The setting up of state-owned manufactories (the Khamovnyi Dvor near Moscow and linen manufactories in Moscow and Iaroslavl') and the subsequent turning them over to private entrepreneurs served as an incentive to other entrepreneurs to set up similar enterprises. By the end of the reign of Peter the Great the total production of the existing linen manufactories reached the figure of about 1.2 million arshins of cloth.[26]

This output was produced in ten manufactories, with a labor force of about 1,900 workers using 842 looms. The output consisted of hemp sailcloth and linen cloth of various kinds. The manufactories differed by the degree of specialization in weaving, or a combination of spinning and weaving. Sailcloth predominated in the total output and a substantial part of it was sold for export at 12 kopeks per arshin. The value of the output around 1725 was thus in the neighborhood of 140,000 to 150,000 rubles. Part of the output was of a higher-value product, and thus the market value of the output of the linen industry was probably in the neighborhood of 160,000 to 170,000 rubles.

The available data do not permit a close following of the growth of this industry, or of the impact of government demand. It is clear, however, that government demand, if at all effective, was influential only upon the production of sailcloth, the share of which in the industry's total output was decreasing. In addition, even the scarce data available on the production and export of sailcloth make it clear that the bulk of production was destined for foreign markets rather than for the Russian navy or the very small merchant marine. The linen industry was a market-oriented industry that responded to a combination of foreign and domestic demand.

The growth of the industry can be inferred (rather than measured) from the growth of the number of manufactories, labor force, looms, and exports.

The number of manufactories increased from 10 in 1725 to 35 in 1741, 79 in 1763, and 318 in 1799. After the abolition of the licensing system of industrial enterprises in 1775, many small manufactories were opened or legalized. Thus the 1799 figure reflects a different mix of enterprises by size than the previous ones. Perhaps 200 enterprises belonged to the same category as the ones reported for the earlier period.[27]

The labor force increased from less than 2,000 workers in 1725 to 13,812 in 1763, 18,247 in 1773, and 29,303 in 1799.

A distinction must be made between the skilled labor force employed primarily in weaving and the semiskilled or unskilled employed in spinning. A distinction also should be made between the force actually working and the number of male peasants attached to the enterprises, of which only a fraction was actually employed. For example, the total labor force reported for the year 1771 was 18,342, of whom serfs numbered 10,541. There can be no doubt that not all the serfs listed as attached to the linen manufactories were actually employed. By the end of the century the absolute number and the relative share of serfs employed in the linen industry declined from over 50 percent during the middle of the century to about 35 percent.[28]

The volume of output reported in terms of sale prices increased almost five-fold, from 1,017,039 rubles in 1763 to 4,928,400 rubles in 1799.[29]

Table 3.12 presents the volume of linen exports in the second half of the eighteenth century. It shows the general rise, as well as the changing assortment of exports, the most marked tendency of which was the secular decline of the share of sailcloth and the increase of Ravenduck in the total exports.

These data show the growth of the export trade of the linen industry but do not indicate the share of exports as a percentage of the total domestic output.

Table 3.12   Average Yearly Russian Exports of Main Linen Products (in 1,000 Arshin)

Year	Flemish Linen	Ravenduck	Sail Cloth	Total
1749	182.7	2.0	1,809.5	1,994.2
1758–60	547.75	1,013.55	1,755.1	3,316.4
1778–80	1,458.95	4,685.9	3,012.55	9,157.2
1790–92	1,633.3	4.990.55	2,313.1	8,936.95
1793–95				14,615.0

Sources: Pazhitnov, *Ocherki*, p. 178; Pokrovskii, *Sbornik svedenii*, p. xxviii.

Table 3.13   Share of Exports of Four Major Products of Linen Industry, 1761–63

Product	% Exported
Sailcloth	87.6
Ravenduck	84.0
Kalamenka	80.6
Flemish	89.6
Average Total[a]	85.0

Source: Pazhitnov, *Ocherki*.

[a]Based upon the number of arshin.

This is shown in table 3.13 for the years 1761–63, when between 80 and 90 percent of total linen output was exported.

It is unlikely that the share of exports in the total production remained so high later in the century. Even if we assume that the nobility and gentry still imported a part of their consumption from abroad, some higher-quality domestic goods probably appealed to them as they did to the growing merchant population. Thus it is logical to assume that the share of domestic consumption in the total output grew secularly, while exports did not decline in absolute terms. The value of exports grew from 2,937,000 rubles yearly during the years 1790–93 to 4,285,000 annually during the period 1793–95, a moderate growth when the declining value of the ruble is considered, but still an increase of more than 20 percent in real terms. By the end of the century, exports of linen goods stabilized at a level above 13 million arshins.

Silk-Weaving

A typical industry dependent primarily upon demand in the domestic market was the silk-weaving industry. Although the initiative to set up manufactories of silk-weaving originally came from the government (the court was a substantial consumer of silk-wares), the industry passed very quickly into private hands. The necessary raw materials were imported from abroad and the skills acquired from foreign specialists. In terms of the quality of output, Russian silk-weaving throughout the century did not manage to reach the high standards of work-manship of either Western Europe or China. The Russians therefore concentrated upon the types of products which could be easily produced by less-skilled workers in relatively large quantities and which found a ready mass market. This was the production of silk shawls, kerchiefs, and ribbons. Velvets and brocades did not occupy a prominent place in Russian output. In fact, most of the silk products with a high value per unit were imported throughout the century. Thus one could assume that the imports of silk-wares were made up primarily of consumption goods for the nobility and gentry, for which the demand-elasticity was low. There was a higher elasticity of demand for the product of the domestic silk industry by the lower- and middle-income groups.

The goal of the government to create an industry which would serve the purposes of import substitution did not entirely succeed. Raising the tariffs on silk products did not deter the wealthy from purchasing high-quality foreign products. Tariff legislation both raised the price to the domestic consumer and provided protection to the domestic manufacturers in the chosen areas of their production.[30] The role of the government as a consumer of the domestic output was negligible. Its impact, apart from the initial stimulus, subsidies, and support, consisted primarily of the tariff legislation on the one hand and the licensing system (until 1775) on the other.

Unlike the linen industry, the development of silk-weaving manufactories was not facilitated by the previous existence of handicrafts or cottage industries. Rather, the situation was the reverse. The silk-weaving manufactories by their dissemination of skills contributed to the establishment and spread of a peasant-type, rurally based cottage industry, thus creating competition for itself. As in many other instances, government legislation and regulation aided the manufactories in their competition against the growing number of illegal, small-scale producers entering the industry.

The silk-weaving manufactories were founded and owned almost exclusively by merchants.[31] Nevertheless, during the first half of the century the silk-manufactory owners received generous permits for purchases of serfs to be employed in the manufactories. The permits were granted on the basis of a decree of January 18, 1721, and skilled laborers were enserfed by government decree in 1736. As a result of this legislation, thirty-nine of the merchant-owned silk manufactories received a right to purchase 9,984 male serfs. However, only twenty-three entrepreneurs utilized the privilege and purchased a total of 3,927 male serfs. Although the permission granted to purchase serfs apparently helped some enterprises to solve their labor recruitment problems, the ratio of

Table 3.14   Labor Force-Composition of Thirty Silk Manufactories (Late 1760s)

	Males	Females	Total
Attached serfs	1,545	416	1,961
Purchased serfs	1,217	527	1,744
Hired workers	861	985	1,846
Total	3,623	1,928	5,551

Source: Volodarskaia, "Naemnyi trud," p. 133.

serfs actually purchased to permitted purchases indicates that serf purchases were not a panacea. Even the labor force data in table 3.14 for thirty silk manufactories that used the labor of serfs permanently attached by the government indicate the insufficiency of serf labor to meet all skill categories.

The abolition of the licensing system in manufacturing in 1775 gave a new impetus to the growth of the industry and resulted in a higher rate of growth of output. (After 1775 a larger portion of the actual output was reflected in the official government statistics, which previously had not included the illegal, clandestine production of nonlicensed producers.) The growth of silk-weaving manufacturing in general can be traced from the available, albeit far from complete and not always comparable, data, which are presented in table 3.15.

Raw silk imports increased in the four decades from the 1760s to the end of the century from about 3,500 poods to over 13,000 poods, or almost fourfold. Output increased as much in terms of stable prices. By the end of the century, almost 85 percent of the total consumption of silk-wares were produced domestically.[32]

One of the characteristics of the silk-weaving manufactories was their declining average size and increasing specialization. The largest enterprises in terms of the size of the labor force and number of looms were those set up early in the century which received allotments of serfs. The manufactories set up later in the century were smaller in size and primarily used hired labor. The smallest enterprises were those

set up by peasants in the rural areas and based entirely upon freely hired labor. Advantages of size apparently were not fundamental for the functioning of the enterprises. The composition and level of skill were more important than the scale of operations. Growing specialization found its expression primarily in the division between silk-spinning and silk-weaving, and within silk-weaving between narrow and broad materials. Specialization on a particular line of production rather than on a broad assortment of goods made it possible to introduce whatever division of labor was possible, given the technological processes available and the quality and types of looms in use. Once again, the quality and availability of skills were the decisive variables in the decisions pertaining to specialization in the production process.

The problem of location for the silk-weaving industry was determined more by the location and availability (historical and actual) of the labor force than by other considerations. Raw material was imported and of high value per unit of weight, and consequently transportation costs were not a decisive locational factor. Neither were the costs of equipment. Moreover, the cost of transporting the finished output to the major population centers was hardly significant as a percentage of the unit sales price. The early silk-weaving manufactories were located in Moscow, and for the rest of the century the city of Moscow and the Moscow district remained the major centers of concentration of the industry. The distribution between the city and the countryside varied from period to period.

The two other regions most likely to compete with Moscow as centers of the silk industry were Astrakhan' and St. Petersburg. Both, however, lacked the advantage of an established source of skills comparable to that provided by the Moscow region.

Attempts to provide the silk-weaving industry with a domestically produced supply of raw materials failed until the 1790s. Domestically produced raw silk started to appear on the market in quantities worth mentioning only during the last years of the century;

Table 3.15   Growth of the Silk-Weaving Manufactories

Year	No. of Plants	No. of Looms	Value of Capital (in 1,000 Rubles)	No. of Workers	Value of Output (in 1,000 Rubles)
1725	9	360		1,300	
1741	27			2,788	157,000
1743	23	1,012			178,258
1745	23	1,086			230,137
1763	48		692.0		645,0
1767	63			4,442	590,9
1797	357	4,701		8,853	3,938,3

Sources: Pazhitnov, *Ocherki*, pp. 307–13; Strumilin, *Ocherki*, pp. 343, 357; idem, *Istoriia*, pp. 299–306, 319–20.

this resulted from special efforts by the government and from Russia's expansion southward and into the Caucasus. The easiest and most "natural" means employed by the Russian government was either to collect taxes in kind in raw silk from state peasants who had been ordered to grow mulberry trees or to oblige foreign colonists settled in the southern parts of Russia to supply silk. The stick was much more trustworthy here than the carrot. By the end of the century the domestic supply of raw silk exceeded the 3 percent mark. Most of the raw silk was imported from Iran, Western Europe (Italy), and China.

Salt Production

The production of salt in Russia was an economic activity in which the government during almost the entire eighteenth century acted as a monopsonist. Production of salt was regulated by the government's marketing quotas.

Changes in the volume of salt production in Russia depended almost totally upon the government's perception or estimate of consumer demand at the given level of regulated retail prices and the desired level of stocks. Consequently, production data represent a close approximation of the volume of sales, including changes in inventories in the channels of the government's monopoly trade. This allows using as a close substitute for missing production data the available annual data on the volume of sales.

In order to understand the main problems of salt production and the marketing of salt in eighteenth-century Russia, it is necessary to review the regional distribution of salt production and first to concentrate on the problems of the supply of salt.

Salt was relatively plentiful in Russia, but the chief sources of salt production were located at substantial distances from the main population centers. (Because of the distance from the sources of production, the Baltic provinces throughout the century imported bay-salt from Spain, Portugal, and France and were excluded from the operation of the Russian state monopoly of the salt trade. Outside of the Baltic provinces, a high tariff erected in the 1750s protected domestic salt production.) The major center of salt production and supply during the eighteenth century, as during the seventeenth century, remained the northern Urals region, with its high concentration around Solikamsk, in Perm' province. The chief advantages of this region were its high concentration of salt in the brine, a huge and relatively cheap (at least during the first four decades) supply of fuel for salt boiling, and easy access to the Volga River basin.

Next to the Perm' region, in terms of its share in the total supply of salt, was the Elton salt lake, east of the lower Volga. That source began to produce salt during the late 1740s. The region was one of low production costs, but relatively high transportation costs, first to the Volga itself, then up the Volga, and finally to the various population centers. The annual data on salt transported from Elton Lake to the government warehouses in Kamyshyn and Saratov for further shipment in the years 1747–99 are presented in table 3.16.

The other producing regions, which at various times represented sizable shares in the production of salt, were the lakes and lagoons around Astrakhan' near or on the shore of the Caspian Sea; the salt-producing tier of the North region that embraced the sources described as Pomor'e (near the White Sea), Seregovsk, Tot'ma, Sol' Vychegodsk, and Kungur; the central tier of sources running from west to east and including Staraia Rusa, Sol' Galitskaia, and Balakhna; the sources in the Ukraine, including Bakhmut and Tor (Slaviansk) and, during the last decades, the Perekop and Crimean salt lakes; east of the Ural mountains the rock-salt mine at Iletsk (Iletskaia Zashchita) and the Western Siberian sources both near the Irtysk River and in the Altai region, plus the small salt sources in Eastern Siberia, all of which made Siberia self-sufficient in salt in the eighteenth century. The sales of salt from these regions in the decade 1765–74 are presented in table 3.17.

The supply of salt in Russia was capable of meeting the demand of the population for salt used in food preparation and preservation, for supplementation in the feeding of animals, and for other uses in fisheries, industrial plants, and agriculture. This did not guarantee an adequate supply, year in and year out, or a smooth, uninterrupted supply for all regions of the country. Scarcities which developed on the supply side were caused primarily by poor organization of the government monopoly of the salt trade rather than by problems arising in the production process itself. The high degree of concentration of salt production, particularly in the Perm' region, a process which was strengthened by the introduction of the salt monopoly in 1705, helped to create shortages in the supply of salt.[33]

An increase in the production of salt depended largely upon two supply factors, fuel and labor. Fuel was crucial for the evaporation of the water from brine. The continuous operation of a saltworks demanded large quantities of firewood and thinned out the forests in the vicinity. The transportation of firewood over great distances was expensive even when performed by serf labor. The importance of an adequate supply of labor was repeatedly stressed both in the case of the skilled labor employed in the evaporation process and in the case of unskilled labor

Table 3.16   Transportation of Salt from Elton Lake to the
Warehouses of Saratov and Kamyshyn (Poods per
year), 1747–99

Year	To Saratov	To Kamyshyn	Total
1747	2,436	10,839	13,276
48	305,003	576,575	881,578
49	372,236	1,259,065	1,631,301
1750	388,875	2,729,543	3,118,418
51	547,326	2,729,543	3,276,869
52	1,196,093	2,870,763	4,066,856
53	675,509	1,602,831	2,278,340
54	1,445,790	569,651	2,015,441
55	1,214,368	1,272,915	2,487,283
56	692,737	1,420,905	2,113,642
57	690,322	2,205,798	2,896,120
58	152,660	3,186,336	3,338,996
59	2,701,347	3,727,973	6,429,320
1760	2,133,426	3,137,109	5,270,535
61	2,298,679	2,494,686	4,793,365
62	2,418,120	3,028,989	5,447,109
63	2,126,392	3,609,911	5,736,303
64	1,978,680	2,648,727	4,627,407
65	1,328,970	1,738,379	3,067,349
66	808,574	2,064,427	2,873,001
67		1,546,437	1,546,437
68	473,563	1,298,857	1,772,420
69	1,186,764	2,407,240	3,594,004
1770	138,677	2,891,914	3,030,591
71	1,429,171	1,807,651	3,236,822
72		3,116,290	3,116,290
73	2,494,420	2,943,653	5,438,073
74		843,213	843,213
75		528,521	528,521
76			
77		1,054,932	1,054,932
78		2,920,142	2,920,142
79	1,201,245	2,098,155	3,299,400
1780	1,574,109	3,137,409	4,711,518
81	1,641,173	3,679,692	5,320,865
82	1,824,878	3,201,351	5,026,229
83	1,799,426	3,869,863	5,669,289
84	2,314,687	4,937,927	7,252,614
85	2,513,627	4,129,165	6,642,792
86	1,891,001	3,610,672	5,501,673
87	2,105,536	1,351,793	3,457,329
88	1,046,388	2,445,251	3,491,639
89	1,067,045	2,261,605	3,328,650
1790	2,111,023	2,736,868	4,847,891
91	2,916,088	2,262,777	5,178,865
92	1,940,194	3,758,015	5,698,209
93	1,350,755	3,317,944	4,668,699
94	1,164,421	3,395,564	4,559,985
95	1,383,209	3,848,414	5,231,623
96	1,261,465	3,618,165	4,879,630
97	1,135,517	2,855,204	3,990,721
98	1,578,145	3,883,126	5,461,271
99	1,611,231	3,875,690	5,486,921

Source: "Materialy dlia statistiki Saratovskoi gubernii."

employed in the gathering and breaking of sedimentary salt in lakes and rock-salt domes and in overland and river transportation services. Sundry petitions to the authorities by salt producers which requested that private and state serfs from various regions be sent to or permitted to work under contract on the transportation of salt bear witness to the labor-intensive nature of long-haul transportation. The increasing volume of salt transported on the Volga River basin waterways competed with the rising volume of iron shipped from the Urals via the same waterway and against the growing volume of agricultural goods destined for the capital cities and the ports. The competition for means of transportation and labor during the ice-free river navigation period tended to raise the costs of transportation, unloading, and storage. A contributing element in raising the costs of transportation was an uncertainty on the part of producers about the size of delivery quotas that impaired their ability to adjust production and inventory levels to the demands of the government. For example, the Stroganovs in a petition to Tsarina Anna Ivanovna dated February 1738 pointed out the importance of sales and demand for the output of salt. They assured the Tsarina that production could always be increased in case sales rose. They requested that future orders be as accurate as possible based upon existing inventories in the state trade offices so that production could be gauged according to expected future sales minus existing inventories to avoid excessive local storage in the salt works and along the transportation routes.[34]

There were probably only two periods in the eighteenth century when serious supply problems threatened the ordinary operation of government salt sales. One was in the early 1740s when the government refused to raise the price paid to the Perm' salt producers, and the Stroganovs offered to sell the government their saltworks in order to convince the government of the seriousness of their demands. The government, caught between the prospect of diminished deliveries of Perm' salt and continuing violation of its forest conservation policies, sent out an expedition to explore Elton Lake as a prospective site for a major source of salt production. The results far exceeded initial expectations, and for a few decades Elton Lake became the primary source of salt. The second period coincided with the Pugachëv rebellion and resulted in a sharp curtailment of both the transports from Elton Lake to the Kamyshyn and Saratov warehouses as well as the shipments up the Volga River from those warehouses. Serious shortages were averted by increasing the output of other sources, which marked the beginning of the recovery of Perm' as the dominating producing region. Moreover, the relative flexibility of increasing production and the decrease of stocks held was sufficient to meet the existing level of demand.

The demand for salt on the part of the population increased from about five million poods per year at the end of the Northern War to about fourteen

Table 3.17   Sales of Salt by Place of Origin (in Poods)

	1765	1766	1767	1768	1769
Elton	4,494,374	4,249,141	4,198,755	3,768,004	3,911,621
Astrakhan'	405,223	454,882	433,738	525,757	600,098
Iletsk	269,950	219,439	186,795	202,814	377,566
Koriakov	57,961	57,516	306,909	169,406	297,187
Total lake salt	5,227,509	4,980,978	5,126,197	4,665,981	5,232,335
Perm'	1,673,127	1,747,771	2,214,023	2,825,685	2,902,472
Pomor'e	194,411	167,152	166,235	176,612	186,002
Seregovsk	159,320	174,512	168,408	188,600	213,499
Bakhmut	168,995	199,853	247,970	263,944	108,918
Total brine salt	2,305,546	2,427,339	2,914,920	3,679,229	3,543,808
Total sales	7,537,466	7,413,616	8,048,062	8,485,964	8,776,143
	1770	1771	1772	1773	1774
Elton	3,407,063	3,714,540	3,123,295	2,813,048	2,932,643
Astrakhan'	672,676	897,810	665,501	1,126,802	984,609
Iletsk	372,041	358,917	321,969	262,672	329,534
Koriakov	190,506	228,448	264,109	295,463	258,011
Total lake salt	4,757,172	5,284,082	4,441,009	4,586,264	4,631,417
Perm'	2,682,498	2,744,361	2,811,486	3,167,545	3,125,845
Pomor'e	155,878	192,588	165,595	176,240	164,947
Seregovsk	139,836	176,493	177,085	201,621	194,601
Bakhmut	15,117	5,179	1,602	8,291	12,222
Total brine salt	3,047,490	3,281,840	3,365,724	3,729,443	3,660,997
Total sales	7,804,662	8,565,922	7,806,733	8,315,707	8,292,414

Source: Chulkov, *Istoricheskoe opisanie*, 8, pt. 1, table to p. 228.

Table 3.18   Distribution of Salt Supply by Major Regions (Yearly Averages in Percentages)

Years	Perm'	Elton	Astrakhan'	North	Central	Bakhmut	Iletsk	Crimea	Accounted for
1737–41	65.92		14.47	4.31	5.80	7.22			97.72
1742–46	55.97		20.67	3.96	5.39	11.36			97.35
1747–51	58.45	3.40	16.51	4.78	5.66	8.99			97.79
1752–56	48.99	26.63	5.61	6.26	3.44	4.55			95.48
1757–61	19.30	60.82	3.47	5.80	1.11	3.92			94.42
1761	18.67	62.59	4.00	5.40		3.32	1.41		95.39
1763–66	20.36	58.76	4.96	5.38		3.12	2.65		95.23
1788	33.25	24.96	16.58	3.60	6.88		5.79	3.86	
1789 planned	40.94	32.30	7.47	4.34	4.31		2.2	3.86	

Source: Svirshchevskii, "Oblozhenie soli," app. 3, pp. 199–207.

million poods in the last decade of the century, or a growth of 180 percent. The population of the territory in which the sales were taking place increased from about 15 to about 36 million, a growth of about 140 percent, and so the per capita consumption of salt increased about 16 to 17 percent, a rise from 12.5 to 16 pounds. The government, using the data from the taxpayers' census, estimated that the demand for salt was about one pood (40 pounds) per male soul of the taxpaying population. However, the population's demand for salt was not totally insensitive to changes in price, especially when they were not gradual but sudden and substantial. A price increase in 1750 from 21.2 kopeks per pood of salt to 35 kopeks, or 70 percent, resulted in a 16 percent decline in sales (a rather low elasticity of .23). A subsequent rise in 1757 from 35 kopeks to 50 kopeks, or 43 percent, resulted

in a 24 percent decline of sales in the following year (a more impressive elasticity of .56).[35]

To the extent that the declines in sales volume were disappointing to the government in terms of revenue increments, which fell short of expectations during the Elizabethan and Catherinian periods, the policy of regional distribution of production and supply should be examined. Table 3.18 provides an approximate distribution of the relative shares of the major producing regions in the total sale of salt for selected periods in annual averages per quinquennium.

The notable feature of table 3.18 is the substitution of Elton salt for Perm' salt, each of which occupied a dominant position in different periods. Although the production costs at the source were higher in Perm', the transportation costs were higher for the Elton salt.[36] The substitutable nature of the output from these two regions is shown in table 3.19. There was another area of substitution in the southeast, between Astrakhan' and Iletsk salt, and the transportation costs to markets were crucial there also. In the absence of additional exogenous factors, the patterns of substitution between these regions produced the changes in the shares of the market among the various producers.

Some understanding of the existing or changing structure of the supply of salt as a response to the demand by particular regions and of the attempts to minimize production and transportation costs per unit of sales can be obtained by looking at the cost of the salt supply by regions. The variation of costs from year to year was probably due to changes in the apportionment to consumption regions of some of

Table 3.19   Supply of Salt from Major Sources

Year	Brine	Lakes, Rock Salt	Total
1737	6,074,550	879,756	6,954,306
38	5,823,164	1,190,401	7,013,565
39	5,541,021	1,737,981	7,279,002
1740	6,077,709	1,231,551	7,309,260
41	6,511,713	1,114,155	7,625,868
42	6,368,248	1,105,830	7,474,078
43	5,327,353	2,445,741	7,773,094
44			7,140,189
1745	5,484,774	1,595,202	7,079,976
46	5,585,235	1,894,163	7,479,398
47	5,596,805	1,721,221	7,318,026
48	5,262,587	1,622,378	6,884,965
49	5,618,278	1,578,094	7,196,372
1750	4,838,002	1,324,885	6,162,887
51	4,691,703	1,689,291	6,380,994
52	4,797,298	1,857,141	6,654,439
53	5,135,721	1,897,270	7,032,991
54	4,207,151	2,615,337	6,882,488
1755	4,425,825	2,783,334	7,209,159
56	3,315,160	3,697,154	7,012,314
57	1,801,173	3,882,143	5,683,316
58	1,957,394	4,329,099	6,286,493
59	1,981,415	4,153,076	6,134,491
1760	1,765,953	4,657,422	6,423,375
61	1,855,820	4,919,383	6,775,203
62	1,632,523	4,941,988	6,574,511

Table 3.20   Cost of Salt Supply to the State by Place of Origin (in Kopeks p. pood)

	1763	1764	1765	1766
Elton	19.20	19.19	18.77	18.25
Perm'	17.83	17.94	17.18	17.01
Pomor'e	15.16	14.99	15.10	15.97
Seregovsk	18.52	14.56	14.63	14.91
Iletsk	11.77	14.79	16.49	17.76
Astrakhan'	4.10	2.71	2.10	3.62
Total European Russia	17.21	17.26	16.68	16.25
Siberia	14.46	14.46	14.87	16.24
Total Empire	17.10	17.15	16.61	16.245
Tax p. pood	21.18	21.17	21.55	21.71

Source: Svirshchevskii, "Oblozhenie soli," app. 3, pp. 194, 208–9.

the changes in the costs of transportation. Table 3.20 serves as an example of the costs to the state of the supply of salt during the period 1763–66, when the retail price was set at 40 kopeks per pood for all consumption regions, excepting Astrakhan', where the price was set at 20 kopeks per pood. The table suggests that in the years 1763–66, adjustments took place involving those regions in which a substitution between Elton salt and Perm' salt occurred. Similarly, there were some changes in the territory supplied either by Astrakhan' or Iletsk salt, and possibly even between Pomor'e and Seregovsk. For the state, those changes resulted in modest but beneficial declines in the supply costs and an increase in revenue per unit of sale.

To apportion the costs of the salt supply, it is necessary to know the costs of production and transportation from the source to the various destinations. The problems of substitution can be resolved by using successive approximations, starting with a particular year in which the supply pattern in terms of quantities and prices is known. Table 3.21 shows the pattern of quantity supply by the consuming regions for the year 1761. A quantity matrix is presented by adding the distribution of supply by producing regions.

The availability of data for the years 1788 and 1803–4 and projected data for 1789 permit the construction of supply and sales matrices for those years as well as a calculation of costs of salts of various origin in the districts of sales.[37] For my purposes, however, it is sufficient to point out the general tendencies of the regional distribution of the salt supply as dictated by the demand of consumers and the government.

The most significant effect upon the regional distribution of salt sales and production was the territorial expansion of Russia westward and southward. This, together with a rise in transportation costs, led to a reactivation of previously closed saltworks in the central region (at Staraia Rusa and Balakhna), the reactivation of the Bakhmut saltworks, and, most important, the exploitation of Crimean salt sources. At the same time production in Siberia, Astrakhan', and Iletsk was expanded to accommodate the increasing population in the east. The two main producing regions, Perm' and Elton, supplied the nonblacksoil zone and the blacksoil zone, respectively, with significant overlaps. While the production of the central region somewhat relieved the supply of Perm' salt, that of the Crimea relieved some of the pressure upon the Elton supply in addition to satisfying the demand of some of the newly acquired territories in the south and southwest.

There are two questions that one would like to answer by analyzing salt production in Russia during

Table 3.21   Distribution of Salt Supply by Production and Consumption Regions in 1761 (in poods)

	Elton	Perm'	Pomor'e	Seregovsk	Astrakhan'	Iletsk	Bakhmut	Total
Moscow	1,717,216	258,705			9,530			1,985,451
Kazan'	633,613	267,371						900,984
Novgorod	313,301	436,403	97,090					846,794
Voronezh	489,916						202,840	692,756
Belgorod	383,757	23,381					22,096	457,139
Nizhnii Novgorod	326,879	98,025			3,126			428,030
Arkhangel'sk	69,974		73,853	142,927				338,916
Astrakhan'	65,527				227,246			292,773
Smolensk	229,422	32,915						262,336
Orenburg	10,649					95,517		159,688
St. Petersburg	139	146,962						148,101
Siberia								258,105
Total	4,240,394	1,264,851	170,942	142,927	270,984	95,517	224,936	6,775,202

the eighteenth century: (1) whether at the given level of prices the supply of salt was adequate and (2) whether, given the institutional framework of the industry, the production and supply of salt differed from that which would have occurred under the conditions of a free market. Any answer to these questions requires some judgment about the existing level of salt prices, which in turn involves an evaluation of the operation of the state trading monopoly and the gabelle.

It appears that the price of salt, as established by the government monopoly (including the tax), was relatively high in terms of the farm-gate prices for agricultural commodities, grains as well as livestock products. Presumably, the monopoly profits, added to the costs of procurement of the salt by the government, helped to keep output below the socially desirable level. This situation existed from the beginning until the 1780s.

As the costs of production increased and consequently the costs to the government of procuring the salt, the government, primarily for political reasons, was reluctant to increase market prices accordingly. As a result, toward the end of the century, what had been a profitable monopoly turned into a subsidy on consumption to the extent that salt prices rose more slowly than the prices of other goods and services.

Under conditions of free trade one would not expect the prevailing uniformity of prices that was introduced in 1750. This raises two issues, one with respect to the distribution of the burden of taxation and the other with regard to the hypothetical regional distribution of production. On the issue of taxation, it is clear that the main burden of the tax was upon the inhabitants of the eastern regions of European Russia, while the inhabitants of the western regions bore a lighter tax burden because of the higher cost of transporting salt to them. On the distribution of

production, one would have expected under conditions of free trade a dominance of the production of Perm' salt rather than of Elton salt.

It is proper to inquire why free trade in salt was not reinstated in 1791 when the first deficit in the operation of the state monopoly appeared. There is no obvious answer to this question. It is possible that the government considered the deficit a temporary aberration in an institution which for most of the century had provided the treasury with substantial revenues, as shown in table 3.22. It is also possible that the government was afraid to institute free trade that might have caused sharp price increases in a number of areas, which would have been considered politically undesirable. It is also possible that the unwieldy bureaucratic machine, with its own interests and its preference for the status quo, had a risk aversion for any radical changes of institutions of long-standing.

The production of salt, an industry tightly controlled by the government, exhibited only limited per capita real growth during the eighteenth century. Although in money terms the output of salt was comparable to the production of iron and copper, it had none of the rapid growth or stagnation of the iron industry. The demand by a growing population for a product as essential as salt neutralized some of the considerations of governmental fiscal and trade policies.

The Armament Industries

The existence of a government monopsony places armaments in the first category of industries, those dominated by the conditions of government demand. (There was no export of armaments from Russia.) For reasons of differentiation it is convenient to divide the armament industry into three branches: the production of small firearms; the production of gunpowder;

Table 3.22   Salt Sales and Government Revenue

I Year	II Quantity (in poods)	III Total Sales (in Rubles)	IV Net Revenue (in Rubles)	V Revenue (in Kopeks p. Pood)	VI Producer's Price (in Kopeks p. Pood)	VII Value in Delivery Prices (in Rubles)	VIII Remarks
1705	2,236,455		186,342	8.33			
06	3,564,086		355,216	9.97			
07	3,649,123		385,554	10.57			
08	3,694,697		440,045	11.91			
09	3,700,450		443,330	11.98			
1710	3,413,481		428,849	12.56			
11	3,691,977		464,561	12.58			
12	3,734,590		472,087	12.64			
13	3,938,884		490,911	12.46			
14	3,750,271		515,158	13.74			
1715	4,439,356		570,264	12.85			
16	4,123,649		544,664	13.21			
17	4,227,759		569,860	13.48			
18	4,417,145		594,071	13.45			
19	4,643,209		569,918	12.27			
1720	4,775,833		570,205	11.94			
21	5,261,225		644,783	12.26			
22	5,197,762		659,527	12.69			
23	5,248,213		648,213	12.35			
24	4,806,587		606,982	12.63			
1725	4,663,926		550,059	11.79			
26	4,889,685		584,907	11.96			
27	4,221,202		510,860	12.10			
28 free sales	4,378,426		218,921	5.0			
29 free sales	4,275,321		213,766	5.0			
1730 free sales	4,319,565		215,978	5.0			
31 free sales	3,706,967		185,348	5.0			
State Sales	+ 830,578		118,070	14.21			
31 total sales	4,537,545		303,418	6.69			
32	4,440,476		612,548	13.79			
33	5,068,301		661,439	13.05			
34	5,585,966		678,325	12.14			
1735	5,798,106		697,547	12.03			
1736	5,986,937		711,741	11.89			

and the production of artillery pieces and ammunition. Although the demand for the production of the three branches was almost a joint demand determined by the necessities of active warfare or war preparedness that provided, for most of the period, a synchronized rhythm of output, shifting military priorities (between the army and navy, for example) introduced meaningful variations.

In spite of the tradition dating from the sixteenth century of state ownership of the armament industries, there was no uniform policy of state ownership in the eighteenth century. Political, economic, and technological factors determined the degree of state ownership in each of the branches.

In small firearms production, a high skill require-

ment determined the continuous employment of the labor force. This, combined with a politically motivated fear of putting firearms on the market, determined the state's monopoly ownership of small firearms production facilities. Consequently the first branch remained firmly and continuously in the hands of the government. The policy for gunpowder production was to maintain a monopsony position with regard to the private producers but, beginning in the 1720s and 1730s, to increase gradually the share of the state sector in total output. Both branches required, for their existence as efficient producers, some degree of government planning in the form of forward contracts.

The relative ease, both technological and economi-

Table 3.22, cont.   Salt Sales and Government Revenue

I Year	II Quantity (in poods)	III Total Sales (in Rubles)	IV Net Revenue (in Rubles)	V Revenue (in Kopeks p. Pood)	VI Producer's Price (in Kopeks p. Pood)	VII Value in Delivery Prices (in Rubles)	VIII Remarks
37	6,954,306		764,593	10.99			
38	7,013,565		783,587	11.17			
39	7,279,002		837,845	11.51			
1740	7,309,260		821,347	11.24			
41	7,625,868		840,720	11.02			
42	7,474,078		804,403	10.76			
43	7,773,094		816,438	10.50			
44	7,140,189		706,103	9.89			
1745	7,079,976	1,504,495	777,747	10.99	10.26	726,406	Average sales
46	7,479,898	1,589,418	813,345	10.87	10.38	776,413	price, including
47	7,318,026	1,555,080	792,654	10.83	10.42	762,538	tax, 21.25
48	6,884,966	1,463,055	753,485	10.94	10.31	709,840	kopeks p.
49	7,196,372	1,529,229	801,255	11.13	10.12	728,273	pood.
1750	6,162,887	2,055,345	1,223,001	19.84	13.51	832,334	
51	6,380,994	2,141,233	1,216,156	19.06	14.50	925,077	
52	6,654,439	2,248,354	1,296,971	19.49	14.30	951,385	Average sales
53	7,032,990	2,378,662	1,392,223	19.80	13.94	980,439	price, 35
54	6,822,488	2,281,858	1,318,348	19.32	14.12	963,510	kopeks p.
1755	7,209,157	2,446,186	1,370,518	19.01	14.92	1,075,668	pood.
56	7,512,313	2,715,716	1,599,092	21.29	14.86	1,116,624	
57	5,683,816	2,763,949	1,887,065	33.20	15.43	876,884	
58	6,281,493	3,076,577	2,117,184	33.70	15.27	959,393	
59	6,134,491	2,988,412	2,012,924	32.81	15.90	975,488	
1760	6,423,374	3,108,406	2,065,177	32.27	16.25	1,043,229	
61	6,775,202	3,280,915	2,182,428	32.22	16.21	1,098,487	
62	6,574,511	2,845,817	1,725,751	26.25	17.04	1,120,166	
63	7,280,555	2,787,117	1,542,246	21.18	17.10	1,244,872	
64	7,318,059	2,804,884	1,549,618	21.17	17.15	1,255,266	
1765	7,848,909	2,998,756	1,695,058	21.55	16.61	1,303,698	
66	7,730,158	2,933,728	1,677,934	21.71	16.25	1,255,794	
67	7,382,500	2,805,350	1,698,000	23.00	15.00	1,107,375	
68	7,387,500	2,807,250	1,700,000	23.01	14.99	1,107,386	
69	6,297,500	2,393,050	1,439,000	22.85	15.15	954,071	
1770	8,237,500	3,130,250	1,900,000	23.07	14.95	1,231,506	
71	9,075,000	3,448,500	1,905,000	20.99	17.01	1,543,658	
72	8,210,000	3,283,200	1,570,000	19.12	18.88	1,550,048	
1773	8,640,000	3,282,200	1,586,000	18.36	19.64	1,696,896	
74							
1775							
76	8,500,000	2,805,000	995,000	11.71	21.29	1,809,650	
77	8,500,000	2,805,000	1,115,000	13.12	19.88	1,689,800	

cal, of expansion of artillery production made it possible to have a certain share of the output in the hands of state-owned enterprises while simultaneously placing contracts with the privately owned iron- and copperworks which would accord priority to the government's armament contracts. There was state and private cooperation in artillery production during peacetime with a distribution of supply between the two sectors. There was a reliance upon the resources of the private sector for output increases. Output capacity was also increased in the state sector in case of emergency. During the second half of the century this tendency to strengthen the state sector's share in artillery production was continued as a result of the decreasing trend of Russian iron exports. An increase in the armament industry's consumption of the state's iron production was one measure to counteract a threatened contraction of output.

Small Firearms Production

The main objective in creating and expanding the armaments industry was to free Russia from dependence upon foreign supplies under conditions of intensified and protracted warfare and to counteract whatever political or economic pressure might emerge from such dependency. The emphasis here is more upon economic than political dependency, for the countries from which arms were purchased, the Netherlands and Saxony, tried to steer away from political involvement with their customers which, however, became increasingly difficult during the eighteenth century.

The modernization of the Russian army under Peter the Great quite logically implied an expansion of the armament industries. The standing army which became the pillar of Russian political strength in Europe was a different institution than the various forms of militia-type gentry formations, musketeer regiments, and even the new formation regiments of the earlier periods.[38] Russia's wars no longer served primarily defensive purposes, and the modernized Russian army could no longer depend upon the goodwill of foreign producers in an era of global, but shifting, military alliances among the nations of Europe. During the Petrine period, major purchases of small firearms from abroad were made only twice. The first occurred in 1700–1701, when after the defeat at Narva and the loss of a major part of both artillery and personal firearms, 11,194 handguns were imported. In 1712 an additional 10,000 handguns were commissioned in the Netherlands. Another major purchase was made during the war in 1735–37, when 17,877 handguns and 2,826 pairs of pistols were purchased from Saxony.

The major supplier of small firearms in the eighteenth century was the cradle of the Russian armaments industry, Tula. The output of firearms was gradually centralized and concentrated by comparison with the early system of craft-like operations, so that a number of operations were carried out in a single factory. Around the middle of the eighteenth century the technical specification and standardization of parts resulted not only in mass production but also in a division of the output of parts between the Tula, Sestroretsk, and Briansk factories. The Sestroretsk factory produced, in addition to complete handguns, also some quantities of the locks which were sent to Tula for assembly with parts produced there. In 1762 and 1763 the Sestroretsk factory sent to Tula 3,200 handgun locks, and the Briansk factory supplied Tula with gun barrels beginning in the 1770s.[39]

The specification of technical details and the standardization of firearms remained almost unchanged during the eighteenth century for the basic army equipment, with the exception of the introduction of new carbines for the cavalry during the late 1760s. The specifications for small firearms, established in 1715, are presented in table 3.23.

Although there are no summary data for small firearms production, they can be estimated for 1714–78 (see tables 3.24 and 3.25) from the available data on Tula production, which amounted to from 85 to 95 percent of the total Russian firearms production. The total known output of Tula during 1714–78 was 1,360,198 firearms. Of these, 872,211 were infantry

Table 3.23   Specifications for Small Firearms, 1715

	Infantry Rifle	Cavalry Rifle	Pistol
Caliber (mm)	19.81	17.27	17.27
Length of barrel (mm)	101.6	45.7	35.8
Length of firearm (cm)	142.2	103.6	
Weight of firearm (kg)	5.74	4.91	1.54
Weight of bullet (gr)	34.13	25.6	25.6
Weight of charge (gr)	14.93	14.93	8.53

Source: Beskrovnyi, *Russkaia armiia*, pp. 94–95.

Table 3.24   Factory Small Firearms Output, 1714–51

	I Infantry Rifles	II Cavalry Rifles	III Total Rifles	IV Pistols (pairs)	V Total
1714	13,753		13,753	1,390	15,143
15	11,000	7,000	18,000	4,000	22,000
1716–19	31,780	14,747	46,527	18,532	65,059
1720	15,720	6,768	22,488	4,110	26,598
1721	15,810	6,486	22,296	4,062	26,358
24	1,186	1,496	2,682	2,592	5,274
25	400	2,385	2,785	1,155	3,940
26	1,548	4,854	6,402	4,392	10,794
28	7,652	4,055	11,707	3,576	15,283
29	4,109	7,285	11,394	2,824	14,218
1730	3,393	5,578	8,971	3,162	12,133
31	4,040	6,939	10,979	2,163	13,142
32	—	—	—	—	22,987
33	21,342	8,295	29,637	12,651	42,288
34	—	—	—	—	32,987
36	25,000	—	25,000	—	25,000
37	14,656	7,434	22,090	6,000	28,089
38	25,000	—	25,000	2,172	27,172
39	—	—	—	—	26,539
1740	—	—	—	—	32,736
42	5,549	2,700	4,104	—	12,453
46	17,057	12,758	7,037	—	36,852
47	—	—	—	—	22,729
48	—	—	—	—	27,528
49	13,576	6,549	20,125	8,284	28,409
1751	13,599	5,432	19,031	7,039	26,050

Source: Beskrovnyi, *Russkaia armiia*, pp. 76–77, 86–87.

handguns, 238,414 cavalry handguns, and 276,573 pairs of pistols.

In addition to the manufacturing of new firearms, Tula and Sestroretsk repaired firearms so that economies on the replacement of the stock could be achieved. During 1737–78, the Tula factory repaired 161,454 handguns and 22,822 pairs of pistols. Complete data on labor and employment at the Tula factory are lacking. The number of registered gunsmiths was 749 in 1704 and 1,161 in 1720, and the number probably rose toward the end of the century to at least 3,000 employed under government firearms-contracts and obligations.[40] Bearing in mind that the Sestroretsk gun factory employed a total of 677 workers after 1724, we probably could assume for the country as a whole that at least 3,500 workers

Table 3.25   Tula Factory Firearms Output, Selected Years

	Infantry Rifles	Cavalry Rifles	Cavalry Carbines	Total Rifles	Pistols	Total
1762	12,274	4,924		17,198	4,376	21,574
63	4,822	252	3,956	9,030	3,646	12,676
1776	16,746	3,387	6,067	26,200	7,704	33,904
77	18,000	11,040	12,843	41,883	25,594	67,477
1786	2,370	7,462	5,000	14,832		
1797				24,438		
98				45,438		
99				43,388		
1714–36[a]	186,248	90,178			76,778	353,204
1737–78	685,963	148,236			199,795	1,033,994
1737	14,656	7,434			6,000	28,089
1738–56	234,190	98,078			82,303	414,571
1757–78	437,117	42,724			111,492	591,333
1714–78	872,211	238,414			276,573	1,387,198

Source: Beskrovnyi, *Russkaia armiia*, pp. 345–48.

[a] Except 1735

were engaged in the manufacturing of small firearms during the second half of the seventeenth century.[41]

Concern in maintaining a skilled labor force for the armaments industries was exhibited in the continuous existence of two armories (*arsenals*) in Moscow and St. Petersburg. The Moscow armory, formerly known as the cannon yard (*pushechnyi dvor*), was the oldest gun factory in Russia and was maintained primarily as armament repair shops and also as experimental (laboratory) shops until 1783, when it was converted into a museum.[42] The St. Petersburg armory, just as the Moscow one, performed repair and experimental jobs during peacetime and large-scale manufacturing primarily during wartime emergencies. Thus the two armories should be considered as a production reserve, the capacity of which might have been underutilized during peacetime, but assured the continuity of skills and emergency capacity for the contingencies of war.

The Production of Gunpowder

The production of gunpowder in Russia can be traced to the sixteenth century. At the turn of the eighteenth century there existed, apart from two state-owned gunpowder mills, at least ten private mills.[43] Some were owned by Russians, and some by foreigners (or foreigners in partnership with Russians). The heavy demand for gunpowder during the continuous wars in the Petrine period prompted the search for and an increase in output of saltpeter and sulphur. The major supplies of saltpeter came from the Volga region and the Ukraine. This imposed major transportation costs on the mills since gunpowder production was concentrated around Moscow, the upper Volga, and later in the St. Petersburg region. Although the private sector made an effort to meet the wartime demand, the state tried to increase its share

Table 3.26   Quality of Gunpowder, Percentage of Component Mix

	Saltpeter	Sulphur	Coal
1st quarter, 18th century	77.4	9.6	13.0
1746 cannon	73.72	11.65	14.53
1746 musket	75.8	11.4	12.8
1766 cannon	70.68	10.58	18.58
1783	70.0	12.5	17.5
1797	66.68	13.90	19.42

Source: Beskrovnyi, *Russkaia armiia*, pp. 98, 363.

in the total output by establishing new state-owned gunpowder mills in the area of St. Petersburg and later in the area of Kazan', closer to the sources of saltpeter.[44]

The objective of assuming an adequate supply of gunpowder was met primarily through the expansion of state-owned mills.[45] A major improvement in the quality of Russian gunpowder was achieved with the help of foreign specialists, chiefly Dutch, in the 1720s.[46] Other improvements were made by the Russians themselves during the 1740s and 1780s. The changes in the quality of Russian gunpowder can be surmised from the data in table 3.26 on the proportion of the particular components. These improvements in quality were important because they economized on the scarce component, saltpeter, and increased the use of the plentiful component, coal. More important from an economic point of view was the gradual decrease of the volume of raw materials used per unit of final output, which was 44 pounds per pood of output in 1722, 43 pounds in 1766, and 41.5 pounds in 1796–97.[47]

Artillery and Munitions

The Russian artillery industry, especially during the early part of the century, was a substantial user of

Table 3.27   Specifications for Russian Artillery

	Guns			Mortars			Howitzers	
Type	3-lb.	6-lb.	8-lb.	12-lb.	40-lb.	80-lb.	10-lb.	20-lb.
Caliber (inches)	3	3.8	4	4.8	7.8	9.7	4.8	7
Weight of gunbarrel (pood)	28	36	50	79		140	26	20
Weight of gun-carriage (pood)	20	30	40	70		100	36	50

Source: Beskrovnyi, *Russkaia armiia*, p. 95.

domestically produced iron and copper. The dramatic sight of Peter the Great's guard regiments hauling down church bells to be recast into cannons remained vivid in the memory of the Russian people, for it symbolized one of the basic shifts in priorities of the state and ruler.

For us such acts signify the urgency of the task of creating an artillery force and the inability of current output to fulfill the task. The development of metallurgical plants enabled the government to have a firm basis for the production of artillery pieces and munitions, which had for quite a while the first claim for metal supply among its various uses. The development of the Urals iron manufacturing during the early part of the century made possible the emergence of Petrine artillery by the end of the Northern War as a formidable force. The number of artillery pieces of various sizes and types reached about 13,000. This remained the approximate numerical size of the Russian artillery until the 1760s. After wars both replacements and repairs were required, and the specialized plants under government contract or ownership produced and repaired guns. For example, after the Seven Years' War, a massive renovation of the Russian artillery was required. Out of the 13,160 guns of all types at the disposal of the army (this excludes the navy), 9,558 needed to be replaced.

The production of guns and munitions was organized on a territorial basis, as far as possible, to reduce the great transportation costs. For example, the Olonets region delivered its output to the Baltic fleet and the Lipetsk region its production to the Azov fleet. The exception was the Urals region, which delivered its specialized production wherever government orders required.

Until the 1770s the government did not attempt to concentrate the production of artillery equipment in state-owned enterprises. It preferred to export the iron output of state-owned enterprises and to realize market profits. Contracts for artillery supplies were mostly distributed among the private ironworks at prices below the market price. Thus some of the artillery supply was delivered in lieu of a commodity tax on iron, or as an additional payment for the use of state-owned serfs in iron production by private entrepreneurs.

To ease the burden of artillery deliveries upon private iron producers the government turned over to them the technological knowledge necessary for the manufacturing of artillery. It also standardized artillery, as shown in table 3.27.

Increasingly the government had to pay private producers a price approaching what would have been the market price, and certainly a price which covered production costs plus a reasonable profit. In its distribution of contracts for artillery equipment among private iron producers the government relied upon the largest entrepreneurs. During the first half of the century the heaviest reliance was on deliveries from the Demidov ironworks.[48] In the second half of the century the deliveries by the Batashev ironworks rose in importance. This was due in part, at least, to their location in the center of the country. Table 3.28 provides a general impression of the magnitude in physical units of the production of the Batashev ironworks.

During the 1770s the government freed the private ironworks from obligatory state orders. Although the government continued to place artillery contracts with private producers, greater reliance was put upon the productive capacity of the state-owned ironworks for crucial military supply. Consequently the former state ironworks in Lipetsk, which in the 1750s had been given to Prince Repnin, were recovered by the state and put into operation, primarily to produce artillery supplies.[49] The Alexandrovskii ironworks in Petrozavodsk was also retooled for

Table 3.28   Artillery Deliveries from the Batashev Ironworks

Year	Quantities
1768	360 falconets for army and navy
69	70 field guns
1770	154 field guns
71	128 field guns and 18 "edinorogi"
72	14 field guns
73	880 field guns and 460 falconets
74	257 guns for the navy
76	148 guns and 902 falconets for the Baltic fleet
1777–79	466 guns for the Azov fleet
1780–86	544 guns for the Black Sea fleet
1787–91	496,762 poods (8,137 metric tons) of guns and ammunition and
	27,786 poods of ship anchors.

Source: Beskrovnyi, *Russkaia armiia*, pp. 352–53.

artillery production. Such measures assured the government of its own production base in artillery supply.

The Wool-Cloth Industry

Another industry which developed primarily under the impact of the government and was dependent almost exclusively upon government demand, at least during the first half of the eighteenth century, was the wool-cloth industry. Government contracts, specifications, and supervision of the production process had a profound impact upon the composition of output, the technology, the type of entrepreneur who entered the industry, and the origin of the labor force. Created for the purpose of assuring a domestic supply of wool cloth for army uniforms, the industry had to create import substituting products and to utilize the domestic supply of raw materials. Government demand was in terms of specific qualities and quantities of various types of goods, and it adopted a mode of forward contracts for particular types of goods. These contracts awarded by the government to the producers were usually coupled with established forward prices and money advances as a fixed proportion of the value of the contract.

It is possible to trace the acquisition of skill by the producers by following the increase in the domestic production of wool cloth as a share of the total output of cloth and of *karazeia*, a wool-cloth lining used in military uniforms. The production of coarse *karazeia* was the easiest to introduce, and the quality of Russian wool cloth for decades was very much inferior to that of foreign cloth, particularly English woolens [50] Uniforms for officers and the guard regiments were still made, during the middle of the century, from imported woolens, while soldiers' uniforms were manufactured from the domestic output. Moreover, apparently the domestic wool-cloth was not even used for the field army, but for the garrison regiments, which were clothed in substandard textiles. The demand for quality was imposed upon the producers by the sending of samples, by the higher-quality producers being ordered to share their knowledge with their inferiors, and by a system of penalties for substandard production.

The government assisted in setting up the woolen mills. It advanced large sums for future output. Serf-owners had government-provided incentives to enter the industry because of the availability of some raw materials on their estates as well as a ready forced-labor supply. These serfowners had an insatiable appetite for liquid funds and avoided the free market. These factors made the woolen industry a typical gentry-owned industrial branch.

According to the data of 1731 presented in table 3.29, the armed forces during peacetime needed each year over half a million arshins of army cloth for consumption and reserves. The regulations pertaining to military uniforms of 1731 virtually repeated Petrine regulations of 1720 and remained in force until the 1760s. The 1731 figures should be compared with those in table 3.30 of quantities purchased for the armed forces from the Berlin Company in the years 1725–33. Before each contract, prior to purchasing from British or Prussian suppliers, the Russian government gave native producers samples of the cloth demanded so that they could present their bids.

It was not until 1735, when the government refused to renew the contract with its Prussian suppliers, that Russian producers started to bid for parts of the army cloth supply. Previously Russian production for the government had been in response to command orders. Since the yearly government expenditures for imported army cloth were substantial and had to be paid for either in specie or in some of the state-monopolized commodities, the attempts to develop a domestic source of army cloth were pursued with varying degrees of energy. One of the additional means of encouraging potential domestic producers was to distribute state serfs among future owners of wool manufactories, or to attach state serfs to manufactories of existing producers. In return for this substantial subsidy, the domestic producers were obliged to supply the military intendants (the so-called Kriegs Komissariat) with army cloth in volume roughly proportional to the number of serfs received from the state. This idea of reciprocity between a quantity of cloth to be supplied and the right to use attached serfs was derived from the relationship between the government and the merchant entrepreneurs, who could purchase serfs only at the discre-

Table 3.29   Distribution Army Cloth by Color and Place, 1731 (in Arshins)

	Moscow	St. Petersburg	Riga	Total
Redcloth	217,280	72,427	36,213	325,920
Green Redcloth	106,900	35,633	17,817	160,350
Blue Redcloth	38,467	12,822	6,411	57,700
Total	362,647	120,882	60,441	543,970

Source: Zhuravaskii, *Statisticheskoe obozrenie*, pp. 61–62.

Table 3.30   Purchases of Army Cloth from the Berlin Company (in Arshins)

Year	Army Cloth	Year	Army Cloth
1725	223,375	1730	59,026
1726	316,792	1731	369,282
1727	365,474	1732	306,226
1728	9,878	1733	314,759
1729	2,313		

Source: Schmoller, "Die Russische Kompagnie," p. 491.

tion of the government and otherwise had no rights to own serfs.

The relationship between the government's demand for wool cloth and the industry's supply response can be presented as an evolutionary process in a few distinct periods. During the first period, roughly until the 1750s, the industry was unable to meet the government demand for wool cloth of all specified varieties. The process of learning Western technology for cloth-making took quite a long time in this industry, especially by comparison with others. Whether any particular difficulties arose because of the quality of the domestically produced raw materials is unknown. It is unclear where the bottlenecks to the special skill acquisitions were located, whether in the spinning, combing, and weaving processes, or in finishing and dyeing. It is possible that the lack of entrepreneurial zeal and initiative by the gentry were to blame for the slow adoption of necessary techniques and skills. Be that as it may, until the end of the 1740s, imports of foreign cloth for the military still persisted, even though the share of imports in the total quantity of woolen cloth purchased by the Russian quartermaster general (Kriegs Komissariat) was steadily declining.

On the eve of the Seven Years' War the Russians became self-sufficient in army cloth. Within the next decade, the output of the industry started to exceed the army's demand. For some reason, the industry was unable to switch to production for the civilian market. Unable to compete successfully with the scattered producers of cheap woolens used by the lower-income groups on the one hand, and with the foreign producers of fine cloth used by the upper income groups on the other, the wool-cloth industry had to go through an adjustment process for at least two decades. Relying upon the government to suppress small-scale production and believing that the government would somehow bail out the gentry entrepreneurs, the gentry themselves did little to make the industry more competitive in the civilian market. The expectations of the entrepreneurs that the government by an increase in the size of the armed forces would come to their rescue were in fact confirmed (at least in the short run) by a decision to shorten the length of time that uniforms were used

by a third, thereby increasing the yearly demand for wool cloth. According to the regulations of 1762, the yearly need of the armed forces increased to 796,866 arshins of army cloth and 331,356 arshins of *karazeia*, and the reserves in the state warehouses were also increased accordingly to 1,078,597 arshins and 456,827 arshins, respectively.[51] The overall increase in demand can be seen in table 3.31.

In the long run, however, the government was unable to provide protection and guarantees of increased demand. In 1779 the government granted legal entry into industrial activity to everybody and abolished the licensing system under which most of the firms operated previously. The wool-cloth manufactories were forced to go through an adjustment process in view of the increased competition in wool cloth for civilian consumption. During the 1780s the manufactories succeeded in establishing themselves within a segment of the civilian market. The rise in the general price level and of textiles in particular made it more profitable for the wool-cloth entrepreneurs to produce for civilian instead of government consumption. This was not a new phenomenon in the industrial sector, but in the wool industry it took place at a later date than in the others. The influence of government demand was beginning to erode as a result of the government's insistence on paying the traditional, rather than the market, price for wool cloth.

An interesting example of the supply of wool cloth by the various producers to the armed forces can be traced to the organization of supply for the year 1791. The total demand for 1791 was estimated in advance at 1,105,193 arshins of cloth. Out of this total the manufactory of Prince Khovanskoi in Moscow promised to deliver 200,000 arshins, almost 478,000 arshins had to be delivered by the Khar'kov factory of Lieutenant General Potëmkin, and around 65,000 arshins by Prince Iusupov. Thus 743,000 arshins or 67.2 percent had to be delivered by wool factories belonging to three members of the aristocracy. The order for the rest was placed among twenty wool manufactories which used attached serfs. The key to the distribution of the volume of cloth among the entrepreneurs was the number of serfs available to each. An important distinction was made between landless and land-using serfs. The yearly production "norm" for a landless serf, assuming full employment in the manufactory, was 105 arshins of cloth. For a serf having an agricultural household, a work norm of three days per week, one-half that of the landless serf, was expected, as was half the output.[52] In the 1791 order for army cloth the government agreed to the manufactory owners' demand for a price rise of 20 percent: for white cloth to 72 kopeks, and for colored cloth to 84 kopeks per arshin. Government demand

Table 3.31   Government Demand for Wool Cloth and Industry's Supply Response

Year	Demand		Supply Response	
	Wool Cloth	Wool Lining	Wool Cloth	Wool Lining
1718			125,000	
1719			200,000	
1725			300,000	
1732			635,663	
1741			287,628	312,281
1742		1,310,400	685,200	
1743		1,043,265	800,000	
1756		1,100,000	1,165,000	
1763	796,860	331,356		
1764	814,960	266,383	1,561,866	283,161
1765	559,673	188,952	1,127,175	367,527
1767	154,883	81,114	1,637,998	542,785
1768	610,638	328,368		
1769	640,000	444,330		
1773	1,338,481	550,557		
1774		2,520,252		
1789		1,380,135		
1790		1,500,000		
1791		1,105,193		
1797	1,533,520	1,299,381		
1798	2,027,677	766,527	2,315,000	645,000
1799	1,500,000	480,000	2,162,000	645,000

Sources: Pazhitnov, *Ocherki*, pp. 11, 17, 19–21, 27–29; Beskrovnyi, *Russkaia armiia*, pp. 98–103, 364–67; Zhuravskii, *Statisticheskoe obozrenie*.

fluctuated widely between years of war and peace, something which often conflicted with the specialization and economic interests of the wool producers when the government demanded more cloth.

By the end of the 1790s the conflict between the wool producers and the government reached such a state that the latter threatened to confiscate the stocks of wool cloth in the manufactories to fill military orders.

The orders distributed for the supply of 1798, predominantly among the "possessional" manufactories for deliveries of 1,857,507 arshins of cloth and 766,527 arshins of *karazeia*, could not be met on the basis of the 1791 production norm per serf. The number of serfs, according to the data of the fifth *reviziia*, increased in the wool manufactories to 2,601 landless and 14,385 landed souls, which "entitled" the government to 1,028,317 arshins of cloth. Above this volume the manufactory owners volunteered another 247,408 arshins. The government was forced to turn to the producers who had statutory obligations to the state, and it obtained from them 533,773 arshins. The rest was obtained from the state-owned wool manufactories located in Ekaterinoslav and Irkutsk. Although the demanded army cloth could be delivered by the productive capacity of the existing wool manufactories, the prices offered by the government did not satisfy the producers, who demanded a 10 percent increase above the 1791 prices. The reaction of the government to the wool-cloth producers' foot-dragging was swift and decisive. By an order of

September 9, 1797, which was repeated in a later decree of March 1, 1800, the government prohibited producers and merchants from engaging in private sales of wool cloth and *karazeia* and also prohibited exports (presumably to China) of those commodities until the orders for the army were fulfilled. In the short run, the government prevailed by using its noneconomic powers.

Ultimately the government felt compelled to raise the wool-cloth prices under government contracts and thereby averted a dramatic confrontation. The sketchy information about the size of the government demand for army cloth can be translated into a ruble figure for some years. The value of the army cloth in rubles can be estimated by using the available quantities and prices. The calculation of the value of the delivery of cloth and *karazeia* for the armed forces yields the following results: 607,456 rubles for 1762; 1,102,270 rubles for 1791, and 1,159,766 rubles for 1798.[53] By the end of the century two-thirds of the output of the wool-cloth industry met the government's total demand and about one-third was for the civilian market.

There are many difficulties in trying to assess the value of output of the wool-cloth industry. The available estimates of output are mostly based upon incomplete reportings of the physical production of cloth submitted by producers. Another problem is presented by the prices used in the calculations producing the estimates. Although it was the convention to value the output of manufacturing industries

Table 3.32   Production of Woolen Headwear by the M. Gusiatnikov Firm, 1754–59

	1754	1755	1756	1757	1758	1759
For army regiments	59,053	62,310	67,900	62,387	120,393	58,394
For garrison regiments	45,448	49,650	57,250	49,828	40,488	27,758
Total for armed forces	104,501	111,960	125,150	112,215	160,881	86,152
For sale to civilians	29,805	43,825	39,100	34,985	45,023	45,127
Total Output	134,306	155,785	164,250	147,200	205,904	131,279
Share of the Armed Forces	77.8%	71.9%	76.2%	76.2%	78.1%	65.6%

Source: Lappo-Danilevskii, *Kompanii*, p. 97.

at their market price or sales price, this was done with some degree of reliability only with respect to the production purchased by the state. Since Russian statistics were primarily fiscally oriented, production which did not yield state revenue was often outside of the field of vision of the official reports. The differences between various published estimates are too large to attempt any reconciliation of the conflicting evidence. On the one hand, there are, for example, the Semenov and Chulkov estimates of 548,958, 733,995, and 1,178,282 rubles for 1761, 1765, and 1783, respectively. On the other hand, Strumilin, using different archival sources, cited estimates of 1,000,000 rubles for 1763 and 1,041,800 for 1767. Chulkov had valued the output at cost, a violation of the accepted statistical conventions. The only solution is to attempt to reevaluate the scattered available data to get orders of magnitude of wool-cloth output for a few benchmark years.

Demand for headwear for army personnel was an additional source of support for the wool industry. Although total military demand can be ascertained by using the size of the armed forces, it is of greater interest to ascertain the share of the military's demand relative to the total output of some of the major enterprises. Unquestionably the demand for headwear by the population was satisfied primarily by home production or production by rural and urban artisans, but nevertheless the production of headwear by large manufacturing enterprises gained ground in the eighteenth century.

The scattered data presented in table 3.32 for one of the firms producing headwear on a larger scale, that of the M. Gusiatnikov company in Moscow, provide an insight into the relative comparative dimensions of production of wool hats for the military and for the civilian market. Although the very high share of the armed forces demand in the total production of headwear by the Gusiatnikov firm was partially a result of demand created by the Seven Years' War, which started in 1756, and although the Gusiatnikov firm's output mix might not be typical for the industry as a whole, the data point to the importance of institutional demand (in this case, the armed forces) for the large manufactories in the wool-cloth and

wool-products industries. The dependence of such enterprises and firms upon large government contracts was a major factor accompanying both their founding and their operations, for government contracts presumably assisted in the achievement of economies of scale which provided the manufactories with an advantage over the small producers in the production of wool headwear. Thus the demand by the armed forces for wool headwear helped to create a distribution of headwear-producing units which was heavily concentrated at both ends of the scale, with the small producers catering to the demand of the civilian market and the large ones relying heavily upon state contracts. This industry, a user of wool cloth, by its relative dependence upon army contracts increased the dependence of the wool industry upon government demand.

The impact of government or army demand for wool cloth was doubtless of primary importance for the development of the wool-cloth manufactories. It helps to explain the type of cloth produced, the social composition of ownership of the enterprises, and perhaps also the composition of the labor force in terms of its different categories. During the last quarter of the eighteenth century, however, when the system of licensing was abolished, and for the seventeen years when the College of Manufactures was not in existence (from 1780 through 1796), market forces presumably exerted a more powerful influence upon the wool-cloth industry than before. For some aspects of the industry the market impact reinforced earlier trends, but for others the market introduced corrections into previous patterns.[54]

In the 1780s and 1790s there were several aspects of continuity in the wool industry. One of them was in the social composition of the owners with its high participation by members of the nobility. This tendency was strengthened by the establishment of new enterprises in the provinces acquired from Poland and the expansion of noble entrepreneurship into such areas as Simbirsk, Nizhnii Novgorod, and elsewhere, where locally produced wool and available serf labor were conducive to that development. With regard to merchant-owned enterprises, the recovery of Moscow as the largest producing center of wool cloth after the devastating effects of the 1771 bubonic plague epidemic, the growth of enterprises in Voronezh guberniia, and, most important, the further increase in the number of merchant-owned enterprises based upon hired labor (19 out of 37 manufactories in 1797) also suggested continuity with earlier patterns.

The aspect of wool-cloth production which was most influenced by market forces was the area and degree of specialization. The existing data suggest that some of the nobility-established enterprises during the last quarter of the eighteenth century did not possess the full technological cycle of wool-cloth production. Apparently a substantial share of production was in the form of unfinished, undyed cloth, which was either sold in its raw form or shipped for finishing and dyeing to merchant-owned enterprises that possessed the necessary productive capacity. According to 1797 data, 383,088 arshins of raw wool-cloth were produced by 19 enterprises owned by nobles, while 462,338 arshins of finished, dyed wool-cloth were produced by 21 other nobility-owned enterprises.

Specialization in the woolen industry made good economic sense. The output of raw wool cloth per unit of capital and per laborer was at least as high as for finished cloth, and it did not require the noble entrepreneurs to make additional outlays for capital and labor to finish and dye the cloth. In fact, in terms of units of cloth, the productivity of the raw-cloth-producing enterprises was higher than that of the finished-cloth enterprises owned by nobles. The difference in the unit value of the product was smaller than the difference in productivity, which would suggest that the production of raw cloth was more profitable than the production of finished cloth. Moreover, in order to take advantage of the opportunities offered by the market and to adjust to its demands, noble owners of enterprises began to lease their manufactories to merchants or to have them managed under contract by merchant entrepreneurs.

During the later part of the century the merchant entrepreneurs, especially the ones who were using hired labor exclusively, were often producing wool cloth of a quality inferior to government or army specifications. There are two explanations of this behavior. One is that the newly established merchant-owned enterprises were lacking the technical expertise which the older enterprises, using foreign specialists and generations of skilled serf-workers trained by those specialists, possessed. The other, and even more plausible, explanation sees the behavior as a response to the civilian segment of the market, which demanded cheaper wool cloth. To the extent that both explanations are not mutually exclusive, they might help us to understand on the

one hand the degree of specialization and the growing variety of wool cloth produced, and on the other hand the difficulties of the Russian army in obtaining domestically produced army cloth when faced with competition of price and quality of output.

A summary view of wool-cloth production in Russia toward the end of the eighteenth century as produced by the existing manufactories (exclusive of small-scale production), presented in table 3.33, is revealing in a number of ways. Less numerous and with less capital and a small labor force, the merchant-owned wool-cloth manufactories produced more than their chief competitors, the enterprises owned by the nobility. The productivity per unit of equipment and per unit of labor was apparently higher in the merchant-owned manufactories. Although the labor data are suspect, the higher labor productivity may be attributed to the status of more than half of the labor engaged in merchant-owned enterprises as hired rather than serf-obligated workers. The highest output per unit of labor was achieved in the enterprises owned by burghers who employed no serfs. This seems to be out of line with other evidence, and may reflect special circumstances. The state enterprises reflect a few important features of their historical role in the development of the wool-cloth industry, providing accumulated capital and accumulated skills. The private enterprises benefited by borrowing the state enterprises' technology and developed skills.

No major deviations from previous patterns can be discerned in the industrial activity of the wool-cloth manufactories during the latter part of the century. This branch remained one in which governmental activity and interference were more influential than in the other branches of the textile industry.

The Paper Manufactories

The Russians had been familiar with the art of papermaking since at least the sixteenth century, and small paper-mills existed prior to the eighteenth century. However, paper manufacturing on a sizable scale commenced only in the eighteenth century. The time pattern of the growth of this industry followed closely that of others, especially the textile industry. The explanation for the time pattern lies in the growth of state and private demand for paper, in government policies encouraging the growth of the industry, and in the growth of the linen industry, a supplier of some raw material for papermaking. From both the technical and the economic point of view there was an interdependency of the papermaking and linen industries in Russia, and consequently one would expect both the time pattern as well as the

Table 3.33 Wool Cloth Production in Russia, 1797 (83 Enterprises)

Category	No. of Producers	Cloth Weaving Machines	Karazei Weaving Machines	Workforce					Output (in Arshins)
				Serfs	Ascripti & Purchased	Total Serfs	Hired	Total	
Gentry producing finished cloth	21	606	58	4217	4829	9046	52	9098	462,338
Gentry producing raw cloth	19	346	—	3310	—	3310	3	3313	383,088
Total gentry	40	952	58	7527	4829	12,356	55	12,411	845,426
Merchants producing finished cloth	36	839	101	959	4302	5261	5848	11,109	1,148,712
Merchant producing raw cloth	1	6	—				54	54	7,500
Total merchants	37	845	101	959	4302	5261	5902	11,163	1,156,212
Burghers	2	n.a.	n.a.				21	21	3,164
Peasants	1	4						n.a.	3,200
State	3	372	44	1376	819	2195	140	2335	57,491
Total	83	2173	203	9862	9950	19,812	6118	25,930	2,065,493

location of the paper mills themselves to be influenced by those of the linen manufactories.

The demand for paper, especially for high-quality paper suitable for printing and writing, increased rapidly beginning in the reign of Peter the Great. The expansion of the military and the bureaucracy, the establishment of new educational institutions, the expansion of book and newspaper publishing and the communications network stimulated the demand for paper. Both governmental and private entrepreneurial activities were directed toward a buildup of the domestic paper industry.

From the outset the government became involved not only in the creation of paper mills, but also in the supply of rags and other raw materials used in paper. In 1714 Peter issued a decree known as "the linen rags" decree (o kholostinnykh loskutiakh) in which he stipulated the payment of 4 kopeks per pood of rags. This was followed by a decree of 1720 on the collection in all government offices of used paper and its transportation to paper mills. The decree also ordered that "it should be widely publicized among the population that anyone who has such used paper should surrender it at the paper mills, where he will obtain in exchange a proportionate volume of new paper."[55] Similar decrees on sending used paper to the mills were repeated in 1739 and 1740.[56] Peter also published on February 5, 1723, a decree about codilla classified as substandard by the quality controllers of hemp-products exports in the ports, ordering them to collect the codilla and send it by the end of each month to the paper mills. Finally, the export of rags was burdened in the 1724 tariff schedule with a 3 percent ad valorem duty. This set a precedent for government interference in the export of rags, and from 1734 to 1757 their export was prohibited. The 1756–57 tariff schedule permitted the export of rags, but levied a 200 percent ad valorem export duty. The prohibition of exports was reestablished in 1782. This record of government measures clearly indicates support for the paper mills trying to obtain necessary raw materials.

Apart from rags, used paper, and other fibrous materials, the mills obtained chemicals for bleaching and glue in the market at competitive prices.

The capital equipment employed in eighteenth-century paper mills was not very expensive. It consisted of a vessel, either in the form of a mortar and pestle to break up the fibers, or later in the century, a roller, moved by hand, by horse-, or by waterpower, in a bathtub-like vat.[57] The use of alternative forms of motive power made a difference in terms of human labor inputs and the time required to complete this particular operation. The application of water and chemicals at this stage determined the color and quality of the fibrous mass and, subsequently, of the

Table 3.34   Time Pattern of Establishment of Paper Mills and Social Position of Owners

Ownership	1700–25	1726–41	1742–62	1763–75	1776–96	1797–99	Total
State	3		1		1		5
Church		1	1				2
Nobles	1	5	5	3	16	2	32
Merchants (possessional)	1	5	6		2		14
Merchants (hired labor)		1	10	2	7		20
Foreigners	1			1	1		3
Tatars					2		2
Total	6	12	23	6	29	2	78

paper itself. The most important part of the capital equipment was the collector (*cherpal'nyi chan*) in which the fibrous mass from the various vessels was collected. The size of the collector determined the production capacity of the paper mill. Other pieces of equipment included small, flat vessels with net-like bottoms (*cherpal'nye formy*) used to take out of the collector a fixed volume of the fibrous mass, which was then put between woolen sheets and laid under a wooden press to have the moisture removed from the fibers. Further treatment of the paper, such as drying, pressing, cutting it to uniform size, and packaging did not require any special machinery and was done by hand with small tools. The capital equipment was not complicated and was, given a model, produced by skilled craftsmen in Russia itself.

The technology of papermaking required a number of operations performed by skilled workers or master craftsmen. The operation requiring the greatest skill was the preparation of the net-like bottom of the vessel in which the fibrous mass was transferred from the collector. This involved the use of silver and copper threads in making the bottom and also entailed the impression of the manufactory's water mark on the paper. The mixing of the fibrous materials with water and the appropriate chemicals to obtain a fine quality of paper took the next-greatest amount of skill.

Although the various operations involved in papermaking were differentiated and labeled as separate skills, they did not require long periods of apprenticeship. This kept the number of truly skilled master craftsmen per paper-mill low. Most of the labor force could be obtained from among people with relatively low skill-levels. This characteristic of the labor force explains why a combination of a linen-producing enterprise with a paper mill provided the entrepreneur not only with the possibility of economizing on some of the supply of raw materials, but also of transferring some of the labor from one enterprise to the other and thus of utilizing labor more efficiently throughout the year.

During the first half of the century most of the labor force, except for some highly skilled craftsmen, was recruited from the serfs. Serfs were employed not only by paper mills established by the state, the church, and nobles, but also by merchant entrepreneurs who were allocated so-called "possessional serfs" by the state to work in such private enterprises. The transfer of some serfs was often tantamount to the transfer of skills. Although the foremost authority on the Russian paper mills of this period, Z. V. Uchastkina, has indicated that there was some resistance on the part of skilled workers to divest themselves of "trade secrets" and to transfer their knowledge and skills to assigned apprentices instead of transferring it to their offspring, the technology transfer, including the highly skilled categories, appears not to have been seriously affected by the existing labor conditions, including the institution of serfdom. During the second half of the century the share of hired workers began to increase more perceptibly within the paper mills' labor force.

With sources of raw materials facilitated by government policies, reasonable costs of capital equipment, and an available supply of serf or hired labor, the paper mills were able to function and produce paper. The market for their products, if not assured, was nevertheless favorably inclined in view of the preference for domestic paper by the major users of paper (government institutions and the church) and by a part of the consumers who opted for the cheaper though inferior domestic paper over the expensive, superior foreign product.[58]

It is necessary to sketch out the time pattern of the establishment of the paper mills and the social composition of the entrepreneurs in order to appraise the response of the Russian entrepreneurs to the favorable conditions that existed both in the market for their products and in the attitudes of the government. The information pertaining to 78 paper mills made available by Z. V. Uchastkina in her masterful study is categorized and tabulated in table 3.34.

This reconstructed time pattern of the establishment of paper mills bears a great deal of similarity to the time pattern of other industries in Russia during the eighteenth century. Perhaps a minor difference can be noted: in the case of the paper mills, there was no abatement of foundations whatsoever during the immediate post-Petrine period, when the number of paper mills established doubled by comparison with the Petrine period. A similar tempo of growth was maintained during the Elizabethan period, except that in those years, 1742–62, the most active element in the establishment of paper mills became the merchants, who came to exceed the noblemen in paper-mill ownership. This was also the period of considerable concentration of paper output in the hands of a relatively small number of producers who owned both linen manufactories and paper mills (the Iaroslavl' manufactory established by Zatrapeznyi, the paper mills set up by Goncharov, Tames, and others).

In Catherine II's reign, especially after 1775, when the freedom of establishing manufactories unhampered by the previous licensing system of the College of Manufactures was proclaimed, a large number of paper mills were established. Noblemen set up mills on their estates, which supplied fibers and labor, and merchants founded mills that increasingly utilized hired labor. The papermaking industry became less concentrated and increasingly decentralized in the territory of Russia, including the provinces which were annexed to the empire. Given the economic advantages of locating mills adjacent to linen manufactures, one would expect to find a high degree of territorial concentration of mills in the traditional regions of linen manufactories. In fact, 35 enterprises out of a total of 78 were found in those very regions: Kaluga, 12; Moscow, 11; Yaroslavl', 6; Vladimir and Kostroma, 3; and Vologda, 3. It is surprising to find six paper mills in Viatka province and a few in the Urals and Siberia. During the latter part of the century there developed a tendency to locate mills closer to some of the major consumption centers. Thus seven paper mills were located in St. Petersburg province, nine in the Ukraine, and six in the Baltic provinces.

The social composition of the paper-mill owners was similar to that of entrepreneurs in other branches of industry. The predominance of merchants (and merchant-industrialists) is a familiar phenomenon of the eighteenth century and is underscored by the prevalence of merchants who relied increasingly upon hired labor. The high proportion of noblemen was commented upon earlier and requires no special elaboration. The shares held by the state and the church are explained on the one hand by Petrine policies and on the other hand by the role of the church as a consumer of paper.

The marginal role of foreigners as entrepreneurs during the eighteenth century can be explained by the general familiarity of the Russians with the technology, in spite of the inability to produce high-grade paper. The one category of private entrepreneurs that is not defined by social position but by nationality is that of the Tatars. The emergence of Tatars as industrial entrepreneurs during the second half of the eighteenth century is an interesting phenomenon related to their activities in the eastern trade of Russia and to the regional developments of the Volga region. It has its counterpart in entrepreneurship in the leather and textile manufactories. It may also be related to the attempts to set up schools and publish books for the Tatars in the Volga region and Siberia, although the latter relationship is difficult to document. To the extent that the case of the paper mills is a direct indication of the entrepreneurial activity of the Tatars, it did not seem redundant to separate them from the other socially defined groups.

There is hardly any global data on the production of paper in Russia. The only estimates cited by Z. V. Uchastkina are 4,000 reams of paper (about 4 tons) for the beginning of the eighteenth century and about 4,000,000 reams for the beginning of the nineteenth century, a thousand-fold growth. Starting from such a low base, the growth, even though spectacular, yields a relatively low figure of paper production for Russia by the end of the eighteenth century. On a per capita basis, it amounted to about 50 standard sheets of paper. From the points of view of skill acquisition and the development of a domestic industry, however, the achievements in building paper mills and producing paper during the eighteenth century are more impressive than the mere production data indicate. Eight of the seventy-eight enterprises established during the eighteenth century have survived to this day and are still producing paper.

The Copper Industry

The demand for copper in Russia during the eighteenth century was a sum of the state's demand for coinage and armaments, the civilian demand for copper in a variety of household goods, and the demand for church bells. Most of the demand during the early part of the century was met by foreign imports, although, regrettably, the extant sources for the seventeenth and the beginning of the eighteenth centuries do not provide adequate information on the volume of copper imports. Were the data extant, one would expect to find copper high on the list of imported commodities. Either for its use in coinage or for its significance in arms production, copper constituted during the eighteenth century an object of policy leading toward autarky in its supply.

Of the two major government uses of copper, there are no data whatsoever on the military use, so that one has to restrict oneself to the demand for copper coinage. The first introduction of copper money in

Table 3.35   Coinage of Copper Money (in Current Rubles and in Poods)

Years	Coinage in Current Rubles	Use of Copper in Poods	Average Yearly Use of Copper
1700–1704	1,354,142	96,038	19,208
1705–24	3,000,000	150,000	7,500
1725–29	3,988,330	99,708	19,942
1730–40	2,936,482	293,648	29,365
1742–57	4,144,364	441,253	29,417
1757–61	10,977,349	686,084	137,217
1761–62	3,859,615	120,613	120,613
1762–96	79,965,039	4,997,815	142,795
1797–1800	4,828,810	301,807	75,452

Source: Calculated from data on coinage and copper weights of coins, in Kaufman, *Serebrianyi rubl'*, pp. 129, 148–49, 151, 160–61, 167, 169, 176.

Russia was an ill-fated affair of the late 1650s and early 1660s in an attempt to derive revenue for war needs. Its use led to the Copper Uprising of 1663 in Moscow during the Thirteen Years' War after nearly a decade of currency debasement, and consequently, until the grave war emergency of 1700, no Russian government dared to renew copper coinage. Even until the late 1750s copper did not constitute more than 10 percent of the total coinage minted. As shown in table 3.35, there was a continuous rise throughout the eighteenth century in the monetary demand for copper. The years 1757–61, during the Seven Years' War, constituted an exception. A massive coinage of copper, at the insistence of Count Shuvalov, was made possible not from current copper production but by the melting down of old copper cannons.

A comparison of the data on copper coinage with the incomplete data of reported copper output presented in table 3.36 suggests that it was not until the middle 1740s that domestic copper production was sufficient to meet the monetary demand for copper. We know, however, that other nonmonetary uses of copper had claims upon the supply from domestic sources. This would imply that, if we took the total demand into consideration, it was probably not before the middle of the 1750s that the monetary demand for copper was actually met by domestic supply. Even during the middle 1750s, when many state-owned ironworks were turned over to private individuals, the copper smelters were exempted from such transfer by the Senate "until certain conditions within the country will be met." It was common knowledge that "certain conditions" meant an adequate supply of copper to the mint.

Russia reached self-sufficiency in copper production in the latter 1760s, and by the end of the century even became an exporter of copper. To the extent that copper was a strategic raw material, the increase in its output was both an economic as well as a political

achievement. There is no doubt that, as in some other branches of mining and industry, the sustained interest, support, and demand by the government played a very significant role in the development of the industry. The right to prospect for copper anywhere, the right to mine copper on private and state land during most of the century, the making of forestry grants, and the supplying of labor in labor-deficit areas by the state were all measures which combined together decisively to create growth in the copper industry. The state not only encouraged private entrepreneurship in the copper industry, but also produced a high proportion of the output itself, as shown in tables 3.37 and 3.38. During the decade of the 1750s seven copper smelters were turned over from state to private ownership, but the state was always willing to take over any of the copper smelters previously owned privately. For example, in 1791 the government purchased from the heirs of M. M. Pokhodiashin the three largest copper smelters in Russia for 2.5 million rubles, which greatly increased the government's share in the total copper output. The demonstrated possibility of producing copper at a profit, in view of the domestic demand for coinage and other uses, or for export abroad, stimulated the growth of copper production and made the ownership of copper mines and smelters attractive to both private and institutional entrepreneurs.

Iron Production

The iron industry, the leading industry in terms of value of output in the eighteenth century, occupied an intermediary place within the industrial sector of the Russian economy with regard to the nature of its demand and its dependence upon the government and the market.

The Russian iron manufactories of the eighteenth century were descendants of the seventeenth-century ironworks set up with the help of foreign entrepreneurs and technical specialists in the 1630s. They were not descendants of the indigenous small-scale, craft-like forges and furnaces, which were destroyed in the eighteenth century to eliminate competition for the many newly built blast furnaces of the large ironworks.

The stimulus for the development of water-powered ironworks and the buildup of a new, major producing region in the Urals came from the Russian government. It was one of the results of the psychological shock of the Narva defeat in 1700, when Peter the Great decided to become autarkic in arms production. The key to self-sufficiency in arms production was the production of pig iron and iron for cannons, small-arms, and ammunition. With a very short period, still during the Northern War (1700–1721), this

Table 3.36   Reported Output of Copper (in Poods)

Year	State	Private	Total	Year	State	Private	Total
1720	336	—	336	1739	10,291	12,633	22,924
22	176	—	176	1740	15,286	14,194	29,480
23	574	—	574	41	19,109	11,018	30,127
24	2,336	—	2,336	42	17,617	17,489	35,106
1725	5,533	—	5,533	43	18,087	14,286	32,373
26	9,475	193	9,668	44	20,960	12,711	33,671
27	10,048	183	10,231	1745	22,810	7,294[a]	
28	9,200	964	10,164	46	20,439	n.a.	
29	10,779	1,703	12,482	1767			197,671
1730	10,153	3,123	13,276	69		173,625	
31	10,297	5,129	15,426	1770		148,521	
32	8,786	4,203	12,989	71		166,110	
33	8,198	4,561	12,759	72		164,334	
34	10,978	6,124	17,102	1780			
1735	8,854	6,970	15,824	85		175,631	
36	9,604	6,977	16,581	1790		156,244	
37	10,143	9,052	19,195	95		89,615	
38	10,349	10,432	20,781				

Sources: Pavlenko, *Razvitie*, pp. 56, 78, 288; idem, *Istoriia*, p. 237.

[a]Reported private output for 1745 is incomplete.

Table 3.37   Output and Utilization of Copper by State Enterprises in the Urals (in Tons)

Year	Output	Factory Use	Sent to Moscow and St. Petersburg	Sent to Ekaterinburg Mint
1720	5.50		5.47	
22	2.88		2.88	
23	9.40		9.40	
24	38.30		38.30	
25	87.35	.80	83.91	
26	155.20		154.95	
27	164.59	.59	154.05	
28	146.29		142.75	
29	172.61	4.16	168.22	
1730	165.75	5.00	152.53	
31	162.87	62.34	100.46	
32	139.79	.41	96.74	
33	134.14	78.51	31.48	24.13
34	179.82	20.75	42.18	116.89
35	145.03			177.46
36	157.31	.74	32.76	123.82
37	165.03		82.39	82.64
38	162.96			162.96
39	160.43	65.03	13.10	82.28
1740	250.38	70.99	15.61	163.65
41	313.00		16.38	290.66
42	288.57		3.87	282.77
43	296.27	.05	12.61	283.44
44	343.32		16.38	326.94
45	373.63			373.63
46	334.79			334.79
Total	4,555.21	310.37	1,276.54	2,826.06

Source: Pavlenko, *Razvitie*.

Note: The totals for the columns do not add up since other uses are not included.

goal was achieved. Thus at the beginning of the eighteenth century the iron industry consisted of a state-owned and a private sector and was basically an armament-oriented industry with a part of its output meeting the demand of the government for military supplies.

The government resorted to a number of measures to raise the output of iron and iron products within a

Table 3.38   Private Copper Output and Distribution, 1726–45 (in Poods)

Producer	Smelter	Years	Total Output	Market Sales	State Deliveries	Tax Total	State Take
A. Demidov	Suksunskii	1726–45	26,457	23,584	1,710	1,036	2,746
A. Demidov	Kolyvan[a]	1730–46	17,056	n.a.	14,294	n.a.	14,294
A. Demidov	Bymovskii	1736–45	15,038	13,864		1,120	1,120
A. Demidov	Shakvinskii	1740–45	2,466	2,220		240	240
A. Demidov	Ashapskii	1744–45	1,022	1,020			
Total A. Demidov			62,039	40,688			18,400
G. Stroganov	Tamanskii	1726–44	23,030	14,870	6,978	1,178	8,156
P. Osokin	Irginskii	1729–44	14,594	8,723	3,418	686	4,104
P. Osokin	Bizierskii	1741–44	3,906	3,601			
Total P. Osokin			18,500	12,324			4,104
G. Osokin	Yugovskii	1733–44	12,432	7,243	4,020	633	4,653
G. Osokin	Kurashinskii	1742–44	3,409	3,379			
Total G. Osokin			15,841	10,622			4,653
A. Turchaninov	Troitskii	1731–44	9,510	6,136	2,858	488	3,346
S. Inozemtsov	Taishevskii	1736–45	7,183	5,795	913	473	1,386
S. Krasil'nikov	Korinskii	1733–45	6,678	4,761	1,029	448	1,477
A. Prozorov	Shurminskii	1733–45	5,036	3,841	936	233	1,169
I. Nebogatov	Shilvinskii	1734–45	2,401	2,166		188	188
Total			150,218	101,203	36,156	6,723	42,879

Source: Pavlenko, *Razvitie*, p. 450.

[a]The data for the Kolyvano-Voznesensk copperworks output are incomplete and therefore its output and the total are probably underestimated by 5,000–6,000 poods. Another estimate of Demidov's copper output gives a figure of 69,291 poods instead of the above 62,039 poods.

short period. Among the more effective were outright grants of state-built ironworks to private entrepreneurs, grants of state-owned serfs to augment the labor force in areas of relative labor scarcity, subsidies and loans for additional investments, guaranteed long-term contracts, and guaranteed delivery prices. That all the benefits were not without costs became apparent later, when the various sets of government controls imposed during the early days of industrial expansion and accompanying the various benefits became burdensome to the entrepreneurs, now firmly established and resentful of the daily interference of the bureaucracy in the conduct of their business. Their resentment was directed against government interference with management decisions, prices, and wages. They felt quite comfortable, however, working within the framework of serf labor, of government policies of protection, and of official obstacles to the entry by others into the industry.

By the end of Peter's reign (1725), when government demand became insufficient to sustain the increased level of production, new markets had to be sought. Foreign demand provided the necessary outlet, and an increasing share of total production went abroad. State-owned enterprises paved the way for private exports. The government preferred to export its production and gain foreign exchange, and it relied upon the system of obligatory deliveries of private ironmakers for the normal (peacetime) supply of armaments. The obligatory deliveries of private entrepreneurs to the state, at prices which already by the 1740s were below the level of market prices, were a form of taxation upon the private producers. They remained in force until the 1770s, nominally a payment for the use of government owned serfs attached to the ironworks. The most efficient iron producers followed the example of the government and engaged in large volume sales to exporters. The civilian domestic demand increased gradually throughout the century. Increases in production occurred in spurts following periods of intensified investment activity and the introduction of new capacity. This increasing capacity in the private sector can be followed from the data presented in table 3.39 on the construction of new ironworks by decades.

Although the number of enterprises is an inadequate measure of productive capacity because of the differences in size among ironworks, these data combined with output data presented below provide a general indicator of changes in capacity as well as of changes in the time pattern of investment over the course of the century. The period of the 1750–60s, followed by the 1740s and 1720s, appears as the period of most rapid growth, while the 1770s and the last decade of the century indicate relative periods of slowdowns in net investment activity in ironworks.

The newly developed Urals region became the dominant iron producing region of Russia because of the high quality of the ore and the availability of fuel and water (as motive power). These factors enabled the Urals producers to decrease their costs of production and to undersell the producers of other regions.

Table 3.39   Construction and Disposal of Private Ironworks

Years	Constructed	Received from Government	Sold to Government	Ceased Production	Active
1701–10	2	1	–	–	3
1711–20	8	–	–	–	11
1721–30	15	–	–	–	26
1731–40	13	–	–	1	38
1741–50	20	15	–	3	55
1751–60	35	–	–	10	95
1761–70	32	–	9	13	105
1771–80	19	1	–	15	110
1781–90	17	–	–	–	127
1791–1800	11	–	4	–	134
Total	172	17	13	42	

Source: Pavlenko, *Istoriia*, p. 462.

Table 3.40   Territorial Distribution of Private Ironworks in the Eighteenth Century

Years	Urals & Siberia		Moscow Region		Olonets Region	
	Constructed	Survived	Constructed	Survived	Constructed	Survived
1701–10			2	2	—	—
1711–20	3	3	5	7	—	—
1721–30	8	11	7	14	—	—
1731–40	6	17	6	19	1	1
1741–50	6	22	14	31	—	1
1751–60	13	41	16	37	—	1
1761–70	20	58	6	33	6	7
1771–80	15	71	2	31	2	—
1781–90	12	83	5	36	—	—
1791–1800	5	88	6	42	—	—

Source: Pavlenko, *Istoriia*, pp. 460, 462, 464.

In addition, some ironworks of the central region were closed by the government under the pretext of forest conservation in the 1750s. The construction and survival of private ironworks in the various regions can be traced in table 3.40.

The share of the Urals region and Siberia in the total output of iron is very much underestimated in table 3.40 because of differences in size and capacity of ironworks in different regions. The share of the Urals and Siberia by the end of the century was 81.76 percent of the total output (8,648,000 poods) and all of European Russia's was only 18.24 percent.

Apart from the territorial concentration of the iron industry, there existed a high degree of concentration of output in a few firms. By the end of the century, the ironworks of four families, the Demidovs, Iakovlevs, Mosolovs, and Batashevs, produced over one-half of the total iron production of Russia.[59] The evolution of this concentration in the second half of the century can be traced in tables 3.41 and 3.42. The phenomenon can be explained not only by the comparative advantage of those producers, who acquired vast, high quality resources of ores, fuel, and labor, but also by the difficulties of entry into the iron industry. The latter factor was the consequence of barriers raised by the large-scale entrepreneurs and

the difficulty of obtaining bound labor, combined with governmental policies of licensing and control over the industry.

The supply of labor was one of the basic problems of the iron industry. Located in sparsely populated areas, where the available labor supply was exhausted early in the development of the industry, entrepreneurs had to rely not only upon freely hired labor, but also upon serf labor either acquired by the entrepreneurs themselves or attached to the ironworks by state ascription. The tight labor market, the increasing distance from the ironworks to the places where serf labor force lived, and the government regulations which first limited the number of serfs per enterprise (1751) and then prohibited nongentry entrepreneurs from acquiring serfs (1762) put merchant entrepreneurs at a disadvantage with gentry industrialists. Consequently the problem of labor supply became a matter of contention between the state and the entrepreneurs.

The peculiarities of eighteenth century labor statistics made it very difficult to present estimates of the labor force for selected years based upon uniform criteria. The main difficulty is that the serf labor used in the production of iron was employed for both skilled and unskilled work. The labor force was often

Table 3.41   Private Production of Pig Iron for Selected Years, and Share of Major Producers (in Metric Tons)

	1750	1760	1770	1780	1790	1800
Total private	23,096	58,367	70,224	97,559	116,888	141,654
Demidovs	14,201	24,161	26,568	29,844	30,123	33,874
% of total	61.49	41.39	37.83	30.59	25.77	23.91
Iakovlev	—	—	8,567	18,313	18,886	28,763
% of total	—	—	12.47	18.77	16.16	20.31
Batashev	704	3,145	6,437	9,828	14,070	14,955
% of total	3.05	5.39	9.17	10.07	12.04	10.56
Mosolov	2,473	1,573	1,507	2,883	3,391	2,654
% of total	10.71	2.70	2.15	2.96	2.90	1.87
Golitsyn and Shakhovskov	—	1,114	1,704	1,851	6,830	8,141
% of total	—	1.91	2.43	1.90	5.84	5.75
Stroganov	1,343	3,784	5,324	5,274	5,045	5,946
% of total	5.81	6.48	7.58	5.41	4.32	4.20
Others	4,374	24,586	20,115	29,566	38,542	47,322
% of total	18.94	42.12	28.64	30.31	32.97	33.41

Source: Strumilin, *Istoriia*, p. 170.

Table 3.42   Private Production of Iron for Selected Years, and Share of Major Producers (in Metric Tons)

	1750	1760	1770	1780	1790	1800
Total Private	15,348	36,462	46,110	56,150	81,278	91,499
Demidovs	9,975	17,330	17,101	17,477	21,261	25,274
% of total	64.99	47.53	37.09	31.13	26.16	27.62
Iakovlev	—	—	5,242	11,810	13,268	18,395
% of total	—	—	11.37	21.03	16.32	20.10
Batashev	475	1,802	5,061	6,585	9,500	6,716
% of total	3.09	4.94	10.98	11.73	11.69	7.34
Mosolov	1,654	786	885	1,736	2,228	1,376
% of total	10.78	2.16	1.92	3.09	2.74	1.50
Golitsyn and Shakhovskov	—	262	1,130	1,589	4,930	5,700
% of total	—	.72	2.45	2.83	6.07	6.23
Stroganov	885	1,867	3,423	2,080	3,636	3,423
% of total	5.77	5.12	7.42	3.70	4.47	3.74
Others	2,359	14,414	13,268	14,873	26,454	30,614
% of total	15.37	39.53	28.77	26.49	32.55	33.46

Source: Strumilin, *Istoriia*, p. 172.

reported in terms of people owned by the entrepreneurs, regardless of their use in actual production. It is also difficult to differentiate between the labor force employed in iron production proper and the workers employed in various ancillary jobs such as ore-mining, coal-burning, and transportation. In addition, the use of hired labor is poorly documented by the entrepreneurs in their official reports, although there can be no doubt that the use of free labor was increasing rapidly by the end of the century. Table 3.43 attempts to present the estimates for the different groups of labor for selected dates and to show the general tendencies of employment within the industry. Representing different categories of labor with varying degrees of work obligations, the figures do not represent estimates of actual labor inputs.

The value of iron output can be estimated for selected years during the eighteenth century by multiplying the quantities of output (shown in tables 3.44 and 3.45) by the reported St. Petersburg prices quoted on the exchange. Given the relatively high proportion of exports in the total output and the fact that St. Petersburg was the main port for iron exports, it is plausible to assume that the St. Petersburg price reflected the pattern of price changes of iron in other domestic markets as well. The actual money receipts from iron production and the sales of iron were below the value of output in St. Petersburg prices because a part of the production was used by the industry itself in various investment goods and because other markets located between the Urals and St. Petersburg (such as Kazan', Nizhnii Novgorod, and Moscow) absorbed production at prices lower than the St. Petersburg one. Moreover, for most of the century iron deliveries to the government were exacted at below-market prices. Nevertheless, as a measure of changes in output and for the purpose of comparison with the production of other industries,

Table 3.43   Estimates of Employment in the Iron Industry by Categories of Employment for Selected Years

	Skilled Labor	Unskilled Labor	III Serfs Attached to Enterprise		IV
	I Iron Masters and Workers	II Purchased Private Serfs	Private	State	Hired Workers
1725					
State	1,095			23,462	
Private	2,295	n.a.	n.a.		
Total	3,390				
1747					
State	2,463			34,514	
Private	9,092	9,423	12,581		
Total	11,555				
1764					
State	1,909			75,521	
Private	13,243	25,572	16,574		12,033
Total	15,152				
1783					
State	3,195			88,450	
Private		54,836			
Total					
1800					
State	3,561			83,308	3,075
Private	20,924	48,381			
Total	24,485				

Table 3.44   Output of Pig Iron (in Metric Tons) for Selected years

Year	State	%	Private	%	Total
1720	2,539	25.41	7,453	74.59	9,992
1725	4,717	35.33	8,633	64.67	13,350
1730	5,307	33.85	10,369	66.15	15,676
1735	7,198	31.36	15,758	68.64	22,956
1740	7,567	30.19	17,494	69.81	25,061
1745	8,124	29.21	19,689	70.79	27,813
1750	9,815	29.82	23,096	70.18	32,911
1760	1,638	2.73	58,367	97.27	60,005
1770	13,410	16.04	70,224	83.96	83,634
1780	12,482	11.34	97,559	88.66	110,041
1790	11,482	8.94	116,888	91.06	128,370
1800	18,673	11.65	141,654	88.35	160,327

Source: Strumilin, *Istoriia*, pp. 166, 173, 175.

Table 3.45   Output of Iron (in Metric Tons) for Selected Years

Year	State	%	Private	%	Total
1710	1,048	41.0	1,507	59.0	2,555
1720	1,605	32.66	3,309	67.34	4,914
1725	1,704	27.69	4,449	72.31	6,153
1730	3,448	38.07	5,610	61.93	9,058
1735	3,674	26.61	10,134	73.39	13,808
1740	4,937	29.55	11,771	70.45	16,708
1745	5,427	30.96	12,100	69.04	17,527
1750	6,485	29.70	15,350	70.30	21,835
1760	747	2.01	36,455	97.99	37,202
1770	6,390	12.17	46,100	87.83	52,490
1780	5,458	8.86	56,149	91.14	61,607
1790	6,981	7.91	81,268	92.09	88,249
1800	9,299	9.23	91,495	90.77	100,794

Source: Strumilin, *Istoriia*, pp. 166, 173.

the accepted measure appears to be preferable to others.

The calculations are presented in table 3.46 in terms of silver rubles to eliminate the impact of the depreciated paper currency at the end of the century. To make the intertemporal comparison more effective, in addition to the estimates in current silver rubles, an adjustment for the change in the value of the ruble in 1762 was calculated so that another column presents an evaluation of the output in constant silver rubles of Catherine the Great.

Brick Production

The organization of brick production in Russia has an interesting history. From the sixteenth century there was a corporation of registered brickmakers *(zapisnye kirpichniki)* which assembled annually on May 10 to receive instructions from the Masonry Chancellery *(Prikaz kamennykh del)* about the current or planned construction sites for churches and government buildings and to be assigned to the various sites for the production of bricks. The second half of the seventeenth century witnessed the establishment of permanent government brick factories under the chancellery's supervision as well as the granting of permission to brickmakers to enter into direct contracts with clients. The creation of brick factories on the outskirts of Moscow (the Danilovskie, Khamovnitskie, Plenitskie, Polevye, and other works) enabled the introduction of a division of labor among three categories of workers: the *iaryzhnye,*

Table 3.46   Value of Iron Output for Selected Years in Current Silver Rubles

Year	Output (Tons)	Price/Ton	Value of Output	Value of Output (Post-1762 Silver Rubles)
1724	5,012	40.8	204,840	235,566
30	9,058	36.6	331,523	381,251
31	11,794	36.6	431,660	496,409
32	10,467	36.6	383,092	440,556
33	9,877	36.6	361,498	415,723
34	11,564	36.6	423,242	486,728
1735	13,808	36.6	505,373	581,179
36	14,480	36.6	529,968	609,463
37	13,399	36.6	490,403	563,960
38	14,709	36.6	538,349	619,102
39	16,970	36.6	621,102	714,265
1740	14,922	36.6	546,145	628,067
49	19,509	43.92	856,835	985,360
1750	21,835	35.38	772,522	888,400
1760	37,202	38.43	1,429,673	1,644,124
64	38,526	43.92		1,692,062
66	50,270	43.92		2,207,858
67	53,643	42.70		2,290,556
1770	59,490	40.565		2,413,212
1780	61,607	44.53		2,743,360
81	71,515	44.04		3,149,664
1790	88,249	61.00		5,383,189
93	91,875	58.56		5,380,200
97	85,929	73.81		6,342,419
1800	100,794	70.455		7,101,441

Source: Calculated from output and price data in Pavlenko, *Istoriia*, and Strumilin, *Istoriia*.

employed in the supply and transportation of clay, sand, water, and fuel; the *kirpichniki*, the brickmakers proper who mixed the clay, formed and dried the bricks; and the *obzhigal'shchiki* or kiln workers, who baked the bricks. By the end of the seventeenth century, a number of kiln workers already owned their own kilns and could work directly for the market. In 1700 the Masonry Chancellery was abolished, the state-owned factories were turned over to the municipality organization *(Ratusha)*, and by 1705 the institution of registered brickmakers was also liquidated.

The profession was soon challenged by the government's resolve to construct the new capital, St. Petersburg. The freedom so recently granted to the brickmakers was soon disturbed by the government mobilization of the skilled workers to be relocated to St. Petersburg, where the government was busy setting up new state brick factories. The demand for both bricks and the labor of brickmakers rose during the construction of the new capital. The brickmakers, bricklayers, and masons made up a very sizable portion of the mobilized skilled labor force.[60] To stimulate brick production, the government in 1712 permitted people of any rank *(vsiakogo china liudiam)* to manufacture bricks and to sell them freely.[61] The response was insufficient, and the government felt compelled as a temporary measure to prohibit the construction of brick kilns anywhere outside St. Petersburg or the production of bricks for the use of any other city.[62] The government encouraged its own institutions and private individuals in St. Petersburg to award brick supply contracts to private entrepreneurs to help meet the annual demand of roughly ten million bricks needed for the capital construction works.[63]

Government policy on brick production had to adjust to the rapidly increasing demand for bricks forced by the timetable of St. Petersburg construction and the inability of the newly established state enterprises to attract a sufficient labor force even while using various forms of mobilization and conscription by the state. The resulting government policy was a mixture of conscription and encouragement of private initiative. The state-owned brick factories in the vicinity of St. Petersburg employed 145 conscripted families at the Neva works (in 1712), 95 families in the Tosnensk works, and 136 workers chiefly chosen from army recruits in the Strel'na works (1720).[64] This number of workers was inadequate to bring the production of the yards up to their capacity, and hundreds of laborers had to be hired yearly to perform the auxiliary tasks.[65] The management problems of the state-operated enterprises became so difficult for the bureaucracy to handle that by the early 1720s the government decided to turn over the works to private entrepreneurs, contractors who for a specific payment per unit of production were obliged to supply the contractual volume of bricks for the various construction sites.

Petrine policies shifted brick production from Moscow to St. Petersburg, and ultimately from state-owned to privately owned or privately administered brickworks. The completion of the first stage of St. Petersburg's construction and the death of Peter the Great relieved the pressure for the production of bricks; St. Petersburg production decreased to about five million bricks per year and brick production returned to the Moscow region. The demand for bricks in Moscow was much more steady than it was in St. Petersburg, where it depended upon governmental decisions to undertake major construction projects, such as the Cathedral of St. Isaac and the Winter Palace.

Apart from some major construction endeavors, the other source for rapid increases in the demand for bricks were the major conflagrations in the capital cities, frequent but random occurrences in the eighteenth century. For example, after the fire in Moscow in 1773, the demand for bricks was estimated at twenty million per year, about six to eight million above the earlier production levels. The available, although fragmentary, data for Moscow brick production permit following the increase of productive capacity, output, and also the approximate production per worker for a number of decades during the eighteenth century. Government demand for bricks slackened during the reigns of Peter the Great's immediate successors, but private demand, mostly for church construction and housing by the great nobles and some rich merchants, grew.

The output of bricks by the Moscow brickworks in 1753 was estimated at approximately 7.1 million and in 1757 at 8.5 million. The Moscow merchant Mitrofan Perepletchikov in 1758 petitioned the Senate to turn over to him all the Moscow state-owned and private brickworks in exchange for a promise to supply twelve million bricks annually, ten million for government needs and two million for sale in the market.[66]

The sources list for 1753 a total of twenty-six functioning private brickworks with a total output of 7,133,000 bricks. The owners of those brickworks can be divided by their status into seven merchants of the first guild; thirteen merchants of the second guild; three merchants of the third guild; two peasants; one provincial merchant; and one nobleman-industrialist.[67] As in the case of other industry branches, the preponderance of merchants among the owners of brickworks points to merchant capital as a major source of investment in industrial activity.

Table 3.47   Output by Private Brickworks in Moscow, 1775–80 (No. of Bricks)

Year	Output	Year	Output
1775	15,070,000	1778	15,957,000
1776	16,802,000	1779	18,355,000
1777	15,190,000	1780	20,000,000 (expected)

Source: Voronov, "Kirpichnoe proizvodstvo," p. 95.

The output of bricks by private brickworks in Moscow continued to rise during the reign of Catherine the Great. This reflected the general rise of building construction during her reign, a revival of both government activity as well as private. The increased production for Moscow is illustrated in table 3.47.

There seems to have been technological progress in brickworking during the eighteenth century. The average size of the brick kilns tended to increase, not only in the state-owned brick yards, but also in private enterprises. The standard size of bricks was decreased from seven *vershki* to six *vershki* already early in the century and this accelerated the process of drying and increased the capacity of even the existing kilns.[68]

The forty-three private brickworks of Moscow during the years 1776–82 had a labor force that varied between 551 and 904, depending upon the year and the number of functioning enterprises. The vast majority of the labor force consisted of private serfs, hired under contract. Former ecclesiastical serfs provided the second largest contingent of workers. The participation of these serfs represented both a continuity of skill acquisition in connection with church construction and the large proportion of money-rent-paying serfs who hired themselves out for work in urban areas.[69]

Although the data for the second half of the century were primarily drawn from the experience of the Moscow enterprises, whatever evidence is available for St. Petersburg supports the generalization of the Moscow experience. The 1770s and 1780s witnessed an increase in the number of enterprises and in the size of the labor force. The entrepreneurs were primarily recruited from the merchant class with an admixture of peasants and even some nobility, and the total productive capacity of the private brickworks exceeded the capacity of the state-owned enterprises, all phenomena familiar from the Moscow experience.[70]

The production of bricks, which was an activity carried on exclusively for the internal market and to a very large extent for the government as the major purchaser of the output, followed the demand with some time lag. The difficulty in adjusting to sudden changes in the level of demand can be illustrated by

Table 3.48   Price of Bricks in St. Petersburg (in Rubles per 1,000)

Year	Price	Year	Price
1740	3.50	1767	3.40
1741	2.00	1770	1.81–2.70
1747	3.40	1775	2.65–3.40
1749	2.25–2.50	1779	5.70
1756	2.30	1782	4.98
1761	3.80	1784	6.00
1764	1.85	1790	6.00

Sources: The data for 1740 and 1790 are from Liubomirov, "Leso-pil'noe proizvodstvo," p. 244. The other data are from Stolpianskii, *Zhizn'*, pp. 20–21.

Note: The prices are for standard bricks (11 × 5.5 × 2.75 inches).

the price behavior of bricks, for which there are quotations for a number of years. The quotations, presented in table 3.48, must be viewed against the general rise in prices for the end of the 1770s and throughout the 1780s, but their fluctuations during some of the previous years tell us something about the capacity of the industry to adjust its supply to the changing demand.

These price data point to fluctuations which could not be explained by anything occurring within the industry and point to the impact of exogenous factors, chief among which were fluctuations in government demand. For example, the decline to the low level of 1764 can be explained by the completion of the Winter Palace in St. Petersburg the previous year. There is no doubt that the government was well aware of the price fluctuations, but, as a consumer, it was primarily concerned with price increases, which made construction activities more costly. The usual reaction on the part of the Russian government was to issue severe decrees, as after the 1737 conflagration in St. Petersburg, when the Senate promulgated a decree on August 9, 1737, threatening with capital punishment anyone who raised the price of construction.[71]

The price fluctuations which occurred in spite of threatening government decrees were much more of a reaction to the short-run demand-supply relationship than to long-run increases in the price of fuel or to increasing wages, especially as the output per worker as measured in the number of bricks per employee tended to rise secularly.[72] The data for twenty-five private brickworks in Moscow for 1781 indicate a labor force of 774 and an output of 16,866,000 bricks, or about 21,800 bricks per worker. At a price of five rubles per 1,000 bricks, the value of output per worker was about 109 rubles. If one assumes an output of a maximum of 50 million bricks for all of Russia, the value of the output was a quarter million rubles and the number employed about 2,294 workers.

To the extent that the work in the brick yards had a typical seasonal pattern and the total labor force required was relatively small, the difficulties in the organization of production are surprising. Toward the end of the century some of the organizational problems may have been resolved as the brickworks began to maintain larger inventories and thus smoothed out the fluctuations in output.

Regrettably, it is impossible to estimate the approximate volume of bricks produced during the century. Among the construction materials, wood remained more prevalent than bricks. Nevertheless, for residential construction in St. Petersburg and Moscow, and for some industrial construction, bricks were of increasing importance. Data on the production of bricks, were they available, could provide an index of capital expenditures in residential and industrial building. The absence of such substitute indicators makes the task of estimating the volume of capital expenditures on construction impossible.

The Glass Industry

The glass industry represents an interesting case of substantial utilization of serf labor combined with large amounts of hired labor. It was an industry in which state intervention exhibited itself only in the form of the general licensing of industrial activity until the 1770s and in the granting of permission to acquire serfs.

There are relatively few data about the growth and economic conditions of the glass manufactories because they were only marginally involved in areas of state control and produced for the domestic market rather than for export or state institutions. Most of the data available are for a short time-period, the 1750s and 1760s, and they pertain primarily to the "possessional" enterprises, the ones which were granted the right to purchase serfs and actually did so under existing provisions until 1762, when merchant-industrialists were permitted to buy serfs with and without land.

The majority of the owners of the glass manufactories were merchants. By the beginning of the 1760s they owned 21 of the 27 manufactories; 3 were owned by members of the nobility, 2 by foreigners, and 1 by a commoner (*raznochinets*). Of this total, 17 were possessional manufactories; of them, 14 belonged to merchants, 2 to foreigners, and 1 to the commoner.[73]

The growth pattern of the number of enterprises until the 1760s is presented in table 3.49, which also shows the number of enterprises which used purchased serfs.

Relatively few glass manufactories existed during the 1720s and 1730s, and consequently this industry did not benefit as much as others from the 1736

Table 3.49   Establishment of Glass Manufactories

	Total Manufactories	"Possessional" Manufactories
1723–25	3	3
1726–40	1	1
1741–45	1	—
1746–50	11	8
1751–55	4	3
1756–60	7	2
Total	27	17

Source: Volodarskaia, "Sotsial'nyi sostav," p. 180.

Table 3.50   Labor Force in Possessional Glass Manufactories by Category

Category	No.	Masters
Ascripti	138	5
Purchased	223	4
Hired	268	9
Total	629	18

Source: Volodarskaia, "Sotsial'nyi sostav," p. 194.

enserfment of the skilled workers. In spite of the owners' clamor for *officinae ascripti*, the government attached no additional workers to the glass manufactories, and only a few entrepreneurs were able to shift this type of personnel from manufactories of other kinds in their possession. By the 1760s the total number enserfed under the 1736 decree, together with the former state serfs that were "attached" to the manufactories, was only 152 males, of whom 138 were actively engaged in the work of the enterprises. The main possible source of labor recruitment for newly established glass manufactories owned by merchants and foreigners was the acquisition by purchase of serfs. Until the decree of 1762 revoking the right to purchase serfs for employment in manufactories, entrepreneurs in the glass industry received permission to buy a total of 1,045 male serfs, of whom 930 were with land and 105 without land. Only a fraction of this permitted number of serfs was actually purchased by the glass entrepreneurs, primarily because of the difficulty of matching the location of the manufactory with the location of available serfs and the constraints provided by their actual available capital. Until 1751 only 96 male serfs with land were purchased; between 1751 and 1760 an additional 144 male serfs, including 47 without land, were purchased. The total reported number of purchased serfs by the possessional glass enterprises was 240.

The most interesting feature was not the acquisition of serfs, but the degree of their utilization in the enterprises. A Senate decree of June 6, 1752, established as one of the conditions for serf purchases by industrial enterprises a minimum employment of one-third of the number in industrial employment.

This was the approximate industrial employment of purchased serfs in the linen industry, and also in the silk industry for "possessional" manufactories. The setting of a minimum norm was clearly a compromise between the negative attitude of the nobility, which did not want to surrender its monopoly of serf ownership, and the government's views on the need for labor by the manufactories, tempered by the government's concern that a massive serf transfer to industrial labor would disrupt agriculture in some regions. The actual utilization of purchased serf labor in the glass manufactories reached the number of 223 serfs out of 240 purchased, a proportion that had no counterpart in any other industry. This indicates that there was a tight labor situation in the glass manufactories and a need for additional sources of labor. This is also demonstrated by the fact that 15 of the 17 "possessional" glass manufactories also employed hired labor. The distribution of the total labor force of the "possessional" glass manufactories in the early 1760s is presented in table 3.50, as estimated by the Soviet historian Volodarskaia.

Although the number of skilled workers among the hired ones was relatively high, there is some evidence that in their policies of training and apprenticeship the glass-factory owners preferred purchased serfs over hired ones to assure stability and continuity in production. An adequate labor supply was considered crucial for the operation of the enterprises.

It is difficult to analyze the production pattern of the glass manufactories on the basis of the available data. The data for the "possessional" manufactories, which were the leading glass enterprises in terms of size and value of output, indicate that the value of the average yearly output per employed worker was in the neighborhood of 60 rubles, a figure which would tend to support the claim of a significant role for the labor component in the total productivity factors.

Cotton Textiles

The cotton industry was represented in eighteenth-century Russia by two of its branches, cotton weaving and cotton printing. The raw material, cotton yarn, was imported from abroad. The Astrakhan' region of cotton-weaving worked on eastern cotton imported from Bukhara, Iran, and the Caucasus. The Baltic and Central regions (Moscow and Vladimir) worked exclusively on yarn imported from Britain. Cotton weaving in Russia started in the 1750–60s, but grew slowly by comparison with other branches of the textile industry. The reasons for the relatively slow growth can be explained by the high costs of raw materials and the competition from other fibers. The Russian climate made wool a preferable choice for winter clothing, and flax was a plausible substitute during the summer. Therefore, as long as cotton cloth or calico was produced by primitive methods and at relatively high cost, no ready market was available.

Cotton weaving benefited relatively little from government support. Most of the entrepreneurs were either merchants or peasants. The lack of government interference meant on the one hand a more limited inflow of resources, but on the other hand a lesser likelihood of monopolistic privileges and freer entrance into the industry. The absence of serf-owners among the entrepreneurs meant a larger share of freely hired labor in total employment by the industry and a wider and freer dissemination of skills. As a result, the growth of the industry depended not only upon supply factors, but also upon the nature of demand. On the supply side, it was the introduction of new technology which enabled cotton goods to compete with other fibers in the market by substantially lowering production costs. On the demand side, the growth of the urban population, the increase in incomes of the rural population, and the switch from homemade to manufactured cloth stimulated the growth of demand for cotton goods.

The data pertaining to cotton weaving do not allow us to follow the various phases in the development process of the industry, primarily because the minimal level of governmental involvement meant that few records were kept. The center of the industry gradually moved from Astrakhan' to the Central and Baltic regions, the volume of equipment increased to over 3,700 looms, and the total labor force rose to 6,566, of which 5,436 were freely hired workers.[74] The value of cotton-weaving output for 1799 was officially estimated at 1,963,000 rubles, exceeding the value of the output of the woolen industry.[75] In terms of the quantity of cotton goods, the output of 1804, which was close to that of 1799, was estimated at 4,287,659 arshins of calicoes, cloth, and other products.[76] The cotton-weaving industry conveys the impression of one that emerged from obscurity and came up fast in competition with the other branches of the textile industry.

Relatively more is known about the cotton-printing branch. It was introduced in Russia during the 1750–60s by foreigners, it was originally concentrated around St. Petersburg, and the printing was done on cloth supplied by clients, primarily importers of mitkal-calico.[77] These first enterprises were highly specialized. Printing was their sole task, and the manufactories had relatively large-scale output. The primitive equipment and the dissemination of skills resulted in the establishment of many craft-like enterprises in the industry. Some of these reached larger output capacities, while others were absorbed as auxiliary shops in cotton-weaving production.

According to official data, the cotton-printing industry comprised 43 enterprises, of which 17 represented larger, specialized enterprises (over 30 workers employed in each). Of them, 5 had more than one hundred workers each. By 1793 about 3,240,000 arshins of mitkal-calico were printed.[78]

During the second half of the 1790s the cotton-printing industry went through a period of severe crisis. Thomas Bell's invention of a mechanical, cylindrical printing press increased the productivity and lowered the costs of British printed-cotton goods, but the Russian techniques remained backward. In addition, the Russian tariff of 1797 raised fourfold the duty on mitkal-calico and left a 40 percent duty on other cotton goods. The result was a sharp decline of mitkal imports and printing. Thus the value of imports of mitkal-calico declined from 2,264,000 rubles in 1795 and 2,141,000 rubles in 1796 to 1,096,000 rubles in 1797. The printing of mitkals declined from 3,240,000 arshins in 1793 to a yearly average for 1797–1802 of 755,000 arshins. On the other hand, the imports of other cotton goods, primarily printed ones, tended to increase.[79]

The crisis had a differential effect upon various types of enterprises. The large-scale manufactories around St. Petersburg were severely affected, but the smaller-scale enterprises in the Vladimir and Moscow regions exhibited a greater flexibility and adaptability to the changing market conditions. The enterprises in the central regions undertook to print the domestically-produced mitkal manufactured by the cotton weavers located in their neighborhood and destined for local markets. In addition, they switched to the printing of other, cheaper calicoes and cotton kerchiefs, and found new outlets for their changing output assortment. The merchant and peasant entrepreneurs of the central regions, who themselves had acquired the skills of cotton-printing in the large manufactories, were the ones who changed the output mix of the industry. They introduced new organizational forms of production by combining manufactories with cottage-type industries and thus were able to weather the crisis better than the older, larger enterprises in the industry.

The cotton-goods industry in eighteenth-century Russia was entirely market-oriented. Even in its role of providing import substitutes it did not receive much assistance from the state. It had to compete with two older, more established, and state-supported industries, wool and linen, which were working with domestic raw materials. The cotton-goods industry owed its development to a large extent to the entrepreneurship of its founders and to the competitive spirit prevailing in it. It drew its labor from among the pool of full-time and part-time nonagricultural labor offered for hire. It operated on the fringes of, or even outside of, the prevailing serf economy. This was probably the central significance of the cotton-goods industry for the economic and social order in Russia during the eighteenth century. Its demonstration effect, slight at the beginning, was to become significantly more important during the nineteenth century.

Large- and Small-Scale Production

Industry and Craft

Industry in eighteenth-century Russia included various types of activity which converted both agricultural and mineral raw materials into semifinished or finished products with the use of tools brought into motion by human, animal, and water power. At this time the older Russian system of urban and rural crafts was challenged by larger-scale industrial production based primarily upon the use of waterpower and concentrated under a unified management and supervision of a large labor force in enterprises in which the division of labor was much more advanced than in the small scale scattered workshops. The large-scale enterprises, often described in the literature as "manufactories," were for the eighteenth century what the factories became in the nineteenth century: the modern, advanced, and dynamic sector in industry. It would be, however, a serious mistake of historical interpretation to assume that for Russia of the eighteenth century the manufactories were the typical or dominating enterprises. The confrontation between the small-scale and the large-scale industrial enterprises is probably the most interesting, although less heralded and poorly researched, chapter in the industrial history of the century.

Contrary to the experience of craftsmen in Western and Central Europe, Russian craftsmen and artisans did not possess an organization, like the traditional guild, that was powerful enough to protect their interests against competition. The existing guild-type organizations were too weak, politically and economically, to offer a meaningful resistance. Moreover, a sizable portion of the resources for the large-scale enterprises were originally provided by the state. The state also provided monopoly rights for the manufacture of various products.

There were clearly areas of industrial activity, and very conspicuous ones, in which the competition between small-scale and large-scale production was soon over. Due to economies of scale, mining and metallurgy turned out to be such industries. But even there it was necessary for the government to intervene in order to assure an early victory for the large-scale enterprises.

In a number of industries, however, small-scale industrial workshops, including rural cottage industry as well as urban artisans' workshops, remained competitive with large-scale production and continued to expand their production.

The relationship between small and large production enterprises described above depended to a considerable extent upon the nature of consumption by the population and upon the structure of various markets. The vast majority of the population consumed a narrow range and limited volume of industrial consumer goods, while much of the articles, even of clothing and footwear, and almost all of processed food products, were produced within the household. The goods acquired by the population in the market were consumed in small quantities. This caused a diffusion over dispersed markets, and some of the advantages of economies of scale in production and distribution were thereby lost. We must also recall that transportation and transaction costs to distant and dispersed markets often offset economies of scale in large-scale production enterprises.

Large-scale production by manufactories required a mass demand and a concentration of consumers in large population centers, something that was largely absent in eighteenth-century Russia. It is no wonder, therefore, why large-scale production did relatively well in cases where output could be either sold abroad in large quantities or delivered to the government under special bulk-purchase contracts, or sent to such population centers as Moscow and St. Petersburg. It performed less well in catering to the provincial and rural markets, in which small-scale cottage-type industries not only survived, but thrived, during the eighteenth century.

The competition between large- and small-scale enterprises varied in intensity, and its outcome differed from one industry to another. In the iron industry, the competition between small forges, operated by village smiths and based upon local bog-ores, and the newly built furnaces and forges in the Urals region at the beginning of the century provided a clear advantage to the Urals ironworks, assisted by the high iron content of the ores, cheapness of fuel, availability of waterpower, and quality of the iron products. Nevertheless, it was the government which not only mobilized some of the small producers, resettled them into the Urals, and attached them as foremen and workers to the large ironworks, but also prohibited small-scale local production of iron outside the government-licensed and the government-owned ironworks, which thereby eliminated the small producers. One cannot be certain whether the new technology and the economies of scale of the large metallurgical enterprises would have been viable without government support or would have succeeded in eliminating small competitors. The large iron producers were certainly aided by the low costs for transportation of iron from the Urals via the waterways to the population centers of Russia.

Two branches of craft and industry in which large-scale production could not compete with small-scale output were the leather and flour-milling branches. In tanning and leather manufacturing the economies of scale in production, given the traditional technology, were not significant; even in the case when foreign production techniques were adopted, quality improved only at an increase in cost. There is evidence on this subject, such as Peter the Great's draconian decrees forbidding the tanning of leather by the use of tar-products instead of by his recommended "foreign" blubber-oil recipes. Most of the consumers continued to buy the cheaper, and perhaps coarser and less durable, old-style leather which hundreds or even thousands of tanneries and leather shops continued to produce, even in the face of threats of severe punishment. In one case involving government military contracts, large-scale production was introduced by pooling small production facilities under a unified management employing "foreign" production methods and producing products of uniform quality. In a few instances similar arrangements were made to meet the consumption needs of the upper classes, but these were limited segments of the market, and in the rural market the small producer maintained his share vis-à-vis the leather manufactories. Even in the case of the foreign market, the demand was strong for the tanned hides and raw leather known as *iuft'* (or *iuften* in German), typically cheap products of small shops. High-quality leather goods were not exported from Russia, but imported into Russia.

Most, if not all, of the commercial flour output came from small mills located on the banks of various rivers and streams. All attempts to increase production resulted in a multiplication of the number rather than of the size of flour mills. If flour had become a major export commodity, attempts might have been made to compel the construction of larger enterprises, particularly in the ports. But even the size of the Moscow and St. Petersburg flour markets did not result in a development of a local flour milling industry, but only in the growth of the number of flour mills along the waterways leading to both markets. The reasons for this pattern should be sought in the costs of storage or in other factors.

What has been said about flour-milling was also true for the processing of most of the other agricultural products, such as vegetable oil. The mills for seed-crushing remained relatively small enterprises and exhibited no tendencies toward rapid growth in size. Perhaps the only branch of food processing in which growth of the producing units is clearly visible was alcohol distilling. It is possible that certain economies of scale could have been realized by increasing the scale of distillery production. Nevertheless, the growth of those enterprises can more likely be attributed to other stimuli. Since contracts for the delivery of alcohol were awarded first to nobles and merchants, and after 1753 exclusively to nobles, the size of the contracts often determined the volume of production of various distilleries. Since neither the raw materials (grain), fuel (wood), and construction materials, nor labor were constraints upon production, and as government advances could provide the necessary capital for equipment, well-connected noblemen were capable of setting up large distilleries with a high degree of certainty of being awarded delivery contracts. Since the transportation facilities were provided by the serfs of the estates, the distribution of production among various cities or concentration in one city did not present any major problem for the noblemen-entrepreneurs. Differential delivery prices by region, depending upon the long-term average costs of grain, further diminished risk. Thus we encounter a situation in which large and small distilleries were not really competing among themselves, but rather followed the award of government contracts. Scale was a function of contract size. When contracts were awarded below the production capacity of some distilleries, that did not affect the capability of the distilleries to produce below-capacity output since the profit margin was sufficiently high to compensate for any underutilized capacity. The general trend in alcohol consumption and sales was upward, with yearly variations. Technological improvements, not related to size, kept on increasing the volume of output per unit of raw materials. Under such circumstances the above-output capacity of distilleries was not necessarily an economic vice on the part of producers who, as a group, were monopolists in the government-regulated market.

The most interesting and significant cases of competition between rural crafts and the newly established manufactories are to be found in the area of textile production. Russia in the eighteenth century relied much more upon flax and hemp than on wool, silk, or cotton in the consumption of fibers. Russia was also a major exporter of hemp and flax to the rest of the world. Linen, particularly of the narrow, coarse type of rural cottage-production, was a standard item in Russian exports even before the eighteenth century. Most of the flax and hemp not exported was processed and either consumed directly within the households or sold by rural craftsmen.

Two basic activities were involved: spinning and weaving. Of the two, spinning was the more labor-intensive, but it was done mostly by female labor at a

time of year when there were no other work opportunities. This basic process, which required no
specialized training and very little in the way of tools
(a distaff and a spinning wheel), created a product,
yarn, which was both transportable and marketable.
Flax and hemp were grown mostly in the north and
northwest of Russia; hemp was grown further south
than flax, and required a more fertile soil, although it
did well also on the gray soils when natural fertilizer
was applied. Consequently the southern provinces of
Russia, while exporting grain and cattle to the north,
imported yarn from the flax and hemp regions.

The cottage-type linen industry in eighteenth-
century Russia, specializing in the production of yarn
and linen for the market, grew at the expense of
production designated for home consumption only.
It is difficult to ascertain the pace of this process,
which involved not only the growth of linen production for the market in the nonblacksoil zone, but also
the growth of linen output in areas which imported
yarn. Scattered evidence suggests that during the
eighteenth century the per capita output of linen
increased for the rural population as a whole and the
volume of the marketable linen produced by rural
crafts was an increasing share of total linen production. For a more detailed analysis, one would have to
add to the volume of yarn produced by small enterprises for home consumption and by cottage industry
a substantial part of the yarn-spinning done for the
manufactories. Such work, under contract between
the manufactories and the rural cottage-industry,
increased the volume of spinning done by the rural
spinners.

It is possible to trace the overall growth of the rural
cottage production of linen by tracing the development of this industry in particular districts. Cottage
industry working for the market grew not only in the
"industrial village," where we have evidence
throughout the century, but in villages not formerly
producing for the market. While the cottage industry
increased its output of yarn, expanded its production
of narrow linen, and supplied increasing quantities to
the market, it encountered intense competition from
the manufactories in a growing segment of linen
output. The competition of the cottage industry with
the manufactories was primarily in the weaving of
broad linen, where the manufactories had a clear
advantage for the simple reason that broad looms did
not fit into most peasant dwellings, and investment
in special buildings and larger looms was beyond the
means of many rural producers and at least tended to
raise the costs of small-scale production.

The production-cost advantage enjoyed by manufactories over small-scale producers of broad linen
was supplemented by an advantage stemming from
the costs of distribution. The manufactories dealt
directly with exporters, government contractors, or
wholesale merchants. This decreased the distribution
costs in comparison with those of small producers,
who sold their output at the local market or nearby
fairs to purchasers who in turn resold the output in
larger quantities to merchants. In spite of the rapid
growth of linen manufactories, their labor force,
number of looms, and size of output, the small
producers appear to have held their ground until at
least the 1770s, when they slowly yielded to the
competition of the manufactories.

The wool industry had a somewhat different pattern of development. In quantitative terms, the domestic output was probably about 20 to 25 percent of
the output of the linen industry. Much of its raw
material was "imported" from the southern and
southeastern regions of the country into the central
and northern regions. Apart from the household
wool production processed for cloth, hats, felt boots,
and other uses, the marketed wool was distributed
between the small-scale producers and the
manufactories. Given the technology of cloth-
making, apart from spinning, larger investments and
more specialized labor of higher skill were required in
the wool industry than in the linen industry. Consequently, one would expect rather early to encounter a
more specialized and trained labor force, one that
would work for the market, local or regional, rather
than for home consumption. Woolens were a higher-
value product than linen, a fact which favored a
higher degree of regional concentration of production
because the wool cloth could be transported over
greater distances with transportation costs amounting to a smaller percentage of the selling price than
for linen transported over the same distance.

Until about the 1760s there was very little competition between the small-scale producers and the
woolen manufactories, which were set up primarily
to assure an adequate supply of army cloth. A fragmentation of the market can be observed. The
manufactories were awarded a segment of the market
and sheltered from competition, worked under long-
term government contracts, and used in many cases
the wool output of their estates and the labor of their
serfs turned into workers. Only when the productive
capacity of the manufactories exceeded their delivery
quotas for army cloth did they begin to compete for
the civilian market with the small-scale producers. In
terms of quality, both groups of producers specialized in coarse woolens (the more expensive woolens
were imported from abroad), and thus competition
might have become fierce had the size of the market
not expanded. But it was expanding, as a result of
territorial expansion, population growth, and rising
incomes, and therefore it cannot be assumed that
small-scale production was decreasing as a result of

the competition from the expanding woolen manufactories.

The silk industry had an interesting but somewhat obscure history. The skill of silk spinning and weaving was imported from abroad by manufactories that were established with state support in the second decade of the century and that specialized in import substitution of expensive silk-wares. By the 1760s and 1770s there were in Moscow province a large number of small-scale craft shops engaged in the manufacturing of ribbons and kerchiefs, items of mass consumption. Although the process of skill acquisition is obscure, we can conjecture that former employees of the manufactories who either hired themselves out or were hired out by their owners acquired the production skills, subsequently left the manufactories, and set themselves up in business. Their number rose quickly, and until the end of the century they dominated the market for relatively cheap silk products used by the rural population.

The cotton-goods industry, including spinning, weaving, and dyeing, was almost entirely represented during the eighteenth century by either commercial small-scale production or by small-scale enterprises in the process of expansion. It largely used the skills accumulated in the linen industry, supplemented by additional training. It located itself in the regions in which such labor skills and resources were available, in the nonblacksoil zone. The few manufactories established prior to the abolition of the license system had only a slight impact upon the industry, and their methods of dyeing cotton cloth could be adopted with relative ease by the small producers.

Most of the entrepreneurs in the cotton industry were of serf origin and remained in the rural areas, where they drew upon the labor of the countryside and sold in the rural markets. Thus the development of the cotton industry was similar to some of the early phases of the linen industry, except that the subsequent transition that took place in the nineteenth century was not one from small-scale producing units to manufactories, but to a more modern factory system based upon steam-powered, capital-intensive technology, a large-scale factory labor force, and supported by a highly developed putting-out system.

Until the 1770s, small-scale production carried on by serfs and using nonfamily labor was prohibited by the government in order to strengthen the monopoly rights granted to the manufactories under the system of licenses introduced by the College of Manufactures and the Mining College. Surviving decrees and other documents show clearly that the government assumed that serfs who did not possess their own juridical identity would not make good entrepreneurs and that their role ought to be limited to toiling on the land or in the manufactories. However, the government was constantly aware of the fact that, in spite of its decrees and actual attempts to suppress the serfs' industrial market activity, small-scale enterprises in the rural areas and even in the urban areas existed and did not cease to function. A special term was coined for the illegally functioning enterprises, (neukaznye). It seems logical to assume that such enterprises paid a price for their de facto existence, one that either raised the cost of their products or reduced their profits, or both. The liberalization of government policies permitting the existence of such enterprises and abolishing the requirement to obtain licenses had the effect of removing some of their disadvantages vis-à-vis their adversaries, the manufactories. It is also possible, however, that the abolition of the licensing system permitted many newcomers to enter the ranks of small-scale producers, thereby decreasing the average return on labor and capital in this particular branch of industry. The available evidence does not permit a firm judgment about the direction of change.

During the first half of the century, given the legal disabilities of the small-scale producers, the process of capital accumulation was slow and the establishment of larger-scale production required, apart from capital, traveling the tortuous road of state licensing, which had set up barriers in the form of requiring the status of either merchant or nobleman. The growth of enterprises was accelerated by the abolition of the licensing and by the guberniia reform, which raised the status of many rural population centers to that of cities. A city charter bestowed upon inhabitants the status of burghers or merchants, and removed further obstacles to the expansion of enterprises. The process of capital accumulation in industry, primarily through plowing profits back into the enterprises, proceeded more smoothly and rapidly.

Expansion of production proceeded along two routes. One was via the putting-out system, which collected the production of diffused small-scale producers through a system of delivery contracts, advances for future production, and the distribution of raw materials and even tools to households and other small producers. The second was by the route of concentration of a labor force in a larger enterprise with more numerous tools or machinery and utilizing waterpower as an energy source, in other words, by establishing manufactories.

The choice between the two routes of transformation of small- into large-scale production enterprises depended not only upon the capital resources of the entrepreneur, the relative availability of labor of different skills, and the risk preferences of the entrepreneurs, but also upon the nature of the industry (the degree of required or preferred integration of the production process), the location with respect to supplies of raw materials, and the distance from markets. Some chose horizontal expansion with or without changing the technology, some vertical integration, and some a combination of both, such as the diffused putting-out system of spinning yarn combined with the establishment of a manufactory specializing in cloth-weaving.

Apart from the economic and organizational features of the transformation of small- into large-scale production, a significant social aspect was present. Capital accumulation in Russian industry was retarded as a result of the nobility status acquired by the outstanding industrial dynasties in Russia during the eighteenth century, the revenues and profits being siphoned off to provide for the life style of Russian aristocrats, as was the case with the Stroganovs, Demidovs, and other families. Intermarriage with aristocratic families led to further alienation of industrial profits from industry and, in some cases, to total withdrawal from industrial activity (the Miasnikovs, Pokhodiashins, and others). Under such circumstances, the process of capital accumulation and the growth of small- into large-scale enterprises which took place at the lower layers of the industrial pyramid acquired additional significance. Thus the degree of capital accumulation achieved in small-scale productive enterprises had not only to provide the funds for the expansion (or transformation) of these enterprises; it also had to compensate at least in part for the decrease in the rate of accumulation that took place among some of the larger enterprises. The social aspects suggest the existence of mobility in and out of industrial entrepreneurship in the eighteenth century, a process which accelerated during the last third of the century.

Manufactories

A manufactory is defined as an industrial enterprise in which waterpower is used as the primary source of energy, a relatively large number of workers are concentrated within a confined area (or buildings), in which the division of labor is more advanced than in the artisan shop, and the work force is employed under a unified system of supervision. The technical management of a manufactory might, or might not, be separated from the business management, but both, whether separately or jointly, are subordinated to a unified set of rules or administrative decisions. Whether ownership is separated from technical management or from business administration is of less importance as long as both of the latter are subordinated to the decisions of the owner, whether the

owner be an individual, a partnership, or the government.

There were no rules establishing the minimum or maximum size of manufactories, but contemporaries readily understood which type of enterprises required state licensing and thus qualified legally as a manufactory. An enterprise using waterpower, and thus requiring land in a particular location, one working for the market and aspiring to monopoly rights, tax exemptions, direct subsidies, labor allocations, and government contracts classified itself as a manufactory.

Manufactories in Russia go back to the seventeenth century and are as much a part of the pan-European phenomenon of Dutch entrepreneurship in many countries on the European continent (France, Sweden, and Denmark were the most significant areas) as they are a manifestation of the Russian desire to lessen industrial dependence upon the rest of Europe. The seventeenth-century experience did not result in continuously functioning enterprises, however, and even the most successful one, the ironworks of Tula and Kashira, became only a shadow of its original self after it was turned over to Russian management. Perhaps the most important reason for the failures of the seventeenth-century manufactories was the continuous isolation of Russia during the period, which did not permit the continuity of skill acquisition and managerial and entrepreneurial talent necessary to sustain the momentum of the development of manufactories.

The founding of manufactories for all practical purposes had to start afresh in the eighteenth century, when the mistakes of the previous century were avoided by making the effort on a larger scale, by providing continuity, and by keeping the door open for a continuous infusion of foreign skills until the native labor force acquired the necessary knowledge and working habits. In the seventeenth century all manufactories were organized by foreign entrepreneurs, but during the eighteenth century the government encouraged Russian merchants, and also some nobles, to enter the field of industrial entrepreneurship. A review of the social origin of eighteenth-century industrial entrepreneurs clearly reveals the preponderance of members of the Russian merchant class in most industries. This represented a transfer of capital from commerce into industrial production. There was also a transfer of capital which originated in the government sector, mostly of agricultural origin, and another transfer of capital from agriculture to industry by the noblemen entrepreneurs.

Given the variety of sources for the capital endowment of industry, one might not assume that there was a dearth of capital for industry. However, given the primitive state of property rights in Russia and the vicissitudes of governmental economic and social policies, the risk factor appears to have been substantial. Unless the government provided guarantees, subsidies, and monopolies, which can be considered almost as a form of government partnership in the industrial enterprises, private capital was not forthcoming. An extreme form, apart from exclusive government ownership, was assumption by the government of all the capital expenditures and the transfer of an equipped enterprise, as a gift, to private ownership. Although such cases were an extreme form of government participation in the capital endowment of manufactories, it would probably be more proper to consider them on economic grounds as a payment for entrepreneurial and administrative talents of individual entrepreneurs in areas of high priority for the government. Although from the point of view of government expenditures the difference between extensive subsidies and outright gifts was of a quantitative nature, qualitatively the practice of exchanging government gifts for valuable service was a commonplace practice. (This was evident in the enormous gifts distributed by the Russian rulers to various favorites, members of the ruling elite, mostly in the form of land grants or grants of thousands of serfs.)

The problem of capital scarcity was serious but not insurmountable. It seems not to have been the limiting factor in the development of manufactories during the eighteenth century.

A much more serious constraint, from time to time, appears to have been the size and skill-composition of the industrial labor force. It is necessary to distinguish at the outset of the century between the supply of unskilled labor, freely available, and the supply of skilled labor. The presence of a large number of Russians still unattached by enserfment legislation to particular lords, individuals, or institutions, made the supply of hired labor adequate for the purposes of the manufactories. The employment of unattached individuals, fugitive serfs, or seasonal workers provided the necessary supply of this type of labor for the manufactories.

This situation changed radically as a result of the Northern War and the first population census (reviziia). Although the Northern War added to the number of fugitive peasants and to a general relocation of population, it was marked also by population losses which diminished the supply of labor. The population census attached most of the population that was still free to private or institutional serf owners and thereby diminished the pool of potential labor for hire. Under the pressure of the serf-owners, the government forbade industrial enterprises to hire fugitive serfs and forced them to return those previously hired to their original owners. (An exception

was made for the serfs who had acquired skills. They could be retained upon payment of compensation to their owners.)

The result was that within a short period labor for the manufactories became scarce to the extent that the government was forced to apportion state serfs to enterprises in lieu of the previously available labor for hire. With the narrowing of the labor market, the supply of labor for the industrial sector had to be met through nonmarket channels, through the application of forced labor. This conclusion could be questioned by asking whether the transfer of labor by the government differed only formally from similar arrangements for hire by serf-owners or by the serfs themselves. There is, however, indisputable evidence that the attachment of labor to the manufactories was accompanied by official (plakat) daily wages below the market wage-rate, even in the case where the obligation of the serfs to the enterprise was limited to the size of their taxes to the government. Additional evidence suggests that the administered wage was below the serfs' opportunity costs of work, for some of them paid double the plakat wage for substitutes. The employment of labor provided by the government to the manufactories clearly involved involuntary labor and a subsidy to the manufactory owners paying this group of employees a below-market wage.

The situation for the supply of skilled labor was somewhat different from that for unskilled labor, although some parallels between the two can be drawn. A special category of skilled labor was that of the foreign specialists working under short-term contracts who were paid very high wages. In some areas, such as mining, manufacturing, and shipbuilding, the wages of foreign specialists were very high indeed to attract skilled men to Russia.

Their wages were high not only in terms of Russian prices for necessities and thus in terms of Russian wages, but also in terms of the higher wage-level abroad. Within a generation or so the wages of foreign specialists began to decrease as a result of the decreasing scarcity of their skills and of the availability of domestic substitutes. Still, foreign specialists were continuously brought to work, to train, and to advise in the production process of the Russian manufactories. The demand for these specialists, although shifting from one industry to another, was sustained during the eighteenth century as a result of the increasing number of Russian manufactories and their spread from one industry to another.

The problem of the Russian skilled-labor force was handled in quite a different way. The general scarcity of industrial labor, the immobility imposed by the population censuses, and the required period of skill acquisition, with the consequent increased competition for skilled labor, led to a solution typical for a serf regime: the immobilization of the skilled laborers and their families at the manufactories where they were previously employed under contracts of hire. Their immobilization not only prevented them from leaving their work places or from obtaining a rise in wages, but it also assured that they would transfer their skills to designated apprentices or, following their preferences, to their own offspring.

After 1736 there was a new category of skilled industrial workers in the manufactories, presumably previously free men, deprived of their freedom of mobility, who were converted into *officinae ascripti*. Assured of a minimum skilled labor supply, the owners of the manufactories were able to recruit additions to this core from among purchased serfs and serfs hiring themselves out under contract.

The labor force of the manufactories consisted almost exclusively of serfs, regardless of skill levels. Some economic historians have found it significant to distinguish between owned serfs and hired ones. It is really significant only to the extent that the hired ones indicate the existence of a suppressed labor market, in which even serf-owners were forced to resort to hire and money wage payments. However, this in and by itself is no indication of the role of money wages, since they were very often paid to the owners of serfs as well. Money wages in the manufactories were used not only as a form of labor compensation but as an incentive for work. With the separation of the industrial labor force from agriculture (which in rural areas did not always involve the confiscation of the workers' land, but rather enabled them to tend only a garden plot either at "home" or at their places of industrial employment, which were too far from their villages to permit them to work in the fields), wages became a necessity. They were often used as an incentive to underscore differential payments. Some owners of manufactories such as the Batashev ironworks preferred to pay the whole wage rather than to deduct the tax payments (of the poll tax or even the *obrok)* and to have the taxes collected separately. In addition, the monetization of the Russian economy obviously stimulated the use of money payments in all kinds of transactions, wage transactions included.

Although the majority of the manufactories' labor force was of serf origin and was an extension of the serf system into industrial labor, toward the end of the century hire contracts became more numerous and some influx of free labor into the manufactories became discernible.

The output of the manufactories was increasing, and one must ask about the contributions they made to the growth, development, and transformation of the Russian economy and society. Did their output constitute a net addition to the industrial production of Russia, or did it merely constitute a substitute for goods produced previously by some other methods or by different types of firms? Focusing on the iron-works and the textile industries, one can answer that most of the addition to the total industrial production contributed by manufactories in those two important industries was a net addition rather than a substitute. Both the location of the ironworks and the size of their production suggest that the small-scale mode of producing iron in Russia would hardly have achieved such a production level within a similar time period under the most favorable conditions, including the presence of government subsidies. This was true for pig iron and bar iron, and also for heavy armaments, such as field and naval guns, which were produced by the ironworks more efficiently than they would have been in small enterprises. Although noneconomic means were used to eliminate small-scale iron production in favor of the newly established iron-works, most of the output of the latter was a net addition, produced at costs which did not exceed the costs of alternative producers.

The case of the textile industry was more complicated. There was a degree of competition and substitution in the spinning and the weaving of narrow linen and coarse wool cloth (*sermiazhnoe sukno*) as well as wool lining (*karazeia*). It is difficult to ascertain whether the costs of production of those commodities were cheaper in the manufactories than in the craft establishments. Be that as it may, the wages in the small enterprises or in the households were obviously lower than in the manufactories, even for the same skill level. Within the manufactory, labor could presumably be utilized more intensively. The technological advantages and the savings on distribution costs of the manufactories obviously had to outweigh the difference in wages in order for the manufactory to produce goods more cheaply than did the small-scale producers.

In the production of other types of textile goods the manufactories made a clear contribution. Russian producers had no natural monopoly outside of the assortment of goods produced by the small-scale producers, and it is reasonable to assume that these goods were largely substitutes or near substitutes for goods imported into Russia from abroad. The ability to produce import substitutes was one of the marks of the manufactories, for even their primitive technology enabled the production of uniform-quality goods to a greater extent than was possible in small-scale production. The output of import substitutes and new types of products very often became the domain of manufactory production and to this extent provided a net addition to domestic industrial output.

The social impact of the manufactories has to be viewed from the aspects of both the industrialists and the laborers. The industrialists represented a privileged stratum within the Russian merchant group whose status was enhanced both by economic power and by contacts with the state bureaucracy. Such exalted status enabled the richest among them to acquire nobility patents or to intermarry with the nobility. They guarded their privileges and operated under the umbrella of state tutelage.

The labor force of the manufactories was set apart socially from the other population groups. In purely economic terms, as measured by incomes, that labor force was not equal to the other serf groups and in many cases was superior; by the standards of social status, however, it was thought inferior. The social attitude grew out of the hierarchy of control, dependence, pressure, or absence of customary obligations between master and dependent. On that scale manufactory workers appeared lower than ordinary agricultural serfs. Perhaps the lack of any property or, to be more precise, the lack of any customary claim to perpetual rights of users, played an important role in downgrading the status of the workers. In this sense, they were a new social group, poorly integrated into the existing social system.

Location Problems of the Manufactories

Economic factors explain most of the decisions made to locate industrial enterprises. Some of the decisions, such as the encouragement to set up various industries in the vicinity of St. Petersburg, however, were directed to noneconomic goals. In competitive industries, the market directed the natural selection of firms that made correct decisions to locate efficiently. These forces acted even on monopolists for whom the saving in costs in locating advantageously was a powerful incentive.

Location decisions involved two fundamental economic considerations: the share of transportation costs in the total sales price of the final product; the share of transportation costs in the costs of production, including the transportation costs of the supply of raw materials and the wage differential between various locations.

Location problems were of considerable importance in Russia both for the agrarian and the industrial sectors of the economy. The enormous size of the country and its uneven population density made overcoming distances and decreasing the costs of transport among the pivotal problems of the Russian economy through the ages. Because of the distances involved, it took Russia much longer to develop a national market than other similarly backward countries which enjoyed a similar degree of population density. In the case of numerous commodities of which a marketable surplus was produced, there existed in eighteenth-century Russia a number of distinct, separate markets with marked differences in price trends. The investment in waterways and roads, a part of the social overhead capital made during the period under review, contributed in some cases to progress toward the formation of a national market, but it was inadequate for the purpose of economic integration of the various regions of Russia. All estimates of the size of employment in transportation exceed the size of employment in the industrial sector of the economy. Because of climatic conditions, waterway transportation as well as road transportation was marked by seasonal patterns, and consequently it is difficult to measure and estimate the size of their labor forces. The sheer bulk of the industrial output and agricultural marketable surplus transported over long distances point to a relatively high input of labor. Apart from the problems of transporting final output to market, whether domestic or foreign, the problem of the distribution of raw materials for industry was particularly acute in Russia.

The raw materials for most of the metal products were located at great distances from the major population centers. The raw materials for some branches of the textile industry were located in more densely populated areas. Taking into account the labor intensity of the production of the two types of raw materials, neither was an accident, but geography nevertheless became one of the determinants of the location of the two most important industries in the eighteenth century.

Iron was a preeminent case of a commodity in which the transportation costs constituted a very sizable portion of the sale price. The distance between the main producing areas, in the Urals, and the consuming areas was compensated for by the high ore content and the availability of fuel resources nearby the ironworks. The high quality and the huge quantities of the Urals ore, in contradistinction to the bog ores in the northwestern and central regions of Russia, and the almost unlimited forest resources which assured capacity output for many decades without an increase in the costs of the ore and fuel compensated for the transportation costs of the iron to the market, which constituted from 20 to 25 percent of the sales price. Table 3.51 illustrates the level of the transportation costs of state-produced iron from the Urals to the St. Petersburg market.

The fluctuations in the costs of transportation were due less to changes in prices or wages and more to the duration of the trip by the "iron caravans" and losses sustained during the navigation and the winter stop, which involved the unloading and loading of the iron on boats. A proper procedure of economic

Table 3.51   Transportation Costs of State Iron Output from
Ekaterinburg to St. Petersburg

Year	Transportation Costs (kopeks/pood)	Transportation Costs as % of Sale Price
1730	9.75	16.25
31	9.75	16.25
32	9.125	15.21
33	8.78125	14.64
34	8.875	14.8
1735	8.25	13.75
36	7.6875	12.8
37	10.25	17.1
38	10.0	16.67
39	10.75	17.92
1740	12.8125	21.35
41	14.625	24.375
42	11.96875	19.95

Source: Pavlenko, *Razvitie*, p. 270.

calculation would require the addition to the direct transportation costs of an interest charge for the capital tied up in the caravans in view of the fact that the journey usually lasted about fourteen or fifteen months. (This capital charge must also be considered when calculating the profit rate of the industry. The government reporting may have underestimated the actual transportation costs since some labor and materials charges may have been excluded from its calculations.)

The data on the transport of iron by the Demidovs, the largest and most efficient private iron producers in Russia, show that the high proportion of transportation costs to sale price was not a phenomenon restricted to the state-owned enterprises and did not change much over the course of the century. The costs of transportation from the Urals to St. Petersburg constituted 20 percent of the sale price in 1744 (12 kopeks of 60 kopeks) and 20.5 percent in 1770 (15 kopeks of 73 kopeks) for the Demidov enterprises. Their average share of transportation costs to all markets was 19 percent.[80]

The relatively high costs of transportation were made bearable because of the availability of waterways. Overland, such costs would have been prohibitive. These transportation costs were compensated for by the proximity of two necessary raw material inputs, ore and fuel, in combination with water resources as the source of motive power. However, this happy combination of raw materials and waterpower would not have been sufficient by itself to compensate for the transportation costs and other charges which had to be added as a result of the location of the ironworks in the Urals. The major additional source of compensation for the Urals ironworks was labor costs, which were kept below the market wage. Labor costs constituted the major portion of the production costs of pig iron and the

overwhelming share of the cost of iron production, and thus "economizing" on production costs in the Urals ironworks meant trying to decrease labor costs.

Transportation costs were significant even in optimal instances when there was a cluster of ore mines in the midst of abundant fuel resources located at a suitable river. Under the most auspicious circumstances of location, such as those prevailing in the Demidov ironworks of Neviansk and Nizhnii Tagil, where both fuel and ore were very close to the ironworks, the charcoal transportation costs comprised from one-quarter to one-third of the costs of charcoal production and the ore transportation costs about one-third of the total costs of ore to the ironworks.[81] We must recall also that the high iron content of the ore enabled producers to use relatively little ore for pig-iron production, and thus held down transportation costs.

The situation was entirely different in the case of silver smelting, where the silver content of the ore was about 2 or 3 percent, instead of the 50 to 60 percent of iron in Demidov's iron ore. The internal transportation costs made up the lion's share of the costs of silver production. Because of the high transportation costs, it paid to subdivide the smelting process into two separate technological processes, that is, to have an enriching plant at the ore mines to produce a reduced volume of ore for transport to the smelters, in cases when the absence of power and fuel did not permit construction of a smelter at the mine sites.

A similar situation prevailed in copper smelting, where the determinants of location were the location of the ores, fuel, and motive power, and where major attempts were made to minimize the internal transportation costs of ore and fuel to the smelter. Contemporaries exclaimed about the location of copper smelters in "nonaccessible, undeveloped regions of the Southern Urals and Bashkiriia," and the notorious lack of roads. Very little attention was paid in the case of copper to the transportation costs of the final product, since the per unit sales price of copper exceeded that of iron by about ten times. With the internal transportation costs of the final product minimized and thus constituting a relatively small share of the sale price, the cost of the labor input became a major limiting factor. The manpower problem of the copperworks was solved without upsetting the location advantages of the other factors of production, considered the determinant ones, by employing either available freely hired labor, which had few alternative opportunities to earn money wages, or serf labor, which was mobile within the gentry estates, or state peasants, whose mobility was limited by their attachment to the copperworks.

In the case of ironmaking (distinct from pig iron production), the availability of motive power to convert pig iron into iron was so important that this became one of the chief determinants of location. Pig iron as a raw material for the manufacturing of the final product was often shipped where waterways existed. Motive power, rather than any potential raw materials supply, usually determined the number of hammers, and thus the productive capacity of a plant. The supply of raw materials was often adjusted to the manufacturing capacity of the ironworks, which was in turn determined by the supply of motive power.

The location problems of the textile industries were determined much less by the transportation costs of the raw materials or the availability of motive power than by proximity to the market for final products and the availability of labor and skills. In the case of silk weaving, the raw material was imported and the transportation costs were negligible by comparison with the value of the products. What really mattered were the skills available, which were found within and around Moscow, which was also one of the largest markets in the country, with relatively easy access to the other major markets. Given the market responsiveness of the silk-weaving industry, it is not surprising that proximity to markets was a primary consideration for the location of the industry.

A similar situation existed in the wool industry, both for domestic wool and, by the end of the century, the increasing quantities of imported wool. The chief determinant of the location of wool-cloth manufactories was the availability of labor in the proximity of the major consumer, chiefly the offices of the quartermaster general in Moscow. In the wool-cloth industry, and to an even greater extent in the linen industry, the location problem was often reduced to the urban versus rural decision. Such a decision depended in part upon the social status of the entrepreneur, whether gentry or merchant. A member of the nobility usually had available his own or purchased serfs, whereas a merchant had to hire labor. The nobleman therefore often had labor of lower productivity. He needed also less operating capital, while the merchant had labor of higher productivity but in turn had higher operating capital expenses. In the case of the linen industry, the preference for rural location could probably also be explained by the availability of labor for spinning either in the manufactories or in the homes of the peasants (a form of cottage industry), combined with the proximity to the source of raw materials supply, the production centers of flax and hemp. Perhaps the only branch of the textile industry which was located near the source of raw materials was cotton printing, set up at the outset in St. Petersburg because it concentrated originally on printing imported white cotton goods. Subsequently, when the cotton industry established itself around Moscow, the cotton printing branch moved there.

In summary, in industries in which the costs of moving raw materials were much higher than the costs of moving labor, the location of the raw materials (including motive power) determined the location of the plants. The silver and copper industries were the extreme cases. In the iron industry, the predominance of the Urals location over the Central Russia location (see table 3.52) was determined by the low costs of raw materials, regardless of the higher costs of transportation and somewhat higher costs of labor.

The Social Origin of the Entrepreneurs

For two major industries in eighteenth-century Russia, textiles and iron, the social origins of the entrepreneurs, the founders of enterprises, can be established with a sufficient degree of accuracy. A study of entrepreneurship in both industries provides broad insights into the economic fabric and social dynamics of the industrial sector. Textiles present a more typical example of the social origins of entrepreneurs for other branches of manufacturing than does the iron industry. The degree of competition was originally greater in the textile industry than in the iron industry, and the degree of concentration (however measured) diminished over time. In addition, with entry into the textile industry requiring smaller, more easily divisible investment, that industry enjoyed a larger number of suppliers of the raw materials and sold much of its output in the internal market. As time passed, the larger number of entrepreneurs had more scope for initiative.

The available data on the social origin of the entrepreneurs in the textile industry can be presented for the industry as a whole, indicating the scope of entrepreneurial activity during the various periods of the eighteenth century. Table 3.53 shows both the number of entrants and their social origin.

The distribution of entrepreneurs by their social origin for the entire textile industry obscures very significant differences existing within the industry among the major branches. These were linen, wool, and silk production, with cotton printing and manufacturing coming into prominence only during the last quarter of the century. The social origins of the entrepreneurs among the major branches for the first three-quarters of the eighteenth century are presented in table 3.54.

The pioneering role of the merchant entrepreneurs is clear. Except for wool manufacturing (in which the state had a particular interest through its demand for

Table 3.52   Geographic Distribution of Private Iron- and Copperworks

Years	Urals and Siberia					Moscow Region					Olonets Region				
	Constructed	Received from State	Sold to State	Ceased Operations	Active	Constructed	Received from State	Sold to State	Ceased Operations	Active	Constructed	Received from State	Sold to State	Ceased Operations	Active
1701–10		1			1	2				2					
1711–20	3				4	5				7					
1721–30	14	1		1	18	7				14					
1731–40	15				31	6				19	1				
1741–50	17		2	2	42	14			1	31					
1751–60	36	19		4	97	16	3		2	40					
1761–70	30		10	8	109	6			10	33					1
1771–80	17	2		6	122	2		3	10	31	6				1
1781–90	12		4	2	128	5			4	36	2			9	1
1791–1800	5		8		125	6				42					7
Total	149	23	24	23		69	3	3	27		9			9	

Source: Pavlenko, *Istoriia*, p. 460.

army cloth), merchants led in the establishment of the great majority of the enterprises of the textile industry. They were able to preserve their leadership, in a somewhat diminished numerical proportion, until the end of the century. During the second half of the century both the gentry and the peasants appeared on the scene in larger numbers, particularly in the linen and wool industries.

The gentry and peasants needed for their entrance into the rank of entrepreneurs two different conditions. The gentry needed capital and an assurance of uninterrupted demand. The peasants needed legal protection as entrepreneurs. Preconditions of the gentry's entrepreneurial activity were previous experience in the marketing of raw materials, government subsidies, and a guarantee of sustained (continuous) demand for the final product.

The spread of entrepreneurship among the peasants hinged both upon the process of capital accumulation within the villages as well as upon the legal protection awarded to them. Two differing patterns can be established for peasant entrepreneurs: one for state-owned and the other for privately owned serfs. Most of the entrepreneurs of state peasant origin somehow managed to advance from the peasantry into the merchant or urban groups, and then as nonserfs to enter the manufacturing business. Landowner-serfs initially set up industrial enterprises legally owned by their masters and at a later stage, in case of spectacular success, bought their freedom from their lords. In the intermediate period legal anomalies such as serf-owning serfs existed for years or generations. (Such practices may have been inherited from the Muscovite period, when elite slaves owned other slaves.) The abolition of the licensing system and of the control by the College of Manufactures over the establishment of manufactories greatly benefited the peasant entrepreneurs, for it diminished harassment of the illegal and "nonrespectable" entrepreneurs.

Inquiry into the social origin of entrepreneurs in the iron- and copperworks of eighteenth-century Russia yields results similar to those obtained in the analysis of entrepreneurship in the textile industry. The similarity ought not to obscure, however, the considerable differences existing between the two, even though they were differences in degree rather than in kind.

Some of the differences reflected the existing differences in the organization of the production processes in the two industries, or the place each industry was assigned in the state's preference scale. In addition, the different degrees of competition within each of the industries influenced both the opportunities for entrance and the success of the new entrepreneurs to a varying extent.

Table 3.53   Social Origin of Entrepreneurs Entering and Leaving Textile Manufacturing

	Merchants	Gentry	Peasants	Foreigners	State-Owned	Total
1700–1725	27	3	1	3	5	39
1726–45	36	1	2	−3	−4	32
1745–65	48	24	2	1	−1	74
1762–75[a]	49	23	11	−1	—	82
1776–99[a]	337	86	228	—	—	651

Sources: Zaozerskaia, *Rabochaia sila*, p. 107, and Bernadskii, "Predprinimatel'stvo," p. 116.

[a]The data for 1762–75 and 1776–99 do not specify the number of foreigners but include them among the merchants. The data for these periods are not entirely comparable with those from the previous ones, since enterprises of smaller size were registered, while during the period prior to the 1780s the licensing system (later abolished) required a certain minimum size of operation and output.

Table 3.54   Social Origin of Textile Manufacturers by Major Branches of the Industry, 1700–75

	Merchants	Gentry	Peasants	Foreigners	State	Total
Linen						
1700–25	9	1	1	—	2	13
1726–45	14	2	1	—	−2	15
1746–65	23	9	—	—	—	32
1762–75	18	4	1	—	—	23
Woolen						
1700–25	6	2	—	3	3	14
1726–45	4	−1	—	−3	−2	−2
1746–65	18	13	1	—	−1	31
1762–75	5	16	—	—	—	21
Silk						
1700–25	12	—	—	—	—	12
1726–45	18	—	1	—	—	19
1746–65	7	2	1	1	—	11
1762–75	14	3	3	—	—	20

Sources: Zaozerskaia, *Rabochaia sila*, pp. 89, 98, 102; Bernadskii, "Predprinimatel'stvo," p. 116.

Note: The figures for 1762–75 are not identical to those in the previous table.

One of the characteristics of the entrepreneurs in the iron- and copperworks was the virtual absence of foreigners. (The only exceptions were the partners of Riumin, the Beloff brothers, and their English partner with his Russified name, Maef.) This was very unlike the textile industry. Apart from whatever anti-foreigner bias that may have existed, or elements of national security involved with an industry which produced most of the Russian armaments, other factors also determined the lack of foreigners among the entrepreneurs in this industry. Given the location of the industry, the Urals, it was inconceivable that any foreign entrepreneur could have operated in the virtually frontier environment. No foreigner in Russia was willing or able to build a private organization that could function under the conditions of such distances and uncertainties. The other element concerned the Russians' own abilities to absorb the Western technology in iron and copper metallurgy. The Russians had already learned some rudiments of the technology from the Dutch in the seventeenth century in the Kashira works near Tula. During the early part of the eighteenth century the technology transfer occurred at the Olonets-region state works headed by Hennin, with the help of other foreigners under the control and auspices of the Mining College. In addition, Russians were sent for training and "industrial espionage" to Sweden and other countries of Western Europe. Although technical specialists were imported by the state and private enterprises, entrepreneurship remained in the hands of Russian nationals.

One of the major differences between metallurgy and textiles was the number of entrepreneurs involved, which was much smaller in iron and copper than in the wool, linen, and cotton industries. (The chronology of entrance into the iron and copper industries is presented in table 3.55.) The reasons are manifold, but a few ought to be mentioned: (1) after a few decades the supply of iron exceeded domestic demand, and the level of production depended upon foreign demand to a large extent. (2) The state, which at a very early stage in the development of textiles withdrew from direct activity in the area of production, maintained an active role in the iron and copper industry to the extent of producing 10 to 12 percent of the total pig-iron output in the second half of the century. (3) The amount of capital necessary for successful entry into iron and copper production

Table 3.55   Entrance of New Entrepreneurs into Iron- and Copperworks

Years	Merchants	Gentry	Total
1701–10	1		1
1711–20	7		7
1721–30	11	1	12
1731–40	17		17
1741–50	32	3	35
1751–60	16	16	32
1761–70	21	10	31
1771–80	4	4	8
1781–90	1	5	6
1791–1800	3	4	7
Total	113	43	156

Source: Pavlenko, *Istoriia*, p. 463.

substantially exceeded the capital requirement for entrance into other branches of manufacturing.

Another notable difference pertaining to the social origin of entrepreneurs in the metallurgical and textile industries is the virtual absence of peasants among the metallurgical entrepreneurs (except for a handful of individual cases such as the Osokins and Miliakovs). This can be explained by the amount of required capital and the different character of technology in metallurgical production. The increased number of small furnaces operated by peasants never challenged the water-powered furnaces and forges, as the expansion of spindles and weaving machines qualified for classification as a manufactory. In ironworks the jump in quantity of craft-type equipment was insufficient to result in a qualitative change from craft to manufacture. Still another difference was the degree to which technical knowledge played a role in the entrance and success of entrepreneurs. In this respect the existence of a subgroup of former iron masters who entered the ranks of the most successful entrepreneurs via merchant status is significant as well as enlightening. Of 227 water-powered iron- and copperworks constructed by private individuals, 81 were built by five iron masters from Tula and their heirs. Of the five, the Demidovs built 50; the Batashevs 14, the Mosolovs 13, the Krasilnikovs 3, and Arekhov 1. The high degree of concentration of ownership in the iron and copper industries is shown in table 3.56.

There was nothing even remotely similar in any of the branches of the textile industry. The degree of concentration had a definite impact upon the conditions of entry into the metallurgical industry. The concentration of productive capacity and output and the high governmental priorities awarded the armament industries (of which the iron industry was an important component since cannons were produced in ironworks) put the entrepreneurs in a special position. They had to submit frequently to government control and to follow orders, but they were able

to exact a high price for it. As a result, the metallurgical industrialists achieved a greater degree of economic power and political influence than any other group of entrepreneurs in eighteenth-century Russia. It is not surprising, therefore, that the majority of ennobled industrialists was recruited from among the owners of iron- and copperworks. There were at least thirteen ennobled families among the top entrepreneurs who owed the privilege of nobility to their role in iron and copper production.

Entrepreneurship in the iron and copper industries differed from other branches of manufacturing in one more important respect. Thanks in part to the location, but even more to the peculiarities of the technological process and the state of the economy, iron and copper producers had to supply their own raw materials. Most of the raw materials for the textile industry were bought in the market through established channels of trade, but the iron and copper producers had to create, each individually, the organization of their raw material supply. In most cases they had to find the labor force (mostly enserfed peasants) to mine the ores, burn the charcoal, quarry the limestone, and transport everything to the work sites. The problem of provisioning the labor force in remote, nonagricultural regions was one that frequently confronted the entrepreneurs. Substantial organizational effort was also needed to transport finished products to the market, often more than a thousand miles from the production site. The metallurgical entrepreneur, in order to be successful, required a well developed organization to synchronize a multitude of production and sale activities

Who were the entrepreneurs and how did they master their difficult tasks?

For the most part, the entrepreneurs were merchants. Entrance into this industry by new entrepreneurs was made possible primarily by a broadening of the geographic area of ore production and by expansion of iron- and copperworks into new areas. Successive waves of entrepreneurial activity can be identified with expansion into particular areas: the period 1700–1730 with the northern Urals, the 1740s and 1750s with the central or Moscow region, and the 1750s and 1760s with the southern Urals region and eastern Siberia. The vastness of territory and the dispersion of natural resources defied the vast power of the giants in the industry in their attempts to prevent entry of new entrepreneurs.

The area of most active merchant entrepreneurship, measured not in terms of success but in terms of effort, was the central Russian region. This was an area familiar to the Russian merchants, of relatively cheap labor, close to local markets, and it offered the possibility of savings on transportation costs and a more rapid turnover of operating capital. During the

Table 3.56 The Share of Six Leading Industrialists in Iron- and Copperworks Throughout the 18th Century

| Owner | Number of Works | | | |
	Constructed	Purchased	Sold and Discontinued	Remained Active
Iakovlev	9	16		25
Demidovs	50	4	25	29
Batashevs	14	4	4	14
Osokins	10	2	1	11
Mosolov	13	2	7	8
Gubin	1	6		7
Total Listed	97	34	37	94
Total Private	227		60	167

Source: Pavlenko, *Istoriia*, pp. 458, 462, 464.

eighteenth century, forty-seven merchant families entered the metallurgical industry in the territory of European Russia (the Moscow and Olonets regions). The majority, however, were defeated in their attempts. This can be explained by a combination of high costs of production (because of the low quality of ores and relative scarcity of charcoal in the Moscow region), insufficient capital, and fierce competition waged by the large producers. By the end of the century only eight merchant families remained in business in this region (families such as the Batashev and Mosolovs were not included in the above figures).

The entrepreneurs in the Urals and Siberia must be subdivided into three groups. To the first group belonged such "old-timers" as the Demidovs (who constructed a total of 50 iron and copper works) and the Mosolovs (who constructed 13 works). The second group consisted of seven merchant families who constructed or purchased a total of 72 enterprises (Iakovlev, 25; Osokins, 12; Tverdyshev and Miasnikov, 12; Luginin, 5; Gubin, 7; Turchaninov, 4; and Pokhodiashin, 4). Most of this group entered during the large upsurge of entrepreneurship in the southern Urals of the 1750s and 1760s. Toward the end of the century, the heirs of Luginin and Pokhodiashin decided to abandon the field. Nevertheless, by 1800 the remaining members of that group of entrepreneurs were producing 48,337 tons of pig iron and about one-third of the private copper output. A third group in this region consisted of merchants who attempted entrepreneurship on a more modest scale. The Soviet historian Pavlenko listed twenty-nine relatively small producers who owned 32 works. For my purposes, I would have to exclude five who bought their enterprises from the state. Of the total of twenty-two active entrepreneurs who constructed iron- and copperworks, only two were able to hold on to their enterprises until the end of the eighteenth century. Of the twenty who were unsuccessful, nine liquidated their enterprises and closed their works, ten withdrew from their ventures by selling out to other industrialists, and one transferred his enter-

prise to his noble son-in-law. Is there an explanation for this high degree of turnover in ownership and relative lack of success of the smaller operations? Pavlenko listed a number of explanations of this phenomenon.[82] One cause was the existing high concentration of ownership of copperworks, accompanied by a rarity of highly productive ore deposits. Another was the summary failure of all enterprises established in eastern Siberia. This region of enormous distances, low population density, and still primitive economy defied every private and governmental attempt to transplant industry to its virgin soil. In the local market, the producers were unable to compete with the peasant-operated furnaces and hand forges producing for local consumption. Still another reason was the scarcity of labor and the unwillingness of the state to allot peasant-serf labor to small and middle-sized enterprises in the iron and copper industries.

The amount of initial capital and the scope of operations appear to have been of crucial importance for survival in the metallurgical industry. The ownership of hundreds instead of a few ore mines and the existence of multi-enterprise firms permitted more effective utilization of the existing labor force and the achievement of a higher degree of specialization within firms. They also allowed firms to engage in the production of many more commodities or types of product, and thereby to react more flexibly to changes in market conditions. The amount of initial capital, under conditions of credit scarcity and slow turnover (two to three years) of operating capital, played an important part. In many cases of smaller entrepreneurs, their capital was insufficient to construct the works, and they encountered difficulties in obtaining working capital. Compounding the problems of the small entrepreneur during the second half of the century were the facts that domestic demand was below the productive capacity of the iron industry and foreign demand fluctuated. All of these conditions make it clear why in the Urals and Siberia, out of sixty-nine enterprises owned by rich merchants, only two were liquidated, but seven of the

Table 3.57   Acquisition by Noblemen of State Owned Iron- and Copperworks during the Late 1750s

I Noblemen	II No. of Works Acquired	III Purchase Price (Rubles)	IV No. of Works Sold	V Sale Price (Rubles)
Shuvalov, P. I.	3	179,689	6	680,420
Chernyshev, I. G.	2	92,493	3	430,000
Vorontsov, M. I.	4	170,975	4	259,505
Vorontsov, R. I.	1	35,712	1	200,000
Gur'ev, A. G.	4	47,864	4	140,000
Iaguzhinskii, S. P.	2	72,582	2	100,000
Repnin, P. I.	2	22,069	3	180,000
Total	18	621,204	23	1,989,925

Source: Pavlenko, *Istoriia*, pp. 373–75, 473.

nineteen enterprises belonging to smaller merchants were closed during the same period.

The experience of the merchant entrepreneurs in the iron and copper industry can be summarized by concentrating on the conditions which contributed to their success as entrepreneurs. Among the elements that determined their success (apart from personal qualities) were: (1) the market situation (the demand for metals in the domestic and foreign markets) at the time of entry; (2) the attitude of the state both in terms of prevailing policies with regard to the demand for metals and concerning subsidies for the industry (particularly by supplying labor); (3) the amount of initial capital and the ability to plow back the profits; (4) the degree of competition in the industry, with particular reference to the type of product and market; (5) the entrepreneur's technical and expert knowledge with regard to choice of location, raw material supply, and degree of reliance upon the expertise of technical personnel.

The merchants were not the monopolists in entrepreneurship. Only 43 out of 156 entrepreneurs (27.5 percent) were members of the gentry. A closer examination would reduce the figure if one were to restrict the concept of entrepreneurship to those who established new enterprises rather than inherited old ones or received them from the state. But even that restriction would leave a sizable group of gentry among the entrepreneurs. For reasons of convenience, the group of gentry entrepreneurs could be divided into three subgroups. The first were members of the aristocracy who were awarded (or received at a price below market value) iron- and copperworks by the state. The second group were members of the gentry who were actively engaged in entrepreneurial activity on their own initiative. The third group consisted of members of the gentry who acquired enterprises through marriage and continued in a business established originally by merchant families.

The precedent-setting transfer of an ironworks into the hands of the nobility occurred when Peter the Great turned over the previously foreign-owned and operated Kashira works (near Tula) to his maternal relatives, the Naryshkins, rather than have them operated directly by the state or put up for sale at an auction. (The latter possibility was in fact quite remote in view of the scarcity of private capital available for such a business venture.) The second transfer, this time on a much more massive scale, took place during the 1750s. (I have omitted the short-lived attempt in 1740 to transfer the state-owned ironworks to a company formed by the foreigner and acting head of the Mining Department, Schönberg, which is considered by most Russian historians as a sellout of Russian interests to foreigners and therefore an act of national betrayal.) During the late 1750s, sixteen state-owned iron- and copperworks in the Urals region were sold at very low prices to six members of the aristocracy. In addition, the state sold the Lipetsk ironworks, appraised at 75,880 rubles, to Prince P. I. Repnin, for 22,069 rubles.

The experiment of turning over metallurgical works at below-market prices to noblemen was short-lived. Only a few of the recipients attempted to expand production by constructing new works. In most cases they restricted their activities to sales of accumulated inventories and to a routine continuation of the existing production pattern. (The only alteration in the routine was a somewhat harsher treatment of the labor force, if the peasant riots at the Shuvalov and Chernyshev enterprises can be used as evidence.) That the initial transactions were primarily subsidies to the elite was revealed when the nobles sold the iron- and copperworks either back to the state or to private industrialists. As is evident in table 3.57, they reaped significant profits when they sold these works. The nobles' lengths of tenure also support this thesis: Shuvalov owned his enterprises for nine years, Gur'ev ten years, Chernyshev thirteen years, Repnin fifteen years, and only the Vorontsovs and Iaguzhinskii over twenty years.

This experiment, quite interesting from the point of view of the direction of the government's economic policy, was a minor and rather insignificant incident in the development of entrepreneurship in Russia. It was indicative of the limited flexibility of the estate organization of the aristocracy, which was unable to integrate and direct large-scale industrial operations with and in addition to agricultural production. The episode itself had a very limited impact on gentry entrepreneurship in the industry.

The most successful noblemen-entrepreneurs were the Stroganovs. As owners of the largest private estate in Russia, located in the Urals region, who had a well-developed managerial organization for their vast salt-producing business, the Stroganovs entered the ranks of the iron entrepreneurs in 1721. They may have been encouraged by the example of the Demidovs, or entered the industry to set limits upon the expansion of the Demidovs. During the eighteenth century the Stroganovs constructed fourteen iron- and copperworks. Six of them remained in the hands of the family until the end of the century. Those of their works which passed into the hands of other noblemen were the foundation upon which the expanding enterprises of the others rested. The businesses of Golitsyn, Shakhovskoi, Vsevolozhskii, and Lazarev were built around works inherited or purchased from the Stroganovs, so that by the end of the eighteenth century eighteen enterprises were in operation on land which at one time or another had belonged to the Stroganov manor. This group of producers was quite significant in terms of output (1,038,000 poods), and its share of total pig iron output in 1800 was 10.5 percent.

Along with the success of the Stroganovs, the history of gentry entrepreneurship in the iron and copper industries includes a number of unsuccessful attempts to add industry profits to agricultural rents as a component of gentry income. Three top bureaucrats, A. I. Glebov, procurator of the Senate, K. E. Sievers, a provincial governor, and P. I. Rychkov, a leading administrator in Orenburg province (south Urals), were unsuccessful. Similar lack of success marked the enterprise started in the 1720s by Prince A. M. Cherkasskii which was inherited by P. B. Sheremetev and finally liquidated by him. (The Cherkasskii and Sheremetev families had been linked as early as the first half of the seventeenth century.) Those experiences indicate that success or lack of it was not determined exclusively by a nobleman's wealth or his rank in government service. I would suspect, on the basis of the experience of both the Stroganovs and the other rich noblemen-entrepreneurs, that their success in the iron and copper industries depended to a very considerable extent upon the availability of the necessary natural and human resources within the boundaries of their estates. Most of them, including the Stroganovs, were either unwilling to expand their operations outside the boundaries of their estates or unsuccessful when they tried. Pavlenko has advanced the view that the labor shortage outside their estates may have contributed to this failure. Be that as it may, success was determined by exogenous factors. Whether the incapacity or unwillingness to engage more actively in entrepreneurial ventures was a result of limited expectations or of an inability to bargain on the part of the notoriously command-issuing noblemen is anyone's guess. The fact remains that they were not immune to failure.

The record of a group of middle gentry (including Tevkelev, Satin Khlebnikov, and Keponov) who became entrepreneurs and were able to remain active until the end of the century without any prospects of spectacular expansion does not help to define any general proposition about the gentry's conditions of success in entrepreneurship. The total number of gentry-entrepreneurs in the second category who entered it voluntarily included seventeen families who constructed 39 iron- and copperworks. Twenty of the works were established by the Stroganovs and their heirs, so only 19 were established by the other twelve families.

The third category of gentry who inherited iron- and copperworks established by merchants included seven families. Four of the families owed their ownership to marriages with the Miasnikov daughters, who inherited the iron- and copperworks of Tverdyshev and Miasnikov. A fifth, Lebchev, inherited it from the Osokin family; the sixth, Rtishev, from Mosolov, and the seventh, Shuvalov, from Chirev. Pavlenko credited them with a large share (10.2 percent) of the 1795 output, the accuracy of which I am unable to establish. The involvement of these gentry was more in ordinary ownership than in entrepreneurship. Their reason for marrying out of their class was probably to improve their economic situation, and the ownership of iron- and copperworks provided such opportunities.

Are there any common characteristics of the textile, iron, and copper entrepreneurs? In the most general sense, both groups contained individuals who responded to government policies encouraging them to set up manufactories. They were also similar in terms of their social origin, although the textile entrepreneurs constituted a more representative sample of entrepreneurs in the total economy, irrespective of the size of the enterprises. The metallurgical entrepreneurs represented the upper strata of entrepreneurs, those with larger accumulations of capital. The differences in the degree of concentration between the two industries (not always identical with the degree of competition prevailing within the industries) were not decisive in terms of entrance and success of the entrepreneurs.

The social origin of the entrepreneurs was important for the shaping of their views of themselves and for establishing their relations with the various social classes and institutions. For peasants and merchants, this was a clear case of social advancement; for the gentry, it was a matter of earning additional income. The internal differences and often diverse interests of those groups, depending upon their social origin, were important in the eighteenth century and not yet subordinated to the feeling of entrepreneurial group solidarity. However, the development was clearly in that direction to the extent that the incomes from industrial entrepreneurship and activity were an increasing component of the total income of the entrepreneurs, regardless of their origin and other activities as merchants or landowners.

The Recruitment of Foreign Specialists under Contract

The intensity and scope of recruitment of foreign technical specialists and skilled craftsmen during the eighteenth century differed from period to period and from one area of employment to another. The numbers recruited and their specialties varied according to the priorities of the government (both as a political institution and as a massive employer of foreign specialists) and to what private entrepreneurs considered to be the chief technological bottlenecks in the achievement of their economic objectives and political goals. Even if it were possible to eliminate entirely the recruitment of army and navy personnel from these considerations,[83] one would expect to find in the pattern of recruitment the powerful impact of political considerations, such as the ones which manifested themselves in the recruitment of shipbuilders for the navy and specialized masters for the armament industries during the Northern War.

The intensity of recruitment of foreign specialists, as reflected in the surviving documentary evidence, appears to the historian as a number of major spurts reflecting successive bunchings of numbers of recruits within short time-periods. During the reign of Peter the Great such spurts were in the years 1698–1700, 1707–8, and 1717–18. The first and last of those spurts were associated with Peter's travels abroad, and the high number of recruits during the other years was dominated by military considerations. Shipbuilders and armaments masters dominated the employment distribution of the early spurts.

In the post-Petrine period, spurts or recruitment drives can be detected in the middle 1730s and the middle 1750s, during the reigns of Empress Anna Ioannovna and Empress Elizaveta Petrovna. The 1760s and finally the 1780s can also be described as periods of increased recruitment activities of foreign specialists for Russia. In general, there was a correlation between periods of Russia's political involvement in European affairs and the periods of recruitment of foreign specialists. Confrontation with Western Europe reminded a small, select, enlightened group in both the Russian government and the Russian business community of the degree of Russia's technological and economic backwardness.

Throughout the eighteenth century the major instrument for recruitment of foreign specialists and skilled artisans generally was the labor recruitment contract. The form of a standard contract drawn up in 1700 and approved by Peter the Great and recommended for general use is available in the Amsterdam Archives. The contract stipulated a time duration, the obligations and nature of the services to be performed, and the remuneration to be paid the individual.

In order to recruit specialists, trained recruitment agents had to be found. The role of recruitment agents during the early drives was performed by members of Moscow's foreign trading community who were delegated and instructed to recruit specialists in a broad spectrum of skills. Subsequently, the recruitment work was often performed by members of the Russian diplomatic service stationed in particular legations.

There were many flaws in these recruiting methods. Knowledge about the actual skills of the hired specialists was often insufficient. Some were hired under false pretenses, and complaints were frequent about the specialists' inadequate knowledge or skills. Unquestionably some of these complaints, which may have been lodged by Russians jealous of the very substantial salary differentials enjoyed by the specialists, must be discounted. On the other hand, even well-qualified specialists found many things lacking in the Russian environment that were needed for them to fulfill their tasks. Some Russians were impatient or incapable of acquiring the skills the specialists had to offer and accused the foreigners either of ill will or of incompetence. On the other hand, a comparative perspective based on the history of "technical assistance" to less developed countries in the twentieth century indicates that many of the Russian complaints may have been made on valid grounds.

Aware that problems existed, the government decided to remedy the situation by introducing stricter procedures. In 1723 Peter the Great instituted the requirement of an obligatory demonstration of skills by newly hired foreign technicians that was to be performed prior to their assignment to and assumption of duties with enterprises or institutions. It is difficult to judge the effectiveness of this innovation, which as a formal arrangement hardly outlived its creator. Perhaps the subsequent decline in the number of "imposters" among foreign specialists was due to the accumulated experience by Russian entrepreneurs and government officials in recognizing true expertise, or to a realization on the part of foreigners that the Russians would not look kindly at attempts to take their ignorance for granted.

In terms of Russian priorities for foreign skills, the demand for civil and military engineers was a long-standing one. These were skills requiring not only training but talent and experience, as well as a social milieu providing conditions for both specialization and cross-fertilization of ideas and techniques. The technology and art of city planning and the construction of churches, monasteries, palaces, fortification systems, canals, and harbors were poorly developed (or did not take hold) in Russia, and the tradition of importing Italian architects and engineers for those tasks goes back to the sixteenth century.[84] Recruitment of these specialists became easier for Russia, as for other European countries, in the eighteenth century.

The next group on the preference scale consisted of mining specialists. Saxony was the traditional recruiting ground for many European countries, Russia included. Specialized techniques within this category also could be obtained from the Swedes, the Dutch (or Walloons), and later from the English. Russian mining and metallurgy enterprises, operating with waterpower, were started by Dutch entrepreneurs and technical specialists in the 1630s, but they failed to keep pace with developments abroad. The limited number of skilled specialists was neither sufficient to modernize the previously small-scale operations in the Tula-Kashira and Olonets regions nor to establish the Urals iron industry. This major task was performed during the first two decades of the eighteenth century by imported specialists. G. W. Hennin and Buhler were vivid examples of the major, pioneering effort of that particular group.

A number of Russians, either apprenticed to foreign specialists or sent abroad for study and specialization, reached a high level of technical and administrative expertise in mining and metallurgy. One such was V. N. Tatishchev, at one time the head of the state ironworks in the Urals, and also a noted historian and statesman. By the middle of the 1730s, however, Russia required another infusion of foreign technical expertise to expand its iron- and copperworks. This task was performed by the importation of massive numbers of Saxon specialists, an operation usually referred to as the Schönberg influx. Kurt Alexander Schönberg, a high mining official in Saxony, became the chief mining official in Russia. He was subsequently removed in view of alleged gross violations of office and illegal activities that enabled him to amass a huge fortune at the expense of Russian state interests. Schönberg's activities and the role played by his large group of mining specialists have been obscured in the Russian historical literature, which also has been influenced by the general Russian reaction against foreigners in the early 1740s. The misbehavior, or even the crimes, of Schönberg ought not to blind objective scholars to the significance of the contribution made by his group. It is very likely that the rapid expansion of Russian metallurgy in the 1740s and 1750s would have been impossible without the services of this group of mining specialists.

Only in the 1760s and later did the Russian mining schools and the system of on-the-job training begin to supply mining specialists with middle and higher skills. The presence of talent and experience within the Russian labor force must be acknowledged. However, in the area of ferrous metallurgy, the training ordinarily produced practitioners of the existing technology rather than pioneers of a new one. (There were exceptions, such as the highly talented and imaginative innovators Palzunov and Frolov.) It is therefore little wonder that when new technology in mining, metallurgy, and machine building was introduced in Western Europe toward the end of the century, Russia again turned to foreign specialists as the transmission belt for the introduction of more modern production methods.

Two other groups of foreign specialists, bearers of high levels of skills, were in demand by Russia in the eighteenth century. One, a relatively small group, involved highly specialized services concentrated around the Academy of Sciences in St. Petersburg and the services for the Russian mint. The specialists servicing the Academy of Sciences were individuals who made their investment in basic science, who either became scientists themselves or serviced its laboratories, museum collections, and libraries. (Excluded from this category are famous members of the Academy, mathematicians and scientists like Euler or de l'Isle who resided for years in Russia and used their connections with the French Academy, the British Royal Society, and numerous universities abroad to facilitate contacts between Russians and their colleagues in other countries.) The foreign specialists working for the mint were individuals with highly specialized skills or with education and training that prepared them for work with instruments of precision.

The other group of foreign specialists in demand were those who could provide the Russian social elite with objects of "conspicuous consumption." This was a group with varied skills and included landscape specialists (creators of gardens), masters in the production of tapestry, china, gold or silver brocade, and even masters of the hunt. The members of this group were hired either for the imperial court or for the estates of the aristocracy. One could include in the same group portrait painters, painters of miniatures, and related artists. The inclusion of artists does raise a number of classification problems. For example, is it appropriate to classify in the same category the famous Rastrelli and an anonymous miniature painter who might have been a good craftsman but was devoid of any artistic talent? If the category of specialists in conspicuous consumption is broadened, it should include at least some of the foreign private tutors, who became very fashionable in the upper circles of Russian society for helping the younger generations of the Russian aristocracy acquire, if not an education, at least some of the paraphernalia of Western culture.

Purchased Serfs

In an economy based primarily upon serf labor, where serfs were the major labor resource, it was natural for manufactory owners to turn to this source of supply when other sources of labor were less remunerative or less available.

Government permission to buy serfs was given to the manufactory owners in a decree of January 18, 1721.[85] The decree allowed the purchase of peasants both singly and in entire villages. The response to this decree by the textile manufacturers was insignificant, and that by the owners of ironworks was modest. A few factors explain this response. First, the chief demand was for skilled rather than unskilled labor. Second, the purchase of serfs involved a substantial initial investment per actual unit of labor service performed, at a time when profits had to be reinvested in the enterprise's working capital rather than in the expansion of the long-term productive capacity of the enterprises. Under such conditions, very few merchant entrepreneurs could afford to buy serfs.

In 1736, along with the grant of the *officinae ascripti*, a decree prohibited the purchase of whole villages and permitted only the purchase of serfs without land. This did not provide manufactory owners with any additional incentive to buy serfs. Most of the textile manufactories were located in the cities, where the costs of maintenance of such serfs were high. The purchase of serfs probably became profitable only after the second census (*reviziia*), when the poll tax was imposed upon the manufactory labor force, and the wage freeze of 1724 (the norms of the *plakat*) began to work to the advantage of the industrialists. The demand of the textile manufacturers to remove the provision of 1736 was granted by a decree of July 27, 1744.[86] A substantial increase in the rate of serf acquisition followed. This not only ameliorated the situation of the labor supply but served as a device for increasing investment in land, the safest form of investment during this period in Russia. The increase of serf acquisitions by merchant entrepreneurs also produced a political effect, an aroused gentry opposition, which led to the decrees of 1752 and finally to the prohibition of further acquisitions of serfs by nongentry in 1762. Table 3.58 attempts to reconstruct the volume of serf purchases in light industry around the middle of the century.

There is less certainty about the use of purchased serfs by the iron- and copperworks. The problems with the data stem from a lack of clarity about the distribution of purchases made by merchant entrepreneurs, by ennobled merchants, and by gentry entrepreneurs. The first reliable data pertain to the year 1747 and indicate purchases of 9,939 male serfs.[87]

During subsequent years the ironworks located in the central metallurgical region bought proportionally more peasant-serfs than did those in the Urals. In part, this can be explained by the availability of serfs in the central region (some of whom in fact might have been sent later to the Urals). It is also explained by the lower rate of grants of state peasants in the central region in comparison with the Urals. As in the case with the textile manufactories, the iron- and copperworks witnessed a rise in the number of serf purchases in the late 1740s and in the 1750s. An official report alleged that prior to 1752 iron- and copperworks bought 19,645 serfs, of whom 8,051 were employed at various auxiliary jobs in the works, while the rest were left in the villages for agricultural labor.[88]

A report of 1764 shows a total of 29,293 male serfs purchased by iron- and copperworks.[89] The total continued to rise in spite of the prohibition against purchasing serfs. Some merchant ironmakers were able to circumvent the law. For example, the ironmaker Batashev managed to purchase a total of 1,856 male serfs during the years 1762–76, mostly in transactions involving him as a silent partner.[90] Others received special privileges from the government that allowed them to acquire serfs. For example, the iron and linen manufacturer A. A. Goncharov received for himself and his heirs such a privilege on February 17, 1763. During the years 1770–83 Goncharov expended the huge sum of 113,632 rubles on the purchase of serfs.[91] By the end of the century, due to purchases and to natural increase, the serfs owned by metallurgical industrialists (excepting hereditary gentry) totaled 48,285 males.[92]

Two matters have to be discussed on the matter of serf purchases. Some groups of the gentry were alarmed by the substantial purchases of serfs by the

Table 3.58   Purchased Peasants (Male Serfs) for Enterprises under the Jurisdiction of the College of Manufactures

	Linen	Wool	Silk	Total Textiles	Other	Total
Prior to 1762						
With land	11,422	2,464	3,355	17,241		
Without land	316	139	275	730		
Total	11,738	2,603	3,630	17,971	1,674	19,645
Working in manufactories	3,863	1,344	1,217	6,424		
Working in agriculture	7,875	1,259	2,413	11,547		
1767						
With land	11,699	2,471	3,359	17,526	2,588	20,114
Without land	314	129	363	806	552	1,358
Total[a]	12,013	2,600	3,722	18,332	3,140	21,472
Working in manufactories	3,999	1,341	1,284	6,624	1,758	8,382
Working in agriculture	8,011	1,259	2,438	11,708	1,382	13,090
1769–70						
Total	12,800	2,520	2,174	17,494	3,165	20,659

Source: Zaozerskaia, *Rabochaia sila*, p. 234.

[a]The document is dated November 25, 1769, but pertains to 1767.

industrialists. One of the results of their reaction was an attempt by the government to establish norms of serf-holdings in the textile manufactories depending upon the capital stock of the enterprise and specific technology of the various branches of the industry, similar to the norms established earlier for the iron and copper workers by Tatishchev, who as an administrator of the state-owned works in the Urals and Siberia was concerned with the problems of manpower in those regions. Such norms were established finally in 1752 by the College of Manufactures. The norms for the textile industry were based upon the assumption that only one-third of the number of male serfs purchased by the enterprise could be employed in agriculture. Given the prevailing use of labor per machine (*stan*), the norms were fixed at 42 workers per machine for wool cloth, 15 for lining, 12 for each linen-weaving machine, and 16 for silk weaving.[93] The results were astonishing. An inquiry by the College of Manufactures into the labor situation of the textile manufactories concluded that, to employ the machines fully, the manufactories needed an additional 76,099 male serfs—42,806 in linen, 24,063 in wool cloth, and 9,230 in the silk manufactories.

The industrial entrepreneurs did not exercise the privileges granted them by the official norms for acquiring serfs. This situation is even more vividly reflected in the fact that until 1762 the government issued specific permissions to textile manufacturers to buy a total of 41,657 male serfs with land and 719 landless males, a total of 42,376. A total of only 17,971 were actually purchased, so that 24,405, or more than half, of the male-serf quota was not exercised. Table 3.59 shows how selected entrepreneurs in the linen and wool-cloth industries exercised their quotas.

There were many reasons for the failure to exercise the purchase options. The most obvious ones were a lack of capital on the part of some of the entrepre-

Table 3.59   Serf Purchase-Quota and Actual Purchase for Selected Entrepreneurs

	Linen			Wool Cloth	
	Quota	Actual		Quota	Actual
Strigalev	240	3	Tulinov	464	23
Ashastin	300	38	Sakharov	100	3
Serebrennikov	250	4	Kuznetsov	500	21
Sivokhin	100	6	Peremyshlev	288	18
Tetiusheninov	200	3	Olesov	450	30
Mitrofanov	120	3			

Source: Zaozerskaia, *Rabochaia sila*, p. 234.

neurs and lack of available opportunities for purchase in the vicinity of the enterprises.

The outcome was that the larger entrepreneurs took advantage of the opportunity to acquire serfs to a much greater extent than did the smaller manufacturers. The former became major serf-owners, a characteristic which made them socially more eligible for joining the ranks of the gentry.

Among the visible effects of the purchase of serfs, which resulted in the acquisition of 50,665 males by the manufactory owners, was a trend for textile manufacturers to establish enterprises in rural areas or to transfer existing ones to such areas. This reinforced the trend to decrease the share of Moscow in the total number of textile enterprises and in the total output. In metallurgy, the acquisition of serfs on the one hand facilitated the relocation of labor closer to the enterprise, and on the other provided a source of labor services and replacement, thus lessening the dependence of the entrepreneurs upon government-supplied labor.

The role of rural serfs as an auxiliary component of the labor force in the ironworks is well known. Agricultural serfs were utilized seasonally at the ironworks in such labor-intensive tasks as prepara-

Table 3.60   Serfs Employed by the Textile Industry in Cottages, 1775

Total Accounted for		Moscow and Moscow-Uezd-Based Enterprises
Linen	9,558	3,331
Silk	2,396	2,396
Woolens	874	452
Total	12,828	6,179

Source: Indova, "Manufaktury," pp. 316–25.

tion of charcoal fuel, mining and transportation of ore to the ironworks, as described in the discussion of metallurgy. Agricultural serfs were not, however, employed as auxiliary labor only in mining and metallurgy. A certain number of rural serfs, attached to or purchased by textile enterprises, performed important tasks such as spinning yarn or even weaving cloth in rural cottages rather than on the premises of the enterprises. The term "auxiliary workers" may understate their function, an inevitable result of differentiating them from the workers employed in the manufactories proper.

Although many documents provide evidence of the existence of such an auxiliary labor force, few are specific with regard to the utilization of such serfs in the industrial labor force. A 1775 report of the College of Manufactures which lists 344 enterprises provides the following breakdown of the enserfed labor force employed by the enterprises: (1) purchased and attached workers—16,052 males, 4,731 females, and 50 not distributed by sex; (2) in addition to these—14,036 "at work in the villages for the enterprises."[94] It is of interest to follow the distribution of this working population among industries.

Of the 14,036 serfs working in their cottages for the industrial enterprises, 12,828 can be identified as employed by textile manufactories, by matching the data for individual enterprises with the reported number of serfs, as in table 3.60.

The auxiliary labor force of the textile industry was employed massively in linen and silk manufacturing. In the latter the proportion of the reported auxiliary workers to those employed directly in the industrial enterprises was the highest. The high concentration of the auxiliary workers in the Moscow-based enterprises also reflects the relatively high overhead of locating industrial establishments in Moscow proper.

These data do not provide an accurate estimate of the size of the auxiliary labor force, for they suffer from serious shortcomings. The government reports omit entirely the serfs employed by entrepreneurial members of the nobility, a procedure which not only reduces the reported totals, but particularly distorts the data for employment in woolen production. The government reports include the serfs who were either purchased by or assigned to merchant entrepreneurs

under the terms of the privileges bestowed by the College of Manufactures to industrial entrepreneurs.

The data on the rural serfs utilized as an auxiliary labor supply for the industrial enterprises are important for the following reasons: (1) They indicate the existence of a division of labor between the manufactories and the cottage-industry type of production, or the possibility of introducing such a division of labor, should it become profitable for the enterprise. (2) They point to the existence of a labor reserve that could be used to adjust the volume of output to the fluctuating level of demand. (3) They explain in part the phenomenon of skill acquisition in the countryside which led to the growth of rural-based small-scale manufacturing enterprises, particularly in the silk and cotton branches of the textile industry, some of which subsequently made an easier transition to the modern factory system than did the large-scale manufactories.

Some of the significant differences between the situation of agricultural serfs working for the textile manufactories and those employed for the ironworks should be noted: (1) In metallurgy, there was hardly any small-scale handicraft-type production (except for the northwest region, a great distance from the centers of Russian metallurgy), while in textiles there existed a large number of craft-type producers. Thus the agricultural serfs working for metallurgy were employed in tasks which required hardly any skills and could neither obtain nor transfer skills within their environment, while for the auxiliary workers in the textiles this was possible. (2) The auxiliary labor services in metallurgy required the absence of the serfs from their households and farms, while those working for the textile enterprises could perform their functions within their households. (3) While the ironworks used predominantly male labor for the tasks of fuel and ore supply, the textile enterprises used the services of women as well as of men in most of the tasks performed by the auxiliary labor force outside of the premises of the enterprise. (4) The skill differentials and differences in the life-styles between serfs performing auxiliary tasks for the ironworks and the labor force employed directly in the ironworks were greater than those existing in the textile industries between the labor force of the manufactories and the auxiliary laborers in the villages. (5) The ironworks, as a result of the above, experienced greater difficulties in substituting hired laborers to do the work of the attached serfs than did the textile enterprises.

In spite of the enumerated differences, the presence of an auxiliary labor force supported the existence of the serf-manned manufactories at a lower level of dependency than the support of auxiliary labor in the ironworks. The differences could be attributed to a considerable extent to the nature of the production process and its location, including the labor supply in the different regions. Nevertheless, an important similarity remains in that in both cases industrial production required a broader labor base than the data on direct employment in the manufactories or ironworks would suggest.

In the case of the ironworks, the employment of auxiliary workers constituted a net addition to industry-wide employment and was an integrated part of the production cycle, not a substitute for small-scale production. Auxiliary workers for the textile manufactories constituted a substitute for small-scale, cottage-type output and were integrated into the production process of particular enterprises rather than into the industry-wide production cycle, for which they represented a substitute input.

The Officinae Ascripti

Contemporary analysis assumes that, with spatial mobility, labor will move from one place to another or from one job to another and that such movements depend upon the marginal value product of labor in different localities and industries as expressed by existing wage differentials and the availability or costs of information, transportation costs, and other factors. This assumes a direct bargaining position between entrepreneurs and workers, constrained by the general legal framework, and equal freedom of choice for both parties entering the bargain.

The situation in the labor market of eighteenth-century Russia differed significantly from our contemporary models. Both parties, the entrepreneurs and the laborers, were not entirely free to bargain over the whole range of possible forms of rendering labor services. The entrepreneurs were often restrained by government regulations concerning the number and status of their employees. The laborers were mostly handicapped by their status of serfdom and seldom could influence the duration of the contracts, the terms of payment, or the conditions of the job, all of which were determined by the serf-owner or circumscribed by existing legislation. As a consequence, the choices available to a particular laborer were much narrower than those available to the entrepreneur and were determined by the choice of his owner.

One might therefore assume that the labor market was dominated by the demand of the entrepreneurs, as mitigated by the constraints put upon them by the owners of labor. To free themselves from the constraints by the owners of labor, the industrial entrepreneurs at times preferred to assume ownership of the labor resources they required. Moreover, the assumption of one labor supply curve facing the

Table 3.61   Indemnity Payments Made in Lieu of Taxes by Employers in the Textile and Iron Industries

Demidov	20,685	Kiskhin	2,560
Zatrapeznov	7,424	Okorokov	2,100
Goncharov	6,020	Solodovnikov	2,100
Bolotin	5,419	Driablov	1,440
Nechaev	2,830		

entrepreneurs is a simplifying device for analytical purposes which is useful to explain the relationships between the entrepreneur and the labor force. This assumption should not preclude paying attention to the fragmentation of the labor market into the skilled and the unskilled.

During the period of the 1730s, characterized as one of a "tight" labor supply, the preference of the entrepreneurs to bind particular categories of labor was revealed most clearly. Their overwhelming preference was for skilled labor. Two examples of petitions by manufactory owners illustrate the problem of protecting investments in the training of the work force: "the landowners and managers of court serfs or monastery serfs recover their former serfs who acquired skills in the manufactory and return them to peasant work or send them away either as army recruits or as fugitives"; and "factory masters and working people should not be hired away either secretly or openly by other industrialists."[95] Thus both the supply of labor and the protection of their investment was of vital importance for the functioning of the enterprises.

As a result of frequent petitioning and pressure by the manufactory owners on the government, a decree was published on January 7, 1763, which enserfed all the skilled workers in the manufactories who were working under contracts of hire.[96] Skilled workers who were previously serfs could be kept at the manufactories upon the payment of a fixed indemnity to their previous owners. The indemnity payment for employees who previously had been taxpayers was 30 rubles for a single male, 50 rubles for a family with small children, and 10 rubles for boys over ten years of age, and 5 rubles for girls over fifteen.[97] The available evidence reveals that indemnity payments of over 62,000 rubles were made, including 42,000 rubles by textile manufactory owners and 20,685 rubles by the iron makers, the Demidovs. Of this total, I was able to find figures for the payment of 50,578 rubles shown in table 3.61. In addition we know that Tames and Seridov paid in excess of 2,000 rubles each and that payments were made by the textile manufacturers Ovoshchnikov, Shchepochkin, and Poluiaroslavtsev.[98]

The number of peasant-serfs among the skilled workers was relatively small, perhaps only 10 percent. The greatest advantage to the manufactory

Table 3.62   Number of Enserfed by Decree of January 7, 1736, in
Textile Manufactories of Moscow (city and county)

Data	Linen	Wool Cloth	Silk	Total
End of 1730s	836	4,226	999	6,061
1740s	910	4,303	904	6,117
1750s	784	4,035	940	5,759

Source: Zaozerskaia *Rabochaia sila*, pp. 215–16.

owners consisted in the enserfment of the previously free skilled workers for whom no indemnity had to be paid. The second census *(reviziia)* established a tax payment of 70 kopeks per head for the skilled workers enserfed by the decree and those enserfed by the census, but the grant by the government to the manufactory owners was still a very substantial one. It provided many of the owners with a guarantee of continuous labor services (and made them into serf-owners), and it also presented a huge subsidy to their business. Thus a new category of workers emerged in Russia with the status of *officinae ascripti* (bound to the factory), a term coined as a parallel with *glebae ascripti* (bound to the soil).

The legal distinction between the category of *officinae ascripti* and conventional serfs consisted in the fact that the former were bound to the enterprise, not to the person of the owner, who exercised jurisdiction over them but only in connection with the enterprise and with the permission of the Mining College or the College of Manufactures.

I shall now present the available data on the number of workers concerned by the decree of January 7, 1736, and similar ensuing decrees.[99] The historian M. N. Artamenkov estimated that 9,872 workers of both sexes in thirty-seven Moscow textile enterprises were enserfed by the decrees of 1736 and 1744; 6,066 were in woolens, 1,702 in silk, 1,484 in linen, and 620 in others. If other information provided by Artamenkov is correct, the total number of those enserfed in the entire textile industry, presumably including family members, was about 17,300.[100] Zaozerskaia, on the other hand, has estimated the number of serfs in the textile industry to be about 12,500, of whom about 10,000–10,500 were employed workers.[101] Her information breaking down those enserfed by the 1736 decree in the Moscow-region textile manufactories is presented in table 3.62.

For the 1750s, the total number enserfed by the decree of 1736 located in fifty-eight textile manufactories was estimated at 11,423. Of them, 2,930 were in the linen industry, 6,825 in the wool-cloth industry, and 1,668 in the silk industry. This total has obvious omissions, and therefore Zaozerskaia assumed the actual number of employed from these groups to have been approximately equal to the estimate of the 1730s (10,000–10,500). This figure involved a transfer

of about 3,000 from previously purchased serfs and therefore implies an actual labor force in the middle 1760s of about 9,500 from this category in the textile manufactories.[102]

F. Sukin, vice-president of the College of Manufactures, estimated in 1764 that there were 13,241 such people in the textile industry. Other documents for the late 1760s provide the somewhat different estimates presented in table 3.63 for all the manufactories under the jurisdiction of the College of Manufactures.

To the extent that the figures of the 1760s involve the 3,000-man transfer, a net figure of about 10,000 workers for the manufactories of the College of Manufactures may be assumed. Of them, about 9,000 were employed in the textile manufactories.

The decree of 1736 was not limited to light industry, but also involved iron- and copperworks. According to incomplete figures, the decrees of 1736, 1746, and 1755 enlarged the dependent labor force of the private iron- and copperworks by 5,716 workers.[103] Government policies, one may conclude, converted about 18,000 skilled laborers into serfs attached to the manufactories by the middle of the eighteenth century.

The main economic advantage of the conditions of transfer to the owners was a prohibition of the workers' mobility and the possibility of employing them at fixed wage rates below the prevailing market rate for labor service.

The category described as *officinae ascripti* included still another group whose origin, like that of those enserfed by the decree of January 7, 1736, can be found in the relationship between the state and the entrepreneurs. This was the group of government-owned serfs who became attached *(pripisnye)* to the manufactories. Responding to the manufactory owners' demand for cheap labor or for government subsidy, the government transferred some groups of state-owned serfs to work in privately owned industrial establishments. No major change in their legal status occurred. They came under the jurisdiction of the entrepreneur and were bound to the enterprise, but they could be recovered by the state, their origi-

Table 3.63   Estimates of the Number of Enserfed by the Decree of January 7, 1736 in Textile Manufactories

	Linen	Woolcloth	Silk	Total Textiles	Other	Total
1767	2,478	8,583	910	11,971	1,217	13,188
1769–70[a]	2,691	8,794	1,139	12,624	1,033	13,657
1760s						12,329

Sources: Strumilin, *Istoriia*, pp. 341, 344; Zaozerskaia, *Rabochaia sila*, pp. 225–26.

[a]In addition, 180 under the jurisdiction of the Office of Manufactories, which makes a total of 13,368 males and lists 78 women separately.

nal owner, upon the liquidation of the enterprise. The actual change was in terms of their economic activity. Serfs included in this group were expected to earn their living from agricultural work in their peasant households and then to pay their taxes and rent in the form of labor services for the manufactories. The grant of such labor to private manufactory owners was in each case an individual act and not by an industry-wide decree.

Very little of this procedure was practiced in the textile industry, which relied either upon the laborers bound to the plants by the 1736 decree or upon purchased serfs to increase its labor force. The few existing instances when state-owned villages were turned over to textile manufactories are exceptions to the rule. Thus the linen manufacturer T. Filatov received the village Tovarkovo, which was later assumed, along with the manufactory, by A. Goncharov. In another instance, in 1718–20 Tamesz received the village Kokhma (in Suzdal' *uezd*) for his linen manufactory.

The government's practice toward the private iron- and copperworks was an extension of its labor supply policy with regard to its own ironworks. Its history goes back to the supply of labor to the oldest ironworks, those of the Naryshkins and Müllers, which in 1720 had 3,626 and 3,063 male serfs, respectively. The government's favorite among the iron and copper producers, Demidov, was able to persuade the government that a grant of state-owned peasants would enable him to increase output. Other copper producers, including Osokin and Mosolov, followed suit. By 1747 the private iron and copper producers had 22,553 male *ascripti* granted them by the government from among the former state peasants. If we deduct the 6,716 granted Naryshkin and Müller (who were not active producers), the effective number at this date was 15,837 state serfs attached to the iron- and copperworks.

The statistics for this category from the 1750s and 1760s reflect grants of state peasants to entrepreneurs and the more important transfer of state enterprises, together with their serf labor, to private ownership and occasionally their return to state ownership. Incomplete data for 1756 point to 12,724 male serfs. In 1764 there were 17,283 attached male serfs in the private ironworks who had previously been state-owned serfs. In addition, 20,815 serfs were acquired by private owners as a result of the transfer of state-owned enterprises. Excluding the latter category, the number of state-owned serfs in the ironworks did not increase until the end of the century because the state did not make any more grants of this type and liquidated enterprises had to return their peasants to the state. The number of state serfs in this category, plus the category enserfed by the

Table 3.64   Ascripti to Metallurgy Works (Males)

Reviziia	Year	State-Owned Works	Privately-Owned Works	Total
1st	1719	63,054	24,199	87,253
2d	1744	99,330	43,187	142,517
3d	1763	104,184	44,402	148,586
4th	1783	209,554	54,345	263,899
5th	1795	241,253	70,965	312,218

Source: Semevskii, *Krest'iane*, 2: 304–5.

Table 3.65   Labor Input by Ascripti in Metallurgical Works (in Full-time Equivalent)

Reviziia	Labor Input
1st	5,933
2d	9,691
3d	10,024
4th	17,945
5th	21,231

1736, 1746, and 1755 decrees, totaled 20,924 in private ironworks, 635 in copper, or 21,559 male serfs in all.[104]

The actual labor input of this group was significantly smaller than its numerical size would indicate. Most of the *ascripti (pripisnye)* were used for auxiliary types of work such as fuel supply, ore mining, and ore transportation. Moreover, their work time was much less than a worker-year equivalent. A coefficient must be used to convert their work obligations into a worker-year equivalent in order to derive their actual contribution to the labor force. To execute all the necessary auxiliary operations in the iron- and copperworks, even in the presence of *ascripti* or of enterprise-owned serf labor, it became necessary, more and more, to contract with outside labor for this type of job. Such labor was paid the market wage. As a result, competition with serf labor belonging to enterprises grew even in areas where serf labor was available because the market provided a means of substituting more productive labor. According to the census data reported by Semevskii, the total number of *ascripti* state serfs in state-owned and privately owned metallurgical works was as shown in table 3.64.

Since this labor force had to work only in order to fulfill its tax obligations, which can be estimated at 17 days per year, the labor input of this usually unskilled labor force can be estimated in terms of 250 days of work, the average for a full-year worker. In terms of full-year equivalents, the labor input of the *ascripti* is shown in table 3.65.

Data are available only for the *officinae ascripti* in the iron, copper, and textile industries, where they numbered in the neighborhood of 40,000 males. It would be erroneous to assume that the specific weight of the labor contribution was the same for all the *ascripti* as it was for those enserfed by the decree of January 7, 1736. Differences in skill, application at work, and average yearly length of service make the two groups within this category noncomparable. They also were not uniform in terms of the subsidy to the sector of manufactories resulting from the government grants of labor.

The surviving documents about the working conditions of the *ascripti* attached to the ironworks speak only of the excesses of the owners and administrators rather than of the normal treatment the workers experienced. Two types of conclusions have been drawn from the documents. Some historians have taken these excesses to be the normal treatment and have vividly described the hardship caused by the working conditions portrayed in the documents. Other historians, understanding that the documents reflect excesses, have assumed that the *ascripti* accepted their "normal" status without much criticism and reacted only against extremely harsh treatment. Both views could stand some modification. It is true that the documents reflect primarily cases of excesses and harsh, arbitrary treatment, but it is also true that even the "normal" treatment evoked resentment and resistance on the part of the labor force of the *ascripti* category.

The two most frequently quoted collections of documents about the conditions of the *ascripti* serfs in the iron industry are the petitions submitted to the A. A. Viazemskii Investigative Commission of 1763–64 and the instructions that the *ascripti* of the Votkinsk and Izhevsk ironworks gave to their delegates to the Legislative Assembly of 1767.[105] The repeated grievances of the *ascripti*, which reoccur when one collates both collections of documents, were the following:

1. The total volume of output, whether in the form of wood cutting, charcoal burning, transportation, or final product expected from them within the number of days of their work obligation (at the Petrine *plakat* norms of pay per day of work) was impossible to achieve within the stipulated period.

2. The work norms were too high because they did not take into consideration the actual conditions of work such as the state of the roads and the nature of the woods.

3. The ironworks administration used arbitrary means and brutal force in the assignment and supervision of work to achieve more than statutory output.

4. The nominal wage calculated in lieu of the poll tax was only half the actual wages the same workers could have earned or at which they could hire substitute laborers. When either they themselves or the administration hired substitutes they were paid double the nominal wage rates of the *plakat*. Thus, they calculated that the system doubled the tax burden.

5. During the years of lowered poll taxes (1757 and 1758, for example), the ironworks administrators still forced them to perform the usual amount of work, and thus pocketed "their money."

6. For work above the statutory requirement they were paid substantially less than the wages of hired laborers, even though the law entitled them to receive market wages for such work. Similar transgressions of the law took place with respect to the travel allowance from their residences to the ironworks.[106]

7. The assigned work reflected the number of *reviziia* (population-count) souls, regardless of the actual number of males currently in the households or their capacity to work. Moreover, the ironworks administration disregarded whatever internal arrangements were made by the serfs and demanded from each the statutory amount of work.[107]

8. The administration mobilized some of their sons for apprenticeship in the skilled trades of the ironworks, but failed to exclude them from their households' tax obligations, at least until the next census. This was viewed as doubled taxation and also deprived the household of effective workers not only for the ironworks, but also for agricultural production.[108]

There is no doubt that the stated grievances reflected some of the conditions of work for the *ascripti* in the ironworks. It is not surprising that the *ascripti* were driven by some of the more arbitrary and brutal acts of the administration to violence and rebellion. A large portion of the grievances, however, were caused by inflation and the gap between their frozen wages and the rising wages of hired labor. This wage lag was characteristic for the entire enserfed factory labor-force. It provided increased profits to the entrepreneurs, and was only in part remedied by government decrees of 1769 and 1779 raising the wage for the *ascripti*. Subsequent rapid inflation played havoc with the government wage policies and led to even greater *ascripti* discontent.

Hired labor

Soviet economic historians have used the two terms "hired" and "freely hired" (*naemnye* and *vol'no-naemnye*) almost interchangeably to describe the same category of labor used in the manufactories, a category outside the various kinds of legal dependency upon the employer. This was a particularly sensitive problem for Soviet economic historians at the time when a rigid periodization of Russian economic development with highly compartmentalized and labeled periods (feudalism, capitalism) and a set of preconceived attributes for economic institutions put their history into a straitjacket. Of the two terms, "hired" appears to be the more appropriate.

From the point of view of the entrepreneur, labor that offered its services for hire possessed a larger freedom of choice in comparison with those laborers legally dependent upon the employer. In fact, the legal status of the suppliers of "hired" labor often limited the area of their choice in response to the demand for their services. Most of the hired labor was not free. Hired laborers were for the most part recruited from among serfs, who for various reasons were able (or compelled) to sell their services in the nonagricultural labor market for different lengths of time.

Even if the majority of the "hired" laborers were themselves the sellers of their services, their entering into negotiations of a labor contract depended upon a previous contractual relationship between themselves and their legal owners. This relationship specified the terms and duration of their separation from the serf economy of which they were an integral part. On numerous occasions the services of serfs for hire were made available in the nonagricultural labor market, without their consent, for the primary benefit of the serf-owners. Consequently the use of the term "freely hired" appears to be somewhat ambiguous as a description of prevailing conditions during most of the eighteenth century.

Several conditions made possible the availability of a relatively substantial group of laborers for hire within the institutional framework of serfdom. The initial distribution of labor resources that became institutionalized under serfdom when labor mobility was curbed did not make sufficient provision or allowance for nonagricultural activities. Consequently the demand for labor by large-scale industrial enterprises had to overcome the sundry institutional barriers set up to preserve the initial distribution of labor resources. The needs of the manufactories were met to some extent by the development of a money economy with its increased demands for money payments from the peasant households on the part of the government (to pay taxes) and on the part of the serf-owner (to pay rent). This posed new problems for the peasant household and proffered at least two solutions. The household could increase agricultural output to raise marketable output, or it could increase nonagricultural activities by its members. Under pressure from the outside and in spite of the lack of investment outlays, the peasant households succeeded in increasing marketable output by accelerating the plowing up of long-term fallow, by some conversion of pasture into plowland in the older agricultural regions, and by an accelerated migration to the southern and eastern regions of the empire. Simultaneously some households released labor resources for nonagricultural activities.

Depending upon the region and other local conditions, the gradual decrease of the land-labor ratio within the peasant economy (not kept in balance by increasing the plowland and migration) and the absence of savings to make technological advancement and increased capital intensity possible forced some peasants to seek employment outside the household. These factors combined with the seasonality of agricultural operations to make possible (and sometimes mandatory) a release of manpower for nonagricultural economic activities by members of the peasant household. The release of manpower resulted in a growth of cottage industries working for household consumption as well as for rural and urban markets. It also generated a flow of labor services into mining and manufacturing enterprises.

The state and the serf-owners did their best to control this flow. Their intervention influenced at least a portion of the market for hired labor in the manufactories. The passport was the basic document stating the serf-owner's approval of the serf's absence from the village. The system of passports both mirrored and regulated the total supply of peasant-serf labor outside agriculture and contributed to the temporary employment of serfs, who remained under the control of their rightful owners.

Many Russian historians have believed that serfs could not be hired out without their consent, but in fact the conditions of serfdom made such a provision a sheer formality and therefore should not be treated as a strong basis for real bargaining between the serf and his owner. In concrete terms, the hiring out of serfs by the serf-owner was as much a part of the operation of the market for hired labor as was the hiring out by the serfs themselves who, having obtained permission to leave the village for a specified period of time, worked for the highest bidder in the labor market.

The evidence available on the hiring of serfs by the manufactories of Moscow indicates a prevalence of contracts between serf-owners and entrepreneurs in the case of child labor and a high percentage (60) of similar contracts for adult serfs.[109]

There was no uniformity in the length of hire contracts. The duration apparently depended upon the demand of the entrepreneur and the age of the workers. Children or youngsters usually were hired out for a longer period than adults, either to acquire skills or for the entrepreneur to recover some of the training costs. The type of work, apart from seasonality, and the degree of skills, as well as the expectations of the hired laborer or his serf-owner, influenced the duration of the hire contracts.

The data assembled in table 3.66 for workers hired by Moscow textile enterprises in the period of the 1740s–1770s by the Soviet historian M. N.

Table 3.66   Percentage Distribution of Contracts by Number of
Years of Work Stipulated by Contract

No. of Years	1740s	1750s	1760s	1770s
2–3	35.0	80.5	90.0	100.0
5–6	40.0	19.5	10.0	
7–8	8.0			
10–12	12.0			
20–25	.5			
For life	4.5			

Source: Artamenkov, "Naemnye rabochie," p. 139.

Artamenkov provide a rough breakdown of the duration for which the hiring contracts were drawn up. This information is of interest not because it may reflect purely institutional arrangements such as the length of apprenticeship, but because it may in fact reflect the market demand for hired labor.

The distribution in table 3.66 shows a shortening of the duration for which hiring contracts were concluded and also indicates a decreasing tightness in the labor market. Apparently there was less need for the industrialists to use hiring contracts as a means to assure a future labor supply or to train more workers, which also lengthened the time period of the hire contract.

Some of the contracts reveal the fact that serf-owners were discouraged in attempts to establish manufactories or, having liquidated their manufactories, hired out their skilled labor force. For example, the serf-owner N. Ogarëv who was listed in 1760 as the owner of a wool-cloth manufactory in 1769 hired out about 125 of his trained serfs to the Moscow manufactory owner S. Kalinin. Prince B. G. Shakhovskoi hired out a part of his industrially trained labor force.[110] There is also evidence that the hiring out of serfs was sometimes practiced with a view to the establishment of gentry-owned, serf-operated manufactories as soon as the necessary skills had been acquired by the prospective workers. Similarly, there were numerous instances of peasant-serfs who hired themselves out with a desire to acquire skills to start small cottage-type establishments of their own. Some of these peasants set up "unlicensed manufactories" not only in rural areas but also in the major urban centers.

The distribution of hired labor among the various skill categories, or the substitution of hired labor for owned serf labor within the scale of skills, is of interest. In the iron industry hired labor was heavily concentrated in the lower skill levels, and particularly within the auxiliary labor category. This may be explained by the prevalence of short-term contracts and the consequent unwillingness of the entrepreneurs to invest in skill-acquisition without a guarantee of recoupment of the additional outlays. Table

3.67 shows the existence of demand for employment in the auxiliary labor category.

State peasants attached by the government to private iron and textile enterprises were heavily concentrated in the auxiliary jobs because of the conflict between their agricultural pursuits and their activities in the ironworks and manufactories. A decree of 1779 prohibited an increase of the total work-load of this category to meet the payments to the state, and thus manufactory owners had to use one of the following solutions: (1) employ the available labor at higher rates of pay; (2) transfer some of the laborers into the category of factory personnel to perform the auxiliary jobs; (3) subcontract some of the work to outsiders; (4) hire workers for jobs to be performed under the supervision of the available supervisory personnel. Depending upon local circumstances and relative profitability, the owners of the ironworks moved in any of these directions. The iron manufacturer Khlebnikov, for example, used only hired workers for auxiliary jobs. Private entrepreneurs probably found hired labor more flexible in terms of its capacity for organization for various tasks (such as subcontracting, where the workers formed *arteli*), more strongly motivated than their own serf labor-force, and consequently of higher productivity. This is likely because of the fact that, at lower levels of skill, effort rather than knowledge and training is a decisive factor in worker performance and worker motivation and attitude are crucial in determining productivity.

The state sector of the growing Russian manufactures hired labor for an increasing variety of tasks in nonagricultural enterprises. As soon as economic analysis of enterprise performance, or more correct accounting procedures, were introduced, the relative costs of using serf or hired labor became more apparent for various tasks and occupations. A report of the Kolyvan Government Chamber of January 19, 1784, indicates that the use of hired labor for the transportation of silver ores resulted in substantial savings during the year 1783 in comparison with the costs of using the labor of government serfs.[111] Consequently, during the 1780s hired labor dominated the auxiliary jobs of the Altai metallurgical plants and silver mines.

Along with the heavy concentration of hired labor in the auxiliary jobs of mining and metallurgy, there was a numerous group of semiskilled and skilled hired workers, particularly in some branches of the textile manufactories. The availability of documentary evidence enables the historian to gain some insight into the hired labor force in the Moscow manufactories, the bulk of which was employed in the branches of the textile industry. The data are of particular interest since they reveal the social origin and previous legal status of the hired workers, and

Table 3.67   Distribution of the Actively-Employed Labor Force of 11 Metallurgical Plants in 1800

	Demidov (4)	Iakovlev (4)	Lazarev (2)	Mosolov	Total
Total working	1,746	1,686	620	244	4,296
Employed directly in plant	778	978	274	113	2,143
% of total	44.6	58.0	44.2	46.3	49.9
Employed in auxiliary jobs	968	708	346	131	2,153
% of total	55.4	42.0	55.8	53.7	50.1

Source: Strumilin, *Ocherki*, p. 382.

Note: The category of labor represented in the table is the one of "masters and skilled workers" (*masterovye i rabotnye liudi*).

Table 3.68   Social and Legal Status of Hired Workers in Moscow Manufactories, 1738–79

Category by Status	No.
Burghers (*posad* population)	688
Diverse origin, nontaxable (*raznochintsy*)	537
Private serf peasant	5,931
Private household serfs	2,391
Church serfs	3,521
Court serfs	1,263
Retired soldiers	107
Wives of soldiers	933
Total	15,371

Source: Artamenkov, "Naemnye rabochie," p. 159.

thus provide us with a picture of social dynamics in the formation of this group.

Moscow was the center of the textile industry during the eighteenth century, and the manufactories there could not rely exclusively upon the recruitment of purchased serfs or upon the skilled labor force that was enserfed by the government decree of 1736. A significant share of the labor force was made up of workers hired by industrial entrepreneurs for various periods of time through contractual arrangements. Where did these workers come from, to which legal and social groups did they belong, did they hire themselves out voluntarily, or were they hired out by their owners? Such questions can be answered approximately for a large group of workers on the basis of surviving documents pertaining to 15,371 cases during the 1738–79 period.[112] In addition, the data explain some aspects of the mechanics of skill acquisition and skill dissemination that originated in the Russian manufactories. The data for the 1738–79 period, which reflect the social and legal status of the hired workers in the Moscow manufactories based upon the documents of hiring arrangements, are presented in table 3.68.

A comparison of the distribution in table 3.68 with the data on the social origin of the labor force of the Moscow manufactories in 1734–37 reveals a decline in the urban elements of diverse social origin, from the taxable and nontaxable population of paupers. The rural element predominates—serfs who became the chief source for the manufactories and for the seg-

ment of the labor force which was hired under various contractual arrangements. The enserfment of the "unattached" strata of the Russian population considerably narrowed the choice of industrialists for hiring workers.

The most interesting feature of the Moscow data is the preponderance of private serfs in the total number of hired workers (about 56 percent, including both agricultural and household serfs). Although at first glance this would tend to be at variance with the observed preponderance of state and institutional serfs among hired workers in manufactories, there seems not to be any contradiction but rather a combination of general and local environmental circumstances which produced the above results. The Moscow region, in terms of serf ownership, was dominated by private rather than institutional ownership; according to the third *reviziia* of 1762, up to 72 percent of the serfs belonged to private rather than institutional owners. Since distance, as well as the duration of leaves granted to serfs, was important in labor migration, including work in the manufactories, the presence of a high share of private serfs appears congruent with the demand for labor in the Moscow manufactories.[113] In addition, two other features are important in interpreting the relatively high share of private serfs in the hired labor force of the Moscow industrial establishments. One is the fact that among the 5,931 private peasant-serfs, only 2,291 arrived at the manufactories of their own free will, while 3,640 found themselves there by order of their owners.[114]

The other feature is the hiring out of household serfs to the manufactories. One could surmise a general trend of a decreasing number of household serfs in Moscow thanks to a number of factors, one of which may have been the migration of the aristocracy and gentry from Moscow to the new capital of St. Petersburg. Although the particular phases of this process are still insufficiently researched, it would be reasonable to assume that the transfer of residence from Moscow to St. Petersburg was a speedy one for courtiers and some bureaucrats, but a gradual one for other members of the gentry, among whom generational change, individual circumstances, and other

Table 3.69   Number of Hired Workers by Legal Status and Time Period

Category	1738–44	1745–52	1753–62	1763–69	1770–79	Total
Private agricultural serfs	206	453	1,288	1,570	2,417	5,931
Private household serfs	45	88	329	793	1,040	2,295
Church serfs	160	251	571	1,161	1,378	3,521
Court serfs	106	206	259	440	216	1,227
Total	517	998	2,447	3,964	5,051	12,974

factors played a role. Assuming a decline of household serfs as a secular trend for the period after the 1750s, one can explain more easily their high incidence in the composition of the hired workers of Moscow. The serf-owners probably found that the hiring out of their previous household serfs to city-based manufactories was a choice superior to the alternative of sending them back to the villages.

Even if one can explain successfully the high percentage of private serfs among those hired by manufactories, it is necessary to note that for the Moscow region this percentage was lower than the share of private serfs in the total serf population, and the percentage of state and institutional serfs among those hired was above their respective share in the serf population. This would tend to support the more general proposition that nonprivate serfs were more mobile and thereby would avoid the apparent contradiction between the Moscow data and the global data.

The data for a part of the hired labor force in the Moscow manufactories presented in table 3.69 enable one to construct an approximate time pattern for the changes in the number of hired workers. The data also suggest a secular growth of hired employment for all categories, although the growth was at different rates.

The time pattern in table 3.69 appears to support the general growth pattern of the Moscow textile manufactories, but one might not expect the growth rate of hired workers to have tapered off during the 1770s. One might argue that the growth rate during the 1760s was exceptionally high because the former ecclesiastical serfs and some court serfs were transferred from service obligations to money rent, and therefore were able to hire themselves out for work in the manufactories more freely. It is also possible that the Moscow plague of 1771, during which a quarantine was enforced, and the Pugachëv uprising affected the process of labor recruitment by contractual arrangements.

Another issue is the one of industrial preferences as expressed by those who hired themselves out or were hired out by their owners. This issue is related not only to the problem of wage differentials, but to the acquisition of skills usable both in the manufac-

Table 3.70   Social and Legal Status of Hired Workers in Moscow Manufactories by Industry, 1738–79

	Silk	Woolens	Linen	Other	Total
Burghers	405	n.a.	n.a.	283	688
Private agricultural serfs	1,396	2,165	1,686	684	5,931
Private household serfs	728	405	1,015	145	2,293
Church serfs	1,386	774	595	766	3,521
Court serfs	415	139	290	415	1,259
Total	4,330	3,483	3,586	2,293	13,692

tories as well as in the small-scale cottage-type industries. Table 3.70 categorizes workers in particular industries by social or legal origin.

The data of table 3.70 indicate a preference for the silk industry by comparison with other branches of the textile industry. This preference is clearly expressed by the group which was the least restrained in expressing its choice, the burghers. They overwhelmingly responded by hiring themselves out to the silk enterprises. Circumstantial evidence makes it possible to arrive at the same conclusion with respect to some of the serf groups. We know, for example, that all the private agricultural serfs and private household serfs employed in the linen industry were hired out by their owners to the manufactories of Johan Tamesz and Ovoshchnikov, and that the serf-owner Iaguzhinskii hired out his serfs to the wool manufactories, both clearly not the choices of the serfs themselves.[115]

This information tends to support the contention that, given a free choice, the preference of the hired workers of serf origin in the Moscow manufactories was the silk industry. Two conclusions can be drawn from the revealed preferences of the hired workers: they responded to the demand for labor in the expanding silk manufactories and their preference was motivated, at least in part, by a desire to acquire skills fundamental to the rapid growth of the rural-based small-scale silk industry in the Moscow region, which for the rest of the eighteenth century provided supplemental income for numerous producers.

The tendencies of growth in the category of hired laborers in the textile manufactories both within and outside of Moscow persisted during the 1780s and 1790s. The growth of the cotton textile industry, one

Table 3.71   Employment of Hired Labor in Private Manufactories in the Eighteenth Century

Manufactories	No. of Manufactories	No. of Hired Laborers
1750s—total	214	25,251
Metallurgy	61	10,775
Manufacturing	153	14,476
1760s—total	578	42,504
Metallurgy	174	21,373
Manufacturing	404	21,131
1799—total	2,256	96,114
Metallurgy	162	37,577
Manufacturing	2,094	58,537

Source: Strumilin, *Ocherki*, pp. 370, 384, 387.

with a preponderantly hired labor force, strengthened the tendencies previously at work. In summary, throughout the second half of the eighteenth century the number of hired laborers employed in mining, metallurgy, and other manufactories was increasing. The Soviet economist S. G. Strumilin provided the estimates presented in table 3.71 on the use of hired labor in private manufactories.

Strumilin estimated that for the end of the eighteenth century the number of hired workers in the state sector of metallurgy was 7,280, which, added to the figures in table 3.71, brings the total of hired workers up to 103,394, of whom 58,537 were employed in manufacturing and 44,857 in metallurgy. The total number of hired workers at the end of the century, as calculated by Strumilin, amounted to 52 percent of his estimated total employment in manufactories for 1799.

Out of the mass of peasant-serfs there emerged a numerous group which derived a large part of its income from industrial employment. This occurred without a change in their legal status. Unless one assumes that the marginal value product of these workers when engaged in agriculture was very low, one might argue that the social costs of supplying labor for industrial employment were relatively high by comparison with the cost when the supply was provided by a hereditary industrial labor force. On the other hand, if the maintenance of other members of the households of hired laborers was derived from work in agriculture, the existing system may have been profitable for the economy as a whole. In any event, whether or not the social costs of the existing arrangements of hired labor exceeded other alternatives, the political framework of Russian society was not ready for change along the lines of unhampered expressions of an economic calculus. The existing forms of hire depended upon serfdom and could not be radically changed as long as other social arrangements and the bulk of the labor resources were controlled by this basic institution.

Recruitment of Women into the Labor Force of the Manufactories

The conditions and circumstances of recruitment of women into the labor force of the manufactories differed to some extent from the conditions of male recruitment. The difference can be accounted for by two considerations: the role occupied by women in industrial employment and the status of women actually mobilized for industrial labor. Women as a group occupied a subordinate role in the industrial enterprises because of their low skills. In the textile industry, the basic employer of female labor, they were primarily spinners of wool, flax, or silk, tasks that were often performed by the cottage-type industries and which were less essential for the functioning of the manufactory as a production unit since the products could be obtained from outside the manufactory. To the extent that women were employed in the manufactory under the supervision of the enterprise's management, there probably existed good reasons for their employment, which was profitable to the enterprises, but other workers were easily substituted for them.

The social status of the women who were allocated to and distributed mostly by force among the manufactories was lower, by and large, than the status of serfs. The status of those women was considered to be the counterpart of the male categories of paupers, vagrants, and beggars. The majority of women sent to the manufactories consisted of soldiers' wives and daughters, mixed with prostitutes and wives of criminals. As a rule, the women were sent to the manufactories by the police, under one of the many decrees against vagrancy.[116]

It is, therefore, of interest to inquire into the government's motive behind its policies of sending specific categories of women into the manufactories. One motive was the industrialists' demand for female labor, the second was the government's attitude toward vagrancy and the consideration of manufactory labor as a penalty for vagrancy, and the third was the consideration of manufactory labor as a source of income for a social group that was deprived of regular, dependable sources of income and in fact was a public charge. Concerning the demand by the industrialists, perhaps it played a role in 1736 when the tightness of the labor market, which led to the enserfment of the skilled workers, might have increased the demand for female labor also. Later, however, industrialists hardly made any specific demands for female labor. The consideration of labor in manufactories as a penalty for vagrancy was based upon the January 7, 1736, decree which prescribed a five-year term of manufactory labor for women attached by the government to industrial enterprises. A

Senate decree of March 26, 1762, specifically assigned "all vagrant soldiers' wives" to be sent through the College of Manufactures to manufactories.[117] Issuing the decree, the College of Manufactures collected data on how many such women could be employed. The most convincing explanation of the government's motive is that labor in the manufactories was viewed as a source of income for specific categories that were unemployed or underemployed.

With respect to the soldiers' wives, a decree of the Senate of August 12, 1762, required removing such women from the border areas, providing them with passports, and sending them to the Moscow textile manufactories. The Moscow industrialists had agreed to employ 1,555 women of this category. Among the 1,764 women employed in the Moscow manufactories in the year 1764, 933 were soldiers' wives. Another piece of evidence supporting this lists the 933 soldiers' wives as possessing passports and working under a hire contract, the proper legal form for employment of persons in the possession of passports.

Female labor in the manufactories was motivated by considerations of welfare, as understood by the eighteenth-century Russian government. The government stipulated that soldiers' wives and daughters ought to be set free by their employers upon the return (or retirement) of their husbands and fathers from the armed forces. The forcible recruitment of women into the labor force of the manufactories was less a result of the demand for female labor and more a combination of government policies to combat vagrancy and to provide employment and income for social groups which found themselves on the fringes of society, outside the regular labor force. There are no known complaints about soldiers' wives remaining in the villages when they found support there, and it is reasonable to assume that most of the women sent to work in the manufactories were living outside the rural areas and were disturbing the sense of social order of the government authorities. Forced labor in the manufactories was one of the forms of making these wives economically productive and assuring them of a livelihood until the males in their lives returned to support them.

The Improvement of the Quality of Labor

A discussion of the labor market for eighteenth-century industrial enterprises in Russia cannot avoid the problem of the quality of labor. The problems of health protection and some rudiments of what are now described as "social services" are discussed elsewhere in a separate context. Here I shall discuss hereditary workers, child labor, education, and skill training. No attempt to compare the relative impor-

tance of these factors has been made because the data do not permit using any system to weigh the likely effects of each of the factors. Together, certainly, they help explain the gradual improvement of the quality of the industrial labor force employed in the Russian manufactories.

Hereditary Workers

A possible way to assure a steady stream of labor into the manufacturing or industrial sector, irrespective of the legal and economic situation of the serfs, was to create a hereditary industrial labor force. Hereditary workers as a social, but not necessarily legal, category encompassed those for whom employment in the manufactories was the main source of income and for whom the acquisition of industrial skills and habits can be traced for more than one generation.

This "hereditary worker" phenomenon was quite important during the preindustrialization phase when both rudimentary technical skills and "industrial habits" were rare. The elements of work discipline cooperation within the manufacturing establishment that are usually associated with industrial employment (or taken for granted in a developed industrial society) are of as much importance as skill itself. The acquisition of such habits was painful, costly, and time-consuming. Thus factory discipline was instilled in the labor force of the Russian manufactories of the eighteenth century literally by whips of overseers, managers, or armed guards. Later, during the nineteenth and early twentieth centuries, raw brutality was often replaced by an elaborate system of fines to enforce discipline and norm fulfillment. This system had its roots in the eighteenth century in a crude form as a method auxiliary to physical coercion.

Data related to the earliest period of the development of manufactories in Russia reflect the situation prior to the general enserfment of the skilled labor force. The first fragmentary data on the social origin of the labor force in manufactures (except iron and copper) that are in any way reliable and indicative are those for the 1730s. Two samples, presented in table 3.72, provide information on the origin of the first generation of workers among whom a continuity of skills might be assumed.

Although the percentage of manufactory employees who were of worker and craftsmen descent appears to be low, its relative size can in part be explained by the rate of growth of manufacturing industries during this period. The high growth-rate of industrial employment called for the absorption into the labor force of descendants of various social groups. Additional information provided by the second sample and presented in table 3.73 suggests that young descendants of workers were given preference

Table 3.72   Origins of Workers in Manufacturing (Percentages) in Two Samples of the 1730s

	Sample I					
	Urban Origin		Worker Descent		Craftsman Descent	
	1732	1737–38	1732	1737–38	1732	1737–38
Total workers	42.4	42.8	9.1	13.3	9.7	9.7
Males	36.5	39.0	9.2	15.0	7.7	
Females	68.3	55.1	8.2	8.2	2.9	2.6

	Sample II		
	Urban Origin[a]	Worker Descent	Craftsman Descent
Total workers[b]	60.6	10.8	1.1
Males		10.9	1.1
Females	27.6	8.2	.6

Source: Tomsinskii, *Sotsial'nyi sostav*, pp. 7–8, 27–29, 112–20.

Note: Sample I represents the employees in linen and wool cloth manufactories of 1732 and 1737–38. Sample II represents employees in linen, sail cloth, wool cloth, glass, pipe and ceramics, paint, and buttons factories for the year 1738.

[a]Percentage of the 6,063 employees who responded to the question.
[b]The total number of workers in Sample I for the two years was 1,535 and 1,954, of which males were 1,116 and 1,367 and females 419 and 587, respectively. The number of employees in Sample II is 6,992, of which 6,405 were males and 587 were females.

Table 3.73   Percentage Distribution of Employees by Age at the Start of Employment in Manufactories, 1738–40

Age	Descendants of Factory Employees	Total Labor Force
Below 11	48.6	32.2
12–14	25.3	22.2
15–19	17.0	22.8
20–24	6.1	9.5
25–29	1.3	5.3
30 and over	1.7	8.0

Source: Tomsinskii, *Sotsial'nyi sostav*, p. 118.

Table 3.74   Percentage Distribution of Manufacturing Employees and Employees of Worker Descent by Prior Means of Earning a Living

	Total Employees	Employees of Worker Descent
Stayed with family or relatives	31.7	67.6
Vagrancy	21.6	9.7
Other wage employment	22.6	8.8
Employment in Other manufactures	13.9	8.8
Trade	2.2	1.2
Crafts	1.8	.9
Other odd jobs	6.2	3.0

Source: Tomsinskii, *Sotsial'nyi sostav*, p. 16.

in the hiring policies of the entrepreneurs, who may have sensed that in numerous instances the inculcation of "industrial habits" and also skill training was provided directly to the young workers by their employed fathers.

The advantage to both employer and employee resulting from the hiring of descendants of manufactory workers is revealed by the record of the workers' prior activities and employment presented in table 3.74.

It follows from the information in table 3.74 that early entrance into manufactory employment, combined with worker descent, spared a number of workers the experience of what is contained in the term "vagrancy" and other, perhaps similar, alternative "opportunities" open to the early urban laboring class. The relative social and employment stability of the worker-descendant group, when compared with that of the other groups, suggests that the process of formation of a stable work-force for the manufactories set in during the first half of the eighteenth century. The process, was, however, both too slow and insuf-

ficient in terms of numbers to meet the demand for replacement and net additions to the labor force.

The absolutist state found a partial solution to this problem by forcing the creation of a "hereditary labor force" by the means of enserfment of the free skilled workers and by assigning enserfed peasants forever to mines, iron- and copperworks, and other manufactories. The government thus assured that the offspring of the enserfed peasants would provide labor services for the industrial establishments. The impact of these policies, originating in the 1730s, which created the category of *officinae ascripti* (*pripisnye*), can be traced in table 3.75.

Of the mass of ascribed and privately owned serfs who were employed by serf-owning entrepreneurs (the so-called *possessionnye* peasant workers), only a relatively small fraction, the skilled workers, could be included in the category of a "hereditary" industrial labor force. For the majority, mostly unskilled, their

Table 3.75   Social Origin of Skilled Workers in State-Owned Iron- and Copperworks, Urals and Siberia

	1726		1745	
	No.	%	No.	%
Peasant serfs	456	29.7	2,780	77.7
Workers	336	21.9	586	16.4
Raznochintsy[a]	500	32.5	170	4.7
Foreigners	30	2.0	9	0.3
Unidentified	215	14.0	34	0.9
Total	1,537	100.1	3,579	100.0

Source: Strumilin, *Istoriia*, pp. 286, 321.

[a]"Raznochintsy" was a term for free members of various service classes.

simultaneous engagement in agriculture and low level of skills in industrial employment appear to be a sufficient reason not to include them in this category. A more definite severing of their ties with agriculture and a minimal level of industrial skill-proficiency constituted the preconditions for their inclusion in the hereditary industrial labor category.

The eighteenth century witnessed the beginning of both a "natural" and a forced development of a hereditary industrial labor force. The existence of serfdom made possible the furthering of such a development, but, on the other hand, many impediments were imposed at the same time by the limitations on the mobility of labor and the forcible binding of many to agricultural activity. As a result, the process of inculcating "industrial habits" was incomplete even for the ones upon whom it was imposed and this explains in part the prevalence of the harsh treatment of labor in the industrial establishments of Russia over a long period of time.

The Problem of Child Labor and Entrance into the Labor Force

Modern historians have inherited from nineteenth-century reformers a critical attitude toward the utilization of child labor in industry. Many familiar arguments were advanced against such practices, from national interest (health deterioration of the younger generation) through a whole array of humanitarian reasons (condemnation of child-labor exploitation) up to the argument against child competition for jobs held by adult members of the labor force. Eighteenth-century figures who thought about labor relations and those who made labor policy were aware of these problems, but nevertheless entrepreneurs did not hesitate to employ children and youngsters. According to the responses to a 1738–40 questionnaire of workers employed in some branches of manufacturing, 10.6 percent were below 15 years of age.[118] Similarly, among 3,432 cases of the hiring out of serfs by their owners to Moscow manufactories in the years 1740–79, there were 637, or 18.6 percent, from

the same age group. Table 3.73 suggests that in the late 1730s over one-half of the workers in some branches of manufacturing began to work at an age of less than 15 years.

Some considerations pertaining more specifically to the eighteenth century than to recent periods ought to be mentioned. The demand for income on the part of the worker's household in which a child was not an income earner (as in agriculture) but primarily a consumer explains a good deal of the behavior of the urban working population. I would add to that the fact of short life-expectancy, which made it advantageous to begin on-the-job training as early as possible in order to be able, after the completion of training, to compensate the household or the employer for the previous outlays.

As long as the income position of workers' households required the early earnings of the younger generation, and as long as technology was more or less stable and general education was a prerequisite for only a few industrial skills, the manufactory owners resisted attempts to make them responsible for educating their young workers or for setting an age floor for their hiring practices. Both demands were refuted by the entrepreneurs on the grounds that the utilization of child labor was economically profitable and the substitution of adult for child labor in some auxiliary operations in the ironworks, for example, would double the wage expenditures for the particular operations and eventuate in an increase in the cost of the final product.[119] The resistance came from entrepreneurs who paid the market wage, which is understandable, but even more vehemently from the ones who by the nature of their privileges paid their workers a below-market wage.

It was plausible for both the household and the manufactory to accept a decrease of child labor only when the government had assumed the direct costs of elementary education, and when developing technology required general education as a prerequisite for some types of skill training or as a partial substitute for others. This, however, was to come much later. In the eighteenth century, early entrance into the labor force provided a visible advantage in terms of skill acquisition and income-earning.

Education

The awareness of the role of education in economic progress of the country can be traced at least as far back as Peter the Great. Peter did not have in mind anything resembling universal education, and he restricted education to the upper classes of society. For the gentry it was imperative, and for the merchants optional. But even this program met with considerable resistance on the part of the intended beneficiaries. Peter's determination is well enough known so that two examples will suffice as illustrations. He prescribed a minimum education for the children of the gentry and government officials and prohibited the clergy from performing marriage rites for them without proof that the educational demands had been met.[120] Another example might be Peter's reaction to the disobedience of a candidate for education abroad, the case of the nephew of Field Marshal Boyarin Sheremetev: the tsar ordered the culprit's mother confined to many months of slave labor in a factory in the company of criminals and prostitutes. While special skill-training was understood by merchants and industrialists to be beneficial, they refused throughout the first half of the eighteenth century to accept formal education as a component of an economic development program. This resistance was epitomized by the 1721 petition to Peter by various urban communities to exempt merchant children from the obligation to attend the newly established "cipher schools" with the explanation that both training for commerce and direct assistance in family business would suffer as a result of compulsory school attendance. The petitioners' request was granted, although probably on other grounds than those they advanced.

It was only in the second half of the eighteenth century that the requirement of education as a vehicle for successful business, for the individual as well as for the state, was recognized. During the 1760s the merchants started to petition the government for the establishment of elementary and secondary schools to provide education that would meet the needs of the business community. Although the clamor for education by the merchant class could conceivably be attributed in part to the demonstration effect of "Westernization" among the gentry, the arguments used were phrased primarily in terms of economic needs for and advantages from education in the area of commerce. The most interesting petition was submitted by the head of the urban community in Arkhangel'sk, Ivan Druzhinin, in 1764. He pointed to the losses suffered by merchants as a result of ignorance: (1) a low level of literacy leads to poor writing in commercial correspondence which results in incorrect interpretation of orders and directives: (2) lack of knowledge of arithmetic leads to an inability to deal with foreign exchange or foreign weights and measures; (3) a lack of knowledge of bookkeeping leads to ignorance about the solvency of the firm or enterprise; (4) lack of knowledge of geography leads to confusion in the area of transportation costs, freight charges, and insurance; (5) the inability to use foreign languages leads to excessive use of Amsterdam firms as middlemen; (6) ignorance of foreign and domestic laws and trade regulations opens many avenues for abuse on the part of government officials,

to the detriment of the merchants. Only education, the author concluded, could remedy the existing ills. Another contemporary author, Vasilii Krestinin, maintained that the establishment of schools would provide for "the teaching of attitudes that would produce good merchants and good citizens."[121]

To determine the contribution of education to the spread of manufactories and the improvement of the quality of the labor force, one must review the effort made during the eighteenth century in the area of technical education and formal general education. Among the higher technical schools, we find three which were instrumental in creating a cohort of Russians familiar with technical problems. Two were mining schools, one established in 1716 at the state ironworks in Olonets and the other in 1721 in Ekaterinburg, in the Urals. The third was the St. Petersburg Art Academy. The mining schools trained technical personnel for the armament industries, the Mining Department, and, subsequently, private industry. The Art Academy prepared specialists in architecture and construction. While the general direction of the educational effort of Peter the Great was "polytechnical," with special emphasis upon the military schools and technical schools and very little emphasis upon the general education component, the policies of Elizabeth and her successors differed somewhat from Peter's. In 1743 Peter's elementary schools, the cipher schools, were converted into schools for children of soldiers. With this pinpointing of the particular category of children for whom the schools were desired and whom they ought to serve, they were set upon a more realistic footing. By 1786 a system of two- and four-year elementary schools was set up.

Considering the nature of the Russian state and economy in the eighteenth century, the achievements of government policies in the field of education were very modest indeed. The data in table 3.76 summarize the state of education in Russia at the end of the eighteenth century.

One hundred years of governmental policies and changing social attitudes produced educational services available to 0.33 percent of the total male population of the Russian Empire. In addition, an approximate distribution of the total number of students between elementary education on the one hand and secondary, specialized, and higher education on the other, indicates that about 53,000 pupils annually were the beneficiaries of elementary education, and about 9,000 received an education above the primary level.[112] The impact of education upon the lower classes, and particularly on the labor force in manufacturing, was probably very slight. The impact of education upon the merchants and entrepreneurs was strong, for the schools served primarily the cities

Table 3.76   Enrollment in Educational Institutions at the End of the Eighteenth Century

Type of Institution	No. of Institutions	No. of Students
Universities and gymnasia	3	1,338
Cadet corps	5	1,980
Gentry boarding schools	8	1,360
Private boarding schools	48	1,125
Art academy	1	348
Medical schools	3	270
Mining schools	2	167
Church seminaries and schools	66	20,393
Schools for soldiers' children	116	12,000
Elementary schools (four-year)	49	7,011
Elementary schools (two-year)	239	15,209
Other schools	9	765
Total	549	61,966

Source: Beliavskii, "Shkola," pp. 110, 119.

Table 3.77   Employee Literacy by Social-Origin, 1737–40

Parents' Social Group	Literacy (%)
Clergy	31.7
Government officials	18.3
Postal employees	15.0
Nonmercantile urban inhabitants	14.1
Merchants and traders	13.1
Inhabitants of craft and mercantile settlements	10.6
Soldiers	7.4
Workers	6.8
Peasants	6.8

and the upper classes in those cities. Certainly one should not exaggerate the level of education and intellectual sophistication of the merchants, a consideration that brings to mind the fact that the three sons of the ennobled merchant and industrialist Turchaninov divided up their father's library by, in turns, each taking every third volume from the shelves. Regardless, whatever education was absorbed probably had a positive effect upon their business performance.

The educational minimum, literacy, was a relatively scarce resource of the labor force in Russia. The only more or less representative data in our possession pertain to the early, formative period of the manufactories' labor force, the years 1737–40, and indicate a 9.9 percent literacy rate among the male employees. The distribution of literacy among the labor force could almost serve as a proxy for its distribution within the social groups that supplied labor to the manufactories during this period. Table 3.77 appears to support this hypothesis.

Additional data on literacy rates in the sample employed in the construction of table 3.77 indicate that for a substantial number of manufacturing oc-

cupations there was a close relation between literacy level and the level of skill. The incidence of literacy among the higher-skilled workers was substantially above that among the less-skilled ones. The data are too fragmentary, however, to argue that literacy was a precondition of higher skills or that the income differential in the past made it profitable to invest in education. The data in table 3.77 hint that that was probably the case.

Skill training

In societies where there was a system of guild organization of crafts, skill training constituted an integral part of the apprenticeship system. Formalized and institutionalized apprenticeship included on-the-job training. There were no guilds in Russia, and consequently eighteenth-century Russian manufactories could not draw upon any prescribed system of apprenticeship and had to provide training within the enterprise itself. The situation was even more complicated in the case of skills that had to be imported from abroad, which was achieved through a two-way traffic of inviting foreign specialists and sending Russians abroad to acquire skills from foreign masters. The major clause in all the contracts with "imported" foreign specialists during the Petrine period was the obligation to train a certain number of Russian nationals in the particular skill or occupation. In fact, the clause was phrased sufficiently to relieve the Russians from their obligations under the terms of the contract even when the production performance of the foreigner was satisfactory. This seems to indicate that the future value of skill acquisition and substitution of domestic production for imports was sometimes placed by the government above the value of current output.

The use of foreigners as the "carriers" of superior skills was almost universal during the Petrine period, but rapidly diminished as the Russians acquired skills. The standard of quality and craftsmanship during the first half of the eighteenth century, as reflected in statements in surviving primary sources, was "as good as that of the foreign [product or work] or even better." Except for the introduction of new industries or new technological processes previously developed in Western or Central Europe, the use of foreigners in the normal operation of Russian manufactories declined. One reason was the high cost of foreign specialists. The salaries of foreigners, almost as a rule, were double those of the indigenous specialists of comparable skill.[123] Of much greater interest is the existence and size of the wage differentials for skilled versus unskilled labor that prevailed in the Russian labor market. The existence of such differentials is not difficult to ascertain, and their approximate size is sufficient to explain the incentive for the acquisition of skills.

It was expensive to acquire skills, and it is not surprising that an entrepreneur who bore the costs would have been interested in extending the time period during which he would be able to recoup his investment in training. Given the life- (or work-) span of a laborer during the eighteenth century, this training consumed a larger part of his active life than it did for workers at later periods in history. This also helps to explain why entrepreneurs resisted mobility between occupations, as well as job mobility within the same occupation. (The workers' attitudes on this subject are unknown.) The private entrepreneurs, to the extent that they paid for their laborers' skill acquisition, emphasized the need for and value of specific training for the production processes of their enterprises. This may have been manifested in the fact that the wage differentials among particular skill levels were more pronounced in private than in state enterprises. The government was in general less concerned with the proper application of the particular skills acquired by trainees. Examples of training with subsequent unemployment in the area of one's acquired skills were numerous but perhaps inevitable in a rapidly expanding and broad program of training such as the one conducted during the Petrine period.

The acquisition and utilization of skills facilitated the spread of manufactories and cottage industries. The manufactories utilized the skills of existing cottage industries (spinning, linen and wool weaving) and crafts (blacksmithing and other metalworking crafts) to include them in the production cycle or labor force of the manufactories. The establishment of the manufactories also greatly contributed to the spread of skills in adjacent areas and thereby created not only an auxiliary labor force which could be contracted for or compelled to render productive services for the manufactories, but also competitors against whom the manufactory owners carried on a bitter fight for decades, such as the linen weavers around Iaroslavl' and the silk weavers of the Moscow region.

As was noted above, there were numerous instances in which state and private peasants entered manufactories to acquire skills and later set themselves up in cottage industries. An example was the employment of 134 peasants from the village of Grebnev in the cottage silk-weaving industry. A few such peasants occasionally rose to large-scale entrepreneurship.

Social Services

The social services provided for the labor force in the eighteenth century should not be measured by the standards of the end of the twentieth century but by the standards and social norms of the times when the services were provided. In most cases, the demand for social services was initiated by the government. The case of medical care and sick benefits can illustrate the prevailing situation. Medical care for employed workers was first introduced in state-owned enterprises. The Admiralty Regulations (*Reglament*) of 1722 provided for the establishment of hospitals in the port cities for its workers, and required the workers to contribute half of their salary as well as the entire food ration during their stay there. The hospitals had to have on their staffs one physician and two assistants (*gezeli*) for each 200 hospitalized. The food ration for those hospitalized was prescribed as 1.5 pounds of bread and 5 *zolotniki* of salt daily, "good kvas always," and 5 pounds of meat, 4.5 pounds of cereals, and a half-pound of butter a week.[124]

A decree of January 27, 1724, established a physician and a supply of drugs in the Sestroretsk armament factories. In 1725 a hospital for the ironworks in Ekaterinburg was established, and in 1734 a hospital for the state armaments factory in Tula was founded. On May 1, 1747, a physician was ordered for the Kolyvano-Voskresensk factories, and the government decreed that by 1752 a hospital had to be established there.[125] In Ekaterinburg and Tula the employees contributed 1 percent of their wages toward the maintenance of the hospital services.

During the negotiations of the government with the owners of the Urals ironworks in 1734–36, the government representatives proposed that a flat rate of sick benefits be paid to the skilled workers. The rate pertained to "legitimate" illness and injuries, while "self-inflicted" disabilities such as venereal diseases, alcoholism, and injuries received in fights were explicitly excluded.[126] The manufacturers, however, refused to assume the financial responsibility and replied that illness and accidents "result from the will of God and not from the negligence of industrialists."[127] Thus the system of medical care which was at least nominally introduced in some state enterprises was rejected by the private entrepreneurs and did not come into being for over a century. (The Mining Statute [*Gornoe polozhenie*] of 1806 prescribed medical service in both state-owned and private mines and ironworks. It was ignored in practice, however, for many more decades.)

Some attention was paid during the eighteenth century to payments to skilled workers during periods of enterprise idleness. Disability pensions and death benefits were also offered upon occasion. The Muscovite government had paved the way by usually paying pensions to surviving widows and orphans of its military personnel. In 1724 the government ordered the payment of a pension in the amount of one-eighth of salary to the widows of deceased masters of the Sestroretsk armaments factories. By the end of the century the state enterprises in Kolyvano-Voskresensk were paying yearly death benefits of 5 rubles to widows of skilled personnel and 3 rubles to their children (boys until school age, girls until the age of fifteen). The same decree established a pension for retired skilled workers. Twenty-five years of employment, disabling accidents, or chronic illness entitled the highly skilled to a pension of 20 rubles per year and the less skilled to 10 rubles per year.[128] As in the case of hospitalization, private entrepreneurs showed no enthusiasm for assuming or sharing the costs of insurance schemes initiated by state enterprises.

The industrialists refused to pay indemnity in the case of loss of life or limb. They also refused to pay any portion of wages during the idleness of the ironworks. They argued that their own losses exceeded the losses of their workers when the works were idle, and that during such periods they did employ the skilled workers as general laborers and paid them the appropriate wage rates.[129]

How is it possible that the views of the private entrepreneurs and the professed views of the government diverged? Is it possible that the greed of profit-seeking entrepreneurs blinded them so much that they were thereby unwilling to follow "enlightened" government policy directed toward improving welfare? The answer is quite simple, and has very little bearing upon degrees of "enlightenment." The attitude of the government and its agencies was not the result of general labor policies but of mechanically transplanting into the armaments industry some of the institutions of the armed forces. Note that all the cases mentioned above pertained to armament factories, naval yards, and the like, all state enterprises closely connected with the armed forces. The issue of pensions for disabled or retired workers was raised by the government in an attempt to ease its own burden of maintaining old-age homes and hospitals, and to shift the burden to the shoulders of the industrialists. The industrialists did not deny the need for such institutions or for provisions to ease the lot of the poor; they just considered that to be the obligation of the government. This may explain both the origin of such "welfare" measures as well as the different positions taken by the state and the entrepreneurs. The real struggle for the welfare of the industrial labor force in Russia properly belongs to the history of the second half of the nineteenth century.

Work Discipline

To the extent that the manufactories of the eighteenth century were enterprises in which a higher level of cooperation and a greater division of labor prevailed than in small craft-establishments, the organization of the production process was much more important than in handicrafts or cottage industries. Another factor was the greater interdependence within the manufactory. These factors required certain habits, a work discipline determined both by the type of machinery and tools used as well as by managerial decisions. The work force employed in the early stages of manufacturing did not enter the enterprises with much knowledge of industrial or work discipline. It had to be acquired. Given the spirit of the age, the background of the labor force, the prevailing social conditions of serfdom, and the existence of an absolutist state, it is not difficult to imagine the tools and methods used for the inculcation of industrial habits.

An early charter (*gramota*) of 1702 issued by Peter the Great exempted the iron-master Nikita Demidov from the jurisdiction of the local administration and provided him with the right "to mete out punishment to his workers in matters of less importance."[130] Peter was much more specific with regard to the instruments of punishment when he wrote in another charter of the same year that Demidov "ought to punish the lazy, depending upon their guilt, with lashes, whips, and irons." Peter mitigated his directive in a moralistic tone: "so that the workers will not flee the ironworks as a result of excessive cruelty, he should not cause rightful tears and slights to the injured, for every offense, particularly when inflicted upon a poor man, is an unpardonable sin."[131] This moralistic tone has led some historians to attribute to Peter the Great a sensitivity to the welfare of labor and almost to make him a champion for the rights of the underdog. Regrettably, this role is ill-suited to Peter when one considers his further instructions and his own behavior.

The formula of the "lazy ones" who have to be punished, introduced by Peter into the field of what we now call labor relations, became a standard explanation that endured for generations among those who were either unable or unwilling to analyze the social conditions and causes of particular situations and were content to find a definition that would put the blame upon the subordinate, the object of individual or social punishment. An order given in 1706 by Peter to the head of the government gunsmiths in Tula prescribed a punishment and lashes and fines for those guilty "of laziness, drunkenness, insubordination, and low-quality production."[132]

The Admiralty Regulations of 1722 made it the business of special overseers to watch "that the workers are busy working honestly and not just having a good time, and to beat the lazy ones with clubs."[133] In the manufactories and ironworks the range of punishments was wider, as witnessed by the Instruction of General Hennin (1724) and V. N. Tatishchev's Factory Statute (1735) issued for the state-owned iron- and copperworks in the Urals and Siberia, but the spirit remained the same. The penalties included money fines, transfer to less skilled, harder, and less remunerative work, wearing chains during working hours, jailing in a cold chamber with or without chains, and relocation to other works or mines. Most of the penalties were accompanied by corporal punishment.

The first attempt at reform, designed to tame the arbitrary rule and brutality of plant managers, guards, and others in the administration, was the introduction of rules for the Izhevsk and Votkinsk ironworks by Prince Viazemskii in 1763. Prince Viazemskii, the future attorney general (Ober Prokuror) of the Senate, had been sent on a mission to investigate the causes of the bloody riots by the laborers, which were subdued by a military expeditionary force.[134] The novelty of the rule introduced for the *ascripti* was the provision of some autonomy for the workers themselves, who were allowed to organize into groups of tens and hundreds and then to elect representatives who dealt with minor disciplinary problems.[135]

The whip did not disappear from the factories, but it was perhaps less arbitrarily used on workers over whom the state retained some form of jurisdiction. It was the Pugachëv rebellion and the mass participation of the Urals factory labor-force in it that prompted the government to recommend the introduction of the Viazemskii reforms in other iron- and copperworks. In an order to the governor-general of Perm' dated January 30, 1781, Catherine decreed that the minor disciplinary problems of the *ascripti* ought to be handled by elected representatives, and major offenses had to be handled by the courts.[136]

Another instrument to enforce work discipline and "good behavior" was the threat of deportation. In 1734, at the request of the Kazan' wool-cloth manufacturer Driablov, fifty-one workers were deported and distributed among various state enterprises or sent into the army. A decree of January 7, 1736, provided entrepreneurs with the right to petition the Commerce College to deport workers guilty of bad behavior to forced labor in Siberia or Kamchatka as an example for and to frighten others. In 1739, fifteen workers of Poluiaroslavtsev's wool-cloth manufac-

tory were deported to Siberia, by decree of the Senate, for drunkenness, cardplaying, and other similar offenses. After the gentry gained the right to deport their private serfs to Siberia or to forced labor (*katorga*) for any term, and by a law of August 22, 1767, became immune against their serfs' appeals to the government, manufacturers with gentry status could do the same to enforce discipline in their enterprises. The merchant-industrialists, however, could only petition the government to do it for them. They also did not possess immunity against workers' appeals to the government comparable to that which the gentry had with regard to the serfs.

Evaluating the impact of such disciplinary measures on the labor force is very difficult. Whether these were the best means to inculcate factory discipline, cooperation, obedience, and high-quality performance cannot be assessed without examining many areas of social relations and making a general study of Russian society's culture in the eighteenth century. Even then it would be uncertain whether or not the student had transplanted his twentieth-century bias into the eighteenth-century context. Be that as it may, one thing is certain: the labor force of the manufactories, iron- and copperworks in Russia did not remain entirely passive. On many occasions they protested, resisted, and revolted against the authorities or the social order.

The workers' strikes and other forms of unrest in the eighteenth century constitute a fascinating chapter in the history of social revolt. By their nature they bore a close resemblance to the peasant revolts of the century and were hardly "anti-capitalist." The most interesting distinction between workers and peasants was the much higher degree of discipline and cohesion displayed by the manufactory workers on such occasions. The process of acquisition of general industrial habits was not without influence on their individual and collective behavior.

Government Policy toward Industry from 1725 to 1740

There was no sharp break between the economic policy of Peter the Great and that of his successors with respect to industrial development. The period is of particular interest because it was one of relative quiescence and minimal stress after Peter's stormy years. Such periods are often ignored by historians because they lack the drama of the more eventful ones. They should be examined, however, because they reveal the consequences of the stormy periods, and in this case because they show what Russian society was capable of doing when it was less goaded by the government.

A major historiographic issue has been the survival of the Petrine innovations, including the survival of the industrial firms created at Peter's instigation. Since industrial equipment was not the largest item in the total investment expenditure of firms, the continuity of one industrial firm was only in part influenced by a desire to maintain the capital stock as a unit. Transfers of capital stock and skilled labor occurred frequently. The latter was more important than the former. Consequently the survival rate of particular enterprises during this period is a poor and inaccurate measure of the success or direction of government policy, or of the economic soundness of particular branches of industry.[138]

Both state and popular demand assured the survival of the industrial sector after the death of Peter. Wars, although less frequent and protracted than during the Petrine period, remained an accompaniment to Russian foreign policy, and the demand for military supplies, even though fluctuating, was a powerful stimulus for maintaining the various branches of the war industries. The demand for luxury and "household type" manufactured goods increased as a result of the growth of incomes and purchasing power of the population following the Northern War.

In order to determine whether there was continuity with, or a break from, the policies instituted during the Petrine period, it is necessary to discuss three major problems: the general attitude toward industry as reflected by official pronouncements and actual policy measures; the choice between state and private enterprise whenever the government was faced with such a choice; the degree of state control and regulation of private enterprise.

The Petrine period was one in which the economic resources of the nation were strained to the utmost, when the burden of taxation grew heavier, the losses in human life and labor were large, and a large part of the country's output was consumed in prolonged wars.

It was also a period during which large investments were made whose gestation period was destined to be long and whose returns were to be reaped at a later period. This was particularly true for the investments in overhead capital or infrastructural projects such as roads and canals. The result was that the Petrine period not only met heavy current expenditures for wars, but also laid much groundwork for future economic activity. A certain volume of fixed capital and both improved and newly introduced skills were created which served as a base for future growth. Looking on the Petrine period as one of overexpansion, one must expect the ensuing period to be one of adjustment and stabilization. It was almost certainly beyond the power of even such a purposeful and resourceful ruler as Peter to continue the drive much longer. A replenishment of used-up resources and a stocktaking of achievements were necessary before a decision could be made on the path to follow after his death. Austerity imposed during Peter's wars had to give way to a possibility for the postwar demand to find its level of supply. A reappraisal of the investment potentials of a peace economy became part of the process of conversion from the previous overwhelmingly war-tainted economy. Last but not least, criteria of profitability had to be introduced to ensure the long-term prospects of enterprises as soon as wartime emergency considerations diminished in importance.

The immediate successors of Peter issued declarations in which their intentions to continue industrial growth were explicitly spelled out. A decree of September 26, 1727, contained the following unmistakable passage: "No customs duties shall be charged on commodities of new Russian factories that are exported from Astrakhan' to Khiva and Bukhara, so that the Russian factories may maintain themselves and expand through the sale of their products."[139] The post-Petrine government went even further than its predecessor in recognizing the need to consult the manufacturers in matters of policy and administration. The Petrine College of Manufactures was dissolved on February 24, 1727, and its role was assumed by the Commerce College and by the Council of Manufacturers.[140]

The idea of self-sufficiency, autarky, in areas assumed to be of importance for national defense was not discarded during the post-Petrine period. A decree of November 18, 1732, clearly stated the objective of "in the future satisfying the army with domestic, instead of foreign, cloth."[141]

It was the need to equip a modern army and navy from scratch that caused the Petrine striving toward self-sufficiency to assume such enormous proportions, to dwarf any measures toward autarky taken by his successors. In this area there was no break with Petrine policies. Such a policy continuity doubtless aided the further development of manufacturing.

Another area of continuity in economic policies was the one of preference for private vs. state-owned enterprises. A distinction must be made between the treatment of the iron and copper industries and the treatment of other industries. In the case of the latter, the issue was clear-cut. The government tried to dispose of deficit-ridden, high-cost production enterprises, working chiefly for a limited market, in branches of industry not competitive with foreign production which Peter did not have the opportunity to transfer to private ownership.

The solution was obvious and rational, even when a giveaway of equipment was involved as an incentive for private entrepreneurs to continue production. The writing off of the original investment as a loss to the state was the price paid for wrong decisions. In cases where a gain in skills was achieved, however, there may have been no loss to the economy at large. Much more complex was the problem of the bulk of the state-owned industrial establishments, the iron- and copperworks. As this was fundamentally a war industry, the choice was not between state vs. private in the abstract, but rather about a vital link in the national defense. The decision was not only economic, in the sense of comparative profitability, but chiefly political in terms of reliance upon private entrepreneurs or direct management by the state.

A discussion on the future of the state enterprises went on for almost a decade. The extreme view in favor of state ownership was presented by members of the state bureaucracy. It was associated with the names of the chief architects of the state-owned complex of ironworks, the able administrators General von Henning and V. N. Tatishchev. Von Henning, the builder and administrator of the Olonets ironworks, became the head of the Urals ironworks and authored the most detailed description of the Urals iron industry during the 1720s and 1730s. Tatishchev, von Henning's successor in the Urals, was even more extreme in favoring state ownership. Author of the proposed "Instructions to the Mining Supervisor" (Nakaz shikhtmasteru) and "Mining Regulations" (Gornyi ustav) of 1734 and 1746, he made an unsuccessful attempt to subject the private iron industry to very strict government controls. The arguments in favor of state ownership, apart from political considerations, used cost data to prove the lower cost of state-produced iron output compared with private output. These price calculations were faulty because they omitted the costs of the employed serfs and also an interest rate for capital. (Some of the elements of this type of calculating costs are still present in the accounts of many governments. The Soviet Union is a faithful follower of von Henning's accounting.)

The Senate questioned the contention that the costs of state enterprises were lower, in spite of the statistics von Henning presented. Its report of 1733–34 pointed to the fact that the state-owned iron industry had almost 35,000 serfs and produced only 160,000 poods of iron in 1732, whereas Demidov with only about 5,000 serfs produced 300,000 poods of iron annually. Demidov obtained a price of 70 kopeks per pood, while the state sold its output for only 60 kopeks per pood. The Senate also questioned von Henning's contention that his costs were 17 kopeks per pood and Demidov's were 25.

The other extreme was represented by those who recommended immediately turning over the iron-works to private entrepreneurs and preferred the transfer to partnerships rather than to single entrepreneurs. The rationale for preferring partnerships was based upon a notion of enlarging the number of participants and preventing the development of a personal monopoly. This anti-monopolistic tendency was combined with an anti-concentration bias to the extent that a 1730 proposal would have transferred only the best ironworks at first to encourage private enterprise. It also proposed dispersing the plants among as many partnerships as possible. One can only speculate whether this anti-concentration and anti-monopolistic bias was influenced by the behavior of the Demidovs.

The policy accepted by the government can be summarized as follows: (1) the higher efficiency of the private ironworks was basically admitted; (2) the state's interests with regard to volume of deliveries, prices for output, and tax revenues had to be safeguarded in any deal involving the transfer of state industry into private hands; (3) the expectation with regard to further capital investment by the private entrepreneurs and an increase in output was both a cause of this favorable attitude toward private ownership and a condition of the transfer.

The conclusion about the relative profitability of the private industrial enterprises compared with those the state owned was further substantiated by a report in 1732 by the Monetary Committee (Monetarnaia kommissiia) to the Senate. At this point, the Senate, which favored distributing the state enterprises to private entrepreneurs, was still hoping to recover in the course of the transfer a part of the invested capital by imposing an obligation to repay the original investment during a ten-year period.[142] Apparently the hope of recovering the original investment was soon given up, for it was not mentioned in subsequent documents. The recommendation that state-owned enterprises be transferred to private ownership was repeatedly stated by the special committee of 1733, the Golovkin Committee report of June 5, 1739, the report of the General Mining Directory, the Council of Ministers report of 1739,[143] the Mining Regulations of 1739,[144], and an instruction of 1740.

While the share of state-owned enterprises in the total output of manufacturing was declining during the post-Petrine period, the degree of state control and regulation of private enterprises apparently increased. This leads me to hypothesize that an idea of substitutability of state ownership and state control was present in the minds of policy makers. Assuming that state ownership in the absence of profits and in the presence of costs might ultimately be more expensive than the administration of state control, the leaders of Russia apparently gave preference to the latter over the former.

The government simultaneously realized that the ownership rights of entrepreneurs constituted a basic precondition of private entrepreneurial activity and found it necessary to define more rigidly the conditions of exercising those ownership rights in the area of industrial activity. (A concomitant feature of government regimentation and control in Russia was the ever-present problem of licensed vs. unlicensed manufacture. This is dealt with more fully elsewhere. In general, the relationship between the state and the private entrepreneurs in Russia was closer to that in the continental countries, France, Prussia, and Sweden, than it was to England. The similarities and differences can in part be attributed to the power relationship between the state and the organized bodies of the commercial and industrial strata in each country.)

The following major areas of government control over private enterprise, applied during the post-Petrine period, can be distinguished: requirement of accurate reporting and punishment for report falsification; control over size of operation; control over some sources of raw materials and labor; control over the functioning of establishments; control to stimulate growth of particular industry branches.

The demand for accurate and detailed data became a major part of the control system. The type and scope of the requested data were designed to meet not only specific fiscal criteria, but to cover the broad area of the overall operations of the particular manufacturers. For example, a Senate document of 1738 demanded the following information from the Iakov Bobrovskii and Co. wool-cloth factory in Irkutsk: dates of establishment and start of operation; list of equipment, purchased and made on the premises; number of masters and workers; specification of yearly wages and other payments; local prices of raw materials; consumption of raw materials (by year); output by type of products; quality of production; costs of production; places of marketing and sales prices of output.[145] Aside from the fact that the aggregated data provided useful information about the manufacturing sector of the economy and its relations with other sectors, and also could serve as a useful source for appraising the general economic situation and for suggesting policy changes, the information gathered provided a control over the particular enterprises sufficient to judge whether those enterprises were living up to the standards set by the government.

Although report falsification apparently was a widespread practice, instances in which such falsifications might have affected national defense were not treated liberally and punishment was meted out. An interesting example was presented by a wool-cloth factory in Putivl'. Organized in 1719 by General Korchmin and Ivan Dubrovskii (a merchant), it failed to report its output until 1726, when it declared its "readiness in the near future to produce cloth and lining for four regiments and more." An inspection by the College of Manufactures revealed that there was no ready-made cloth in stock, and only 2,300 arshins (about 1,700 meters) of undyed cloth, in spite of the fact that 476 workers (mostly state peasants) were at the disposal of the enterprise. In response to a Cabinet decree of August 12, 1726, Dubrovskii was sent under guard to St. Petersburg, his property was confiscated to collect tax debts, and the enterprise was taken over by the state (to be managed by the assessor Neelov). The confiscation of the enterprise was justified because of the offense of "providing an untrue report about cloth."

Entrepreneurs were strongly motivated to falsify reports because of the privileged status enjoyed by those manufacturers who had the right to purchase land and serfs, plus the freedom from compulsory services they possessed that ordinary merchants did not. The failure to maintain certain standards of production expected by the government led to a revocation of the privileges and the striking of the entrepreneurs from the list of manufacturers. (Genuinely intensive striking from the lists began during the Elizabethan period and will be dealt with separately below.) Accurate reporting was considered a form of control over the degree to which entrepreneurs conformed with the state standards.

The state's review of the size of operations consisted basically of control over the applicability to particular enterprises of the concept of manufacturing plant as distinct from small-scale operations of the handicraft type. The state had no awareness of the concept of optimal size, but its image of a manufacturing plant was of a place that maintained a certain level of operations or volume of output and used mechanical (water) power. In order to influence, if not impose upon, the entrepreneurs with the aim of maintaining a high level of output, control over the size of operations was stressed and the enjoyment of privileges was mandatorily conditioned upon meeting that size. A decree of June 28, 1731, announced a purge of manufacturers and an annulment of the privileges enjoyed by "pseudo-manufacturers" (fal'shivye fabrikanty), defined as those who pretended to establish manufactories but only "maintained small plants as a front." They were to be treated as ordinary merchants.[146]

In some cases control over the size of operations went beyond the simple principle of distinguishing between a handicraft and manufacturing establishment. The government demanded that the entrepreneurs work at maximum capacity. An example was an order given to Akinfii Demidov to return from

Moscow to Siberia because the government had received a report that the Demidov ironworks were operating at only one-quarter capacity in the owner's absence. There was also a shortage of funds on the spot. Demidov was ordered to "return from Moscow to Siberia to improve his ironworks, or to send there the necessary amount of money for their maintenance."[147]

Control over the current functioning of the enterprises was exercised by the government agencies (Mining College, College of Manufactures, Commerce College) that were supposed to supervise them. Although the supervision in general was quite superficial and the routine was not too burdensome for the entrepreneurs, attempts were made by some officials of the agencies to introduce a permanent control apparatus over the daily functioning of the manufacturers. A set of proposals for the iron industry, "Instructions to the Mining Supervisor," advanced by V. N. Tatishchev was characteristic of the tendency toward increasing government control. The project envisaged the establishment of an institution of government experts attached to the private enterprises which would report upon all irregularities and impose government policy goals.[148]

Tatishchev proposed that the enterprises would pay the experts' salaries. In turn, the entrepreneurs would benefit by obtaining technical expertise and advice from the officials. The major private iron producers, and most notably the Demidovs, were up in arms against such extensive interference in the conduct of their business. They succeeded in fighting off that menace to their entrepreneurial independence "at the summit," which rejected the proposed innovation. Tsarina Anna acted after the Commerce College had presented its view "that the subordination of the entrepreneurs to the commands of outsiders will decrease their desire to produce," and thus recommended rejection of the extreme position of increased controls.[149]

The above proposal was accompanied by a more sweeping one, that a code of economic behavior for the mining and metallurgical industries should be established. This proposal was Tatishchev's project for "Mining Regulations."[150] Tatishchev hoped to control the routine operations of the enterprises by subjecting them to an agreed code covering a wide range of activities including output norms, pricing, marketing, and wage policies. A heated controversy resulted from the discussions conducted between Tatishchev and the iron manufacturers in the Urals in which a clash between private and etatist interests can be observed. The discussion also caused the divergent views within the government to come out into the open. The united forces of the private entre-

preneurs and "liberals" within the government defeated the proposals.

The proponents of stricter government control advanced an argument which became a recurrent theme and was utilized in attempts to impose controls. This was an argument pointing to existing low quality of output and the necessity to impose quality standards in manufacturing. Just as the attempt of Peter in 1714 to train specialists and disseminate knowledge about new methods of tanning leather was related to a desire to achieve higher quality, so the attempts of the 1730s to send samples of higher quality wool cloth to the cloth manufacturers can be considered an expression of a desire to achieve higher quality and an attempt to interfere with the freedom of entrepreneurship. The latter contention is made on the basis of the typically Russian (or mercantilist) practice of declaring that absence of conformity with new quality-standards was a punishable offense.[151]

Repetition of the same decrees and the attempts to remedy the low quality of output indicates that either the controls were enforced leniently or that they were quite ineffective. The resistance to quality standards was reinforced by the market, for the entrepreneurs responded to the market within the range of prices they could obtain, and new technology could be introduced by private entrepreneurs only if they expected higher returns. In the absence of positive market signs, even intensified government controls were rendered ineffective.

Another feature of government controls and interference was the attempt to assure and stimulate growth of particular branches of industry. Here a scale of preferences can be detected for the post-Petrine period that did not deviate from the preceding one. A distinction should be made, of course, between general, long-run policies, where the tools were tariffs, fiscal measures, and subsidies, and short-run measures designed to meet on short notice urgent governmental demands, chiefly in the area of military supplies. The latter type of measures concern us at this point.

On the stimulation of growth, the division between the two existing philosophies within the government was as marked as it was on other issues. One group believed in the omnipotent role of bureaucratic controls as a means to achieve higher levels of output and investment. Such belief was expressed in a special decree to the Commerce College ordering an increase in the supervision by its officers of the wool-cloth manufacturers in order to achieve higher output and improved quality.[152] The other group tried to combine controls with incentives for entrepreneurs, but was willing to use controls if they appeared to have the desired effect. Thus a decree posed for the entrepreneurs the alternative of either selling excess serfs or "employing them in *newly* constructed ironworks." The decree was issued as a measure to compel entrepreneurs to increase their output and investment. In another case, the government tried to solve a gunpowder problem that resulted from a price increase by the Dutch by stimulating additional private domestic output. But in case the private entrepreneurs did not respond and build additional gunpowder plants, the government intended to build them at its own expense, with their subsequent transfer into private ownership in mind.[153]

These various government decrees reflect the prevalence of each of the groups at particular junctions of government policy. One of the measures intended to stimulate further private investment in plants and expansion of output was the extension of long-term government contracts for supply to the state. This also increased the area of government controls. An example was the decree of November 12, 1735, which prescribed six-year contracts for the wool-cloth industry.[154] There can be no doubt that such contracts, apart from increasing the state's power and control over the private entrepreneurs, were advantageous to the state, for they assured government departments of a part of necessary supply and made it easier to meet emergency needs. Price decreases may have occurred in the market later, but the government benefited nevertheless.

The benefits for private entrepreneurs of state controls in the marketplace depended upon a number of conditions: advance payments, which helped the entrepreneur to bridge the time gap between his own expenses on current account and his proceeds from sales; stability of prices, which precluded an increase in his costs while the prices of his future deliveries under contract were usually fixed; an assumption that the government would not lag in the payment for supplies beyond the entrepreneurs' normal expectations; no excessive uncertainties in the market that threatened the entrepreneur with losses or might slow down substantially the turnover of his capital (meaning additional costs to him). In case these conditions were not present, long-term government contracts, which were imposed upon the entrepreneurs, were likely to discourage rather than induce increased output and additional investment.

To the extent that a judgment can be formed on the basis of official policy pronouncements and enacted legislation on the one hand and actual performance on the other, the range and scope of government controls over private enterprises exhibited a tendency to expand, to become more penetrating, and possibly more refined, in comparison with the Petrine period. It is true that most were applied and concentrated in industries that were related to national defense, but those were branches prominently represented in the total value of output and the labor force of the manufacturers, the leading industries of this period.

The substitution of controls for state ownership passed its test during the post-Petrine period, and the government apparently settled for this form of substitution without relinquishing its command post in the national economy, or even in the industrial sector, where it appeared not as a competitor of private entrepreneurship or as an example-setter, but as the supreme supervisor, comptroller, and large consumer, attempting to dictate the quality, set prices, and regulate the supply.

4
FOREIGN TRADE

Russian foreign trade in the eighteenth century mirrored the country's emergence from political and economic isolation and its growing involvement in the affairs of Europe and the world. In real terms, foreign trade increased approximately fifteenfold from the beginning to the end of the century. Table 4.1 shows a twelvefold increase in exports between 1742 and 1797, years for which relatively reliable data are available. The growth of foreign trade was a reflection of the capability of the commercial sector in Russian agriculture and industry to supply increasing volumes of commodities at the very time when the foreign demand for them was rising. As one would expect, the prospect of higher prices brought an increased supply of goods.

The basket of exports from Russia, consisting basically of the staples of the Baltic trade, was not unlike that of Sweden, Poland, and Prussia. It was made up primarily of low price-per-unit-of-weight bulky commodities, agricultural goods, forest products, iron, and other raw materials. Transportation costs were relatively high, for imports (finished industrial and luxury goods) were of high value per unit of weight and had to be imported on ships that came into the Baltic half empty or in ballast.

Russia had to compete with other countries in most exports and thus was in no position to create monopoly positions. Exports that could not excel in quality had to compete in price. The development of foreign mass markets in the eighteenth century created a strong demand for Russian goods. Among Russia's customers were not only the shipbuilders of Western navies and merchant marines, not only the producers of ironwares, of soap and candles, linen and ropes, but also the New World slaveowners, who clothed their slaves in coarse linen shirts made in Russia.

Until the British had perfected the new technology that enabled them to replace their imports with domestically produced iron, the Russians supplied the metal. Until the cotton industry had gone through its successive stages of absorbing the new

inventions in weaving, spinning, and ginning, the Russians supplied hemp, flax, and linen. Russia's contribution to the Industrial Revolution was its support for a process of capital accumulation that occurred without a major deterioration in Western living standards.

There were important and inevitable backward linkages between the demands of the Russian export trade and domestic production. The high level of demand for hemp and flax caused the expansion of those crops in northwestern Russia, as well as further south, and created areas of specialization in which those crops not only constituted a sizable share of the planted area but absorbed most of the labor of farming households. Likewise, without foreign demand the output of Russian iron probably would never have risen beyond the level that it achieved by the middle of the century. Such examples can be multiplied. Foreign trade in Russia during the eighteenth century was one of the important engines of economic growth. It had a major impact on the commercialization of agriculture, the growth of industry, the expansion of the money supply, and the accumulation of capital.

Russia's import trade grew as well. It reflected the distribution of purchasing power among the various groups of the population. Apart from imports by the government itself, it consisted primarily of commodities to satisfy the demand of upper-income groups for luxury goods. Also in demand were industrial commodities such as metals and dyestuffs for textiles.

The degree of government interference in trade ranged from direct state trading monopolies for both exports and imports to virtually no interference whatsoever. The prevailing tendency, in accord with mercantilist principles, was to stimulate an increase of exports and to diminish the volume and value of imports as much as possible through tariff legislation and direct subsidies to import-substitution industries. The favorable balance of trade that Russia reportedly enjoyed during most of the century was perhaps due less to government measures and more

Table 4.1   Exports from Russia in Current Rubles

Year	Total	St. Petersburg	Narva	Revel'
1742	4,567,423	2,479,650		
1743	4,240,548			
1744	5,916,408			
1745	5,249,366			
1746	5,267,811			
1747	5,401,934			
1748	4,624,306			
1749	5,536,374	3,153,988		
1750	7,152,829			
1751	6,595,576			
1752	7,931,559			
1753	7,458,250	3,451,383		
1754	7,240,649	3,577,939		
1755	8,182,770	4,550,060		
1756	8,005,237			
1757	8,195,496	4,598,120		
1758	8,662,596			
1759	9,601,836	3,530,614		
1760	9,875,014	3,194,353		
1761	9,724,277			
1762	12,762,493	5,217,006	464,502	
1763	11,139,713	5,156,943		
1764	11,493,803	5,885,243	630,341	155,198
1765	13,098,824	6,912,790		249,628
1766	11,608,181	5,775,357		197,864
1767	11,609,607	6,184,300		124,729
1768	12,971,542	6,630,248		133,422
1769	14,518,024	7,640,302		192,203
1770	14,989,135	7,522,502		204,877
1771	17,136,353	8,937,798		479,839
1772	15,670,308	6,451,495		
1773	18,141,676	8,900,575	245,930	106,534
1774	17,603,964	9,530,627	314,881	204,195
1775	18,557,279	8,299,586	458,645	420,380
1776	17,968,372	8,966,156	367,711	209,654
1777	20,486,358	11,116,938	451,493	107,502
1778	19,173,568	10,210,488		
1779	18,791,358	11,216,898		
1780	19,656,714	10,941,129		151,416
1781	22,690,493	12,954,440		
1782	21,059,167	11,467,347		
1783	23,503,632	10,098,798	614,127	
1784	26,295,034	12,941,513	494,400	323,622
1785	25,373,593	13,497,645	776,756	443,146
1786	22,904,403	13,411,408	746,440	247,203
1787	26,113,849	16,086,800		
1788	28,721,196	20,351,937	495,038	113,000
1789	31,053,757	21,735,662	421,872	144,477
1790	32,754,734	21,641,779	573,806	81,934
1791	34,290,225	20,048,697	721,375	104,351
1792	40,696,733	22,224,331	536,966	108,327
1793	43,481,089	23,757,954	238,555	109,897
1794	45,474,331	25,565,767	457,315	152,002
1795	53,772,284	31,367,953	321,401	417,349
1796	67,670,464	37,110,333	688,139	657,468
1797	56,683,560	32,450,911	526,776	359,535
1798	63,378,920	36,552,476	631,439	346,533
1799	68,996,982	38,169,935	556,540	417,108

Riga	Pernau	Vyborg	Arkhangel'sk	Kiakhta	Year
			411,256		1742
					1743
			273,681		1744
					1745
					1746
			230,161		1747
					1748
			339,794		1749
			310,492		1750
					1751
					1752
			288,440		1753
					1754
			351,255		1755
					1756
					1757
					1758
					1759
			530,866		1760
2,029,585					1761
			689,602	522,477	1762
			694,232	302,798	1763
			521,271	137,493	1764
			649,875	694,232	1765
2,266,191			753,297	28,489	1766
		73,121	687,879		1767
		77,619	842,409	50,095	1768
		72,076	886,340	1,074,651	1769
			877,773	1,351,978	1770
		65,095	1,446,079	1,246,410	1771
		58,306	1,727,932	1,002,519	1772
3,738,860	110,205	100,357	2,058,535	1,140,183	1773
4,896,615	159,165	77,370	1,453,660	1,227,760	1774
4,619,798	280,675	51,437	1,367,926	1,365,826	1775
4,422,013	188,431	78,024	1,535,362	1,638,791	1776
4,433,544	200,184	83,032	1,261,327	1,440,546	1777
4,515,435		85,220	1,582,058	794,540	1778
4,647,957		85,642	1,129,445		1779
3,861,869		48,727	1,474,592	2,700,187	1780
3,696,775		47,413	1,373,855	3,735,312	1781
		55,343	1,183,668	3,520,343	1782
5,864,816		178,261	1,121,433	2,789,177	1783
6,392,422		213,026	1,460,427	2,713,357	1784
5,214,415		121,387	1,553,999	1,805,926	1785
4,337,896	298,624	143,724	1,661,833		1786
4,199,786		134,998	1,671,020		1787
4,199,780		130,222	1,687,111		1788
4,436,687	447,859	97,438	2,371,546		1789
6,690,580	378,623	79,416	1,830,063		1790
7,997,730	382,855	161,655	1,843,978		1791
8,642,251	433,505	177,357	2,335,198	2,467,280	1792
8,985,929	189,131	124,832	2,548,667	3,549,432	1793
9,888,916	334,801	99,358	2,411,846	2,522,942	1794
11,050,332	357,610	70,344	2,749,845	2,720,286	1795
14,053,652	768,004	138,160	4,479,859	2,551,764	1796
10,412,384	729,698	154,132	2,420,657	2,378,750	1797
11,849,184		104,625	2,521,425	2,783,943	1798
11,251,409		16,988	2,555,252	3,677,824	1799

to the relatively low purchasing power of the mass of the Russian population and the high prices of most imported goods. The actual balance of payments is difficult to calculate, and it is probable that illicit trade, expenditures of the Russian nobility abroad, and payments for invisibles used up the foreign funds that the surplus provided.

At the beginning of the century, the Dutch were Russia's most important trading partners, but by the 1730s and 1740s they were succeeded by the British, who occupied first place throughout the rest of the century. England was not only the chief exporter to Russia and the main importer of Russian goods, but also one of the major carriers of Russian goods to southwestern Europe and the Mediterranean. The positive trade balance of Russia with Great Britain and the Netherlands was to some extent neutralized by a negative balance with the Hanseatic cities and other areas.

The great bulk of Russian trade was directed through the Baltic ports acquired or constructed in the eighteenth century and through the old port of Arkhangel'sk on the White Sea. By the end of the century a new outlet for Russian goods, the ports on the Black Sea, began to rise in significance after the liquidation of the Crimean Khanate. The Black Sea ports had an advantage of proximity to the Mediterranean, an area in which there was an increasing market for Russian grains, primarily wheat.

Despite the increased number and capacity of the Russian ports, the Russian merchant marine was nonexistent, except for domestic coastal trade. The high cost of capital, a lack of skills and supporting institutions made it unprofitable for Russian merchants to ship their goods in Russian bottoms. A Russian version of the Navigation Acts would have been a folly, for the Russian foreign maritime trade suffered from shortcomings that were difficult to overcome: the lack of standardization of goods, the lack of quality specifications, and, most important, the relative lack of capital. These facts made it necessary for merchants to obtain loans or merchandise on credit from their foreign trading partners. Thus trade with Europe was financed to a large extent by foreign capital, a situation that was advantageous to the Russian economy but offended the sensitivities of the Russian merchants striving for economic independence.

Trade relations between Russia and its eastern neighbors, the Chinese, and the nomads of Asia were somewhat different. In the trade with China, political considerations were more important than in the case of the rest of Europe, and for a long period trade involved a bilateral clearing of accounts so that exports would equal imports. Tea, silks, and textiles were imported into Russia; textiles, furs, and rhubarb were exported to China. Significant mutual benefits resulted from the Russo-China trade, a trade conducted primarily at the border. (Only in the first quarter of the century did state-organized caravans of Russian merchants reach Peking.) The benefits derived were so substantial that the Russians even imported furs from England to transport them eastward for resale. The trade with the nomads from Asia and indirectly with Central Asia grew during the second half of the eighteenth century. Russia re-exported textiles to meet the demands of its trading partners along the steppe frontier and received wool, sheep, cattle, and horses in return.

It was through the channels of foreign trade that Russia received much of the silver needed for coinage; the silver came as shipments of specie (especially German Reichstalers) to pay for the excess of exports over imports and for duties. The imports of silver for minting provided the government with a source of income, and the trade surplus enabled the Russian silver monetary unit, the ruble, to remain during most of the century above its intrinsic value in terms of silver. By the end of the century, the increased use of copper and later of paper money, coupled with some deterioration in Russia's terms of trade with Western Europe, diminished the flow of silver from the West to Russia. A decrease in the price differential for agricultural products and raw materials between Russia and Western Europe became noticeable. Foreign demand increased Russian prices of traded commodities, and decreases in the costs of handling and transportation of goods, primarily of shipping in Western Europe, contributed to the narrowing of the price differential. Inflationary pressures in both Russia and Western Europe had an impact on the relative movements of the general price levels in both areas as well as on the changes in the relative prices for foods and raw materials.

The Russian merchants specializing in foreign trade can be divided into four categories, each characterized by a particular set of attitudes. The first group consisted of foreign merchants or representatives of foreign firms residing or operating in Russian ports who were generally considered high in status and were accepted as members of the highest Russian commercial corporate group, the *gosti*. Specializing primarily in Baltic exports, including a variety of goods such as hemp, flax, iron, forest products, and grains, they usually raised their original capital prior to their arrival in Russia. For the most part they were organized in partnerships or in family businesses that achieved a remarkable continuity over several generations.

The second group consisted of merchants of foreign origin who were either assimilated culturally or participated in the Russian corporate structure. Some were merchants of the Baltic provinces annexed by Russia. Their traditional contacts with the trading communities of northcentral and northwestern Europe and their contacts with suppliers from the territory of Poland-Lithuania were a major asset in the development of their business in both the export and the import trade. This group, like the first, represented a high degree of concentration of commercial capital, but it was organized in family firms rather than in partnerships, less specialized in terms of commodities traded, and less concentrated in a particular market. In terms of its residence pattern, this group was more widely dispersed. Possessing both smaller organizational units and quantities of capital, the merchant firms in this second group had to be closer both to the markets and the sources of supply. Lacking an outside base, but maintaining cultural relationships with their Russian counterparts, the merchants in this group were closer than those in the first one to most of the indigenous merchant groups with whom they did business.

The third group consisted of indigenous merchants who resided in the ports and were registered in the city guilds. They constituted the core of the traders in the Baltic ports which were annexed by Russia during the eighteenth century. They also included the St. Petersburg merchants who settled there as residents early and had advantages over other Russian merchants.

The fourth category was made up of outsiders, registered merchants of other cities designated as "trading in the ports." Although perhaps the lowest of all groups in terms of status, their participation in the actual trade was very significant in the ports of St. Petersburg and Arkhangel'sk. Their only real disability vis-à-vis the resident trading firm was in access to sources of credit. In an era when credit extension involved substantial risk, residence status was viewed as an element that diminished the possibility of default.

Although credit scarcity was a perennial problem in Russian foreign trade, and relatively high interest rates tended to diminish the real rate of profit, Russian merchants clamored not only for cheaper sources of credit, but also for tariff protection and special privileges in their competition with foreigners. However, the incentives provided for Russian merchants to develop shipping facilities and the differential customs duties were insufficient to make them either more aggressive or more competitive. Their low social status and their dependence on foreign capital did not help to raise their morale and self-esteem. It was only toward the end of the century, when the process of capital accumulation in the trading sphere came to include the Russian merchants and when credit eased in the Russian economy under inflationary pressures brought about by the expansion of the money stock, that the port merchants both as individuals and as groups in a number of regions became active participants in, or promoters of, economic expansion.

In the expansion of Russian foreign trade during the century the merchant class provided the producers with indications of increased demand and also served as a supportive element. As the other branches of the economy began to grow and the Russian market demonstrated its ability to absorb a greater volume of imports, the merchants became more active. Although they did not excel in the search for new foreign markets, much of their energy found an outlet in meeting the demands of their home market, the one they knew best.

The Composition of the Export Trade

A study of the composition of the Russian export trade reveals the shifts that took place during the eighteenth century in the relative strength of certain commodity groups. The paucity of data available on the exports of the period complicates the task of detecting such shifts.

Accumulated knowledge about the development pattern of the various branches of the Russian economy during this period, and a certain familiarity with the economic development of Western Europe suggest areas of likely shifts. Given the evidence of population increase, a growth in agricultural production, and development in mining and manufacturing, one would expect a relative decline in the share of forest products and an increase in the share of manufactured goods, as well as in the products of mining and metallurgy. The export of manufactured goods grew at the expense of agricultural commodities. One would expect a general shift toward an increase in exports of commodity groups that had a higher share of value added in their cost structure and also, in view of the slow increases in the efficiency of goods transportation, movement toward an export mix that would maximize the price per unit of weight of exports. Most of those changes took place in the first half of the eighteenth century. The second half of the century saw changes in the commodity groups subject to shifts in the relative prices in the world market.

The commodity classification adopted to reveal the changes in the composition of Russian exports suggests itself because of the linkages of export commodities with the relevant sectors in the economy. By way of illustration in table 4.2, the chosen years reflect the share of commodity groups in the total value of Russian exports (in current prices) for the beginning, middle, and end of the century. (The data for 1710 reflect the private trade through the port of

Table 4.2   Shares of Commodity Groups in the Total Value of Russian Exports For Selected Years

	1710	1769	1793–95
Crops	37.8%	50.5%	43.1%
hemp	34.4	18.8	20.2
flax	3.3	11.3	12.6
linseed and hempseed	.04	3.5	3.4
grains	2.9	16.9	6.9
Livestock products	50.4	12.5	18.1
tallow	11.4	5.0	11.3
hides	39.0	7.5	6.8
Forest products	5.1	4.5	4.2
Industrial goods	3.3	22.8	22.2
iron	—	9.8	12.0
linen textiles	3.3	13.0	10.2
Accounted for	99.4%	90.3%	87.6%

Source: Kozintseva, "Vneshnetorgovyi oborot," pp. 124–25; Storch, *Supplementband*, p. 38.

Arkhangel'sk and exclude government sales amounting to about 12 percent of total exports. Including government sales changes only slightly the composition of exports by the enumerated commodity groups. Considering transportation costs, the Baltic trade had a different structure of exports. In addition, the war that raged during 1710 unquestionably influenced the composition of exports.)

Table 4.2 supports expectations about the direction of the shifts of the various commodity groups in the total value of exports over the course of the eighteenth century. It also underscores the continuously overriding importance to the export trade of the industrial crops, hemp and flax, and of the products derived from their production and processing. Hemp and flax, rather than grains, were the cash crops par excellence for eighteenth-century Russia. The data in table 4.2 dispel notions about the importance of forest products, such as pitch, tar, potash, and even wood products, in the total value of Russian exports. Such notions arose because of the importance of those commodities as strategic materials for shipbuilding in Western European countries, and also because for a long time the Russian government either was actively involved in the trade of or exercised control over those exports. In the totality of Russian exports, the economic role of forest products appears to have been marginal. The role of manufactured goods, iron and linen textiles, reflected not only the spectacular growth of those industries, but also the increasing demand for those goods in foreign trade. The data also reflect the early stage of the Industrial Revolution in Western Europe, and especially in England, when imports of raw materials were not only increasingly used in the manufacturing branches of the developing industries, but also the time when the growing demand for textiles could not be met by domestic production and the major technological break-throughs in iron production and cotton manufacturing had not yet taken place.

Thus Russia helped to sustain the Industrial Revolution in Western Europe not only by its exports of agricultural raw materials, especially the naval stores that facilitated the maintenance of huge merchant marines, but also by its exports of industrial raw materials that assisted industrial change in Western Europe.

The Russian Foreign Trade in Grains

A number of characteristics of the Russian grain trade in the eighteenth century are worth exploring, even on the basis of data which are still incomplete. Two features of the grain trade prior to the 1760s have to be kept in mind. First, grain exports from some of the Baltic ports, particularly Riga, were primarily of Lithuanian and Belorussian origin, and therefore were from outside the political boundaries of Russia. Prior to 1772, Russian grain exports from the port of Riga amounted to only a fraction of the total. Second, the relationship of Russian grain exports and grain prices cannot be understood without knowing how the Russian government intervened to prohibit exports. Until the 1760s, exports were usually prohibited when the price of a *chetvert'* of rye in Moscow province exceeded one ruble. Lacking data on grain prices in Moscow, we cannot judge the responsiveness of exports to price fluctuations.

Still another important characteristic of the grain trade was the scarcity of off-farm storage facilities for grain, which meant that the volume exported must have been highly dependent upon the size of the current grain crop. Since, however, the volume of exports was such a small fraction of the size of the yearly grain crop, that volume depended primarily on the prevailing grain prices in the European market. It was only when a short-run rise in European grain prices (due to unfavorable weather conditions in Europe) coincided with a similar rise in Russia that there was no major rise in exports (due in part to prohibitive government policies). In most cases, when the data permit correlation of short-term price rises in the European market with Russian exports, the response in the form of growth of volume exported can be observed.

An examination of the volume of Russian grain exports during times of famine in Western and Central Europe reveals that it was the demand of Western Europe rather than the domestic supply of grain in Russia that was decisive in determining the level of Russian grain exports.[1] Lack of reliable data forces omission of the famines during the first decade of the century, the time when Russia was in the critical phase for it of the Northern War. The behavior of Russian exports to Western Europe (excluding ex-

Table 4.3   Grain Shipments through the Sound 1738–42 (in Lasts)

Year	Total Shipments		Shipments from Russian Ports		Russian Ports as % of Total	
	Rye	Wheat	Rye	Wheat	Rye	Wheat
1738	11,951	6,410	4,171	425	34.9	6.6
1739	41,337	12,088	13,357	782	32.3	6.0
1740	67,841	21,830	24,616	1,320	36.3	6.0
1741	33,728	14,757	19,025	1,145	56.4	7.8
1742	12,539	5,951	30			

Sources: P.R.O. (London), BT 231; Bang and Korst, *Tabeller*, 2: 1.

Table 4.4   Grain Shipments through the Sound 1768–73 (in Lasts)

Year	Total Shipments			Shipments from Russian Ports			Russian Ports as % of Total		
	Rye	Wheat	Other Grains	Rye	Wheat	Other Grains	Rye	Wheat	Other Grains
1768	37,246	23,354	8,548	2,050	668	171	5.5	2.9	2.0
1769	46,251	15,389	5,594	4,934	427	217	10.7	2.8	3.8
1770	60,021	30,841	14,488	4,798	1,763	1,120	8.0	5.7	7.7
1771	30,955	20,385	6,131	12,430	3,060	2,597	40.1	12.7	42.4
1772	50,221	20,102	9,414	25,923	3,426	2,522	51.6	17.0	26.8
1773	27,902	14,212	14,112	9,167	2,572	2,351	32.8	18.1	16.7

Source: The same as in table 4.3.

ports to Sweden and other regions around the Baltic) during the severe famines of 1739–41 and 1770–72 can be adequately documented. The data in tables 4.3 and 4.4 on the grain shipments westward through the Sound clearly indicate the prominence of Russian grain sales and the pattern of their rise.

The data indicate that the Russian grain-export trade responded to the demand by Western European markets, but with somewhat of a lag. The delay was caused partly because of the distances involved in transporting Russian grain from the interior to the ports and partly because of the state of navigation from Russian ports. Once the stimulus provided by the high prices for grains had set in motion the mobilization of relatively huge volumes of marketable commodities, the supply in response to the famine of 1739–41 was at a very impressive level for two years, 1740–41. The lag of only four to five months between the movement of prices and the volume of grain shipments indicates a relatively high degree of sensitivity in the organization of Russian grain exports. The response of the Russian grain market to the famine of 1770–72 was quite similar to its response to the earlier famine.

Table 4.4 illustrates another feature of the role of the Russian marketable grain supply for Western Europe in the eighteenth century, its use as a supply of last resort in times of extreme shortages. The data for 1770 exports suggest that other, geographically closer, regions were used in the first instance to mobilize an adequate grain supply for Western Eu-

rope. The Russian supply possibilities were tapped only when the other suppliers were unable to meet the demand. A Russian market in high gear was capable of supplying huge quantities of marketable grains. An examination of monthly price movements indicates that the lag encountered during the early 1740s was substantially diminished if not entirely eliminated later in the century. The movement of grain shipments from Russian ports responded almost perfectly to the movement of monthly grain prices. The change could be interpreted as a growing sophistication and more efficient operation of the Russian grain export market in responding to Western European demand.

This relatively rapid response of the Russian suppliers of grain to price rises bears witness not only to a sensitivity to changing market conditions, or the ability on the part of traders to organize the supply, but also to the small size of the exports relative to the total output of grain. It would be erroneous to assume that in the eighteenth century exports constituted a serious alternative to domestic human consumption, as came to be the case in the nineteenth and twentieth centuries. For rye and barley, a choice existed between their use as food and their use in alcohol distilling, with the latter consistently absorbing a larger volume of grains than foreign trade. The export of oats affected the Russian level of grain consumption even less because of its limited size and its primary use as a fodder crop. The only truly commercial grain crop was winter wheat. It was the growth of wheat exports, concentrated primarily in the last third of the century, that was the most interesting feature of the Russian grain trade.

The policy of distributing exports among the various ports of the country was implemented by Peter the Great by the use of special inducements, such as lower export duties, as well as by the use of prohibitions. St. Petersburg was unable to function as a port for grain exports until the Ladoga Canal was completed and the southern and eastern waterway connection was adjusted for the mass transportation of bulk commodities. Consequently the government tried to concentrate the grain trade in Arkhangel'sk, thereby rerouting the streams of grain which otherwise would have moved toward the Baltic, most conveniently toward Riga. The decision was a political one, for transportation costs were higher to (and out of) Arkhangel'sk than they would have been for the Baltic ports. The desire to maintain Arkhangel'sk as a viable outlet for Russian trade, combined with misgivings about turning over the bulk of the grain exports to an alien merchant group, kept this policy very much intact until 1762, when some of the more blatant prohibitions against Russian grain exports through Riga were lifted. The gradual movement away from Arkhangel'sk as the chief outlet for Russian grain and the growth of exports through St. Petersburg, Riga, and later in the century increasingly through the Black Sea ports, were effected by the shift of the grain-producing regions, and primarily the wheat region, toward the south and southeast of the country.

So far, discussion had centered around the problems of the Russian grain trade as it moved through the port of Arkhangel'sk and the Baltic ports. For subsequent economic history, however, the opening of the new trade route during the last quarter of the eighteenth century was of no less momentous importance than had been the opening of the Baltic at the beginning of the century for Russian trade in general. The opening up of the Black Sea and the Azov Sea trade provided vastly greater opportunity for the grain producers in the chernozëm region and had a profound impact on the development of agricultural production in southern Russia. Although the grain producers of the northern tier of the chernozëm zone (Voronezh and Belgorod) had shipped some of their grain, at considerable expense, to the Baltic ports during the eighteenth century, their neighbors further south lacked export opportunities. It is not surprising, therefore, that conversion of grain into alcohol and a limited amount of utilization by the armed forces provided the only market demand for the grains of the fertile steppe lands. The result was that livestock production was the prevailing branch

Table 4.5 Grain Exports through Black Sea Ports (Yearly Averages in Chetvert')

Grains	1776–80	1781–90	1791–1801	1776–1801
Wheat	182	14,136	77,277	38,201
Barley	—	5	4,246	1,798
Rye	—	314	3,150	1,454

Source: Mironov, "Eksport khleba," pp. 164–65.

of agriculture, and population growth in the region was slow.

The opening of the trade in the Black Sea ports dramatically changed both the economic outlook and the social realities of southern agriculture. Many factors were coincidentally at work: the opening of the Black Sea trade, the conquest of the Crimea, the general land cadastre (*general'noe mezhevanie*), and the final enserfment of the peasant population of the Ukraine. The general land cadastre was marked by an increased acquisition of large land-tracts in the south by the land- and serf-owners of the central Russian provinces, a process which enabled the nobles to resettle their serfs on new land. A simultaneous active colonization policy by the government attempted to attract foreign colonists to Novorossiia. Both developments, coupled with the final enserfment of the local indigenous peasant population, led to a rapid growth of the cultivated area and to an upsurge of wheat production that could be exported profitably through the Black Sea ports. The opening of the Black Sea ports even had an impact on the volume of grain production of such distant areas as northern Podolia and southern Volynia, provinces of the former Polish state, which began to export grain through the Dnestr, Dnepr, and Southern Bug waterways to the new ports.

The data on grain exports through the Black Sea ports presented in table 4.5 reflect this development in both the quantity and composition of exports. With respect to the latter, the overwhelming bulk of exports consisted of wheat. Barley and rye were in very distant second and third places, and oats were totally absent. "Southern exports" of wheat through the Black Sea ports during the last decade of the eighteenth century exceeded the wheat exports of Riga and St. Petersburg, the major grain-exporting ports on the Baltic, and Arkhangel'sk. The pattern of the nineteenth and twentieth century dominance of Black Sea wheat exports had already emerged

The overwhelming bulk of the wheat in the total grain exports of the Black Sea and Azov ports reflected not so much the composition of grain output in the southern region as the demand and price relationships (including transportation costs) of the various grains. Wheat brought the highest return to the producers and merchants.

Merchants trading in the Black Sea ports received a bonus from the government in the form of lower export duties (about a one-quarter reduction in the general tariff duty) and the right to pay the duties in Russian currency, measures that were designed to stimulate foreign trade in that region. In fact, the trade hardly required special incentives, except for conditions of peace. The hostilities between Russia and the Ottoman Empire were responsible for the below-capacity volume of exports during the early period when trade began. Interruptions in trade due to war and political tensions were frequent and serious in terms of their economic consequences. Although trade began in 1758 in the small port of Temernikov, it was paralyzed during the years 1768–75 because of war. The trade through Taganrog that began in 1776 and looked so promising was interrupted for the years 1778–83. Lastly, the war of 1787–91 that led to the treaty of Jassy resulted in an interruption of trade for at least four years.

The opening of the southern ports and the growth of the grain trade did not automatically assure access to Mediterranean markets for Russian exports. It was necessary first to gain access to the market of Istanbul and the Ionian Islands. It would be a mistake to attribute the initial difficulties of establishing a foothold in southern Europe for Black Sea exports exclusively to any "staple" policy on the part of the Turks. Much more serious was the competition encountered by the exporters and shippers of wheat to those regions, and therefore the free passage through the straits (the Bosporus and Dardanelles) was a relatively minor problem. Like the previous Russian experience in the Baltic and consonant with the pattern of the development of markets during the eighteenth century, the buildup of new trade networks required time, skills, and capital. These were provided by Western European firms and foreign residents of the southern ports, Greeks and Armenians, who began to play an important role in the grain trade of the region.

The new trade route provided an alternative for Russia's grain trade to those already existing. In addition, the new outlets helped to develop a hinterland, a supply base which in terms of commercial output was more promising than many of the old grain-producing regions. Thus the opening up of the southern route for Russian grain exports marked four developments. First, by making new markets accessible it helped to adjust the potential and actual supply of commercial grains to the foreign demand and, while having a stimulating effect upon commercial production, increased the total domestic grain output as well. Second, it accelerated the growth of the marketable share of Russian grain production in general, but especially in wheat, the

most valuable and highest-priced grain, thereby increasing the value of grain exports more than the increase in volume of exports would indicate. Third, it lessened the dependence of Russian grain exports both upon the political conditions of northern Europe, particularly around the Baltic Sea, and upon the climatic conditions of central and western Russia. (Not only did transportation costs and insurance rates fluctuate widely, depending upon the political conditions in the Baltic, such as the wars with Sweden, the Seven Years' War, and the Dutch-British conflicts, but often naval convoys were necessary to bring Russian exports to England.) Fourth, the development of the Black Sea trade in grains helped to introduce a degree of specialization into the eighteenth-century grain trade which was responsive not only to production in the hinterland but also to the demand of particular regions in Europe. While the countries of northern Europe most easily accessible through the Baltic ports and Arkhangel'sk purchased Russian rye and oats, the countries of southern and southwestern Europe demanded wheat. The demand in Turkey, Spain, Portugal, Italy, and occasionally France for Russian grain depended on the transportation-cost differential between Black Sea, Mediterranean, and Baltic routes. Specialization leading to cost decreases in the production and transportation of wheat was a benefit of the new trade route for Russian grains.

Grains were not among the most conspicuous items of Russian export during the eighteenth century and certainly lagged behind such "traditional" export commodities as hemp and flax, pitch and tar, iron and some cheap textiles. Nevertheless, the history of the grain trade is tied to the larger problem of the gradual growth of commercial grain output and the territorial and structural shifts that characterized Russian agriculture of that period.

Estimates of the commercial output of Russian agriculture point to an interesting relationship between the different components of the commercial output and the estimates of foreign trade in grains: the volume of grain exports was smaller than the other components of the commercial output. Nevertheless, the growing share of winter wheat appears to be positively correlated with the territorial shift of grain cultivation in Russia toward the chernozëm zone, toward the southern and southeastern provinces of the empire. The territorial shift toward the end of the century of exporting grain through the newly established southern harbors on the Black Sea inevitably had a stimulating effect on the increase of wheat cultivation. The figures on the size of Russia's grain exports (primarily from Arkhangel'sk and the Baltic ports, as revealed in tables 4.6–11), when combined with the available price data, are indicative

Table 4.6   Rye Exports from Russia (in Chetvert')

Year	Baltic Ports	Arkhangel'sk	Total	Year	Baltic Ports	Arkhangel'sk	Total
1710	632	34,519	35,151	1755	36,912		
11	14,576		14,576	56	16,912		
12	11,840		11,840	57	4,472		
13	66,384	56,999	123,383	58	5,224	99,348	
14	18,992	195,085	214,077	59	896	99,385	
1715	89,064	171,674	260,738	1760	21,056	2,840	
16	44,736	169,720	214,456	61	242,797	6,500	249,297
17	9,728	17,989	27,717	62	330,479	27,469	357,948
18	1,195	11,118	12,313	63	182,402	4,804	187,206
19	992		992	64	176,232		
1720	144		144	1765	163,665	21,873	185,538
21				66	72,737	68,093	140,830
22	1,637			67	50,852	1,814	52,666
23	800			68	71,065	160	71,225
24				69	95,934	8,400	104,334
1725				1770	110,784	15,359	126,143
26	24			71	287,508	163,535	451,043
27	480			72	628,563	235,282	863,845
28	13,072			73	228,280	254,442	482,722
29	53,232			74	266,180	154,713	420,893
1730	55,936			1775	387,464	76,394	463,858
31	87,112			76	64,624		
32	14,920			77	203,176	56,104	259,280
33	7,296			78	193,088	98,254	291,342
34	71,712			79	173,866	19,093	192,959
1735	23,952			1780	99,848	10,928	110,776
36	10,816			81	188,989	60,995	249,984
37	24,248			82	272,046	41,173	313,219
38	66,432			83	528,129	67,498	595,627
39	210,032	29,841	239,873	84	648,238	153,090	801,328
1740	376,080	115,543	491,623	1785	237,932	56,009	
41	286,992	120,000		86	183,414	64,668	
42	480			87	4,845	4,676	
43	912			88	30	6,254	
44				89	31,770		
1745	18,176			1790	171,900		
46	8,432			91	191,220		
47				92	213,300	268	
48				93	237,495		
49		1,152		94	83,430		
1750	2,800			1795	73,305		
51	1,152			96	284,340		
52				97	191,565		
53	39,248			98	164,235		
54	18,512			99	259,155		

of two characteristics of the Russian grain trade: first, the foreign demand was more decisive in determining the volume of exports than was the size of the actual or potential domestic supply; second, the supply of Russian grains during ordinary years was quite elastic, responsive to changes in price.

Exports of Livestock Products

Russian agriculture supplied the export markets not only with its crops, but also with some of its livestock products. These were not the primary products, but the by-products of animal husbandry. Archival sources mention exports of beef tongues and dried meat to Western Europe, but the quantities were minute. Butter exports started toward the end of the

century in the trade with the Ottoman Empire. Meat and dairy products found few buyers in the international market, but there was a thriving market for tallow, hides, bristles, and horse manes.

The steppe regions of southern Russia provided meat animals for the central and western regions of the country but developed no major exports except to neighboring Poland. An important source of income, the trade in animals was a regional rather than an international trade.

The most important item in terms of export value was tallow. The British production of soap and candles depended to a very considerable extent upon the Russian exports of tallow. The basic suppliers of tallow were the peasants and the landowners who,

Table 4.7 Wheat Exports from Russia (in Chetvert')

Year	Baltic Ports	Arkhangel'sk	Total	Year	Baltic Ports	Arkhangel'sk	Total
1710		2,205		66	5,887	14,633	20,520
11	200			67	8,993	30,116	39,109
12				68	12,615	30,946	43,561
13	285			69	43,411	42,392	85,803
14	168	14,381	14,549	1770	29,975	13,066	43,041
1715	320	17,565	17,885	71	70,088	23,196	93,284
16		12,102		72	69,025	9,522	78,547
17		3,766		73	54,933	39,585	94,518
1723	16			74	95,644	52,871	148,515
29	48			1775	54,223	16,334	70,557
1731	32			76	11,143	20,300	31,443
32	48			77	54,340	44,865	99,205
33	493			78	57,815		
34	1,376			79	100,979	85,396	186,375
1735	5,896			1780	86,105	58,265	144,370
36	968			81	47,339	41,345	88,684
37	2,624			82	41,814	39,114	80,928
38	6,800			83	89,132	41,890	131,022
39	12,512			84	99,904	9,510	109,414
1740	21,152			1785	42,603	18,074	60,677
41	27,312	20,000		86	19,295	18,328	37,623
43	1,360			87	2,565	15,398	17,963
1745	32			88		13,381	
48	928			89	16,608		
1750	160			1790	42,316	10,669	52,985
53	2,816			91	45,860		
54	576			92	56,052	11,861	67,913
1755	336			93	75,781	24,078	99,859
56	48			94	81,057	27,853	108,910
1760	736			1795	103,400	46,172	149,572
61	944			96	213,411	56,194	269,605
62	5,245			97	86,168	14,839	101,007
63	3,098			98	51,452		
64	5,305			99	72,111	7,237	79,348
1765	6,732	1,505	8,237				

using peasant intermediaries, engaged in the collection of this commodity. As in the case of other agricultural commodities, a network of suppliers and merchant intermediaries was engaged in this trade, whose terminals were the ports of St. Petersburg and Arkhangel'sk. Most of the supplies were brought to the ports through the waterways.

Exports of tallow, like most of the other major agricultural commodities, fluctuated widely. In the case of tallow it is difficult to establish whether the fluctuations reflected changes in demand or changes in supply. Demand relationships were especially significant in the case of tallow exports, for contemporaries observed that "sheep from the Kirgiz steppes" were an auxiliary source of tallow supply, that from 25,000 to 40,000 were imported each year for the animal fat they provided.[2] Given favorable conditions of demand from Western Europe, the Russians had an outside source of tallow and the possibility of adjusting the supply to the current or expected demand.

The price of tallow in the foreign market was favorable for Russia, where the relative prices of livestock (relative to grains and other crops) were lower than in Western Europe. This price differential stimulated exports. A comparison between the price changes and the fluctuation of the volume of exports of tallow indicates that significant price changes in the foreign market affected the volume of exports very strongly: they rose when prices increased, and declined when they fell.[3]

Lacking annual data for exports from Arkhangel'sk, one can project only a limited series of figures for tallow. The annual data for the exports of tallow from the Baltic ports going through the Sound (see table 4.12) provide only a general and imprecise view, although they do indicate a period of rapid growth. These data are also summarized in terms of five-year averages for the period 1720–80 in table 4.12. The data on British imports of tallow for the period 1771 through 1799 are presented in tables 4.13–14 and indicate the importance of this product for the British market.

Other important export items among the livestock products were hides and leather. The most significant in terms of bulk and value within this group were the roughly processed hides known as *iufti* (or *iuchten* in German), sometimes translated as "Russian leather."

Table 4.8   Barley Exports from Russia (in Chetvert')

Year	Baltic Ports	Arkhangel'sk	Total	Year	Baltic Ports	Arkhangel'sk	Total
1711	1,522			1767	4,798		
1712	320			1768	5,480		
1713	8,464			1769	6,403		
1714	4,032			1770	17,964		
1715	512			1771	32,321		
1728	2,320			1772	41,930		
1729	613			1773	33,331		
1730	16			1774	44,638		
1731	736			1775	46,504		
1733	624			1776	9,440		
1734	1,512			1777	2,720		
1735	1,664			1778	4,720		
1736	2,720			1779	14,192		
1737	16,792			1780	8,448		
1738	25,744			1781	6,816		
1739	17,024			1782	8,378		
1740	54,656			1783	44,812		
1741	4,552			1784	88,938		
1743	880			1785	27,259		
1745	6,496			1786	8,106		
1746	6,160			1787	80		
1750	6,192			1788			
1751	1,760			1789	208		
1753	840			1790	17,920		
1754	5,200			1791	45,344		
1755	4,288			1792	93,472		
1756	2,856			1793	49,312	47	49,359
1760	1,680			1794	44,064	160	44,224
1761	773			1795	10,976	689	11,665
1762	14,266			1796	54,640	3,256	57,896
1763	11,131			1797	56,912	5	56,917
1764	6,641			1798	30,128		
1765	4,742			1799	59,253		
1766	1,740						

Their tanning of these hides was primitive and handled by small-scale tanneries in the countryside. A rather low-quality product, their main attractiveness to the foreign market was their low price. Peter the Great made numerous attempts to force Russian tanners to adopt a new, more modern technology that would also improve their product. He failed abysmally in this endeavor, just as succeeding Russian tsars failed in forcing the rural weavers to broaden their linen. As long as both domestic and foreign buyers were willing to buy the Russian *iufti* at a price that secured their producers a reasonable profit, there was no reason to change to a finer product whose profitability and marketability were questionable. Under such circumstances, the Russian tanners, like the rural weavers, acted with greater economic sense than their "enlightened" rulers and avoided some of the mercantilist follies of governmental policies.

Bristles were still another by-product of Russian livestock output that found a ready market in Western Europe. The production of pork in Russia ran a distant second to cattle production, and we know relatively little about the commercial production of this commodity, although there is evidence that the leading export market was St. Petersburg, followed by Arkhangel'sk. There were two grades of the product and they differed significantly in price (the price ratio between the two grades was in the neighborhood of 35:1), but the export duty was virtually the same on both.

The opening of the Black Sea trade increased the variety and volume of livestock product exports. The market for Russian butter in the Ottoman Empire was a welcome addition to the minute demand for Russian butter in Western Europe. It provided an outlet for the dairy production of southern Russia, which in the second half of the eighteenth century was beginning to be transformed from a livestock-raising to a grain-producing region. The Ottoman demand for butter provided Russian producers with an additional source of income derived from foreign trade.

The opening of the Black Sea trade also provided a strong boost for the export of wool, produced in the southern steppe zone of Russia. According to the customs office accounts, over 90 percent of the butter exports and almost all of the wool exports were

Table 4.9   Oat Exports from Russia (in Chetvert')

Year	Baltic Ports	Arkhangel'sk	Total
1725	32		
1727	32		
1729	1,048		
1730	112		
1737	8		
1739	832		
1740	416		
1754	2,016		
1756	80		
1761	11,504		
1762	22,859		
1763	9,820		
1764	443		
1765	7,184		
1766	1,105		
1767	3,242		
1768	3,455		
1769	1		
1770	3,477	150	3,627
1771	32,676	150	32,826
1772	46,507		
1773	12,101	543	12,644
1774	17,588		
1775	2,512		
1776	64		
1777	20		
1778	4,960		
1779	10,000		
1780	40		
1781	20		
1782	31,620		
1783	45,784		
1784	117,412	1,363	118,775
1785	36,208	1,363	37,571
1786	41,076		
1787	80	250	330
1789	40		
1791	28,700		
1792	17,540	10	17,550
1793	5,200		
1794	80	5,157	5,237
1795	7,780	767	8,547
1796	19,940	3,621	23,561
1797		17	
1798	8,260		
1799	5,520		

Table 4.10   Mironov Data on Other Grain Exports from Riga (in Chetvert')

Year	Other Grains
1762	4,110
1763	964
1764	381
1770	33
1771	1
1774	200
1776	0
1777	2,736
1778	4,704
1779	6,704
1780	10,816
1781	7,376
1782	10,112
1783	28,800
1784	140,864
1785	30,576
1786	16,384
1787	9,856
1788	4,000
1789	1,680
1797	240
1798	22
1799	51

Source: Mironov, "Eksport," p. 166.

A common characteristic of the two industrial crops was labor intensity. The relatively small volume grown on each farm and the need for special care meant that they were grown on serfs' farms rather than on landowners' estates. The two fibers (particularly flax) supplied the serfs' households with raw materials for homespun yarn, home-woven linen cloth, rope, and other domestic goods, and consequently a large share of the crop was not marketed or was marketed within the rural areas and therefore was not available for foreign trade or domestic large-scale manufacturing. Both as a material source for homemade clothing and as a cash crop, the two fibers were very important for rural producers.

The commercial output of flax came from the Baltic provinces, the northwestern provinces of Russia, Belorussia, and Lithuania. The non-Russian areas supplied the larger share of exports while the Russian provinces largely supplied the fiber used in both domestic, cottage-type industry and in larger-scale manufacture. Riga dominated the flax trade.

The areas of commercial hemp production were the central and southcentral provinces of Russia. St. Petersburg gained primacy early in the century in the hemp trade, and Arkhangel'sk and Riga were relegated to lesser roles.

Although exporters of the two crops had to compete with both household consumption and domestic industry, most of this competition with the domestic market was confined to the Russian provinces proper. The task of collecting the marketable share

shipped through the Black Sea ports by 1793. They brought in an income of 150,000 rubles.

Trade in Hemp and Flax

In terms of market value, the most important Russian exports during most of the eighteenth century were hemp and flax. These two industrial crops were exported as raw materials: as seeds, their by-products were a source of vegetable oil, and in processed form as linen, the major textile export. It is both permissible and convenient to treat these distinct aspects of the hemp and flax trade as one.

Table 4.11 Mironov Data on Exports from Arkhangel'sk and St. Petersburg Rye and Wheat Flour (in Poods) (1762–1800)

Year	Rye Flour	Wheat Flour
1762		55
1764		25
1765	16,000	
1766	3,796	7,353
1767	37	
1768	100	1,520
1769	50	3,102
1770	2,492	2,627
1771	150	8,204
1772	690	517
1773	10,413	675
1774	10,947	1,286
1777	11,702	3,270
1778		13,160
1797		192
1798		89
1799		298
1800		2,246

Source: Mironov, "Eksport," pp. 155–57.

Note: The rye data are exclusively for Arkhangel'sk, the wheat data are primarily for St. Petersburg.

Table 4.12 Tallow Exports from Russia through the Sound, 1720–83 (in Shippounds)

Year	Tallow	5-yr. Average	Year	Tallow	5-yr. Average
1720	700.2		1755	280.5	
21	76.5		56	3,845	
22	10.8	875.9	57	4,241.8	2,857.6
23	1,951		58	3,016.2	
24	1,641		59	2,904.3	
1725	4,044		1760	2,658.4	
26	2,084		61	3,025.5	
27	304	3,257	62	4,584.3	3,431.7
28	4,402.3		63	4,123.0	
29	3,811		64	2,767.4	
1730	2,397		1765	2,798.5	
31	1,933.1		66	5,318	
32	2,997.1	3,442.1	67	12,216.5	9,333
33	6,923.5		68	11,991.4	
34	2,959.8		69	14,340.8	
1735	3,919.8		1770	16,070.4	
36	2,461		71	23,695.9	
37	167	1,632	72	19,166.4	24,072.9
38	521		73	28,582.3	
39	1,090		74	32,849.5	
1740	1,754		1775	25,760.8	
41	1,680.7		76	30,215.4	
42	3,733	2,339	77	30,979.4	26,940
43	1,071		78	22,504.5	
44	3,458		79	25,239.7	
1745	2,566.5		1780	43,872.4	
46	300		81	45,001.0	
47	440	902.1	82	9,837.0	
48	429		83	31,481.0	
49	774				
1750	1,000.5				
51	3,043.5				
52	591	1,820.1			
53	623.8				
54	3,841.6				

was time-consuming and expensive. A market network in the rural areas collected the supply. An organization of fairs and other means enabled wholesalers to assemble larger shipments and to arrange transportation to the ports, where the commodities were sold to foreign merchants.

The lack of standardization was a perennial problem for foreign buyers. The situation at Riga, with its older tradition and the higher quality of available fibers, was somewhat better. In spite of the efforts of the Russian government to institute *brackers*, or officials charged with the responsibility of enforcing and certifying uniform standards, the complaints of foreigners persisted. This neglect or lack of understanding of standardization procedures on the part of the Russian merchants plagued Russian foreign trade in numerous commodities and gave rise to reciprocal acrimony and recrimination between trading partners.

In spite of ill feelings, inconveniences, and additional costs, trade was carried on to the mutual advantage of the trading parties. The spectacular growth of flax and hemp exports, in competition with the growth of the domestic linen industry and a growing population that consumed more household-produced linen, provides conclusive evidence of Russia's interest in exports and their profitability. The rising population, its growing textile industry (prior to the mass production of cotton goods), and the strategic importance of the building of sailing ships for merchant marines and navies were served by

Table 4.13 British Tallow Imports from Russia (in Cwt)

Year	Imports from Russia		
	England	Scotland	Total
1771	69,039	1,343	70,382
1772	65,867	1,734	67,601
1773	82,246	2,386	84,632
1774	91,094	5,169	96,263
1775	51,984	5,591	57,575
1776	95,112	3,722	98,834
1777	72,967	10,034	83,001
1778	50,882	6,825	57,707
1779	76,920	7,357	84,277
1780	126,956	14,150	141,106
1781	116,865	5,053	121,918
1782	78,864	2,758	81,622
1783	68,553	7,540	76,093
1784	144,559	15,323	159,882
1785	226,955	34,032	260,987

Source: P.R.O. (London), BT 6/231.

Table 4.14   British Tallow Imports (in Cwt)

	Total British Tallow Imports			Tallow Imports from Russia			
Year	England	Scotland	Total	England	Scotland	Total	%
1786	200,743	46,579	247,322	186,535	46,561	233,096	94.2
1787	292,116	64,365	356,481	260,162	63,733	323,895	90.9
1788	327,017	28,028	355,045	313,858	27,928	341,786	96.3
1789	235,645	24,481	260,126	212,167	24,098	236,265	90.8
1790	218,079	37,842	255,921	191,413	37,549	228,962	89.5
1791	139,087	25,775	164,862	121,429	25,340	146,769	89.0
1792	175,663	26,193	201,856	124,154	25,268	149,422	74.0
1793	211,479	23,529	235,008	195,660	23,794	219,454	93.4
1794	176,299	25,873	202,172	164,335	25,854	190,189	94.1
1795	129,088	51,719	180,807	109,923	51,681	161,604	89.4
1796	287,483	43,500	330,983	248,924	43,027	291,951	88.2
1797	205,953	38,088	244,041	174,161	37,059	211,220	86.6
1798	386,290	53,621	439,911	355,447	51,221	406,668	92.4
1799	373,262	76,955	450,217	344,057	73,778	417,835	92.8

Source: P.R.O. (London), BT 6/231.

Russian exports. Sails and ropes were considered "strategic" naval stores, and until the nineteenth century, when jute began to be used in rope making and packaging materials, no readily available substitute existed.

The Russians knew better than to try to create a monopoly, even in hemp, the one crop in which their share of the overall European supply was dominant. Their restraint, however, was less a matter of policy than a function of internal conditions. Any attempt to withhold supplies of the two industrial crops would have adversely affected the producers or sellers of the crops, whether peasants or gentry, who were in many areas dependent for their cash incomes upon the sales of their hemp and flax. Moreover, any serious interruption of the trade would have jeopardized both the tax revenues of the state and the incomes of the gentry, and thus would have been unacceptable economically as well as politically. Thus for all practical purposes the trade in both commodities was regulated by competitive forces. Harvest fluctuations were important, but more significant were the effects of foreign demand and market prices. Flax was imported into England until 1788 duty free, and the tariff on hemp was about 10 to 12 percent ad valorem and did not influence the market in any major way.

The available data do not permit an estimate of the total value of Russian exports in flax and hemp. The only continuous yearly series for most of the century pertains to those exports from the Russian ports on the Baltic that passed westward through the Oresund (the Sound), presented in tables 4.15–19. Trade within the Baltic Sea and exports through Arkhangel'sk as well as other border outlets are not included. Only for the period 1758–77 do we have estimates by M. M. Chulkov supposedly accounting

Table 4.15   Hemp Exports from Russia (in Shippounds) 5-Year Averages

Years	Baltic Ports through the Sound	Total Russian Exports	St. Petersburg Total Exports
1730–24	41,354.4		
1725–29	79,623		
1730–34	68,776.4		
1735–39	84,674		
1740–44	101,259.2		
1745–49	117,020.6		
1750–54	145,659.4		
1755–59	176,376.2		
1760–64	134,001	188,954	
1765–69	145,463.8	184,732.6	130,096.6
1770–74	189,111.8	248,818.4	162,905.4
1775–79	212,174.6		179,916.2
1780–84	224,607		187,216.8
1785–89	223,880		186,992.7
1790–94	259,300		219,821.8
1795–99			208,837.7

Sources: Chulkov, *Opisanie*, 8, bk. 1, table 3; Bank and Korst, *Tabellor*, 2, pts. 2/1, 2/2; Johansen, *Sund*; P.R.O. (London), B/T 6/231, 6/232, 6/233.

for all the trade in hemp and flax.[4] The credibility of Chulkov's data is established by comparing the Sound toll accounts for St. Petersburg and the volumes of hemp and flax which, according to his sources, were graded in the capital between 1762 and 1782 (see table 4.20). Some of the differences can be explained by the gap between grading and passing through the Sound. Moreover, some difference might arise from the conversion of poods into shippounds in St. Petersburg and the Sound.

Most of the differences between the total volume of exports and the exports through the Sound can be explained by intra-Baltic exports from the port of Riga, for which the published data are very sparse. We know only that by the middle of the century about half of all the hemp and flax exports of Riga went to ports on the Baltic. A forthcoming study by

Table 4.16   Hemp Exports from Russia (in Shippounds)

Year	Baltic Exports through the Sound	Total Exports According to Chulkov	P.R.O. Data for St. Petersburg, Riga, and Arkhangel'sk	Year	Baltic Exports through the Sound	Total Exports According to Chulkov	P.R.O. Data for St. Petersburg, Riga, and Arkhangel'sk
1720	23,024			1760	130,028	187,658	
1721	33,296			1761	94,386	134,270	
1722	39,784			1762	170,767	253,647	
1723	55,763			1763	128,667	185,731	
1724	54,905			1764	146,157	183,464	
1725	101,286			1765	151,373	186,365	
1726	101,476			1766	117,867	158,278	
1727	73,358			1767	146,040	183,983	
1728	67,824			1768	145,284	187,278	
1729	54,171			1769	166,755	207,659	
1730	82,520			1770	157,497	204,458	
1731	73,270			1771	213,697	251,263	
1732	54,222			1772	141,118	180,019	
1733	80,738			1773	210,042	302,820	
1734	53,132			1774	223,205	305,532	
1735	96,373			1775	146,821	196,284	
1736	53,923			1776	179,523	225,474	
1737	82,514			1777	222,351	280,919	
1738	88,464			1778	250,006		
1739	102,096			1779	262,172		232,868
1740	88,731			1780	202,161		232,868
1741	101,090			1781	263,566		298,418
1742	115,487			1782	260,625		294,060
1743	65,688			1783	143,383		184,598
1744	135,300			1784	253,300		
1745	92,966			1785	230,900		259,373
1746	136,358			1786	166,000		
1747	155,182			1787	1,930,000		196,573
1748	95,892			1788	288,900		311,230
1749	104,705			1789	240,600		
1750	139,048			1790	304,500		
1751	114,473			1791	214,800		
1752	180,568			1792	276,300		
1753	134,375			1793	231,000		
1754	159,833			1794	270,000		
1755	177,386			1795			250,753
1756	187,503			1796			302,528
1757	177,702			1797			264,888
1758	138,461	193,894		1798			340,488
1759	200,829	235,998		1799			330,394

Professor Doroshenko of the Institute of History, Latvian Academy of Sciences, may fill the gap in our knowledge about the commercial activities of Riga in the eighteenth century.

Some data on St. Petersburg's intra-Baltic trade are known for the period from 1765 to 1799. They account for about 10,000 shippounds of hemp yearly for the second half of the century. Although there is sufficient evidence to corroborate Chulkov's data, it will probably take some time and effort before we will have a continuous yearly series of the total hemp and flax exports from Russia. The series offered here covers only 65 to 70 percent of the total exports and gives a clear indication of the general order of magnitude and pattern of growth.

Linseed and hempseed were also in demand in Central and Western Europe. Linseed for sowing was heavily sought because the varieties of flax grown in the Baltic region of Russia were superior and the seed produced gave a higher yield than did the seed of the same variety produced in Central and Western Europe. Varieties such as Rakitzer, Drujana, and Marienburg were used along the southern coast of the Baltic as far as the Netherlands. Crushed linseed, the larger part of the linseed exports, went to the oil mills of Western Europe for the production of vegetable oil and oil cake. The use of vegetable oils for nonfood purposes, such as paints and chemicals, was much more important in the eighteenth century than later. The use of vegetable fats was also widespread, particularly among the urban population (and also the rural population, especially during seasons when the

Table. 4.17   Flax Exports from Russia (in Shippounds) 5-Year Averages

Years	Baltic Ports through the Sound	Total Russian Exports	St. Petersburg Total Exports
1720–24	11,258.2		
1725–29	15,781.6		
1730–34	18,015		
1735–39	23,916.4		
1740–44	20,990.2		
1745–49	39,531.4		
1750–54	44,155.6		
1755–59	46,295.6		
1760–64	51,597.8	78.079.6	16,298.1
1765–69	53,338.2	70,480.4	11,640.4
1770–74	61,462.8	75,224.8	16,298.1
1775–79	80,848.4		24,981.1
1780–84	88,192.4		27,075.8
1785–89	122,140		46,293.9
1790–94	131,200		52,226.7
1795–99			45,233.3

use of meat was prohibited), more so than in later periods which witnessed the rise of a well-functioning dairy industry. All of the exported hempseed was used for crushing. The totals of exports of linseed and hempseed which passed through the Sound are presented in tables 4.21 and 4.22.

Domestically produced linseed oil was in strong demand by the Dutch and the British. Russia was without any doubt the major linseed oil supplier to Western European markets throughout the eighteenth century. The fluctuations of linseed exports mirrored the fluctuations of marketable flax to a large extent because weather conditions similarly affected both. Such was not the case with hemp and hempseed: the share of domestic consumption of hempseed exceeded that of hemp, and the price effects upon the quantity of hempseed exported were stronger than upon the exports of linseed.

Until the middle of the 1760s, the total Baltic exports of both hempseed and linseed were tantamount to the exports of the port of Riga. Only later did the share of St. Petersburg and other Baltic ports in linseed exports begin to rise. The diversification of hempseed exports by ports was an even slower process. The port of Arkhangel'sk was also continuously engaged in the export of linseed and hempseed. It is difficult to determine whether its ascendancy was determined by earlier commercial contacts or other economic advantages over St. Petersburg, but at the time when hemp exports were so heavily concentrated in the capital's port, there must have been good reasons why hempseed was transported to Riga and Arkhangel'sk. The preference of the Dutch, the chief customer for hempseed, for the other ports is not a sufficient explanation.

This review of the hemp trade is incomplete without including tow. Tow was a lower-quality product of hemp cultivation, or, using the terminology of an industrial society, a by-product of hemp processing. Although its price per unit was three to four times lower than that of clean hemp, it was used not only in agricultural households but was marketed for industrial use in the manufacturing of tow-cloth. It was separated from the higher-quality groups of hemp by the producers, but since tow itself was not uniform, it was classified into two grades by specially appointed graders in the ports of St. Petersburg and Riga. Tables 4.23 and 4.24 present the total exports registered in the Sound toll accounts. The data reveal a long-term growth of tow exports to Western Europe. They clearly reflect both the increased production of hemp in Russia as well as the growth of marketings of this product, depending upon foreign demand. The development of a Russian market that specialized in organizing the collection of tow, arranging for transportation to the ports, and dealing with exporters increased the benefits from hemp cultivation.

The Trade in Finished Linen

Discussion of the Russian trade in hemp and flax would not be complete without considering the export of semifinished and finished linen. The German territories engaged in large-scale exports of linen yarn and finished linens to England, the Dutch primarily exported finished linens, and Russia predominantly supplied the primary products. This particular pattern was a consequence of the technical backwardness of Russia and an economic and political structure that favored agricultural exports and hindered the development of industry.

The less than favorable conditions for the development of Russian exports of finished linen did not prevent such exports from taking place. The two major sources of Russian linens were the rural cottage industry and the large-scale linen manufactories, whose development is discussed above in chapter 3. The older, more traditional type of linen in the seventeenth and eighteenth centuries was a narrow, coarse linen referred to in the early British customs sources as "Muscovy narrow." Alongside his efforts to induce the establishment of linen manufactories, Peter the Great tried to "improve" the quality of the products of the cottage industry by requiring by decree that the serfs produce broader linen, especially for export. To produce broader linen, larger looms were needed of a size that would not fit into existing peasant dwellings. Moreover, the means for this kind of capital investment were not available to an overtaxed peasantry. Consequently Peter's threatening decrees remained unenforced, and the narrow linens continued to be supplied to the market. The

Table 4.18 Flax Exports from Russia (in Shippounds)

Year	Baltic Ports through the Sound	Total Exports According to Chulkov	Year	Baltic Ports through the Sound	Total Exports According to Chulkov
1720	3,835		1755	50,218	
1721	5,970		1756	40,584	
1722	16,837		1757	38,800	
1723	15,990		1758	43,110	54,455
1724	13,659		1759	58,766	66,033
1725	14,204		1760	32,270	59,671
1726	17,028		1761	46,375	72,842
1727	8,600		1762	49,672	82,700
1728	19,055		1763	71,135	95,903
1729	20,021		1764	58,537	79,282
1730	19,934		1765	40,356	54,163
1731	14,261		1766	52,564	68,824
1732	21,025		1767	43,012	68,373
1733	13,082		1768	63,259	77,288
1734	21,773		1769	67,500	83,754
1735	14,718		1770	68,738	86,319
1736	19,768		1771	70,339	82,506
1737	35,988		1772	66,905	77,692
1738	25,356		1773	41,568	55,965
1739	23,752		1774	59,764	73,642
1740	22,885		1775	87,396	100,771
1741	29,280		1776	78,096	95,554
1742	28,536		1777	90,136	97,878
1743	13,974		1778	77,406	
1744	10,276		1779	71,208	
1745	24,364		1780	87,394	
1746	33,001		1781	86,904	
1747	47,022		1782	82,531	
1748	56,114		1783	82,533	
1749	37,156		1784	101,600	
1750	45,143		1785	161,200	
1751	40,517		1786	124,300	
1752	39,251		1787	119,800	
1753	39,462		1788	131,300	
1754	56,405		1789	74,100	

Table 4.19 Hemp and Flax Exports from Russia (in Shippounds) Not Separated in the Sources of the Sound-Tolls

Year	Exports	Year	Exports
1720	3,498	1739	348
1721	5,661	1740	30
1722	7,633	1741	651
1723	7,283	1743	126
1724	16,116	1747	37
1725	5,701	1749	97
1726	12,344	1750	231
1727	4,892	1752	514
1728	10,967	1753	745
1729	12,840	1755	572
1730	23,104	1757	405
1731	9,686	1758	50
1732	10,753	1762	12
1733	1,907	1763	197
1734	2,260	1764	1,365
1735	2,575	1767	1,713
1736	2,232		
1737	1,558		
1738	226		

output of the manufactories (sailcloth, some table napkins, toweling—known as diaper in the English terminology—and bleached linens), lower in quality to be sure than that of their Western European counterparts, became important items of export.

Data on the volume and distribution of Russian linen exports by type and by country of destination are lacking for the first half of the eighteenth century. The Sound toll accounts indicate that much was sold to various countries of Western Europe such as the Netherlands, England, and the former Hansa towns, but this provides little evidence on the final destinations of the Russian finished linen, except for the products used in sail making. Although for single products such as "Muscovy narrow" British sources confirm some of the reports of the Sound toll accounts, the data are spotty. It is only from 1753 on that more systematic and comprehensive data are available for British imports. These statistics, however, account for only a part of the exports. Data for Dutch and other imports are virtually nonexistent and consequently it is difficult either to verify or to

Table 4.20   Comparison of Accounts of St. Petersburg Flax and Hemp Exports (1762–82), in Shippounds.

	Flax		Hemp	
Year	Sound Toll Account	Chulkov's Account	Sound Toll Account	Chulkov's Account
1762	11,368	10,134	115,903	117,014
63	17,269	18,061	81,936	89,400
64	11,886	12,093	110,385	135,170
1765	8,566	9,184	121,280	122,200
66	7,389	12,943	100,070	124,272
67	11,413	12,499	124,031	146,881
68	15,243	16,077	124,718	147,665
69	14,227	14,404	141,665	173,958
1770	17,486	18,406	126,982	128,121
71	17,038	16,474	185,053	207,452
72	13,821	14,589	108,254	125,823
73	8,969	10,805	176,883	217,860
74	17,797	16,736	168,912	172,767
1775	21,444	27,460	108,474	138,255
76	23,062	20,261	140,579	141,214
77	29,623	31,272	186,454	210,518
78	22,527	29,988	204,616	227,826
79	23,522	18,914	207,709	230,919
1780	23,515	25,695	137,273	183,554
81	28,436	26,713	199,120	218,131
82	26,501	22,543	218,164	231,310

Source: Chulkov, *Opisanie*, vol. 4, bk. 5, pp. 719–20.

Table 4.21   Russian Exports of Linseed and Hempseed (in Lasts) from Baltic Ports Through the Sound (Annual Averages)

Years	Linseed	Hempseed
1720–24	1,621.9	1,001.8
1725–29	4,283.5	5,056.8
1730–34	1,823.0	3,276.2
1735–39	3,015.6	4,165.6
1740–44	1,283.9	2,391.4
1745–49	2,340.0	2,401.8
1750–54	1,965.0	2,911.7
1755–59	2,025.7	1,722.4
1760–64	2,208.3	2,317.9
1765–69	2,596.6	1,825.3
1770–74	3,774.5	2,204.2
1775–79	5,726.8	2,170.3
1780–84	5,323.6	
1785–89	7,486.4	
1790–94	7,319.0	

refute the estimates of total exports of finished linen provided by M. Chulkov for the period 1758–77 (see table 4.25). For subsequent years, apart from the British import data, the export data for the ports of St. Petersburg and Arkhangel'sk provide information on some products within the category of finished linen for selected years, but no systematic, consistent, and continuous series can be constructed. Although the data provide only limited quantitative information about the finished linen exports, some qualitative

information is useful for understanding the problems the Russians encountered in their foreign trade in linens.

Russian exports were primarily in the category of lower-quality linens, those that required less specialized skills, such as sailcloth. Within the general category of sailcloth three major subcategories can be distinguished: sailcloth proper, ravenduck (a lighter type of sailcloth used for upper masts), and Flemish cloth, a cloth broader than sailcloth, that was used also for bedding and, according to H. Storch, was very popular for shirts for slaves on the plantations of Central and South America.[5] A second category, well represented in Russian exports, included white flat linen cloth, both broad and narrow, as well as printed linens of the same variety. The latter were often mentioned in the sources as a separate item. A third category included sack and packing linen materials, of which *khriashch* was the more expensive and *deriuga* the cheaper variety. A fourth category of linen products, *diaper*, included table and towel napkins and serviettes, which were classified by width.

Russian exports of finished linen encountered competition in the foreign markets from the previously established French, Dutch, and German producers. They also had to overcome the tariff which England had imposed in an attempt to protect its own Scottish and Irish industries. Russia itself had a tariff on linens, which only the higher-quality Western producers could surmount, and therefore it was not in a position to bargain for a reduction in the tariffs on Russian finished linen. Only gradually did Russian exports of finished linen enter the markets and establish their reputation as quality goods (at the given price) which made up in durability what they lacked in appearance. Initially they were confined to the coarser varieties of linen that were still (prior to the development of cotton) an object of consumption for different uses.

Relatively early in the century England became the chief outlet for Russian exports, and it was within the vicissitudes of that market that the Russian exports had to survive. A search inevitably began for wider markets. The specialization in particular items of finished linen permitted Russia not only to retain a foothold in the British market for linen goods, but also to gain access to the American market through the reputation and connections that were established earlier in the century. Like the Russian iron and hemp that reached the colonies prior to independence, linen goods, especially sailcloth, ravenduck, and Flemish linen continued to play a significant role in the American-Russian trade.

The data in table 4.26 on the St. Petersburg exports to Great Britain and the United States for the three categories of linen goods provide both a yardstick of

Table 4.22   Russian Exports of Linseed and Hempseed through the Sound (in Lasts).

Year	Linseed	Hempseed	Year	Linseed	Hempseed
1720	1,139	270	1770	4,159.2	1,899.5
1721	1,476.5	1,955	1771	2,270.3	1,269.9
1722	1,060	181	1772	3,207.8	2,197.5
1723	2,773	1,323	1773	3,636.3	2,081.3
1724	1,661.2	1,280	1774	5,599	3,600.3
1725	2,688.6	1,911.7	1775	8,863.8	5,905.6
1726	3,553.8	2,627	1776	4,577	1,020.3
1727	3,411.7	6,156	1777	5,522.3	1,520.2
1728	4,954.7	4,578	1778	5,197.3	1,236.9
1729	6,808.9	10,011.3	1779	4,473.5	1,168.4
1730	4,321.2	9,502	1780	6,010.5	1,030.5
1731	1,301.7	3,098	1781	3,281.3	1,458.7
1732	591.5	246	1782	3,269	034
1733	1,566.8	2,314	1783	5,212	2,141
1734	1,334	1,221	1784	8,845	
1735	2,744	2,411	1785	7,728	
1736	2,160	2,467.2	1786	6,451	
1737	4,623	7,258.5	1787	3,321	
1738	2,967.5	3,454	1788	7,188	
1739	2,583.5	5,237.5	1789	8,122	
1740	1,948.2	3,398.8	1790	7,910	
1741	1,826	3,347.4	1791	7,018	
1742	801.4	1,818	1792	8,204	
1743	553.3	900	1793	6,751	
1744	1,290.5	2,492.9	1794	6,713	
1745	1,860.6	1,918	1795	8,538	
1746	3,219.4	2,374			
1747	2,192.4	4,035.7			
1748	2,395.3	1,771.1			
1749	2,032.5	1,904			
1750	2,722.7	1,509			
1751	1,787.6	2,923			
1752	1,993	3,131			
1753	1,148.8	2,762.7			
1754	2,173	4,232.9			
1755	2,128.4	1,536.5			
1756	2,586.8	3,225			
1757	2,435.3	1,718.2			
1758	427	159			
1759	2,550.8	1,973.5			
1760	1,302.5	1,535			
1761	2,154.8	1,133			
1762	2,904.4	2,277.6			
1763	2,644.2	2,297			
1764	2,035.8	2,373.4			
1765	1,451.4	2,207.2			
1766	1,995.7	1,618.7			
1767	2,459.7	1,386.6			
1768	3,453.7	1,975.5			
1769	3,522.7	1,938.6			

Source: Bang and Korst, *Tabellar*.

comparison and an approximation of the Russian exports to both countries. The list in table 4.27 of selected goods designated as Russian in the British exports to the North American colonies for 1771 reveals an awareness that the goods were actually Russian. The much higher proportion of sailcloth in the American imports can be explained by the lower state of linen manufacturing in the U.S. at the time.

The higher share of Flemish linen supports the notion by H. Storch about their use by the slave population on the plantations.

Although most of the commercial yarn in the Baltic basin was exported by German towns, the data in table 4.28 reveal that the Russians also sent a small volume of yarn and cordage through the Sound in the eighteenth century. Exports of yarn reached their

Table 4.23   Tow Exports from Russia through the Sound, 1720–79 5-Year Yearly Averages (in Shippounds)

Years	Exports
1720–24	3,970.0
1725–29	2,985.3
1730–34	4,498.2
1735–39	9,781.2
1740–44	10,878.5
1745–49	9,895.8
1750–54	7,900.2
1755–59	10,373.4
1760–64	14,594.2
1765–69	19,456.4
1770–74	18,739.1
1775–79	23,868.5

Source: Bang and Korst, *Tabellar.*

peak just after the death of Peter the Great, and declined almost continuously to the end of the century. The volume of cordage exports, on the other hand, rose quite dramatically in the same period.

Exports of Iron

During the eighteenth century iron production in Russia grew from insignificance to a leadership position among European iron producers. By the end of the century Russia became the major exporter of iron.

During the first half of the century domestic demand was the major force in iron output, but the expansion of iron production during the second half of the century occurred under conditions of rising foreign demand. Besides relatively stable prices and steadily increasing demand in foreign markets (especially on the part of Great Britain), the lavish grants of land and labor by the Russian government to the iron producers created a rapid expansion of ferrous metallurgy during the 1750s and 1760s.

The number of iron producers in Russia was relatively small during the eighteenth century. There was a high degree of concentration in the number of producers, particularly those engaged in foreign trade. The main suppliers of iron for export were a few major industrialists in the Urals region and the Russian government itself through its state-owned ironworks.[6] Relatively early in the century, sometime in the 1740s, iron export items became standardized, and purchasers were able to determine the origin and quality of a product through identifying seals. The seal of the Demidov ironworks, a Siberian sable, became a famous trademark for Urals bar iron. The export of Russian iron became heavily concentrated in the port of St. Petersburg, the outlet for the waterway connecting the Urals with the Baltic Sea through rivers and canals. It took the iron caravans one or two seasons to reach their destination by way of the waterway. The concentration in St. Petersburg was for both economic and political reasons. The purchasers as well as the producers were small in number and dealt in large volumes. Long-term contracts and forward buying that involved large advances to the supplier against future deliveries, along

Table 4.24   Tow Exports from Russia through the Sound (in Shippounds)

Year	Baltic Ports	Year	Baltic Ports	Year	Baltic Ports
1720	2,517	1745	13,767.3	1770	18,795.8
1721	3,553	1746	9,236.1	1771	15,442.6
1722	2,702	1747	12,071.6	1772	19,672
1723	6,331.3	1748	4,365.7	1773	17,034.1
1724	4,741.5	1749	10,038.2	1774	22,780.8
1725	2,726.5	1750	6,783.9	1775	17,732.8
1726	7,686	1751	5,828	1776	26,120.4
1727	2,443.5	1752	10,321.6	1777	32,734.2
1728	1,479.5	1753	8,563.8	1778	21,995.7
1729	590.9	1754	8,003.7	1779	20,759.2
1730	3,930.6	1755	12,933.7	1780	26,746.2
1731	4,329.5	1756	7,590.6	1781	16,341.6
1732	5,008.5	1757	7,681.9	1782	22,965
1733	4,160	1758	13,083.3	1783	23,707
1734	5,062.2	1759	10,577.5		
1735	5,312.2	1760	11,732.1		
1736	9,849.5	1761	7,720.9		
1737	11,104.2	1762	21,695.4		
1738	11,163.2	1763	18,006.3		
1739	11,477	1764	13,816.4		
1740	8,566.5	1765	24,772.3		
1741	12,842.4	1766	13,254.8		
1742	11,201.3	1767	21,203.3		
1743	5,411.8	1768	17,372.5		
1744	16,370.5	1769	20,679		

Table 4.25   Exports of Linen from Russia (in Arshins)

Year	Printed	Dyed	"Pestriad"
1758	32,751	236,750	84,126
1759	5,113	570,889	76,837
1760	576,141	588,134	91,415
1761	10,659	557,603	129,161
1762	10,468	1,015,337	105,589
1763	10,287	564,767	82,018
1764	49,438	396,130	90,142
1765	260,524	248,409	91,150
1766	99,265	187,152	53,083
1767	123,085	381,604	87,414
1768	144,416	255,152	112,263
1769	146,465	168,775	93,169
1770	266,126	208,256	115,390
1771	170,412	125,748	123,091
1772	139,589	179,361	87,818
1773	117,921	225,228	145,306
1774	124,013	124,453	237,805
1775	78,003	396,579	244,840
1776	99,162	236,711	210,009
1777	104,352	199,407	199,514

Source: Chulkov, *Opisanie*, 7, pt. 1, table 3.

with the size of the market, provided for substantial price stability.

Russian iron was relatively cheap, in spite of the significant transportation costs, because of the ironworks' low labor costs. Surmounting both the Russian export duty and English import duties, Russian iron was capable of underselling British iron in England. With expanded productive capacity, the Russian ironworks were capable of increasing the volume of exports when given sufficient advance notice for transportation to the ports. While domestic demand in Russia increased slowly in view of the limitations

upon the growth of the purchasing power of the enserfed population, and although government demand for war materials was related to events exogenous to the industry, exports assumed an increasing share of total iron production during the second half of the century. The growth in foreign demand for Russian iron lasted from the 1760s to the 1780s, and Russia displaced Sweden as the chief foreign supplier in the British market. The British government preferred Swedish iron for its armaments, while private producers and consumers replaced Swedish bar iron with the cheaper Russian product. Table 4.29 shows Russian exports of iron through the port of St. Petersburg between 1736 and 1759 and the dramatic decline of state-produced exports in that period. During the 1790s Russian exports to England reached a plateau and then began to decline because of the impact of the technological revolution in the combined use of coke and steam engines for iron smelting. Rapidly rising British production capacity, in conjunction with the transition from charcoal to coke, prevented a further increase of demand for Russian iron in its most important market.

Russia became the bulk supplier of iron to the British market, but it did not acquire a monopoly. In fact, during the 1780s, when the Russian government attempted to obtain from the British a reduction of import duties and preferential treatment for its iron exports in the British market to offset rising domestic costs of iron production, it was unable to prevail.[7]

Estimating the volume of Russian iron exports in the eighteenth century is a difficult task in view of the incompleteness of published production and trade data. Although no complete series of data can be

Table 4.26   St. Petersburg Exports to Great Britain and the U.S. in Arshins[a]

Year	Sailcloth		Ravenduck		Flemish Linen	
	Great Britain	U.S.	Great Britain	U.S.	Great Britain	U.S.
1783	54,200	25,000	2,380,550	28,500	1,236,000	21,850
1784	140,000	18,500	3,813,050		1,210,200	
1785	127,800	203,700	3,629,550	15,600	806,100	135,450
1786	104,750	342,500	2,496,700	73,200	864,100	30,050
1787	110,800	458,200	3,699,100	138,450	1,519,900	84,400
1788	147,100	388,550	4,449,250	87,600	2,026,400	93,850
1789	246,650	583,350	4,864,800	81,750	1,473,450	28,250
1790	42,550	490,200	4,960,150	123,150	1,207,250	42,800
1791	111,900	259,200	3,134,100	167,700	745,550	26,650
1792	33,650	778,850	3,355,900	299,650	1,207,750	135,550
1793	2,100	669,550	3,948,900	253,100	1,888,950	292,200
1794		1,289,350	5,045,050	707,150	1,079,050	752,750
1795	10,550	591,400	5,734,700	538,400	1,411,750	334,100
1796	8,500	466,400	4,888,450	511,250	1,835,300	287,150
1797		396,300	5,659,850	392,650	1,341,400	539,250
1798	8,200	1,777,000	5,545,800	711,900	1,791,850	935,100
1799	182,700	1,102,850	6,307,950	997,600	3,079,450	1,048,950

[a]The data in tables 4.26 and 4.27 on exports to Great Britain and North America are presented in terms of the Russian measure of arshins, on the assumption of 50 arshins per piece of goods exported.

Table 4.27 British Re-exports of Russian Goods to North American Colonies, 1771

Diaper Russia Tabl.	275 yards
Diaper Russia Narrow	6,194 yards
Duck pieces 7,103	161,977 yards
Russia broad centums	2,386 yards
Russia drilling centums	553 yards
Russia narrow centums	430 yards
Russia printed	145,013 yards

Source: P.R.O. (London), BT/232

presented, combining available sources permits a presentation of data that are a closer approximation to the probable export volume than anything presented heretofore. A comparison of three long-term series (the Sound toll reports, S. G. Strumilin's list of St. Petersburg exports, and a series on exports from St. Petersburg in the London Public Record Office [see tables 4.30 and 4.31]) permits an estimate of the approximate exports of iron through the Baltic ports, especially as there is a high correlation among the data of the three series.[8]

The data on the exports through the Baltic ports, or even from St. Petersburg alone, are sufficient to confirm the trend of Russian iron exports. Nevertheless, the paucity of data for the port of Arkhangel'sk creates some problems, particularly for the earlier period, and prevents the construction of a well-documented, continuous, and systematic series.

Two observations about Russian iron exports are in order. Although Russian iron was exported chiefly to England, it also reached other parts of Western and southwestern Europe. At various times Russian iron was imported into France, Portugal, Italy, and, after the opening of the Black Sea trade, also into the Ottoman Empire. Beginning at least in the 1760s, Russian iron even reached the American colonies. During the second half of the century iron amounted to about 10 percent of the total value of Russia's maritime exports. The relative stability of prices and the increased volume of iron exports, and consequently the rising receipts and customs duties, were comforting both to the producers and to the Russian government.

Table 4.28 Exports of Yarn and Cordage from Russia through the Sound, 1720–83 (in Shipppounds)

Year	Annually		5-yr. Average		Year	Annually		5-yr. Average	
	Yarn	Cordage	Yarn	Cordage		Yarn	Cordage	Yarn	Cordage
1720	30	153			53	20.0	730		
21	1	42			54	233.4	626		
22	357		377	81	1755	130.0	253		
23	579	27			56	192.0	44.5		
24	919	184			57	464.0	69	170.4	124.2
1725	1,046	276			58	.8	175		
26	929	304			59	65.0	79.7		
27	1,236.5	190.3	969	200	1760		110.6		
28	857	86			61		46		
29	775.8	143			62	.5	117.8	8.7	270.3
1730	1,523.3	476.3			63	3.0	388.7		
31	489	803			64	39.8	688.5		
32	258.7	654	481.1	530	1765	2.7	828.8		
33		103			66	8.3	860.8		
34	134.5	616			67		107.8	4.0	694.5
1735	117.7	76			68	9.0	1,171.0		
36	533.5	1,040			69		504.1		
37	120.5	1,279	333.3	666	1770	15.4	951.9		
38	573	383			71	2.9	566.7		
39	322	550			72	17.3	1,245.4	8.3	1,171.0
1740	158.8	885			73	2.5	799.2		
41	92.4	112			74	3.6	2,291.7		
42	458.5	163.1	208.3	291.3	1775	4.8	1,447.3		
43	117	62			76	16.1	1,902.9		
44	214.8	234.5			77	6.6	1,128.3	6.3	1,884.0
1745	949.0	405			78	2.7	1,322.6		
46	33.1	685			79	1.4	3,619.0		
47	54.9	913	207.7	790	1780	2.1	4,548.7		
48	1.6	153			81	66.0	6,138.0		
49		1,796			82	8.0	9,040		2,508.9
1750	15.7	665			83		9,970		
51	201.0	767			84				
52	.8	1,144	94.2	786					

Source: Bang and Korst, *Tabellar*, vol. 2, pts. 2/1 and 2/2.

Table 4.29   St. Petersburg Iron Exports (in thousand poods)

Year	Private	State-Owned	Total
1736	114.3	170.7	285.1
37	135.9	148.5	284.4
38	220.0	120.0	340.0
45	81.4	108.4	189.8
46	210.4	106.4	316.8
47	177.6	150.1	327.7
48	146.2	22.3	168.5
49	361.1	167.3	528.4
50	568.2	636.8	1,205.0
51	402.2	242.0	644.2
52	610.8	332.4	943.2
53	482.5	67.0	549.5
54	417.8	227.6	645.4
55	735.5	132.8	868.3
56	393.8	87.0	480.8
57	397.5	38.0	435.5
58	608.5	9.5	618.0
59	873.7	7.3	881.0

Source: Strumilin, *Istoriia*, pp. 199–200.

Russian iron exports were made up almost entirely of the bread-and-butter iron product, bar iron, and the country continued to import through most of the century some types of wrought iron and also steel. Although Russia became one of the leading world producers of bar iron, it did not achieve self-sufficiency in other areas of iron making. Even in the area of bar iron, the volume of exports of so-called "assorted iron" (bar iron manufactured according to special orders or nonstandardized sizes) was very small. This indicates that the level of technical proficiency was lower in Russian iron production than in Western European production, or that the organization of production to meet customers' demands was worse. Specialization in particular products within an industry is, however, by no means a condemnation of either the rationale or the skills of the producers. In the case of Russia, it is indicative only of the conditions of an industry relying heavily upon serf labor and vast forest resources, an industry that was under little pressure to change its technology or adjust to the preferences of the market as long as the concentration on its basic product was yielding profits. That those conditions led to a subsequent rapid decline in Russia's activity as an iron producer and exporter is best illustrated by the fact that Russia's leading role in the eighteenth-century European iron market is largely a well-kept secret known primarily to specialized historians.

The data presented in tables 4.30 and 4.31 represent at least two independent series of iron export data. One reflects the volume of exports through the Sound and thus underestimates the total Baltic ports' export volume by the amount of the intra-Baltic trade. To provide a check on the Sound toll data and to demonstrate the underestimation of the volume of exports, the St. Petersburg data are singled out for a comparison between the Sound estimates and the Russian sources on the total exports from St. Petersburg. For this purpose the series by S. G. Strumilin is used for the years for which it is available. To check the Strumilin estimates, two series of data reproducing figures from the St. Petersburg customs office that have been preserved in the Public Records Office in London have been used. The discrepancies between the customs office series are minor, but they were helpful in detecting at least two errors in the Strumilin series, one for 1765 and another for 1772.

Table 4.30   Iron Exports from the Baltic Ports and Arkhangel'sk (in Shippounds)

Years	Through the Sound		Strumilin Estimate St. Petersburg	P.R.O. Estimate St. Petersburg	Exports through Arkhangel'sk
	Baltic Ports	St. Petersburg			
1720–24	2,493.2	2,148.4			
1725–29	9,413.8	8,558.0			
1730–34	19,091.2	18,079.2			
1735–39	22,487.0	21,304.6			
1740–44	28,060.4	27,088.0			
1745–49	31,291.4	29,481.4	30,640		
1750–54	77,692.6	75,827.8	79,740		
1755–59	66,694.6	65,925.6	65,660		
1760–64	95,820.6	93,133.0	101,100		
1765–69	160,225.8	158,107.6	n.a.	158,480	
1770–74	222,733.2	220,488.2		233,420	
1775–79	199,473.2	198,030.8		204,980	
1780–84	243,583.8		244,440	243,534	7,443.2
1785–89	207,560.0		210,760	210,747	
1790–94	241,800.0		233,600	233,654	
1795–99	232,139.6			227,094	13,211.4

Sources: Bank and Korst, *Tabellar*; Strumilin, *Istoriia*; Johansen, *Toll Accounts*; P.R.O. (London), BT 6/231.

Monopolies in the Export Trade

The problem of monopolies in Russian foreign trade during the eighteenth century is one of the more widely discussed topics in the historical literature. On the whole this subject has been treated within the framework of trade or fiscal policy rather than by indicating or estimating the impact of monopolies upon the volume or pattern of Russian foreign trade, especially in exports. In order to focus on this neglected aspect of the trade monopolies, it is convenient to distinguish between two kinds of trade monopoly that were operative during the eighteenth century. Monopoly was fostered by government policy in two ways: exclusive privileges were assigned to an individual merchant or group of merchants for a stipulated period of time, often in exchange for a payment or some form of service rendered to the government. This included even the granting of monopoly trading rights to a favorite of the ruler and could be considered as a form of exchange for particular services rendered, or as a substitute for a money or land grant. Alternatively, the government exercised the trading monopoly it created, perhaps by appointing agents to act on its behalf. In the language that was used, commodities that were traded by government monopoly were called "government commodities" (kazennye tovary).

For the most part the commodities involved in the trading monopolies were products of forests and fisheries, branches of the economy in which there was a virtual absence of private-property rights and which required the mobilization of considerable labor resources for the production of goods. The role of the government in defining common rights to forestry and fishing resources and also its ability to mobilize and control the labor supply in particular areas made such products an obvious and logical target for trade monopolies. This explains the presence and preponderance of such goods as pitch and tar, potash and caviar, blubber oil, fish glue, and walrus tusks. The presence of wood products for shipbuilding, such as masts and wainscot logs, is but an extension of the previous list.

The share of the "government commodities" in the total export trade was in fact much smaller than the attention paid to such monopolized exports in primary and secondary sources would lead one to suppose.

It was never possible for the Russian government to subject to monopoly-type controls the trade in hemp, flax, iron, and tallow. Very rarely did it attempt to control the exports of grain: the only attempt to monopolize grain exports by granting export licenses to high government officials at times of general embargoes on grain exports took place in the 1750s, when Vorontsov and Co. were granted such licenses, but they were not very successful in utilizing them. With all of these commodities excluded, it follows from the discussion of the composition of exports that the share of "state commodities" in the total volume of exports was not substantial. Direct trade by government grants of monopoly trading rights was most extensive during the reign of Peter the Great (for fiscal reasons—to finance the Northern War), and thus the data from that period should provide an upper-bound estimate of the share of monopolized exports in the total. Such estimates are found in the meticulous study of the Soviet historian R. I. Kozintseva and are presented in table 4.32.

The share of "state commodities" of total exports varied within the range of 10 to 15 percent, depending upon the success of the government in mobilizing the necessary volume of commodities and its success in marketing, either in Arkhangel'sk or in Amsterdam and London. In instances when the sales were made abroad, rather than in a Russian port, the Russian government frequently used foreign merchants, who served as supply agents for the Russian embassies in the Hague or London, to dispose of the shipments of "state commodities." The prevailing view of the impact of the sale of "state commodities" on foreign trade ought to be revised. There can be no doubt that the monopolization of trade in particular commodities had a detrimental effect not only upon that specific branch of trade but also, because of the likelihood of uneconomical shifts in capital and human resources, upon other branches as well. That such effects were probably smaller than presumed by earlier students of the subject becomes apparent when the proportion of monopolized trade to the total is assessed.

The significance of the state monopolies should be seen not so much in their size as in the opportunity they presented to the government to transfer funds abroad directly and conveniently. Foreign exchange needed to purchase supplies and defray other expenditures abroad was earned through the sale of government commodities in a manner considered more efficient that the use of other revenue channels.

The monopoly profits derived by the state in exporting particular commodities seldom could be attributed to the real monopoly position of Russia in the foreign markets. Perhaps a monopoly price could be established in such commodities as rhubarb (obtained by the Russian government in its trade with China and re-exported to Western Europe) and caviar (monopolized at the source, the Caspian Sea fisheries) by limiting the supply. However, in most cases monopoly power (perhaps better expressed as monopsony power) was used to obtain products

Table 4.31   Iron Exports (Sound Toll Data) for Baltic Ports

Year	Exports through the Sound (in Shippounds)		St. Petersburg Strumilin Data (in 1,000 poods)	St. Petersburg P.R.O. (in 1,000 poods)	St. Petersburg P.R.O. (in poods) St. Petersburg	Arkhangel'sk and Riga (in poods)
	Baltic Ports	St. Petersburg				
1720	1,228	605				
1721	446	446				
1722	2,626	2,449				
1723	2,714	2,523				
1724	5,434	4,719				
1725	3,599	3,066				
1726	5,618	5,133				
1727	9,654	8,103				
1728	15,392	14,238	155			
1729	12,806	12,250				
1730	6,440	5,911				
1731	20,842	20,418				
1732	26,953	25,047				
1733	24,246	22,703				
1734	16,975	16,317				
1735	22,981	22,656				
1736	21,248	20,146	295			
1737	20,283	18,926	284			
1738	22,664	20,328	340			
1739	25,259	24,467				
1740	28,524	28,014				
1741	26,353	25,845				
1742	34,998	34,220				
1743	27,207	25,541				
1744	23,220	21,824				
1745	23,076	20,312	190			
1746	30,595	29,914	317			
1747	30,880	29,831	328			
1748	19,873	17,731	169			
1749	52,033	49,619	528			
1750	117,893	116,279	1,205			
1751	60,868	57,115	644			
1752	87,931	84,679	943			
1753	57,650	57,003	550			
1754	64,121	64,063	645			
1755	83,244	82,876	868			
1756	52,170	51,642	481			
1757	43,558	43,190	435			
1758	61,708	60,903	618			
1759	92,793	91,017	881			
1760	70,283	68,851	785			

within Russia at a price below the market level. The monopoly resulted in an income redistribution from the Russian population to the state that tended in some cases to depress the level of supply of such commodities. In such instances the level of supply tended to increase at the time of the abolition of the monopsony. In a few cases (potash is the prime example), the long duration of the state monopoly in exporting commodities can in part be explained by a calculation of production costs by the Russian government, which underestimated the opportunity costs of labor and raw materials and showed a larger "profit" than was actually obtained.

During the Petrine period direct state monopolies were established for a number of export commodities for fiscal purposes, but the Elizabethan period was marked by a series of grants of monopoly rights for sundry commodities to members of the Empress's entourage. Some of those monopoly rights were then sold by the courtiers to Russian or foreign merchants for a flat fee or for a commission. An example of such a practice was the monopoly of the sale of flax seed through Arkhangel'sk granted jointly to Vorontsov and Glebov in 1757. The following year they resold their license to the prominent merchant Evreinov for a fee of 50 kopeks per *chetvert'* of seed exported. During the following three years (1759–61), Vorontsov and Glebov received 62,700 rubles. An-

Table 4.31, cont.   Iron Exports (Sound Toll Data) for Baltic Ports

Year	Exports through the Sound (in Shippounds)		St. Petersburg Strumilin Data (in 1,000 poods)	St. Petersburg P.R.O. (in 1,000 poods)	St. Petersburg P.R.O. (in poods) St. Petersburg	Arkhangel'sk and Riga (in poods)
	Baltic Ports	St. Petersburg				
1761	107,561	105,517	994			
1762	98,013	96,219	994			
1763	85,841	80,344	964			
1764	117,405	114,734	1,318	1,316.9	1,317,617	
1765	175,032	170,052	2,347	1,724		
1766	81,245	79,798	n.a.	904.3		
1767	143,587	143,257	n.a.	1,282		
1768	166,083	162,432	n.a.	1,674		
1769	235,182	234,999	2,340	2,341		
1770	237,571	236,953	n.a.	2,384		
1771	231,507	226,259	2,780	2,400		
1772	183,938	182,753	2,759	1,759		
1773	242,827	241,792	2,560	2,452		
1774	217,823	214,684	2,247	2,176		
1775	169,588	167,737	1,775	1,651		
1776	217,449	214,487	2,354	2,223		
1777	257,727	256,950	2,735	2,616		
1778	142,219	141,897	n.a.	1,590		
1779	210,383	209,083	2,184	2,169	2,092,378	
1780	198,229	194,379	2,014	2,107	2,013,530	
1781	352,839	340,063	3,560	3,571	3,560,116	
1782	171,037	164,910	1,733		1,733,021	
1783	187,914	180,434	1,875	1,822	1,874,517	
1784	307,900		3,040	2,995.5	2,995,517	
1785	225,600		2,266.4		2,266,415	
1786	198,700		2,019		2,018,925	
1787	165,700		1,699.5		1,699,478	
1788	241,100		2,480		2,479,982	
1789	206,700		2,073		2,072,596	
1790	195,400		1,999		1,998,556	
1791	257,800		2,646		2,646,132	
1792	264,800		2,235		2,234,780	
1793	263,600		2,630		2,630,239	
1794	227,500		2,173		2,173,006	
1795	246,300				2,358,000	2,729,781
1796					2,329,766	2,498,904
1797					1,857,710	2,040,375
1798					2,689,842	2,878,766
1799					2,019,379	2,119,690

Source: The same as in table 4.30.

other example was the ill-fated Gomm enterprise of the Onega forest monopoly, one of the largest commercial enterprises undertaken at the middle of the eighteenth century to develop the export of forest products from Russia. The license to export forest products on a large scale from the Onega region was originally granted in 1752 to Shuvalov, who sold it to the British merchant Gomm in 1760 for a period of thirty years at the annual fee of 10,000 rubles. The enterprise was set up on a grand scale with ships constructed to carry the timber abroad. Gomm claimed that by 1763 he had already invested 243,947 rubles of his own capital, and he requested a government subsidy. The enterprise was liquidated in 1783 with a total indebtedness to the Russian government of 1,569,111 rubles.

The Catherinian period witnessed the demise of both state trading monopolies and monopoly grants to individuals. Many historians see the eclipse of monopolies as a consequence of a general governmental liberalization policy, but a closer analysis of the performance of some of the monopolies points to changing market conditions and unprofitability. The meager revenues received by the state from the foreign trade monopolies were of declining importance to the state budget and may not have warranted even the administrative expenses involved. Thus practical considerations, rather than governmental

Table 4.32   Exports of "State Commodites" during Peter's Reign

Year	Caviar (in Poods)	Fish Glue (in Poods)	Potash (in Poods)	Pitch (in Barrels)	Tar (in Barrels)
1701	3,946	669	80,156	14,488	4,621
1702	7,074	244	64,794	6,680	3,912
1703	6,302	937	3,334	10,510	2,039
1704	5,248		21,492	9,710	1,302
1705	7,282	1,512	22,298	12,085	1,405
1706	8,062		22,310	45,938	3,788
1707	5,312	2,013		5,785	4,899
1708	5,467		27,878	10,740	2,830
1709	3,513	1,191	20,019	25,321	24
1710	4,806	364	20,019	30,000	
1711	11,496	718	4,820	20,084	660
1712	7,644	1,040	49,649	30,000	1,906
1713	7,290	845	30,974	25,000	480
1714	5,439		n.a.	22,000	354
1715	4,000	1,344	6,968	29,000	270
1716	n.a.	n.a.	n.a.	30,300	273
1717	4,123	828		29,352	1,669
1718	2,790	1,913	94,005	25,819	881
1719	5,699	1,029			727
1720	1,693		50,416	6,038	1,000
1721	333				
1722	4,767	2,385	44,697	18,403	
1723	7,128	130	28,180	60,000	
1724	1,670		37,086	50,000	4,679
1725			23,886	40,000	1,385

Source: Kozintseva, "Uchastie," pp. 300, 304, 308, 315, 317.

Table 4.33   Indexes of Grain and Livestock Product Exports (1765–69=100) Yearly Averages for 5-year Periods

Year	Rye[a]	Wheat	Oats	Barley	Tallow	Iuft[b]
1710–14	71.95	8.74		61.91		
1715–19	93.08	17.11		2.20		
1720–24	4.65	negligible			9.40	
1725–29	12.05	negligible	7.41	12.67	34.90	117.7
1730–34	42.73	.99	.73	9.28	36.88	81.9
1735–39	60.49	14.50	5.60	276.06	17.49	76.7
1740–44	187.50	35.40	2.77	259.42	25.06	97.1
1745–49	5.01	.49		54.63	9.67	109.4
1750–54	11.13	1.80	13.44	60.40	19.61	99.2
1755–59	47.46	negligible	.46	30.85	30.62	98.9
1760–64	179.34	7.77	29.78	148.90	36.77	103.4
1765–69	100.00	100.00	100.00	100.00	100.00	100.0
1770–74	422.80	232.17	755.25	734.73	257.93	118.2
1775–79	229.37	225.83	117.13	334.91	288.65	83.6
1780–84	373.41	281.10	1,209.40	679.49	393.20	100.6
1785–89	106.31	74.15	527.22	153.93		
1790–94	167.58	190.40	378.23	1,080.69		
1795–99	175.37	330.06	306.30	931.92		

[a]Grains are inclusive of the Baltic trade and the trade of the port of Arkhangel'sk.
[b]Iuft is low-quality tanned leather.

policy shifts, may have been responsible for the phasing out and abolition of the existing monopoly grants, some of which were allowed to expire rather than being abolished outright. The demise of the trade monopolies was probably as much a result of the increasing participation of Russia in the world market, the realization of the insignificance of the government commodities in the expanding trade, and awareness of some of the detrimental effects of the monopolies as of a reversal toward a more liberal foreign-trade policy.

A Recapitulation

As a postscript to the discussion of Russian exports, it would be useful to recapitulate some observations on the time pattern of export growth of the major com-

Table 4.34   Index of Exports of Industrial Crops through the Sound (1765–69=100) Yearly Averages for 5-year Periods

Years	Hemp	Flax	Tow	Hempseed	Linseed
1715–19					
1720–24	28.43	21.11	20.40	54.8	62.46
1725–29	54.74	29.59	15.34	277.04	164.97
1730–34	47.28	33.78	23.12	179.49	70.21
1735–39	58.21	44.84	50.27	228.21	116.14
1740–44	69.61	39.35	55.91	131.01	49.45
1745–49	80.45	74.11	50.86	131.58	90.12
1750–54	100.13	82.78	40.60	159.52	75.68
1755–59	121.46	87.36	53.32	94.36	78.01
1760–64	92.12	96.74	75.01	126.99	85.05
1765–69	100.00	100.00	100.00	100.00	100.00
1770–74	130.01	115.23	96.31	120.76	145.36
1775–79	145.86	151.58	122.68	118.42	222.30
1780–84	154.41	165.35	115.33		206.60
1785–89	153.91	228.99			254.70
1790–94	166.90	252.70			284.10

Table 4.35   Indexes of Iron and Forest Product Exports through the Sound (1765–69 = 100) Yearly Averages for 5-year Periods

Years	Iron	Iron to England	Potash	Ashes
1720–24	1.56		286.14	41.66
1725–29	5.88	4.04	534.46	218.50
1730–34	11.92	13.03	331.09	169.01
1735–39	14.03	13.49	227.59	237.68
1740–44	17.51	18.22	403.46	219.69
1745–49	19.53	20.04	334.65	144.61
1750–54	48.49	39.60	282.55	126.56
1755–59	41.63	41.34	125.93	114.98
1760–64	59.80	62.52	120.50	94.67
1765–69	100.00	100.00	100.00	100.00
1770–74	139.01	133.13	137.70	47.33
1775–79	124.50	105.84	120.56	138.54
1780–84	152.03	147.81	268.07	160.84
1785–89	129.54	122.06	693.45	
1790–94	150.90	129.13	727.70	
1795–99		124.85		

Table 4.36   Index of Physical Quantity of Russian Lumber Exports through the Sound (1765–69 = 100.0)

Years	Deals	Planks	Boards	Balks	Masts
1720–24	7.3	.9	.9	21.4	47.7
25–29	6.2	.6	6.1	47.2	67.6
1730–34	11.7	2.8	46.2	90.6	57.3
35–39	8.4	5.9	113.2	72.1	85.7
1740–41	8.5	15.9	85.7	81.8	132.1
45–49	9.1	12.8	28.5	68.6	105.7
1750–54	63.9	66.5	72.2	95.0	158.2
55–59	50.6	11.8	79.8	47.7	151.6
1760–64	22.6	53.4	85.6	61.5	126.8
65–69	100.0	100.0	100.0	100.0	100.0
1770–74	144.8	107.3	86.0	91.0	152.3
75–79	117.7	98.9	1.0	96.2	177.4
1780–84	179.8	84.5	3.3	58.7	417.9
85–89	375.9	97.8	28.9	117.9	
1790–94	270.2	152.4	18.5	128.2	

modity groups. For this purpose I have used the data of selected Russian exports to Western Europe through the Sound, even though they underestimate the total volume of exports in instances when the Arkhangel'sk and Black Sea trades are omitted. Most serious is the omission of the Black Sea export of wheat, which became massive toward the end of the century, but the lack of yearly data cannot be overcome. The data on the physical volume of exports were used to construct indexes for the trade of the Baltic ports through the Sound running from 1720 to 1789 for most commodities, the bulk of Russian exports (see tables 4.33 through 4.36).

It may be unfair to judge the Petrine period in foreign trade by relying primarily upon the years 1720–24, which were years of famine. Nevertheless, that evidence, when combined with other information, strongly suggests the limited scope of foreign trade under Peter the Great in comparison with the scale of exports under his successors.

The period 1740–44 is notable for an upsurge of grain sales in response to a famine in Western Europe, but it is also characterized by a general slackening of Russian exports of other commodities because of weather conditions and political disturbances that affected the volume of trade. During the late 1740s the growth of exports resumed, but was interrupted by the Seven Years' War. The return of peace in Europe stimulated an increased demand for Russian exports. This was spurred on by the European famine of the early 1770s that raised grain exports to an unprecedented level. The early 1780s witnessed a new spurt in exports, which reached higher levels for most of the enumerated commodities. Subsequently the growth rate of the export volume diminished, and exports tended to level off.

The indexes portray not only a time pattern of uniformity, but also a degree of volatility of exports that differed among the various commodities. The

Table 4.37   Imports of Russia (in Rubles)

Year	St. Petersburg	Riga	Narva	Revel'	Pernau
1760					
1761					
1762	4,091,606			298,711	
1763	5,042,494				
1764	5,459,522			420,979	
1765	5,071,082			440,219	
1766	5,256,521	1,211,914		437,896	
1767	4,779,837			414,469	
1768	6,328,113			482,506	
1769	6,795,096			376,064	
1770	6,546,734			369,267	
1771	6,810,123			414,527	
1772	7,342,724				
1773	8,493,815	1,761,570	38,738	384,194	
1774	8,829,591	1,482,803	44,422	334,788	
1775	6,892,834	1,950,803	37,211	556,985	88,155
1776	7,006,730	2,027,780	44,278	369,267	
1777	7,626,220	2,915,954	56,761	534,852	
1778	6,592,144	3,166,790			
1779	8,651,601	2,848,070			
1780	8,656,379	2,251,085		473,241	
1781	9,582,352	1,970,212			
1782	12,204,482				
1783	11,674,120	1,448,486	113,215		
1784	12,172,345	1,422,717	63,302	564,666	
1785	10,033,785	1,503,824	63,501	735,117	
1786	11,775,577	1,491,167	66,463	755,424	69,684
1787	15,564,553	1,489,667			
1788	15,474,396	1,314,185	55,372	759,292	
1789	15,371,105	1,308,555	81,500	1,212,623	107,408
1790	22,964,618	1,828,112	169,912	3,806,949	241,856
1791	25,140,632	2,498,183	137,631	2,464,031	1,399,342
1792	22,114,025	2,432,813	142,275	2,934,919	2,354,360
1793	14,580,569	1,797,375	152,938	1,477,261	899,615
1794	21,741,176	1,697,778	104,935	1,747,403	926,475
1795	23,019,175	1,520,446	37,950	1,765,294	1,275,410
1796	26,355,890	2,166,838	148,526	1,879,979	1,624,664
1797	19,366,059	2,490,641	121,006	1,505,719	932,800
1798	25,936,020	4,150,783	150,222		
1799	19,290,778	2,803,390	61,022		
1800	20,070,935	5,075,001			
1801	27,074,118	5,132,234			

Source: Storch, *Supplementband*, pp. 1–2.

differences can be explained not only by changing demand-conditions (a high elasticity with respect to price is assumed) but also by the supply-conditions, including governmental policies, of particular exports, such as grains and seeds. The most stable commodities in terms of their growth were iron and flax. Iron reflected the growth of industrial capacity and flax presumably reflected the growth of the sown area.

The Composition of Russian Imports

Although there are serious gaps in our knowledge of Russian commodity exports during the eighteenth century, data on imports are truly terra incognita.

Apart from the general value of total imports as recorded by the Russian customs office, plus scattered data for the value of imports at particular ports (see table 4.37), there are few indicators of the commodity composition of imports and their changes over time. Since Russian historians have traditionally been much more interested in the exports of Russia than in the country's imports, relatively little of the archival materials pertaining to imports has been published. For major export commodities continuous and consistent time series can be compiled for about thirty to forty years of the century, and this data can be verified by the Sound toll accounts; the available data for commodity imports both cover a shorter time-period and represent a smaller fraction of the total traded imports. Last, but

Vyborg	Arkhangel'sk	Kiakhta	Total	Year
94,316	177,325	658,331	7,358,052	1760
65,353	183,637	619,598	7,180,794	1761
82,205	260,638	553,186	8,162,236	1762
88,301	380,233	401,607	9,190,358	1763
124,875	306,216	158,236	9,670,619	1764
109,560	315,360	244,478	9,200,465	1765
84,243	268,322	15,715	9,175,175	1766
83,141	404,410		8,893,298	1767
64,299	392,775	45,300	10,856,162	1768
63,231	336,420	928,984	11,679,577	1769
88,569	310,626	1,271,739	11,374,259	1770
144,216	256,483	1,142,511	10,726,897	1771
	309,227	934,121	15,562,653	1772
166,966	374,506	1,153,992	13,571,433	1773
153,086	335,132	1,120,870	13,595,945	1774
113,584	285,748	1,278,584	12,469,373	1775
107,087	316,859	1,401,916	13,007,186	1776
150,138	292,070	1,342,127	14,644,420	1777
96,084	341,255	667,253	12,704,237	1778
162,791	282,844		14,368,748	1779
95,881	321,398	2,700,187	15,477,114	1780
91,451	373,158	3,735,312	16,297,954	1781
128,479	384,368	3,520,343	19,292,287	1782
118,149	351,386	2,789,177	19,251,477	1783
128,680	427,388	2,413,357	18,396,303	1784
	414,922	1,805,926	16,432,543	1785
89,172	519,662		17,070,892	1786
	440,665		22,752,795	1787
	540,565		18,920,719	1788
133,590	894,980		21,513,157	1789
157,931	923,917		31,132,268	1790
176,558	799,790		35,113,195	1791
142,275	978,842	2,467,280	37,521,116	1792
110,011	461,347	3,549,432	26,118,764	1793
116,607	676,388	2,522,942	34,529,757	1794
113,034	822,641	2,720,286	36,652,092	1795
139,319	666,744	2,551,764	41,878,566	1796
95,150	574,910	2,378,750	35,002,733	1797
	646,892	2,783,943	48,188,285	1798
	460,028	3,677,824	41,051,175	1799
	264,157			1800
	444,393			1801

not least, the Sound toll accounts were less accurate in recording the true destination of imports by countries around the Baltic than they were in recording the origin of exports by country and port. This last fact means that the researcher is deprived of an independent, reliable source that checks and controls native data.

A superficial glance at the trade balance of Russia should convince the reader that, at least in terms of the commodity trade, the official data (which do not include any estimates of illicit trade) show the trade balance to have been an active one during most of the years for which such data exist. This observation, made under the assumption that it reflects the historical economic reality, raises a number of interesting issues. First, did Russia's role in providing Western Europe with the raw materials and other goods that fed the Industrial Revolution provide for the Russian Empire, in turn, the means to support a high level of consumption by the nobility and an aggressive military policy on the part of its government?

A second issue, one that primarily concerns me here, involves the capacity of the Russian market to absorb foreign goods. The general impression one gathers in reviewing the data on Russian imports is that purchasing power was highly concentrated. Thus few imported commodities, other than articles such as needles and nails, were sold to a mass market. It is no exaggeration to state that the vast majority of Russians were not in the market for imports. A large number, however, benefited from the use of foreign components in the

Table 4.38   Classification of Selected St. Petersburg Imports (in Rubles)

Commodity	1768	1769	1770	1771	1772	1773	1774	1775	1776
Total imports	6,328,113	6,745,096	6,546,734	6,810,123	7,342,724	8,493,815	8,676,339	6,756,043	7,006,730
Ale and beer	84,611	102,358	186,874	163,466	117,170	107,382	189,475	194,078	144,080
Wine	267,652	289,770	437,971	429,900	407,205	415,828	513,959	395,132	418,480
Sugar	880,293	819,213	626,899	810,021	967,455	559,982	477,888	755,125	1,013,722
Coffee	131,666	131,212	50,896	167,799	186,080	126,504	108,314	85,629	82,160
Oil	98,239	11,919	33,166	70,321	120,461	107,020	176,732	56,318	88,160
Total beverages and colonial products	1,462,461	1,365,472	1,335,806	1,641,507	1,798,371	1,316,716	1,466,368	1,486,282	1,893,001[a]
% of total	23.11	19.93	20.40	24.10	24.49	15.50	16.90	22.00	27.02
Silks	329,882	270,638	237,290	612,252	476,055	829,809	780,406	344,806	338,125
Woolens	1,441,716	1,865,444	1,816,939	1,634,910	1,385,158	2,132,810	2,050,012	2,286,129	2,286,686
Total textiles	1,771,598	2,136,082	2,054,229	2,247,162	1,861,213	2,962,619	2,830,418	2,630,935	2,747,639[b]
% of total	28.00	31.44	31.38	33.00	25.35	34.88	32.62	38.94	39.21
Cochineal	143,569	332,659	15,122	9,724	74,818	148,853	290,453	245,715	114,612
Indigo	452,309	308,843	283,323	251,686	369,551	338,720	387,764	316,086	279,598
Logwood	64,829	74,733	99,920	91,826	3,365	41,101	36,869	13,706	24,105
Total dyes	660,707	716,235	398,365	353,236	447,734	528,674	715,086	575,507	418,315
% of total	10.44	10.54	6.08	5.19	6.10	6.22	8.24	8.52	5.97
Alum	59,426	33,214	24,265	17,387	11,784	57,528	55,367	36,184	8,178
Tin	97,396	184,853	138,324	62,413	24,601	116,323	207,782	117,713	229,185
Lead	82,538	79,280	63,554	39,896	44,906	93,159	176,980	52,429	75,038
Total minerals	239,360	297,347	226,144	119,696	81,291	267,010	440,129	206,326	312,401
% of total	3.78	4.38	3.45	1.76	1.11	3.14	5.07	3.05	4.46
% of total accounted for	65.33	66.29	61.31	64.05	57.05	59.74	62.83	72.51	76.66

Commodity	1783	1784	1785	1786	1787	1788
Total imports	11,481,900	12,723,345	10,063,211	11,775,577	15,504,553	15,474,396
Beer, ale and porter	212,850	262,198	312,172	208,782	185,054	283,639
Wines	737,000	936,786	890,652	756,508	880,007	894,810
Sugar	1,638,200	2,270,574	1,770,244	1,560,802	1,915,594	2,274,088
Coffee	248,850	143,270	323,886	293,802	558,003	632,214
Pepper	115,300	17,187	50,224	84,320	41,229	41,573
Fruits	91,400	164,534	140,212	102,705	130,565	174,449
Tobacco	49,300	77,466	72,829	46,861	74,965	75,181
Total beverages and colonial products	3,092,900	3,872,015	3,560,219	3,053,780	3,785,417	4,376,008
% of total	26.94	30.43	35.38	25.93	24.42	28.28
Cotton goods	746,650	657,027	310,163	586,358	996,286	796,056
Linen goods	57,050	52,518	50,603	76,956	61,661	65,765
Woolens	2,383,050	2,050,617	1,741,465	2,078,008	2,827,655	3,186,837
Silks	583,900	461,044	467,046	519,191	447,079	243,082
Total textiles	3,770,650	3,221,206	2,569,277	3,260,513	4,332,681	4,291,740
% of total	32.84	25.32	25.53	27.69	27.95	27.73
Including indigo	599,850	548,895	211,784	457,762	595,183	513,712
Total dyes and raw silk	1,026,700	1,213,323	611,757	1,054,671	1,199,791	799,674
% of total	8.94	9.54	6.08	8.96	7.74	5.17
Lead	123,700	115,791	43,478	88,932	141,008	286,492
Tin	98,100	108,328	77,050	128,977	189,807	162,735
Total minerals	304,100	287,713	147,807	228,836	464,334	607,700
% of total	2.65	2.26	1.47	1.94	2.99	3.93
Total % accounted for	71.37	67.55	68.46	64.52	63.10	65.11

[a]Includes spices for 146,148 rubles.
[b]Includes embroidery for 122,828 rubles.

Table 4.39   Shares of Various Commodity Groups in St. Petersburg Imports (in percent)

	1768	1769	1770	1771	1772	1773	1774	1775	1776	Average for 1768–76
Beverages and colonial	23.11	19.93	20.40	24.10	24.49	15.50	16.90	22.00	27.02	21.24
Textiles	28.00	31.44	31.38	33.00	25.35	34.88	32.62	38.94	39.21	32.80
Raw materials for textiles	10.44	10.54	6.08	5.19	6.10	6.22	8.24	8.52	5.97	7.43
Other industrial inputs	3.78	4.38	3.45	1.76	1.11	3.14	5.07	3.05	4.46	3.38
Total accounted for	65.33	66.29	61.31	64.05	57.05	59.74	62.83	72.51	76.66	64.85
Total imports (in rubles)	6,328,113	6,795,096	6,546,734	6,810,123	7,342,724	8,493,815	8,676,339	6,756,143	7,006,730	7,195,080

	1783	1784	1785	1786	1787	1788	Average for 1783–88
Beverages and colonial	26.94	30.43	35.38	25.93	24.42	28.28	28.23
Textiles	32.84	25.32	25.53	27.69	27.94	27.73	27.84
Raw materials for textiles	8.94	9.54	6.08	8.96	7.74	5.17	7.67
Other industrial inputs	2.65	2.26	1.47	1.94	2.99	3.93	2.65
Total accounted for	71.37	67.55	68.46	64.52	63.09	65.11	66.39
Total imports (in rubles)	11,481,900	12,723,345	10,063,211	11,775,577	15,504,553	15,474,396	12,837,164

production of Russian goods, rather than from the purchase of foreign-made products themselves.

Despite limited factual knowledge and less data than one would wish for, it is incumbent upon anyone dealing with the subject of the Russian commodity trade to classify the major categories of imports, which reflect the tastes and demand of that segment of Russian society which had sufficient purchasing power to buy them. Imports also point to the areas in which domestic production was incapable of satisfying domestic demand at existing prices.

The skewed income distribution of Russian society of the eighteenth century meant that imports were substantially dominated by high-quality (and high-priced) consumer goods. One can assume (or expect) to find a relatively high proportion of imports in the areas of so-called "colonial goods" and high-quality textile goods. In other words, the foods, beverages, and attire of the upper classes which reflected their changing tastes and high social status were inevitably prominent in the totality of Russian imports. Some of those items were of foreign origin and were processed abroad because of Russia's inability (technical and economic) to produce them competitively.

A second category of imports included some foreign raw materials, such as raw or wrought silk and, notably, dyes for the textile industry, whose rise reflected the growth of Russian textile production. Several commodities, such as lead, tin, and alum, were imported by various industries for further processing in Russia.

Another group of commodities could not be included in the general categories because the price data were too scattered and incomplete to make a consistent and consecutive run, even for the few years for which the other data are available. This group consists of substitutes for Russian goods that were in demand by a broad stratum of the Russian population and ranges from salt to black tea, which was gaining popularity with the consuming masses by the end of the century. Although there were some substitutes for black tea for the population of European Russia, there were no substitutes for "brick tea" in the Far East and Siberia, or for green tea in other parts of Asiatic Russia. Many such commodities were not uniform in quality. Upper-income groups often demanded better products than did the broader stratum of consumers. Herring is a case in point. Dutch and English herring commanded a high price, but Swedish herring, of inferior quality, was demanded in larger quantities, was purchased by a broader population stratum, and was becoming a substitute for some domestic fish products.

The imports of St. Petersburg, which accounted for over half of all licit imports into Russia, have been analyzed in table 4.38 to test the hypothesis about the composition of Russian imports. Bias must be admitted in choosing the capital and seat of the central government and court. The data on imports into St. Petersburg during the years when the court was in Moscow show unmistakably the depressing effect the absence of the court had on the volume of imports. Moreover, the correspondence of English merchants makes it clear that for at least some imported commodities, the absence of the court meant a substantially reduced volume of sales.[9] Although there was a difference between the products imported into St. Petersburg and those that came into Riga and Arkhangel'sk, the difference is not of significant magnitude.[10]

The available data on the detailed composition of St. Petersburg imports permits their classification into categories and a determination of their relative share in the import total. Since it is possible to compile such data for two periods, for the years 1768–76 and for 1783–88, there is also an opportunity to note some of the changes that occurred over a longer period. The first group included beverages and some colonial goods: beer and porter, wines, coffee, sugar, pepper, oranges and lemons, and tobacco. (Tea was excluded because much of it was imported via Kiakhta, although after 1785, when the Sino-Russian trade was interrupted, St. Petersburg's imports of tea became significant.) The second group of commodities included dyestuffs such as indigo, cochineal, and logwood, raw material inputs for the domestic textile industry. The fourth group includes lead and tin, sulphur and alum, materials used in Russian manufacturing. The results are presented in table 4.38 and summarized in table 4.39.

The social and economic elite consumed the following shares of imports (primarily beverages, colonial products, and textiles): 41 percent for the years 1768–76, and 45 percent for 1783–88. About 40 percent of the imported textiles were not consumed by Russians at the top economic levels. A more meticulous analysis of import data for other periods and ports would certainly reveal that imported foods, beverages, colonial products, and textiles for consumption by the Russian aristocracy and upper gentry constituted at least half of all imports.

The tables of both periods reveal a significant change from textiles to beverages and colonial goods. It is possible that colonial goods and wines came to be substituted for different types of textiles. It is also possible, however, that decreases in the price of textiles resulted in a lower level of expenditures on them and thus permitted greater expenditures on foods, beverages, and tobacco. The causes of the shift cannot be explained.

The data also indicate that from 7.6 to 11.8 percent of imports were made up of raw materials and other inputs for Russian industries, the lion's share of which went to the textile industry. The data from British sources, especially the summary tables presented below on British exports to Russia, indicate very clearly a rising trend of dyestuff exports to Russia. Imports of indigo, for example, quadrupled during the last decade of the century, and the import of cochineal doubled, bearing witness to the growth of the Russian textile industry. The share of this particular group of imports exhibited a tendency to increase by comparison with the level of the 1780s, which, on the basis of scattered evidence, was higher in turn than during the 1760s and 1770s. When an attempt was made during the 1790s to curtail imports into Russia, this group was hardly affected by the policy.

The composition of St. Petersburg's imports reflected the taste and demand of the economic elite, and their tastes reflected certain economic changes and cultural adjustments.[11] Several additional aspects of the problem are worth mentioning. For one, after almost a century in which a particular pattern of imports was developed, no domestic substitutes for imported textiles satisfied the needs of Russia's upper classes.

The importation of raw materials for Russian industry did not proceed at a faster rate than the growth of the value of total imports. Since the growth of imports depended upon population growth and an increase in the incomes of the serf-owning elite, there could not have been a rapid rise of imports without corresponding spectacular rises in the productivity of Russian agriculture. The growth in imports was moderate and the import of raw materials for industry as a share of total imports remained largely unchanged. If we assume that the growth of certain raw materials approximated the growth rate of certain related domestic industries, the rate of growth of manufacturing industries showed only moderate growth rates.

The Trading Partners

The Trade with Britain

The primacy of Great Britain in Russian foreign trade from the 1730s and 1740s to the end of the century has already been mentioned. England was also the chief carrier of Russian goods and imports, and analysis of Russian eighteenth-century trade must be made against the backdrop of English maritime and industrial ascendancy.

Russo-British trade has a special significance for two basic reasons. First, because Great Britain established itself during the period as Russia's most important trading partner and market, and second, because the trade relations between Great Britain and Russia can be considered as a model for the latter's relations with the more advanced Western European countries. The assumption that the Russo-British trade can serve as a model describing the relationships between Russia and the other Western European countries is a gross oversimplification, and no one would argue that the Russo-Dutch or Russo-French trade by any means followed this particular model in every detail. Yet the basic elements that shaped the pattern of Russo-British trade were present in the trade relations with other Western countries. All Western European countries were actual or potential customers for Russian hemp, flax, iron, wood products, and naval stores. Each of them was capable of supplying Russia with colonial goods or textiles consumed by the upper classes of Russian society. Most of them, when called upon, could provide capital and services as well as "technical assistance" to Russia's government or private industry.

What distinguished Great Britain from the other Western European countries in trade relations with Russia was the presence of strong political interests, the availability of organizational means to mobilize or direct the flow of resources necessary to maintain its position in Russia's trade, and an acute sense of competition with other Western European countries, such as the Netherlands or France. The consciousness that, in order to compete, one has to overcome the deficiencies of one's resource endowment, or reorganize, innovate, and utilize the totality of available resources more efficiently, was more pronounced in Great Britain than among its competitors. Once Great Britain realized that Russia had forced its entry into the arena of European politics and economy and set in motion a process that could not be reversed, it acted accordingly and tried to adjust its policies to the new reality. It fashioned its trade relations with Russia not by criteria of taste, but by principles of self-interest.

This is not to say that the British and Russians formed an *entente cordiale* during the eighteenth century. Far from it. Such concepts were alien to the two partners, and their political interests diverged more often than not. Their relationship could be described as primarily a businesslike one in spite of fluctuations in the degree to which their political interests converged. Both partners valued the economic benefits that accrued from their trade relationship, and each tried to use it to achieve their particular ends, to satisfy their own objectives and short-term needs.

It was fortuitous for the Russo-British trade relationship that the two truly competed with one another in few areas of production or commodity trade. In cases where a conflict existed, the partners were convinced of the implacability of each other. It was clear to the British that the Russians would not lower the tariffs on bar iron or on coarse linen, either because of national interests or for the lack of a quid pro quo. The British therefore tried to export to Russia wrought-iron products or fine linens, commodities in which they had a comparative advantage and which did not evoke any negative reaction. But by and large the pattern was one of mutual interdependence, with one partner supplying raw materials and primary processed goods, and the other industrial products of a broad variety, in addition to some colonial products.

In 1734 Great Britain made a faint attempt to fashion its commercial treaty with Russia according to the Methuen Treaty (1703) with Portugal, but the nature and conditions of trade with Russia differed very substantially from that with Portugal and its colonial markets, and the British changed their position. Through most-favored-nation clauses and the British Navigation Acts, British textiles captured the market from most of their competitors. The British benefited also as a reexporter of Portuguese wine, salt, and colonial goods, and thus achieved a trade balance with Portugal that resulted in a very substantial and steady flow of Brazilian gold to England.

The Russians, on the other hand, enjoyed a favorable balance of trade with England. While the English market was capable of absorbing an increasing volume of imports from Russia, the Russian market had a very limited absorption capacity. Moreover, the British faced stiff competition from the Dutch, the North Germans, and others in the Russian import trade. The trade with Portugal made the British partners affluent; the Russian trade, although profitable, had convenient and useful strategic features (for the British navy) and provided raw materials important for England in maintaining its economic growth and furnishing employment for a part of the British labor force during the crucial period of economic transformation known as the Industrial Revolution. Although some historians love to describe the Industrial Revolution in terms of a series of technological, economic, and social discontinuities, the pattern of Russo-British trade reveals the evolutionary aspects of its early period. It is fascinating to watch the period prior to the jumps that enabled Great Britain to forge ahead at great speed and overwhelm the rest of Europe, at least for some decades, in its cotton production or its iron and machinery output. However, the buildup to this qualitative change took place only gradually, and the exports of Russian goods to Great Britain played a significant role in this process. The British trade with Portugal was related primarily to the commercial interests of England (which doubtless had a number of important secondary, or spillover, effects on other segments of the British economy); the trade with Russia was directly related to the interests of the British manufacturing industries and the British government.

The British government took its trade relations with Russia seriously and did not bemoan the fact of a negative trade balance, which required remittances of specie to Russia in considerable quantities. During the early part of the century most of the money transfers took place via the Amsterdam money market through such well-established firms as Pels, Hope, Clifford, deSmeth, and others, who handled bills of exchange to and from Russia; but during the second half of the century the role of the London money market in making transfers to Russia increased substantially.

The British merchants engaged in the Russian trade were recruited from among a prestigious, wealthy, and well-connected stratum of the merchant class. The British merchants, a minority within the foreign trading community in Russia, were highly regarded during most of the period by Russian government officials and traders, as well as by the other foreign merchants. A famous early case seems to have taught the British a lesson. In 1724 British merchants were accused of trading in shoddy goods and lost their contract for delivery of army cloth. The contract was awarded to the Royal Woolen Factory in Berlin, which supplied the army cloth at a lower price and manufactured fabric presumably of better quality.[12]

The Russia Company, a flexible, relatively efficient, and well-disciplined organization, facilitated the capturing of an important share of Russian trade for the British. Although the Russia Company in the eighteenth century did not possess the monopolistic features of power of the East India Company or similar organizations, it was superior to what Britain's competitors could produce during that period for the Baltic region. The Russia Company was a rather loose association, but one that had significant connections with the textile industry and traders, with the metal trade, with the Bank of England, and with the British government, including the Board of Trade as well as the Admiralty.

The British merchants had to work hard to maximize their profits in the trade with Russia. Most of the Russian claims of extraordinarily high profits earned by foreigners belong to the realm of fairy tales and are a result of uncritical nationalistic bias or profound ignorance.[13] Transportation costs were high because most ships came to Russia in ballast for lack of cargo. Capital was tied up in advances to Russian merchant-suppliers, and insurance costs were high because of frequent wars and uncertain weather. Among the uncertainties of the weather one would have to include the possibility that a certain number of ships might be frozen in and would have to winter in the port of Kronstadt.[14] Yet the profit rate was sufficient to make calculating and profit-conscious British traders persist in their activity, even though myths that Russia was an El Dorado for

foreign merchants in general and for the British in particular were quickly dispelled.

To succeed and maximize profits, British merchants could not rely exclusively upon a formal, umbrella-type organization such as the Russia Company. Each of the major firms or "middle" merchants trading with Russia had to provide a structure for their own enterprises. While large firms usually relied upon junior partners or salaried employees who in turn dealt with Russian merchants, smaller trading firms in England relied upon contractual relations with a group of semi-independent or independent British commission-traders stationed in Russia. Typically, these firms or traders worked with credits extended to them by English wholesalers in foreign trade, and occasionally with credit extended by British industrialists. They in turn extended credit to their Russian trade partners or to individual purchasers.[15] In both exports and imports, these firms conducted their trade at both the wholesale and retail level, and consequently had conflicts with Russian traders and the Russian authorities. For example, one Mr. Edward Fowell reported in a letter from St. Petersburg, March 5, 1743: "We have had a dangerous affair hapned here by a Raning goods & having em seated & I with 20 Dutch Mercht have been kept in Arrest 5 Weeks, & not a Friend, paper, pen, nor Ink admitted to us."[16] There is no question that this group was engaged in small-scale wholesale and retail trade, areas which by Russian law were reserved for Russian merchants and from which foreigners were excluded by treaty. Regardless, in the 1740s the livelihood and effectiveness of these British traders still depended upon their ability to sell goods in their residences. Much anguish was caused by decrees such as: "The sale of anything in your house will be punishable by death,"[17] and jubilation ensued when trade within the residence was later permitted.

The activities of this group clearly stimulated British firms in other areas of trade (such as imports of furniture, glassware, cutlery, various household items, and apparel) and provided more specific information about the demand of various population groups in Russia. A typical complaint was the bemoaning of the absence of Elizabeth's court from St. Petersburg as the cause for a standstill in trade of particular types of luxury goods.[18] These Englishmen established direct contacts with members of the aristocracy, Russian merchants, and the foreign trading and service community in St. Petersburg to whose tastes that type of import trade was catering. For example, a list of debts outstanding signed by Samuel Swallow in St. Petersburg for May 1756 reads like a directory of the highest-ranking nobles and office-holders at the time, with Peter, Catherine, Count Shuvalov, and Vorontsov leading the roster. Although the turnover of each of the British commission merchants was not spectacular, it was quicker, and the activity more aggressive and probably more energetic, than that of their actual or potential competitors. The lists of outstanding accounts varied. The largest one in the Public Record Office collection FJ370 was for 52,270 rubles, and that included subaccounts of other British traders.

Until about the middle of the century a significant portion of British-Russian trade required the presence of intermediaries for it to function at maximum capacity, but toward the end of the century, thanks to the learning process and the forces of competition, Russian merchants assumed this particular function. The expansion of the participation by Russian nationals in Russo-British trade occurred by the gradual elimination of the foreigners from the commission trade. The force of decree was ineffective in the process, which was propelled by the acquisition of skills, new attitudes, and capital. This particular development was a normal process of adjustment and organizational change conditioned by and resolved as a result of the development of the trade, its uninterrupted duration and growth. The substitution of Russian merchants who ultimately performed a function originally undertaken by the British shows the way in which adversary interests and attitudes expressed ancillary but not fundamental relationships. That this substitution by Russians for certain functions of the British commission traders was accompanied by a simultaneous growth of the trade turnover per merchant points to the growth and concentration which was the overwhelming characteristic of Russo-British trade in the second half of the eighteenth century.

That trade can be divided into three broad categories: Russian exports; Russian imports of British textiles; and Russian imports of colonial products and items of "conspicuous consumption." The growth rates of the three categories were in the same, descending, order. While Russian exports were growing most rapidly during the second half of the century, the import of British textiles grew moderately. The imports of the third category, while increasing, were derived not only from Great Britain, but also from the Netherlands, Hamburg, and other centers of European trade.

A Russian source provides data, presented in table 4.40, on the participation of British firms in the St. Petersburg trade and compares it with data on the participation of Russian merchants in both export and import transactions during the 1760s. The data, broadly confirmed by the reported distribution of trade in St. Petersburg by nationality of the merchants, vividly illustrate the growth of the volume of transactions of the British firms.

Table 4.40 Participation of Russian and British Firms in St. Petersburg Trade, 1764–69 (in rubles)

	British Firms		Russian Firms	
	Exports	Imports	Imports	Exports
1764	3,429,626	1,815,779	1,727,653	580,248
1765	4,063,735	1,598,912	1,543,099	614,758
1766	3,423,705	2,918,908	1,461,697	354,913
1767	3,888,806	1,683,880	1,386,378	460,523
1768	3,927,050	1,696,030	1,906,772	429,234
1769	5,370,782	1,571,345	2,673,543	514,613

Source: Ministerstvo finansov, *Istoricheskii obzor*, p. 124.

In addition, one must reckon with the phenomenon of concentration of trade among the British. The process of concentration on the part of the British merchants led to large-scale contracts, with special emphasis on bulk commodities. Catering to the personal tastes of small groups of individuals was less profitable for those operating on a grand scale. Tables 4.41–43 illustrate the size of some of the ten largest English firms involved in the St. Petersburg trade in the years 1795, 1797, and 1799 and compare them with the operations of the ten largest Russian firms engaged in foreign operations. Note should be taken of the changes in the rank order of the various firms even for those few years, a fact indicating that competition among the firms was quite intense.

The Russo-British Trade in Hemp and Flax

Great Britain established itself early in the eighteenth century as the largest importer of Russian hemp and flax. Although the choice of import sources of flax was relatively wide, with Poland, Prussia, and other North German lands offering feasible alternatives to Russia, hemp sources were more restricted. As a maritime power and a major textile producer, Great Britain was aware of its dependence upon Russian supplies of those vital industrial crops and fibers. The significance of hemp as a "strategic material" for shipbuilding has already been noted; it was important also for the cordage and ropes used as transmission belts to put in motion most of the machinery of the time.

After the Seven Years' War and some inevitable interruptions of supply, the British government began to search for a more secure source of hemp. Hemp cultivation in the American colonies was encouraged. Incentives in the form of a special bounty were effective in stimulating production, and the export from the colonies to England reached about 6,400 cwt. of hemp in 1767, still a negligible quantity in comparison with the 271,200 cwt. of imports from Russia in the same year. The exports from the colonies declined during subsequent years, and, especially after the outbreak of hostilities between the colonies and England, the attempt by the British

Table 4.41   Value of Exports and Imports of Major British and Russian Firms in St. Petersburg, 1795 (in Current Rubles)

British Firms	Exports	Imports	Russian Firms	Exports	Imports
Paris, Warre, Harvey & Co.	3,294,057	1,197,394	Ivan Kusov	46,733	432,286
Thompson, Peters, Bonar & Co.	2,883,758	1,032,072	Piotr Pishchalnikov		366,718
Cattleys, Prescott & Co.	1,587,893	181,703	Ivan Laptev	11,285	279,002
Thorntons, Smalley, Bailey & Co.	1,512,952	252,321	Fedor Zaitsev	1,672	276,636
Thorntons, Cayley Jun & Co.	1,031,760	250,350	Semen and Fedor Sitnikov		145,095
Shairps & Co.	746,996	233,915	Ivan Filipov	18,924	124,200
Jones & Co.	807,572	112,305	Avet Kalustov		130,000
W. Glen & Co.	910,421	—	Martin Glukhov	16,964	107,750
Porter, Brown, Wilson & Co.	692,036	217,957	Alexei Shadimerov		124,500
Th. Raikes	612,620	77,578	Vassilii Iroshnikov		118,750
Total	14,080,071	3,555,595		95,578	2,104,936

Total exports and imports for St. Petersburg: exports 31,767.952, imports 23,019.175

Table 4.42   Value of Exports and Imports of Major British and Russian Firms in St. Petersburg, 1797 (in Current Rubles)

British Firms	Exports	Imports	Russian Firms	Exports	Imports
Paris, Warre, Harvey & Co.	3,013,961	1,117,298	Feodor Zaitsev	6,278	416,157
Thompson, Peters, Bonar & Co.	3,152,528	705,981	Ivan Kusov	71,865	303,141
Cattaleys, Prescott & Co.	1,628,193	73,214	Semen & Fedor Sitnikov		369,006
Thorntons, Smalley, Bailey & Co.	1,668,586	13,015	Piotr Pishchalnikov		256,841
Thorntons & Cayley	1,016,783	59,476	Osip Belenkin		229,863
Shairps & Co.	748,436	218,011	Ivan Filipov	96,652	95,763
Anderson, Brown, & Moberley	564,427	368,981	Vassilii Iroshnikov		187,792
Jones & Co.	609,662	166,947	Ivan Laptev		151,922
Bayley, David	737,921		Grigorii Kiriakov	20,000	131,185
Smith, Edw. Jones & Co.	597,328	119,462	Alexei Shadimerov	154	122,644
Total	13,737,825	2,842,385		123,084	2,264,314

Total exports and imports for St. Petersburg: Exports 32,450,911; imports 19,366,059

Source: Tooke, *View*, 3: 524–29.

Table 4.43   Value of Exports and Imports of Major British and Russian Firms in St. Petersburg, 1799 (in Current Rubles)

British Firms	Exports	Imports	Russian Firms	Exports	Imports
Thompson, Bonar & Co.	3,919,017	1,162,411	Ivan Kusov	278,631	20,836
Paris, Warre, Harvey & Co.	3,484,908	1,067,216	Feodor Zaitsev	279,314	
Cattleys, Prescott & Co.	2,301,371	295,411	Piotr Pishchalnikov	213,500	
Thorntons, Smalley, Bailey & Co.	1,633,796	189,781	Osip Belenkin	209,627	
Anderson, Brown, & Moberley	2,280,541	479,996	Peter Kozhevnikov	205,559	
W. Glen & Co.	1,323,172	133,659	Grigorii Kiriakov	203,788	
Jones & Co.	1,321,884	85,570	Ivan Laptev	190,518	
Shairps & Co.	818,809	406,715	Semen & Feodor Sitnikov	183,069	
Porter, Brown, Wilson & Co.	1,137,416	96,887	Alexei Shadimerov	156,983	
Hubbard & Co.	733,367	489,716	Vassili Shigarev	103,685	
Total	17,954,281	4,407,362		2,024,674	20,836

Total exports and imports for St. Petersburg: Exports 38,169,925; imports 20,173,263

Source: Tooke, *View*, 3: 526–41.

government to gain relative independence from Russian exports failed. The production of hemp in America must have been uneconomic, for America imported Russian hemp after independence.

The London prices for St. Petersburg hemp that are available for the years 1764 and later indicate a relative stability in the hemp market in which variations in supply were mitigated by inventories maintained in England.[19] Those inventories were not large enough to prevent seasonal fluctuations of prices or the secular upward trend of raw-material prices during the last two decades of the century, a pan-

European phenomenon. The data in table 4.44 illustrate the relative price stability in the hemp market between 1764 and 1783.

Under conditions of relative stability, British imports of Russian hemp and flax gradually increased, as shown in tables 4.45 and 4.46. Neither the Russian nor the British government was capable of monopolizing the trade and denying its partner access to foreign markets. For both, the trade in hemp and flax constituted not only an economic necessity, but also an important source of fiscal revenue. Therefore each side was careful not to tamper with the market

Table 4.44   Average Yearly Price for St. Petersburg Hemp

Year	Pounds	Year	Pounds
1764	30.10	1774	23.0
1765	29.7	1775	27.10
1766	30.10	1776	29.10
1767	30.0	1777	33.0
1768	38.0	1778	33.10
1769	27.0	1779	34.0
1770	25.10	1780	31.18
1771	25.0	1781	37.0
1772	23.10	1782	38.10
1773	25.0	1783	38.10

Source: P.R.O. (London), BT 6/231 #35.

beyond the measures considered acceptable and legitimate in eighteenth-century trade relations.

The Russo-British Trade in Forest Products

Of the three groups of Russian forest products, two are pertinent to the study of Russo-British trade: timber, and pitch and tar. (The third group includes primarily potash and ashes.)

Although less important in terms of overall monetary value, pitch and tar exports had the more dramatic significance because of their strategic value in shipbuilding, the lack of available substitutes, and the acute shortages that England suffered during the earlier part of the eighteenth century. During the Northern War in the Baltic, two major producers, Russia and Sweden, were locked in a protracted war, communications were obstructed, and the British admiralty experienced a scarcity of those critical products. This experience prompted the British government to be attentive to the market in those goods and to seek substitutes for imports from the Baltic. The interaction of political and economic considerations, coupled with the long-standing government control and monopoly of the trade in pitch and tar (a consequence of the high share of direct government production) on the part of the Russians, elevated the trade in those commodities to a degree of British governmental attention and scrutiny unwarranted by the monetary value of this trade alone.

Tables 4.47 through 4.50 present the data reporting the Russian exports to Great Britain. The data are available primarily for the last third of the eighteenth century, a period for which data for the total British imports of pitch and tar are available for comparison. Sweden was the chief competitor of Russian exports until the very end of the eighteenth century.[20] In this period the United States also emerged as a serious competitor for Russia, lessening Britain's dependence for its supply on the stability in the Baltic. During most of the period 1786 through 1799, American exports of tar exceeded those of Russia, and only huge shipments in 1794, 1798, and 1799 caused

Russia's exports to exceed America's by about 8 percent. Although Finland under Swedish rule was a very valuable source of forest products, Sweden's advantage lay not so much in possession of superior resources but in a superior organization of supply and trade. Even though Russia had been traditionally a supplier of tar and pitch, very little progress was made in the eighteenth century to improve the exploitation of its vast forest resources. Arkhangel'sk remained throughout the century the important center for this trade and had to rely on a hinterland that was less well developed than Finland and some Swedish provinces obviously were. As a result, Russia lagged behind Sweden, at least in the British market, and acquired a real competitor in the U.S.

Exports of timber were of major importance in relation to Russian exports in general. Yet it was difficult to expand the trade because of problems of transportation costs, technology, and organization. Because the transportation of timber overland was uneconomical, the exploitation of those resources that lay along rivers and waterways was required. Proximity to ports and major rivers proved to be a decided advantage to the owners of forests in such locations. Russian timber producers relied for a very long time on manual labor rather than upon sawmills, and Russian peasants were more skillful in using the axe than they were in using the large saw. Entrepreneurship also was poorly developed under conditions in which forests were owned exclusively by the gentry or the state.

It is no wonder that in the first half of the century at least, the exports of timber from the Baltic provinces through the ports of Narva, Riga, and Reval exceeded the exports of timber through St. Petersburg. Merchants in the Baltic provinces had traditionally established relations with the gentry of Belorussia and Lithuania, where sawmills could process the wood to foreign specifications and capital was available. The merchants of the Baltic provinces also had long-standing business connections with Western importers of timber along with a reputation for supplying high-quality products.

The Russian government was not unaware of the state of affairs in its timber trade. However, besides an effort to conserve oak forests for naval construction and a prohibition against felling timber for industrial purposes within a 200-verst radius of Moscow, little attempt was made to improve the timber economy. Neither government nor private forests were replanted, and although foresters were appointed in the government domains, they were more interested in prosecuting poachers than in administering the forest economy.

As in many other areas of the Russian economy, an attempt was finally made "to go to the school of the

Table 4.45   British Hemp Imports (in Ctw)

Year	Total Imports England	From Russia			Year	Total Imports England	From Russia		
		England	Scotland	Total			England	Scotland	Total
1718	146,243				1755	416,307			
1719	98,638				1756	455,944			
1720	137,777				1757	258,871			
1721	139,809				1758	207,345			
1722	72,467				1759	544,287			
1723	109,586				1760[a]	220,785			
1724	144,238				1761	285,611			
1725	157,830				1762	272,822			
1726	165,622				1763	276,390			
1727	163,340				1764	345,621	321,599	11,022	332,621
1728	154,241				1765	337,244			
1729	157,822				1766	207,172			
1730	181,849				1767[b]	279,693	259,919	11,332	271,251
1731	76,704				1768	266,197			
1732	140,903				1769	341,105			
1733	201,786				1770	360,692			
1734	153,325				1771	502,509	469,753	11,296	481,049
1735	149,749				1772	270,276	252,869	17,924	270,793
1736	150,179				1773	342,816	339,381	12,192	351,573
1737	218,858				1774	418,997	410,003	17,282	427,285
1738	178,062				1775	298,374	282,741	13,600	296,341
1739	237,477				1776	315,216	302,113	13,970	316,083
1740	188,902				1777	348,220	341,088	13,691	354,779
1741	228,500				1778	342,807	341,617	10,113	351,730
1742	229,633				1779	518,716	490,707	11,901	502,608
1743	111,031				1780	375,882	367,648	18,199	385,847
1744	243,957				1781	419,071	411,886	22,306	434,192
1745	239,119				1782	502,441	501,351	20,273	521,624
1746	212,678				1783	247,014	246,288	20,019	266,307
1747	241,920				1784	355,576	353,287	24,508	377,795
1748	313,456				1785	304,550	301,951	24,499	326,450
1749	169,534								
1750	299,177								
1751	136,656								
1752	297,017								
1753	211,937								
1754	240,199								

Source: P.R.O. (London), BT 6/232.

[a]Elisabeth Schumpeter gives the figure of 68,029 (*Trade Statistics,* table 16, p. 55).
[b]Schumpeter gives the figure of 152,677 (ibid.).

foreigners." The negotiations and twenty-year concession granted to the English entrepreneur Gomm (with Count Shuvalov perhaps as a silent partner) for the exploitation of timber in the vast Onega region has already been mentioned. Exploitation of the Onega timber was envisaged on a major scale, but documentary evidence is insufficient to evaluate its performance.

More is known about the conventional methods employed in the trade of an important component of the timber exports, masts, which involved the inspection, choice, and marking of suitable trees; supervision of the felling of the trees; the handling of the trunk, and its transportation overland and by water to its port of destination. The careful and meticulous handling of masts was motivated by the relatively high price of this commodity, and masts from Russia were at a premium because of their size. Tables 4.51 and 4.52 show the volume of British imports of masts in the last third of the eighteenth century.

Three other types of timber were also important in Russian exports. The Russian share of Baltic exports of fir timber was significant, although, as shown in table 4.53, that share declined toward the end of the century because of competition from other supply sources. Deals (fir or pine boards and planks) were another item of mass consumption in the West, and, as shown in table 4.54, Russia was able to maintain and even increase its share of the trade because of technical improvements, primarily the establishment of new, large sawmills. The third forest product in which Russia (actually, the Baltic provinces) was able to hold its own was in the production of wainscot logs.

The Russian Iron Trade with Great Britain

Among manufactured goods, iron exports occupied a special place in Russia's trade with Britain. In terms of value, iron constituted the most important manufactured export. The emergence of Russia as a poten-

Table 4.46   British Flax Imports (in Cwt)

	Total Imports			From Russia		
Year	England	Scotland	Total	England	Scotland	Total
1718	38,161					
1719	44,453					
1720	37,310					
1721	36,703					
1722	50,750					
1723	37,661					
1724	61,761					
1725	50,340					
1726	59,160					
1727	35,048					
1728	58,719					
1729	52,534					
1730	61,397					
1731	72,324					
1732	73,221					
1733	57,369					
1734	80,346					
1735	56,885					
1736	68,441					
1737	103,454					
1738	87,035					
1739	77,555					
1740	69,572					
1741	75,933					
1742	96,016					
1743	56,302					
1744	51,722					
1745	74,464					
1746	62,615					
1747	97,677					
1748	119,250					
1749	84,625					
1750	124,646			24,435		
1751	101,651			29,769		
1752	80,718			26,640		
1753	117,970			60,014		
1754	119,254					
1755	113,833					
1756	102,568					
1757	91,859					
1758	107,826					
1759	168,312					

tial producer of iron was less surprising than its appearance in the world market as an exporter, a fact that did not pass unnoticed by the English trading community. It is true that prejudices against Russian iron products persisted for a long time, especially among the purchasers for the Royal Navy. As early as the 1730s the English firm of Schiffner and Wolf was engaged in wholesale purchases of iron from St. Petersburg and contracted for the commercial output of the Russian state-owned ironworks. (Schiffner and Wolf combined its purchases of Russian state-produced iron with sales of British-produced army cloth to the Russian government.) Both the early recognition of the significance of St. Petersburg as the chief outlet for Russian goods, underscored by the leading role of English shipping into that port, as well

as the conclusion of the Russo-British Treaty of 1734 with its "most-favored-nation" clause for Britain, facilitated a growing number of iron export transactions.

The iron trade with England began with the extension of credits to the Russian producers and a system of long-term contracts. In view of the general credit scarcity in Russia, the system of long-term contracts appears to have been advantageous to the Russians because the credits granted for future deliveries helped to offset the time-consuming transportation of iron from the Urals to the ports. Later, iron was sold at auctions in St. Petersburg. It is difficult, however, to ascertain whether the prices obtained there were appreciably higher than were the long-term contract prices, particularly when one considers the high

Year	Total Imports			From Russia		
	England	Scotland	Total	England	Scotland	Total
1760	73,059					
1761	113,014					
1762	102,436					
1763	157,124					
1764	164,288			127,499	30,707	158,206
1765	120,413					
1766	128,605					
1767	122,840			89,318	24,552	113,870
1768	145,643					
1769	137,756					
1770	121,683					
1771	188,905			162,239	39,788	202,027
1772	140,278			117,445	37,798	155,243
1773	64,487			52,393	28,468	80,861
1774	118,651			100,203	42,026	142,229
1775	169,165			138,702	44,849	183,551
1776	113,983			98,354	54,671	153,025
1777	148,120			126,192	57,827	184,019
1778	123,174			101,585	30,588	132,173
1779	124,702			102,839	43,104	145,943
1780	145,591			112,774	59,902	172,676
1781	102,450			88,864	58,286	147,150
1782	94,013			85,417	58,468	143,885
1783	117,020			101,821	61,619	163,440
1784	112,355			98,660	61,536	160,196
1785	193,307			167,643	84,486	252,133
1786	158,333	85,637	243,970	137,695	54,508	192,203
1787	164,935	104,738	269,673	127,326	76,133	203,459
1788	149,781	112,190	261,971	133,997	77,008	211,005
1789	80,079	59,415	139,494	67,141	39,144	106,285
1790	145,056	112,166	257,222	110,153	71,000	181,153
1791	172,096	136,005	308,101	142,801	96,396	239,197
1792	137,799	105,525	243,324	116,894	65,485	182,379
1793	165,381	105,868	271,249	139,654	69,077	208,731
1794	190,925	157,442	348,367	148,119	117,705	265,824
1795	122,912	102,941	225,853	98,171	84,896	183,067
1796	165,435	155,804	321,239	114,214	114,002	228,216
1797	122,685	86,997	209,682	94,149	57,227	151,376
1798	221,716	168,271	389,987	168,082	122,959	291,041
1799	227,513	191,224	418,737	178,620	165,378	343,998

Sources: P.R.O. (London), BT 6/232; Schumpeter, *Trade Statistics*.

degree of collusion in bidding at least among the English iron importers.

The growth of Russian iron exports to Great Britain was a gradual one, as indicated by the data in tables 4.55 and 4.56. Those exports grew at a rate that exceeded the rate of increase of total British iron imports, an indication that the share of Russia in the foreign supply of iron to Great Britain was rising through most of the century. The data also make it abundantly clear that the rate of growth of Russian exports was not equal in all periods. Economic crises in England, production-capacity problems in Russia, and the behavior of Russia's main competitor, Sweden, were all factors influencing the volume of iron exports. It was the relatively low price of Russian iron that enabled exports to continue along an upward

trend in spite of the year-to-year, or even decennial, fluctuations during the second half of the century. Russian exports reached a virtual plateau when the costs of production in Russia began to increase at the same time that British iron producers became seriously engaged in the technological reconstruction of their industry. The export data reflect this tendency quite vividly for the 1790s, a decade that witnessed an accelerated growth of British iron consumption accompanied by a stable level of imports.

Tariffs, as well as market factors, influenced the volume of Russian iron exports to Great Britain. For most of the century both import duties in Great Britain as well as export duties in Russia did not change, but beginning in the 1780s the tariff became an issue for negotiations between the two govern-

Table 4.47   British Imports of Pitch and Tar (in Lasts)

Year	Total Imports			From Russia		
	England	Scotland	Total	To England	To Scotland	To Great Britain
1720–24	5,474					
1725–29	5,610					
1730–34	6,635					
1735–39	6,860					
1740–44	6,218					
1745–49	6,101					
1750–54	8,102					
1755–59	6,548					
1760–64	7,464					
1765–69	12,650					
1770–74	8,822					
1775–79	8,779			2,172	193	2,365
1780–84	8,249			3,274	319	3,593
1785–89	8,753			2,894	361	3,255
1790–94	9,635	930	10,565	3,378	554	3,932
1795–99	11,341	1,287	12,628	4,211	690	4,901

Sources: P.R.O. (London), BT 6/231; Schumpeter, *Trade Statistics*, pp. 53–59.

Table 4.48   British Imports of Pitch and Tar (in Lasts)

Year	Total Imports			From Russia		
	England	Scotland	Total	England	Scotland	Total
1771	9,177			624		
1772	9,141			356		
1773	10,393			838		
1774	8,362			445		
1775	13,800			775	1	776
1776	4,330			1,450	102	1,552
1777	7,692			2,815	398	3,213
1778	9,402			3,839	167	4,006
1779	8,669			2,001	299	2,300
1780	7,246			3,457	331	3,788
1781	10,985			3,594	180	3,774
1782	7,438			3,506	413	3,919
1783	5,129			2,582	316	2,898
1784	10,445			3,231	353	3,584
1785	8,014			2,499	227	2,726

Table 4.49   British Imports of Tar (in Lasts)

Year	Total Imports			From Russia		
	England	Scotland	Total	To England	To Scotland	Total
1786	7,115	1,077	8,192	2,648	601	3,249
1787	9,754	1,556	11,310	2,557	783	3,340
1788	7,810	837	8,647	3,244	109	3,353
1789	7,044	784	7,828	1,306	67	1,373
1790	12,616	1,246	13,862	2,535	744	3,279
1791	6,734	958	7,692	2,639	316	2,955
1792	8,536	1,500	10,036	2,366	403	2,769
1793	9,004	706	9,710	1,514	224	1,738
1794	11,286	1,119	12,405	5,899	1,050	6,949
1795	9,823	361	10,184	1,897	164	2,061
1796	11,281	750	12,031	2,782	466	3,248
1797	6,961	973	7,934	1,750	528	2,278
1798	11,405	1,586	12,991	5,005	1,168	6,173
1799	17,233	1,320	18,553	7,264	1,089	8,353

Table 4.50   British Imports of Pitch (in Lasts)

Year	Total Imports			From Russia		
	England	Scotland	Total	To England	To Scotland	Total
1786	830	25	855	420	1	421
1787	1,754	28	1,782	927	10	937
1788	698	20	718	385	6	391
1789	745	8	753	165	2	167
1790	1,177	70	1,247	459	11	470
1791	917	70	987	747	1	748
1792	832	64	896	270	2	272
1893	978	19	997	226	3	229
1794	746	15	761	236	15	251
1795	1,018	5	1,023	426	0	426
1796	1,981	26	2,007	330	7	337
1797	1,050	43	1,093	498	12	510
1798	1,135	33	1,168	582	8	590
1799	1,252	13	1,265	519	6	525

Table 4.51   British Imports of Masts, 1786–99

Year	Total Imports			From Russia		
	England	Scotland	Total	To England	To Scotland	Total
1786	15,035	179	15,214	2,802	28	2,830
87	11,808	421	12,229	2,494	37	2,531
88	11,711	326	12,037	2,523	36	2,559
89	12,554	472	13,026	3,537	83	3,620
1790	13,907	560	14,467	1,888	39	1,927
91	15,979	779	16,758	3,740	163	3,903
92	16,788	1,157	17,945	3,857	284	4,141
93	17,140	836	17,976	2,441	45	2,486
94	22,448	338	22,786	5,585	36	5,621
1795	15,885	377	16,262	3,014	40	3,054
96	19,497	1,121	20,618	2,613	23	2,636
97	10,763	672	11,435	3,255	159	3,414
98	14,613	1,390	16,003	2,015	209	2,224
99	16,138	1,725	17,863	1,014	115	1,129

ments, and during the 1790s the British tariff was raised. During the 1780s the British customs duty was 2 pounds 16 shillings 2 pence per ton on an average price of 13 or 14 pounds per ton. The duty in 1796 was raised to 3 pounds 1 shilling 19 pence and then to 3 pounds 4 shillings 7 pence per ton in 1797, when prices before duties were about 19 and 20 pounds per ton, respectively. In percentage terms, the ad valorem duty was not significantly higher. In 1798 the duty was raised further to 3 pounds 15 shillings 5 pence on top of a price of about 20 pounds per ton.[21]

The rise in the duty must be attributed to fiscal motives and to Britain's attempt to protect domestic industry from foreign competition while British prices were rising. In the short run, Russian iron output was elastic with respect to price, and each rise in the British customs duty resulted in a temporary decrease of Russian iron imports into Great Britain. British tariff policy, or at least its protectionist features, turned out to be an anachronistic response to fundamental technological change in the iron in-

dustry, a change that soon made British iron competitive in the world market even without tariff protection.

The Russo-British Trade in Finished Linen

Considering the British imports of linen goods, one must first correct the view expressed by the eminent British historian of the eighteenth century, T. S. Ashton, who referred to English imports as follows: "Next in importance in 1700 came a group of textile materials, among which the first place was occupied by linens. These consisted largely of yarn from Germany and the 'East Country' where the labor costs of preparing and spinning the flax were well below those in this country; but substantial quantities of finished linen cloth also came in, at first from Holland, but later chiefly from Ireland."[22] This ranking of yarn above finished linen occurred because Professor Ashton had not carefully examined the data on finished linen imports and compared them with the value of the yarn imports. Although the data in table

Table 4.52   British Imports of Masts 1771–99

	Large			Middle			Small		
	England Total	From Russia		England Total	From Russia		England Total	From Russia	
		England	Scotland		England	Scotland		England	Scotland
1771	4,246	3,233	12	4,046	713	1	7,007	514	5
72	3,186	2,006	1	3,251	573	2	3,691	321	—
73	2,221	1,027	8	2,842	431	—	3,188	691	4
74	1,572	863	4	2,336	470	5	3,086	364	13
75	1,459	561	—	3,261	227	3	5,102	340	3
76	1,780	1,200	—	3,084	245	—	4,769	276	21
77	1,923	1,574	2	3,316	164	—	4,854	279	15
78	4,083	3,690	12	3,279	652	2	4,847	507	11
79	6,303	5,745	2	2,880	798	7	3,805	664	30
1780	4,045	3,409	42	5,761	1,263	—	5,113	423	2
81	3,601	3,025	2	4,691	702	—	5,293	388	—
82	5,203	4,485	2	3,724	1,384	—	3,113	486	4
83	11,225	7,830	74	3,956	683	—	10,228	576	—
84	2,681	1,305	14	2,174	146	52	3,486	402	7
85	1,613	754	8	2,799	196	10	4,006	372	13
86	2,158	1,526	20	4,620	332	2	8,257	944	6
87	2,335	1,676	16	4,307	211	4	5,166	607	17
88	2,774	1,481	16	4,513	363	1	4,424	679	19
89	3,234	1,986	46	4,205	496	6	5,115	1,055	31
1790	2,804	1,240	2	5,282	180	19	5,821	468	18
91	4,115	2,147	44	4,995	350	97	6,866	1,243	22

	Large		Middle		Small	
	Britain	From Russia	Britain	From Russia	Britain	From Russia
1792	3,617	1,859	6,727	1,127	7,601	1,155
93	2,496	1,474	7,163	337	8,317	695
94	5,706	4,087	7,856	691	9,219	843
95[a]	12,249	(10,770)	6,207	560	7,904	882
96[a]	21,419	17,659 (17,665)	8,855	1,361	11,748	1,488
97[a]	19,101	14,150	6,015	2,218	5,344	1,196
98[a]	7,936	5,936 (5,941)	8,055	1,563	7,935	661
99[a]	5,935	3,082 (3,086)	9,114	513	8,749	616

Sources: P.R.O. (London), BT 6/231; Schumpeter, *Trade Statistics*.

[a]For the years 1795–99 the number of large masts imported is estimated from the total value of imports. This is necessary because of the "alteration in the manner in collecting the duty" and the reporting procedures of the Customs Office, which entered not the number but the "load and feet" of imported masts.

4.57 apply only to a relatively short period, they may be helpful in correcting Ashton's mistaken impression of the importance of yarn and finished linens in the British import trade.

Ashton was certainly correct in assigning to Ireland the role of primary supplier of finished linens to England. After 1742, when a new tariff raised the duty for foreign linen in the English market and the revenue generated was applied as a bounty for Irish and British exports of linen, the share of Irish exports in the English market was on the rise. Later, in the second half of the century, the principal exporter of linen among the foreign countries was Germany, in this case not the "East Country," meaning Prussia, but the region of Silesia and Bohemia. The ties of this most important producing region with both the Neth-

erlands and with England represent an interesting chapter in European economic history, one which reflects the interregional economic relationships typical of the eighteenth century. This was a case of interdependence which developed gradually and which demonstrates not only differences in labor costs, as Ashton has pointed out, but also, and more interestingly, transfers of technology and adaptation to distant markets.

It is therefore much more important for the study of Russian exports of finished linen to determine their share of the total non-Irish exports, even though in terms of quality the Russian linen exports were more similar to the Irish than to the German ones. Although some of the data on Russian exports of finished linens go back to 1729, the comparisons

Table 4.53   Fir Timber Imports (in Loads)

Year	England	From Russia to England	From Russia to Scotland	Year	Britain	From Russia
1771	91,574	28,121	741	1792	260,923	34,965
72	100,387	31,961	1,312	93	188,276	29,093
73	96,968	21,571	864	94	159,632	24,065
74	86,025	14,115	607	1795	141,901	12,715
1775	101,304	13,084	834	96	183,838	16,268
76	117,200	9,488	243	97	117,936	11,518
77	94,675	9,477	366	98	136,831	6,978
78	102,455	16,335	806	99	142,880	5,303
79	68,690	11,112	255			
1780	63,433	9,169	68			
81	56,886	5,687	148			
82	64,657	6,798	13			
83	92,988	12,148	536			
84	119,699	10,994	509			
1785	91,660	6,909	455			
86	151,498	16,462	405			
87	155,871	22,811	947			
88	161,971	18,160	702			
89	144,276	19,185	785			
1790	181,563	10,884	620			
91	170,529	21,225	1,750			

Table 4.54   British Imports of Ordinary Deals (in Pounds sterling Custom Valuation)

Year	Total Imports Great Britain	From Russia England	From Russia Scotland	Year	Total Imports Great Britain	From Russia England	From Russia Scotland	Total
1771		6,427	4,856	1792	104,546	19,543	12,929	32,472
72	49,403	8,295	3,871	93	85,643	18,820	8,461	27,281
73	46,878	8,647	4,366	94	76,283	11,898	4,030	15,928
74	46,265	7,003	5,016	95	69,723	13,672	4,657	18,329
1775	43,253	5,520	2,863	96	92,384	19,477	10,766	30,243
76	52,950	6,426	3,038	97	65,877	14,265	7,879	22,144
77	55,137	5,616	6,074	98	79,492	10,921	11,439	22,360
78	43,318	5,544	3,008	99	76,116	6,136	1,063	7,199
79	34,455	4,970	2,928					
1780	38,493	3,496	2,902					
81	36,521	4,145	2,964					
82	36,873	2,567	1,557					
83	55,269	10,463	3,225					
84	53,781	8,532	6,274					
1785	46,614	7,320	3,075					
86	58,745	14,979	3,872					
87	52,427	9,412	7,413					
88	53,541	13,924	8,821					
89	48,443	15,386	4,359					
1790	53,892	14,378	6,556					
91	47,765	19,239	9,288					

Source: P.R.O. (London), BT 6/231.

made in table 4.58 assist an assessment of Russia's place in the British market with respect to its main competitors. Table 4.58 replicates an account by the inspector general of the Customs Office of May 20, 1786, and differs only slightly from the data in table 4.57. The data enable us to present the total imports of finished linen and the respective shares of Ireland, Germany, and Russia. The data reflect, not current market prices, but the "stable prices" of the English Customs Office.

A distinct feature of Russian exports of finished linen to England during this period is the lack of significant growth, as revealed in tables 4.59–61. This was largely due to the competition of Russian-finished linens with those from both Ireland and Germany. Enjoying no significant cost advantage

Table 4.55   British Iron Imports (in tons) 1725–99 (5-year averages)

Years	Total Imports			Imports from Russia		
	England	Scotland	Total	England	Scotland	Total
1725–29	19,214.2			843	53.8	896.8
1730–34	23,727.4			2,890.8		
1735–39	27,329.6			2,964.4	30.2	2,994.6
1740–44	21,091.8			3,959.4	84.0	4,043.4
1745–49	23,904.4			4,359.4	88.6	4,448.0
1750–54	29,278.2	1,640.0	30,918.2	8,620.8	166.4	8,787.2
1755–59	30,019.2			8,958.4	214.6	9,173.0
1760–64	36,772.4			13,457.6	416.6	13,874.2
1765–69	42,742.8			20,838.8	1,352.0	22,190.8
1770–74	47,144.4			27,798.0	1,744.4	29,542.4
1775–79	41,763.8			22,216.6	1,270.4	23,487.0
1780–84	44,342.4			30,420.0	2,380.8	32,800.8
1785–89	44,099.8	4,368.6	48,468	25,190.4	1,894.8	27,085.2
1790–94	48,039.6	5,072.4	53,112.0	26,797.4	1,857.2	28,654.6
1795–99	42,937.2	5,067.8	48,005.0	25,746.4	1,959.4	27,705.8

Sources: P.R.O. (London), BT 6/231, BT 6/232; Schumpeter, *Trade Statistics*; Scrivenor, *Iron Trade*, appendix, tables 1, 5, 8, 10, 12, 13.

over Irish linens and offering quality unequal to that of the German and Dutch linens, the Russian exports had a hard time in the British market in an industry that was not growing rapidly anyway in this period. In fact it is remarkable that Russia was able to stay in the British market at all. Its survival there can be explained in part by the composition of its exportable finished linen. Packaging cloth, drills, crash, diaper, Flemish, and ravenduck were the standard items, and specialization helped them to remain competitive.

By the end of the eighteenth century manufactured goods, particularly iron and linen textiles, played a significant role in Russia's exports to Great Britain. The British market exerted an increasing impact upon different areas of Russian agricultural, forest, and industrial production. The economic meshing of Russia and Great Britain was of mutual advantage.

The Import Trade With Britain

An important indicator of the changes and pattern of Russian imports during the last three decades of the eighteenth century can be derived from the British data on the Russo-British trade. There are problems with the data because the British customs office officially recorded both exports and imports at stable prices, established at the beginning of the century, until 1797. Valuations thus reflect changes in the quantities of each of the goods rather than changes in the relative market prices. Nevertheless, the information presented in tables 4.62 and 4.63 is valuable, although it may overstate somewhat the share of industrial goods, whose prices did not rise as rapidly as did the prices of the colonial goods. The information is especially valuable because it distinguishes between British manufactured and mining products

and colonial goods, primarily food-consumption items and dye products. The figures are rounded to the nearest pound sterling.

Two simultaneous processes aid interpretation of the secular growth of the share of colonial products in Russian imports: the growth of the taste for colonial goods among the members of the Russian gentry, an aspect of the cultural Westernization of this particular social group that coincided with the growth of their money incomes; more specifically, the growth of Russo-British trade at the expense of the Russian trade with the Netherlands, which increased the share of colonial products obtained from London at the expense of those previously obtained from Amsterdam. The data for the late 1790s also may reflect a reevaluation of Russian imports from Britain at prices more in line with prevailing relative market prices than did the set of prices recorded for the earlier period.

Trade and Competition With Sweden

Russian trade with Sweden is not as well documented as is the Russo-British trade. Nevertheless, it is of interest for two primary reasons. At the beginning of the eighteenth century Sweden was Russia's chief political adversary and the two countries engaged in a war that lasted an entire generation. Russia and Sweden also were competitors in some of the main items of their export trade. The competition in forest products such as pitch, tar, ashes, and wood products was of long standing. During the first half of the eighteenth-century Russia succeeded in breaking Sweden's monopoly in iron exports, and, although producing lower-quality iron, the latecomer made inroads into Sweden's iron trade with England and the Netherlands. In the space of three decades

(1720–1750) Russia turned from a consumer of Swedish iron into a formidable competitor. The trade rivalry between Russia and Sweden in foreign markets, particularly in the English market, was fierce over Sweden's traditional export commodity, iron.

Sweden's monopoly was broken during the lifetime of Peter the Great, when Russian iron produced in the Urals region began to reach the ports of Arkhangel'sk and St. Petersburg. The English, weary of the Swedish monopoly, seem to have encouraged the Russian export trade by entering into long-term contracts for delivery of iron both with the major private iron producers and with the Russian government, which preferred to export its own iron production and to use the output of the private producers for its armaments.

The entrance of Russian iron into the world market coincided with the growth of demand for iron in Western Europe. Therefore Sweden's attempts to thwart the development of the Russian iron industry by guarding Swedish technological secrets and to undersell the Russians and block their access to markets were unsuccessful. The share of Russian iron exports to England rose throughout the period from the 1720s to the 1750s, but only in the late 1760s did Russia succeed in overtaking Sweden in the export of bar iron to the British market. The British data in tables 4.64 and 4.65 on imports of iron from Sweden and Russia illustrate the long-run relationship between English imports from both countries.

The rivalry in the iron market does not exhaust the story of Russo-Swedish trade relations. Table 4.66 presents the share of Russia (including Livland and Kurland) in the total Swedish imports during much of the eighteenth century.

The basic characteristic of Russo-Swedish trade was Russia's favorable balance, as is shown in tables 4.67 and 4.68. This characteristic marked most of Russia's trade with Western Europe, but the reasons are somewhat different for the Swedish case. In the trade with Western Europe the demand for Russian primary goods exceeded Russia's demand for the manufactured goods and colonial products supplied by Western Europe, but in the Swedish case both countries were exchanging raw materials or semiprocessed goods. After the loss of Livonia Sweden became a net importer of industrial fibers and grain, and it had little comparative advantage, except perhaps for high-quality iron and steel, in the goods it was selling to Russia.

Sweden attempted to find suitable exports that would diminish its trade deficit with Russia. It was not particularly successful in substituting for the Dutch or the British as a supplier of colonial products or even of salt, the category labeled in table 4.69 as "re-exports." Fish, and especially herring, was the

only commodity in whose export Sweden succeeded in gaining a firmer position. The substitution of Swedish for Dutch herring was a result of both a shift of the fishing grounds and a substitution of the cheaper Swedish product for the higher-value product exported by the Dutch at a time when herring consumption in Russia was increasing.

Another means employed by Sweden to decrease its deficit in the commodity trade was to increase its earnings from the shipping that serviced the Russo-Swedish trade. The data in table 4.70 on the earnings of Swedish and foreign shipping, which are incorporated in the overall trade balances, as well as other evidence, suggest that the balance of payments deficit was smaller than the deficit on commodity trade, but the shipping earnings could not make up more than a small fraction of the deficit. The size and commodity composition of the Russo-Swedish trade clearly suggest that Russian exports to Sweden were of greater significance for the Swedish economy and import trade than were imports from Sweden for the Russian foreign trade.

The composition of Russian exports to Sweden (table 4.71) shows a primacy of industrial fibers as represented in the table under the heading "raw materials" (flax, hemp, and hemp oil). They continuously constituted a very substantial share in the total exports; variations depended primarily upon fluctuations in the share of grains.

The share of grains was the item of the greatest variability, for it depended upon the relative sizes of the harvest in both countries and the supplies available to Sweden from other sources outside Russia. The available data provide some measure of the extent of Sweden's dependency upon Russian grain during the eighteenth century. The data in table 4.72 for five-year intervals provide some insight into this problem. The Swedes obtained from Russia relatively little of their wheat imports, usually half or less of their rye imports, and usually a quarter or less of their barley imports.

Russian historians have tended to overemphasize the importance of grain imports from Russia for the Swedish economy and polity. There is perhaps some truth to the assertion that the Russian government viewed its grain exports to Sweden as a tool of international diplomacy, and thus the export of nontaxable grain or a guarantee of a minimum level of exports during famines in Sweden might be considered as a gesture of good will on Russia's part. The data, however, do not support claims that Russia enjoyed a monopoly position in the Swedish grain market. Even in the case of rye, Russia's role was important, but imports from Poland and Prussia were perfect substitutes for Russian grain. Moreover, most of the Swedish grain imports came from the Baltic

Table 4.56   British Imports of Bar Iron (in tons)

Year	Total Imports			Imports from Russia		
	England	Scotland	Total	England	Scotland	Total
1716	14,857			74		
1717	7,122			121		
1718	17,053			334		
1722	22,624			34		34
1723	18,878			210	15	225
1724	20,919			569	13	582
1725	18,178			148	26	174
1726	21,206			264	73	337
1727	15,652			945	115	1,060
1728	21,774			1,522	28	1,550
1729	19,261			1,336	27	1,363
1730	21,772			714	32	746
1731	24,442			1,627		
1732	23,282			4,456		
1733	24,248			4,119		
1734	24,893			3,538		
1735	26,289			2,650		
1736	23,987			2,864	26	2,890
1737	29,554			2,831	32	2,863
1738	28,321			3,132	27	3,159
1739	28,497			2,345	36	2,381
1740	23,028			3,065	45	3,110
1741	23,126			3,727	142	3,869
1742	19,817			5,384	44	5,428
1743	15,427			3,792	77	3,869
1744	24,061			3,289	112	3,401
1745	29,297			3,291	72	3,363
1746	21,896			4,146	110	4,256
1747	19,698			4,419	62	4,481
1748	25,976			2,615	141	2,756
1749	22,655			7,316	58	7,374
1750	35,051	1,570	36,621	14,976	178	15,154
1751	26,495	2,022	28,517	5,632	183	5,815
1752	24,946	1,488	26,434	8,599	189	8,789
1753	28,824	1,376	30,200	7,286	194	7,480
1754	31,075	1,744	32,819	6,611	88	6,699
1755	29,449	1,590	31,039	9,949	120	10,069
1756	30,062			7,534	158	7,692
1757	26,717			5,175	268	5,443
1758	30,719			8,162	300	8,462
1759	33,149			13,972	227	14,199
1760	27,718			9,954	305	10,259
1761	42,323	2,140		16,692	296	16,988
1762	32,342	1,700		11,934	284	12,218

provinces, areas that had been connected to the Swedish market during the seventeenth century, and not from the Russian lands proper.

The pattern of Russo-Swedish trade in the eighteenth century was a continuation of the trade relationships established earlier between the Scandinavian region and the Baltic provinces annexed by Russia as a consequence of the Northern War. No new pattern of trade emerged in the eighteenth century. Both economies were at approximately the same level of development and both produced an exportable surplus in many identical commodities. This left little room for a large volume of trade between them.

The Russo-French Trade

France was the one Western European power during the eighteenth century for which trade with Russia was marginal, even unimportant. This is not to deny that France was importing flax, hemp, seeds, iron, and even tobacco from Russia, or that French wines, salt, and textiles were exported to Russia. Rather, both countries treated their trade with each other as limited, as providing goods for which substitutes were readily available from other trading partners. Neither of them made any concerted effort to capture a larger share in the other's markets. At no point did

Table 4.56, cont.   British Imports of Bar Iron (in tons)

Year	Total Imports			Imports from Russia		
	England	Scotland	Total	England	Scotland	Total
1763	37,577	2,389		11,693	545	12,238
1764	43,902	2,600		17,015	653	17,668
1765	51,413	2,694		25,273	588	25,861
1766	32,397	2,423		11,420	823	12,243
1767	36,507	2,511		17,470	1,155	18,625
1768	44,748	2,922		22,136	1,568	23,704
1769	48,649	3,355		27,895	2,626	30,521
1770	46,020	2,612		29,340	1,000	30,340
1771	45,953	3,277		26,920	990	27,910
1772	51,919	2,601		27,268	1,637	28,905
1773	46,476	3,480		29,519	1,034	30,553
1774	45,354	2,877		25,943	1,816	27,759
1775	41,888	3,039		19,214	1,066	20,280
1776	50,192			26,470	1,285	27,755
1777	43,106			25,995	1,654	27,649
1778	31,547			16,324	1,235	17,559
1779	42,086			23,080	1,112	24,192
1780	37,223			24,394	1,729	26,123
1781	51,738			37,265	1,891	39,156
1782	39,940			27,052	2,403	29,455
1783	43,972			28,671	2,557	31,228
1784	48,839			34,718	3,324	38,042
1785	40,387			25,293	2,775	28,068
1786	44,330	4,235	48,565	21,829	2,084	23,913
1787	42,407	4,342	46,749	26,029	1,268	27,297
1788	46,864	4,634	51,498	27,816	1,725	29,541
1789	46,511	4,532	51,043	25,005	1,622	26,627
1790	43,812	5,429	49,241	22,440	1,664	24,104
1791	51,575	5,609	57,184	29,972	2,581	32,553
1792	52,452	5,240	57,693	26,892	1,693	28,585
1793	54,780	4,182	58,962	33,512	1,473	34,985
1794	37,578	4,902	42,480	21,171	1,875	23,046
1795	44,831	4,696	49,527	26,215	1,958	28,173
1796	48,276	5,001	53,277	29,083	1,899	30,982
1797	33,135	3,825	36,960	20,537	1,082	21,619
1798	45,965	5,964	51,929	29,446	2,496	31,942
1799	42,479	5,853	48,332	23,451	2,362	25,813

Note: The data reflecting the growth of foreign imports of iron into England are from Schumpeter's *Trade Statistics* for the period 1716–85. Although they exceed some of the existing data provided by Scrivenor (*Iron Trade*) or by the custom house inspector (P.R.O., BT 6/321), they were chosen for their consistency and availability to readers. The data for Scotland's imports are from the two other sources. For 1786–99 the custom house inspector's data were accepted. For the Russian exports Scrivenor's and the custom inspector's data were combined with that of the Sound tolls. The discrepancies usually do not exceed 5 percent and could be in part explained by the conversion coefficients of the Russian poods into shippounds and tons.

France for economic or political reasons engage in the type of competition that existed at various times between the British and the Dutch in the Baltic. Neither the French nor the Russians possessed the type of institutions or merchant associations set up for trade in the Russian or French markets which would pursue expansionist trade policies independent of or alongside their governments, as the Dutch and British did. Paradoxically, perhaps, regardless of the low level of commercial relations, the Russian elite borrowed French culture wholesale in the second half of the eighteenth century.

Peter the Great was interested in French achievements in the areas of science, manufacturing, and naval and military technology and sent Russians to be trained in France. The French navy not only followed with considerable interest the progress and rise of Russia's navy. It also exhibited real concern for access to supplies of naval stores at times when it was upgrading its fighting capacity. Although the French were politically active and tried in various ways to influence Russian foreign policy, trade was seldom an incentive they seriously held out to win the Russians over to their side. Perhaps they perceived that the Russian merchants had little influence with the makers of foreign policy.

Walther Kirchner's interesting study of Russo-French trade makes it clear that the volume of trade,

Table 4.57   Imports of Linen Manufactures and Linen Yarn 1772–85 (Custom Valuation in Pounds sterling)

Year	Linen Yarn	Linen Manufactures
1772	326,452	1,337,606
1773	228,739	1,069,921
1774	306,597	1,258,165
1775	361,041	1,250,577
1776	371,305	1,265,044
1777	422,964	1,233,957
1778	351,582	953,104
1779	383,090	969,281
1780	450,382	1,160,683
1781	436,760	1,029,216
1782	404,163	968,865
1783	389,191	1,129,054
1784	323,641	1,298,918
1785	360,017	1,283,102

Sources: P.R.O. (London), BT6/231; Schumpeter, *Trade Statistics*, table 17, pp. 56–77.

as reported in French sources, was growing over time.[23] Professor Kirchner, who published the data in table 4.73 based upon the declarations of French merchants and recalculated by the customs officials, has observed that their precision is questionable, but certainly the general tendency of growth ought not to be challenged. The available Russian estimates of exports from St. Petersburg to France for the years 1764–98 correlate poorly with the French data but nevertheless support conclusions that there was a growth of trade from the late 1760s through the 1780s.

Through the 1770s the Russian trade with France occurred almost exclusively through the Baltic (with some occasional French visits at the White Sea port of Arkhangel'sk) to the French ports of La Rochelle, Rouen, Nantes, and Bordeaux. The 1780s marked the opening of a new trade route through the Black Sea into the Mediterranean and the port of Marseilles. The direct connection between Kherson and Marseilles heralded the nineteenth-century development of trade relations between Odessa and various French ports.

The composition of French exports to Russia was not affected by the shift in the trade routes. Textiles, wines, and colonial products were dominant. The opening of the Black Sea route added to the traditional Russian exports (industrial fibers, naval stores, tallow, and iron) a new commodity, avidly sought in the Mediterranean, wheat and wheat flour. The demand for wheat, combined with the lower costs of shipping through the Black Sea, served as a powerful stimulant for the expansion of wheat cultivation in the southern steppe regions annexed by Russia. Already in 1793 wheat constituted over one-half of the reported value of the Black Sea trade, and France was considered an important potential customer.

The Baltic basin (including Russia) was marginal for French trade in the eighteenth century and the French did not develop the intricate organization of supporting services, such as shipping, insurance, and capital transfers, which were necessary for the conduct of trade in that part of the world. Although the French built up those services for other trade routes, they did not specialize in the Baltic region to the extent that the Dutch and British did. It was therefore natural that both the Dutch and the British at various times during the century served to some extent as intermediaries in the Russo-French trade.

French exports were directed to a relatively small

Table 4.58   Linen Imports into England 1772–85. (Custom Valuation in Pounds sterling)

Year	Total Imports	From Ireland[a]	Non-Irish Imports	From Germany	From Russia	Share of Russia in Non-Irish Imports
1772	1,338,701	648,212	690,489	485,981	143,379	20.9
1773	1,069,941	596,829	473,112	267,697	149,145	31.5
1774	1,618,165	717,647	900,518	304,008	150,464	16.7
1775	1,250,558	732,992	517,566	321,452	130,680	25.3
1776	1,265,050	699,852	565,198	364,020	131,556	23.3
1777	1,230,878	703,544	527,334	330,195	127,073	24.1
1778	953,719	630,337	323,382	154,330	132,331	40.9
1779	969,393	511,267	458,126	275,782	136,445	29.8
1780	1,160,428	651,082	509,346	328,844	128,577	25.2
1781	1,029,212	538,158	491,054	325,257	106,699	21.7
1782	968,881	541,619	427,262	264,919	114,571	26.8
1783	1,169,051	691,442	477,609	279,814	108,620	22.7
1784	1,298,115	819,901	478,214	281,624	139,511	29.2
1785	1,283,096	819,446	463,650	296,701	112,130	24.2

Source: P.R.O. (London) BT 6/232.

[a]Also includes imports from Guernsey and the Isle of Man.

Table 4.59   Linen Goods Imports from Russia (Custom Valuation in Pounds sterling)

Year	England	Scotland	Total
1764	163,497	948	164,445
1767	131,185	47	131,232
1771	134,921	205	135,126
1772	143,379		
1773	149,145		
1774	150,464		
1775	130,680		
1776	131,556		
1777	127,073		
1778	132,331		
1779	136,445		
1780	128,577		
1781	106,699		
1782	114,571		
1783	108,620		
1784	139,511		
1785	112,130		
1786	100,833	1,192	102,025
1787	140,076	4,897	144,973
1788	177,230	8,149	185,379
1789	169,637	6,488	176,125
1790	162,637	5,024	167,661
1791	98,255	6,305	104,560
1792	138,751	11,870	150,621
1793	158,032	9,356	167,388
1794	101,529	8,118	109,647
1795	200,779	10,375	211,154
1796	203,435	12,083	215,518
1797	169,669	9,809	179,478
1798	179,184	11,260	190,444
1799	253,111	20,496	273,607

group of consumers in Russia and the volume of their exports depended upon the development of a taste for their goods among the Russian elite. The volume of exports depended to some extent also upon the level of the customs duties on their products. The availability of close substitutes which were taxed at a lower rate or were less expensive prevented the French from gaining a greater share of the Russian market. The Russian government was able to proceed less gingerly when taxing French goods than English ones as it kept in mind the retaliatory power of the chief importer of Russian goods. There is here the paradox mentioned earlier, the fact that the cultural influence of France on Russia had only a very small impact on the trade relations of both countries. On the other hand, the Dutch and British, so prominently represented in foreign trade, had only a slight cultural impact upon Russia. Apparently the Russians learned not to mix business with pleasure, or pleasure with politics.

The Russo-Iranian Trade

The Muscovite annexation of the Kazan' and Astrakhan' khanates in the 1550s created opportunities for direct commercial relations with Iran after the estab-

Table 4.60   Exports of Finished Linen to Great Britain from St. Petersburg

Years	Diaper Broad (Arshin)	Diaper Narrow (Arshin)	Linen Broad (Arshin)	Linen Narrow (Arshin)	Crash (Arshin)	Drills (Pieces)	Flemish (Pieces)	Ravenduck (Pieces)	Sailcloth (Pieces)
1755–59		215,590		2,212,246	342,751	44,772	9,823	20,283	7,682
1760–64	145,917	265,691	158,324	1,926,630	681,553	55,173	15,785	29,007	7,807
1765–69	214,686	322,230	166,465	1,640,869	748,729	45,969	17,895	41,182	9,059
1770–74	197,536	224,992	63,345	1,237,550	843,351	34,205	21,438	45,662	8,572
1775–79	182,799	319,331	75,563	933,951	875,601	24,719	22,868	57,536	1,296
1780–84	212,782	288,557	66,807	555,162	695,733	15,753	20,211	58,105	1,062
1785–89	162,475	240,583	59,426	675,780	1,133,587	16,012	26,760	76,558	2,948
1790–94	168,492	286,347	61,448	282,401	1,230,407	11,646	24,514	81,776	761
1795–99	200,741	305,372	91,367	419,961	1,646,963	9,314	37,839	112,547	840
Total St. Petersburg Exports of Finished Linen									
1790–94		547,353	391,531		1,318,926	25,395	38,443	105,923	48,078
1795–99		601,385	573,787		1,778,154	16,939	65,335	155,037	58,681
Share of English Imports in the Linen Export of St. Petersburg, in %									
1790–94	83.1		87.8		93.3	45.9	63.8	77.2	1.6
1795–99	84.2		89.1		92.6	55.0	57.9	72.6	1.4

Table 4.61   Flax and Hemp, and Goods Made from These Fibers, Exported to Great Britain from St. Petersburg

	Unit	1753	1754	1755	1756	1757	1758	1759	1760	1761
Hemp, clean	Poods	545,661	736,476	1,202,302	1,117,018	736,639	839,111	1,352,166	803,182	549,797
Hemp, outshot	Poods	4,997	3,891	17,399	6,569	2,637	3,804	6,757	1,040	13,108
Hemp, half-clean	Poods	15,736	11,716	33,897	12,642	6,330	6,349	5,665	5,332	2,075
Total hemp	Poods	566,394	752,083	1,253,598	1,136,229	745,606	849,264	1,364,588	809,554	564,980
Flax, 12 heads	Poods	47,026	32,808	58,242	58,979	63,906	98,559	166,995	63,604	92,348
Flax, 9 & 6 heads	Poods	18,027	15,573	29,009	21,833	18,520	28,820	28,818	19,827	21,701
Total flax	Poods	65,053	48,381	87,251	80,812	82,426	127,379	195,813	83,431	114,049
Diaper, broad	Arshins	—	—	—	—	91,369	77,546	141,134	116,185	115,814
Diaper, narrow	Arshins	554,319	107,177	194,662	152,555	252,994	208,901	268,839	260,175	309,033
Linen, broad	Arshins	—	—	—	—	13,900	20,774	2,511	213,624	211,997
Linen, narrow	Arshins	3,106,448	2,122,773	4,797,253	3,683,672	1,503,334	793,047	283,925	2,049,092	2,774,284
Crash	Arshins	979,061	393,531	594,171	303,673	99,657	552,945	163,308	366,822	1,229,989
Drills	Pieces	48,155	49,496	50,191	51,361	44,319	37,426	40,562	44,992	74,029
Flemish	Pieces	10,009	7,540	8,782	8,534	9,350	10,505	11,943	8,904	12,360
Ravenducks	Pieces	18,442	15,523	19,036	15,108	17,685	24,323	25,263	22,103	24,289
Sailcloth	Pieces	3,093	4,472	9,135	5,423	7,202	11,583	7,069	11,242	13,361

	Unit	1762	1763	1764	1765	1766	1767	1768	1769	1770
Hemp, clean	Poods	819,886	600,591	876,338	876,074	672,599	822,339	757,154	910,499	931,162
Hemp, outshot	Poods	83,237	56,507	44,110	55,887	35,993	33,845	83,870	98,825	25,739
Hemp, half-clean	Poods	16,050	22,632	36,060	12,854	6,981	20,765	13,326	26,718	23,027
Total hemp	Poods	919,173	679,730	956,508	944,815	715,573	876,949	854,350	1,036,042	979,928
Flax, 12 heads	Poods	66,206	107,939	88,198	50,104	42,650	82,098	95,852	83,878	87,650
Flax, 9 & 6 heads	Poods	32,891	52,869	18,375	16,921	14,839	10,063	20,980	14,171	1,998
Total flax	Poods	99,097	160,808	106,573	67,025	57,489	92,161	116,832	98,049	89,648
Diaper, broad	Arshins	132,551	225,582	139,451	108,678	163,706	348,349	190,865	261,834	338,418
Diaper, narrow	Arshins	190,469	345,063	223,716	142,653	255,806	413,808	344,992	453,890	423,207
Linen, broad	Arshins	49,516	204,902	111,581	248,269	180,566	95,247	51,904	256,340	59,620
Linen, narrow	Arshins	575,580	1,604,481	2,629,714	3,013,207	1,639,642	1,067,750	1,014,369	1,469,379	2,127,426
Crash	Arshins	237,689	172,089	1,401,178	1,575,897	492,267	349,997	535,006	790,476	1,349,070
Drills	Pieces	72,099	41,052	43,692	42,148	34,994	49,776	48,906	54,019	25,631
Flemish	Pieces	13,888	19,127	24,644	23,555	18,612	19,071	16,767	11,469	15,749
Ravenducks	Pieces	20,236	38,332	30,074	35,870	40,225	39,501	51,267	39,049	41,067
Sailcloth	Pieces	1,406	2,483	10,541	13,889	12,039	1,286	6,772	11,309	13,574

	Unit	1771	1772	1773	1774	1775	1776	1777	1778	1779
Hemp, clean	Poods	1,384,081	589,453	1,023,713	1,132,767	798,435	767,472	1,104,299	939,693	1,380,605
Hemp, outshot	Poods	72,823	10,341	31,844	53,644	65,424	161,910	92,950	86,432	91,209
Hemp, half-clean	Poods	42,089	5,046	21,489	43,089	28,490	46,516	32,735	90,092	54,093
Total hemp	Poods	1,498,993	604,840	1,077,046	1,229,500	892,349	975,898	1,229,984	1,116,217	1,525,907
Flax, 12 heads	Poods	113,488	97,473	39,935	112,190	147,224	135,232	208,135	156,137	150,419
Flax, 9 & 6 heads	Poods	16,761	12,147	5,214	7,068	16,387	21,084	27,544	18,391	8,083
Total flax		130,249	109,620	45,149	119,258	163,611	156,316	235,679	174,528	158,502
Diaper, broad	Arshins	206,533	79,967	145,711	217,051	128,988	295,058	152,834	190,824	146,289
Diaper, narrow	Arshins	242,082	146,744	146,760	166,169	176,925	454,715	337,683	313,682	313,649
Linen, broad	Arshins	21,000	79,940	66,331	89,833	157,085	98,535	82,155	—	45,042
Linen, narrow	Arshins	2,871,210	527,374	257,505	404,237	865,483	1,045,061	1,596,716	687,211	475,286
Crash	Arshins	1,150,247	615,714	575,572	526,153	753,727	1,777,580	1,143,440	558,771	744,487
Drills	Pieces	39,225	27,554	51,059	27,558	21,145	22,379	28,243	28,614	23,212
Flemish	Pieces	16,496	26,607	21,366	26,976	24,895	17,293	23,483	27,741	20,927
Ravenducks	Pieces	47,951	37,910	55,302	46,080	49,444	53,837	56,494	58,629	69,274
Sailcloth	Pieces	7,832	3,714	4,914	9,910	2,915	2,059	1,205	141	158

	Unit	1780	1781	1782	1783	1784	1785	1786	1787	1788
Hemp, clean	Poods	810,982	1,310,967	1,163,570	590,557	1,209,231	1,038,791	638,000	900,763	1,481,264
Hemp, outshot	Poods	96,786	192,021	29,452	22,494	71,342	37,382	74,040	56,504	49,852
Hemp, half-clean	Poods	32,987	80,941	14,137	11,376	38,993	18,374	56,228	67,003	47,248
Total hemp	Poods	940,755	1,583,929	1,207,159	624,427	1,319,566	1,094,547	768,268	1,024,270	1,578,364
Flax, 12 heads	Poods	145,280	189,193	155,648	248,100	168,063	378,606	299,150	324,417	443,441
Flax, 9 & 6 heads	Poods	8,482	13,739	9,874	10,698	1,695	9,049	26,296	34,886	19,787
Total flax		153,762	202,932	165,522	258,798	169,758	387,655	325,446	359,303	463,228
Diaper, broad	Arshins	261,475	201,172	182,237	244,010	175,467	198,074	171,028	219,132	111,049
Diaper, narrow	Arshins	228,410	155,774	197,554	410,026	351,022	310,861	156,930	284,672	217,900
Linen, broad	Arshins	191,790	46,286	19,695	38,667	37,599	75,969	135,369	44,206	23,379
Linen, narrow	Arshins	786,989	302,564	259,405	834,713	592,137	529,472	491,040	876,987	481,288
Crash	Arshins	94	1,201,444	496,279	738,840	1,042,006	894,066	676,274	1,213,572	1,739,820
Drills	Pieces	21,833	13,961	12,790	14,901	15,280	20,890	15,343	12,430	14,203
Flemish	Pieces	17,500	19,210	15,423	24,720	24,204	16,122	17,282	30,398	40,528
Ravenducks	Pieces	77,793	51,793	37,069	47,611	76,261	72,591	49,934	73,982	88,985
Sailcloth	Pieces	428	272	724	1,084	2,800	2,556	2,095	2,216	2,942

Table 4.61, cont. Flax and Hemp, and Goods Made from These Fibers, Exported to Great Britain from St. Petersburg

	Unit	1789	1790	1791	1792	1793	1794	1795	1796
Hemp, clean	Poods	1,306,594	1,499,476	865,731	1,582,252	1,290,867	1,492,533	1,050,680	1,340,063
Hemp, outshot	Poods	48,752	48,617	30,224	52,395	56,804	43,703	77,467	146,898
Hemp, half-clean	Poods	27,646	44,908	14,026	13,754	24,198	37,453	7,396	70,801
Total hemp	Poods	1,382,992	1,593,001	909,981	1,648,401	1,371,869	1,573,689	1,135,543	1,557,762
Flax, 12 heads	Poods	263,709	370,367	523,682	344,917	389,018	488,607	413,494	388,795
Flax, 9 & 6 heads	Poods	7,931	5,125	1,729	5,638	7,603	8,594	22,526	31,863
Total flax	Poods	271,640	375,492	525,411	350,555	396,621	497,201	436,020	420,658
Diaper, broad	Arshins	113,092	207,227	112,376	265,810	106,418	150,628	128,485	175,849
Diaper, narrow	Arshins	232,554	233,562	248,408	563,798	205,817	180,152	239,614	186,250
Linen, broad	Arshins	18,208	54,409	36,399	122,463	50,102	49,868	71,339	45,518
Linen, narrow	Arshins	640,114	227,338	69,934	384,124	309,115	421,492	329,773	289,154
Crash	Arshins	1,144,204	990,278	1,036,875	2,034,876	1,088,089	1,001,916	1,077,277	1,606,650
Drills	Pieces	17,193	10,223	10,645	11,790	12,902	12,670	11,164	3,235
Flemish	Pieces	29,469	24,145	14,911	24,155	37,779	21,581	28,235	36,706
Ravenducks	Pieces	97,296	99,203	62,682	67,118	78,978	100,901	114,694	97,769
Sailcloth	Pieces	4,933	851	2,238	673	42	—	211	170

	Unit	1797	1798	1799	1800	1801	1802	1803	1804
Hemp, clean	Poods	1,145,392	1,491,614	1,267,245	694,128	1,195,208	743,860	1,313,912	1,092,055
Hemp, outshot	Poods	7,500	151,150	346,615	180,895	207,475	102,092	194,411	134,026
Hemp, half-clean	Poods	15,264	35,393	162,721	177,474	105,564	99,640	232,442	217,348
Total hemp	Poods	1,168,156	1,678,157	1,776,581					
Flax, 12 heads	Poods	291,970	468,018	341,927	231,966	283,133	180,094	176,471	268,323
Flax, 9 & 6 heads	Poods	12,173	14,552	85,090	27,282	50,720	15,183	7,527	18,034
Total flax	Poods	304,143	482,570	427,017					
Diaper, broad	Arshins	165,376	253,558	280,437	86,575	209,398	175,300	75,976	50,209
Diaper, narrow	Arshins	345,644	445,978	309,372	77,604	270,216	153,241	140,675	155,476
Linen, broad	Arshins	99,008	107,552	133,416	23,570	63,611	194,714	106,471	1,838
Linen, narrow	Arshins	465,881	515,197	499,801	72,977	256,383	734,753	327,352	71,397
Crash	Arshins	1,848,303	2,110,134	1,592,453	—	1,161,286	1,663,279	1,443,294	967,900
Drills	Pieces	7,490	17,255	7,424	5,812	9,082	—	6,578	6,532
Flemish	Pieces	26,828	35,837	61,589	24,140	21,021	28,881	20,009	21,339
Ravenducks	Pieces	113,197	110,916	126,159	91,965	76,950	100,894	85,943	89,564
Sailcloth	Pieces	—	164	3,654	60	338	—	160	95

Table 4.62   Composition of Russian Imports from Great Britain (in Pounds sterling)

Year	British Products	Colonial Products	Total	Year	British Products	Colonial Products	Total
1764	59,316	8,909	68,225	1782	159,247	48,496	207,743
1765	64,067	12,353	76,420	1783	160,069	59,797	219,866
1766	39,639	20,773	60,412	1784	162,253	64,208	226,461
1767	101,071	24,713	125,784	1785	168,792	65,206	233,998
1768	90,323	37,160	127,483	1786	206,747	88,939	295,686
1769	115,565	46,371	161,936	1787	206,855	100,998	307,853
1770	108,297	38,902	147,199	1788	273,032	85,459	358,491
1771	109,992	41,973	151,965	1789	212,793	95,726	308,519
1772	130,295	30,562	160,857	1790	265,920	188,369	454,289
1773	158,579	49,924	208,503	1791	281,243	292,114	573,357
1774	170,816	91,209	262,025	1792	400,493	371,987	772,480
1775	142,012	74,787	216,799	1793	197,684	123,144	320,828
1776	180,548	71,326	251,874	1794	240,520	255,387	495,907
1777	148,657	57,735	206,392	1795	393,501	468,767	862,268
1778	150,483	52,251	202,734	1796	393,933	372,965	766,898
1779	270,330	59,709	330,039	1797	256,483	217,723	474,206
1780	129,537	38,593	168,130	1798	360,068	311,712	671,780
1781	104,849	39,034	143,883	1799	428,611	341,099	769,710

lishment of diplomatic relations between both countries. Formal diplomatic relations were established during the 1580s and envoys sent out of the two countries were accompanied by goods for exchange primarily between the two sovereigns. During the seventeenth century the major component of trade was the exchange of goods by the Russian treasury for goods exported or commissioned by the Shah of Iran. The state trade did not exhaust the total trade turnover between the two countries. Merchants acting on behalf of their states also engaged in private trade. Such Russian merchants in the seventeenth century traded in Iranian cities such as Derbent, Shemakha, Tabriz, Rusht, and even Isfahan. Iranian merchants travelled not only to Astrakhan', but also to Kazan', Nizhnii Novgorod, and Moscow for their business. The state trade involved primarily raw silk, carpets, and jewels from Iran in exchange for Russian furs, metals, and foreign textiles. The merchants trading on their own account imported Iranian silk wares, cotton goods, and leather goods in exchange for Russian and transshipped foreign goods that were not subject to the state monopolies.

An important institutional development during the 1680s was the granting of special privileges to an Armenian company of merchants organized in Dzhulfi (a suburb of Isfahan) to conduct a transit trade in silk through Russia. The granting of trading privileges to a foreign company had a precedent in Russia's earlier grants to the British Muscovy Company, but the novelty in the case of the Dzhulfi Armenian Company was the grant to conduct a transit trade, especially since earlier attempts in this direction by the English and Danes had failed. The activities of the Dzhulfi Armenian Company was the

first successful venture in the transit trade, and the legacy of this activity was strongly felt during the first half of the eighteenth century.

The eighteenth century witnessed a further expansion of trade. Private trade began to dominate and substituted for state trade. About the only remnant of the state trade by the middle of the eighteenth century was the declaration of some Iranian merchants that they were trading on the account of the Shah and therefore should be exempt from customs duties.

Among the distinct institutional and economic features of the Russo-Iranian trade were a few which, even if not unique, should nevertheless be mentioned because they differed from the general pattern. One was the existence of corporate bodies, or trading companies. Apart from the Dzhulfi Armenian company, which by 1711 obtained a confirmation of its previous privileges and whose role in trade was acknowledged by the Russo-Iranian treaty of 1715, there were attempts during the 1720s to set up a similar company in Astrakhan' during a Russo-Iranian war that cut off relations with the Dzhulfi company. The idea of substituting a domestic company (although made up in its majority also by Armenian merchants) for a foreign-based one was not only motivated by mercantilist-type policies, but was consonant with the military expansion of Russia into the Caspian region after the occupation of Iranian provinces bordering on the southern and western Caspian littoral. The Astrakhan' company officially expired in 1725 when relations with the Dzhulfi company were reinstated. Apparently the Astrakhan' company was moderately successful. Its records do not survive and there is no real record of

Table 4.63   Russian Imports from Great Britain 1764–99

	1764	1767	1771	1772	1773	1774	1775	1776
Alum (cwt=112 lb)	355–87	1,179–102	992–96	617–4	1,934–14	1,555–49	6–0	—
Coals—Newcastle meas. (1 chalder=72 bush)	239–	361–	464–	396–	745¼–	620–	599½–	300
Coals (cwt=112 lb)		1,347 cwt	720	852	1,500	800		5,420
Copper—wrought (1 cwt=112 lb)	—	0–28 lb	25–28	–84 lb	28 lb	3–0	4–91	29–28
Iron—cast (cwt=112)		—	—	337,047–12	183,606–0	4,595–0	2,579–44	5,581–96
Iron—wrought (1 cwt=112 lb)	1,565–28	824–84	1,860–42	3–0			3–0	3–0
Steel (cwt=112 lb)	5–0	14–0	1–0					
Lead	5,925–54	7,137–77	10,369–4	10,575–24	21,658–8	30,566–0	12,069–77	15,908–96
Tin	766–109	3,504–17	2,424–36	1,110–26	4,660–92	8,256–80	4,924–44	9,555–32
Glass & earthenware (pieces)	59,975	37,579	194,812	155,555	228,950	175,412	161,800	280,685
Skins—total value	—	—	—	—	197–14	—	21–13–6	72–8–1
Leather—tanned	62–52	175–104	215–49	212–91	197–14	230–49	116–54	273–32
Cottons & linens—dimity	—	—	—	—		—	—	—
Stuffs—plain		—	328–	1677–				
Printed linen (yds)	—	982			5,413	17,985	9,253	7,166
Calico	3,045	553	762		6,647	6,240	14,354	13,582
Woolen goods—		—						
Spanish cloth (pieces)	8		1	11	12	10	4	27
Flannel (yds)	3,370	49,040	37,712	64,662	25,679	53,746	46,510	44,796
Northern—single dozens (pieces)	8,212	6,600	9,035	6,083	6,790	12,648	7,027	8,991
Stuffs (lbs)	31,140	180,210	127,410	88,430	93,140	105,080	130,530	122,704
Salt—rock (bushels)	23	28	8,000	41,480	16,300	5,702	2,000	—
Sugar—refined (cwt/lbs)	14–64	41–20	34–7	29–32		29–56	4–88	77–49
Cochineal (lbs)	262	814	709	1,644	9,348	12,685	14,467	2,277
Indigo (lbs)	1,169	69,333	51,007	48,950	69,347	92,416	62,800	63,984
Logwood (cwt=112 lb)	3,320	2,600	14,770	1,800	5,200	4,940	1,000	8960–
Coffee—foreign (cwt/lbs)	—	—	22–72	—			37–16	753–56
Coffee B.P. (cwt/lbs)	—	121–65	92–59	286–101	95–63	1,656–63	827–102	766–74
Furs—total value (£-s-p)	2,560–10–8	484–10–0	7,727–9–0	7,199–6–0	6,748–10–7	13,357–10–5	15,360–15–9	12,869–7–7

	1777	1778	1779	1780	1781	1782	1783	1784
Alum (cwt=112 lb)	428–30	605–98	2,462–56	98–0	24–63	4,787–91	4,564–28	731–98
Coals—Newcastle meas. (1 chalder=72 bush)	383	4,655	2,068	803	589	312¾	902	1,156
Coals (cwt=112 lb)	3,800	13,530	75,001–56	10,753	15,521–0	12,351	8,246	9,507
Copper—wrought (1 cwt=112 lb)	18–77	722–4	591–76	12–28	1–0	393–0	13–44	20–0
Iron—cast (cwt=112)	—	6,400–0	—	—	6,400	—	—	—
Iron—wrought	2,714–91	2,867–52	3,713–18	3,731–28	1,973–56	2,277–84	1,568–77	74,224–68
Steel (cwt=112 lb)	—	—	4–0	—	13–0	—	—	7–0
Lead	26,256–51	19,767–38	6,754–33	17,274–70	19,242–43	23,408–51	24,013–7	22,676–29
Tin	6,507–13	16,620–52	5,910–27	2,740–44	4,378–76	6,478–36	4,455–76	4,562–108
Glass & earthenware (pieces)	391,600	358,445	490,185	313,680	245,140	464,060	411,725	273,075
Skins—total value	71–10–6	123–14–8	—	162–	185–2–6	73–6–3	35–2–8	361–2–0
Leather—tanned	313–16	312–42	334–10	209–80	211–105½	319–68	392–93	201–10
Cottons & linens—dimity	—	—	—	—	—	—	—	—
Stuffs—plain								
Printed linen (yds)	5,202	10,759	5,957	8,464	1,033½	2,495	10,743	5,792
Calico	20,382	33,718	23,487	11,319	9,513	20,237	12,832	5,813
Woolen goods—								
Spanish cloth (pieces)	22	125	287	319	155	472	727	947
Flannel (yds)	11,470	17,198	62,885	17,348	13,470	21,820	25,071	890
Northern—single dozens (pieces)	9,120	8,465	28,682	9,655	6,371	10,431	10,990	8,027
Stuffs (lbs)	71,140	98,130	119,864	116,690	58,530	114,880	79,054	130,156
Salt—rock (bushels)	—	26,280	94,244	8,000	37,168	33,905	52,800	22,320
Sugar—refined (cwt/lbs)	45–56	78–95	87–5	103–55	407–80	93–35	2,087–20	5,676–76
Cochineal (lbs)	4,854	3,712	2,540	1,890	1,596	5,070	9,990	12,769
Indigo (lbs)	68,815	36,212	57,020	13,372	56,523	33,515	45,366	45,177
Logwood (cwt=112 lb)	3,712–86	3,260–	5,000–	6,268–	10,033–21	12,549–28	2,540–	602–12
Coffee—foreign (cwt/lbs)	218–84	—	2–76	112–24	—	126–11	36–4	432–110
Coffee B.P. (cwt/lbs)	306–100	—	107–77	—	—	—	—	—
Furs—total value (£-s-p)	11,020–6–0	15,124–4–2	7,643–0–10	8,155–19–8	8,694–15–0	12,411–19–4	14,690–4–6	12,232–2–2

Table 4.63, cont.   Russian Imports from Great Britain 1764–99

	1785	1786	1787	1788	1789	1790	1791	1792
Alum (cwt=112 lb)	12–56	3,792–16	6,414–28	9,138–105	10,900–30	6,072–78	1,955–33	194–71
Coals—Newcastle meas. (1 chalder=72 bush)	1,256	1,176–57½	1,062–53	980–33	476–18	1,468–	1,090–17	1512–18
Coals (cwt=112 lb)	10,058	26,594–0	57,092–0	83,315–0	79,089–0	55,626–0	76,634–0	84,945–0
Copper—wrought (1 cwt=112 lb)	87–56	11–28	5–0	138–56	61–0	213–56	160–56	232–56
Iron—cast (cwt=112)	12,580	3,820–56	412–0	27,665–16	17,844–91	251–56	—	465–32
Iron—wrought	2,011–88	4,115–98	4,983–35	3,344–11	3,322–52	3,409–83	3,191–76	5,446–88
Steel (cwt=112 lb)	40–0	10–0	14–0	22–0	80–0	60–0		—
Lead	9,980–41	22,451–85	11,417–6	36,902–5	28,767–3	33,013–86	2,727–87	17,235–53
Tin	4,375–24	6,125–12	7,724–35	8,028–44	6,687–103	5,051–64	2,504–13	3,810–79
Glass & earthenware (pieces)	203,725	351,806	273,931	508,903	249,553	215,468	814,145	1,056,355
Skins—total value	—	—	442–11–2	8–2–0	90–6–0	—	27–0–0	101–5–0
Leather—tanned	396–56	431–67	440–103	519–11	396–102	499–74	789–19	699–23
Cottons & linens—dimity	—	600	1,200	500	1,000	—	—	6,000
Stuffs—plain	8,040	104,103	49,368	142,022	107,446	224,974	88,422	217,550
Printed linen (yds)	7,007	6,783	992	130	10,906	1,041	—	12,353
Calico	5,813	25,384	39,141	19,287	13,197	50,891	86,791	136,653
Woolen goods—								
Spanish cloth (pieces)	997	1,180	1,244	1,295	1,534	1,494	2,829	1,998½
Flannel (yds)	10,000	8,546	10,415	25,341	24,000	12,554	4,630	1,760
Northern—single dozens (pieces)	4,941	8,356	11,851	11,511	10,356	11,673	7,549	—
Stuffs (lbs)	135,810	133,185	124,100	224,800	120,754	163,810	469,337	447,602
Salt—rock (bushels)	24,800	80,500	71,000	20,780	71,320	115,400	77,800	85,880
Sugar—refined (cwt/lbs)	8,664–23	3,489–110	3,083–26	1,971–63	2,427–72	9,231–77	7,113–85	17,502–86
Cochineal (lbs)	17,544	27,773	14,028	100	10,708¾	10,068	25,176	11,967
Indigo (lbs)	36,545	38,581	52,949	53,296¼	103,364	164,177	171,299	126,058
Logwood (cwt=112 lb)	4,100–	13,056–	14,752–	1,680–	4,400–	960–	3,150–	21,170–84
Coffee—foreign (cwt/lbs)	—	—	—	—	—	—	76–31	21–37
Coffee B.P. (cwt/lbs)	830–105	120–32	842–1	461–106	605–39	77–40	744–50	1,082–9
Furs—total value (£–s–p)	8,642–15–5	7,678–3–8	14,675–11–7	6,997–16–5	10,614–9–6	11,793–10–6	3,497–17–8	20,970–

	1793	1794	1795	1796	1797	1798	1799
Alum (cwt=112 lb)	626–43	2,392–0	5,446–109	6,632–53	4,305–85	4,582–71	5,066–6
Coals—Newcastle meas. (1 chalder=72 bush)	1,182–0	1,143–0	2,228–9	1,791–34	416–0	886–26½	1,156–6
Coals (cwt=112 lb)	—	56,160–0	46,161–56	41,349–0	30,520–0	103,191–70	23,257–0
Copper—wrought (1 cwt=12 lb)	152–0	15–0	10–0	—	148–61	9–42	115–0
Iron—cast (cwt=112)	—	—	—	—	85–84	—	—
Iron—wrought	2,179–	1,872–0	1,656–56	2,154–56	1,409–68	2,085–104	4,368–94
Steel (cwt=112 lb)	3–0	—	—	130–0	50–0	21–0	22–56
Lead	—	23,117–5	41,166–88	24,662–14	14,863–55	28,714–10	27,537–23
Tin	2,757–8	4,726–100	7,250–77	3,974–69	2,854–104	4,983–61	3,294–3
Glass & earthenware (pieces)	1,088,300	702,450	1,191,511	461,300	1,210,424	901,130	1,292,069
Skins—total value	66–18–0	—	1,039–5–5	115–14–0	—	—	—
Leather—tanned	117–73	3–95	22–32	11–89	—	7–14	—
Cottons & linens—dimity	—	—	—	—	1,000	87	—
Stuffs—plain	171,800	211,796	17,960	15,270	10,480	11,150	5,020
Printed linen (yds)	6,800	77,310	72,000	62,260	55,932½	101,175¼	196,610
Calico	31,717	63,475	100,244	90,859	44,533	28,292	75,433
Woolen goods							
Spanish cloth (pieces)	1,104	867	1,047	1,509	1,553	1,677	2,951
Flannel (yds)	1,100	2,730	1,028	—	100	9,995	8,230
Northern—single dozens (pieces)	64	—	—	—	—	—	100
Stuffs (lbs)	157,300	43,395	67,053	73,452	45,284	95,854	153,916
Salt—rock (bushels)	40,600	79,048	126,920	536,440	129,880	49,800	83,520
Sugar—refined (cwt/lbs)	2,845–83	10,710–28	16,328–42	12,944–5	4,852–52	20,236–86	28,203–36
Cochineal (lbs)	15,127	31,486	66,704	13,302	10,709	1,769¾	25,746
Indigo (lbs)	58,836	151,663	204,999	229,367	101,572	188,439	296,878
Logwood (cwt=112 lb)	2,000	10,768–104	8,432	4,620–84	3,534–10	1,582–56	10,253–57
Coffee—foreign (cwt/lbs)	—	—	1,064–82	539–1	711–19	1,291–46	50–76
Coffee B.P. (cwt/lbs)	—	1,277–44	5,427–99	3,483–108	2,727–21	8,376–95	2,100–12
Furs—total value (£–s–p)	10,285–18–9	16,310–0–4	20,231–0–11	5,090–13–8	12,280–11–4	4,098–3–2	3,661–4–8

Table 4.64   The Share of Sweden and Other Exporters in the English Market, 1750–65 (in Tons), Iron

Year	Total Imports	Share of Sweden	Others	Of Which Russian
1750	34,751	17,575	17,176	15,148
51	26,005	17,859	8,146	5,814
52	33,308	13,859	10,660	8,789
53	28,351	20,004	8,347	7,469
54	30,694	22,424	8,270	6,696
1755	29,321	17,762	11,559	10,069
56	30,062	18,669	11,393	7,534
57	26,025	19,769	6,256	5,125
58	30,719	22,252	8,467	8,162
59	32,607	17,045	15,562	13,972
1760	27,383	16,328	11,055	9,954
61	40,735	23,484	17,251	16,692
62	32,342	17,816	14,526	11,934
63	36,856	21,708	15,148	11,693
64	43,210	23,517	19,693	17,015
65	50,978	21,973	29,005	25,273

Sources: P.R.O. (London Cust.), 3/50–70; Scrivenor, *Iron Trade*, app.; Kent, *War and Trade*, app. 3.

Table 4.65   British Imports of Bar Iron from Sweden and Russia, 1766–85 (in Tons)

Year	Sweden	Russia	Year	Sweden	Russia
1766	18,179	11,420	1776	20,950	27,743
67	16,451	17,471	77	15,244	26,470
68	19,361	22,137	78	14,498	16,588
69	17,164	27,895	79	18,031	23,221
1770	12,275	29,340	1780	11,503	23,572
71	14,652	26,920	81	13,738	37,358
72	17,789	27,268	82	12,457	27,052
73	15,161	29,518	83	14,677	28,671
74	17,663	25,943	84	13,449	34,718
1775	20,723	19,415	1785	14,480	25,273

Source: P.R.O. (London), BT 6/231.

its activities, but it is known that it conducted business on a larger scale than did most of the trading and industrial-commercial companies established during Peter's reign. After Russia was forced in 1732 to give up its recent conquests in Iran and relied upon the Dzhulfi company, a new attempt was made in 1755 to set up another trading company and combine its activities with those of the Armenian company. By 1762 this new company was dissolved, simultaneously with the abolition of the other state trading-monopolies. Free trade was introduced in the trade with Iran.

Table 4.66   Share of Russia in Sweden's Imports (in Percent)

1738–40	13.3	1771–75	19.9
1741–45	8.0	1776–80	18.8
1746–50	11.7	1781–85	23.5
1751–55	12.6	1786–90	10.3
1756–60	17.5	1791–95	13.0
1761–63, 65	20.1	1796–1800	19.3
1766, 1769–70	17.8		

Source: Heckscher, *Sveriges Ekonomiska Historia*, 2: 46, table 26.

Wide fluctuations make it difficult to judge the effect of the domestic or foreign trading companies upon the volume, composition, or terms of trade. Although the trading companies certainly exhibited monopolistic tendencies in terms of entry into the trade by individual merchants, it is possible that the existence of the companies prevented the respective governments from discriminating in an even more restrictive manner. The existence of the trading companies also may have lowered some of the transactions costs, or the transportation and insurance costs, because they organized shipping convoys and obtained protection against the arbitrariness of local bureaucrats. Regardless of what those net effects were, the existence of trading companies in which Russian merchants participated introduced techniques of foreign trade previously unknown to those merchants, from which they could learn and benefit in the long run.

Another feature of the Russo-Iranian trade was the transit trade in silk. The Sound toll accounts which registered the silk exports from St. Petersburg to

Table 4.67   Russian-Swedish Trade as Calculated by Sweden (in 1,000 thalers)

Year	Russian Exports	Russian Imports	Swedish Trade Deficit
1731/32[a]	1,002.5 (817.8)	647.2 (500.2)	355.3 (317.5)
1734/35	1,455.9 (1,041.8)	373.2 (280.0)	1,082.7 (761.8)
1735/36	1,545.0 (1,091.9)	322.2 (231.0)	1,222.8 (860.9)
1736/37	4,022.0 (3,200.6)	646.4 (507.7)	3,375.6 (2,692.9)
1738[b]	605	233	372
1739	1,351	344	1,007
1740	713	224	489
41[c]	513.3	139.9	373.4
42	397.3	95.0	302.2
43	555.9	183.2	372.6
44	784.9	292.3	492.5
1745	1,040.9	319.4	721.4
46	1,015.5	333.8	681.7
47	893.8	220.5	673.3
48	1,257.0	199.1	1,057.9
49	1,073.9	202.1	871.8
1750	741.5	231.8	509.7
51	831.1	239.3	591.8
52	738.8	438.0	300.8
53	1,658.0	339.5	1,318.5
1756	3,060.4	310.7	2,749.7
57	1,557.0	337.4	1,219.6
58	1,475.4	497.1	978.2
59	1,202.7	489.6	713.1
1763	4,434.2	923.5	3,510.7
1769	492.7	159.6	333.1
1770	501.9	109.6	392.3
71	692.2	92.2	590.0
1774	455.5	231.5	224.0
75	385.0	170.1	214.9
76	532.6	154.5	378.1
77	590.2	174.9	415.3
1778	651.3	231.7	419.6
79	719.0	194.2	524.8
1780	699.1	174.8	524.2
81	1,135.5	249.9	885.6
82	1,090.5	279.1	811.4
87	597.8	175.3	422.5
88	280.6	126.5	154.1
1790	293.0	81.2	211.9
91	515.5	161.1	354.4
92	476.2	163.4	312.8
93	347.0	197.3	149.6
94	521.0	204.8	316.2
1795	479.5	174.3	305.2
96	516.0	148.4	367.6
97	696.1	205.9	490.2
98	924.6	278.7	645.9
99	823.1	246.5	576.6

Note: The data are inclusive of trade with Kurland. The data in parentheses are for Russia only.

[a]For 1731/32–1736/37, data from April 1 through March 31, source is Boethius and Heckscher, *Svensk Handelsstatistik*, pp. 596–97, 606–7.
[b]For 1738–40, Statistika Centralbyran, *Historisk Statistik*, pp. 154–55.
[c]For 1731–1799, Kommerskollegii Arkiv Stockholm. DC3, Ukrikeshandeln Serie 3, 1739–1799.

Western Europe (see table 4.74) and the St. Petersburg data on the transit trade with Iran via Astrakhan' both point to the significance of the transit trade during some periods of the first half of the eighteenth century. During the second half of the century the transit trade in raw-silk became insignificant because of its irregular nature and diminished volume and the growth of other branches of trade. Although the raw silk transit trade was only one distinct legal form of re-exporting, the characteristics

Table 4.68 Russian-Swedish Commodity Trade as Calculated by Sweden (in 1,000 Thalers) (1741–99)

Year	Russian Exports	Russian Imports	Excess of Exports
1741	485.6	135.1	350.5
42	344.6	94.2	250.4
43	529.2	179.1	350.1
44	760.2	275.1	485.0
1745	1,026.0	303.2	722.8
46	1,008.8	322.7	686.1
47	883.0	213.4	669.6
48	1,248.1	193.5	1,054.7
49	1,057.9	192.0	865.9
1750	727.9	222.3	505.6
51	819.8	231.6	588.2
52	732.1	431.1	301.0
53	1,638.3	324.1	1,314.2
1756	3,050.4	277.6	2,772.8
57	1,531.0	307.4	1,223.6
58	1,464.5	497.1	967.4
59	1,195.3	421.1	774.2
1763	4,425.8	923.5	3,502.3
1769	490.2	148.4	314.8
1770	501.2	100.0	401.2
71	682.0	86.6	595.4
74	454.4	217.8	236.6
75	383.7	158.7	224.9
76	531.1	137.5	393.6
1777	588.8	153.9	435.0
78	649.7	210.7	439.0
79	716.3	164.4	551.8
1780	697.6	157.4	540.3
81	1,132.9	187.8	945.1
82	1,085.4	204.5	880.8
1787	596.2	165.7	430.5
88	269.2	122.8	146.3
1790	285.9	80.7	205.2
91	506.6	147.3	359.3
92	470.9	156.9	314.0
93	341.8	186.5	155.3
94	515.3	183.5	331.8
1795	473.5	132.9	340.6
96	506.3	128.3	377.9
97	673.7	157.0	516.7
98	887.8	224.7	663.2
99	785.4	180.3	605.1

Source: Kammerskollegii Arkiv, Stockholm DC3, Utrikeshandeln, Serie 3, 1739–1799.

Table 4.69 Swedish Commodity Exports to Russia (in 1,000 Swedish Thalers)

Year	Metals	Fish	Re-exports	Total
1741	87.3	.2		135.1
42	91.7			94.2
43	166.7		4.1	179.1
44	228.6	.4	13.7	275.1
45	250.2	.2	23.0	303.2
46	243.5		12.4	322.7
47	177.2		27.0	213.4
48	155.6	.2	16.8	193.5
49	159.6		24.0	192.0
1750	152.3		54.6	222.3
51	169.5	.2	24.7	231.6
52	383.6		19.5	431.1
53	245.0	.1	39.1	324.1
1756	195.2	1.5	23.4	277.6
57	198.9	1.1	34.9	307.4
58	289.5	24.5	39.5	497.1
59	125.0	120.2	64.8	421.1
1763	389.9	292.6	50.1	923.5
1769	37.2	69.3	21.0	148.4
1770	29.6	54.7	3.1	100.0
71	37.9	21.8	11.9	86.6
74	57.0	105.9	28.8	217.8
1775	49.6	64.1	18.2	158.7
76	47.1	51.6	20.3	137.5
77	55.2	50.2	14.7	153.9
78	84.9	41.1	25.7	210.7
79	52.8	28.4	29.7	164.4
1780	46.7	37.1	28.7	157.4
81	54.3	69.2	29.6	187.8
82	55.0	86.8	10.0	204.5
1787	29.1	81.6	26.6	165.7
1788	11.8	80.9	8.3	122.8
1790	24.9	41.7	8.7	80.7
91	53.6	66.7	3.6	147.3
92	36.1	72.4	10.2	156.9
93	53.9	74.3	22.7	186.5
94	28.8	47.5	40.0	183.5
1795	22.8	26.6	34.9	132.9
96	6.5	57.1	17.9	128.3
97	14.0	59.8	36.1	157.10
98	40.4	83.7	46.6	224.7
99	8.7	84.1	29.4	180.3

differed from other forms of re-exporting practiced by Russian merchants. The use of "foreign goods," notably Western European textiles in the trade with China, the Asian steppe regions (the so-called "Orenburg trade"), and Iran, was widespread and almost standard practice. In the case of raw silk, however, the movement went in the other direction. In the other cases Russia exchanged "Western goods" for "Eastern goods," most of which were consumed in Russia. But in the case of the silk trade, much of it was re-exported in exchange for the goods demanded by the Iranians. Under such circumstances, one should not be surprised to learn that most of the transit trade was handled not only by the Armenians and other Iranian merchants, but also by British merchants. The data for the years 1737–44 in table 4.75 provide some order of magnitude for the transit trade relative to the rest of the trade with Iran and also relative to the estimated turnover of Russian imports and exports.

The Russian exports to Iran included a large assortment of Western textiles, fine woolens (preferably dyed red), and also smaller quantities of coarser, cheaper Russian cloth. Iran also imported textile dyes such as cochineal, madder, and black dyes. Russian furs were in demand and were exported to Iran, although earlier in the century fur exports were not always registered in the customs books because they were a state monopoly. Russian merchants also

Table 4.70   Swedish and Foreign Proceeds from Shipping in Russian-Swedish Trade (in 1,000 Swedish Thalers)

Year	Swedish	Foreign	Total	Swedish Balance
1741	4,735	27,690	32,425	−22,955
42	852	52,640	53,492	−50,788
43	4,075	26,639	30,714	−22,564
44	17,195	24,701	41,896	−7,506
1745	16,206	14,841	31,047	1,365
46	11,088	6,715	17,803	4,373
47	7,044	10,812	17,856	−3,768
48	5,580	8,857	14,437	−3,277
49	10,068	15,980	26,048	−5,912
1750	9,528	13,617	23,145	−4,089
51	7,668	11,254	18,922	−3,586
52	6,906	6,752	13,658	154
53	15,456	19,754	35,210	−4,298
1756	33,090	10,026	43,116	23,064
57	29,930	25,940	55,870	3,990
58		10,846		
59	68,490	7,392	75,882	61,098
1763		8,382		
69	11,214	2,538	13,752	8,676
1770	9,602	665	10,267	8,937
71	5,587	218	5,805	5,369
1774	13,691	1,151	14,842	12,540
1775	11,351	1,332	12,683	10,019
76	16,970	1,354	18,324	15,469
1777	21,001	1,501	22,502	19,647
78	21,039	1,506	22,545	19,473
79	29,715	2,673	32,388	27,042
1780	17,466	1,410	18,876	16,056
81	62,109	2,600	64,709	59,509
82	74,553	5,064	79,617	59,489
1787	9,605	1,573	11,178	8,032
88	3,671	11,382	15,053	−7,711
1790	504	7,185	7,689	−6,681
91	13,737	8,927	22,664	4,810
92	6,558	5,327	11,885	1,231
93	10,847	5,200	16,047	5,647
94	21,297	5,681	26,978	15,616
1795	34,430	6,005	40,435	28,425
96	20,081	9,721	29,802	10,360
97	48,902	22,413	71,315	26,489
98	53,977	36,742	90,719	17,235
99	66,291	37,747	104,038	28,544

Source: Kammerskollegii Arkiv, Stockholm DC3, Utrikeshandeln, Serie 3, 1739–1799.

traded in a variety of metal goods, household goods, and writing paper.

Russian imports included raw and manufactured silk, cotton, fine leather, copper, jewelry, rice, and fruits. The share of Russian imports of raw silk in the trade turnover increased relative to the transit trade as raw silk was used increasingly by the Russian cottage industries and silk manufactories as a raw material input. For a number of years Russia's trade balance with Iran was negative, at least according to the official surviving records presented in table 4.75.

The volume of trade between Russia and Iran is difficult to estimate because of the gaps in the published data, and because after 1754 the official valua-

tions of the commodity trade were based largely upon 1754 prices.[24] At best, the post-1754 data can be considered as an approximation of a quantity index. Until archival data yield a commodity breakdown of the Russo-Iranian trade, judgment must be reserved about significant changes in the trade pattern over time.

It is possible to say something about the shares of the trade turnover in the Russo-Iranian trade held by particular merchant groups. The data for 1778–81 presented in table 4.76 illustrate existing patterns. According to such data, the major shares in the trade turnover belonged primarily to Armenians, then to

Table 4.71   Russian Commodity Exports to Sweden (in 1,000 Swedish Thalers)

Year	Raw Materials	Grain	Other Foods	Total
1741	263.4	196.2	16.5	485.6
42	152.0	136.6	43.7	344.6
43	193.5	230.2	81.0	529.2
44	262.2	415.2	40.8	760.2
1745	517.9	304.0	133.8	1,026.0
46	605.2	219.4	137.7	1,008.8
47	572.8	176.7	86.8	883.0
48	635.5	91.4	102.9	1,248.1
49	753.8	148.8	114.9	1,057.9
1750	653.9	31.3	286.6	727.9
51	461.3	58.4	235.9	819.8
52	474.4	68.4	105.7	732.1
53	512.9	776.4	266.9	1,638.3
1756	575.3	2,013.3	358.6	3,050.4
57	318.7	960.4	199.4	1,531.0
58	740.2	511.1	171.3	1,464.5
59	704.6	189.2	233.1	1,195.3
1763	1,223.3	2,699.6	525.3	4,425.8
1769	183.1	208.2	86.5	490.2
1770	228.9	185.8	68.8	501.2
71	197.7	391.9	60.3	682.0
74	220.3	148.8	68.8	454.4
75	238.6	45.0	60.8	383.7
76	239.5	221.4	38.9	531.1
1777	252.4	296.7	18.2	588.8
78	241.7	286.7	70.3	649.7
79	293.0	316.7	57.9	716.3
1780	340.5	238.5	71.3	697.1
81	311.9	731.3	55.8	1,132.9
82	389.4	581.2	74.9	1,085.4
1787	309.5	187.1	65.7	596.2
1788	183.7	38.9	26.9	269.2
1790	160.3	69.7	23.0	285.9
91	283.9	138.5	53.1	506.6
92	305.1	62.9	37.3	470.9
93	239.3	32.7	38.5	341.8
94	417.2	5.6	39.6	515.3
95	333.5	.9	56.6	473.5
96	335.6	41.9	43.6	506.3
97	322.7	194.5	60.7	673.7
98	328.1	422.0	37.3	887.8
99	266.6	404.2	23.4	785.4

Persians and subject Azeri, the Central Asians, finally Russians, and lastly, Indians.

The Russo-Lübeck Trade

A short discussion of the Russo-Lübeck trade is warranted for a number of reasons. Although Russia's foreign trade during the eighteenth century was dominated by a few trading partners such as Great Britain and the Netherlands, the trade with other partners was also important, and for some commodities could be considered a possible substitute for the trade with the major trading partners. The trade with Lübeck during the eighteenth century constituted a continuation of an age-long demand by both parties. During the latter part of the century Lübeck appears to have had an active trade balance

Table 4.72   Imports of Selected Grains into Sweden (in 1,000 Barrels, Yearly Average)

Years	Total			From Russia		
	Wheat	Rye	Barley	Wheat	Rye	Barley
1738–40	9.4	116.6	38.8	.7	52.0	14.4
1741–45	30.9	193.8	84.0	.5	37.5	5.3
1746–50	31.9	124.8	77.1	.2	13.6	8.2
1751–55	40.3	150.9	56.1	.3	61.1	10.7
1756–60	27.6	112.1	55.5	2.5	47.0	15.2
1761–65	22.4	269.5	76.0	.6	142.8	33.6
1766–70	29.0	288.8	63.3	.7	122.6	9.6
1771–75	25.1	159.7	58.4	3.6	101.3	12.1
1776–80	17.7	221.6	55.0	.5	116.3	3.0
1781–85	38.9	600.4	106.6	4.6	285.1	27.8
1786–90	36.2	337.9	124.9	1.6	60.4	5.8
1791–95	33.2	101.0	42.8	.5	22.3	.6
1796–1800	18.0	223.9	80.1	2.6	92.0	20.5

Source: Statistika Centralbyran, *Historisk Statistik*, p. 138.

Table 4.73   Russian French Trade (in Livres) (5-year averages)

Years	Russian Exports	Russian Imports
1745–49	161,946	307,204
1750–54	951,829	511,881
1755–59	1,133,835	828,888
1760–64	565,597	695,116
1765–69	1,414,288	1,190,213
1770–74	3,343,314	9,170,821
1775–79	3,434,669	2,689,333

Source: Kirchner, "Franco-Russian Economic Relations," pp. 164–66, 168.

Table 4.74   Silk Exports from St. Petersburg, 1721–83 (in Lbs.)

Year	Volume	Year	Volume
1722	23,000	1746	97,234
23	18,300	47	105,635
24	32,100	48	55,050
1725	47,000	49	63,415
26	96,150	1750	124,907
27	133,050	51	41,368
1730	100,400	52	34,769
31	140,300	53	50,594
32	109,900	1754	36,044
33	20,400	1755	2,550
34	24,400	56	17,019
1735	39,300	57	30,832
36	49,537	58	23,745
37	33,600	59	3,446
38	42,600	1760	811
39	15,000	1763	2,630
1740	50,200	64	400
41	80,600	1767	11,555
42	60,300	1769	37
43	82,972	1770	260
44	261,750	1776	1,122
1745	162,626	77	102

with Russia, a phenomenon markedly different from the pattern of the Russo-British or Russo-Dutch trade. Russia's trade with Lübeck was part of the

Table 4.75   Russian Trade with Iran (in Rubles)

Year	Commodities		Custom Duties		
	Exports	Imports	Export	Import	Total
1737	233,029	374,099	12,632	21,473	34,105
38	396,055	203,920	22,514	12,214	34,728
39	360,940	639,078	20,910	38,313	59,223
1740	437,739	601,024	25,199	35,976	61,175
41	498,443	347,562	28,289	21,291	49,580
42	571,423	299,400	36,359	17,200	53,559
43	745,327	941,974	43,992	58,963	102,955
44	908,407	920,983	57,693	56,812	114,505
1750	847,600	48,500			6,300
51	437,900	22,400			6,800
52	485,300	410,900			14,300
53	813,139	588,606			16,400
54	313,150	444,020			46,000
1755	339,657	355,336			37,600
56	207,789	239,303			13,800
57	239,800	249,500			17,700
58	241,700	362,200			
59	129,700	212,500			5,400
1760	180,500	210,500			26,400
61	115,700	138,000			17,700
62	269,100	207,000			28,600
63	392,100	156,800			26,800
64	482,600	256,100			40,600
1765	254,500	283,000			38,200
66	282,100	92,800			
67	240,400	251,600			13,500
68	438,500	318,500			23,300
69	408,800	317,500			21,900
1773	456,207	245,576			
74	16,010	516,420			
1775	635,892	316,800			
76	561,327	237,224			
77	347,519	226,865			
78	380,161	196,192	9,311	27,762	37,073
79	169,884	312,267	3,114	22,323	25,437
1780	169,682	326,756	3,554	25,596	9,150
81	400,320	178,586	7,590	10,230	17,820
1787	792,039	548,315			68,892
88	543,929	477,092			46,143
89	488,424	567,771			41,499
1790	473,433	423,755	[7,400]	[56,000]	57,741[63,400]
91	413,618	425,799	[5,000]	[37,000]	38,074[42,000]
92	418,833	520,030	[13,300]	[75,400]	81,484[88,700]
93	291,037	428,508			43,966
94	276,756	450,275			48,931
1795	472,423	306,919			46,457
96	395,541	317,074			27,307
97	368,178	396,759			24,873

Sources: Storch, *Supplementband*, pp. 18–23, 33, 55; Markova, *Rossiia*, pp. 77–79; Kukanova, *Ocherki*, pp. 142–43, 158.

intra-Baltic trade and was therefore largely not registered in the Sound toll accounts, and thus significantly supplements and broadens our knowledge about the real scope of Russian imports and exports. The Lübeck data on Russo-Lübeck trade provide a useful check upon some of the Russian data on St. Petersburg exports and help in correcting erroneous impressions about the scope of trade created by the Russian data.

Although the Russo-Lübeck trade never exceeded a 5 percent share of the total Russian foreign trade volume, both its growth pattern and its commodity composition were typical for large segments of Russian foreign trade with the European countries.

Table 4.76   Percentage Shares in Trade Turnover, 1778–81

Russian merchants	9.65
Persians and Azeri	30.88
Armenians from Iran	26.51
Armenians from Russia	8.92
Bukharans and Turkomans	12.80
Indians	9.01

Table 4.77   Russian Trade with Lübeck (in Lubisch Marks) Yearly Averages

Years	Exports	Imports
1716–20	67,810	89,800
1721–25	659,000	131,680
1726–30	500,625	165,570
1731–35	561,940	245,775
1746–50[a]	907,300	532,467
1756–60[b]	1,262,131	508,775
1761–65	976,650	545,270
1766–70	831,715	430,985
1771–75	849,640	467,040
1776–80	953,460	979,110
1781–85	968,130	951,400
1786–90	638,220	1,080,705
1791–95	981,245	1,218,510
1796–1800	1,589,720	2,137,552

[a]Three-year average for 1748–50.
[b]Four-year average for 1756–60.

Source: Harder-Gersdorf, "Handelskonjunkturen," pp. 20, 22, 24–25, 27.

The trade between Lübeck and the Russian lands, and the trade in commodities originating in Russia, go back to the thirteenth- and fourteenth-century tradition of the Hanseatic trade with Novgorod, and then with the eastern Baltic ports of Narva, Revel', and Riga. Such Baltic commodities as furs, wax, flax, hemp, pitch, and tar were supplied through the Hanseatic trade to Western Europe. Lübeck, which had been a major center of the Hanseatic trade, kept this tradition alive after later powers such as the Netherlands, Great Britain, Denmark, and Sweden had taken over the old Hanseatic trade. At the end of the seventeenth century Lübeck, thanks to its shipping facilities and old trading connections in the eastern Baltic, still played an important role in the trade of the commodities originating in Russia, Livonia, and Estonia.[25] Lübeck's trade clearly suffered when the Northern War disrupted Baltic traffic and diminished the flow of those raw materials to the West because of its inability to find substitute sources on short notice.

The period of the early 1720s was one of pent-up demand for Russian goods. The relationships that Lübeck re-established with the eastern Baltic ports were supplemented by the developing trade with the new capital and port of Russia, St. Petersburg, which was granted favorable treatment by the Russian customs authorities. The relatively high level of Russian exports of the early 1720s, shown in table 4.77, could not be maintained in the long run, and the trade turnover for two decades settled on a somewhat lower level. For the rest of the century the trade between Lübeck and Russia displayed a rising tendency affected by economic fluctuations and by political events. Political events had a mixed impact on the volume of trade: although the Northern War was clearly detrimental, the Seven Years' War had a stimulating effect. The later politics of armed neutrality had no harmful effects on trade.

While the volume of Russian exports to Lübeck was rising, the composition of the exports underwent changes similar to those affecting imports of other trading partners. In addition to the traditional "Baltic exports" of raw materials originating in Russian agriculture and forestry, later in the century there were increasing quantities of primary processed goods such as iron, copper, hemp-seed oil, soap, candles, linen, and sailcloth. The Russo-Lübeck trade supports the contention made earlier that the component of value added, the application of labor either in small-scale processing enterprises or in larger manufacturing enterprises, was increasing in Russian exports.

The composition of imports changed to a lesser extent. Perhaps there was a greater assortment of the same categories of fine textiles, housewares, wines, and food products, fundamentally items for consumption by the upper classes of Russian society. Those imports from Lübeck were substitutes for the imports from other countries, but perhaps were lower in price due to lower transportation and transaction costs. The volume of imports from Lübeck increased rapidly during the last quarter of the century; this created an export surplus for the old Hansa town which had to be covered by a transfer of bills of exchange. Given the trade balance of Russia with its major European trading partners, covering the deficit with Lübeck created no problems as far as the licit trade was concerned.

There are problems with the available estimates of the Russo-Lübeck trade because they are derived almost exclusively from customs-duty data, not from actual trading reports. Regardless, the estimates reflect some of the processes shaping the trade pattern of Russia during the eighteenth century and help check other data.

The Orenburg Trade

The trade along the Asiatic border with the nomadic tribes inhabiting the area from the southern Urals to the Mongolian border was both very interesting and somewhat exotic.

The Russian policy of establishing military posts, attaching military settlers to them, and policing thereby the uninhabited areas of the Asiatic steppes was intensified during the eighteenth century, when relations with China became tense. Both unwilling and lacking the resources to get involved in a head-on collision with China, the Russian government watched closely the spread of Chinese influence in Dzhungaria and tried to win allies among the confederations of Kirgiz tribes populating the vast areas over which the sovereignty of the neighboring states was at best nominal. One of the ways to establish a foothold in the borderlands and also to maintain good relations was to organize orderly trade. As if by design, from the late 1730s, when the Russians built the border towns of Orenburg, Troitsk, and Semipalatinsk, trade began to develop with the nomadic tribes.

Data concerning the duties collected at a few trading points have survived from the early trade, and more general data are available for the late 1760s and the beginning of the 1770s, and then for the 1793–97 period.[26]

The data presented in table 4.78 on the volume of customs duties collected indicate a very rapid growth of trade after the establishment of Orenburg. The lack of a breakdown of exports and imports make the data less comparable with those for the subsequent periods. Scattered information is available on the types of commodities traded and on the variety and origin of some of the merchants, but it is descriptive material unsuitable for quantitative analysis. There is, however, an impression of bustling commercial activity. Trade estimates for much of the 1738–65 period are presented in table 4.79, but they may not be very reliable.

According to Governor Rychkov, the data on the customs duties collected after 1748 do not fully reflect the trade turnover, for an edict of that year permitted the duty-free importation of gold, silver, and jewels. He estimated that between 1748 and 1755 about 50 poods of gold and about 4,600 poods of silver were imported, besides the specie that was smuggled in. Another source estimates the imports for the longer period of from 1748 to 1767 to have been 54 poods 2 pounds of gold and 6,330 poods of silver.[27] These observations are important, for they help to explain the negative balance of trade in Chulkov's table for the late 1760s and beginning of the 1770s. In view of the price differential for specie between Russia and the steppes of Asia, they also shed light on the incentive for Russian merchants to bring so many imported goods, particularly European textiles and possibly imported metal goods, to the southeastern frontier. The advantage to the merchants of Bukhara, Tashkent, Samarkand, Khiva, and other locations in

Table 4.78   Custom Duties Collected in Orenbrug, 1738–76 (in Rubles)

1738	547	1758	20,099
1739	688	1759	24,545
1740	3,083	1760	21,224
1741	3,872	1761	21,137
1742	3,385	1762	40,795
1743	4,183	1763	35,516
1744	4,806	1764	32,453
1745	6,893	1765	27,473
1746	8,028	1766	33,185
1747	12,628	1767	37,283
1748	19,689	1768	65,040
1749	44,189	1769	64,697
1750	52,507	1770	43,839
1751	85,124	1771	49,073
1752	73,233	1772	60,805
1753	33,884	1773	55,145
1754	50,363	1774	15,911
1755	20,449	1775	52,396
1756	17,847	1776	47,835
1757	24,129		

Source: Apollova, *Sviazi*, pp. 265, 303.

Table 4.79   Available Estimates on the Size of the Orenburg Trade 1738–46, 1761, 1763–65 (in Rubles)

Year	Exports	Imports
1738	17,997	13,049
39	22,597	3,487
1740	31,338	64,522
41	50,933	58,104
42	35,600	58,637
43	59,195	5,992
44	54,130	72,301
45	108,604	105,708
46	110,436	67,166
1761		117,167
1763		63,815
64		64,217
65		125,489

Note: The estimates for 1738–46 are of the Orenburg Customs Office only. The estimates of imports for 1761 and 1763–65 include Orenburg and Troitsk.

Sources: Apollova, *Sviazi*, pp. 265, 303; Akademiia nauk Kazakhskoi SSR, *Otnosheniia*, p. 349.

Central Asia of paying in specie or exporting it for Russian and foreign goods is clear. An exchange of goods required Russian import duty payments, while specie payments did not. The imports in this caravan trade from Central Asia were specie, silks, and cottons. The Kirgiz tribesmen exported horses, camel hair and skins, wool, and sheep. (The Russians imported sheep to meet the demand for a cheap source of tallow to export to Western Europe.)

The Orenburg customs house data provide a continuous series on the "exchange" (import) of horses and sheep at that segment of the border. Table 4.80 presents the numbers involved in the trade in quin-

Table 4.80   Russian Imports of Horses and Sheep through Orenburg (Yearly Averages)

Years	Horses	Sheep
1745–49	6,529	19,699
1750–54	6,247	17,059
1755–59	4,262	14,820
1760–64	3,148	63,370
1765–69	2,036	112,693
1770–74	718	134,017
1775–79	3,232	147,500
1780–84	4,578	200,011
1785–89	3,254	276,737

Source: Apollova, *Sviazi*, pp. 248–49.

Table 4.81   The Share of Horses and Sheep in the Reported Imports of the Orenburg and Troitsk Custom Offices

Year	Total Imports (in Rubles)	Imports of Horses and Sheep (in Rubles)	%
1768	354,737	175,863	49.6
1769	338,625	171,584	50.7
1770	219,331	91,300	41.6
1771	205,498	128,140	62.3
1772	281,697	161,188	57.2

Source: Chulkov, *Opisanie*, vol. 2, pt. 3, p. 268.

quennial groupings. The dramatic rise in sheep imports between 1760 and 1789 is patent.

The data on the import of horses and sheep via the Troitsk customs house are available for seventeen of those years. The most striking feature of the combined Orenburg and Troitsk data is the wide amplitude of annual fluctuations, from 950 to 13,773 for horses and 12,202 to 411,791 for sheep.

The importance of the trade in horses and sheep in the total Orenburg trade can be grasped from the data provided by Chulkov for the years 1768–72. For the entire five-year period imports of horses and sheep constituted 52 percent of the total reported value of imports through the Orenburg and Troitsk customs offices. As shown in table 4.81, the annual percentage fluctuated between 41.6 and 62.3.

The data in 4.82 provided by Chulkov for the 1760s and 1770s show exports and imports not only for the total of the Orenburg trade, but specifically for three locations (Orenburg itself, Troitsk, and Semipalatinsk) where the trade took place. (The decline of trade during 1774 was caused by the Pugachëv rebellion and the siege of Orenburg by Pugachëv's troops.) In addition, for the Russian merchants' exports, the data distinguish between foreign goods and those originating in Russia proper over a period of a few years. Foreign goods were predominant in Russian exports to the Asiatic borderland. The strength of Russian demand for the products of the

steppes was such that not only were foreign goods brought across the entire territory of Russia, but the Russians ran a deficit on account of the commodity trade.

In the last quarter of the century changes occurred in the trade along the Asian steppe frontier that are difficult to explain. Perhaps a monetary and trade mechanism was at work. Perhaps there was a shift in markets. Whatever the reason, the influx of specie through this frontier either greatly diminished or stopped entirely. In the latter 1780s the trade with Central Asia increased substantially. The commodity trade as reflected in the data for the 1790s presented in table 4.83 settled down and maintained itself on a relatively high plateau.

The presence of Bukhara and Khiva merchants in the steppe frontier trade was notable in the import of silks and cotton goods. The participation in a caravan trade to the Russian frontier constituted an alternative to the route overland to, and then via, the Caspian Sea, or via the northern Iranian region and then the Caspian Sea to Astrakhan'. It is difficult to determine whether economic preferences or safety considerations caused by political circumstances were at work in the choice of the routes for those merchants. The trade via Astrakhan' was more convenient for most Russian merchants, but they nevertheless were willing to travel further to obtain the valuable goods brought by the Bukhara and Khiva merchants.

Published documents provide both the total and the shares of Bukhara and Khiva imports and exports in the steppe frontier trade for the years 1793–96. The share of those Central Asian merchants was about one-third of the total. The data, presented in table 4.84, exhibit an excess of Russian imports over Russian exports (including foreign goods in transit).

Had the Orenburg trade been reported in current prices, its growth by the end of the century compared with the 1770s still would be larger than that of the trade along the European border. However, there is evidence that the Orenburg trade data were compiled in 1774 prices, and therefore the growth rate apparent in the data reflects an approximate growth in real terms.

The China Trade

The trade with China is significant not because of geography or because of commodity composition, but because of the conditions under which Russian merchants, like most other foreign merchants, had to conduct it. No other Russian trading partner controlled the location of trade, directed its size, and subjected it to state regulation as much as did China.

As Professor Foust demonstrated in his excellent study, the circumstances of this trade were unusual

Table 4.82   Volume of Trade in Orenburg, Troitsk, and Semipalatinsk (in Rubles)

	Orenburg			Troitsk			Semipalatinsk			Total Orenburg Trade (in Current Rubles)			
Year	Imports	Russian Exports	Foreign Exports	Imports	Russian Exports	Foreign Exports	Imports	Russian Exports	Foreign Exports	Imports	Exports	Including Russian Goods	Including Foreign Goods
1768	246,435	66,554	91,203	90,306	26,859	72,042	15,114	5,173	72,090	315,855	333,921	98,586	235,335
1769	264,060	49,774	207,458	74,565	15,221	52,312	97,812	6,860	77,293	436,437	408,918	71,855	337,063
1770	170,020	23,604	131,984	49,303	5,267	36,543	78,286	4,228	65,556	297,618	267,183	33,100	234,083
1771	188,391	37,641	133,824	17,107	1,956	12,672	51,808	2,159	52,572	257,306	240,824	41,756	199,068
1772	245,969	39,863	195,473	35,727	7,814	14,835	40,258	2,140	30,691	321,954	290,816	49,817	240,999
1773	205,789		199,732	48,759		42,646	19,959		63,574	273,507	307,952		
1774	72,575		9,621	1,478		95	4,690		834	78,743	10,550		
1775	207,243		206,215	34,339		31,137	—		—	241,582	237,352		
1776	182,365			10,626			—		—	192,991	188,008		
1777	222,364		241,325	13,847		14,995	18,621		34,860	254,832	291,180		

Sources: Chulkov, *Opisanie*, vol. 2, pt. 3, p. 268; Akademiia nauk Kazakhskoi SSR, *Otnosheniia*, p. 84.

Table 4.83   The Orenburg Trade, 1793–97 (in Rubles)

	Imports					Exports				
	1793	1794	1795	1796	1797	1793	1794	1795	1796	1797
Orenburg	1,249,967	1,274,372	1,539,761	1,218,910	1,003,299	1,128,904	1,143,119	1,238,633	1,037,695	886,574
Troitsk	134,483	121,712	101,814	113,821	131,098	136,124	152,894	136,922	139,554	187,775
Semipal	54,992	47,622	59,999	88,381	88,185	40,893	54,745	55,549	78,440	115,159
Petropavlovsk	58,152	47,466	41,185	49,512	100,827	33,411	30,003	27,547	30,060	71,789
Ust Kamenogorsk	17,907	16,576	32,591	29,240	44,414	9,560	13,890	22,374	28,932	38,983
Jamushevsk	6,464	8,224	9,866	14,074	10,094	5,775	7,472	8,882	11,024	8,141
Presnogorov	2,952	3,617	2,125	2,079	2,620	2,339	2,749	1,788	1,839	2,378
Sheleshensk	1,853	1,172	413	1,883	1,643	1,553	801	320	1,387	1,243
Total	1,526,768	1,520,761	1,787,754	1,517,900	1,382,180	1,358,559	1,405,673	1,492,015	1,328,931	1,312,042

Source: Storch, *Supplementband*, pp. 10–19.

Table 4.84　Bukhara and Khiva Merchants' Participation in Orenburg Trade (in Rubles)

	Exports from Russia			Imports into Russia		
Year	Bukhara	Khiva	Total	Bukhara	Khiva	Total
1787	341,176	7,450	348,620	379,084	8,278	387,362
88	176,993	25,183	202,176	198,868	28,295	227,163
89	443,834	27,892	471,726	493,148	30,992	524,140
1790	346,896	54,241	401,137	365,153	57,096	422,249
91	420,821	67,886	488,707	467,579	75,428	543,007
92	305,159	8,090	313,249	381,449	10,112	391,561
93	440,783	37,091	477,874	479,112	40,316	519,428
94	366,751	107,153	473,904	407,500	119,059	526,559
95	426,653	34,522	461,175	501,945	40,614	524,559
96	411,805	43,651	455,456	484,477	51,355	535,832
Total	3,680,870	413,159	4,094,024	4,158,316	461,545	4,601,860

Source: *Arkhiv gosudarstvennogo soveta*, 2 (1888):653–54.

by European standards.[28] Until 1727, under the terms of the Treaty of Nerchinsk (1689), trade in Peking was reserved for Russian government-organized caravans only. Trade at the border was sporadic. There were Russian state monopolies over many of the significant items, and without doubt some private merchants engaged in both licit and illicit trade activities. After 1727, according to the Treaty of Kiakhta, the trade was limited to the border, primarily the city of Kiakhta, the counterpart for the Russians of Canton for Western Europeans. The Russian government began to withdraw slowly and gradually from active participation in and control of the China trade. There were two reasons why the relaxation of government regulations and controls proceeded more slowly than might have been expected. The first was the length of time it took to learn to choose long-term gains over short-term advantages. The Chinese market was profitable both for Russian-made goods and for re-exported Western European goods. It was also advantageous for Russia to import from China silks, cotton goods, and tea, all goods that yielded not only a profit in the domestic and foreign markets, but also revenue for the customs office. Given fiscal considerations and the existence of state monopolies at least until the 1760s, the liberalization of the Russian trade with China was slow indeed.

Another reason for state intervention and supervision of the China trade may have been the delicate nature of political relations between Russia and China. Involved in European power politics and still trying to establish itself on the Black Sea at the expense of the Ottoman Empire, Russia could have gained nothing from conflicts with China. The government's preoccupation with the problems of the trade with China may be viewed as an attempt to prevent any conduct that might have irritated China.

The most important Russian commodities exported to China were furs and textiles. Furs made up about half of the total. The demand by the Chinese for Russian furs was strong, and the prices were high enough not only to absorb most of the fur exports, but also to impel importation of pelts from Western Europe and their transportation across European Russia and all of Siberia to China. The exchange of goods between Russia and China was marked by Russian exports of primary products and Chinese exports of specialized manufactured goods.

Siberia and the Russian Far East (Primor'e) benefited from the relative proximity of the Chinese market and shared the profits between the hunters and merchants. This did not, however, lead to any further economic integration between Siberia and China because Siberia's requirements for food products and manufactured goods continued to be met by imports from European Russia.

The first Russian joint-stock company, the Russo-American Company, was chartered in the last years of the eighteenth century to exploit the fur resources of Russian America in order to meet China's demand for furs.

The official data on Sino-Russian trade, presented for what they may be worth in table 4.85, are available for most of the years between 1755 and 1799. The notable omission of 1785–91 was caused by Chinese suspension of the trade with Russia. The data help to narrow the gap between the official figures for the total trade of Russia and the Baltic and White Sea trade, for which documentary evidence is more readily available.

Tariff Policy

No discussion of foreign trade can avoid consideration of tariff policy. Russian eighteenth-century trade policy inevitably reflected the economic realities and political philosophies of the times. Historians dealing with this policy have found it convenient to write about two systems: the Petrine, which stood for a mercantilist model, and the Catherinian, which has

Table 4.85   Volume of Russian-Chinese Trade at Kiakhta, 1775–99 (in Rubles)

Year	Export of Russian and Foreign Goods	Import of Chinese Goods	Total Volume	Total Duties Collected
1755	606,084	230,982	837,066	193,173
1756	450,768	241,253	692,021	157,184
1757	421,879	418,811	840,689	147,216
1758	526,000	511,071	1,037,071	178,877
1759	718,145	698,985	1,417,130	230,482
1760	699,940	658,331	1,358,272	238,156
1761	391,469	619,598	1,011,067	230,840
1762	522,417	553,186	1,075,603	199,671
1763	302,798	401,607	704,405	179,066
1764	137,493	158,236	295,730	59,525
1765	149,875	244,478	394,353	90,472
1766	28,489	15,715	44,205	ca. 10,000
1767	—		—	—
1768	50,095	45,300	95,395	11,025
1769	1,074,651	928,984	2,003,636	401,708
1770	1,351,978	1,271,739	2,623,715	495,291
1771	1,246,410	1,142,511	2,388,921	451,343
1772	1,002,519	934,121	1,936,640	389,270
1773	1,140,183	1,153,992	2,294,175	397,420
1774	1,227,760	1,120,870	2,348,630	444,998
1775	1,365,826	1,278,584	2,644,410	453,279
1776	1,638,791	1,401,916	3,040,707	500,460
1777	1,440,546	1,342,127	2,782,674	479,061
1778	794,540	667,253	1,461,793	277,600
1779	—	—	—	—
1780	2,700,187	2,700,187	5,400,375	545,979
1781	3,735,312	3,735,312	7,470,624	706,219
1782	3,520,343	3,520,343	7,040,686	662,850
1783	2,789,177	2,789,177	5,578,354	509,148
1784	2,413,357	2,413,357	4,826,713	431,601
1785	1,805,926	1,805,926	3,611,852	347,579
1786–91	—		—	—
1792	2,467,280	2,467,280	4,934,559	509,830
1793	3,549,432	3,549,432	7,098,864	515,581
1794	2,522,942	2,522,942	5,045,884	527,070
1795	2,720,286	2,720,286	5,440,571	532,394
1796	2,551,764	2,551,764	5,103,529	488,320
1797	2,378,750	2,378,750	4,757,501	414,278
1798	2,783,943	2,783,943	5,567,885	509,685
1799	3,677,824	3,677,824	7,355,647	698,487

Source: Foust, *Muscovite and Mandarin*, p. 332.

been considered basically a physiocratic, if not a free-trade, approach. Such characterizations, with their appeal to symbols familiar to every student of Russian history, have had more organizational than analytical value. They have, however, suggested a range of policies, from extremely restrictive to liberal, that determined economic policy from the beginning to the end of the century.

The difficulty in applying Petrine and Catherinian concepts as analytic devices resides in the fact that neither of the so-called systems constitutes a pure and consistent model. Each was a hybrid version incorporating common elements. Both represented changes and oscillations in trade policies rather than ideological commitments. The swing of the pendulum toward mercantilist-type policies in the reign of

Peter the Great was not a result of philosophical conviction so much as it was an outgrowth of an activist attitude toward the role of government. The "liberalization" tendencies of the Catherinian system sprang from a realization of the limits of government, a periodic awareness of the hazards of favoritism, and the consequences of Elizabeth's uneconomic policy of granting trade monopolies, rather than from trust in a free market. Consequently, the use of the Petrine or Catherinian designations is of questionable analytic and interpretative value and will not be pursued.

Instead of using labels, I will attempt to explain the origin and characteristics of trade policies, the degree to which they achieved their state objectives, and the extent of their impact upon both foreign trade and the development of the industrial sector of the Russian economy.

A description and analysis of eighteenth-century trade policies must commence with the general observation that Russian foreign trade policies during the preceding century were liberal, with moderate tariffs within the bounds of 3 to 5 percent ad valorem. There was very little economic discrimination against foreign traders, who were taxed primarily on the excess of their sales over their purchases in Muscovy. An overall favorable balance of commodity trade stimulated an in-flow of specie into the country. Both the tsar and the state were involved in foreign trade as exporters and importers, and each additional requirement of specie was met by an increase of state trade exports. The New Trading Regulations (*Novotorgovyi ustav*) of 1667 gave the government the right to interfere in foreign trade and to apply protectionist policies, but after the successful overcoming of the monetary crisis of the 1660s there was no need to apply them for any discriminatory purposes.

In the case of the Petrine tariff, which dates from 1724, the last year of his reign, many of the changes and departures from the seventeenth-century pattern notable in that edict had already been enacted piecemeal in earlier years. The 1724 tariff represented on the one hand a codification of Peter's accumulated trade policy experiences, including monopolies in trade and industry and the use of trade policies in warfare, and on the other hand Peter's perception of the economic progress enjoyed by Russia during the years of his reign.

The Petrine tariff of 1724 can be characterized as the "poor man's" mercantilism. This term is used because the Western European variety of mercantilism presupposed certain conditions common to the states that pursued those policies. The common preconditions of Western European mercantilism were: the existence of a relatively commercialized sector within agriculture; a relatively well-developed and specialized commodity and money market; the existence of a colonial empire, or free access to one; the existence of a merchant marine; the availability of industrial skills that could be molded with relative ease into various forms of industrial organization; and a relatively educated and efficient bureaucracy.[29]

The "building blocks" for a mercantilist system in Russia were either missing or so imperfect that the first task was to create them. Russia's ruler could no more enact anything resembling the Navigation Acts in the absence of a merchant marine than he could follow Colbert's industrial policy consistently without the skills of the weavers of Lyon and other centers of manufacturing.

I would therefore classify Peter as a proto-mercantilist, i.e., as one who tried to create conditions that would eventually allow a mercantilist policy and who pragmatically and selectively used some of the measures of the cameralist and mercantilist arsenal. The typical goal of the mercantilist policies of the more economically advanced countries of this period was to achieve a favorable balance of international trade by developing the manufacturing export industries. Peter realized that this could eventually be achieved by Russia but only in a very distant future.

For Russia a successful trade policy sought to attempt to maintain a high volume of primary-product exports, preferably processed primary products. Peter saw the key to a favorable trade balance in import substitution. The tariff of 1724 therefore ought to be judged primarily in terms of its effectiveness as a tool to assure import substitution and to protect both the older and newly founded industrial enterprises, which had to meet the domestic demand for manufactured goods imported largely from abroad. Protection for domestic manufactured goods serving as substitutes for imports, according to the tariff of 1724, was awarded by the use of an upward-sliding scale which related the ad valorem rate of tariff to the ratio of domestic output to imports. The higher the domestic production capacity of a particular commodity, the higher the tariff rate applied to imports.

It was a strange and curious formula of protection, to say the least. Under ordinary market conditions, such a formula should have raised the prices of products instead of lowering them and provided more protection the further an industry moved away from its infancy stage. How can one explain the introduction of such an import substitution policy? Was it Peter's misunderstanding of the operation of markets? Or, was it meant perhaps as an assurance for domestic producers that, given the existing wide cost-differentials and in spite of existing losses, they would be rewarded with lucrative profits when they increased output? Or was it an attempt to secure monopoly profits for a class of entrepreneurs in the hope that they would continue to invest in the manufacturing of import substitutes? We may never find out about Peter's motives, although we do know that his immediate successors at the policy-making level did not believe that his formula of protection was a viable solution. Peter's successors also disagreed with his optimistic evaluation of the state of Russian manufactories and their capability to increase production under the umbrella of protection. Lastly, Peter did more than set his import customs duties high on an ad valorem rate, for in fact the state rate had to be doubled in real terms because of the requirement that the duties be paid in Reichstalers at an exchange rate set at 50 percent of the market exchange rate.

The Petrine tariff set the protective rates on an ad valorem basis, rather than as specific rates. The high level of the tariff defeated the benefits and convenience that are usually related to moderate ad valorem rates. The high level of the tariff combined with ad valorem rates led to the practice of lowering the declared value of the commodities by the importers, thereby depriving the state of substantial revenues. The attempts to control the situation through the creation of a customs office bureaucracy resulted in collusion between the importers and the poorly paid customs officials, who could be bribed easily.

A more threatening effect of the high tariff rates was the development of illicit trade, of smuggling. The long and poorly guarded border provided many opportunities for smuggling as soon as it became profitable, and no administrative measures at the disposal of the government could stop it. Moreover, the Petrine and some of the post-Petrine governments used the institution of tax farming to collect customs on various segments of the European border. The government farmed out the collection of specific taxes for a specified lump sum which the tax farmer had to recover along with his profit by collecting the revenue. When faced with illicit trade, the tax farmer preferred to collect at least part of the customs duty rather than none at the stipulated tariff rates. This led in some instances to collusion between the tax farmers and importers at the expense of the state. Interested in maximizing their revenues and not in law enforcement, the tax farmers provided, for a price, the legal cover for goods that were smuggled into the country in quantities higher than officially reported.

The Petrine tariff, designed with the idea of import substitution in mind, was not very successful. The rates of protection, set at a much higher level than a realistic appraisal would suggest was necessary—on some manufactured goods at the 75 percent level—failed to provide meaningful protection and invited a host of consequences against which both the government and the domestic producers were helpless.[30] One of the more rational features of the tariff, one designed to promote import substitution, was the introduction of a high export duty on raw materials deemed essential for domestic manufacturing enterprises. In a number of cases the duty may have caused foreign demand to decline and thus made it easier for domestic producers to obtain raw materials.

Peter's successors lost little time in trying to correct some of the extreme features of his tariff policies. The turning away from some of the Petrine policies was instigated by the "young birds from Peter's nest" (*ptentsy gnezda petrova*), his lieutenants and assistants, his lifelong confidants and chosen pupils. No insinuations by ultranationalist Russian historians, who

termed this a sellout of Russian national interests to foreign powers, can change the facts: the post-Petrine tariff of 1731 was prepared and introduced by those brought up by and exposed to the political logic and goals preached and acted on by Peter the Great. The leading characteristic of the 1731 tariff was again the idea of import substitution.

A much more realistic approach to the degree of protection required for efficient domestic producers was introduced, however. The legislators assumed that a combination of a 20 percent customs duty plus the payment of transportation costs by the foreigners, with freedom from internal tolls on raw materials and the attachment of state peasants to domestic manufactures, ought to be sufficient at least to equalize the prices for imported and domestically produced goods. Thus the *Sturm und Drang* characterizing the Petrine period of industrial entrepreneurship with its forced pace came to an end, and a period of more gradual, solid, and careful entrepreneurship was in the making.

The commercial treaty with Great Britain was concluded in 1734 under the auspices of the 1731 tariff. Chauvinist Russian historians have tried to characterize this treaty as a sellout, as an attempt to make a colony out of Russia. Nothing could be further from the truth. The Russo-British treaty never reminded anyone of the Methuen treaty between Great Britain and Portugal, perhaps because the Russian negotiators were familiar with that particular treaty and insisted on a maximum of reciprocity and economic independence. An important addition to the wording of the treaty that provided the British merchants with a limited version of most-favored-nation status was a sense of mutual benefits. The British learned during the period from 1725 to 1733 that Russia could find substitutes for British woolens (in the famous case of Russia's refusal to buy army cloth from English merchants who delivered poor-quality products and to rely instead upon a long-term contract with the Prussian Cloth Company, which supplied most of the needed army cloth during the late 1720s and early 1730s). The Russians in turn realized that it was to their advantage to gain access to the growing British market to sell their hemp, flax, iron, and other goods. They also understood that it would be folly to assume that they had a virtual monopoly on many products of vital importance just because their share in the European trade was substantial and that they would pay a high price if they acted under such beliefs. Thus the Russians seem to have been ready to give up some short-term revenue gains for the opportunity to expand their trade in the long run.

Given the slow rise in world demand for the "typical" Baltic goods, Russia might have expected to gain in a competition with the other countries around the eastern Baltic, notably Sweden and Poland, and the struggle in the existing markets was fierce. Russia conducted a "passive" trade and did not export in its own bottoms, and therefore it had to assume a waiting attitude of winning over the trade with countries such as England and the Netherlands which not only imported for themselves, but also carried Russian goods to other countries.

The 1731 tariff was in effect for a long time because the policy considerations upon which it was based were long-term considerations. In a government like Russia's, it was inevitable that the ruler infringed upon policy matters. During the Elizabethan period, when a great deal of lip service was paid to the memory of Peter the Great in a reaction against the "rule of the Germans" during the previous reign, and xenophobic policy advisers had the ear of the empress, a retreat to more protectionist policies would have been a possibility. In spite of that fact, during the first part of Elizabeth's reign the only visible retreat to Petrine policies in the area of trade was a revival of some trade monopolies (such as the one on blubber oil in the north), which were distributed to the empress's favorites, and the dismantling of the state ironworks economy and the distribution of the best ones to money-hungry courtiers.[31]

A substantial change in foreign trade policy occurred under the impact of two important events: the abolition of internal tolls in 1753 and the outbreak of the Seven Years' War. In an attempt to compensate for the loss of revenue resulting from the abolition of the internal tolls, a 13 percent increase in duties on foreign trade was decreed; since less than 13 percent was levied on export products, the rise in duties on imports was more than 13 percent. This revenue was intended to compensate for the loss of internal tolls, and one ought not to assume that the prices of foreign imports paid by Russian consumers increased by the same amount. A redistribution took place in which some goods became more expensive, others less.

The rise in duties on foreign trade which took place in 1754 was incorporated in the new tariff of 1757, which increased revenues to help in financing the war. The 1757 tariff, branded by some economic historians as the most protective of the century, appeared to be so primarily because of the added rates, not because of its other, non-revenue-maximizing attributes.[32] A closer examination of the 1757 tariff suggests that raising the import duties on already well-protected goods, such as iron, copper, and linen cloth, did not make the tariff more protective in and of itself. Raising the rates on foreign goods provided additional revenue, but it did not help to develop any domestic substitutes. Widening the customs duty differential between raw sugar and refined sugar probably benefited the domestic sugar refineries. The significance of the 1757 tariff lay primarily in its continued protection of domestic industries, and secondarily in its demonstration of the intent or ability to raise the tariff rates.

The Catherinian tariffs that gave rise to the cliché about a Catherinian system require close scrutiny. They represented a mixture of a continuity of protection for domestic industry and attempts to get rid of duty payments when they became nominal, rather than effective or real. There is no evidence whatsoever that would permit one to point to instances where domestic industrial interests were sacrificed for the principles of physiocratic or free-market policies.

Catherine's tariffs introduced certain criteria for the level of protection into Russian protectionist policies. A tariff of one-third above the world market-price was considered sufficient to protect a domestic industry, especially when it was coupled either with the availability of domestic raw materials, export duties for such supplies, or duty-free imports of the raw materials. Another innovation in Catherine's tariff policies was the broadening of the term *industry* to cover both large-scale manufactories as well as small-scale enterprises.

Catherine's tariffs clearly rejected the notion of government abandonment of an active role in influencing the patterns and conditions of foreign trade. By their customs-rate policies, her tariffs not only reflect a clear awareness of changing conditions in particular branches of production, in various industries and areas of trade, but also display an awareness of rising prices and of the necessity to adjust the level of specific rates to changes in the price level. This attempt to make the tariffs more flexible was certainly a step in the right direction. So was the provision of greater freedom for rate changes; thus the prevalence of or an increase in smuggling of a particular product was accepted as a legitimate reason for lowering the import duty.

An additional feature, if not of the tariffs themselves, then certainly of the tariff deliberations, was an increased concern not only with the balance of trade but also with the balance of payments. The first trace of a discussion of the balance of trade issue dates to a meeting in 1747 at which Prince Trubetskoi presented trade data for St. Petersburg indicating a deficit in its trade balance.[33] Beginning in the 1760s and increasingly during the subsequent period, the tariff issue in the deliberations of government committees was linked to problems of the trade balance, the balance of payments, and the exchange rate of the ruble.

The first of the Catherinian tariffs was that of September 1766. Its guidelines were defined by a specially appointed committee under Catherine's supervision. The central feature of the tariff on the issue of imports was the placing of 206 items of manufactured and processed goods, which had a domestic near-equivalent, under an umbrella of a 30 percent ad valorem tariff. Imports of primary products and raw materials that constituted equivalents of Russian exports were either prohibited or taxed at a 200 percent rate. Raw materials for Russian industry were exempt from duties or had to pay a minimum duty of 4 or 5 percent. Imports of expensive, luxury products were taxed by a 100 percent duty, and imports of near-luxury goods (155 items of foods, silken goods, and other commodities) were taxed with only a 20 percent duty. Catherine seems to have been drawing a distinction between what the gentry could afford or aspired to and the kind of luxury goods accessible to the large landowners and court circles only. One was a demonstratively anti-luxury provision enacted with no expectation that consumption would be diminished; the other was not prohibitive but, given the sense of the demand elasticity for such goods, it reflected the determination that excesses of consumption had to be prevented.

There was little doubt that, while retreating somewhat in the formal sense (e.g., in the level of import duties) from the protective tariff of 1757, the 1766 tariff retained the basic protective features of Russia's foreign trade policy. Perhaps the most significant differences between the 1757 and 1766 tariffs can be found in the lowering of export duties, which made Russian products more attractive to foreigners and provided a boost for the growth of the export trade. Another notable difference was in the provision that duties could be paid by Russian or British merchants either in Reichstalers or in Russian money at the less discriminatory exchange rate of 1 Reichstaler = 1.25 rubles.

The 1766 tariff did not eliminate some of the pernicious effects of protectionist policy, such as illicit trade, or some of the still-remaining monopolies operating in the foreign trade area. By the elimination of some of the vestiges of existing regulatory agencies and government control practices, a further amelioration of duty rates was being prepared for the next tariff revision. The time interval between 1766 and the next tariff (of 1782) witnessed important changes in the institutional framework of the industrial and trading sectors in Russia. By 1773, the government monopoly on potash sales was abolished, together with the few other remaining trade monopolies. In 1775 freedom of manufacturing production was announced. By 1779 the chief licensing agency for industrial production, the College of Manufactures, was abolished. Finally, in 1782, all noblemen were granted the right to set up industrial enterprises in the countryside, merchants were allowed to develop manufactories in the cities, and all craftsmen were granted the freedom to acquire and install machinery for craft production.

It was against this background and momentum that the 1782 tariff was announced. This tariff further ameliorated and decreased import and export duties without changing the proportions between protected and nonprotected imports. The most noteworthy feature of the tariff was the incorporation of the Livonian and Estonian ports in the Russian system. By eliminating this low-duty region, the Russian government not only simplified the administration of duty collection but also closed a loophole through which foreign imports could legally arrive at a lower duty and be transported into Russia proper at a lower risk while avoiding the higher Russian duty.

The other major alteration of the 1782 tariff was its granting permission to all foreign traders to pay half of the duty in Reichstalers and half in Russian money, while Russian merchants were allowed to pay it all in Russian money. A second-order consequence of this measure was to diminish the advantage over other foreign merchants enjoyed by the British, who previously had the privilege of paying duties applicable to Russians.

To provide special encouragement for the developing Black Sea trade, the duties in the Black Sea ports were lowered by 25 percent from the level applicable in all other Russian ports. (Some exceptions also were made for the port of Astrakhan'.) In general, the tariff of 1782, although it moderated the level of duties, did not renounce protectionist aims. In fact, the combination of an internally liberalized attitude toward industry coupled with a measure of protection against foreign competition had a beneficial effect on the development and growth of Russian industry.

The period following the enactment of the 1782 tariff was marked by very strong inflationary pressures on the Russian economy. The issuance of paper money, initiated in 1769, coupled with an increased minting of copper, relieved the demand for money in the Russian economy for a time; but after about a decade, the printing and minting of nonsilver currency exceeded demand and caused Russian prices to rise and the value of the Russian ruble to decline in the foreign money markets. This had an impact on foreign trade because of its timing: inflation in Russia started about ten years before it commenced independently in Western Europe.

The declining exchange rate of the Russian ruble in terms of foreign currencies made Russian goods attractive to foreign buyers and explains to a considerable extent the expansion of Russian exports. Imports, which became more expensive in terms of Russian currency, lagged behind the export expansion and may have encouraged the manufacture and consumption of Russian substitutes. This situation began to change drastically in the 1790s when Western Europe experienced its own rapid inflation. The advantages temporarily enjoyed by Russia began to diminish. Technical progress in a number of Western European, especially British, industries caused the real price of manufactured goods to decline. The Russian government became concerned about the effectiveness of tariff measures to protect its own industry.

Concern about the protection of industry became combined with alarm over the decline of the exchange rate. This was compounded by the political effects of the French Revolution: in 1793 Russia announced an embargo on trade with France, which was extended in 1795 to include the Netherlands. The result was the Catherinian tariff of 1796. It was somewhat more protective than the 1782 tariff, although fundamentally it attempted to adjust the various duty rates to the rising price level. Its most distinct feature was discrimination against trade with France.

The 1796 tariff was never put into effect because Tsar Paul I, Catherine's son and successor, disagreed with her anti-French policies, as he disagreed with nearly all her other policies. Instead, in 1797 a new tariff was enacted without most of the discriminatory anti-French provisions. This made it more like the 1782 tariff. By requiring all merchants to pay the customs duties in Reichstalers at the exchange rate of 1 Reichstaler for 40 rubles, the 1797 tariff once again abolished the special privileges of the British merchants as well as the incentive for foreign merchants to assume Russian citizenship as a means of gaining a tax advantage. To diminish the volume of illicit trade, Paul's tariff provided that various categories of imported goods could be brought in only through selected ports rather than overland.

It was typical for the last few years of the century that political considerations permeated Russian trade policies, regardless of stated tariffs. This may have been an important element contributing to the palace coup that removed Paul from the Russian throne in 1801 in favor of his son Alexander. The politicization of commercial matters was inevitable, given the titanic political struggle taking place in Europe. The result was that the existing tariff became much less decisive than earlier ones had been, either as a policy instrument or as an explanatory device for understanding the pattern of trade.

Any attempt to summarize the totality of Russian tariff policies during the eighteenth century would have to include the continuity of protectionist concerns for the developing industrial sector, the measures designed to expand the exports of raw materials or primary products, and the desire to maximize state revenue from customs duties. The government took the interests of powerful groups into account in shaping its tariff policies, but it did not create a conflict with the national interest as defined by the policy-makers themselves. Foreign trade was considered an important sector of the economy and an engine or major instrument for economic development, but the primacy of political objectives was preserved.

The historian writing retrospectively must view the tariff as a policy instrument primarily designed to enhance the national interest in political terms. In evaluating the success of Russian tariff policy, however, one cannot have sympathy with arguments based on economic nationalism. The development of import substitutes cannot be considered beneficial in and of themselves. What is important is whether they impart new, useful skills, or have some other external economies. Thus one must ask: What was the effect of the Russian tariff on producers and consumers? What were the benefits, if any, to the Russian producer of exports, and what were the approximate costs added by the tariff to the Russian consumers of imported goods or import substitutes?

The overwhelming impression conveyed by the customs tariffs is that they were, primarily, of fiscal significance for the government. Their protectionist elements, although important in a number of cases, were basically secondary in the minds of the decision-makers. By the same token, because the Russian government was interested in a favorable balance of trade and in an influx of specie from abroad, it was concerned with the export duties and their level in order to balance the considerations of fiscal interests with the interests of maximizing the volume and value of exports. Such concerns overrode desires for import substitution or for the protection of domestic industry.

This observation should not surprise any student of eighteenth-century Russia who bears in mind the fact that we are considering a preindustrial society and an economy in which the significance of the industrial sector was growing slowly, and in which the interests of the industrial classes carried relatively little weight with governmental decision-makers. In addition, so long as the industrialists articulated their interests in parochial or group-interest terms, rather than in terms of *raison d'état*, their effectiveness with either the government or public opinion was rather limited.

Customs Revenues and Export Duties

Data underlying Russian customs revenue estimates are available on a continuous basis only for the years 1742–97.[34] In view of the depreciation of the value of

Table 4.86 Changes in Customs Revenues 1742–96 (5-year averages)

| Years | Custom Revenue | |
	in Rubles	in Reichstalers
1742–46	936,519	844,780
1747–51	999,678	876,636
1752–56	1,829,566	1,689,520
1757–61	2,554,302	2,150,024
1762–66	2,893,648	2,495,372
1767–71	3,023,934	2,455,711
1772–76	3,369,139	2,723,567
1777–81	3,518,315	2,793,033
1782–86	5,068,963	3,800,276
1787–91	6,216,080	3,830,174
1792–96	6,145,864	3,282,849

Table 4.87 Customs Revenues, 1742–97 (in Albertustalers)

Year	Collected Albertustalers	Collected Rubles	Rubles in Albertustaler Equivalents	Total
1742	559,589	255,816	236,867	796,456
1743	634,546	267,581	238,912	873,458
1744	583,326	272,558	250,053	833,379
1745	595,216	287,826	256,987	852,203
1746	620,815	279,777	247,590	868,405
1747	593,574	208,650	186,295	779,869
1748	523,943	233,706	205,005	728,948
1749	600,073	302,436	260,721	860,794
1750	723,500	323,383	281,203	1,004,703
1751	750,461	291,995	258,403	1,008,864
1752	822,398	399,642	356,823	1,179,221
1753	804,870	454,317	420,664	1,225,534
1754	756,405	1,189,004	1,121,702	1,878,107
1755	727,859	1,502,927	1,417,856	2,145,715
1756	751,293	1,381,827	1,267,731	2,019,024
1757	757,704	1,607,221	1,385,535	2,143,239
1758	729,085	1,648,280	1,408,786	2,137,871
1759	762,173	1,701,833	1,442,231	2,204,404
1760	726,870	1,716,450	1,430,375	2,157,245
1761	749,235	1,707,394	1,388,125	2,137,360
1762	870,756	1,740,286	1,426,464	2,297,220
1763	993,157	1,831,211	1,620,541	2,613,698
1764	960,142	1,768,987	1,524,989	2,485,131
1765	965,632	1,919,650	1,698,805	2,664,437
1766	968,543	1,665,005	1,447,830	2,416,373
1767	425,391	2,132,167	1,791,737	2,217,128
1768	379,487	2,356,114	1,963,428	2,342,915
1769	324,930	2,799,944	2,314,003	2,638,933
1770	334,219	2,773,224	2,183,641	2,517,860
1771	358,407	2,820,238	2,203,311	2,561,718
1772	778,458	2,253,878	1,817,644	2,596,102
1773	735,735	2,694,683	2,121,798	2,857,533
1774	729,144	2,628,396	2,037,516	2,766,660
1775	730,440	2,377,621	1,996,323	2,726,763
1776	575,164	2,495,876	2,095,614	2,670,778
1777	610,768	2,466,450	2,058,806	2,669,574
1778	641,323	2,174,842	1,794,424	2,435,747
1779	679,820	2,278,546	1,846,472	2,526,292
1780	782,662	3,099,622	2,179,762	2,962,424
1781	656,741	3,563,987	2,714,385	3,371,126
1782	763,524	3,581,249	2,658,685	3,422,209
1783	949,199	3,776,928	2,803,955	3,753,154
1784	895,322	4,255,860	3,117,846	4,013,168
1785	819,128	4,261,771	3,204,339	4,023,467
1786	610,277	4,069,257	3,179,107	3,789,384
1787	867,041	4,384,952	3,168,318	4,035,359
1788	740,066	4,262,478	2,913,519	3,653,585
1789	693,263	4,621,367	2,707,303	3,400,566
1790	793,452	5,966,477	3,495,300	4,288,752
1791	816,042	5,505,130	2,956,568	3,772,610
1792	839,368	6,179,500	3,228,579	4,067,947
1793	520,739	4,205,218	2,032,488	2,553,227
1794	551,246	4,437,712	2,361,741	2,912,987
1795	475,282	4,701,530	2,594,663	3,069,945
1796	790,408	5,242,251	3,019,730	3,810,138
1797	2,231,413	2,460,331	1,424,627	3,656,040

the Russian monetary unit, the estimates of the customs revenues are represented in two series, one for current rubles and the other for the silver coins that were most commonly used in commercial transactions by partners in the Baltic trade, Reichstalers. The data report the customs revenues in silver by weight and in Russian money, and therefore each of the components was brought under a common denominator by the use of linked indices of the Reichstaler:ruble and stuiver:ruble exchange rates. The Reichstaler:ruble exchange rate of Riga was used for 1742–74 and the stuiver:ruble average exchange rate for bills for 1775–97. The growth of the customs revenue by quinquennia is shown in table 4.86, a summary of the data in table 4.87 and 4.88.

Although the comparison of the changes in the size of the customs revenue achieved by using both measures is by no means an accurate index of the rate of inflation, thanks to the changing shares of silver and Russian currency in the customs revenues, it does represent an attempt to measure revenue in terms of a stable currency in addition to the current value of the Russian ruble.

Apart from its fiscal importance (discussed in the essay on taxation in chapter 8), customs revenue was used as a device to obtain foreign currency and was thus linked to the government's concerns in the area of monetary policies. In view of the inability of domestic silver production to meet the mint's demand for coinage and the relatively small (during the first half of the century at least) export surplus, the customs revenues paid in silver were an important source for the state mint. This dependence diminished in the second half of the century as both export surpluses and domestic silver output increased. The demand for a sizable, steady, and continuous supply of foreign currency did not disappear in Russia for reasons as much external as internal. This helps to explain the government's insistence on having the customs duties paid in silver, even during the last

two decades of the century when it was increasingly relying upon the printing press to finance the budget deficit, when it obtained foreign loans to repair its

Table 4.88   Customs Revenues, 1742–97 (in Rubles)

Year	Collected in Albertustalers	Albertustaler Exchange Rate	Albertustalers in Rubles Equivalents	Collected Rubles	Total
1742	559,589	108	604,356	255,816	860,172
1743	634,546	112	710,692	267,581	978,273
1744	583,326	109	635,825	272,558	908,383
1745	595,216	112	666,642	287,826	954,468
1746	620,815	113	701,521	279,777	981,298
1747	593,574	112	664,803	208,650	873,453
1748	523,943	114	597,295	233,706	831,001
1749	600,073	116	696,085	302,436	998,521
1750	723,500	115	832,025	323,383	1,155,408
1751	750,461	113	848,021	291,995	1,140,016
1752	822,398	112	921,086	399,642	1,320,728
1753	804,870	108	869,260	454,317	1,323,577
1754	756,405	106	801,789	1,189,004	1,990,793
1755	727,859	106	809,068	1,502,927	2,311,995
1756	751,293	109	818,909	1,381,827	2,200,736
1757	727,704	116	844,137	1,607,221	2,451,358
1758	729,085	117	853,029	1,648,280	2,501,309
1759	762,173	118	899,364	1,701,833	2,601,197
1760	726,870	120	872,244	1,716,450	2,588,694
1761	749,235	123	921,559	1,707,394	2,268,953
1762	870,756	122	1,062,322	1,740,286	2,802,608
1763	993,157	113	1,122,267	1,831,211	2,953,478
1764	960,142	116	1,113,765	1,768,987	2,882,752
1765	965,632	113	1,131,924	1,919,650	3,051,574
1766	968,543	115	1,113,824	1,665,005	2,778,829
1767	425,391	119	506,215	2,132,167	2,638,382
1768	379,487	120	455,384	2,356,114	2,811,498
1769	324,930	121	393,165	2,799,944	3,193,109
1770	334,219	127	424,458	2,773,224	3,197,682
1771	358,407	128	458,761	2,820,238	3,278,999
1772	778,458	124	965,288	2,253,878	3,219,166
1773	735,735	127	934,383	2,694,683	3,629,066
1774	729,144	129	940,596	2,628,396	3,568,992
1775	730,440	119.1	869,954	2,377,621	3,247,575
1776	575,164	119.1	685,020	2,495,876	3,180,896
1777	610,768	119.8	731,700	2,466,450	3,198,150
1778	641,323	121.2	777,283	2,174,842	2,952,125
1779	679,820	123.4	838,898	2,278,546	3,117,444
1780	782,662	142.2	1,112,945	3,099,622	4,212,567
1781	656,741	131.3	862,301	3,563,987	4,426,288
1782	763,524	134.7	1,028,467	3,581,249	4,609,716
1783	949,193	134.7	1,278,571	3,776,928	5,055,499
1784	895,322	136.5	1,222,115	4,255,860	5,477,975
1785	819,128	133.0	1,089,440	4,261,771	5,351,211
1786	610,277	128.0	781,155	4,069,257	4,850,412
1787	867,041	138.4	1,199,985	4,384,952	5,584,937
1788	740,066	146.3	1,082,717	4,262,478	5,345,195
1789	693,263	170.7	1,183,400	4,621,369	5,804,769
1790	793,452	170.7	1,354,422	5,966,477	7,320,899
1791	816,042	186.2	1,519,470	5,505,130	7,024,600
1792	839,368	191.4	1,606,550	6,179,500	7,786,050
1793	520,739	206.9	1,077,409	4,205,218	5,282,627
1794	551,246	187.9	1,035,791	4,437,712	5,473,503
1795	475,282	181.2	861,211	4,701,530	5,562,741
1796	790,408	173.6	1,372,148	5,242,251	6,614,399
1797	2,231,413	172.7	3,853,650	2,460,331	6,313,981

balance of payments, and when customs duties (including the income derived from the reminting of foreign coins) became a relatively small source of government revenue.

Before discussing some additional aspects of customs revenues in conjunction with tariff policies and the pattern of Russia's foreign trade, we must recall that the data reflect an institutional arrangement. As

Table 4.89   Custom Duties on Exports and Total Customs Revenue, 1758–68

Year	Duty in Reichstalers	Russian Money Substituting for Foreign	"Internal Duty"	Total in Rubles (Reichstalers at the 1.25 Ruble Exchange Rate)	Total Custom Revenue
1758	415,345	34,118	644,251	1,197,550	2,559,763
59	362,063	74,789	694,060	1,221,428	2,654,550
60	334,208	90,300	659,577	1,167,637	2,625,036
61	332,506	81,780	623,663	1,121,076	2,669,139
62	483,691	88,586	718,677	1,411,877	2,881,232
63	420,144	85,866	748,809	1,359,855	3,072,658
64	424,169	61,819	694,398	1,286,428	2,969,165
65	418,864	66,984	740,617	1,331,181	3,126,690
66	364,335	50,343	602,083	1,107,845	2,875,674
67	178,828	392,790	454,406	1,070,731	2,663,905
68	193,641	418,997	494,301	1,155,349	2,823,473

Note: The custom duties to support the Ladoga Canal, on the average of about 50,000 rubles yearly, are omitted.

Sources: Chulkov, *Opisanie*, vol. 7, pt. 1, p. 946; Storch, *Supplementband*, p. 3.

mentioned earlier, there existed in Russia, prior to 1754, internal tolls that were levied both upon goods destined for export and upon imported products. The loss of revenue stemming from the abolition of those internal tolls in 1754 was compensated for by an increase of external tariffs on imports and exports. It would therefore be logical to assume that during the pre-1754 period the total tax derived from exported and imported goods was actually higher than the reported customs revenue as the commodities crossed the internal toll barriers. Unfortunately, it is now impossible to estimate the amount. Even if we ignore this important consideration, the data on directly reported customs revenues indicate that their growth lagged behind the growth of the volume of trade turnover and that the ratio of the customs revenues either to the volume of imports or to the total trade turnover was declining secularly. In view of this, the gradual decrease of the customs revenue as a percentage of the total trade turnover may represent a liberalization drift as far as the tariff is concerned. Regardless of the government's intent, such a drift certainly was conducive to the growth of Russian foreign trade.

One of the most convincing pieces of evidence on the nature of the Russian tariff is the distribution of customs revenue between the revenues from exports and from imports. Import revenue exceeded export revenue, but for a number of the years for which such data are available the export revenue was a substantial portion of the total customs revenues and cannot be ignored.

Unquestionably the Russian authorities, in both the Commerce College and the customs offices, made a distinction between export and import revenues. The authorities certainly used such separate accounts at times when tariff issues were debated. Unfortunately almost no comprehensive accounts from the

surviving documents have been published, and whatever was published in eighteenth-century secondary sources has been summarily ignored by scholars.

One attempt to treat the size of the export customs duties separately was made by M. Chulkov in his well-known study of the years 1758–68, the time preceding the rapid growth of the Russian overseas trade. Chulkov distinguished three components or categories of duties according to the schedule of the 1757 tariff: export duties paid in foreign currency (*efimki* or Reichstalers); export duties paid in rubles as a substitute for foreign currency; so-called "internal tolls," a compensatory payment for the abolition of internal tolls in 1754, which was added to the export duties. Table 4.89 illustrates both the total amount and the composition of the export duties reported by Chulkov as well as the share of export duties of the total customs revenues.

A small body of evidence points to the existence of calculations of the export duties for the port of St. Petersburg which tend to support Chulkov's data. A document in the French National Archives estimates the export duties (*Droits de Sortie*) for St. Petersburg as 585,771 rubles for 1777, 400,911 rubles for 1778, 486,447 rubles for 1779, and 428,730 rubles for 1780.[35] An English document credits the St. Petersburg customs office with collecting 1,112,415 rubles on exports in 1783.[36] The English figure is just over a third of the total customs duties collected in St. Petersburg in 1783, according to the data in table 4.90.

Another crude method of determining the amount of export duties is to estimate the volume of exports of various commodities for particular time periods and then to multiply by the average tariff duty. An exercise for illustrative purposes with a few commodities yields the results presented in table 4.91. This table does not include the duties on tallow

Table 4.90   Customs Duties (in Rubles)

Year	I Total	II St. Petersburg	III Riga	IV Revel'	V Arkhangel'sk	VI Vyborg	VII Kiakhta
1752	1,427,640						
1753	1,460,405						
1754	2,134,511						
1755	2,412,750						193,173
1756	2,320,941				87,925		157,184
1757	2,516,851						147,216
1758	2,559,736						178,877
1759	2,654,550						230,482
1760	2,625,036						238,156
1761	2,669,139						230,840
1762	2,881,232						199,671
1763	3,072,657						179,066
1764	2,969,165						59,525
1765	3,126,991						90,472
1766	2,875,674				194,588		
1767	2,663,905						
1768	2,823,473						11,025
1769	3,206,107						401,708
1770	3,190,999						495,291
1771	3,268,245						451,343
1772	3,226,951						389,270
1773	3,614,352	2,077,004	520,155		224,198		397,420
1774	3,539,827	2,056,161	537,257		146,360		444,998
1775	3,290,671	1,699,213	590,213		145,064		453,279
1776	3,214,831	1,686,421	435,008		147,555		500,460
1777	3,229,909	1,768,449	490,975		124,009		479,061
1778	2,976,497	1,729,051	505,033		140,585		277,600
1779	3,128,325	2,162,872	495,922	25,253	128,731		
1780	4,078,702	2,434,204	615,082	36,783	169,805		545,979
1781	4,384,913	2,541,833	527,899	24,478	229,302		706,219
1782	4,535,655	3,074,826	569,328	57,138	164,451		662,850
1783	4,963,427	3,236,409	974,682	92,626	183,099		509,148
1784	5,375,013	3,157,215	997,743	137,200	189,435		431,601
1785	5,285,680	3,147,213	933,451	162,628	208,486		374,579
1786	4,832,103	3,343,984	705,675	180,396	245,047		
1787	5,468,753	3,984,250	680,059	173,049	238,765		
1788	5,187,561	4,035,743	661,807	161,822	233,339		
1789	5,487,947	3,897,866	592,874		344,879		
1790	6,958,291	4,761,902	709,738	985,674	238,204		
1791	6,525,183	4,514,745	805,506	535,038	207,221		
1792	7,228,712	4,109,074	992,485	400,294	147,239		509,830
1793	5,017,339	2,752,147	625,455	297,823	157,192		515,581
1794	5,294,374	2,959,899	671,180	259,723	186,932		527,070
1795	5,424,027	3,229,065	561,531	250,955	169,773		532,394
1796	6,470,586	3,504,643	779,248	270,930	215,971		488,320
1797	6,090,687	3,149,071	844,122	207,774	144,312		414,278
1798		4,219,325					509,685
1799		4,684,184					698,487

(287,000 rubles for 1793–95), *iufti* (123,000 rubles in 1793–95), hemp and linseed products (116,000 rubles in 1793–95), and most important, wood and forest products (the greatest source of duties), and thus Chulkov's figures appear logical and consistent.

The changes in the amounts and composition of the export duties reported by Chulkov can be explained by the volume of exports and the changes introduced by the tariff of 1766. The problem that one has to resolve, however, is that of the relative reliability of the order of magnitude of Chulkov's data, which indicate that at least from a third to a half of the total customs revenue originated from export duties.

Yet another source points to the importance of export duties in the total reported customs revenue. H. Storch in his work on Russian trade calculated the customs duties paid in specie for the period 1793–96. That they were collected primarily in the port of Riga is important for Riga's role in Russia's foreign trade but immaterial for the present purposes. Here the issue is the share of export duties in the total customs collections. Although Storch's data, presented in ta-

Table 4.91 Estimated Export Duties for Selected Commodities (in 1,000 Rubles)

Years	Hemp	Flax	Iron	Total
1760–64	208	195	77	480
1770–74	350	232	83	665
1780–84	408	280	93	781
1793–95	422	327	91	840

ble 4.92, account for only a part of the export duties, their order of magnitude—always over half—is instructive.

There are at least two implications in the data in table 4.92 on the dimension of export duties. First, by levying the export duties, the Russian government was collecting an immediate tax from the domestic producers in a most direct fashion, in addition to cutting the prices the producers received for their goods in the long run because of the fact that entrepreneurs could not raise their prices to cover the tariff costs in a competitive world market. Second, if the amount of the export duties was as high as Chulkov and Storch indicate, the duties on imports must have been smaller than generally assumed. Russian historians habitually calculated the rate of import duties as the ratio of total customs duties to the value of imports. The correction in this "traditional" estimate

of protection is quite substantial in view of the Chulkov evidence presented in table 4.93 on the size of the export duties. A further implication of this picture is that entrepreneurs, whose efforts were dampened by the consequences of the tariff, must have paid a larger portion of government revenues and the gentry consumers of imported luxury products a lesser portion than is generally assumed.

The tariff of 1724 established export duties for most Russian products in the range of 5 percent ad valorem. When this rate is multiplied by two, in view of the foreign currency exchange rate, the real duties were at the 10 percent level. The Petrine tariff had very strong fiscal overtones and was designed to obtain revenues that would help Russia to overcome its balance of payments difficulties. An extreme example of high export duties is those on the export of grains, but one must appreciate the high grain prices within the country in the years 1723–24 to comprehend the almost prohibitive tariff. In view of the amelioration of the grain supply situation and declining grain prices, the next tariff (of 1731) lowered the export duties on that commodity drastically.

The beginning of the 1730s witnessed a general decline of prices not only in Russia, but all over

Table 4.92 Export Duties Paid in Specie and Their Share in Total Customs Collections, 1793–96

Year	Export Duties in Specie (Converted into Rubles)	Total Reported Duties in Specie (in Rubles)	Total Customs Duties	Export Duties in Specie as % of Total Customs Duties
1793	2,582,508	4,205,218	5,017,339	53.46
1794	3,171,633	4,437,712	5,294,374	59.90
1795	3,576,924	4,701,530	5,424,027	65.95
1796	3,668,527	5,242,251	6,470,585	56.70

Source: Storch, *Supplementband*, pp. 3, 22.

Note: the export duties were converted from the weight of silver coins into rubles by using their shares in total specie and applying it to Storch's data in rubles.

Table 4.93 Ratio of Customs Duties to Imports

	Estimated Customs Revenue of Imports	Value of Imports	Ratio of Customs Duties to Imports	"Traditional" Calculation of the Ratio of Customs Duties to Imports
1758	1,362,186	6,353,119	21.44	39.37
1759	1,433,122	8,002,980	17.91	32.50
1760	1,457,399	7,358,052	19.81	35.18
1761	1,548,063	7,180,794	21.56	36.61
1762	1,469,355	8,162,235	18.00	34.34
1763	1,712,803	9,190,358	18.64	32.14
1764	1,682,737	9,670,619	17.40	29.81
1765	1,795,509	9,200,465	19.52	33.17
1766	1,767,829	9,175,175	19.27	30.28
1767	1,593,174	8,893,298	17.91	29.67
1768	1,668,124	10,856,162	15.36	25.90

Sources: Chulkov, *Opisanie*, vol. 7, pt. 1, p. 946; Storch, *Supplementband*, p. 3.

Europe. Thus the tariff of 1731 had to be lower than the 1724 tariff in order not to jeopardize Russian exports. For this and other reasons already mentioned, the 1731 tariff was not a sellout of Russian interests by foreigners ruling Russia. In fact, it was a shrewd policy that not only kept Russian export goods in the foreign market but even increased the volume and value of exports abroad and helped to create a steady demand for Russian goods. This policy facilitated the growth of exports from the Baltic ports in competition with the older exporting areas such as Poland, Prussia, and Sweden. A glance at the export customs duties of 1724 and 1731 provides convincing evidence of a careful process of downward adjustment of the tariff rates. This was particularly true in grains, and also in linseed, tallow, hemp, flax, vegetable oil, and iron. The rates for some commodities, such as tanned hides, remained unchanged. Thus the downward adjustment was neither a random one nor an automatically uniform one. While the customs duties were reduced in 1731, payments in the ports for various services such as fire prevention were introduced. They were payable in Russian currency and computed as surcharges on top of the customs payments.

The tariff of 1757 consisted of two parts. One was made up of the export duties in the ports and on the customs border and the other was the internal customs abolished in 1754 but added to the tariff duties. Although Russia needed the customs revenues to refill the treasury's coffers that had been emptied by participation in the Seven Years' War, the duties on such important export commodities as hemp, flax, and iron were not raised at all. This may have been an ancillary reason why Russian exports became more attractive to foreign buyers during the 1760s. (The main reason was the devaluation of the ruble by 13 to 14 percent, which made Russian commodities cheaper in terms of foreign currencies.) The attractiveness of Russian export commodities increased to such an extent that the tariff of 1766, although it raised most of the export duties except that on iron, did not exercise any dampening effect on the growth of Russian exports.

The tariff of 1782 was introduced under conditions of international tension in European politics that involved, particularly, France, England, and the Netherlands. Lengthy diplomatic exchanges and debates went on not only in St. Petersburg but also in London, Paris, the Hague, and Vienna. Yet the tariff introduced no major changes in the export duties. The rate increases introduced in 1766 and maintained in 1782 were offset by the provision that one-half of the amount had to be paid in foreign currency, rather than the total as before. The real gain for the mer-

chants engaged in foreign trade was the provision raising the exchange rate of the Reichstaler (efimka) from .50 ruble to 1.25 rubles. This brought it much closer to the market value of the ruble and diminished the actual rate of the customs duties by eliminating the discriminatory exchange rate.

Following the tariff of 1782 and the rapid growth of Russian exports, a number of developments of significance for exporters of Russian commodities occurred. One was the general price inflation in Russia caused by the increasing issue of paper money (assignats). The second was the privilege granted to Russian merchants to pay the entire customs duties in Russian currency instead of half in foreign coins, as foreigners were obliged to do. This, together with the falling exchange rate of the ruble-assignats, made it palatable and profitable for many of the foreign merchants in St. Petersburg to respond favorably to the government's pressure to become Russian merchant-gosti, members of the highest corporation of the Russian merchant class, and to be registered as such for the purposes of local taxation and statistics by various nationalities in the account books of the customs office. These facts made it possible to increase the share of "Russians" in the export trade of St. Petersburg in the two years from 1786 to 1788 by more than four times.

A secondary aspect of the tariffs of the second half of the century was their impact on the destination of exportable commodities to different ports. In a fashion reminiscent of the competition between St. Petersburg and Arkhangel'sk during the Petrine period, the tariffs of 1755 especially and also 1766 attempted to provide incentives to the merchants trading in the Azov and Black Sea ports. Not only could the duties be paid in foreign currency, but the customs rates were reduced for a number of commodities in demand by partners of the Black Sea trade. To some extent, as in the case of iron exports, for example, the reduction of the export duty can be attributed to a recognition that transportation costs to the Black Sea were higher than to the Baltic. In the case of tanned hides (iufti), the reduction may have been helpful in encouraging a rerouting of exports to less certain and underdeveloped markets.

The abolition in 1766 of the separate tariff on ports in Livonia and Estonia seems not to have had any major distorting effect on the trade in those ports, except perhaps for indirectly strengthening the position of St. Petersburg vis-à-vis those ports. However, the special conditions set up for the port of Riga and the insistence that everybody, even Russian merchants, pay duties in Reichstalers rather than in Russian currency had the visible effect from 1790 to 1796 of redirecting much of the import trade from Riga to the nearby ports of Revel' and Pernau, where the duties were collected in depreciated Russian currency. Consequently substantial volumes of imports were rerouted as a result of a discriminatory policy, or perhaps because of exaggerated expectations of stability in the old pattern.

The highest increase in nominal terms was enacted by the tariff of 1796. (It may have been less extreme than it appears in terms of the real price of commodities.) Moreover, the requirement that the customs duties be paid in Reichstalers at the old rate of 1.25 rubles per Reichstaler, which was much below the market exchange rate, indicated the fiscal nature of the tariff under conditions of constant, mounting budget deficits which were largely being covered by the printing of paper money.

Fortunately for Russia's foreign trade, the 1796 tariff was replaced by a new one in 1797 that reinstated the 1782 rates, with minor upward adjustments. (They appear almost as though they were a rounding of the rate to the next tenth of a ruble.) Although the tariff schedule preserved the payment of duties for imported goods in Reichstalers (at an exchange rate of 1.40 rubles per Reichstalers), it permitted the payment of export customs duties in Russian currency.

With the exception of the first (1724) tariff and the 1796 aberration, the export duties in the Russian tariff, although fiscally motivated and yielding a revenue that was increasing with the growing volume of exports, did not jeopardize the interests of the export trade. The Russian government realized quite early that its bargaining position in the export trade was far from that of a monopolist, and it behaved accordingly. Unable to compete in quality against the other suppliers of Baltic goods, it had to rely upon the attractiveness of lower prices and an ability to mobilize huge volumes of commodities to meet sudden upsurges of demand from Western and southwestern Europe. The tariff policy was by and large sensitive to the nature of foreign demand, and the government learned gradually to restrain its short-term fiscal appetite, which was somewhat placated by the decision to issue paper money, in favor of the longer-term interests of its export trade. That this evolution of Russian tariff policies has found very little recognition in the writings of economic historians was not the fault of the statesmen who directed Russian policies, but of the preoccupation of the former with import trade tariffs.

The Russian Port Cities

Since the foreign trade of Russia was predominantly a seaborne trade, it is instructive to take a closer look at the major ports of the Russian Empire.

The Port of St. Petersburg

St. Petersburg's history and development as a port offer a rare example, at least for the eighteenth century, of how a ruler's vision and will created new realities and shaped the lives and activities of masses of people of both present and future generations. The will of Peter the Great determined not only the shift of a capital city and seat of government, not only the single most massive Russian investment of the century, but also the development of what became in a short time the largest Russian port and the most significant center of Russian foreign trade. This is not to suggest that Peter's feat bordered on the miraculous, or that he undertook to achieve what King Canute intended. It is, however, a splendid example of the will and ability to mobilize the resources of a country to achieve what is politically necessary and symbolically important. The costs of achieving those goals could be assessed only in terms of a time frame that spanned at least a few generations.

St. Petersburg, the port on the delta of the Neva River in the Finnish Gulf of the Baltic Sea, had to overcome many obstacles in order to become what it was expected to be. Although St. Petersburg did not replace Moscow as the economic center of domestic commerce and industry, it became the outlet for the largest portion of an increasing flow of goods from and into Russia. Moscow remained the center of domestic commerce and industry because of its location, its radial transportation network, and its position as the seat of the textile industries.

A system of waterways connecting the city and the port with a sufficiently large hinterland constituting a supply base had to be constructed in order for St. Petersburg to survive and to perform its function. The first part of this system was the Ladoga Canal, a waterway parallel to the southern shore of Lake Ladoga, which connected the Neva River with the Volkhov River through the stormy and treacherous Lake Ladoga. The canal, started in 1719 and finished in 1730, was 104 versts long and provided a connection between Lake Il'men and the Volkhov River. It was supplemented in the 1730s by the Vyshnii Volochëk Canal, which connected the Msta and Tveritsa rivers and thus the Baltic with the Volga basin.

For the rest of the century this remained the most important water artery of Russia and the main collector of commercial agricultural and industrial production in the country. It was also the lifeline for the St. Petersburg foreign trade. Given a hinterland that, theoretically at least, not only embraced central Russia, but reached the foothills of the Urals and the shores of the Caspian Sea, St. Petersburg had a vast trade zone to serve. In addition to the economic

Table 4.94   Distribution of Exports from St. Petersburg by Foreign Subjects and Russians (in Rubles)

Year	England	Holland	France	Italy	Spain	Portugal
1764	3,947,244	423,188	25,500	108,208		
1766	3,499,864	359,779	216,638	112,868		
1768	4,339,840	391,375	225,251	155,767		
1769	5,370,782	350,186	82,087	220,686		
1770	5,208,975	351,748	114,329	223,349		
1771	6,383,862	417,905	46,302	249,195		
1772	3,566,944	307,017	111,716	202,858	118,786	
1773	4,725,232	525,535	256,558	124,395	156,340	
1774	5,140,039	507,021	346,325	197,429	99,432	
1775	5,061,709	375,127	177,962	94,713	119,064	
1776	5,581,463	293,292	417,710	182,397	60,209	
1777	7,518,147	486,495	432,426	298,598	53,076	
1778	6,156,745	396,723	702,459	233,093	8,843	
1779	6,072,602	354,405	595,859	335,952	128,768	
1780	6,403,427	361,699	490,108	305,801	14,837	29,260
1781	8,653,084	116,269	111,251	333,900	75,789	105,796
1782	6,269,341	229,570	296,697	241,674	185,460	92,096
1783	5,639,875	207,428	128,694	109,948	153,266	156,435
1784	8,390,755	182,059	181,404	330,534	135,476	121,935
1785	9,035,846	184,196	328,265	278,295	166,249	78,069
1786	9,029,533	62,269	357,740	201,226	113,145	66,904
1787	8,188,324	76,254	575,201	13,203	107,747	69,140
1788	8,307,434	178,201	1,169,058	16,531	119,847	160,044
1789	9,618,823	133,536	545,430	1,226	159,890	220,400
1790	9,745,595	80,172	695,328	2,410	145,452	200,340
1791	7,902,558	133,747	671,523	7,467	174,118	170,298
1792	7,378,319	134,330	417,809	3,510	179,458	112,866
1793	13,121,788	100,371	151,111	2,210	49,509	
1794						
1795	19,123,940	2,373	5,256	50	71,445	247,372
1796	23,077,891	190	862	185	195,557	373,377
1797	19,749,180		10,831		66,327	205,459
1798	24,880,372	129,990	252,428	418	15,597	103,487
1799	29,229,057			50		175,932

boundaries of the hinterland, the connection established between local markets, there was another element: by government regulation certain areas were administratively assigned to support the growth of St. Petersburg's trade with their exports. Administrative interference did not stop with monopoly assignments of product supply. In the early years of the St. Petersburg trade, the body of Russian merchants in the city was collected or selected by direct assignment from the various trading communities of Russia, from Moscow, Arkhangel'sk, Iaroslavl', Kaluga, and other centers of the existing regional markets.

The growth of the St. Petersburg trade cannot be explained exclusively in terms of its export base or the size of its hinterland as a supplier of goods. Another very important factor was the concentration of population and that population's income. St. Petersburg was the place where such incomes, though not necessarily originating there, were actually spent. As the capital of Russia, the seat of the government and the court, and garrisoned by the prestigious guards regiments, St. Petersburg was the center for the consumption of foreign goods, the locale where the demand for imports was the strongest. It was in St.

Petersburg that the standards for consumption by the wealthy classes were set, where fashions were established to be emulated by the aristocracy, gentry, and merchants of other regions, where consumption by the rich was considered a virtue. Foreign trade became one of the chief vehicles by which the new life-styles were introduced. The evidence supporting these contentions is contained in the data pertaining to the composition of St. Petersburg imports, which show the high share of food, beverages, colonial products, and foreign textiles that were imported into the capital.

The evidence for the traders in the port of St. Petersburg, their origin and the volume of trade turnover, bears witness to the predominant role of foreign merchants there. The actual share of foreigners probably was even higher than is obvious from a first glance at table 4.94, which is based on data in the archives of the Public Record Office in London; regulations of 1787 provided special treatment for Russian nationals that were a strong inducement for foreigners to accept membership in Russian merchant guilds during the period from 1787 to 1796. Those regulations certainly were responsible for much of

	Total Germany	Switzerland	Austria	Denmark	Sweden	Armenia
1764				89,069	52,065	
1766	836,152	3,306	1,656	69,044	1,772	4,325
1768	703,054	74,947	1,558	32,866	9,053	1,134
1769	829,988	512	279	40,542	12	3,311
1770	751,027	1,696	849	34,555	3,583	710
1771	775,805	3,160	52,032	24,612	5,654	1,369
1772	644,055	26,340	8,761	32,521	939	7
1773	1,103,322	37,004	35,213	32,355	818	671
1774	1,763,887	8,495	22,055	9,053		
1775	932,978		7,218			
1776	661,092		2,847	28,939	32,339	3,104
1777	899,290	424			45,327	20,018
1778	924,944				49,322	2,546
1779	1,152,081	19,604			53,767	270
1780	894,103		1,941	36,618	68,135	
1781	519,209	28,068	4,347	24,128	64,492	
1782	1,134,876	66,965	4,017	34,248	228,480	
1783	501,573	7,659	3,149	648,061	78,457	
1784	148,570	4,546	5,427	340,730	157,513	
1785	188,490	2,662	1,344	541,977	45,688	1,380
1786	73,815		290,151	502,735	65,946	
1787	134,484		9,869	454,074	89,919	
1788	34,458		10,345	329,155	33,354	
1789	13,327		23,974	994,361		
1790	12,435		54,506	404,237		
1791	5,710		86,703	390,349		
1792	8,547		65,288	201,726		
1793	10,802		65,288	126,252	200	
1794						
1795				71,990	3,191	
1796	7,011	1,309	18,389	7,498	506	
1797	32,516		370,131	13,124	1,870	
1798	289,694	7,535	143,395	389,179	2,275	
1799			30,580	272,916		
1791	5,710		86,703	390,349		
1792	8,547		65,288	201,726		
1793	10,802		65,288	126,252	200	
1794						
1795				71,990	3,191	
1796	7,011	1,309	18,389	7,498	506	
1797	32,516		370,131	13,124	1,870	
1798	289,694	7,535	143,395	389,179	2,275	
1799			30,580	272,916		

the great upsurge of trade by *Russians* from 1786 to 1787 and again from 1787 to 1788 and also for the declines in the shares by merchants of other nationalities at the same time. Both the Russian merchants and the merchants of foreign origin who were involved in foreign trade operated through networks of agents and suppliers, employed large numbers of hired hands for the transportation of goods, and provided credit advances. In other words, they created a demand for labor and capital to carry on and expand the trade turnover. My discussion of the population size, its rapid growth, and its social composition can be found in chapter 1 of this work. Unfortunately there is no readily available material on direct employment in the St. Petersburg port.

The rapid growth of the population, which rose from about 0 in 1701 to at least 200,000 by the end of the 1790s created very serious supply problems, for St. Petersburg was at the end of a long supply line for most of its foods and raw materials. In spite of the considerable transportation costs, the city relied on domestic sources of supply that came to it overland and by the inland waterways from the east and south. St. Petersburg took relatively little advantage of what might have been a favorable coastal trade because of regional price differentials. The exceptions were alcohol and grains from Livonia at times when supply by the normal river routes was disturbed. Both the size of the St. Petersburg population and its composition were due less to its role as a port and more to its role as the capital. Therefore it was less typical as a Russian port city in the eighteenth century than were some of the other port cities.

Table 4.94, cont.   Distribution of Exports from St. Petersburg by Foreign Subjects and Russians (in Rubles)

	Hamburg	Lübeck	Rostock	Prussia	Saxony	Danzig
1764	287,587	294,136	139,513			
1766	321,157	250,924	112,700	149,723	1,648	
1768	190,209	274,664	121,762	116,380	39	
1769	160,238	407,715	131,105	130,618	312	
1770	165,528	329,567	115,635	140,271	26	
1771	132,220	388,928	111,550	140,824	2,283	
1772	154,104	250,950	126,547	107,167	5,287	
1773	335,163	551,612	92,552	118,501	5,494	
1774	204,116	499,137	944,550	111,387	4,697	
1775	365,302	332,836	158,678	69,497	6,665	
1776	229,628	177,390	202,309	42,100	9,665	
1777	373,102	283,090	195,894	32,495	14,560	
1778	448,651	218,877	184,677	34,644	18,613	19,482
1779	668,826	183,692	209,963	48,480	13,110	28,010
1780	245,197	243,404	216,879	175,501	13,122	
1781	57,020	98,127	42,949	317,132	3,484	497
1782	375,481	157,838	305,578	288,780	7,199	
1783	128,277	80,422	138,031	8,850	146,173	
1784	89,752	42,740	9,688	6,390		
1785	113,861	72,123		1,005		1,501
1786	20,744	51,260		302	1,509	
1787	33,404	33,252			924	
1788	320	34,138				
1789		13,327				
1790		12,435				
1791		5,710				
1792		8,547				
1793	4,022	6,780				
1794						
1795		3,892				
1796		7,011				
1797	12,603	19,623	290			
1798	95,013	108,636	86,045			
1799			2,040			

The Port of Riga

The trade of the port of Riga, the second port in terms of foreign trade turnover during most of the eighteenth century, deserves special mention not so much because of its size but because of its special status and function in Russian foreign trade.

Even though Riga was conquered by Russia during the Northern War in 1709, it preserved much of its internal autonomy for most of the century: its own system of customs duties until 1766, when it had to adjust to the Russian tariff system; its own system of taxation, inherited as part of the Swedish system of the seventeenth century; its own system of weights and measures; and the use of its traditional monetary unit, the silver Albertustaler.

Riga's special significance in the foreign trade of Russia did not stem from its leading role as the largest port of Livonia, but from its position as a Hanseatic stronghold and a port of non-Russian transit trade. Consequently the largest part of its hinterland was for most of the century outside the borders of the Russian Empire. The origins of the commodities exported from Riga as late as the years 1767–82 are shown in table 4.95. Eastern Belorussia was incorpo-

rated into the Russian Empire in 1773, western Belorussia and Lithuania in 1795, and Kurland in 1796, so that in 1767 only about a third of Riga's exports originated in the Russian Empire.

The goods originating from the territory of Russia proper were heavily concentrated in hemp, textiles, and iron, plus some shipments of grain and flax seeds. In all other commodities Russia's share was negligible.

The overall composition of Riga's exports was similar to that of the other major ports on the Baltic, but differed from St. Petersburg's in its conspicuously low level of iron and tallow exports. The commodity composition of exports from Riga in broad categories remained stable for most of the century and can be represented as shown in table 4.96 for the 1767–82 period.

The exports of Riga were directed to the Netherlands, Great Britain, Denmark and Sweden, Spain, Portugal, France, Hamburg, Bremen, and Lübeck. Of these trade partners, the Dutch and the Danes were mostly engaged in the re-export trade and also in carrying a substantial share of the Riga imports. Notable among the imports were bulk products such

	America	Russians	Ships	Merchants	Total
1764		580,248			5,885,243
1766		512,097	157,854	157,854	5,775,356
1768		476,607	48,495	170,298	6,630,248
1769		514,673	35,939	191,364	7,640,302
1770		541,780	24,638	255,312	7,522,502
1771		471,742	20,912	485,248	8,937,798
1772		1,150,381	20,520	260,649	6,451,494
1773		1,471,836	56,843	333,252	8,859,408
1774		1,269,270	28,411	544,794	9,086,215
1775		890,196	18,200	622,421	8,299,585
1776		1,086,279	26,968	589,602	8,966,156
1777		1,058,394	31,154	644,302	11,116,937
1778		1,001,629	26,661	707,523	10,210,488
1779		1,840,400	29,478	633,722	11,216,898
1780		1,087,708	34,059	1,242,701	10,941,129
1781		2,367,727	28,827	598,087	12,954,440
1782		2,598,469	25,335	48,239	11,467,347
1783		2,374,178	104,818	49,413	10,098,798
1784		2,841,997	49,387	16,677	12,941,513
1785	204,938	2,556,307	30,166	14,840	13,497,645
1786	252,092	2,480,504	71,806	32,688	13,359,993
1787	279,636	6,357,498	67,344	12,872	16,086,800
1788	252,240	10,021,083	49,848	13,485	20,351,937
1789		10,002,933	153,441	6,939	21,735,663
1790		10,179,262	95,569	6,411	21,641,779
1791		10,349,611	109,766	8,802	20,040,697
1792		13,579,337	100,656	23,002	22,224,331
1793		9,937,776	69,291	10,490	23,757,954
1794					25,565,767
1795		11,881,182	151,776	123,175	31,767,952
1796		13,077,000	170,551	17,852	37,110,333
1797		11,827,209	154,369	19,893	32,450,911
1798		10,064,371	235,742	37,993	36,552,476
1799		8,254,643	197,188	7,519	38,169,925

Source: P.R.O. (London) BT 6/232, BT 6,233.

Table 4.95   Distribution of Exportable Commodities from Riga by Various Regions of Its Hinterland, 1767–82

Region	% of Supply
Eastern Belorussia	29.4
Western Belorussia and Lithuania	26.6
Kurland	11.1
Russia	25.5
Livonia	7.4

Source: Data supplied by Professor Vasilii V. Doroshenko to the Copenhagen Congress of Economic History (August 1974). Eastern Belorussia was incorporated into the Empire in 1773, Western Belorussia and Lithuania in 1795, and Kurland in 1796.

Table 4.96   Supply of Exportable Commodities to the Port of Riga, 1767–82

Commodities	% share
Flax, hemp, seeds	50.4
Grains	25.2
Forest products	18.3
Manufactured goods	6.1

Source: V. V. Doroshenko, at the Copenhagen Congress of Economic History, 1974.

as salt and herring. In this respect the case of Riga was typical of the problems of the Baltic trade with Western Europe. The Baltic supplied bulky goods, such as forest products, grain, hemp, and flax, while importing high-value products such as colonial goods and textiles. This compelled many ships from Western Europe to sail into the Baltic in ballast instead of being fully loaded. Salt was the one commodity which often supplanted ballast, in an attempt to decrease the cost of transportation services. In addi-

tion, the Baltic provinces were exempted from the government salt monopoly.

The chief advantage of Riga's trade for the Russian revenue derived from customs duties plus the export surplus by which Riga earned foreign exchange. Riga became a convenient place to acquire silver and bills of exchange. Peter the Great ordered Riga merchants to acquire bills of exchange drawn for him on Amsterdam in 1712. A difficulty arose when Peter paid in copper money at the nominal rate of exchange. Consequently the Riga merchants concluded this operation at a substantial loss and refused any further transactions at nonmarket rates. For many years Riga, which collected and transferred revenues in silver coins rather than in depreciating rubles, was the chief source of supply for silver coins (Reichstalers) for the Russian mint.

The port of Riga was far from ideal in terms of convenience and safety for vessels. Major investments to rebuild the port and to regulate the delta of the Dvina River were undertaken in the second half of the century, but no major improvements were achieved. Nevertheless its relative position vis-à-vis the ports of St. Petersburg and Arkhangel'sk during the second half of the century was by and large maintained, at least until the 1790s. This can be gauged from the data on the trade turnover of the ports and the number of ships that frequented the respective harbors.

Riga in its eighteenth-century trade exhibited a great deal of continuity with the seventeenth century, for which far more data have been published.[37] Such continuity can be explained by the relatively minor economic changes that took place in the hinterland, which included a continuous growth of commercialized agriculture.

Riga's trade doubtless gained from its access to the hemp-producing regions of Russia. Its observed growth was due to the commercial traditions of the port, its reputation for the quality of its products, the readiness on the part of foreign merchants to grant credits, the ability of the Riga merchants to provide credit to its suppliers, and the increased output of the hinterland which was coupled with a growing demand for "Baltic goods" in Western Europe.

The trade of Riga suffered, however, from the government tariff policy, which maintained high rates of customs duties. Those relatively high customs rates were designed originally to provide a stimulus to shift trade toward the port of St. Petersburg. They had a detrimental effect not only on the Riga trade, but on the trade of Russia in general. The government originally expected merely a transfer of a part of the Riga trade to St. Petersburg. It hoped to influence the distribution of trade between the two ports, but not the total volume of trade, which, it was assumed, would remain constant. Overlooked by the policy-makers was the competition of Riga with the ports of Kurland (Libau and Windau) and with the Prussian ports of Königsberg and Memel. The actual effect of the governmental policy of maintaining high customs rates is vividly described by the famous Russian publicist A. N. Radishchev in a memorandum he authored in his official capacity as a counsellor at the St. Petersburg Customs House in 1790.

A difference in customs duties in two neighboring states is harmful to the one in which they [the duties] are high, and profitable to the one in which they are low. That is the situation with respect to the city of Riga, between Russia and Kurland. All Kurland products are sent to [the port of] Libau.... For the same reason even the Kurlanders who bring their exports to Riga and earn their money there do not purchase any foreign goods there, but purchase them in Kurland ports, where they are cheaper. Riga's trade suffers and the volume of money in circulation diminishes.

The Riga trade finds itself in the same situation with respect to the Prussian ports because the latter's customs duties are considerably lower than the ones existing in Riga. The consequences are similar to the ones for the Kurland trade. The Poles and Lithuanians, instead of following the usual pattern of carrying their products to Riga, carry them in increasingly large volume to Königsberg and Memel. Even the money they earn from their greatly diminished export trade in Riga they do not use for purchases of foreign goods in this port; instead, take their money or bills of exchange to Königsberg, for foreign imports there are considerably cheaper than in Riga.[38]

The population of Riga went through a traumatic experience in 1709 at the time of the siege by the Russian army. The bubonic plague struck the besieged Swedish garrison, the besieging Russian regiments, and the civilian population. Forty percent of the population died from the plague, and the population of Riga recovered very slowly. Livonian peasants were bound to the land and were not accepted in the alien environment of the town of Riga. It took about a century for Riga to reach its previous population size. The trade that made the city prosperous continued, but its income was shared by the merchant elite, which cherished and guarded its position of power and wealth.

Riga was the urban center for the Livonian nobility which divided its life between study in Germany and service in St. Petersburg while drawing its income from landed estates. It was a city of predominantly North German culture and Protestant spirit. The economic interdependence between the merchants, the regional nobility, the local artisans, and the Protestant clergy recommended rational cooperation, if not harmony, as long as each group knew its place in the social hierarchy. As a port city and commercial center, Riga was not as dynamic as St. Petersburg, not as boisterous and exotic as Astrakhan', and less subdued than Arkhangel'sk, but it was more businesslike and solid than any of the Russian ports, an enclave of Western Europe in an environment that was going through the early states of Westernization.

Table 4.97   Riga's Trade through the Sound (in Albertusthalers, 1761 Prices) (5-year averages), 1765–69 Base

Years	Exports	Index	Imports	Index	Imports as a % of Export
1710–14	192.0	14.4	52.6	9.25	27.4
1715–19	475.6	35.7	271.4	47.7	57.1
1720–24	686.2	51.6	302.2	53.1	44.0
1725–29	1,259.4	94.7	369.0	64.9	29.3
1730–34	977.4	73.5	388.0	68.2	39.7
1735–39	1,506.3	113.2	382.2	67.2	25.4
1740–44	1,238.6	93.1	394.0	69.3	31.8
1745–49	1,317.4	99.0	338.0	59.4	25.7
1750–54	1,792.0	134.7	443.6	78.0	24.8
1755–59	1,399.4	105.2	742.0	130.5	53.0
1760–64	1,562.4	117.4	579.0	101.8	37.1
1765–69	1,330.4	100.0	568.0	100.0	42.7
1770–74	1,894.4	142.4	566.6	99.6	29.9
1775–79	2,100.2	157.9	551.0	96.9	26.2
1780–83	2,606.25	195.9	553.5	97.3	21.2

Source: Dunsdorfs, *Latvijas Vesture*, pp. 466–69.

Table 4.98   Distribution of Exports by Major Commodity Groups, 1761 Prices (in Percent of Total)

	1710–31	1731–70	1771–83
Fibers	61.2	58.5	50.3
Forest Products	21.4	27.1	30.3
Seeds	14.6	8.3	6.4
Grains	1.6	4.9	11.5
Other	1.2	1.2	1.5

Source: Dunsdorfs, *Latvijas Vesture*, p. 476.

Note: Fibers include hemp, flax, and tow; forest products include timber, masts, potash, and tar; seeds include hemp and linseed.

Table 4.99   Distribution of Imports by Major Commodity Groups, 1761 prices (in Percent of Total)

	1710–30	1731–70	1771–83
Textiles	44.7	44.5	30.2
Salt	30.2	31.0	34.7
Colonial goods	14.1	11.1	13.0
Beverages	7.1	7.9	16.3
Herring and other fish	2.4	2.8	3.1
Metals and coal	1.5	2.7	2.7

Source: Dunsdorfs, *Latvijas Vesture*, p. 476.

The availability of the Sound toll data has enabled the Latvian historian Professor Edgar Dunsdorfs to estimate the value of the Riga exports and imports through the Sound, valued in 1761 prices, for the period 1710–83.[39] That enormously valuable labor permits insight into the pattern of Riga's trade with the countries outside of the Baltic in terms of stable prices. The share of Riga's trade through the Sound fluctuated widely. There was also a great deal of price variability over the period, aside from the decline in the value of the Russian ruble, relative to the more stable currency of the albertustaler in Riga itself. Table 4.97 reconstructs in the form of five-year averages the basic features of Prof. Dunsdorfs's yearly estimates.

The same scholar also attempted to distribute the exports and imports through the Sound by major commodity groups for various periods, as presented in table 4.98. The changes in the distribution of Riga's exports to Western Europe reflected both changes in demand and competition from other exporting areas. The relative decline of the demand for fibers and seeds may indicate a slackening of demand for linen and hemp goods in competition with other fibers,

notably cotton, but also finer woolens. The increase in the share of forest products is indicative of the growing demand in Europe for construction materials and, during certain periods, for naval stores.

Dunsdorfs also calculated the structure of Riga's imports through the Sound, which is presented in table 4.99. The changes in the distribution of imports into the port of Riga mirror the shift in tastes and the sources of supply of both the Livonian and Belorussian hinterlands. The relative decline in the imports of textiles resulted in part from the development of the domestic textile industry in Russia, which after 1772 gained direct access to the Belorussian markets. The spectacular rise of the beverage imports may be explained for the decade of the 1770s by the diversion of trade in beverages from Polish or Prussian ports to the port of Riga.

Regardless of the changes in the structure of Riga's trade with Western Europe, noted by sundry historians and calculated by E. Dunsdorfs, the overwhelming impression is one of continuity and specialization. Both the hinterland which supplied Riga with its exports and demanded goods and currency in exchange and the clients in Western Europe who main-

Table 4.100 Exports from Riga (in Rubles)

	1766	1783	1785	1787	1788	1789	1790	1791	1795	1796	1797	1798	1799
Great Britain	755,967	1,098,640	1,357,090	1,586,526	1,590,956	1,143,329	2,103,756	2,461,063	4,850,810	6,497,393	3,053,420	4,922,214	6,115,149
Netherlands	551,566	1,520,374	1,138,363	755,861	964,944	1,354,600	1,885,072	1,601,823					
France	54,230	303,731	295,826	198,773	267,117	175,787	238,709	53,963					
Spain	85,312	420,041	440,972	396,305	399,712	339,851	342,155	592,784	583,156	901,042	1,576,338	915,941	322,543
Portugal	69,239	206,496	305,979	109,937	168,610	312,690	335,303	855,853	508,210	615,332	1,025,403	1,137,983	1,005,663
Italy		157,230	213,508	71,455	127,137	78,407	244,593	242,035	873,043	172,055	192,396	7,363	
Sweden	190,285	1,135,486	554,436	299,300	95,166	63,337	82,346	498,515	462,366	692,498	749,084	1,320,104	1,097,569
Denmark	371,382	612,449	451,479	445,676	435,071	415,115	675,710	736,693	2,421,855	3,094,986	1,350,275	1,461,175	1,751,768
Lübeck, Rostock	112,287	198,106	221,833	215,728	273,796	260,798	301,169	328,491	789,663	589,106	638,224	634,511	951,302
Flanders			38,294	66,289	108,083		56,181						
Prussia	3,937			54,350			72,942		449,813	1,185,346	1,638,158	1,235,955	940,751
Hamburg, Bremen	68,735			69,586			187,872		107,374	276,238	189,086	213,938	631,705
Total	2,266,193	5,864,816	5,214,415	4,199,786	4,536,995	4,436,688	6,325,714	7,997,731	11,275,777	14,023,996	10,412,384	11,849,184	11,251,409

tained a preference for goods from Riga were stable constituencies during the eighteenth century who were interested in maintaining trade relations through trusted and expert intermediaries. These generalizations are supported by the data in tables 4.100 and 4.101, which trace the value of exports from Riga to its Western trading partners in the years 1766 to 1799 and the volume of commodities shipped between 1758 and 1799.

The Port of Arkhangel'sk

Arkhangel'sk was distant from the hinterland where most of its exports originated and distant from the markets that absorbed its imports. It was not a port of convenience, but a port of necessity. Its origins go back to the mid-sixteenth century, when Muscovy was barred from the Baltic and when control of the Baltic coast adjacent to Russian lands was in the hands of Muscovy's chief competitors in the West, Sweden and Poland. During the seventeenth century, when a lively and extensive overland trade was still carried on through the Livonian cities, the port of Arkhangel'sk became the chief outlet of Russian goods to the West and the gateway for many of the imported goods. The Arkhangel'sk trade fair attracted both Russian and foreign merchants, who conducted most of the foreign trade transactions involving Muscovy. The only commodities in which Arkhangel'sk enjoyed a comparative trade advantage were some forest products, naval stores, and Siberian furs. Other commodities had to be brought overland and by river transport in tortuous journeys at considerable expense. This political and economic necessity forced Muscovite trade into a constant search for alternatives. Such alternatives were created and made available as a result of the outcome of the Northern War and Peter the Great's decision to build a new capital on the Baltic.

The data on Arkhangel'sk's volume of trade in the first decade of the eighteenth century have a special significance, for they represent the bulk of Russian exports abroad at a time when that city was the only port for trade with Western Europe. Table 4.102 presents the export data for the few years for which they are available.

This particular period in the history of the Arkhangel'sk trade was marked by the active participation of the Russian state in foreign commerce through trading monopolies administered by state officials or farmed out to merchants. The state also actively competed with private entrepreneurs in some segments of the export market. During the first fifteen years of the century Arkhangel'sk was a bustling port, a place where merchants and government officials were engaged in relatively large-scale transactions, and through which mercantile and financial flows fed parts of the Russian economy and government. During the Northern War Arkhangel'sk was a lifeline through which necessary supplies were delivered. Arkhangel'sk's supremacy as a port came to a sudden standstill as a result not only of the comparative geographical advantage of St. Petersburg and Riga, but also following a government decree that lowered St. Petersburg's customs duties relative to the ones in Arkhangel'sk and reapportioned a number of export commodities from the hinterland to other ports. The impact of those government regulations is evident in table 4.103, which shows the number of ships calling at Arkhangel'sk and the amount of customs duties collected during the second and third decades of the eighteenth century. Volume peaked in 1715–16 and then declined dramatically.

The export trade of Arkhangel'sk almost immediately fell to third place among that for Russian ports. Trade was greatly diminished and had to rely on a much higher degree of regional specialization than before. The outlet of the Northern Dvina River basin, the port had an extensive territorial hinterland that was sparsely populated. The previously established overland and river routes were still used but less frequently and with lighter loads. Although St. Petersburg and Riga outdistanced Arkhangel'sk in exporting the major bulk commodities such as hemp, flax, iron, and even certain types of wood products, reduced exports of those goods found their way abroad via Arkhangel'sk. The sea lanes to England and Scotland, to the Netherlands and the North Sea German cities were used by ships coming into and leaving for Arkhangel'sk, especially because these lanes could not be as easily blocked during periods of European wars as were the approaches to the Baltic ports. This factor explains much of the rise of the Arkhangel'sk trade that began during the Seven Years' War (see table 4.104).

For both Russia and its trade partners Arkhangel'sk was a form of insurance against the vicissitudes of European politics that infringed on the flow of goods to and from Russia. Throughout the period, although its share of the total Russian foreign trade declined, the Northern Dvina port held on tenaciously to its role as an exporter of several products. Pitch, tar, and other forest products were naturally on the list because of the economic characteristics of the hinterland, but it is somewhat surprising to discover that linseed, tallow, and grains were regularly exported in large quantities, as shown in table 4.104. Perhaps this can be explained by the demand of the foreign countries that traded in Arkhangel'sk and by some economies of scale involved in Arkhangel'sk shipping. Of the various commodities mentioned, the case of grain exports from Arkhangel'sk is an interest-

ing one, for the value of grain exports from Arkhangel'sk over the century exceed that of St. Petersburg. This persistence is due not only to the demand by the Netherlands and North German cities, but also to the location of the grain marketing regions in Russia proper and the availability of transportation facilities. Economies of scale in shipping were possible because of the larger ships needed for the Arkhangel'sk sea route in comparison with those that plied the Baltic. The data in table 4.105 show that activity was depressed during the 1720s–1760s, increased during the 1770s and 1780s, and rose substantially during the 1790s. (Part of the reported increase for the 1790s was a manifestation of the general rise in the price level during that decade.)

The population and employment profile of Arkhangel'sk followed closely the status and role that were assigned to that port by the government in the arena of foreign trade. From a bustling port during the first two decades of the eighteenth century Arkhangel'sk declined to a supporting and second-rate position in comparison with St. Petersburg and Riga. It was kept very much alive due to contacts established in the previous centuries with Dutch and British firms, its ability to carry on trade when political events made the Baltic less accessible to a trading partner, and its competitive position with respect to the transportation costs of selected commodities such as forest products and furs.

The growth of Arkhangel'sk's population ceased around the time of the first population census. Those censuses, which reported the taxpaying, urban-estate, male population, are a poor indicator of the size of an urban population that included military garrisons, officials, clergymen, and peasants settled in the cities and employed in trade and crafts—all social groups that either were not accounted for in the urban population rolls or were exempted from the censuses as nontaxpayers. Therefore conclusions on the population size of Arkhangel'sk must be drawn from population reports by local police authorities and from accounts on the number of residence buildings in the city. A count of houses for 1739 that included those which survived a major conflagration and those newly built listed 1,609 houses in Arkhangel'sk.[40] The 1779 description of Arkhangel'sk by the local municipality (*magistrat*) estimated the number of houses at 1,857, or 248 more than in 1739.[41]

Military personnel were a high proportion of the Arkhangel'sk population. The 1739 list of houses reported a total of 722 dwellings of the 1609 (or almost 45 percent) as belonging to the military and admiralty personnel (including those retired). The population estimate for 1785 listed 3,622 males of various groups of military and naval service among 7,537 male inhab-

Table 4.101   Commodity Exports from Riga, 1758–99

Commodity	Unit	1758	1759	1760	1761	1766	1774
Clean hemp	shp.	34,049	41,215	31,425	30,042	8,436	50,515
Hemp outshot	shp.						
Hemp pass	shp.	14,936	16,701	17,031	16,077	12,058	16,129
Total hemp	shp.	48,985	57,916	48,456	46,119	20,494	66,644
Flax tow	shp.	562	704	804	558	1,327	919
Total flax	shp.	30,978	37,010	26,439	34,390	37,777	30,657
Hemp tow	shp.						
Hemp seed	shp.	7,478	47,854	37,331	27,190	39,791	
Linseed sowing	shp.	13,795	30,667	12,101	23,334	32,428	45,520
Linseed crushing	shp.	8,945	27,999	22,642	31,409	25,301	34
Linseed total	shp.	22,740	58,666	34,743	54,743	57,729	
Veg. oil	Oxhoft	59		64	35		
Cordage	shp.	548	660	694	692		938
Iron total, incl. Swedish	shp.	662	174	211	170		
Leather							
Wax	shp.	263	187	100	155	166	196
Tallow and candles	shp.	163		44	55		321
Potash	shp.	472	2,492	1,498	1,063	1,191	1,616
Weed ash	lasts	90	70	116	73	222	122
Masts	number	3,070	1,014	1,558	1,411	984	1,446
Sailcloth	pieces	1,100	2,780	1,544	1,358		844
Ravenduck	pieces	416		535	668		251
Flemish	pieces						173
Assorted linen	Arshin	62,869	47,018	35,482	48,592		29,855
Mats	pieces						

Commodity	1780	1781	1782	1783	1784	1785	1786	1787
Clean hemp	56,901	61,050	43,373	40,327	47,088	49,050	38,925	39,142
Hemp outshot								
Hemp pass	22,770	18,168	18,005	15,259	22,433	16,168	13,371	16,900
Total hemp	79,671	79,218	61,378	55,586	69,521	65,218	52,296	56,042
Flax tow		625	533	1,586	660	456	734	815
Total flax	53,906	37,645	38,723	44,652	57,353	68,763	57,494	52,493
Hemp tow	28,871	17,590	23,985	21,593	24,500	18,385	10,809	16,523
Hemp seed	35,434	36,258	7,318	54,281	30,541	49,450	33,318	48,248
Linseed sowing	30,162	32,332	31,803	53,394	53,670	23,716	45,719	38,403
Linseed crushing	83,134	41,108	46,420	80,820	101,455	101,328	62,051	47,765
Linseed total	113,296	73,440	78,223	134,214	155,125	125,044	107,770	86,168
Veg. oil	286		18					
Cordage	1,369		1,991					
Iron total, incl. Swedish	3,270	5,738	4,788	5,815	3,150	1,938	184	281
Leather	20,690	21,270	16,460	5,590		7,190	7,500	8,160
Wax		216	230	526	222	92	99	130
Tallow and candles								
Potash	1,762	1,927	1,659	1,310	1,904	1,538	1,243	1,127
Weed ash	110	114	105	101		178	158	95
Masts								
Sailcloth	1,470		2,620					
Ravenduck	404		781					
Flemish	83		47					
Assorted linen	17,058		10,261					
Mats	163,627		273,648					

itants of the city, or 48 percent. This population estimate probably did not include the suburban parish of Solomba, for another source for 1786 estimated the male population as 9,363.[42] P. I. Chelishchev, on his voyage in 1791, estimated the population as 13,570. Regardless of what the precise population of Arkhangel'sk was, the reported high share of military and naval personnel is a feature common to many Russian ports during the eighteenth century.

For the purposes of this work, other population groups besides the military are of greater interest, such as those actively engaged in the commercial activities of the port and in the annual trade fair, at which much of the import-export business was con-

Table 4.101, cont.   Commodity Exports from Riga 1758–99

Commodity	1788	1790	1793	1795	1796	1797	1798	1799
Clean hemp	50,625	72,331	50,210	61,424	62,051	48,268	68,252	61,708
Hemp outshot	*	2,287	5,998	7,831	12,499	7,142	14,471	11,142
Hemp pass	11,013	9,108	18,847	13,027	13,587	12,536	15,519	20,247
Total hemp	61,638	83,726	75,055	82,282	88,137	67,946	84,282	93,097
Flax tow	696	496	530	987	697	548	678	1,065
Total flax	50,895	45,185	55,414	45,275	59,651	63,919	64,834	69,362
Hemp tow	16,262	21,547	13,561	19,462	22,650	21,755	27,559	26,470
Hemp seed	13,579	31,322	21,250	21,345	19,412	11,473	7,764	15,161
Linseed sowing	40,941	41,691	90,601	49,635	68,479	68,202	41,989	34,695
Linseed crushing	79,928	96,756	81,077	96,545	61,861	78,178	99,697	79,338
Linseed total	120,869	138,447	171,678	146,170	130,340	146,380	141,686	114,033
Veg. oil		104	690	941	231	266	130	610
Cordage				1,851	1,692	191		
Iron total, incl. Swedish	179	75	4,292	16,206	1,631	700	3,125	3,130
Leather	5,870	2,720	4,840	10,185	1,067	5,930	1,680	1,390
Wax	58	50	88	113	68	62	25	15
Tallow and candles			91	647	1,055	212	580	710
Potash	1,215	1,476	2,198	2,126	708	1,695	1,789	1,387
Weed ash	114	60	788	455	531	795	903	643
Masts	4,275	4,113	739	1,865	1,790	1,962	867	250
Sailcloth					1,364		3,517	
Ravenduck					745		2,240	
Flemish					294		611	
Assorted linen					12,817		12,937	
Mats					212,876			

ducted. Such groups were the merchants, foreigners, and craftsmen. A distinction must be made between merchants and petty traders. The merchants, organized earlier as such in the urban tax commune (*posad*), and later in the guilds, constituted a minority of the trading population, although they dominated the volume of trade. The merchants constituted between 25 and 35 percent of the local trading population, and the rest were petty traders. Only some of the merchants were engaged in wholesale trade; the majority were retailers.

Most of the trade at the fair and in the port was not conducted by the local Arkhangel'sk merchants. The Arkhangel'sk trade, especially after the 1720s, assumed the characteristics of a regional commerce. Arkhangel'sk was the gateway for foreign goods entering the North Russian (and by extension, part of the Siberian) market and served as an outlet for the goods of a sparsely populated but geographically extensive region. The regional character of the Arkhangel'sk trade was underscored by the withdrawal of many of the Moscow commercial firms and trading dynasties which had actively participated in it during the first two decades of the century.[43] The participation in the Arkhangel'sk trade by the merchants of Vologda, Velikii Ustiug, and Tot'ma, all centers established along the roads and waterways leading from different hinterlands, underscores the way in which the port served a vast region with capital dispersed over a large area and human resources exceeding those of Arkhangel'sk itself by a large margin. River transportation alone on the Northern Dvina employed about 9,000 workers by the end of the century.

The merchant population in the second half of the century was larger in both Vologda and Velikii Ustiug than it was in Arkhangel'sk, as is evident in table 4.106. The merchants of those cities were also very active, if the trading in ports may be used as an indicator of activity. The merchants of those cities not only participated in the trade fair and port trade, but also owned residential buildings in Arkhangel'sk.

The composition of the artisanal and industrial population illustrated three features: a demand for craft services by the local population; the large proportion of the military; and the demand for employment in small-scale enterprises engaged in the processing of export commodities.

The demand on the part of the local population for services by local craftsmen was met by the relatively large share of cobblers, tailors, and others listed in table 4.107. These data reveal not only the large demand for varied craft services but also the improvement in the economic situation and the growth of the population that occurred some time during the late 1780s.

The processing of export commodities can be surmised from the presence of a number of small-scale

Table 4.102   Value of Exports from Arkhangel'sk (in 1,000 Current Rubles)

Year	Value
1704	1,581
1705	1,696
1706	1,212
1707	1,558
1709	1,775
1710	1,760

Source: Kozintseva, "Uchastie," p. 328.

Table 4.104   Arkhangel'sk Trade (In Current Rubles) 5-Year Annual Averages

	Exports	Imports
1725–29	283,176	96,982
1730–34		
1735–39	315,410	136,845
1740–44	428,363	236,102
1745–49	274,953	116,141
1750–54	310,910	177,706
1755–59	375,763	129,919
1760–64	573,495	261,610
1765–69	772,971	343,457
1770–74	1,511,597	317,195
1775–79	1,343,397	322,253
1780–84	1,423,433	400,952
1785–89	1,789,454	565,258
1790–94	2,205,874	770,018
1795–99	2,962,629	642,971

Table 4.103   Arrival of Ships and Collections of Customs Duties at Arkhangel'sk 1710–30, in Current Rubles

Year	No. of Ships	Internal Customs	Port Customs	Total Customs Duties
1710	159	153,154	84,329	237,483
1711	184	156,228	(89,540)	245,768
1712	132	135,416	(70,827)	206,243
1713	169	161,634	80,974	241,908
1714	155	164,822	96,549	261,371
1715	230	182,773	103,824	286,597
1716	208	168,526	104,452	272,978
1717	146	159,442	62,560	222,002
1718	116	123,995	63,728	187,723
1719	119	120,234	66,155	186,389
1720	122	121,134	75,397	196,531
1721	110	101,090	72,195	173,285
1722	60	40,634	29,210	69,844
1723	40	25,535	13,135	38,670
1724	22	19,041	1,557	20,598
1725	19	14,095	892	14,987
1726	29	16,665	1,743	18,408
1727	45	29,730	4,531	34,261
1728	41	30,789	4,252	35,041
1729	26	24,716	2,646	27,362
1730	38	26,568	4,286	30,854

Source: Ogorodnikov, *Ocherki.*

enterprises: 70 rope makers; 30 tar makers; 50 tallow makers; 15 wood distilleries; and a number of enterprises involved in the curing and drying of meat. The enterprises involved in processing were referred to not as "craft shops," but as "industrial enterprises." The operators catering to domestic consumption were referred to as "artisans."

The foreign colony of Arkhangel'sk was one of the oldest in Russia, although in numbers it lagged far behind St. Petersburg and Moscow. The number of foreigners was estimated at 253 in 1764 and 283 in 1791. They enjoyed a certain autonomy, worshiped in two churches, and had their own school. Their contacts with the local business community seem to have been correct and businesslike. Their role in the economic life of the city was limited, and increasingly so as Arkhangel'sk's share in Russia's foreign trade declined. A higher proportion of the Russian merchant houses were engaged in foreign trade than was the case with the foreign firms, the largest of which departed for St. Petersburg. Business contacts were long-lasting (in many cases for generations). There was less cutthroat competition, less of a sense of foreign dominance, and less of the characteristic antipathy that the Russian merchants of other trading centers felt toward foreigners.

The size and composition of the Arkhangel'sk population were more typical of Russian ports and commercial cities than they were in St. Petersburg. The population size was sufficient to handle the trade turnover of the port and the employment composition was adequate to meet the needs of the local economy. The fact that Arkhangel'sk had use for capital supplied from outside and for seasonal labor employed in river transportation bears witness to a lively exchange with its hinterland, the mark of a commercial city.

Extant information also touches on the working of the municipal authorities and their relationship to the state bureaucracy, and the struggle of the lower-income groups against the oppression by the municipality which represented a commercial oligarchy. Such information does not describe the life and work of the lower classes, the laborers in the port, the peasants coming into the city to work on the wharves and docks, loading and unloading the river barges and foreign ships. Thus we can obtain a sketchy view of the commerce and crafts of the port and city of Arkhangel'sk, but we lack material on life and labor in a port city of the eighteenth century that would enable a fuller reconstruction of the reality of the place.

The Port City of Astrakhan'

Most of the major Russian cities in the eighteenth century, although differing from one another, could still be classified as European cities. Each of them had its counterpart in Western or Central Europe. St. Petersburg had features in common with Stockholm,

Riga with some of the former Hanseatic cities of North Germany, and even Arkhangel'sk could be compared with some northern European cities. The one among the commercial and port cities of Russia which had no counterpart in Europe, not even among the Mediterranean cities, was Astrakhan'. A port on the Volga River and the Caspian Sea, Astrakhan' remained throughout the eighteenth century a frontier city, a Russian gateway to the east, perhaps more eastern than Russian in spite of the numerical predominance of its ethnic Russian population. As the major port for the Russian trade with Iran and Transcaucasia, and even Central Asia, Astrakhan' preserved its character as a meeting place of civilizations.

Astrakhan' was located on an ancient trade route that for over a millennium had served the fur trade between the interior of the Russian heartland and Western Asia. Its proximity to various branches of the ancient spice routes and the silk roads that have crisscrossed the Eurasian continent left an imprint upon Astrakhan' and made it a congenial place for merchants of various regions and different nationalities and cultures. In Astrakhan' the fur hats of the Russian merchants mingled with the Moslem turbans of the Bukhara merchants, as well as with the headgear of the Persians and northern Indians. Armenian merchants spoke their own language, or freely used either Persian or Russian. The marketplace of Astrakhan' blended the characteristics of the eastern "bazaar" with those of the Moscow "riady" (rows of stalls and shops), plus an admixture of the warehouses and countinghouses typical for European commerce of this period.

Although Russian rule was firmly established by the middle of the sixteenth century, the risks of banditry in the vicinity and corsair raids on seaward shipping lanes were still alive in the collective memory of the eighteenth century. Also present were the experiences of the plebeian participants in the rebellion led by Stepan Razin in the 1670s and in the urban uprising in Astrakhan' itself in 1705-6.

A bustling metropolis with an immediate hinterland lightly populated, but attracting people and goods from broad and culturally diverse areas, Astrakhan' preserved its frontier spirit and its inner spiritual autonomy throughout the eighteenth century as the third largest urban area of Russia after Moscow and St. Petersburg.

Carrying on such a diverse trade and other economic activities on the fringe of the multinational Russian Empire was beyond the capacity and skills of the Russian merchants alone. The multinational character of the city made it possible. Besides the composition of the indigenous population, the group of foreigners residing there temporarily was a varied

one. The Cabinet prescribed a population count on August 31, 1738, which revealed the composition of the 1,126 foreigners in Astrakhan'. There were 543 Armenians and people of the "Roman denomination"; 273 Bukharians; 183 Kazan' Tatars; 78 inhabitants of Gillian province (not distinguishing between Persians and Armenians); and 49 "Agryzhantsy."[44] The Russian census data are not necessarily the best source for estimating the actual number of foreigners, which fluctuated in harmony with the volume of trade. For example, according to a count of 1746 there were 52 Indian merchants staying at the Indian Merchants Court who had been registered there in the 1744-45 census, plus another 23 who had come after the census was taken.[45] The sizable presence of foreigners aroused concern among the indigenous population, who demanded that the foreigners share with them the city's tax burden, for the foreigners who paid duties on their wares paid only a small fee for the use of the trading courts assigned to different groups of foreign merchants. The jealousy of the local population was understandable, for in Astrakhan' the general prohibition against foreigners' engaging in retail trade operations which was applied in most cities of the Russian Empire was not enforced. For the foreigners to share in the local fiscal burden, they had to be permitted or compelled to join the urban tax commune (the *posad*), the guilds, and other urban institutions. In 1745 the *Glavnyi Magistrat* in St. Petersburg, the chief office for urban affairs, permitted foreigners in Astrakhan' to acquire the right of burghers. When the Senate was requested to approve the decision of the *Glavnyi Magistrat,* real incentives for the foreigners in Astrakhan' were added, such as a guarantee for freedom of worship. (The only known case of infringement upon the religion of some foreigners occurred when the city authorities complained to the government in St. Petersburg against a display of animal statues in front of what was alleged to be a "pagan temple" kept by Indian merchants.) The Senate also guaranteed the foreigners the right to be tried according to *their* laws in special courts.[46] Thus it appears as though the central authorities in St. Petersburg tried to provide the multinational trading community of Astrakhan' and foreign merchants visiting there with encouragement and incentives for the conduct of trade.

As a trading center Astrakhan' depended upon the reciprocal demand of the available trading partners for "eastern goods" and Western European as well as Russian goods. The volume of trade turnover depended not only on the economic conditions and the relative profitability of the trade, but also upon the complex set of political relations and circumstances of the broader region including Iran, Transcaucasia, and Central Asia, as well as Iranian, Ottoman, Russian,

Table 4.105   Commodity Exports from Arkhangel'sk

Commodity	Unit	1760	1761	1765	1767	1778	1779	1780	1781
Iron	pood	18,033	23,983	151,901	27,710	51,165	26,393	41,574	33,979
Hemp	pood	37,005	20,080	37,923	58,260	72,806	51,072	30,267	25,226
Flax	pood	4,558	5,215	353	11,430	358			432
Linseed	chetvert'	45,723	38,690	52,347	42,334	57,422	58,867	61,861	52,299
Hides	piece	10,804	8,920	10,785	7,399				11,919
Tallow	pood	70,046	59,880	85,344	69,293	107,494	98,824	161,364	80,797
Candles	pood	5,375	6,414	15,993	8,240	4,352	10,086	12,507	14,040
Soap	pood	465	64	3,721	1,407				
Wax	pood	1,801	187	237	26				1,402
Tar	barrel	25,868	28,692	53,067	75,095	118,357	32,048	104,849	52,710
Pitch	pood			661	1,521				124,774
Train oil	pood	6,797	2,540	2,819	1,811				69,094
Matts	piece	374,710	502,300	1,038,569	721,612	669,310	430,146	809,060	1,050,742
Cordage	pood	4,891	8,354	26,820	11,248	2,075	2,928		8,249
Sailcloth	piece	1,124	501	289	601	40	754	100	250
Ravenduck	piece	23	15	86	25				385
Flemish linen	piece	45	19						17
Diaper	arshin			355,815					
Rye	chetvert'	2,840	6,549	21,873	1,814	98,254	19,093	9,473	
Wheat	chetvert'			1,505	28,886	76,650	85,396	56,265	41,345
Barley	chetvert'								
Oats	chetvert'								
Wheat flour	pood								
Rye flour	pood								

Commodity	Unit	1782	1783	1784	1784	1785	1786	1787	1788	1789	1790
Iron	pood	108,601	69,485	104,811	95,638	144,867	154,796	124,998	93,569	114,597	105,300
Hemp	pood	21,686	20,359	21,236	20,767	6,864	6,698	6,601	11,111	23,141	9,749
Flax	pood	2,595	1,909	2,031	2,448		2,678	6,700	10,268	30,165	6,779
Linseed	chetvert'	31,352	69,098	27,270	27,468	46,786	45,243	67,301	83,696	85,260	43,926
Hides	piece	8,805	9,402	10,003	11,098		14,912	18,782	18,894	26,687	19,578
Tallow	pood	148,606	105,564	118,587	113,804	192,777	133,742	155,990	126,384	93,780	133,780
Candles	pood	11,347	9,485	10,319	11,185		9,818	10,239	11,315	11,070	3,701
Soap	pood		48		422			151	60	1,149	117
Wax	pood	569	518	427	390		390	195	234	1,247	518
Tar	barrel	98,107	89,601	89,355	86,272	47,730	82,052	94,041	81,713	79,881	70,966
Pitch	pood	108,772	50,987	17,693	28,869	55,540	96,171	63,463	47,507	3,695	63,148
Train oil	pood	45,604	40,248	50,643	53,837		53,256	51,953	43,462	42,668	26,185
Matts	piece	703,456	677,483	1,411,182	1,373,771		806,220	1,521,426	673,293	840,715	574,100

Cordage	pood	3,277	12,736	8,129	17,467	17,467	1,297	1,936	3,050	3,719	2,089
Sailcloth	piece	78	370	526	841		132	390 (604)	65	150	382
Ravenduck	piece		50	84	160			176 (249)	230	25	264
Flemish linen	piece		25	44	44			8			
Diaper	arshin	39,360	72,459								
Rye	chetvert'	41,173	60,995	150,995		56,009	64,201	4,656	6,254	395	
Wheat	chetvert'	39,114	41,345	9,510		18,074	18,163	15,398	13,381	5,662	10,669
Barley	chetvert'										
Oats	chetvert'										
Wheat flour	pood	2,340	445	32				1,991			
Rye flour	pood	13,448	17,228	3,122			18,910				

Commodity	Unit	1792	1795	1796	1797	1798	1798	1799
Iron	pood	14,425	93,701	152,553	175,542	157,127	153,000	68,463
Hemp	pood	12,791	1,306	27,553	29,719	30,549	30,994	47,661
Flax	pood	15,990	16,779	18,661	12,289	6,852	7,000	14,349
Linseed	chetvert'	55,376	53,625	76,946	35,963	32,261	34,307	34,515
Hides	piece	17,673	13,450	20,675	7,751	3,249	3,452	3,598
Tallow	pood	145,458	120,365	184,070	98,341	103,373	107,147	148,776
Candles	pood	11,010	12,651	23,380	12,731	8,425	919	
Soap	pood	653		5,292		1,344	1,543	
Wax	pood	200	470		306	166	150	
Tar	barrel	68,185	44,309	71,389	44,713	112,806	120,498	116,270
Pitch	pood	4,356	70,540	5,731	7,951	10,662	92,000	7,186
Train oil	pood	17,873	37,400	82,657	47,100	36,877	36,715	23,552
Matts	piece	1,082,281	420,729	1,109,873	63,811	1,017,683	1,500,000	
Cordage	pood	7,134	22,226	39,303	49,140	34,107		
Sailcloth	piece	355	464	1,076	580	3,457	3,760	
Ravenduck	piece	248	361	300	160	100	153	
Flemish linen	piece		152	200	190	110	173	
Diaper	arshins						148,256	
Rye	chetvert'	268						
Wheat	chetvert'	11,455	46,172	56,194	16,062			7,259
Barley	chetvert'		689	3,256	5			
Oats	chetvert'	10	767	3,621	17			
Wheat flour	pood	1,073	10,200		192		89	298
Rye flour	pood							

Source: P.R.O. (London), BT 6/232, BT 6/233.

Table 4.106   Employment of Males in Trade, Craft, and Industry (Russian North)

1764	Arkhangel'sk	Vologda	Velikii Ustiug
Merchants	963	1,439	1,893
Craftsmen	200	279	441
1791			
Merchants	951	1,921	1,170
Petty traders	2,611	2,852	3,852
Crafts	261	494	417
Industry	219	82	48

Source: Ogorodnikov, *Ocherki*, pp. 218, 244, 247–48.

Table 4.107   Employment Distribution of Craftsmen in Arkhangel'sk

	1764	1785	1791
Cobblers	40	35	47
Tailors	25	22	29
Hatters	8	8	n.a.
Joiners	n.a.	11	25
Carpenters	4	19	19
Window-makers	4	6	10
Silversmiths	13	11	20
Coppersmiths	11	14	20
Blacksmiths	12	n.a.	22

Source: Ogorodnikov, *Ocherki*, pp. 218, 244, 247–48.

and Western European diplomatic relations. The tendencies of successive periods of Russian territorial expansion and retrenchment and the strengthening and weakening of central authority in Iran affected the volume and conditions of trade. Russian attempts to develop land routes for the trade with Transcaucasia through Kizliar or through Baku have to be seen against the background of the difficulties encountered in the direct trade with Iran.[47] Closely related to the trading activity in Astrakhan' was the development of shipping services. Unlike the prevailing tendencies in the Baltic and White Sea trade, on the Caspian Sea the Russians provided the bulk of the shipping facilities during the eighteenth century. In addition, there was the shipping on the Volga River, for which Astrakhan' was one of the most important terminals. The Volga brought huge riverboats to Astrakhan' loaded with bulk goods from the Russian interior. Imported goods made their way up the Volga on long, tortuous journeys of months' duration to the great Russian fairs, to Moscow, and as far as the Baltic. Consequently, shipbuilding and shipping services provided employment for a fraction of the Astrakhan' population.

Astrakhan' was not only a major trading and shipping center, but also a craft and manufacturing center. Silk weaving became one of the city's leading industries. However, the Astrakhan' organization of silk weaving differed from the typical bipolar Russian pattern. For most of Russia silk weaving was concentrated at both ends of the spectrum, either in peasant-type cottage enterprises or in large-scale manufactories. In Astrakhan' silk weaving was a well developed urban craft with a tendency to grow into medium-scale manufactories employing freely hired labor. Other branches of industry and craft were leatherworks specializing in high quality products and silversmith shops. In all of those branches of production there was a very substantial proportion of employment of Armenians, who were also active in the trade of those branches' raw materials and finished goods. They established a high degree of vertical integration in those skilled trades. In 1759 about 91.5 percent of all weavers in Astrakhan' were Armenian, as were 71.3 percent of the silversmiths and 48.3 percent of the leatherworkers.[48]

Data on the volume of trade in Astrakhan' are not voluminous. Table 4.108 presents a few figures for the second quarter of the eighteenth century from the 1745 Astrakhan' customs house records. They show a surprising variability from year to year, and also the general importance of the transit trade to the volume of trade through Astrakhan'.

The Role of the Merchants

Special attention must be paid to the role of the merchants in Russian trade in the eighteenth century, for their position in the trade picture has evoked a debate that has persisted through the succeeding centuries. To a large extent the problem has been due to semantics, definitional unclarities, and the cultural attitudes one brings to the question: "Who was a Russian merchant?" In the prevailing contemporary popular opinion, in the higher culture of the eighteenth and nineteenth centuries, and also in the official view, a "Russian merchant" was defined as an individual member of the commercial corporate body (or guild) of the Russian Orthodox faith who professed undivided loyalty to the state, the church, and the Russian land. A foreigner, or a merchant of foreign origin, was not considered a "Russian" as long as he was a Protestant or Catholic, regardless of his degree of language assimilation or of the history of his ancestors' residence in Russia. Cultural assimilation was recognized as complete only when it was accompanied by baptism in the Orthodox church.[49]

Contrary to traditions in other European countries where the foreign element among the merchant group was slowly absorbed, in Russia foreigners and aliens were distinguished from "Russian merchants" and continued to be regarded as a separate category for an inordinately long time.

Table 4.108   Astrakhan' Trade and the Share of Transit Trade via St. Petersburg, 1737–1745 (in Rubles)

Year	Astrakhan' Trade		Transit Trade		Total Trade via Astrakhan'	
	Imports	Exports	Imports	Exports	Imports	Exports
1734	106,181	39,480				
37	274,752	80,937	99,347	142,092	374,099	223,029
38	149,028	63,354	54,892	332,701	203,920	396,055
39	449,717	91,297	189,361	269,643	639,078	360,940
1740	360,756	164,026	240,268	273,713	601,024	437,739
41	102,878	92,786	244,684	405,657	347,562	498,443
42	233,556	58,971	65,844	512,452	299,400	571,423
43	448,152	162,860	493,822	582,467	941,974	745,327
44	345,712	97,785	575,271	810,622	920,983	908,407
1745	159,759	104,162				

Source: Akademiia nauk SSSR. Institut narodov Azii. *Russko-indiiskie otnosheniia*, pp. 211–34.

When Russian merchants began to free themselves from some of their phobias about foreigners, the task of perpetuating the cleavage between the nationals and aliens was taken over by historians and other nationalist-minded members of the Russian intelligentsia. Even now the problem of foreigners and nationals in the foreign trade of Russia occupies the attention of contemporary Soviet historians.[50]

Two aspects of the nationality of merchants in Russia's trade must be considered: first, the extent of the participation of Russian merchants in foreign trade; and second, the significance for various historical interpretations of the debate on the participation of Russian merchants in foreign trade.

There is a consensus among historians that the policy of Peter the Great to mobilize Russian merchants, to resettle them by force from the cities of the interior to the port cities, and to press them into "the service of foreign trade" failed to resolve the problem of creating a social stratum large enough and endowed with the necessary skills and capital to operate effectively in the area of foreign trade. Peter, as he did in a number of other cases, transferred his belief in the possibility of a *perpetuum mobile* (one of his pet projects) into the area of social and economic relations. He believed that, once given the initial momentum, a process would continue of its own accord. Peter opened up avenues of upward social mobility into the merchant class, but neither force nor incentives assured success in the short run.

The policy of permeating the area of foreign trade with Russian merchants could not be effected either under Peter or his immediate successors. During the reigns of his successors there were often clear signs of appreciation of the success of individual merchants engaged in foreign trade that resulted in the ennoblement of the most prominent Russian merchants, acts that helped them escape the world of business for a life of government service and leisure congruent with the status and life-style of the older hereditary nobility. Whereas Peter had made possible upward mobility into the merchant class, his successors opened up avenues of escape from that class.

There was a very rapid turnover of personnel among Russian merchants operating in the area of foreign trade. This reflected, inter alia, a perpetual capital scarcity. There were no "dynasties" of Russian merchants that lasted for more than two generations in foreign trade, and even families lasting two generations were not numerous. The initial lack or scarcity of capital was not remedied by a long-term process of capital accumulation.

Economic historians of Russia who have argued about the nature of Russian participation in foreign trade and have characterized it variously as either passive (in the sense that Russians were not carrying their exports to the importing countries) or as essentially a type of collection and commission trade performed on behalf of foreign exporters and importers were describing a situation in which the Russian traders could not perform independently. The Russian merchants lacked capital. They had no knowledge or ability to arrange insurance, shipping facilities, or quality control. They had no network of information-gathering and other important ancillary services necessary for efficient trading in a world market.

In contrast, their foreign competitors had the means, the skills, and the elaborate organization required to supply the services at an appropriate price. Moreover, they also had a longer time-horizon. The foreign merchants residing in Russia, and also the foreign firms trading with Russia, displayed a much greater continuity in their business activities than did most of their Russian counterparts. A glance at the membership lists of the Russian company in London, at the lists of the foreign merchants residing in St. Petersburg or Arkhangel'sk, or at the reproduced archival miscellanies pertaining to trade reveals foreign trading families as well as firms constantly reappearing from the 1730s to the last decade of the century.

It is insufficient to characterize Russian merchants engaged in foreign trade purely in terms of relative economic disabilities without referring to the other aspects of their social milieu. It is also not enough to point out the heavy fiscal burden under which the merchants labored, or even to emphasize the degree of competition to which they were subjected by trading peasants, enterprising nobles, and merchant industrialists who preferred to trade directly with the foreigners and avoid the Russian middleman. It is much more important to realize that the risks involved in trading activities were relatively high because of the condition of the judicial system and the insufficient protection awarded to nonlanded property.

Still another disability of Russian merchants was the prevailing set of social attitudes that the nobility and bureaucracy created for them. This stimulated a sense of anxiety among the merchants, who accumulated grievances. The spirit of the grievances came to the fore in the deliberations of the abortive Legislative Assembly of 1767. The Russian merchants not only complained about their low social status there, but actually demanded the use of some of the trappings of nobility, such as the right to wear swords or drive in coaches, as symbols of their actual economic, rather than social, status. One would suspect that, for the merchants engaged in foreign trade and residing in the port cities and coming into contact with Dutch, British, or Hanseatic merchants, the difference between their own and the foreigners' sense of self-esteem and social standing in their respective societies drove the point home with even greater force. The presence of foreigners served as a reminder to the Russian merchants of their dependency relationship, but even more as a reminder of their inferiority and low status in their own society.

To all the economic disabilities of the Russian merchants, one must add the institutional constraints under which they labored and the psychological impact of their own sense of economic dependence and social inferiority. If this set of assumptions is realistic, the problem of actual competition between Russian merchants in foreign trade and foreign residents or foreign firms could only have arisen seriously during the nineteenth century. It was not expressive of the reality that characterized most of the eighteenth century in the area of foreign trade.

For the eighteenth century, the real yardstick by which the relative strength of the Russian merchants could be measured was their ability to monopolize the retail and wholesale branches of internal trade in imported goods and in the collection of exportable commodities. A real issue was the elimination of foreigners from the positions acquired in the commission trade. The most important of all issues was the

ability of the Russian merchants to build up their capital assets in order to provide themselves with both credit and a degree of independence vis-à-vis the merchants of foreign origin and the foreign firms. It was not easy to achieve even those limited objectives in view of the Russian economic milieu and the governmental fiscal and trade policies.

The available data for the second half of the century indicating the scope of economic activity and the expansion of foreign trade support the impression of a rising accumulation of capital among Russian merchants in foreign trade. The data also show their growing role as the sole collectors of exportable goods. To a lesser extent they became exporters in their own right. The increasing activity of Russian merchants in the wholesale trade in imported commodities, in ordering sizable consignments of foreign goods from foreign suppliers of textiles and colonial products is also discernible.

Given the special conditions of the Baltic trade, one can also observe the simultaneous engagement of the foreign firms in export-import operations. This allowed them to minimize their transportation costs and also to benefit from the fluctuating exchange rates of the Russian and foreign currencies. In contrast, the Russian merchants, even when gaining a foothold in one of the branches of trade, were much more specialized and rarely engaged in both import and export operations.

In summary, the bulk of Russian foreign trade in the eighteenth century was carried on by either foreigners or residents of foreign origin. Native Russians of Orthodox persuasion played a subordinate role. This does not present any major economic problem for us, and it is not much of an issue except in terms of extreme economic nationalism, a phenomenon that was not typical of foreign trade in the eighteenth century.

That this has been an issue for some Russian and Soviet historians, however, is not surprising. It is the mark of most historians and economists of the neomercantilist persuasion. What is often obscured both in the writings and in the thinking of the neomercantilists is the tacit assumption that the formation of an indigenous, national bourgeoisie is a process that justifies a sacrifice of the welfare of the rest of the population because such a formation is in itself a valuable national asset. Such writers assume that the achievement of a monopoly position in exploiting the national resources by the national bourgeoisie is a positive factor in the historical process. With respect to the eighteenth century one profoundly wishes that some of the historians would ask, "When would the prices for hemp obtained by the Russian peasants have been higher, under conditions of competition between Russian and foreign

Table 4.109   Growth of Russian Foreign Trade on a Per Capita Basis

Years	Annual Trade Turnover		Estimated Population 1,000s	Per Capita Trade	
	Rubles	Reichstalers		Rubles	Reichstalers
1745–46	9,304,627	8,270,325	18,206	.51	.45
1763–64	20,747,247	18,118,400	23,236	.89	.78
1782–83	41,553,282	30,848,762	28,410	1.46	1.09
1796–97	100,582,142	58,076,536	37,414	2.69	1.55

merchants, or when the Russian merchants had no competition?'' The probable answer to that question reveals why I find it valid to argue in terms of capital accumulation for a Russian bourgeoisie who would compete with foreigners, and leave the impossible task of arguing illogically from the vantage point of mistaken national welfare (a monopoly enjoyed by the Russian bourgeoisie) to the representatives of a neomercantilist, extremely nationalist school of historians.

Conclusion

The growth of Russian exports between 1742 and 1793 was spectacular, whether measured in current rubles or in a series of ruble values deflated by the Reichstaler exchange rates as an approach to a measure of real values. In current rubles exports increased from 5 million in 1742–46 to 53 million in 1793–97, a growth of 1,058 percent. In Reichstalers, exports grew from 4.5 to 29 million, 644 percent, during the same period. Imports rose from 4 to 35 million current rubles, 877 percent, and from 3.6 to 19 million Reichstalers in the same period. An even better perspective on the growth of Russia's foreign trade is apparent in the per capita terms presented in table 4.109.

Russia's spectacular foreign trade growth was a response to the growth of Western European demand for forest products, for agricultural raw materials (especially for industrial crops), and for iron. Western Europe's demands could not have been met easily by the traditional Baltic sources, Sweden and Germany. Western Europe's demand coincided with the sudden end to Russia's isolation, its eagerness to promote commercial relations, and its acquisition of Baltic and then Black Sea ports. These ports brought a considerable reduction in transportation costs.

Russia's response to the opportunities of trade was facilitated by the low level of agricultural wages and the resulting low prices of agricultural products relative to industrial products. Improvements in internal waterways extended the internal market and the regions from which exportable goods could be drawn. This orientation to production for the market was facilitated by governmental policies that con-

verted a growing number of Russian nobles to the desirability of producing for the market.

Russian exports were stimulated by a rise in Russian demand for foreign imports, especially on the part of the social elite, the government, and the entrepreneurs of the developing industrial sector. The life-style prescribed by the government for the Russian aristocracy and gentry emphasized the consumption of foreign goods, and the search for additional sources of money incomes naturally led to an increase of production for the market and to an increase in money rents paid by the serfs. The demand by the government for imports for the military and for luxury goods for consumption at court induced the government to employ fiscal policies and government trading monopolies to raise additional revenues. The fiscal measures had the effect of stimulating market production. The trading monopolies, confronted with a price-taker's international market, could realize profits only at the expense of domestic producers. Part of the government's demand also was for specie for the mint. Industrial demand was particularly strong for dyestuffs, both for domestic production and for production intended for export.

The rapid growth of Russian foreign trade required an increase in capital to finance those trading operations. To a very large extent this capital (or credits), together with some of the ancillary services such as shipping, insurance, and brokerage, was provided by foreign firms trading in Russian ports or by foreign residents. Given the relative scarcity of capital in Russia, it was profitable for the foreigners to provide it. It was simultaneously beneficial for the Russian traders to increase their volume of transactions at no extra cost, without making investments in ships and the working capital needed for foreign trade.

Extending credit and supplying services enabled foreign merchants to occupy a commanding position in Russian foreign trade throughout the century. Simultaneously Russian nationals were gradually accumulating capital and expanding their share of foreign trade. Toward the end of the century Russian nationals not only replaced foreigners in the area of commission trade, but also increased their share in direct import transactions. The slow process of penetration of foreign trade by Russian merchants was due in part at least to the imprecision of legal norms regulating movable property rights, to the low social status of the Russian merchants, to their relative ignorance of foreign markets, and to the dissipation or transfer of their capital out of foreign trade into industrial entrepreneurship or into landed estates once the merchant obtained a patent of nobility.

Because the Russian merchants were unable to create an efficient foreign trade organization, foreign merchants had to provide a substitute, one that required substantial investment. Only the major trading partners found it profitable to build up organizational structures and networks. In this respect Russia was fortunate in having the most economically advanced countries in Europe, the Netherlands and Great Britain, as its chief trading partners. The two accounted for the bulk of Russia's European trade, and the decline of the Netherlands coincided with the growth of the British share.

Russia's association with the most economically dynamic country in Europe was clearly beneficial and assured a rising demand for its goods. The Russo-British relationship was of mutual benefit, for Russia provided both strategic goods for British shipbuilding as well as other raw materials for British industries both prior to and during the period of the industrial revolution. Russian supplies of flax, linen, iron, and tallow to Britain's "old" industries released British resources for the production of new products.

The available price data are insufficient for judging the movement in the terms of trade between Russia and its major trading partners. Given the general trend of the relative prices of agricultural and manufactured goods during the century, one might surmise an improvement in Russia's terms of trade. To the extent that colonial goods were an important component of Russian imports, one cannot be certain about the terms of trade without a closer scrutiny of such prices relative to the prices of the Baltic goods. There can be no doubt, however, that during certain periods, when the exchange rate of the Russian ruble declined in terms of silver, the demand for Russian goods and consequently the volume of Russian exports rose.

Although numerous factors contributed to the rapid expansion of Russian trade, other factors constrained it. Disposable income was heavily concentrated in the hands of the nobility and the upper level of the merchant class, groups that consumed an inordinately high share of imports. This top-heavy concentration of incomes, advantageous for the import of luxury and colonial goods, limited the import of goods produced for mass consumption.

Governmental trade policy and, to be more precise, tariff policy, also imposed constraints upon foreign trade. Although every government was in favor of extended foreign trade, the formally pro-trade policies were circumscribed by other policy considerations that adversely affected foreign trade. A conflict arose between the encouragement of trade and the protection awarded to domestic manufacturing industries. Another conflict arose in the matter of export duties, which raised the prices of Russian goods in foreign markets and thereby limited the volume of exports. Last, but by no means least, there were customs duties and prohibitions that drove goods away from the legal trade channels into illicit trade channels, thereby defeating the intentions of the tariff legislation. There are reasons to believe that the volume of illicit trade was considerable, which might indicate an even higher growth rate of the actual trade than the one indicated by the data of the recorded trade.

The composition of both Russian exports and Russian imports exhibited a great deal of continuity. This points not only to the relatively stable pattern of foreign demand, but also to the areas of Russia's specialization. There also existed a considerable degree of uniformity in the growth pattern which is prominently displayed by the data on the physical volume of exports to Western Europe from the Russian ports on the Baltic. This does not imply that the export demand for different commodities was always of the same intensity, that relative prices remained unchanged, or that the composition of exports did not reflect such changes. In fact, both the data on the physical volumes of traded commodities and the data on the value of trade are very helpful in explaining some of the specific changes that occurred. Beyond those changes that can be explained by specific circumstances, general economic forces worked steadily to expand Russia's foreign trade.

5
INTERNAL TRADE

The old dictum by Adam Smith that "the division of labor depends upon the extent of the market" is of crucial importance for an understanding of the structure of the eighteenth-century Russian economy. The closest indicator of the extent of the market in any country is the volume of internal trade. This was particularly true for the period before the dramatic expansion of Russia's foreign trade.

Reliable estimates of the volume of domestic trade are lacking, but there is sufficient indirect evidence to presume that there was a very substantial growth of internal trade during most of the century. The economic historian desires to know the sources of that growth of internal trade, besides population growth and territorial expansion. The answer lies in an analysis of the structure and composition of the internal trade.

The size of the internal market was limited because of the predominance of the agricultural population and the small size of the urban and rural non-agricultural population. Most rural households consumed the agricultural products produced within the household, and many rural inhabitants produced much of their clothing and footwear, and even utensils and agricultural tools.

The shift from home-produced goods to goods produced by rural or urban specialized producers was one of the chief sources of the market expansion. This process proceeded along a number of lines. One of them was the expansion of intrarural trade, which was of two types. One involved an exchange of goods within single villages or between adjacent villages in particular micro-regions. The other type was between distant rural areas, involving goods produced by the rural population, but it was carried on by specialized traders and could be considered as an intervillage trade. Very little of both types of trade was recorded by the fiscal authorities or even described by observers. It is clear, however, that any shifts away from home-produced goods toward specialized production leading to a marketable surplus of either agricultural products or rural crafts found their way in the first

instance exactly into those two types of markets, ones that left almost no trace.

A parallel movement of an increasing volume of goods can be observed in the exchange between the countryside and the towns. This movement of goods was predicated upon an increasing differentiation of production between the two as well as upon the development of regional specialization. This trade differed from the intravillage and intervillage trade which, although extensive, consisted of very numerous small transactions with a large component of barter, transactions that were transformed into money exchanges only by the subsequent increasing monetization of the economy. The town-country trade was based on money transactions, and the "balance of trade" was probably maintained by the active participation of the serf-owning class and by the sales and purchases of the serf population.

Cloth and yarn, iron and ironwares, salt, alcohol, and some other goods of agricultural or forest origin were among the commodities that entered the town-country trade and were therefore traded over considerable distances. These were goods produced by both small-scale enterprises, cottage-type industries, and by large-scale enterprises such as mines, ironworks, and manufactories.

To understand this growth of longer-distance, intervillage and village-town trade (both of which were varieties of interregional trade), one must recall the pattern of industrial growth and specialization in Russia. Specialized production of hemp and flax, tallow and leather in particular agricultural regions was one of the features of this process. Another feature was the development of cottage-type, small-scale, rural enterprises that specialized in primary processing and the subsequent production of consumer goods; wool and hides, flax and hemp were used, yarn and linens, cloth and agricultural tools were made—all activities absorbing an inordinate volume of labor.

It was one of the characteristics of the Russian economy, in contrast with that of Western Europe, that many crafts were originally located and grew up in rural rather than in urban areas. The absence of a developed guild system prevented a monopolization of the crafts and the curtailment of the growing cottage industries. Competition within the cottage industries led to an increasing concentration and specialization by regions in the production of various goods. Examples were Pavlovo village and environs which specialized in the output of iron products, Ivanovo village (linen goods), Khimry village (leather footwear)—all growing industrial centers that were located outside designated urban areas and that succeeded in capturing for their goods large regional markets.

Both the industrial growth and the creation of regional markets in those industries cannot be attributed to the conventional heroes of eighteenth-century Russian industrialization such as Peter the Great, Demidov, and Shuvalov, and therefore these developments defy the one-sided analysis made by some Russian historians who have been fixed exclusively on large-scale production. This does not deny the significance for interregional domestic trade of the production by Russian manufactories or large-scale enterprises. The available estimates of Russian internal trade for the middle of the eighteenth century have not included the sales of salt and alcohol because they were exempted from internal tolls, even though their magnitude is known from direct evidence.

The volume of internal trade grew very rapidly during the eighteenth century, and particularly during its second half. This can be surmised from the growth of the money supply and the movement of prices. Both sets of data, even when incomplete, indicate that the volume of production and trade was larger than has been assumed by previous historians. Moreover, that volume increased very substantially and thus mitigated the inflationary impact of the growth of the money stock, at least until the second half of the 1780s.

Apart from the impact of monetization on the growth of internal trade, the real increases were a result of the increased real output of agriculture, craft, and industry, of a shift from household production for home consumption to production for the market, and of the expansion and regional specialization of markets. Growing foreign demand resulted in the collection of marketable surpluses, stimulated the production of new goods, and involved an increasing population in market activities. The demand by both the state and the serf-owning social class for additional income forced the tax and rent payers to increase their money incomes by working for hire or selling their output, thus driving them toward market activities. The last, but not least, factor in the growth of internal trade was the expansion of the social stratum directly involved in exchange transactions, the merchants.

The Institutional Setting

Analyzing eighteenth-century Russian internal trade is one of the most difficult tasks in Russian economic history. Two factors have contributed to our ignorance of this important topic. One is the paucity of available data: there are only three major published contemporary sources on Russian internal trade.[1] The second is the unwillingness on the part of Soviet historians to publish additional archival data on market activities. This can be explained by the accepted periodization of the history of the Russian economy and by the minimization of the role of market forces in Russian economic development. Until recently only N. L. Rubinshtein, S. G. Strumilin, I. D. Koval'chenko, and L. V. Milov tried to discuss some aspects of market formation. Fortunately in 1981 B. N. Mironov published a book on the internal market in which he cited many archival sources.[2]

The lack of congruence between our knowledge of Russia's foreign trade and its internal trade has been one of the most disturbing features of the state of the art in Russian economic history. It has obscured our understanding of the system of distribution that prevailed in Russia. We are still ignorant about Russian internal trade during the first half of the century,[3] and limited in ability to describe or analyze the dynamics of internal trade during the second half of the century. Nevertheless, it is possible to argue that a process of market expansion was occurring during the eighteenth century and that tendencies of market integration through interregional markets and the formation of a national market network were highly visible. I would therefore argue that there is no need for Soviet historians to deny the existence of extensive regional markets in the sixteenth century. Moreover, the working of the market ought to be "rediscovered" for the seventeenth century, if we are to achieve a realistic view of the history of the Russian economy and its continuity.

The system of goods distribution had to be very flexible to fulfill its economic function, because of the following factors: the general low population density; the existence of a moving agricultural frontier that expanded southward and eastward and thus created huge migratory population movements; the relatively low share of the urban population; the impact of serfdom upon occupational choices; the huge distances even within European Russia and the consequent high cost of goods transportation; and the high cost of transactions and high interest rates.

Table 5.1   The Growth of Fairs in Russia

Decade	In the Whole Territory			In a Comparable Territory		
	Urban	Rural	Total	Urban	Rural	Total
1750s	244	383	627	244	383	627
1760s	487	1,143	1,630	447	1,046	1,493
1790s	864	3,180	4,044	749	2,698	3,447

Source: Mironov, *Vnutrennii rynok*, pp. 62–63.

The backbone of the goods distribution system in eighteenth-century Russia was made up of periodic *fairs* located in a number of urban and rural settlements. They constituted the institutional arrangement for most of the wholesale trade and a substantial portion of the retail trade. *Bazaars* for markets with appointed market days during the week were another institutional arrangement in which some wholesale trade and much of the retail trade was conducted. Two additional arrangements that facilitated the supply of goods to consumers were stationary trade in stores and stalls, especially in the major cities, and the itinerant trade of peddlers in the countryside. These last two types of trading institutions were less developed than might be expected.

The most interesting feature of the two major institutions of trade, the fairs and the bazaars, was their simultaneous service as wholesale and retail channels and as centers of selling as well as the buying of goods. They combined the sale of imported goods with the mobilization of Russian goods for export abroad. The fairs are a good example of the mosaic of Russian internal trade. The available data lend support to a categorization of their trading activities. The data in table 5.1 assembled by the Soviet economic historian B. N. Mironov from various archival sources reflect the growth of the number of fairs in the second half of the eighteenth century.

The data in table 5.1 help to distinguish the growth of the fairs in the earlier territory of Russia from the growth of the fairs in the territory that resulted from the military and political expansion of the imperial boundaries, especially during the 1770s and 1790s. They also show the important distribution between fairs in urban and rural areas. The distribution of fairs

Table 5.2   Settlements with Fairs

Decades	Urban	Rural	Total
1750s	144	323	467
1760s	244	615	839
1790s	366	1,795	2,161

Source: Mironov, *Vnutrennii rynok*, p. 56.

Table 5.3   Number of Settlements with Fairs and Number of Fairs

Years	Settlements	Fairs	Fairs per Settlement
1770	836	1,623	1.94
1800	2,152	4,028	1.87

by the type of settlements is provided in table 5.2. Comparing tables 5.1 and 5.2, one discovers not only the faster growth of the number of fairs located in rural areas, but also the growth of the number of fairs per rural settlement, something that indicates the growing scope and intensity of rural trade.

The growing intensity of rural trade becomes especially apparent in a comparison of the total number of fairs and the total number of settlements for two dates, 1770 and 1800. The data indicate that the number of fairs per settlement remained quite stable throughout the last third of the century.

The growth of fairs in the rural areas can also be discerned by comparing the distribution of rural fairs by location with the distribution of the various groups of the Russian serfs by ownership. The data in table 5.4 permit the derivation of the approximate size of the "hinterland" of the rural fairs, but also a comparison of the density of the fairs for the various groups of serfs.

Table 5.4   Rural Fairs and the Composition of the Serf Population

	Fairs		Male Serfs (in 1,000)		Male Serfs per Fair	
	1760	1800	1778	1795	1760s	1790s
Private serfs	413	1,615	5,612	9,788	13,588	6,061
State serfs	539	1,153	2,781	4,548	5,160	3,944
Court serfs	22	54	524	521	23,818	9,648
Former church serfs	95	167	1,061	1,465	11,168	8,772
Unknown	74	191				
Total	1,143	3,180	9,978	16,322	8,730	5,133

Table 5.5   Geographic Distribution of Settlements and Fairs by
Major Regions

	Settlements		Fairs	
	1770	1800	1770	1800
Nonblacksoil	176	583	244	852
% of total	21	27	15	21
Ukraine	169	231	507	730
% of total	20	11	31	18
Blacksoil, northwest	125	237	213	445
% of total	15	11	13	11
Blacksoil, southeast	84	224	123	396
% of total	10	10	8	10
All fairs, Incl. above	836	2,172	1,623	4,028

Source: Mironov, *Vnutrennii rynok*, pp. 74–75.

The increased density of the fairs, in terms of population, and their increasing frequency did not necessarily lead to a decrease in the trade turnover. If my assumptions about the growth of the planted area and the agricultural output of the last third of the eighteenth century are correct, both the growing marketability and the increasing purchasing power compensated for the growth of the density of the fairs. In fact, the increasing number of fairs was a response to the growing marketability of agriculture.

The growth of settlements with fairs and of the number of fairs per se proceeded at different paces which depended upon population changes and economic growth in the various regions of Russia. During the period 1770–1800 the highest growth rate, both in absolute terms and as a share of the total, took place in the nonblacksoil zone. It was the result of increasing urbanization and the development of craft and industry. As is evident in table 5.5, the share of the southern provinces (Malorossiia, the Ukraine) declined relative to the nonblacksoil zone.

The geographic or regional distribution of fairs is not the only important factor in assessing their role in internal trade. Also necessary is a sense of their distribution by the volume of their sales. The majority of fairs during the 1790s were small ones with a trade turnover of less than 10,000 rubles. There were 2,202 such fairs or 69.7 percent of the total 3,195. In the middle range were 590, or 18.7 percent of the fairs, with a turnover of from 11,000 to 100,000 rubles. The large ones, 367 or 11.6 percent, had a turnover of over 100,000 rubles. At both extremes of the distribution were 23 percent of the fairs, with sales of less than 1,000 rubles, and 3.7 percent, with sales of over a million rubles. On the basis of the distribution of all fairs in the 1790s by the size of their turnover, B. N. Mironov estimated the average at 15,700 silver rubles. When that figure is multiplied by the estimated total number of fairs (4,044), one derives a total volume of sales amounting to 63,491,000 rubles, or Mironov's estimate of 64,000,000 for the 1790s.[4]

Only a limited number of fairs at the end of the eighteenth century have left records on the number of their participants. Mironov, trying to estimate participation, reduced the number of the participants in his sample by a third and estimated their number as about 1,400,000 during the 1760s and 5,800,000 for the 1790s.[5] If one accepts his estimate, the purchases per participant in the fairs were 10.95 rubles. The estimated number of participants in the fairs for the two periods constituted, respectively, 9 and 16 percent of the population, and one can derive from that the per capita purchases.

The fairs attracted sellers and buyers from beyond the county in which they were located. In fact, only 278 of all of the fairs were exclusively county fairs. About one-third of all fairs attracted participants from counties located within a particular province (*guberniia*); 638 fairs attracted participants from the counties of adjacent provinces and 558 from adjacent districts and, therefore, should be considered regional fairs. Seventy-six fairs attracted participants from various regions and from abroad, which made them truly national in scope. An interesting feature of the fairs was their relatively short duration: 2,455, or 77.7 percent, lasted from 1 to 3 days and 545, or 17.3 percent, lasted from 4 to 7 days. Only 5 percent of the fairs on which there are data lasted more than a week.

There was no strict specialization of the fairs in terms of the commodities sold or purchased. Nevertheless, depending on their location, the season, and the sellers and buyers they attracted, some of the fairs gained a comparative advantage over others in the trade of certain commodities. Food products were traded at two-thirds of all the fairs (or 2,146 fairs), but 42 fairs specialized in the trade of industrial crops such as flax and hemp. At 149 fairs large-scale purchases of goods destined for export were made. At 2,639 fairs domestic goods were sold, and at only 271 fairs were imported goods traded in bulk. At 1,974 fairs, chiefly rural ones, Russian peasants sold their own output, whether agricultural or handicraft, and at 332 fairs professional traders traded with one another.

The fairs presented a broad and varied panorama of goods-exchange. They were differentiated in size and some degree of specialization appeared. The smaller fairs were connected to the middle-sized ones, the middle-sized ones to the larger ones. It would be a mistake to apply central-place-theory analysis to Russian fairs and then view them primarily as a system of clusters in which a certain number of major fairs were operating and each had its supply source and hinterland consisting of concentric rings of middle and smaller fairs. It would be much more correct to view the fairs as a well-functioning network fed by two streams of commodity flows. One stream moved from the wholesalers dealing in manufactured goods and imports and got thinner as it moved from the major to the minor fairs. The other stream flowed in the opposite direction and supplied agricultural goods and raw materials for domestic and export use. The second stream grew and swelled as it moved from the local to the regional and national fairs. The two were not necessarily in equilibrium at each level and therefore could not necessarily have conducted barter transactions. Besides those two flows, there were others. One was from the grain surplus to the grain deficit regions within the country, and there were still others. Money was important in facilitating trade in the multiple directions; it was spent, withdrawn from the market, and lent on different terms.

The operation of the fairs as a network in which there existed as much horizontal as vertical interdependence becomes much clearer when one considers the timing of the fairs. Their timing reminds one of a train schedule in which the main trunk lines are synchronized and the feeder lines are then adjusted in their schedules to the trunk lines. Although the government decreed the schedules of fairs in the eighteenth century, unquestionably they developed gradually, organically, and were based on the proved behavior of sellers and buyers, rather than on the whims of bureaucrats.

"Ecological" elements, such as interruptions in fieldwork (between plowing and hay mowing, between hay mowing and grain harvesting, and right after the harvest), had an impact on the timing and frequency of fairs. The presence of major church holidays (in May, Boris and Gleb, Nicholas the Miracle Worker, Constantine and Helena; in June, the Vladimir and Tikhvin Holy Virgin, Peter and Paul; in September, the Mother of God, St. John) facilitated the scheduling of fairs. It was also crucial that the roads and waterways be passable, which explains why two-thirds of all fairs were held from May through September. June had the largest number, 610 of 3,159 whose dates are known. Moreover, by June and July the peasants who hired themselves out for various kinds of work were sending home the first installments of their earned wages. Wages earned later were in part spent to pay rents and taxes (the latter were payable semiannually on December 15 and March 1).

The timing of the fairs underscored the patterns and directions of the commodity flows. It also determined the itinerant nature of the trade required of traders, who were on the move for large parts of the year. A few major fairs which served the region of the northern Ukraine and a part of the Russian blacksoil provinces and which constituted a part of the total integrated network of fairs illustrate their interde-

pendence, the relative efficiency of their operations, and the manner in which they provided the participating merchants with an opportunity to achieve a higher annual turnover of their capital. The timing was as follows (dates in parentheses): goods received from Moscow were brought to the fair in Sumy (22 November to 6 December), from there to Khar'kov (6 January to 6 February), from there to Maslianskaia in Romny (17 to 30 February), from there to Elizavetgrad (21 to 29 April), from there to Voznesenskaia in Romny (20 July to 1 August), from there back to Khar'kov (15 August to 1 September), from there to Krolevets (14 to 26 September), and from there back to Khar'kov (1 October to 1 November).

Another aspect of the location of the fairs points not only to their location in the context of their hinterland, the population inhabiting the area which supplied and purchased goods at the fairs, but also to the location of the major fairs with respect to their distances from one another. Normally only about 60 to 65 percent of the goods brought to a major fair were sold there. The rest was transported to other fairs, where it had a chance of being sold. Thus the distances among the major fairs had to be reasonable in terms of travel time and transportation costs.

A list of the twenty-seven largest fairs points to their location along an internal ring that covered the territory of the central areas and lines that connected the central area with the boundaries or fringes of the empire. The list includes the following fairs and their general locations.

1. Makar'evskaia—near Nizhnii Novgorod on the Volga.
2. Irbitskaia—east of the Ural mountains in western Siberia.
3. Korennaia—in Kursk.
4–7. Kreshchenskaia, Pokrovskaia, Uspenskaia—in Khar'kov, Ukraine.
8–10. Maslianskaia, Voznesenskaia, Il'inskaia—in Romny, Ukraine.
11. Sbornaia—in Rostov, Iaroslavl' province.
12. Vvedenskaia—in Sumy, Ukraine.
13. Kontraktnaia Kievskaia—Kiev, Ukraine.
14. Krestovozdvizhenskaia—in Krolevets.
15. Vseednaia—in Nezhin, northern Ukraine.
16. Syrnaia—in Novgorod-Seversk, Ukraine.
17. Svenskaia—in Briansk.
18. Blagoveshchenskaia Vazhskaia—in Vaga.
19. Uriupinskaia—in Uriupinsk.
20. Troitskaia—in Troitsk, near the Urals.
21. Orenburg—in Orenburg, Siberia.
22. Rizhskaia—in Riga, Baltic port.
23. Arkhangel'skaia—in Arkhangel'sk, White Sea port.
24. Irkutskaia—Irkutsk, Siberia.
25. Eniseiskaia—in Eniseisk, Siberia.

Table 5.6   Settlements with Bazaars, and Market Days per Week

Decades	No. of Settlements with Bazaars			Total No. of Market Days per Week		
	Urban	Rural	Total	Urban	Rural	Total
1750s	209	165	374	398	177	575
1760s	278	193	471	428	209	637
1790s	513	570	1,083	722	608	1,330

26. Iakutskaia—in Iakutsk, Siberia.

27. Kiakhtinskaia—in Kiakhta, Chinese border.

The dating of four of them serves as an example of accommodation to an existing interdependence among the major fairs. In 1728 the dates for the Makar'ev fair were reset for June 29 to July 8, instead of the earlier dates of July 25 to August 1. The government explained that the change was required by the merchants' need to arrive at the Svenskaia fair by August 1, and then to proceed from there to Krolevets for the opening of its fair on September 15.[6] While the dates for the Makar'ev fair were changed, the dates of the Korennaia fair in Kursk were moved ahead two months to enable the merchants participating in it to make themselves ready for the Makar'ev fair. In 1749 the date for the Krolevets fair was changed "to give the Makar'ev and Svenskaia fairs more freedom."[7]

Similar accommodations taking into account both the distance and the travel time were made with respect to the route between the Makar'ev and the Irbit fairs, and the intermediary fairs located along the Siberian trail all the way to Kiakhta. These two examples illustrate the existence of the interdependence which was one of the marks of the system of fairs. Such routes, complete with supply schedules, sources of resupply, and easily arranged outlets for transportation in various directions are among at least a dozen that harmoniously made up the system of fairs in eighteenth century Russia.

No description of the fairs and their characterizations as a part of the distribution system would be complete without mentioning the role of Moscow and St. Petersburg. St. Petersburg was the main gateway through which imported goods entered Russia and exports left. Peter's capital was the destination of most of the flax, hemp, seeds, tallow, furs, and forest products gathered in the various regions of Russia, as well as the port of entry for foreign cloth, dyestuffs, and luxury items that were disseminated through the fairs. Moscow, on the other hand, was the center of distribution through which domestically produced manufactured goods were assembled and whence they were injected into the system of fairs through the main trunk lines of goods movement described above. Consequently the two capitals were vital links in the chain of operation of fairs.

Besides the fairs, the so-called *bazaar* or market was the second important institutional arrangement of internal trade. These were markets that operated during certain days of the week in places especially designated for transactions between buyers and sellers of goods. The data presented in table 5.6 indicate the number of settlements, urban or rural, in which such markets existed, as well as the number of market days per week on which the bazaars functioned.

The data in table 5.6 suggest a gradual pattern of growth of urban bazaars and an accelerated growth of rural bazaars during the decades of the 1760s to 1790s. The number of bazaars grew in the smaller urban centers, in which one market day per week was sufficient. The rural bazaars rarely lasted more than one day, which resulted in a slower growth of market days than of the number of markets. During the 1760s and 1770s Fridays and Sundays were the most popular market days and accounted for 30 and 18 percent of all the market days, respectively.

Retail trade prevailed in the bazaars, which served as loci for the sale and purchase of foodstuffs and handicrafts by urban and rural craftsmen. Merchants of the second corporation purchased the agricultural surplus at the bazaars to resell to the wholesalers at fairs. Sales of grains, vegetables, livestock products, and domestically manufactured goods, produced to meet peasant demand, dominated the bazaar trade.

That trade, far more than the fair trade, was affected by seasonal fluctuations. Its peaks were during the early autumn and middle winter months. It declined precipitously during the seasons of heavy agricultural work. It was attuned to the rhythm of agricultural work and life. It was affected by the life-style of the smaller cities and towns in which the urban population made its purchases of foodstuffs in season, at lower prices and in large quantities. This seasonal distribution of the bazaar trade had additional significance because it differed from the seasonal features of the fair trade, which thereby tended to spread out trade, and the earnings from trade, more evenly during the year than otherwise would have been the case in view of the domination of the fairs. This also increased the velocity of money and capital engaged in trade.

As in the case of fairs, the bazaars were stratified by size. Alongside small rural markets there were huge markets serving the inhabitants of adjacent counties, bazaars with a relatively high volume of trade, and bazaars in major cities which drew large crowds of buyers and sellers. The large city-bazaars had a greater assortment of goods and attracted not only peasants but also members of the local nobility, local officials, army officers from neighboring military garrisons, and other figures not of lower-class origin. At such bazaars the sale of industrial and imported manufactured goods constituted a higher percentage of sales than at the bazaars of the smaller towns or in the rural markets.

It is almost impossible to estimate the number of participants in the bazaar trade, or even the number of sellers in those markets. Since neither the peasants bringing their products to the market (surprisingly, much grain was sold in such markets) nor the craftsmen selling their wares had to pay any fees, data for their turnover do not exist. It is known, however, that the bazaar market trade, not the fairs, was the domain of the second corporation merchants. Their number was relatively small: the best estimate for the years 1764–66 is about 13,200 men. In general, however, there is no information on how many active, steady participants there were in the bazaar trade nor what the trade turnover was at that institution for goods distribution.

During the last third of the eighteenth century the bazaar trade-network became more evenly distributed over the territory of the empire. This was partially the result of territorial expansion and partially the consequence of increasing urbanization. For example, in 1770 the nonblacksoil and blacksoil zones and the Ukraine accounted for 67 percent of the settlements with bazaars and 64 percent of the number of bazaars; by 1800 the share of those regions in the total was only 51 and 52 percent, respectively. This was a period of relatively rapid growth of bazaars, which more than doubled their number.

Still another form of goods distribution was the itinerant trade in the Russian countryside. During the eighteenth century the bearers of this trade were primarily the merchants of the smaller provincial towns and their agents, for whom several bazaars and infrequent rural fairs provided insufficient income. What started for some of those merchants as an auxiliary activity later became full-time. The economic rationale for the itinerant trade was the opportunity to bring directly to the villages goods for the peasants' household needs and to obtain some of the agricultural surplus that the peasants decided to sell or barter, but were not because of the costs involved. By saving the peasants both time and transportation costs, those merchants justified ob-

taining an appropriate price differential on the traded goods. The transactions involved both cash and barter, and less often, credit arrangements. The last became more widespread during the nineteenth century, when peasants themselves began on a larger scale to perform the functions of the itinerant merchants. Knowing more intimately the customers of their own or adjacent villages, such peasant-merchants were able to extend credit even against future crops at prices often dictated by the lenders.

The itinerant merchants, recruited from the small towns and rural areas, traveled in wagons with their wares or walked with their boxes as peddlers. They were referred to by different names and distinguished by a number of characteristic traits. Some, called *ofeni*, traveled in wagons and dealt primarily in cheap cottons, costume jewelry, needles, buttons, small mirrors, and similar items. Their travels started in August or September and brought them home in May or June. Others who traveled by foot and peddled out of boxes they carried were called *korobeiniki* (in reference to the boxes), operated within a smaller radius and on a smaller scale, and had to replenish their wares more often that did the *ofeni*. A third group, called *slobozhanie* (from *slobody* or settlements of Old Believers), traveled considerable distances from their homes. They constituted a special network, which consisted of a wealthy merchant, a certain number of overseers, and many petty traders. The last were supplied with merchandise and received a 10 percent commission on the value of goods sold.

The itinerant trade supplemented the other institutional forms of internal trade. It reached the female members of peasant households and helped to bring into the market the rural goods which were the domain of female labor but, because of their small volume, otherwise would have remained outside the market sphere. The activities of the itinerant traders caused such goods to be sold or bartered for commodities for which there was a household demand. In the newly acquired Polish territories located in Belorussia, Lithuania, and the right-bank Ukraine, the function of the itinerant traders was performed by local Jewish traders and peddlers from the small towns who traveled into the countryside to reach their customers. The itinerant trade required no license and the range of incomes from this activity varied; consequently an estimation of the scope or value of this form of trade is impossible.

The last form of institutionalized trade was the stationary retail trade in stores, continuously operating trading establishments. During the period under consideration, such establishments were located almost exclusively in urban centers, predominantly in the large cities. Information exists on retail stores in

209 urban settlements for the 1750s, 278 urban settlements for the 1760s, and 578 urban settlements for the 1790s. In 1790 a total of 14,060 retail stores were reported by 151 cities, an average of 93 stores per city. Such an average clearly obscures a bipolar distribution. Moscow and St. Petersburg had a large number of stores. Already in the seventeenth century Moscow had approximately 4,000 trading establishments. Kazan' had about 850 stores by the end of the eighteenth century, while Simbirsk had only 223.[8] The county-seat towns of Moscow *guberniia* in 1785 reported a total of 902 stores for 12 towns, or about 75 stores per town. Once again, the variance was great: Kolomna and Serpukhov each had more than 200 stores, Podol'sk and Zvenigorod had only 13 and 9 stores, respectively.[9]

There were no retail stores in the countryside for the following reasons: the limited purchasing power of the peasantry combined with a relatively high degree of self-sufficiency, an access to fairs, bazaars, and itinerant traders; and the seasonal nature of income receipts and expenditures by the peasantry. A prohibition imposed in 1755 on the operation of rural stores by nonrural residents made it more difficult to transfer capital from the traders to entrepreneurial peasants and thus to set up stores even in the larger villages. The rarity of stores in the smaller towns can be explained not only by the presence of and competition with the other institutions of trade, but also by the fact that the inhabitants of such places produced vegetables, dairy products, and often meat within their households; they purchased other products quasi-wholesale. Clothing items lasted for a long time and fashions hardly changed (except perhaps for the nobility), and thus retail trade in small towns could not support the owners of such establishments.

Only the major cities, whose populations were separated from agricultural activities and possessed sufficient purchasing power to demand a broad assortment of domestic and foreign manufactured goods in addition to food and other products of agricultural origin, could support continuously functioning and even specialized retail outlets. The urban stores catered to the tastes of the more affluent strata of the population and also supplied goods of perhaps inferior quality to the relatively large numbers of household servants, craftsmen, and laborers living in the cities. In the major cities the stores were located in the traditional Russian manner in special rows (*riady*), concentrated in and near the merchants' inns (*gostinyi dvor*), and also were distributed among the extended neighborhoods. The reported turnover in the retail stores (*lavki*) by the end of the century ranged from 200 to 4,000 silver rubles per establishment, a fact which suggests great variation in the size of such stores. The size and growth of sales through those urban stores depended both on the degree of urbanization and to a more limited extent on the competition with the other forms of trade, such as the bazaars and fairs.

There were other institutional arrangements of goods distribution besides those discussed above. A sizable part of the internal trade was carried on by the government. Examples are the sale of alcoholic beverages through the government ale houses (*kabaki*) and the sale of salt, another state monopoly. Although a discussion of the internal market should include both the functions and the effects of alcohol and salt sales to the population, government trade has been omitted from this section. Those topics have been discussed elsewhere with emphasis on their fiscal aspects because market decisions were primarily administrative, even when they were not devoid of economic rationale. Omitting government sales as a special form of internal trade poses no serious methodological problems so long as their dimensions are considered.

A problem to be considered is whether the institutions of internal trade—the fairs, bazaars, the itinerant country trade, and the urban retail trade establishments—constituted an integrated network, or whether they acted as different functional or territorial units that were poorly integrated with one another. There are two schools of thought in Soviet historiography on whether there was a unified national market for commodity trade during the eighteenth century. One views the second half of the eighteenth century as the time when a national market for many commodities was formed.[10] The other school until very recently assumed that there was an identity between an integrated market and a full-blown capitalist formation. Consequently the adherents of the latter school claimed that the first view clashed with the fundamental Soviet periodization of Russian history, which has placed the development of capitalism in Russia in the post-emancipation period, after 1861.

I have a bias in favor of recognizing market forces in the Russian economy and reject the myth that the Russian state successfully put the entire economy into a Procrustean bed of state controls and that things happened only because of exclusive state initiative. I therefore view the process of market formation during the eighteenth century as much more advanced than official Soviet historical doctrine would allow.

The leading official historians have modified their stand somewhat and now argue that a development of capitalism in Russia presupposes the existence of well-developed commodity markets. They also portray the eighteenth-century market formation process as a very slow one in which the forces of market integration required another century to achieve the goal of a unified market. A recent empirical study of grain prices by two leading Soviet economic historians, I. D. Koval'chenko and L. V. Milov, presented such weak grain price-correlations that it was almost impossible to argue for the existence of an integrated national grain market.[11] When one discovers the incompleteness of the primary data upon which the grain price-correlations were based, however, one's confidence in an analysis based upon economic logic is restored and one can embrace the conclusion that, for most of the major commodities, the internal market achieved a high measure of integration.

The available evidence on the trade contacts existing among the fairs and between the fairs and the bazaars, the frequency of those contacts, the choices available, the existing degree of competition, the relationship between internal and foreign trade, the dependence of price responses and commodity movements on changes in disposable income and seasonal variations in the volume of money in circulation, all point unmistakably in the direction of rapid progress toward market unification and integration in the second half of the eighteenth century. To be sure, high interest rates, high transaction costs, and high transportation costs acted as brakes on the process of market integration, but they could not stop the process.

The Composition of the Merchant Class

Russian domestic trade, unlike foreign trade, was the domain of the local, native merchants. The struggle of the Russian merchants for a monopoly in domestic trade not only against foreigners, but also against members of other estates, had an old history. By the middle of the eighteenth century the Russian merchants had lost their battle against the nobility, and also against the serf traders who operated their own businesses in the names of their masters. Nevertheless, they won against the foreigners, who were barred from internal Russian trade.

What did the Russian merchants represent as an employment group and as a social class? They were defined as the preponderant urban element of Russian society, and therefore the term "merchant" as commonly used was broader than the one describing individuals pursuing independent private activity in the distribution of goods. It was a reference term for the urban estate and included, in addition to merchants proper, also craftsmen and plebeian elements of the urban population in some way connected with commerce and crafts.

As members of an estate, merchants were liable to carry out some compulsory state-service obligations. In return, they were granted protection, certain im-

Table 5.7   Distribution of Guild Membership in Moscow by Trade and Hired Labor

	Trade	Hired	Total
1761			
1st guild	637	150	787
2d guild	2,072	1,723	3,795
3d guild	911	3,452	4,363
Total	3,620	5,325	8,945
1764			
1st guild	614	8	622
2d guild	1,846	1,412	3,258
3d guild	901	2,203	3,104
Total	3,361	3,623	6,984

Source: Vartanov, "Kupechestvo," pp. 276–77.

munities, and a trade monopoly. The merchants, unlike members of the so-called "service class," paid taxes. As a group, the merchants were not directly obligated to perform continuous government services, although its members could and were called upon to perform individual services on an irregular basis in some of the areas of their expertise, such as collecting customs duties.

One of the difficult tasks of the economic analysis of eighteenth-century Russian merchants is to separate the merchants engaged in trade from the population legally defined as merchants but not employed in trade.

Even the registration of the urban population in separate merchant and craft "guilds" or corporations did not succeed in separating the trading from the non-trading population. The vast majority of urban residents preferred to be registered in the merchant "guilds," even though they did not trade but hired themselves out for all kinds of work. This tendency is illustrated in table 5.7 by an example of the Moscow guild membership in the years 1761 and 1764.

The Moscow data suggest what is confirmed by the evidence from other cities and towns: the official estimates of the trading population are an inaccurate guide to the actual number of traders in Russia. On the one hand, the officially designated number of traders includes a large number of non-trading individuals. On the other hand, it excludes a large group of trading peasants, whose role in trade was increasing rapidly after the 1750s.

One should logically expect that the real merchants must have attempted to separate themselves from those who were merchants in name only but who shared with them their privileges and general status. Unfortunately, there are no documentary sources reflecting such an inner struggle within the officially defined merchant class. One can therefore judge only on the basis of later events.

During the fourth quarter of the century a successful attempt was made to separate the actively trading

Table 5.8   Guild Capital Requirements

Year	1st Guild	2d Guild	3d Guild
1775	10,000	1,000	500
1785	10,000	5,000	1,000
1794	16,000	8,000	2,000
1807	50,000	20,000	8,000

Source: Ryndziunskii, *Gorodskoe grazhdanstvo*, p. 42.

merchants from the rest. It was in part at least carried out by increasing the capital requirement (table 5.8) that entitled one to be included in a particular guild. In real terms, the significant increase was enacted during 1785 for the second guild, a fact best seen in table 5.9 by correcting the data for changes in the value of money by using either of the two existing indexes (the Brzhevskii ruble-silver ratio or the Strumilin grain price-index) as deflators. The 1785 move probably resulted in some elimination of the "inferior" elements from the second guild and their transfer into the third.

The capitalization increase for the third guild both in 1785 and in 1794 probably served as a deterrent which prevented some outside elements from trying to get into the category of merchants. During the subsequent years of the eighteenth century the change in the value of money eroded most of the increase enacted in 1794, and the increases of 1807 were promulgated to maintain the barriers to entrance and to modify the differentials between the guilds.

The attempts by the merchants to draw a line of distinction between their group and the general urban dwellers (described by the newly introduced term *meshchane*) perhaps can be explained by the merchants' lack of success in their fight against the gentry and the industrial entrepreneurs for the maintenance of their previous trading monopoly. Consequently the merchants tried to decrease the upward mobility into their class for the urban plebeians and thereby decrease the number of competitors.

Regardless of the effectiveness of this effort, the attempts to prevent the upward mobility of the trading peasants into the merchant class were certainly not very effective. Generally speaking, during the eighteenth century such upward mobility went through certain phases: substantial mobility existed at the beginning of the century, it was diminished around the middle of the century, and it intensified at the end of the period. The patterns of mobility of the early and middle parts of the century are supported by evidence available for one stratum of the rural population, the court peasants.

Upward social mobility was tantamount to overcoming existing legal and institutional barriers, primarily by accumulating capital. This was congruent with the attitudes of the state, which determined the legal requirements for entrance into the merchant class. For example, a Petrine decree of April 13, 1722, admitted into the ranks of the merchants the *raznochintsy* and trading peasants whose annual total sales exceeded a minimum of 500 rubles or who possessed a minimum of 300 rubles of their own capital.[12]

Opportunities to cross the status boundary by engaging in nonagricultural activities and accumulating capital were by no means equal for all groups of the Russian peasantry. The relative success of the court peasants was facilitated by their concentration in areas of high population density, a situation conducive to the development of trade. Moreover, legislation and procedures concerning court peasants were more specific (if not more lenient) on the possibilities of changing their legal status than they were for private serfs.

A decree of 1699 permitted court peasants "engaged in trade and possessing property" (*torgovye i pozhitochnye liudi*) to register in towns and cities.[13] This set the policy pattern for the Petrine period. Only later did a change occur, when post-Petrine legislation made former serfs liable to deportation from the cities should they lose their initial capital. The tax burden on peasant-merchants was a double one that included both the poll tax and the merchant tax. Elizabethan legislation required that the double taxes be paid not only by the first generation, but also by their heirs.[14]

The mere availability of capital in 1747 was declared insufficient for entrance into the merchant class, and ownership of urban real estate or urban-located businesses became a requirement. Once the acquisition of urban real estate became mandatory for merchant status, a legal vicious circle prevented the peasants from entering the merchant class. Both the opposition of the merchants against entry into their class and, even more important, the gentry's demand for uniform treatment of state and privately owned serfs gradually forced the government to depart from the Petrine attitudes and policies on change of status by state and court serfs. In 1750 a decree was published which prohibited court peasants from changing their status without specific personal permission from the monarch.[15] Moreover, all court peasants who in the past had changed their status by other procedures had to be returned to the jurisdiction of the "Court Administration" (*Dvortsovoe vedomstvo*). (Of course governmental policy was not absolutely consistent. While a real tightening occurred with regard to court serfs' mobility, some ecclesiastical serfs from the village of Ostashkovo were admitted to the status of urban dwellers.)[16]

Table 5.9 Guild Capital Requirements, Deflated by Brzheskii's Ruble-Silver Ratio and by Strumilin's Grain Price Index

Year	Brzheskii's Index			Strumilin's Index		
	1st Guild	2d Guild	3d Guild	1st Guild	2d Guild	3d Guild
1775	10,000	1,000	500	10,000	1,000	500
1785	10,000	5,000	1,000	6,660	3,330	666
1794	11,460	5,730	1,433	8,000	4,000	1,000
1807	27,000	10,800	4,320	n.a.	n.a.	n.a.

Sources: Brzheskii, *Gosudarstvennye dolgi*; Strumilin, *Istoriia*.

The general change in government policy from a recognition of economic advancement as a sufficient reason to change an individual's status to a virtual prohibition against the entrance of court peasants into the merchant class is reflected in quantitative data surviving from the first quarter of the century and the 1760s. During the years 1722–28 3,426 court-peasant households were registered in merchant and urban craft guilds, or about 3.3 percent of the 101,651 court-peasant households. For the period around 1760, however, there were only 1,869 court-peasant members in the guilds. The second document provides an interesting territorial distribution: the capitals accounted for 731 households (Moscow, 577; St. Petersburg, 154); the central region, 661; the Volga region, 169; the North, 105; the blacksoil region, 93; the eastern region and Siberia, 83.[17] The decrease in 1760 reflected both the attrition stemming from the failure of some to make the transition to the higher status a permanent one and the forced reconversion to their previous status of some who had succeeded.

The fourth quarter of the century provided new opportunities to peasants striving to elevate themselves to the status of merchants or burghers. Trade expanded, licensing in areas of industrial entrepreneurship was abolished, and some villages and settlements (*slobody*) acquired urban status. The largest conversion of such settlements into urban and administrative centers occurred at the time of the 1775 *guberniia* reform, which designated many new county seats (*uezdnye goroda*) whose inhabitants automatically obtained the status of burghers or merchants.[18] The Soviet historian E. I. Indova listed 3,422 court peasants in eight new towns whose status was changed to that of urban dwellers on this occasion, more than was accomplished during the entire first half of the century. That did not mean that all the former peasants in those towns turned into merchants, but that opportunities for unhampered trading activities were opened formally to thousands of those who had been rural inhabitants.

Upward mobility was not limited to peasants rising into the merchant class. Members of the merchant class also had avenues of upward mobility into the superior estate, the Russian nobility. Economic fac-

tors and means in this case played a role similar to the one they played in the case of lower elements entering the merchant class. Money was able to overcome the barriers between the estates, regardless of how jealously the nobility protected its exclusive status. The government in some cases was instrumental in such mobility and assisted such status transitions in the name of "recognizing benefits to the economy and general welfare." This formula was used more often in cases of merchants turned industrial entrepreneurs or tax farmers than for those still engaged directly and exclusively in trade. It was also applied to merchants who combined trading activities with government service. Table 5.10 classifies ennobled merchants in terms of their occupations at the time of the awarding of nobility patents and in terms of their previous occupations. The prevalence of industrialists and tax farmers becomes evident from the twenty-six cases classified in table 5.10.

From an economic point of view there was a fundamental difference between the upward mobility at the one extreme of the merchant class and that at the other extreme. At one end was an influx of an energetic element, perhaps poor in capital resources, but one which was climbing the economic ladder. At the other end there was a decline of entrepreneurial drive, often accompanied by a withdrawal of very substantial capital resources from industry and trade, and sometimes a conversion to a life of spending and conspicuous consumption. Politically, the transfer of a part of the elite to another estate had a detrimental impact on the struggle of the merchant class for recognition of its economic role and its legitimate economic interests. Transfer into the nobility also caused a weakening of the merchant elite and all the social and psychological consequences that ensue from such a development.

There were at least three "generations" of merchant elites in the eighteenth century. The first generation, a transitional one from the seventeenth century, involved a group recruited from the urban (*posad*) population, hierarchically organized, with the provincial merchants at the bottom and the merchants in the capitals near the top of the pyramid. The very apex of the pyramid was occupied by the

Table 5.10   Recipients of Nobility Patents by Industrialists, Merchants, and Tax Farmers During the Eighteenth Century

Name	Occupation	Previous Occupation
N. A. Demidov	Industrialist	Merchant and artisan (Tula)
A. Batashov (1788)	Industrialist	Merchant and artisan (Tula)
A. N. Goncharov (1789)	Industrialist	Merchant and artisan (Kaluga)
I. S. Miasnikov (1758)	Industrialist	Merchant
I. B. Tverdyshev (1758)	Industrialist	Merchant
P. G. Krasilnikov (1790)	Industrialist	Merchant
Pokhodiashin	Industrialist	Merchant
Luginin	Industrialist	Merchant (Tula)
F. Maltsev (1775)	Industrialist	Merchant and artisan (Tula)
A. F. Turchaninov (1783)		
Nechaev	Industrialist	
M. P. Mosolov (1790)	Industrialist	
L. Lazarev (1774)	Merchant	
Rukavishnikov	Merchant	
Evreinov	Merchant	
Varentsov	Merchant	
Solov'ev	Merchant	(Arkhangel'sk)
Kurochkin	Merchant	
Ustinov	Tax farmer	Merchant
Riumin	Tax farmer	Merchant
Rogovikov	Tax farmer	Merchant
S. Iakovlev	Tax farmer	Merchant (Ostashkov)
Orlov-Denisov	Tax farmer	Merchant
Shemiakin	Tax farmer	Merchant
Khliustin	Tax farmer	Merchant
Loginov	Tax farmer	Merchant

merchants of the first corporation (the *gosti*) and then the members of the second and third corporations, the "merchants'" and the "woolen cloth hundreds" (the *gostinaia* and *sukonnaia sotni*). (The second and third corporations remind one of the merchants-adventurers and the mercers guild in London at an earlier time.) These corporations embraced and distinguished the richest merchants. In addition to being singled out in terms of prestige, they were often targets for government service, which, as they often complained, ruined their private business during their absence on government assignments. (Their complaints contained a kernel of truth, but were highly exaggerated. Their service was not excessively frequent, their firms were elaborately organized, and they were often appointed to serve precisely in those places with which they were familiar because of their business experience. The consequence was that they probably had ample time to carry on at least part of their trade. These calculations, of course, do not take into consideration the fact that sometimes merchants on government assignment were called upon to make up official shortfalls out of their personal means.)

This elite, defined primarily in terms of its relative wealth, was devoid of most of the attributes of the patriciate of early modern Western European cities. Its members also lacked the scope and wealth of the later Western European commercial princes. Operating under conditions of market uncertainty and shift-ing governmental trade policies, the Russian merchant elite generally did not exhibit an ingrained aversion to risk. The Siberian fur trade and the trade with such areas as Bukhara and China demonstrate as much enterprising spirit as did the activities of their counterparts in other countries. On the other hand, the degree of uncertainty forced them to spread their risk, to avoid specialization, and to prefer investment in land to industrial investment. When forced by the government, or enticed by an expectation of high profit rates, they invested in industrial plants, but still they did not surrender their commercial activities.

Even the richest of that particular generation, the ones who built up quite elaborate and well-functioning trade organizations in their firms, were engaged in both wholesale and retail trade. Their degree of specialization, in terms of either separation of wholesale from retail trade or concentration on a limited number of commodities, was not very high. This generation of merchants, from among whom Peter the Great selected his servants for special tasks such as organizing new institutions (the *ratusha* or *magistrat*), for managing new areas of state and private activity (trade in St. Petersburg, customs collections in the Baltic ports), or for initiating industrial entrepreneurship (the iron and textile industries), passed from the economic scene with the achievement of the special tasks for which they were selected.

This old elite proved to be quite ineffective in providing leadership to the merchant class as a whole and in adapting to changing circumstances. It therefore had to abdicate its leading role in favor of a different group, one whose members were more aggressive in expanding their businesses and thereby served as a different model for the majority of Russian merchants.

The new "generation" of Russian merchants brought to the forefront a new elite, one made up of army suppliers, tax farmers, and individuals from varied backgrounds. Many of them were former state peasants who made their fortune in the grain trade, alcohol distilling, or government contracts. Many of them rose fast in their status and wealth as a result, of a large extent, to their connections with the government bureaucracy. Although some of the old traditions of the previous Russian merchant estate may have been alien to this new generation, its members nevertheless demanded an umbrella of protection against competitors, whether foreign or domestic, as soon as they themselves had reached a level of affluence and status. As individuals, their aspirations were shaped by the tastes and life-styles of the Russian nobility. Although few of them actually were ennobled, many more hoped to achieve that status by being "useful" to the government and to the ruling elite.

The third "generation" of Russian merchants was the one which had the good fortune to operate in a much more stable environment. Cases of rapid advancement and the creation of new fortunes were still numerous, but the general tenor of the time was one of normalcy and steady, perhaps still selective, growth of trade and industry. This merchant elite was conscious of its economic power and the lack of willingness on the part of the government and nobility to treat it with a minimum of respect and recognition. Therefore these merchants became more demanding not only in the area of profits and protection, but also with regard to safety, security, and the rudiments of civil rights.

The sense of social stability, the demonstration effect of foreign merchants as high-status members of their respective societies, the numerous instances of the nobility's guarding of the hierarchical structure of Russian society in which the merchants both politically and socially occupied a subordinate role, and the merchants' own sense of their growing economic place in the state imbued at least some of them with a more critical attitude toward existing social institutions. Catherine II's 1767 legislative assembly provided a forum for airing some of the merchants' social grievances. Those grievances, recorded in the local

instructions to the participants of the assembly or pronounced in the speeches to the assembly, were directed against the members of the nobility and against the existing hierarchy of laws that excluded merchants from some of the privileges of the nobility. The grievances revealed a fundamental dissatisfaction with and resentment against their subordinate status and a desire that their social functions be acknowledged and their status approximated to that of the gentry.

This generation, perhaps because of its educational level and greater sense of social stability, was much less docile and more demanding in its relationship with the political elite. Deriving its self-confidence from the general territorial and economic expansion of both foreign and domestic commerce, the merchant class took a more active stand in demanding collectively an alleviation of its status. Nevertheless, it considered itself very much a part of the existing social order in Russia. Its criticism was directed against deficiencies in its status in comparison with that of the nobility rather than against the existence of institutions such as serfdom. An improvement of the merchants' status appeared to them to be perfectly compatible with the existence of serfdom, and all the more so if the merchants were to be granted the privileges of owning serfs and agricultural estates.

The government's grants of freedom of entry into trade and industry were met with a mixed reaction by the merchant class. Such actions promised them a broadening of opportunities, but the likelihood of increased competition did not evoke much enthusiasm. These facts coincided with the political refusal to upgrade their status and the increased competition from the "trading peasants." The merchants were trying to diminish the social distance between themselves and the nobility while increasing the socioeconomic distance between themselves and their competitors. The future held out no significant promise for them, they were left frustrated in their social ambitions, and they could find solace only in their professional functions.

There was a hierarchical structure based on wealth and economic differentiation within the merchant class. The data for wealth differentiation are sketchy and scattered, but the available documentary evidence illustrates wide income-differentials within the merchant class. An example are the data in table 5.11 on the distribution of volume of sales in 1721. The data include both craftsmen and merchants. Even if merchants are considered only those who had sales of over 100 rubles per year, the spread among the merchants was very substantial, between 161 and 2,389 rubles per year. If the persons with sales between 51 and 100 rubles annually are included, then the spread was even wider.

Table 5.11   Distribution of Merchants and Craftsmen by Size of Sales in Novgorod, 1721

Size of Sales (in Rubles)	No. of Merchants	% of Total	Sales (in Rubles)	% of Total Sales	Average Sales (in Rubles)
0–10	176	29.4	1,191	1.4	6.8
11–20	94	15.7	1,782	2.1	18.9
21–30	44	7.3	1,265	1.5	28.6
31–40	16	2.7	620	.8	38.75
41–50	66	11.0	3,275	4.0	39.5
51–100	80	13.4	7,320	8.9	91.5
101–200	44	7.3	7,076	8.6	160.7
201–300	26	4.3	7,120	8.6	273.8
301–400	13	2.2	4,612	5.6	354.8
401–500	15	2.5	7,400	9.0	493.3
500–1000	10	1.8	7,325	8.9	732.5
Over 1000	14	2.4	33,450	40.6	2,389.3
Total	598	100.0	82,436	100.0	137.8

Source: M. Ia. Volkov, "Materialy," p. 282.

Other inferences about income differentials can be drawn from the tax records of the smaller cities, where one would expect the differentials to be less pronounced than in the large trading centers. The data for the cities of Balakhna and Cheboksary for the second decade of the century indicate that in the former city 5 percent of the merchants paid 30 percent of all the taxes, and in the latter only 2 percent of the merchants paid 25 percent of all the taxes.[19]

The stratification of the merchant class was reflected in the distribution of the merchants according to their engagement in retail, wholesale, and foreign trade. The last category is actually a misnomer, since by definition the merchants engaged in export and import transactions. This category, however, involved a group of wholesale merchants who specialized in the trade of commodities designated for export and in the trade of imported goods. Their specific designation was that of "merchants trading with the port cities" (*torguiushchie k portam*), rather than ones "trading at the ports." The fact that the majority of those merchants were not inhabitants of the port cities is indicative of their role and function as middlemen in internal rather than foreign trade. The number of those wholesale merchants who specialized in the collection of exportable goods or in the dissemination of imports within the Russian market was relatively small, but they were dispersed over a wide territory. The total number of merchants "trading with the ports" in 1764 was officially estimated at 3,167, of whom 762 were located in the central provinces (*gubernii*) and 93 in the city of Moscow.[20] The Soviet historian N. L. Rubinshtein published a table of merchants "trading with the ports" and their home bases for the year 1769. Table 5.12 presents only the cities of the interior having more than fifty "merchants trading with the ports."

The participation of the merchants of a few cities of the interior in the St. Petersburg import and export trade is presented in table 5.13. The data in table 5.13

Table 5.12   Merchants Trading with the Ports, 1769

Home Base	No. Trading
Tula	199
Velikii Ustiug	193
Olonets	150
Ostashkov	138
Vologda	102
Kaluga	99
Moscow	93
Kursk	90
Tver	89
Lal'sk	84
Kiev	75
Rostov	73
Roslavl'	73
Gzhatsk	66
Rzheva	63
Tot'ma	59
Kolomna	57
Toropets	55
Smolensk	53

Source: Rubinshtein, "Vneshniaia torgovlia," p. 353.

Table 5.13   St. Petersburg Trade by Home Base of Merchants

	Imports (in 1,000 Rubles)			Exports (in 1,000 Rubles)		
	1772	1773	1774	1772	1773	1775
Moscow	797.1	1,407.0	878.2	15.1	97.5	44.1
St. Petersburg	304.7	568.1	531.6	87.8	219.3	120.4
Tula	454.8	497.5	436.1	175.5	293.1	265.5
Kaluga	113.9	113.9	141.5	11.6	11.6	19.7

Source: Rubinshtein, "Vneshniaia torgovlia," p. 353.

illustrate the very high share Moscow merchants had in the dissemination of imported goods. This is not surprising, for Moscow, the major trade center of Russia, demanded more imported goods than any other city. More surprising is the high degree of participation of the Tula and Kaluga merchants in the imports from St. Petersburg. This indicates that neither the merchants of the port cities themselves nor the merchants of Moscow possessed a monopoly position in the domestic trade of imported goods, and that in the second half of the century the wholesale merchants of the provincial cities purchased imported goods at the source, directly in the port cities.

This evidence compels one to question some of the attributes of the Moscow trade as they have been presented by Russian historians. Moscow has often been represented as the all-Russian depot for the internal market, as the magnet that attracted the main flow of goods and served as the major distributor of goods. This image of Moscow does not entirely fit eighteenth-century reality and has to be qualified to some extent, and certainly enough to account for the role of fairs in goods distribution. (It is likely that this image was borrowed from another era, perhaps from the later railway age, when Moscow appeared very much as the center of a star-like, or wheel-hub, network.)

Two factors require a qualified version of the role of Moscow. First, although Moscow was nearly centrally located and close to the major waterways, the fact of high transportation costs made the movement of bulk goods back and forth almost prohibitive. Second, the high share of some provincial cities in the collection of exportable commodities illustrates that an opportunity existed to obtain imported goods in the port cities rather than in Moscow. Moscow did have a major role supplying imported goods of high value per unit of weight with relatively low transportation costs to areas which did not trade directly with the port cities. Moscow's wholesale trade was concentrated on the ports, the major fairs, and the western and southern borders during the first half of the century. During the later period, provincial merchants increasingly traded directly with the outlying areas. Moscow merchants behaved passively in the matter of smaller transactions. They expected the provincial merchants to arrive in Moscow and exchange their goods, mostly raw materials, foodstuffs, and goods manufactured in the cottage industries, for quantities of imports or manufactured goods in the warehouses and shops of the Moscow merchants. This relationship between the Moscow and provincial merchants, as well as the structure of the Moscow trade, led to an interesting bifurcation of the distribution between a relatively small group of wholesale merchants and a very large group of retail merchants. The latter primarily serviced the population of Moscow.

The middle level of Russian merchants, that which combined both wholesale and retail transactions, was represented predominantly by provincial merchants. They were a very mobile group. They traveled to Moscow and frequented the fairs. They sought other sources of supply and provided the regional as well as the local markets with the goods which were in demand.

The scope of this group of merchants' activity can be inferred from the fact that in 1764 a total of 19,458 registered merchants from 202 towns bought passports to travel outside their home bases. This was a high portion of the 188,602 total registered merchant population, especially when one considers that many non-trading individuals were formally registered as merchants.[21] From the central region 7,980 merchants bought passports, a figure that indicates a high level of participation. From Moscow city itself there were only 213 who obtained passports.

The provincial merchants occupying the leading position within the middle level of the merchant class were the ones who experienced most of the consequences of upward mobility. The data on the merchant elite and its personnel turnover support the impression that its new recruits came from the provincial merchants. Their social advancement proceeded by acquisition of status in the prestigious merchant corporations, by a change of their residence to the capital cities, and by their intermarriage with the existing elite.[22]

The largest numerical group of the urban merchant population comprised retail merchants who traded in their stores, little shops, or market stalls during most of the year. They also participated at bazaars and the seasonal fairs, whenever these were held.

The lowest level in the merchant hierarchy was occupied by peddlers and other distributors of goods within the urban areas who worked not out of any trading establishment but who sought out their customers at home or at their places of employment. This was a marginal group from the point of view of trade whose members were infirm or impoverished traders who had to compete also with the registered and nonregistered urban dwellers and with the rural serfs seeking income in the urban areas.

This cursory sketch of the differentiation within the merchant population provides a cross-sectional view of this employment group as it existed throughout the eighteenth century, irrespective of the dynamic forces that influenced social mobility between the various layers within the group. The data are too fragmentary to undertake a thorough study of the impact of the dynamic forces.

For the economic historian a merchant is not only an individual engaged in a particular type of activity, but also an owner of a firm, an economic organization. The organizational framework within which most of the merchants operated was the single-family firm based on the capital and labor of the merchant household. Although the typical urban merchant household was much smaller than the peasant household, its labor resources were sufficient to carry on retail trade. In instances of multiple retail outlets owned by one merchant, the labor of relatives and helpers was necessary. The apprenticeship type of employment, although less formalized legally than industrial or craft apprenticeships, was widespread and included both young people of the urban estate and even rural origin (trading peasants).

For the wholesale merchants, the trading firms involved a larger number of employees. Most were hired, but some were serfs.[23] The employees of merchants can be divided roughly into three categories:

1. Those employed in transportation, warehousing, and services requiring no specialized skills.

2. Helpers and clerks, including assistants who ran a particular retail outlet and substituted for the owner in his absence.

3. Agents entrusted with specific tasks who represented the owner in certain transactions, sometimes referred to as stewards (*prikazchiki*).

Of the three categories, the third provided employees with some prospects for advancement into independent business under favorable conditions, both because of the skills (literacy) and experience previously acquired and the acquaintances with other merchants made during careers as agents or stewards.

Elements of continuity in the merchant estate were significant. Inheritance of status, employment, and ownership played an important role. On the other hand, there was also a great deal of mobility into and out of this estate. Besides the short periods of institutional change caused by state legislative or executive means, there was a gradual acceleration of social mobility in the merchant stratum, one related to economic expansion and change.

This discussion of two selected aspects of Russia's internal trade during the eighteenth century, the institutional forms of trade and the social mobility of the merchant class, does not exhaust the topic. Rather, it underscores the need for further inquiry. The following observations only suggest an approach to problems that might facilitate the task and make it more rewarding for the scholar and student. One might argue that some of the most interesting features of eighteenth-century domestic trade reveal themselves during inquiry into what happens to domestic trade in relation to activities in other branches of the economy.

We can safely assume, and test the hypothesis, that the basic dynamic of internal trade was inexorably tied to the growth of agricultural production, especially its marketable share. The growth of marketability of agricultural production was responsible not only for the supply for the growing export trade, but also for expanding domestic consumption. The growth of a marketable surplus helped to increase the disposable income of the population and stimulated the demand for domestic and foreign goods. The import trade was thereby affected as well. Apart from the growth of agricultural production, the growth of industrial output enlarged the volume of commodity production which the market in turn had to distribute.

The growing volume of trade put pressure on the transportation network, which responded by growing both in size and in quality. The latter means particularly the improvement of the waterways, which represented a cheaper and more efficient means of transportation than overland transport. There were additional links between internal trade and other production and service branches of the economy. The Russian government's momentous decision to abolish the system of internal tolls in 1754 had a significant impact on the development of domestic trade. That points to a need to examine the performance of internal trade in conjunction with the prevailing economic policies.

From the viewpoint of an economic historian, one of the most important features of eighteenth-century Russian internal trade was its increasingly integrated network. The relative efficiency of the network, which was in a state of increasing integration, was due to its dual role as a simultaneous distributor and collector of goods. Given the existing population density, the distances involved, and the high transportation costs, this efficiency was probably the most important single contribution of the trade network to economic growth in that period. This helps to explain the relative progress in the formation of both regional markets and a national market for many domestically produced commodities. The fixation of attention by Soviet historians on grain prices as a measure of market integration does not fit eighteenth-century reality, when the marketable output of industrial crops and livestock products exceeded the value of commercial grain. On the other hand, even grain prices, when they are properly organized, not according to simple physical proximity of markets, but according to the existing market patterns and trade routes, show a higher correlation than the Soviet historians found.

Internal trade during the eighteenth century was not a lagging sector in the Russian economy. It was growing *pari passu* with the other sectors. Its own dynamics exhibited elements of quantitative and qualitative change that affected other branches of the economy and the life of the people.

6
TRANSPORTATION

For a country as large and as sparsely populated as Russia was in the eighteenth century the overcoming of distance was a major economic task. The progress which was achieved in the development of mining and manufacturing, in the development of areas of agricultural specialization, and in the growth of regional markets and foreign trade was accompanied by growth of transportation facilities and services.

One cannot possibly attribute the profound changes in volume and value of goods produced for the market to any set of factors which would not include improved transportation. Many of the new economic opportunities that arose in the eighteenth century were based on the widening of the transportation networks and decreases in the costs of transportation services. Many students of European economic history have observed the price differential between Western European and Russian goods, but few have stressed the fact that much of the differential was attributable to the great differences in transportation costs between the two regions. The period witnessed a narrowing of the price differential, and one may assume that this resulted from an expansion of trade between the two regions as well as from a reduction of transportation costs. A similar development is observable within Russia, where regional price differentials began to decrease and previously separated local markets were integrated into major regional markets.

The eighteenth century was marked by a development in the area of transportation in which decreasing costs helped to increase demand for goods exchanged in internal and foreign trade. This is not to claim that there was a revolution or major technological breakthrough in transportation services, but it does suggest that gradual reductions in the cost of transportation services, along with cost reductions in the production of goods, made the economic progress of the eighteenth century possible.

Most transportation services were overland. The horse-drawn sleigh or wagon was the mainstay not only of the short distance haul of commodities (up to

50 kilometers), but also of what might be called the middle-distance haul (50 to 80 kilometers). In addition to household and intravillage transportation services, the hauling of products from the farms and craft shops to the local and urban markets within a radius of up to 150 kilometers was carried out by the owners of horses, the rural population of a particular vicinity. Payments for such services constituted an additional income for the agricultural population during times when the horses were not used in farm work, or when such service was not a part of the serfs' obligations to their masters. It is impossible to estimate the volume of such services or the employment involved. Be that as it may, this segment of transportation services made little contribution to the progress of the economy.

The economies in transportation costs were made by substituting transportation on the waterways for overland transportation. The waterways of Russia were, historically speaking, crucial for the development of the Russian state and society. The "route from the Varangians to the Greeks" connected the Baltic with the Black Sea already at the dawn of Russian history. The Volga route, connecting the Russian central plain with the Caspian Sea, was also important throughout most of the recorded history of Russia. It was only during the eighteenth century, however, that the Russian state secured its outlets to the Baltic and Black Seas, and was able to exploit the internal waterways to an extent larger than before. It became a mark of the eighteenth century (and of the first half of the nineteenth century) that waterways played an outstanding role as a substitute for overland transportation, before yielding primacy to the railroads. The bulk of Russia's exports, and also the majority of its bulky mining, forest, and agricultural commodities, that entered into the channels of interregional domestic trade were transported by water. The century witnessed both the extension of navigable waterways and the growth of the volume of goods transported on the major rivers.

The waterways of the Volga and its major navigable tributaries, the Western Dvina, and the Northern Dvina were the outstanding river routes for the transportation of goods to the ports. They also accounted for most of the goods hauled by water, including all of the timber, iron, and salt, as well as a major portion of the marketable grain, flax, and hemp, and the foodstuffs and manufactured goods. The territorial expansion of Russia westward and southward increased the distances hauled as well as the volume and variety of the goods transported by the waterways.

Students of Russian history are familiar with the public investments in canal building during the eighteenth century, the construction of the Vyshnii Volochëk and Ladoga canals. Also well known is the growth of traffic on the waterways, evident in the fact that the annual employment in the transportation services of the internal waterways rose from about 60,000 to about 220,000 during the century. Such mere description of the waterways and recitation of data on the traffic of goods fail, however, to explain fully the economic nature of internal waterway transportation as a service industry.

On the supply side, service of internal waterway shipping depended on the availability of capital for riverboat construction, on the availability of a certain volume and specific categories of labor, and on a degree of specialization of entrepreneurs (shippers) familiar with the demand for the services. The demand for shipping services fluctuated and depended upon changes in the volume and composition of marketable production. To adjust the supply of shipping facilities to the short-term changes in demand for transportation services, the market organization had to be flexible and capable of quickly expanding or contracting its services.

A closer examination of this market structure, especially the markets for riverboats and crews, reveals their existence already in the seventeenth century. Thus the eighteenth century witnessed not the initial organization of such markets, but rather their expansion and growing sophistication. The social locus of the market for riverboats was the area of cooperation between the merchants and the peasants. The capital outlays for riverboat construction were moderate in terms of cost per unit, and thus capital could be provided either from the milieu of "trading peasants" or in partnerships with the mercantile capital of the provincial towns. Knowledge of the market was important in providing the link between the multiple locations of riverboat construction and the areas where the flow of transportable cargo originated. Market signals had to be interpreted in a manner that permitted the proper mobilization of capital and labor resources for riverboat construction.

The supply of labor to man the riverboats and to carry the cargoes to their destinations depended both upon market demand and upon the institutional arrangements for the hiring of labor. The recruitment of labor to work on the internal waterway vessels was feasible because of the institutional arrangement of granting passports to serfs to work outside the village or estate. This arrangement enabled a sizable part of the serf population to earn cash income not from the sale of their agricultural production but from the hiring out of their labor on a seasonal or other short-term basis.

Only a small stratum of specialized boatmen could be considered as employed exclusively in river transportation. They were recruited from among the population adjacent to the waterways, often from families in which the skills were transferred from generation to generation. They were the ones who supplied the skills and often also the organizational facility to hire the majority of the labor force, the nonskilled crew members. The nonskilled labor was drawn from a wide area, including localities distant from the shipping routes. To the extent that there existed certain points of origin for large flows of cargo, such places served also as major centers of labor recruitment. Increases and decreases in the demand for labor depended on the volume of cargo, and information about employment possibilities was disseminated from those larger markets for transportation services.

For those serfs who had passports and were thus relatively mobile, the labor market in riverway transportation operated as one in which the demand for and supply of labor determined the wage. The wage was specified in the same contract that listed the laborers' obligations. Both the seasonal nature of the work (limited at best to one navigational season) and the heterogeneity of the work force in terms of its residence, or even nationality, required a degree of supervision and enforcement of labor discipline that could be rather costly to the entrepreneurs.

The *artel'* arrangement was one of the solutions found to minimize the costs of supervision and also to ease the problems of discipline and cooperation. This arrangement enabled a labor recruiter to assemble a team of workers who cooperatively shared the work and remuneration. It was self-governed, and thereby avoided the costs of additional supervision. The *artel'* had a hierarchical system and differentiated earnings, but its existence as a labor team could accommodate other desires of the labor force, such as to be among one's own "landsmen" or, if the numbers permitted, one's own villagers. (The *artel'* arrangement was also widely used in another industry that relied heavily on seasonal labor—construction. There also it helped to create labor teams homogeneous in skill and territorial origin and thereby diminished the problems of labor organization and discipline enforcement.)

Two more characteristics of the labor force employed in riverway shipping are worth mentioning. One is that, in spite of differences in the territorial origins of the laborers, and because of their mobility and common experience, they succeeded in creating a subculture dominated by the influence of the common laborers using their muscle power to tow cargoes up the Volga. The subculture of the Volga boatmen, the *burlaki*, provided elements of commonality to an otherwise heterogeneous labor force. Remarkably, much of the folklore and subculture of that particular employment group was absorbed in the common culture of the Russians. Hard toil and harsh working conditions were the other characteristics of this employment group. The work was demanding in terms of the sheer physical effort, but if one is to judge by the lack of complaints about a labor shortage, the supply of labor was plentiful and the wages were relatively remunerative.

Russian internal waterways were backward and inefficient by Western European navigational standards and the risks to the cargoes were much higher, but nevertheless the contribution of those primitive waterways to the economic expansion of Russia was by all accounts higher than the contribution of internal waterways to the economic expansion of Western Europe in the eighteenth century. This was largely attributable to the peculiarities of the location of Russian natural resources. The known rich iron ore deposits were located on the eastern slope of the Ural mountain range; some of the most valuable forest resources were in the far north; the most fertile grain lands were on the southern and eastern peripheries of the populated areas; and the ports were at the extreme west, north, or south of the country.

In the eighteenth century the rivers and canals of Russia became the arteries through which goods flowed from the fringes of the empire to the population centers and port cities, and back. Any technological improvement, any extension of the waterways augmented this flow of goods and brought into the realm of the market economy an increasing number of households and firms. Shipping by water substituted for overland transportation, and there were real increases in the productivity of the shipping services. Services were offered on a competitive basis to those demanding them. The benefits of increased productivity appear to have been passed on to the consumers.

Transportation services were provided not only on land routes but also on internal waterways for a substantial volume of goods moving across the land frontiers or by water to distant markets. We know that Russians very seldom accompanied their exports across land frontiers and participated only marginally in long-distance maritime shipping. There was, however, active Russian participation in the maritime coastal trade.

The Russians possessed the necessary technology in shipbuilding to the extent that the ships used in the coastal trade in size and mode of operation were similar to the larger riverboats or smaller naval vessels. The skill requirements in coastal shipping were minimal for most of the crew members, and this made it possible to use mostly native crews. Coastal shipping was cheaper than land transportation, and therefore some of the distribution of imports, as well as the collection of goods for export, took place via coastal shipping. One would expect a demand for coastal shipping in the ports of the Baltic, White Sea, and later also the Black Sea, and that the services would be provided by Russian nationals rather than by foreigners. Unfortunately, most of the published sources are not specific and do not permit distinguishing between intra-Baltic shipping and coastal shipping on the Baltic. Often one can gain an impression of the scope of coastal shipping only from incidental evidence.

Fortunately direct evidence about the Baltic coastal trade at the port of Viipuri (Vyborg) exists. Moreover, data on the coastal trade of Arkhangel'sk give an accurate picture of this important sector of shipping services, one that provided employment to Russian capital and labor. Although it is possible that the relative success of the Russians in overcoming their disadvantages in both shipbuilding and crew recruitment for coastal shipping occurred with subsidies from the government, the achievement of a competitive position in coastal shipping was important for the Russian merchant-entrepreneurs because it showed that Russian backwardness in shipping, compared with shipping practice in Western Europe, was the result primarily of economic causes, not psychological or "racial" ones, as some contemporaries argued. Some of these contemporary observers, commenting on the reasons why the carriers of Russia's export commodities were almost exclusively foreigners, tried to imply that the landlocked Russians had a "fear of the sea." This view not only contradicted some of the historical evidence of Russian shipping on earlier centuries, but also ignored the economics of the shipping industry.

The record of eighteenth-century shipping is unmistakably clear. Wherever the Russians encountered an inferior technology, inferior skills, and a capital market more primitive than theirs, they provided the shipping services or competed successfully with the others in maritime shipping. This was the record of the maritime trade on the Caspian Sea, and also on the Black Sea. However, vis-à-vis Western Europe, with its superior technology in shipbuilding, its highly developed skills of captains and crews, and its developed capital markets of Amsterdam and London, the Russians were in no position to compete. Not only were the Western ships better constructed, they were also cheaper. Not only were Western services more varied and reliable, their costs were lower, as were the insurance rates and the interest rates at which the entrepreneurs, merchants, and shippers borrowed money. No reasonable subsidy would have been sufficient to equalize the costs between the Western and Russian shippers on most of the heavily traveled trade routes.

The significance of this state of affairs for the Russian economy was that the Russians hardly earned any direct income from the transportation services used in long-distance maritime trade. They did not receive any income from ships built to provide shipping services, any wages for employed sailors, or any commissions on insurance for the simple reason that they did not provide the services. The reasons were mentioned above.

Was this state of affairs detrimental to the Russian economy? An economist would clearly think not. He would point out that the Russians were charged the competitive price, the lowest price, for shipping services, that the competition between the Dutch, British, German, and Scandinavian shippers excluded the possibility of collusion and discrimination against Russian exports and imports. It was a business which each one of them desired for himself, but which was too large to monopolize. Under such circumstances, economists argue, the benefits to the Russian producers and exporters, as well as to the importers, were the highest since they could charge the highest price for their goods by using the cheapest transportation.

Any substitution of Russian shipping for that provided by Western European shippers had one immediate consequence: the costs of transportation to the Russian economy rose and the current net gain decreased. Consequently the reasons for changing the status quo on the part of the Russian policy-makers could not be economic in the short-run sense of the term. A Russian policy pursuing substantial increases in the Russian share of the long-distance shipping of its exports and imports would have been motivated either by very long-term goals of economic nationalism or by motives of political prestige. The discussion of such goals is beyond the scope of eighteenth-century economic history.

The fascinating details of eighteenth-century shipping between Western Europe and Russian ports, the history of Russian exports being carried to the major depots of the world before being distributed all over the globe, properly belong to the history of Western Europe rather than Russia. The year-after-year phenomenon of hundreds and later over a thousand sailing ships entering Russian ports with little cargo and often in ballast and departing loaded with hemp and flax, grain and seeds, iron and timber, tallow, hides, furs, pitch, and tar is relevant to the economic history of Russia primarily in terms of the costs of the transportation services and the regularity or interruptions of the flow of services. The regularity of these services was highly valued by the countries whose merchant marines provided them. This is evident in the armed convoys of the British navy that protected the sea lanes into the Baltic for British shipping against those who tried to interrupt it. An additional benefit to the Russian economy from the growth of shipping was a growth in foreign demand for Russian exports of commodities used in shipbuilding.

Russia survived the period of mercantilist ideology and pressures upon government policies without seriously trying to substitute its own shipping services for the ones of a basically competitive market. It thereby escaped heavy expenditures which would have yielded a negative economic return. If one cannot attribute this correct decision to the wisdom of the eighteenth-century Russian policy-makers, perhaps one can attribute it to their lack of capital or energy. Whatever the reason, it was beneficial to the Russian economy.

Transportation on Internal Waterways

In view of the considerable distances between the major areas of production of agricultural, forest, and mining products and the ports that were the major outlets for Russian foreign trade in the eighteenth century, a very substantial part of the transportation of goods took place on the Russian waterways. From an economic point of view, a waterway, just like an overland trade route (a forerunner of modern highways) represented a form of public capital. Rivers had to be regulated and either broadened or deepened. Canals had to be dug. Locks and sluices had to be constructed to maintain an acceptable water level. They all required both initial investments and constant maintenance, like other forms of capital.

The services were paid for in part by a system of tolls. The Russian government experimented with both private and public authorities to collect the tolls and to maintain the facilities of its major waterways until it decided definitely in favor of stateownership and strict governmental control. For example, the tolls on the Vyshnii Volochëk Canal were originally collected by the entrepreneur Serdiukov, who had constructed the locks near the Borovichi rapids. Later the government took it over and collected the following tolls: 1764, 5,855 rubles; 1781–83, 32,111 rubles yearly; 1784, 53,844 rubles; 1785, 41,984 rubles; 1786, 54,368 rubles; 1787, 60,111 rubles; 1788, 50,109 rubles; 1789, 41,095 rubles; 1790, 65,321 rubles; 1791, 71,144 rubles; 1792, 59,365 rubles; 1793, 43,585 rubles; 1794, 50,434 rubles; and 1795, 47,672 rubles. In addition, costs (whether public or private) were incurred in providing the necessary services for the passing freight and accompanying personnel. Along the waterways, at certain intervals, river ports, docks, storage facilities, and amenities were constructed and maintained.

To the extent that some waterways influenced the direction of goods transportation, they affected the economic role of particular urban settlements participating in the trade or in providing services for the transportation of goods. The waterways also provided opportunities for the use of labor in goods transport for particular areas and thereby influenced the interregional flow of seasonal labor.

The major Russian rivers (in descending order) were the Volga, the Western Dvina, the Northern Dvina, and the Don River basins. Arkhangel'sk was the port of the Northern Dvina, Riga of the Western Dvina, and Taganrog and Azov were the ports of the Don. Astrakhan' on the Caspian Sea was not the outlet for most of the goods of the Volga basin but rather St. Petersburg was, via a circuitous route from the Volga to the small rivers and a system of canals, of which Vyshnii Volochëk Canal and the Ladoga Canal were the most used. To the extent that the data represent the waterway traffic to the St. Petersburg port, they can be compared for some of the export commodities with the Customs House data for St. Petersburg exports and with the Sound Toll data for the port of St. Petersburg.

The data in table 6.1 for the major export commodities shipped to St. Petersburg indicate the close relationship of the volume of goods moving through the waterways on the way to the capital and the volume entering foreign trade. The importance of the waterway transportation, given the bulk nature of the goods and the savings in costs achieved by water in comparison with land transportation, is supported by the available data of the period. Some of the differences between the incoming volume and the quantity of exports can be explained by the domestic use of the goods, either for further processing and export or final consumption.

The upstream movement of goods was the more significant for the Volga waterway. The downstream movement of shipping on the Volga included mostly grains, manufactured goods, and floats of timber as well as other, secondary forest products. Upstream movements along the Astrakhan'-Nizhnii Novgorod route consisted primarily of salt and foodstuffs, such

Table 6.1 Ladoga Canal Shipments into St. Petersburg and St. Petersburg Exports of Selected Commodities

Year	Wheat (in chetvert')		Flax (in poods)		Hemp (in poods)		Iron (in poods)		Tallow (in poods)	
	Incoming	Exports	Incoming	Exports	Incoming	Exports	Incoming	Exports	Incoming	Exports
1768	15,030		116,814		1,341,091	1,791,447	1,442,350	1,674,000	154,618	
1774	76,708	68,399	140,200	184,295	1,699,264		2,813,697	2,176,000	48,951	
1775	32,578	27,715	242,250	213,965	1,399,815	1,191,186	1,446,846	1,651,000	301,013	
1776	12,473		171,580	242,180	1,446,803	1,443,060	1,939,675	2,223,000	345,999	
1777	35,325	36,468	245,150	313,898	2,044,245	1,922,767	4,132,500	2,616,000	443,465	
1778	50,566	22,750	218,050	251,239	2,446,613	2,227,408	1,112,605	1,590,000	238,644	
1779	46,849	62,659	152,350	227,774	2,293,128	2,211,381	2,703,350	2,092,378	284,420	302,342
1780	4,520	17,790	194,045	215,601	1,989,120	1,492,877	2,509,298	2,013,530	472,044	527,454
1781	3,724	12,094	178,050	275,871	2,172,674	2,166,769	2,424,292	3,560,116	529,280	529,928
1782	11,401	8,566	115,215	271,407	2,371,925	2,305,120	3,604,201	1,733,021	449,862	427,436
1783	18,625	17,452	168,170	347,003	1,425,080	1,271,497	585,275	1,874,525	378,570	420,865

Table 6.2   Ladoga Canal Shipping, 1774–83

Year	Barks	Half-Barks	One-Mast Boats	Other Small Boats	Floats
1774	3,255	732	424	1,053	3,347
1775	2,327	667	515	995	7,848
1776	1,987	624	452	1,087	6,473
1777	3,605	655	505	1,232	5,425
1778	2,595	744	587	1,075	8,022
1779	2,746	763	663	1,216	5,775
1780	2,913	896	756	1,134	8,317
1781	3,034	1,009	546	1,087	8,174
1782	3,525	869	460	1,110	8,823
1783	2,626	1,018	771	1,232	5,189
Yearly Average	2,861	797	568	1,113	6,739

Source: Hermann, *Statistische Schilderung*, app., table 8.

as fish, vegetables, fruits, and also hides and wool. Near Kazan', the flow of goods from the south merged with the flow of goods coming downstream from the Kama River basin, a flow consisting of salt, iron, and forest products. The combined flow of freight continued upstream on the Volga. En route it was augmented by goods produced in the nonblack-soil region such as leather, textiles, and wood products on the way to Rybinsk and Kolomna. There the goods flow destined for Moscow turned into the Oka River basin. The rest, reinforced by grain shipments from the northwestern part of the blacksoil region, continued toward and then through the Vyshnii Volochëk Canal en route to St. Petersburg.

Iron caravans originating in the Urals made their way along the Russian rivers and canals to the capital. They followed the same routes used for the transportation of hemp, flax, tallow, and finally huge timber floats. It is no exaggeration to maintain that the strategic factor for the exports of St. Petersburg, and in fact for the existence of St. Petersburg as a capital in the eighteenth century, was the waterway system that included the Ladoga Canal. This canal, which was started in 1718 and completed in 1732 (it was built by Count Münnich), enabled St. Petersburg to play its political and economic role during the eighteenth century.

The shipping volume of this major waterway can be inferred from the data pertaining either to it or to the Vyshnii Volochëk Canal. Although the figures differ both in terms of coverage and the periods they represent, they give in tables 6.2 and 6.3 a roughly comparable picture of the yearly volume of the shipping involved.

Taking into account the fact that the Vyshnii Volochëk Canal was located southeast of the Ladoga Canal and at a greater distance from St. Petersburg and thus accounted for a smaller volume of shipping through the Ladoga Canal, the two data sets appear to be consistent. Both reflect the order of magnitude

of the shipping volume, which one would expect to be greater on the Ladoga Canal at the same period. The case of the number of floats of wood (assuming an approximately equal size) serves as an illustration of a commodity that was transported chiefly from the vicinity of St. Petersburg and for which we could assume that only the more expensive varieties of wood would be transported over longer distances. The labor inputs involved in navigating floats through a canal were considerably greater than navigating them downstream on a major river. Still another explanation of the decrease of the number of floats from table 6.2 to table 6.3 might be the deforestation of the adjacent countryside.

The difference in the number of half-barks and one-mast boats between the Vyshnii Volochëk Canal and the Ladoga Canal is indicative of the volume of shipping that originated in the Russian northwest. It may also be accounted by a variety of commodities, such as flax and forest products which the larger ships coming from the Volga River had to carry through the Vyshnii Volochëk Canal before they entered the Ladoga Canal. The volume of freight passing through the waterway to St. Petersburg did

Table 6.3   Vyshnii Volochëk Canal Shipping

Year	Barks	Half-Barks	One-Mast Boats	Floats
1787	2,914	357	178	1,984
1788	2,846	317	264	2,719
1789	3,812	253	249	1,560
1790	2,927	339	166	1,390
1791	4,025	305	178	1,485
1792	2,553	456	168	1,107
1793	3,480	439	179	2,005
1794	2,945	402	167	1,964
1795	3,149	375	212	1,562
1796	2,983	260	218	1,665
1797	3,958	382	248	1,676
Yearly Average	3,235	353	202	1,738

Source: Storch, *Supplementband*, p. 59.

not decrease during the second period. It may have decreased beginning in 1801, when the Mariinskii Canal was completed through Lake Onega and provided an alternative route from the Volga basin to the port of St. Petersburg. In fact, the mere construction of an alternative route indicates that there must have been a rising volume of freight.

The second water artery, in terms of economic significance, was the Western Dvina which supplied the port of Riga. In the eighteenth century the Western Dvina was a "capricious river," insufficiently regulated, and therefore required both higher expenditures on labor and greater navigational skills in the transportation of goods than did other waterways. One unsuccessful attempt to regulate the Western Dvina was the so-called "Weissman project."[1] On the other hand, one of the Western Dvina's advantages as a commercial waterway lay in the fact that it drew supplies from outside its own basin. In addition to serving the provinces along its tributaries, it drew supplies from the upper Dnepr basin as well. The Dnepr route past Orsha and Dubrovna was 35 versts (about 20 miles) from the Luchesa River, a tributary of the Western Dvina.[2]

The proximity of the upper Dnepr basin connected by a relatively short land route (ford) to the Western Dvina broadened the base for the supply of goods from eastern Belorussia to the Dvina. The composition of the exports of the Western Dvina supply region (the Baltic provinces, northern Lithuania, eastern Belorussia, and the bordering Russian province of Smolensk) was almost uniform for each of the provinces: substantial volumes of flax, hemp, grains, pitch and tar, and timber for shipbuilding. In the case of timber, the winter months were used for overland transportation and then, during the navigational season, the journey was completed by river.

The waterway to Riga provides an interesting case of the impact on the transportation patterns of two adjacent regions, eastern and western Belorussia. Eastern Belorussia gravitated toward the Dvina basin and the port of Riga for dispatch of its bulk products. For grain sales, eastern Belorussia preferred to use the route through western Belorussia which gravitated toward the Wilja and Nieman waterway and the ports of Königsberg and Memel. In the last decades of the century Riga tried to improve the Western Dvina waterway to cheapen the transportation costs for eastern Belorussian grain and to reroute its flow. It did not manage to change the transportation cost-differential because in the 1780s the Oginskii Canal was constructed which connected the Dnepr with the Nieman basin and provided an opportunity to circumvent the Dvina waterway.

No systematic data have been published on the supply of goods shipped through the Western Dvina

Table 6.4   Total Supply to Riga of Selected Commodities (Yearly Averages)

	1766–73	1774–84
Flax (in shippounds)	32,603	41,491
Hemp (in shippounds)	49,880	85,445
Linseed (barrels)	67,625	100,509
Hempseed (barrels)	42,862	44,864
Grain (lasts)	13,762	19,704
Masts (pieces)	5,950	8,264
Balks (pieces)	179,837	156,791

Source: Data courtesy of Professor V. V. Doroshenko of the Latvian Academy of Science.

to Riga. (Such data are available in the Riga archives and there is hope that they will be published in the near future.) Nevertheless, some inference can be made on the basis of the supply of selected bulk commodities to Riga (table 6.4) and the high share in the supply of both the Belorussian-Lithuanian provinces and, in the case of hemp and grain, of the Russian provinces. Given the distance, such commodities could only travel by water if they were to be sold at a profit.

The rising volume of commodities shipped to Riga is clear. Whether the rise took place primarily in the volume transported by the waterways cannot be ascertained because data separating water from overland transport are lacking. The second period (1774–84) coincided with the incorporation of eastern Belorussia into the Russian Empire, and its trade via the Dvina to Riga certainly increased as a result.

The difference in the volume of freight that traversed the Western Dvina waterway and the Vyshnii Volochëk and Ladoga Canals system is due less to their volumes of exportable commodities (the huge quantities of iron and other products give a clear edge to the Ladoga Canal), and more to the size of their port cities (Riga's population was smaller than St. Petersburg's). The supply of commodities shipped for urban consumption made the greatest difference in terms of the volume handled by both waterways.

The technological backwardness of riverboats made development of waterways transportation during the eighteenth century difficult. Traditional Russian riverboats were made of wood hewn by ax, not properly dried and not watertight. Consequently they were heavy and had a low freight-to-weight ratio. They required deep waters, were difficult to maneuver, and were of limited use at times of low water-levels. They were easy targets for stormy waters (on lakes) and swift currents.

To the extent that waterways transportation was both economically important and an area of direct state participation (transportation of state-produced iron and salt, and products monopolized by the state), government regulation became an issue early in the eighteenth century. Peter the Great's intervention in the construction of riverboats started in 1715 and had as its goal the substitution for the old models of riverboat (*topornye*, or ax-hewn) new, lighter types built with sawn planks and boards, with a prescribed rigging and water-tightening. Peter sent models of the new boats to various river wharfs, imposed fines on the builders of the old-type boats, and threatened to banish anyone who disregarded his orders. In view of the scarcity of sawmills, of the proper skills, and the reluctance of the shipbuilders, however, his orders remained largely on paper. Moreover, Peter lacked an apparatus of control to enforce his orders, even if the conditions to institute the technological change had existed.

Government decrees followed in quick succession, but with minimal results. About a half-century after the first decree, a new prohibition against building the *topornye barki* was issued in 1762.[3] Only a half-year later, at the end of 1762, permission was granted to use the *topornye barki* until 1766 "in view of the scarcity of sawn timber and sawmills, to prevent delays in the supply of materials and goods to St. Petersburg and the other ports."[4]

A decree of 1781 tried the carrot rather than the stick and promised premiums ranging from 10 to 50 rubles for "new types" of barks and half-barks bringing cargo to St. Petersburg. The premiums depended on the distance of the journey. The old prohibition against barks longer than 17 arshins also was repeated.[5] The construction of new, improved models of other types of riverboats was also encouraged, especially for the transportation of bulk commodities. Special premiums were established for designs and models of various categories of riverboats: 75 rubles for barks, 120 rubles for flatboats (*lodki*), 300 rubles for grain boats, for large boats used in the transportation of iron (*strugi*), boats used for salt transportation (*vodoviki*), and riverboats which also could be used for coastal transportation (*galioty*).

The various governmental attempts to introduce new and improved types of riverboats to make the transportation of goods speedier, safer, cheaper, and probably less labor-intensive indicate the difficulties of introducing new technology under conditions of scarcity of skills and lack of visible economies. When economic factors, such as increasing costs of timber and rising labor costs in transportation, began to dictate a change in riverboat construction technology, the objectives of the government and the interests of the shippers started to coalesce. The demand by the industry was clearly more persuasive and more effective for the shipbuilders than all the government's threatening decrees. The technological change took place following a different timetable than the one prescribed by the government: when the sawmills began to produce not only for export but also for the domestic market, when the shipbuilders acquired new skills, and when the demand for riverboats increased sufficiently to guarantee a market for boats specialized in the carrying of different types of cargo. This confluence of factors occurred during the last quarter of the eighteenth century.

Employment in River Transportation

Employees in transportation were the third largest group, following agriculture and the small-scale, domestic cottage industry. There are no estimates of overland transportation employment, and this discussion of necessity will be limited to river transportation employment only.

Employment in river transportation, even more than employment in the other two leading sectors of the economy, was circumscribed by seasonal factors. Overland transportation employment had a very clear peak during the winter months, and river transportation employment was limited almost exclusively to the navigation season. The duration of employment in river transportation usually extended beyond the navigational period proper because it included the loading of freight on the boats preceding the journey as well as unloading and putting the freight into storage after the end of the navigational season. The often-extensive travel time from and to places of employment precluded alternative employment for an additional time period.

The major difference between employment in river transportation and in agriculture and domestic industry was the institutional framework. Agriculture involved the institution of serfdom and cottage industry involved household production for the market. In river transportation the service was performed for wages, under contract, and in what appears to have been a competitive market.

There are no exact data on the size of the labor force employed in river transportation. Estimates range from less than 60,000 employed at the beginning of the century to around 220,000 at the end of the century, when about three-quarters of the total were employed on the Volga route, 10 percent on the Western Dvina route, and about 5 percent on the Northern Dvina.

The demands for labor in waterway transportation depended primarily on the movement of freight. The term "freight" is a composite measure involving the total volume of freight, the composition of freight by types of goods, and the desired direction of this volume and composition of goods, whether upstream or downstream. For the main artery, the Volga, the upstream movement of goods involved bulk commodities destined for consumption and export. The upstream movement was the one which absorbed the most labor effort and has left the most traces in the documents of the period. The downstream movement from Vyshnii Volochëk to St. Petersburg did not permit any substantial reduction of labor due to the conditions of the waterway.

The increasing and changing composition of the volume of freight had some impact on the demand for labor. Specialized types of vessels had differing manpower requirements relative to the volume of freight. The composition of the freight also meant differences in the origin and destination of shipments, a phenomenon that required adjustments in the hiring of crews for particular segments of the waterway.

The demand for labor differed (and fluctuated) from one segment of the route to another as well as for different distances along the waterway. It also varied in terms of the required skill composition. A part of each crew had to consist of relatively skilled people who knew the route, could avoid dangerous river turns, and were capable of working the small boats carrying heavy anchors toward which the barge-like freight-carrying vessels were pulled by ropes. A skilled nucleus of the crew was required which was relatively well paid. It was recruited from the river-region population and hired separately from the bulk of the labor force that provided primarily muscle-power.

The unskilled laborers were known as *iaryzhniki* or, more often, as *burlaki*. Documents about the freight carried per boat and the government regulations on the shipping of salt and iron indicate that the load per worker was within the neighborhood of 200 to 250 poods, or 3 to 3.5 metric tons. Most of the workers were adults concentrated in the 20- to 40-year-old age group, and the load per worker was more or less standardized. As noted above, the laboring crews were often organized in *arteli*. At least two elements were instrumental in the formation of such voluntary associations bound by a collective work responsibility as well as a collective contract. First, the collective contract involved a collective guarantee of the presence and behavior of the members of the crew, an important fact under conditions where supervision by the shipowners of serfs or fugitive serfs might be a difficult and costly task. Second, the *artel'* organization of the crew involved its own hierarchy as well as a division of functions in the work process, which also resolved problems of labor organization and discipline.

Although the *artel'* form of labor hiring and labor organization was preferable to individual hiring, it was not the only, or even prevailing, form or organization during the eighteenth century. The labor market was too fragmented, and uncertainty of labor supply predominated. Consequently preference was given to individual hiring and the formation of crews by the employers, who demanded collective responsibility for those crews, withheld the passports and a large part of the wages due until the end of the job, and used whatever other methods were available to enforce labor discipline.

The demand for the unskilled, general labor of the *burlaki* depended on the particular segments of the route, the composition of the freight, and the length of the journey. When the intensity of demand for labor is compared either with the population density of particular regions or the supply of labor otherwise available for nonagricultural labor, the variations in the wage rates observed become much more intelligible.

The supply of labor for waterway transportation was influenced by the distance of population concentrations from the rivers. Also important were the legal and employment composition of the population that had access to the areas of labor recruitment. Given the long span of the Volga and its main tributaries, as well as the span of the Western and Northern Dvina rivers, distance was not a limiting factor for skilled labor and only increased the costs to the unskilled labor recruits from the blacksoil zone. As a result, the labor force in river transport was heterogeneous with respect to region and even to national groups. It included not only Russians but also Tatars and members of Finnic groups. This made the already noted common experience and folklore of the Volga *burlaki* not a local phenomenon, but an element of culture shared by many regions of Russia, even by regions a considerable distance away.

From the legal point of view, the dominant groups laboring on the rivers were serfs and members of the urban estates. The relative shares of the two groups in the total labor force are difficult to determine because of changes over time and in the different segments of the river routes. At the beginning of the century the share of the serfs may have been at least 80 percent; toward the end of the century that share increased.[6]

Among the employed serfs, the group paying quitrent (*obrok*) to their owners clearly prevailed. This suggests not only a relatively high share of state and church serfs, but also private serfs from regions where quitrent payments predominated. Given the seasonal coincidence of employment in river transport and agricultural work, one must assume that rendering labor services on an estate (*barshchina*) was incompatible with work as a *burlak*. Under the system of agricultural-estate labor service, it was only possible for someone to work in river transportation who came from a very large household or a combination of households that deliberately clubbed together for the purpose of freeing an individual for such employment.

The supply of labor was usually directed toward one of the existing areas of hiring, which coincided either with the origin of some commodity flows or with the institutionalized changes of crews. Such places were Kamyshyn and Saratov, where the salt transports from Elton Lake reached the Volga; Nizhnii Novgorod, where many of the salt caravans terminated at government storage facilities; and Rybinsk, where freight was redirected according to destination and carrier. Long cruises taking up the whole navigation season without interruption were more convenient for the labor force, and probably also for employers. They paid less on a per diem basis than some of the shorter journeys, where wages depended on the short-term interaction of supply and demand. It is difficult to determine the extent of choice available to labor about the place of hire except for the element of distance the laborers had to travel from home.

The length of the season was from seven to seven and a half months per year. Ships during the first half of the century traveled 15 versts per day, which meant a distance of over 3,000 versts per season, or less than the distance from Astrakhan' to St. Petersburg (4,064 versts). It is unknown how the 15 versts per day had to be covered, whether in one or two shifts. During the first half of the nineteenth century, the established norm per shift was 10 versts; that enabled the hiring of a double crew to work in two shifts around the clock and an accelerated movement of freight when time was of the essence. No such data are available for the eighteenth century, and speed can be estimated only from the documents about the number of days various caravans were on the move.

In the 1720s the movement of freight from Astrakhan' to Nizhnii Novgorod (2,170 versts) took about 155 days, and a century later it took only about 90 days. The journey from Nizhnii Novgorod to Rybinsk was reduced from 30 to 17 days, and from Astrakhan' to Saratov from about 60 days to an average of 30 days in the same time period.[7]

The scarce wage data indicate an average wage for unskilled laborers of about 6 kopeks per day in the 1720s. It rose to 9 kopeks in the early 1740s, 13 kopeks in the 1760s, and 18 kopeks in the 1780s. By the end of the century, the average wage was over 20 silver kopeks per day.[8] This was a wage that exceeded the rates paid to unskilled workers in Russian industry.

The inflationary pressures operating in the Russian economy had a strong effect on the rise in the level of wages in water transportation. Another important consideration in the rise of wages was undoubtedly the increase in productivity as measured by the speed of moving the freight over the waterways. This increase in productivity was achieved by a combination of factors rather than by a spectacular technological breakthrough. As noted above, there were improvements in the construction of riverboats, some improvements in the maintenance of river routes by installation of markers and warning signals, and some gains in the efficiency of the use of various boats for specialized cargoes. There were also improvements in the efficiency of the labor market, in the changes of crews and supply of labor at the different segments of the routes, that helped to avoid stoppages and delays. Finally, there also may have been some improvement in the organization of the work process itself.

It was not only in the interest of the merchants to move cargoes at a faster pace, to avoid expenditures for storage and to reduce the costs of capital tied up in the freight en route, but also of the government, which was concerned about the timely supply of foodstuffs, raw materials, and export commodities destined for the population of the major urban centers, the industrial establishments, and the foreign trade interests. Given the relative scarcity of labor for hire, wage incentives were the only solution to attract labor and to spur it on to greater efforts. This may explain, in part at least, the rising trend of wages in the river transportation sector of the Russian economy during the eighteenth century.

The growth of the labor force in river transportation had a number of significant effects on the development of the Russian economy. It provided money incomes for a part of the total labor force. It indirectly strengthened the quitrent sector of Russian agriculture as well as the commercial sector of the economy. The increase in the employment and productivity of this sector of the labor force contributed to the long-term decrease of transportation costs in Russia and, last but not least, demonstrated both the feasibility of a labor market for hire and its economic advantage over serfdom arrangements in the area of transportation services. The government itself, although it had at its disposal huge reserves of serf manpower, gave up, after some experience with serf-type arrangements, the idea of using coercion and stipulated nonmarket wage rates in favor of contracts and hiring arrangements which involved both market-level wage rates and market-type profits for entrepreneurs in river transportation. Relevant in this context are the conclusions arrived at by a special committee set up in Astrakhan' in 1744 to deal with the shipping services for the transportation of Astrakhan' salt and fish. The committee reviewed the existing wage rates, recommended wage increases,

Table 6.5   Vessels and Their Crews Passing Through the Vyshnii Volochëk Canal

Year	Boats	Floats	Boat Crews (Men)	Float Crews (Men)	Total Men
1787	3,499	1,984	68,980	7,396	76,376
1788	3,427	2,719	68,540	10,876	79,416
1789	4,314	1,560	86,280	6,240	92,520
1790	3,432	1,390	68,640	5,560	74,200
1791	4,508	1,485	90,160	5,940	96,100
1792	3,177	1,107	63,540	4,428	67,968
1793	4,098	2,005	81,960	8,020	89,980
1794	3,514	1,964	70,280	7,856	78,136
1795	3,736	1,562	74,720	6,248	80,968
1796	3,461	1,665	69,220	6,660	75,880
1797	4,588	1,676	91,760	6,704	98,464

Source: Storch, *Supplementband*, p. 59.

and as a special incentive recommended the free transportation of cargoes belonging to the workers that the workers could sell, presumably at a profit, up the river. A few years later a special Senate decree of February 23, 1761, recommended using hiring contracts, stipulated a maximum wage, but permitted raising the maximum by 20 percent "as long as this is kept secret."[9]

The sight of the Volga *burlaki* evokes an image of beasts of burden. Unquestionably the working conditions were harsh and treatment was often brutal. Nevertheless they worked under conditions that might be termed a voluntary form of "wage slavery" rather than serfdom, something that was considered "progress" by members of subsequent generations.

Rodin calculated that average boat crews consisted of twenty persons and float crews four persons on the route from Rybinsk through the Vyshnii Volochëk Canal. His estimates were based on data for selected years during the period 1753–81.[10] Using the same coefficients and Storch's traffic data, I have estimated in table 6.5 the labor supply required for the Vyshnii Volochëk Canal. Using the traffic data of Herman and von Reden, I have done the same in table 6.6 for the Ladoga Canal.

Coastal Shipping

The experience of the Russians in transporting goods over the extended river routes had a clear spillover effect in coastal shipping. The ships used and the seamen's skills were of a higher order than on the internal waterways, and during the eighteenth century the Russians were able to overcome some of their relative disadvantages in the coastal trade and to establish themselves firmly in that branch of maritime shipping.

A clear distinction between coastal shipping and long-distance shipping must be made if we are to understand the development patterns of Russian shipping. Coastal shipping served two purposes: the territorial distribution of goods for the domestic market and service for foreign trade. The shipping along the coast of grain, alcohol, or other goods from Livonia to St. Petersburg was a clear example of the cost advantage of water over overland transportation. The problems become somewhat more complicated, however, when one has to classify the broad variety of goods involved in coastal shipping that were destined for export.

Although most accepted conventions include coastal trade in the category of domestic trade, in fact it is difficult to classify. This is particularly true for eighteenth-century Russia. Formally speaking, trade between two ports within national boundaries is primarily an internal, domestic trade. However, what is the significance of bringing iron from St. Petersburg to Riga, if not to facilitate the iron trade of Riga? One cannot assume that a Dutch ship sailing to Riga for a cargo of hemp or flax would have traveled to St. Petersburg to purchase iron that it could not find in Riga. A visit to a Swedish port in search for iron was a plausible alternative to going to St. Petersburg. Thus the coastal trade played an important role in distribution, depending on the foreign demand for the stocks of iron among different Russian ports. It could be surmised from the export pattern of various commodities that, apart from supplying goods for internal consumption to different cities, the coastal trade as a substitute for land and river transportation was significant in the process of accumulating and distributing exportable goods in and between various ports. Quite often during the later part of the navigation season, imports were unloaded at the most accessible ports, and reshipped to their final destinations by land or, when the weather permitted, by coastal vessels.

Unfortunately there are no published data on the coastal trade of Russian ports during the eighteenth century. Most of the descriptive literature refers to the Black Sea ports, but even this is rare. A systematic body of data is extant for the port of Viipuri (Vyborg), a small port in the Gulf of Finland, for which the movement of all ships is registered and is accessible to students. The shipping trade of Viipuri with the Russian ports on the Baltic represents a typical coastal trade, ancillary to foreign trade. The capacity of the ships reported in the port of Viipuri was considerably lower than the average capacity of vessels engaged in long-distance shipping, indicating the high share of coastal shipping in the Viipuri total. The shipping services employed in the coastal trade ranged from as few as 29 vessels arriving annually in the five-year

Table 6.6   Vessels and Their Crews Passing Through the Ladoga Canal

Year	Boats	Small Boats	Floats	Boat Crews (Men)	Small Boat Crews (Men)	Float Crews (Men)	Total Men
1774	4,411	1,053	3,347	88,220	10,530	13,388	112,138
1775	3,509	995	7,848	70,180	9,950	31,392	111,522
1776	3,063	1,087	6,848	61,260	10,870	27,392	99,522
1777	4,765	1,232	5,425	95,300	12,320	21,700	129,320
1778	3,926	1,075	8,022	78,520	10,750	32,088	121,358
1779	4,172	1,216	5,775	83,440	12,160	23,100	118,700
1780	4,565	1,134	8,317	91,300	11,340	33,268	135,908
1781	4,589	1,087	8,174	91,780	10,870	32,696	135,346
1782	4,854	1,110	8,823	97,080	11,100	35,292	143,472
1783	4,415	1,232	5,189	88,300	12,320	20,756	121,376
1788[a]	5,723	1,531		114,460	15,310		129,770
1789	6,156	2,155		123,120	21,550		144,670
1790	5,949	2,018		118,980	20,180		139,160
1796	5,962	2,424		119,240	24,240		143,480
1797	4,968	2,104		99,360	21,040		120,400
1798	5,512	3,872		110,240	38,720		148,960
1799	7,045	2,704		140,900	27,040		167,940

[a]It is not clear whether the data pertain to the Ladoga Canal only.

Sources: Hermann, *Statistische Schilderung*, app., table 8; Reden, *Russland*, p. 389.

Table 6.7   Shipping in the Coastal Trade of Vyborg With Some Selected Russian Ports (Ship Arrivals, 5-year Averages)

Years	St. Petersburg	Kronstadt	Revel'	Narva	Dagdon	Riga	Total
1725–29	168	7	43	4	6	—	228
1730–34	263	5	33	6	18	—	325
1735–39	94	23	16	9	11	—	153
1740–44	134	4	8	1	—	—	147
1745–49	111	2	35	3	19	—	170
1750–54	124	1	17	—	37	—	179
1755–59	142	4	12	1	93	1	253
1760–64	106	—	22	—	28	—	156
1765–69	99	3	48	3	41	5	199
1770–74	152	5	28	11	41	8	245
1775–79	248	—	12	—	26	2	288
1780–84	259	5	23	7	30	2	326
1785–89	530	21	30	52	7	50	690
1790–94	698	15	30	23	—	9	775
1795–99	462	—	25	17	14	2	520

Source: Soikelli, *Wiipurin Kaupungen*, vol. 6.

period 1740–44 to 135 per year in 1790–94. For a port the size of Viipuri, one of the smallest in terms of trade turnover on the Baltic, the figures are very significant. The leading role of St. Petersburg as a partner in the coastal trade of Viipuri is explicable both in terms of its size and proximity. The shares tended to be highest among the cities between which the distances were the shortest, as shown in table 6.7. Thus voyages from Revel' and Dagdon were usually more frequent than from Riga to Viipuri. The Viipuri record indicates that Russian coastal trade was extensive, that it presumably employed a large portion of the available Russian ships, and that the key to its role in both domestic and foreign trade is in the hands of the keepers of the Soviet archives.

The only other body of published data pertaining specifically to shipping employed in the regional coastal trade is one that reports on the coastal trade of the North, centered around Arkhangel'sk. The official data for the last years of the eighteenth-century coastal trade of the port of Arkhangel'sk are presented in table 6.8.

The data portray an extensive network of coastal trade. Shipments of fish and salt came into Arkhangel'sk, grain and manufactured goods were dispatched from it to other coastal areas. The coastal shipping is considerable not only in terms of the value of the cargoes, but also in terms of the number of ships and crew members involved. This traditional area of Russian fishing and shipping continued

Table 6.8   The Arkhangel'sk Coastal Trade, 1797–1800

Year	Incoming			Departing		
	No. of Ships	No. in Crews	Value of Freight (Rubles)	No. of Ships	No. in Crews	Value of Freight (Rubles)
1797	545	3,364	500,580	498	2,402	413,590
1798	611	3,867	701,799	572	2,698	493,446
1799	558	3,341	451,254	444	2,409	325,557
1800	445	3,000	432,377	402	2,335	347,683

Source: Poschman, *Opisanie*, 2: 142–44.

throughout the century to support the coastal trade with its regionally available resources.

Both the Viipuri and the Arkhangel'sk data imply voluminous coastal shipping services in which relatively large capital outlays and skilled labor resources were involved and which served the needs of both the domestic and the foreign trade of Russia.

Shipbuilding in Russia

The Russian failure to develop a domestic shipbuilding industry that could provide its foreign trade with sea-going vessels of domestic production can be explained by a number of factors:

1. The scarcity of skills in the preparation of raw materials and in shipbuilding.

2. The predominance of government shipyards and the scarcity of private shipyards, and the preference given by the former to military naval construction over the construction of merchantmen.

3. The high costs of shipbuilding in Russia relative to costs in other countries.

4. The difficulties of staffing Russian-built merchantmen with competent crews.

5. The high insurance costs and high risks ensuing from operating poor quality Russian-built vessels.

6. The high costs and oppressive procedures of bureaucratic control over the construction and operation of Russian merchantmen.

The eighteenth-century Russian experience in the construction of seagoing vessels began with a virtual *tabula rasa*, if one ignores the construction of small ships for use in the coastal trade on the White and Caspian Seas. The truly heroic attempts of Peter the Great to import foreign specialists and to send Russians abroad to acquire skills in the shipyards of the Netherlands, England, and France, as well as his effort to create a Russian navy, are well known. Peter considered the task so important that he paid the chief foreign specialists engaged in the construction of naval ships higher salaries than were paid even top military specialists and other recruited experts.

The massive Petrine investment in an industry which had a clear military purpose was congruent not only with his overall policies, but also with the policies of many other countries in Europe in which investments in the acquisition of recognized important skills and in capital equipment were made directly by governments or with the help of government subsidies.

Shipbuilding skill acquisition was insufficient. It could not be effective without the creation of sawmills and without the proper treatment of raw materials. In other words, Russia also needed an overhaul of the infrastructure, the auxiliary activities that provided the shipbuilding industry with the required inputs. This turned out to be a serious bottleneck and was not removed for decades following Peter's reign. Giving highest priority to military naval construction under direct government administration and control, Russian officials left merchantmen to be built as by-products of government yards. The government shipyards, hard-pressed because of limited budgets and a scarcity of skilled labor, and also insulated from the private demand for ships, were in no position either to stimulate or to respond to any demand for merchantmen.

Private shipbuilding occurred only in the vicinity of the ports of Arkhangel'sk and Astrakhan'. In the vicinity of Arkhangel'sk, in Vavchug, a shipyard was set up at the beginning of the century by the Bazhenin family's merchant firm of Arkhangel'sk. It specialized in fishing boats, small vessels for the coastal trade, and occasionally engaged in the construction of larger merchantmen. In Astrakhan', on the Caspian Sea, some of the larger Volga riverboats were remodeled for the coastal trade. Small seagoing vessels were built from materials shipped there from the upper Volga and Kama basins. Another important consideration in the Caspian Sea was the negligible competition provided by the Iranians.

The lack of effective foreign competition in shipbuilding on the Caspian Sea caused the Russian government to be more responsive to the demands by the Astrakhan' traders and the local government for the leasing and sale of ships to private mercantile firms. In 1747 the port of Astrakhan' was served by 47 government-owned and 37 privately-owned ships.[11]

There is a paradox for the rest of Russia, especially for the burgeoning Baltic trade. There was a repetitive stream of government decrees apparently designed to stimulate demand for Russian-built vessels by reducing taxes for goods transported in Russian bottoms. Yet there was a virtual absence of construction of merchantmen in the major Russian ports. The government was aware of this, even if its decrees on the subject were published for "educational" purposes only. The government was also aware of the scarcity of skills and knew that the technology of constructing riverboats and small coastal-trade vessels could not be applied to larger, seagoing ships. Consequently there was a plethora of decrees stressing the necessity of building ships according to the new, foreign models and threatening with severe punishment those who built along the lines of the "old models." Such decrees had the effect of preventing private experimentation and inhibited a gradual improvement in shipbuilding. The result was a general passivity.

Even the ships built by the government and private yards according to the "new models" were of poor quality, and therefore of high risk for both crew and freight. The result was a substantial differential of insurance costs and crew wages on Russian-built vessels. The differentials tended to nullify the tariff tax advantages for merchandise carried in Russian bottoms. As a consequence, transportation costs tended to be higher on Russian-built vessels, at least for the longer trade routes, on which the risk premium and crew wage-costs constituted a larger fraction of the total costs than for coastal, short-distance transport.

Private shipbuilding activity did not cease entirely. It operated in the shade, on the sidelines. Most of the record survives because of some government involvement. For example, in 1729 the Berheuen shipyard received a privilege of tax exemption on the purchase of raw materials and the sale of its output.[12] Another Arkhangel'sk merchant, Nikita Krylov, was encouraged to establish another yard in 1732, an example followed by the British merchant Frazer at some later date. During two later periods, short-lived stimulae to engage in private shipbuilding were offered. One was related to the monopoly on forest export development in the Onega region granted to Count Shuvalov in 1752 and resold by him to the British merchant and entrepreneur Gomm. Using his own capital, as well as lavish loans provided by the St. Petersburg government, Gomm constructed many sawmills and port facilities in Onega. A part of the scheme consisted of the construction of vessels which would transport wood to England; it is not clear whether the ships were constructed for multiple voyages or just for a single voyage, after which they would be used for wood. During the years 1761–68 Gomm constructed eighteen ships and six galliots in Onega for his venture; an additional three or four ships were constructed annually for his enterprise in the former Frazer shipyard in Arkhangel'sk. Shipbuilding was only a minor by-product of Gomm's major enterprise. This is evident in the fact that wood exports from Onega in 1762–68 engaged a total of 251 ships, and then 95 ships in the years 1768–74.[13] Nevertheless, his activity amounted to a temporary increase in shipbuilding.

A second period of intensified private shipbuilding activity occurred in the 1780s. The government raised the premiums for transporting merchandise in domestically built bottoms. A special yard for the construction of privately owned merchantmen was established in St. Petersburg in 1784. Perhaps most important, the outlook for expansion of the Black Sea trade became much more real with the acquisition of the Crimea and the development of a number of new port facilities. To the extent that competition with foreigners in the Black Sea was less fierce and that the Russians had good prospects not only for Black Sea shipping but also for future shipping to Mediterranean ports, a strong stimulus to shipbuilding was provided. This led to a virtual leap in the share of Russian ships participating in the Mediterranean trade during the 1790s. Although the leap involved a rise in the share of Russian ships from less than 5 percent to less than 10 percent (and much less as a share of the freight tonnage), it was nevertheless significant, for it provided a base for activity in the subsequent periods.

Attempting to evaluate the causes of the failure of the shipbuilding industry in Russia, the government and the merchants engaged in foreign trade diverged in their views. The government habitually considered the backwardness of Russia to be at the heart of the problem. The merchants blamed interference by the bureaucracy. Reproduction of both views in some detail is worthwhile, for they provide an insight into the economic and social realities of eighteenth-century Russia.

The government evaluation, although directed toward military shipbuilding, is even more cogent when applied to the construction of merchantmen.

During the forty years since 1762, the Admiralty here [in St. Petersburg] constructed eight one-hundred-cannon ships, eighteen seventy-four-cannon ships, nine sixty-four-cannon ships, and fifty-one small sailing ships. For labor alone 4,361,945 rubles were expended. In England, where labor is more expensive, the construction [of such ships] would have entailed expenditures of 3,294,547 rubles, or 1,067,397 rubles less. There [in England] a seventy-four-cannon ship is built by 150 people within a year. With us, 600 people won't finish it within two years. Moreover, [the ship] will not last even six years without repairs.[14]

The government's emphasis was on high labor costs and low quality, both functions of "economic backwardness."

The position of the Russian merchants engaged in foreign trade was elaborated in the instruction given by the merchants of Arkhangel'sk to their deputy to the 1767 legislative reform commission. The instruction given to the deputy Sveshnikov makes it clear that:

A shipbuilder desiring to construct a new vessel is obliged to obtain from the Admiralty experts a plan [for the vessel] and also an estimate of how much timber will be required for its construction. Subsequently he has to obtain from the port office a certified report that a requisition has been made from the provincial chancery to secure permission given to the foresters [the *Waldmeisters*] to fell the necessary timber. The next steps are the following: the blueprint must be submitted to the port office for its agreement and approval. Then it must be given to the shipwright for certification and requisition of the timber. The documents must be returned to the chancery office with a new application for a construction permit and timber allocation. This has to be approved by the chancery and the permit officially announced. Then the owner of the constructed vessel must submit affidavits from the shipwrights that the vessel was constructed according to the blueprints and an affidavit from the rigging-master that it was properly rigged. The order to obtain and to present the above-mentioned affidavits is regulated by the procedures of the port office on reports and opinions. After obtaining the certification of the documents [from the port office], one has to petition the municipality [*magistrat*] to receive a registration permit. This requires special procedures, although less elaborate ones. In such a manner the construction of a vessel is accompanied by official procedures which require petitions and reports. All must be written on stamped paper, require payments, and are finalized by the municipality's registered permit, [copies of] which were submitted to the chancery, to the customs office, and to the port office.

If the constructed vessel is intended for use in the transportation of commercial cargo from the local [Arkhangel'sk] port to the ports of Kola and Onega, or for the loading of vessels engaged in long-distance trade, it is necessary to obtain from the *guberniia* chancery a permit for passage beyond the port barriers for each voyage, or for the whole summer, renewable each year. This permit describes the vessel, the captain, and the members of the crew on the basis of their passports presented to the police. It grants passage beyond the Novodvinsk fortress to the Berezovsk outlet, but forbids entrance into other outlets. In addition, the permit prohibits the crew from carrying any prohibited commodities, bootlegged drink, and unspecified French powders called *dies-poudres*. It also prohibits voyages in Finnish waters or to Finnish cities, under threat of fines.

This permit [from the *guberniia* chancery] must be presented to the port office and customs house. Then a customs declaration [must be presented]. [The vessel] must be loaded in the presence of a sworn appointed customs official to obtain a permit [to ship the cargo]. Having loaded the ship and prepared for the voyage, one has to appear in the port office, file a petition to obtain a permit to pass the firewatch [*brantvakhta*], and then obtain a passport. The latter must be presented at the first nearby firewatch, without raising anchor. Thus begins the voyage, which is free of stoppage for 10 versts up to the Novodvinsk barrier, where one must stop and present the customs permit. Finishing there, one may continue the voyage for another verst and stop across from the Novodvinsk fortress. One must wait until daybreak, if it happens to be night, to present the chancery permit granting the right of passage. Weighing anchor, one must sail to the Admiralty firewatch located at the outlet to the Dea, where, having lowered anchor, one must present the pass issued by the port office. Having done that, one meets no further barriers, the river comes to an end, and the exit to the sea is open.[15]

The demand for Russian-built vessels and the ship-owners' and clients' actual experiences remain unintelligible without comprehension of the problems of manning the vessels. There were difficulties in recruiting Russian sailors because of the scarcity of trained personnel and the requirement that they not be serfs (in view of a perceived risk of desertion while in foreign ports). The solution, a partial staffing of vessels by skilled seamen directed to the merchantmen by the navy, turned out to be a mixed blessing. The merchants reported insulting behavior, scandals, and destruction of property perpetrated by the sailors. It is possible either that the navy tried to get rid of unruly, troublesome, and incompetent elements by assigning them to the merchantmen, or that the attitudes toward the merchant class inculcated by a nobility-oriented navy found an expression in the haughty and rough treatment of the owners of merchantmen and their clients by the naval personnel. Whatever the cause, the contrast between the behavior of the efficient Dutch and British captains and freight agents and that of the crude Russians was too obvious to increase the enthusiasm for a Russian-built and operated merchant marine in the eighteenth century.

Long-Distance Shipping

The story of long-distance shipping in Russia's foreign trade in the eighteenth century belongs only marginally to the economic history of Russia. To a much greater extent it is part of the economic history of Western Europe, of that fascinating period of sail-power and the great struggle between two powerful merchant marines, the Dutch and the British, for mastery of the seas.

By and large the Russians did not carry their own goods to distant markets and they did not travel abroad to obtain their imports. For the majority of Russian exports, Russian nationals did not deal with the shippers. Foreign firms and residents in Russia were the chief exporters. They contracted with independent shippers to carry the goods abroad. Shipping in the Baltic ports was as competitive an industry as one could expect to find in the eighteenth century. Fierce competition among the Dutch, British, Danes, Swedes, and North Germans tended to lower shipping rates on all commodities throughout the century.

It is possible that the Russians missed opportunities in shipping. However, lacking knowledge of superior shipbuilding, skilled seamen, and the enormous capital required to finance a merchant fleet, and being well served by highly efficient and competitive foreigners, the Russians seem to have been served well by the absence of a policy to promote long-distance shipping.

Allegations of exploitation and losses because of foreign "domination" of Russia's carrying trade ignore the great saving in costs that foreigners brought through ship design, sailors with high skills, and lower interest rates. The resulting lower freight rates brought higher incomes to the Russian exporters and producers.

The allegations of discriminatory behavior by foreign shippers and insurers against Russian nationals are not based on relevant evidence. For one, shippers very seldom dealt directly with Russian nationals, and the only ones that they could have discriminated against would have been their own nationals trading in Russia. As far as the higher insurance rates charged to Russian-operated ships are concerned, anyone familiar with the level of skills, training, and discipline of the Russian crews on merchant vessels

in the eighteenth century can only wonder how any insurance was made available to them.

The virtual absence of a Russian merchant marine in sea lanes served by efficient foreigners can be explained adequately by the economic conditions of long-distance shipping. This did not constitute a loss to the Russian economy, as nationalist historians would want us to believe. Moreover, the presence of foreign shippers in Russian trade helped to sustain the high level of foreign demand for Russian goods used in European shipbuilding. The Russian economy benefited from the sale of shipbuilding materials to those who built ships more efficiently and cheaply than the Russians could themselves.

Last but not least, the foreign trade of Russia required shipping services that only a highly organized market could provide. Such a market existed abroad, but not yet in Russia. This explains why Russian merchants engaged in the import trade preferred to use the services of foreign shippers. Foreign services were speedier, more reliable, and cheaper—all good reasons for the correct choice made by the Russian merchants.

The available documentary evidence supports the thesis that the carriers of Russian foreign trade during the eighteenth century were of foreign origin and also explains this phenomenon.

Shipping

Annual data for practically the entire eighteenth century are available on the main Russian trade route, the Baltic-North Sea route that passed through the Sound (Oresund). In addition data for a number of years are available, derived from Russian sources, on the total shipping for different ports including both the shipping along the route of the Baltic trade with Western and Southwestern Europe and the inner Baltic trade between Russia and its neighbors along the Baltic coast.

The following topics can be considered to the extent that the data permit:

1. The share of Russian ports in the total westward shipping from the Baltic.

2. The participation of various ports on the Baltic under Russian control in the total shipping of goods from Russian ports.

3. The participation of the major commercial Western European countries, England and the Netherlands, in the shipping of Russian goods.

4. The relationship between the Russian Baltic ports and the port of Arkhangel'sk in terms of the number of carriers.

5. The extent to which the records on shipping are indicative of the changes in the volume of Russian trade during various periods.

The pattern of shipping was determined by the chief characteristics of Russian commodity trade in the eighteenth century: by the import of high-value manufactured and luxury goods and by the export of raw materials of forest, agricultural, and mining origin—many of which, such as wood, grains, and iron, were exported in bulk. Consequently most of the ships coming to Russian ports from Western Europe arrived with small cargoes. Their chief cargoes were unloaded in other ports en route, or they sailed directly in ballast. This explains the huge difference in the statistics of the Sound tolls between the number of ships giving Russian ports as their destination and the much higher number of ships reporting Russian ports of embarkation. Given the bulk of the Russian cargoes, it is understandable why so many ships used Russian ports as the ultimate ports of departure for their voyages back to Western Europe.

The volume of shipping as measured by the number of ships either frequenting the ports under Russian control or by the number of ships departing from Russian ports on their return voyage to Western Europe fluctuated widely. In part, the fluctuations can be explained by random variables, such as political conditions in Western Europe or the Baltic, which increased greatly the risk factor involved in long-distance shipping. To some extent the volume of shipping from Russian ports (table 6.9) was determined during particular years by special circumstances influencing Russian trade policies, such as embargoes on the export of grain because of Russian crop failures. By and large, however, the upward trend in the volume of shipping was indicative of the growth of the Russian economy, and especially its marketable output, which provided an increasing supply of commodities for its foreign trade.

The growth of Russian foreign trade, as reflected by the rising volume of shipping from Russian ports, explains most of the increase in shipping. There is one important caveat, however: the size of the ships. Contemporary sources occasionally insist that the average size of the ships leaving the port of Riga laden with grains, hemp, and flax was smaller than that of the ships leaving St. Petersburg laden with iron, pitch, and tar. This proposition could be tested by examining the original Sound toll accounts. It is also possible that the average ship size increased during the century, which would make the number of ships a less accurate indicator of the volume of trade.

For some trade routes and ports the number of ships and their export tonnage are available; this makes it possible to establish a correlation between the two changing orders of magnitude. However, the correlation between the volume of shipping ex-

Table 6.9   Departures of Ships From Russian Ports to Western Europe, 5-Year Averages

Years	Ships	Years	Ships
1700– 4	110.8	1750–54	884.8
1705– 9	158.8	1755–59	747.0
1710–14	223.8	1760–64	808.6
1715–19	331.6	1765–69	965.2
1720–24	366.2	1770–74	1,329.0
1725–29	563.2	1775–79	1,260.4
1730–34	n.a.	1780–84	1,317.4
1735–39	727.2	1785–89	1,419.2
1740–44	799.2		
1745–49	646.0		

Note: figures include the departures from the Baltic ports through the Sound and from Arkhangel'sk. They do not include the shipping of Vyborg and the ports of Kurland.

pressed by the number of ships and the value of Russia's exports is a weak one for the years in which data are available.

For most of the eighteenth century the ratio of ships carrying exports from Russian ports westward through the Sound to the total number of laden ships leaving the Baltic can be established. In spite of year-by-year fluctuations, the striking feature of the ratio is its relative stability over the period and its tendency to decline slightly (or to stabilize at a slightly lower level) in the second half of the eighteenth century. By the 1730s more than one-third of all ships sailing westward through the Sound were employed carrying cargo from Russian ports. In the 1740s the ratio declined to slightly below one-third, and then continued its slide to about one-quarter of total shipping. In part, at least, this can be explained by the rapid growth of trade in the lands under Prussian control, enhanced by both the annexation of Silesia and some territories of Poland.

Of greater significance for our topic is the problem of the shares of the various ports in the Russian Baltic trade. A glance at table 6.10, which provides a breakdown of the westward shipping through the Sound for Riga, Narva, St. Petersburg, and the ports of Livonia and Estland, reveals a number of interesting tendencies. One is the commanding place occupied at least until 1775 by Riga, which was primarily an outlet for goods produced in the territory of Livonia, Lithuania, and Belorussia, rather than in the Russian provinces proper. One must also remember that until 1762 Riga was discriminated against in the exportation of Russian goods in favor of St. Petersburg to protect a part of the St. Petersburg hinterland from inroads by Riga merchants.

The amazing feature, however, was Riga's ability to maintain its level of exports in view of its competition with Königsberg as well as in the face of the discriminatory policies of the Russian government favoring St. Petersburg. The maintenance of Riga's

Table 6.10   Westward Shipping through the Sound from Major Ports under Russian Control

	Riga	Narva	St. Petersburg	Livonia and Estland	Total	Kurland
1700	24	144		96	264	68
01	56	18		65	139	96
02	129	13		53	195	24
03	135	11		23	169	19
04	193			17	210	39
1705	45			12	57	24
06	47			16	63	35
07	76			8	84	24
08	100			8	108	25
09	69			4	73	23
1710	14		1	7	22	17
11	29			9	38	15
12	46			4	50	10
13	95		5	25	125	28
14	59		5	11	75	65
1715	155	2	59	32	248	9
16	115		16	22	153	10
17	78	1	18	1	98	1
18	102	3	53	4	162	4
19	118	14	40	6	178	15
1720	114	29	36	10	189	10
21	145	62	28	3	238	11
22	145	65	78	10	298	16
23	178	43	106	7	334	17
24	197	109	102	6	414	17
1725	281	154	145	3	583	37
26	243	146	175	4	568	28
27	256	149	94	5	504	20
28	227	154	119	11	511	27
29	260	118	76	22	476	32
1730	299	192	148	33	672	45
31	264	236	127	36	663	47
32	189	301	135	17	642	27
33	231	292	127	6	656	33
34	226	279	123	18	646	40
1735	286	182	131	8	607	44
36	249	119	133	18	519	38
37	306	196	165	29	696	35
38	319	243	174	41	777	49
39	385	172	170	68	795	92
1740	404	132	182	110	828	94
41	451	151	222	67	891	95
42	313	179	203	26	721	47
43	229	233	111	25	598	29
44	258	124	191	22	595	39

export position is even more remarkable in view of its continuous balance-of-trade surplus. That required much greater cash outlays by foreign importers than in a port such as St. Petersburg where a larger portion of foreign imports was paid for by proceeds from exports to Russia. As a source of specie import, the port of Riga was of utmost importance to Russia. Its large volume of shipping could best be explained by the relatively higher quality of its export commodities compared with those emanating from other ports and by the traditional ties of its merchants with the Western European flax, hemp, grain, and wood markets.

The rise of shipping from St. Petersburg, although continuous, appears less meteoric in the systematic data than the secondary literature on the subject sometimes insists. Unquestionably, governmental policies, special incentives, and administrative measures helped in this development, while perhaps retarding the shipping in rival ports. In addition to government measures, the growth of St. Petersburg as a population center, as the seat of court and government, and as the location of a huge garrison, coupled with improved river and canal networks covering distant regions, played a dominant role in attracting shipping to St. Petersburg. The growth of a colony of foreign merchants and agents of foreign trading firms facilitated sale and purchase trans-

Table 6.10, cont.   Westward Shipping through the Sound from Major Ports under Russian Control

	Riga	Narva	St. Petersburg	Livonia and Estland	Total	Kurland
1745	241	165	121	37	564	48
46	314	109	166	23	612	34
47	310	126	223	33	692	30
48	278	85	131	45	539	37
49	315	157	162	42	676	82
1750	336	206	180	24	746	65
51	315	184	181	32	712	63
52	389	184	259	51	883	92
53	375	194	254	40	863	79
54	470	205	250	34	959	70
1755	361	169	300	27	857	75
56	385	26	265	16	692	52
57	335	20	238	5	598	55
58	323	54	218	1	596	36
59	376	93	275	12	756	38
1760	341	19	204	12	576	120
61	451	32	173	37	693	157
62	449	68	249	48	814	99
63	486	132	202	39	859	64
64	456	148	243	24	871	81
1765	430	123	315	44	912	68
66	416	156	215	37	824	83
67	361	102	304	26	793	121
68	403	122	345	22	892	157
69	479	123	439	33	1,074	85
1770	447	115	405	34	1,001	156
71	527	112	465	66	1,170	145
72	697	99	410	71	1,277	129
73	531	82	496	49	1,158	135
74	601	89	504	87	1,281	212
1775	637	91	385	138	1,251	195
76	430	89	485	75	1,079	118
77	466	101	568	66	1,201	159
78	457	73	469	55	1,054	204
79	460	55	526	60	1,101	196
1780	491	56	453	47	1,047	236
81	439	33	595	33	1,100	153
82	524	46	446	56	1,072	139
83	717	78	420	84	1,299	245
84	649	103	586	69	1,407	214
1785	555	146	528	85	1,314	176

Note: The actual control of Russia over the Baltic ports such as Riga, Narva, and the other ports in Livonia and Estland did not start until 1709–10. Kurland was an autonomous duchy under Russian sovereignty until 1796, and is not included in the totals.

actions carried out in St. Petersburg and increased its attractiveness as a port.

An examination of the exports of St. Petersburg reveals clearly that in a number of commodities, notably iron, but also leather, hides, skins, and furs, it was the leader almost from the start. It also dominated in flax and hemp exports originating in the Russian provinces proper. Curiously enough, its major early rival, Narva, for a very long time retained its position in the export of wood. (Riga relied upon a different hinterland.) The rivalry between St. Petersburg and Narva for second place in shipping volume among the Russian Baltic ports, at least until the 1740s, has not been seriously studied or even mentioned in the secondary literature.

A noteworthy eighteenth-century development was the decline of the smaller ports on the Baltic (grouped under the heading "Other Livonian and Estland" in table 6.10). These ports, including Revel', Pernau, and others, played a much more important role in shipping prior to their incorporation into the Russian Empire. The emergence of St. Petersburg and the expansion by Riga explain the relative and absolute decline of the other ports.

To the extent that the trade in commodities (for example, iron) was concentrated in St. Petersburg, it

Table 6.11   Arrival of Ships and Collection of Custom Duties at Arkhangel'sk 1710–1730

Year	No. of Ships	Internal Customs	Port Customs	Total Customs Duties (in Rubles)
1710	159	153,154	84,329	237,483
1711	184	156,228	89,540	245,768
1712	132	135,416	70,827	206,243
1713	169	161,634	80,974	242,608
1714	155	164,822	96,549	261,371
1715	230	182,773	103,824	286,597
1716	208	168,526	104,452	272,978
1717	146	159,442	62,560	222,002
1718	116	123,995	63,728	187,723
1719	119	120,234	66,155	186,389
1720	122	121,134	75,397	196,531
1721	110	101,090	72,195	173,285
1722	60	40,634	29,210	69,844
1723	40	25,535	13,135	38,670
1724	22	19,041	1,557	20,598
1725	19	14,095	892	14,987
1726	29	16,665	1,743	18,408
1727	45	29,730	4,531	34,261
1728	41	30,789	4,252	35,041
1729	26	24,716	2,646	27,362
1730	38	26,568	4,286	30,854

Source: Ogordnikov, *Ocherki*, p. 13.

was natural for the British, given their demand for those commodities to establish themselves at the source of the export trade in them. The British did not neglect the port of Riga as the main source of Russian grain exports and the major outlet for flax, hemp, and oil seed, but, given the nature of their demand, they could not dislodge the Dutch from the Riga trade. The port of Narva was used by both the Dutch and the British, and the ports of Livonia and Estland remained throughout the period a stronghold of Dutch shipping, neglected by the British except during wars and famines. English ships carrying salt entered those ports, but then called on other ports to receive export cargo for the westward passage.

The two chief carriers of the Russian foreign commodity trade not only brought Russian exports to their home countries for processing and consumption, but also for re-export. Although there are no data on the resale of Russian goods leaving the ports of the Netherlands and the British Isles, there is a great deal of evidence that the Dutch and English served as carriers of Russian exports to France, Portugal, Spain, and Italy. The Dutch, as a rule, accounted for at least half of all the ships leaving the Baltic for France; smaller shares went to the Portuguese and Spanish trade. Denmark was another important carrier of goods to southwestern and southern Europe. Given the demand of southwestern Europe for naval stores and other typical Baltic commodities, it is not surprising that Russian goods were

carried in ships under different flags in the absence of direct trade relations between the Russians and those countries.

Only a part of the shipping of the Russian ports on the Baltic has been considered, that between those ports and Western Europe ports reported in the Sound records. Those toll records do not report the number of ships which visited Russian ports as a part of their voyage before sailing to their home ports, or the number of ships visiting the ports as a result of intra-Baltic trade. The available data indicate that during particular periods a third of all ships visiting Russian harbors on the Baltic were engaged in either coastal or internal Baltic trade. The size of such ships was on average smaller than the ones passing through the Sound, and thus perhaps not over 15 to 20 percent of Russia's Baltic trade was with the countries around the Baltic.

The average-sized ship used on Arkhangel'sk voyages had at least 1.5 times the capacity of ships in the Baltic trade. If that is true, then until about 1720 the shipping through Arkhangel'sk exceeded the total combined shipping through the Baltic ports. This is an impression which also makes sense when considering the duration of the Northern War with Sweden. The emerging domination of the Baltic ports was aided by government policy favoring St. Petersburg while discriminating against Arkhangel'sk. The decline of shipping at Arkhangel'sk is evident in table 6.11. The share of that port was reduced to a range of 8 to 15 percent of the combined shipping, with wide fluctuations within that range. As has been shown earlier in this book, throughout the century Arkhangel'sk remained a major outlet for the commercial output of the northern provinces of Russia and specialized in the exports of forest products such as pitch, tar, and potash. A sizable part of the fur from Siberia was exported through Arkhangel'sk, and also a substantial portion of the grain. It remained important for the trade of the Russian North. Although it declined in favor of Baltic and Black Sea ports, its potential importance at a time of war in the Baltic must not be overlooked.

What do the shipping data tell us about particular aspects of foreign trade during the eighteenth century that is not apparent from other types of data? For one, the data on the number of ships sailing through the Sound (see table 6.10) should dispel any doubts about the impact of the Northern War upon the trade and shipping of the Baltic ports. It was not until the years 1724 and 1725 that the number of ships leaving the Baltic returned to the lowest level of the period 1680–99. For all practical purposes, an analysis of shipping that serviced the foreign trade of Russia in the eighteenth century might as well start with 1724–25. Any earlier data, either for the last decades of the seventeenth century or for the beginning of the eighteenth century, would require estimates (which do not exist) of Russian exports through the territories controlled by Sweden.

The volume of shipping during the post-Petrine period, roughly the period 1725–40, requires attention. If we assume that by 1724–25 the volume of foreign trade out of Russia and the Baltic provinces was restored to its pre-1700 level, the shipping data indicate two developments: a definite shift of foreign trade from Arkhangel'sk to the Baltic ports; growth in the total volume of shipping. Such growth should come as no surprise to students of European economic history, except to those who have uncritically swallowed the nationalist line of interpretation of the immediate post-Petrine period of Russian history. For generations Russian historians interpreted the post-Petrine era as one of economic decline caused by the "ruling of Russia by foreigners." Russian historians of a nationalist persuasion even designed a pejorative name for the leading statesmen of the time, such as Münnich, Ostermann, and others, who have been called "time-servers" (vremenshchiki) in an attempt to ascribe selfish behavior and exclusive interest in self-aggrandizement at the expense of the vital interests of Russia and its people. The paucity of economic documentation permitted this myth to survive until it became almost a dogma in the interpretation of Russian history. The shipping evidence provides additional support for a claim that there is a need to reexamine this period from the aspect of economic performance.

Shipping in Amsterdam

The shipping of the Russian ports to one of the two major centers of the Russo-Western European trade, Amsterdam, was recently analyzed and described in great detail by the young Canadian scholar Jake Knoppers of McGill University in his dissertation "Dutch Trade with Russia from the Time of Peter I to Alexander I. A Quantitative Study of Eighteenth-century Shipping."[16] Although the shipping to Amsterdam was only a part of the shipping from Russian ports to the entire Netherlands, it is significant for at least three reasons. First, it indicates direct intercourse with the major European commodity market of the first half of the eighteenth century. Second, it provides data on the volume of the cargoes carried from the various Russian ports to Amsterdam on a yearly basis for most of the century (see tables 6.12 and 6.13), and thus constitutes a continuous long-run series of data. Third, by providing both the registered tonnage of the ships utilized in trade as well as the volume (tonnage) of cargo actually carried, it supplies an index of utilization of the shipping

capacity of laden ships engaged in the trade with Amsterdam for various periods during the century.

Even for students of Russian history, the results of the distribution of tonnage between the various ports trading with Amsterdam have a few surprises. Although it was well known that Riga, rather than St. Petersburg, held the first place in the Amsterdam trade, the constantly high share of Narva certainly must surprise even those aware of its position in the trade of forest products and also of its continuous exports of flax. Perhaps even more surprising is the tenacity of the port of Viipuri in the trade with Amsterdam. This indicates stability in the "traditional" trade contacts between Amsterdam and some Russian ports, including Arkhangel'sk. Amsterdam's trade network, established during earlier centuries with the port cities of the Eastern Baltic and with Arkhangel'sk, was able to survive the vicissitudes of the early eighteenth century and continue its operation. Shipping, together with information and trading capital, played a strategic role in the trade network continuity. The reliability, skill, and efficiency of the Dutch shippers were important ingredients not only in the earlier success story of the Netherlands, but also in the fierce competition with England for primacy in European trade, in slowing down the process of political and economic decline in the United Provinces.

It is therefore instructive to compare in table 6.14 the tonnage of the Dutch shipping from Russian ports to Amsterdam with the tonnage of British shipping from Russian ports to Great Britain. The only years for which this can be done are 1787–98.

The comparison is not overwhelmingly enlightening, and may not be typical for other periods in the century. First, it is limited to the period of Dutch shipping decline and British superiority not only in the number of ships and total tonnage, but probably also in terms of efficiency of utilization of shipping space for the available cargo. The absence of British data on the actual cargoes carried make any comparison with Amsterdam incomplete. There is also a possible upward bias in the British data used in the comparison to the extent that those data include the shipping from Arkhangel'sk, which used larger ships than the Baltic trade, while the figures in table 6.14 for Amsterdam do not include Arkhangel'sk shipping.

Be that as it may, for the period 1787–90 the average tonnage of the ships arriving in British ports was 210.2, while in Amsterdam it was more, 243.6 tons. For the years 1791–94, the average was 231.8 tons for the British and 221.2 tons for Amsterdam. For the period of France's annexation of the Netherlands, there was a very substantial decline to 129.5

Table 6.12   Percentage Distribution of Cargo Shipped to Amsterdam from Russian Ports on the Baltic, 1712–99

Year	St. Petersburg	Narva	Riga	Vyborg	Other	Total Tonnage
1712			68.60		31.40	726
1713			97.48		2.52	6,818
1714	4.50		76.78		23.91	5,198
1715			92.41	6.58	1.01	4,744
1716	7.08		61.18		31.74	22,630
1717	3.62		79.16	6.83	10.39	27,465
1718	8.05		70.85	18.45	2.65	22,974
1719	7.69	12.44	60.38	14.83	4.66	23,598
1720	8.75	20.38	39.18	26.73	4.97	39,952
1721	3.53	41.37	37.89	16.96	.26	41,858
1722	5.05	38.05	37.76	18.16	.97	36,608
1723	8.57	30.33	43.24	11.30	6.56	36,608
1724	10.42	50.41	31.24	7.36	.56	51,128
1725	6.30	53.86	33.24	6.21	.38	75,540
1726	11.37	44.55	34.70	9.08	.29	73,830
1727	6.45	49.93	34.06	9.45	.12	58,794
1728	9.10	50.19	33.37	5.31	2.03	65,242
1729	3.96	46.56	37.33	6.13	6.02	57,540
1730	4.74	47.07	34.77	7.08	6.33	82,316
1731	6.07	51.82	29.09	5.21	7.80	87,810
1732	5.13	69.10	15.93	7.39	2.45	86,466
1733	3.21	69.69	18.95	7.40	.75	83,716
1734	5.56	61.33	23.26	6.23	3.63	94,578
1735	4.75	51.42	32.10	10.89	.84	76,952
1736	7.25	36.62	36.51	17.56	2.07	72,662
1737	13.22	45.90	25.85	11.89	3.15	81,020
1738	16.79	46.73	25.50	5.32	5.67	107,732
1739	6.92	44.36	32.63	4.82	11.27	89,380
1740	7.85	31.04	38.15	2.16	20.80	104,390
1741	25.13	32.01	30.12	3.89	8.85	96,674
1742	12.30	41.55	35.09	4.21	6.85	77,624
1743	7.81	64.34	18.88	5.22	3.74	90,158
1744	12.35	40.47	32.86	7.31	7.01	67,022
1745	5.63	55.18	22.80	6.09	10.38	70,142
1746	9.54	44.69	30.59	5.71	9.48	63,290
1747	14.69	38.06	27.30	5.62	14.33	58,714
1748	8.15	36.86	28.92	5.45	20.62	55,208
1749	7.30	47.39	24.40	4.88	16.02	64,378
1750	4.70	60.94	19.64	6.52	8.20	65,078
1751	9.81	63.46	13.33	2.93	10.48	60,098
1752	10.56	52.40	22.86	3.57	10.61	62,252
1753	10.79	52.00	26.34	6.20	4.67	61,882
1754	7.22	52.24	32.50	4.82	3.23	64,682
1755	5.69	58.36	25.15	7.53	3.26	49,486
1756	17.52	4.55	49.63	20.63	7.68	34,520

tons per ship entering Amsterdam, while the figure remained high, 214.6 tons per ship, for those entering the British ports. The available data thus seem to suggest that it was not so much commercial competition or, for that matter, the English Navigation Laws, but the political demise of the Netherlands that established the unquestionable superiority of the British in the shipping of goods from Russia at the end of the eighteenth century.

The Russian Share in Shipping

The data of the Sound toll accounts, the scattered reports of shipping in various ports, and the shipping data on the British and Dutch ships calling in Russian ports taken together reveal the general tendencies of the growth of shipping paralleling the growth of the volume of trade.

Precise quantitative data are lacking on the share of Russian shipping in the total. It is insufficient to say that the share of Russian shipping was "negligible" or "minuscule." Although the Russian archives might provide an answer to the problem, the few published data and the theorizing based on them have further obscured the subject. The authority on eighteenth-century Russian commerce, Heinrich

Table 6.12, cont.   Percentage Distribution of Cargo Shipped to Amsterdam from Russian Ports on the Baltic, 1712–99

Year	St. Petersburg	Narva	Riga	Vyborg	Other	Total Tonnage
1757	21.97		64.07	9.46	4.50	38,706
1758	14.36	18.59	60.45	3.59	3.02	44,312
1759	12.36	27.99	50.02	3.76	5.87	62,342
1760	10.74	4.51	72.30	6.50	5.94	54,486
1761	5.59		85.36	2.51	6.55	59,478
1762	11.81	14.14	59.18	3.07	11.79	64,972
1763	13.75	31.84	45.23	2.87	6.31	61,236
1764	6.38	35.67	50.19	2.80	4.96	65,660
1765	10.11	30.36	51.06	4.68	3.80	61,722
1766	9.03	36.35	46.46	4.08	4.09	73,870
1767	18.27	33.67	41.18	1.13	5.76	52,260
1768	13.36	39.89	37.59	2.24	6.93	67,636
1769	13.07	26.59	49.68	2.34	8.33	80,492
1770	7.83	29.60	50.55	1.93	10.10	64,252
1771	13.01	21.76	48.42	.60	16.23	44,328
1772	9.47	17.31	59.09	.19	13.94	76,782
1773	10.38	22.72	51.53	1.52	13.86	72,412
1774	9.43	20.80	53.61	.98	15.19	85,316
1775						
1776	4.31	33.68	42.30	1.44	18.27	64,082
1777	10.51	24.61	50.11	.49	14.27	70,822
1778	19.10	17.58	48.73	1.75	12.85	72,778
1779	17.60	16.77	47.19	4.01	14.44	61,934
1780	16.65	18.43	53.95	.67	10.31	67,798
1781	17.46		67.89	4.68	9.97	20,480
1782	12.14	5.57	67.18	5.65	9.46	45,318
1783	7.86	21.90	55.86	2.36	12.03	68,020
1784	20.42	35.67	35.83	1.61	6.47	72,298
1785	4.08	45.22	38.96	2.12		65,678
1786	6.39	50.00	38.13	2.68		62,718
1787	5.42	55.76	32.54	2.44	3.84	64,504
1788	12.09	53.73	29.86	1.61	2.71	62,542
1789	14.04	47.57	31.68	1.78	4.93	72,274
1790	9.50	50.46	36.73	.65	2.66	74,762
1791	13.13	59.53	24.18		3.16	66,258
1792	6.90	55.36	33.17	1.70	2.87	66,886
1793	13.23	14.80	62.43	6.95	2.59	37,422
1794	7.47	52.96	30.93	3.99	4.65	60,472
1795	8.42	4.92	86.66			8,336
1796	8.39	15.49	53.14	1.24	21.74	47,008
1797		28.74	48.12	1.34	21.80	40,050
1798		16.50	57.19	2.61	23.70	20,498
1799			33.53	18.68	47.79	1,360

Storch, provided data on ships under the Russian flag, data which are mechanically reproduced and indiscriminately used in the historical literature.[17] For the years 1773–77 he reported a yearly average of 227 Russian ships out of a total of 2,175, or 10.4 percent, that frequented the Russian ports. For 1793–97 he reported an average of 350 out of the 2,923 ships, or 12 percent.

Storch did not list the home ports of the Russian ships, the ports in which they carried on their trade, their size, or their cargo potential. By giving a list of the Russian ships participating in the shipping of the port of St. Petersburg, Chulkov's voluminous history of Russian commerce provided some of the informa-tion omitted by Storch.[18] Chulkov provided the names of 28 shipowners and listed 153 ships. The ships were constructed in the following years: 1763, 2; 1765, 1; 1766, 3; 1767, 3; 1768, 8; 1769, 10; 1770, 24; 1771, 30; 1772, 35; 1773, 21; 1774, 16. In terms of tonnage, they were distributed as follows: below 50 lasts (1 last = 4,000 pounds), 24; 51–60 lasts, 96; 61–70 lasts, 17; 71 lasts and above, 16.

Their size provides at least a partial answer to the puzzle of Russian ships. A report of the British Customs office noted the sizes of British and foreign ships coming from Russia. The averages per British ship (in tons) for 1773–75 were 186.6; for 1783–85, 207.6; and for 1786–87, 225.5. The foreign ships were

Table 6.13   Cargo Shipped to Amsterdam from Russian Ports (in Tons) 1717–96

Year	Cargo from Baltic Ports	Cargo from White Sea Ports	Total Cargo from Russian Ports
1717	27,465	2,518	29,983
1718	22,974	19,476	42,450
1719	23,598	12,922	36,520
1720	39,952	15,762	55,714
1721	41,858	9,576	51,434
1722	36,608	8,330	44,938
1723	36,608	9,002	45,610
1724	51,128	6,872	58,000
1725	75,540	1,352	76,892
1726	73,830	7,232	81,062
1727	58,794	3,644	62,438
1728	65,242	4,174	69,416
1729	57,540	4,962	62,502
1730	82,316	3,642	85,958
1731	87,810	3,910	91,720
1732	86,466	4,480	90,946
1733	83,716	7,520	91,236
1734	94,578	10,372	104,950
1735	76,952	8,724	85,676
1736	72,662	8,284	80,946
1737	81,020	6,430	87,450
1738	107,732	6,612	114,344
1739	89,380	13,052	102,432
1740	104,390	22,570	126,960
1741	96,674	19,686	116,360
1742	77,624	11,824	89,448
1743	90,158	9,414	99,572
1744	67,022	7,064	74,086
1745	70,142	4,534	74,676
1746	63,290	6,722	70,012
1747	58,714	7,522	66,236
1748	55,208	6,912	62,120
1749	64,378	6,552	70,930
1750	65,078	9,560	74,638
1751	60,098	3,550	63,648
1752	62,252	10,540	72,792
1753	61,882	9,782	71,664
1754	64,682	10,980	75,662
1755	49,486	10,358	59,844
1756	34,520	15,712	50,232

even larger, and probably were used for the Arkhangel'sk trade.[19] A comparison of the sizes of the British and the Russian ships listed by Chulkov in the port of St. Petersburg reveals that the latter were at best only a little more than one-half the size of the former. This suggests that many of the Russian ships were used in the coastal trade, that some were used for trading within the Baltic Sea, and that very few could venture a long-distance voyage.

That only a small fraction of the reported Russian merchant marine even conceivably could have been involved in direct Russo-British trade can also be inferred from available data in the Sound toll reports. A similar inference can be drawn from a copy of a list of Russian ships engaged in the export trade of St. Petersburg for 1780.[20] Finally, table 6.15 summarizing the published Sound toll reports for the years 1725–86, shows that the share of Russian ships in the total volume of shipping westward was very small in comparison with the traffic listed in, for example, table 6.10.

A 1780 list of Russian ships exporting goods from the port of St. Petersburg included 29 ships which made 37 voyages during the navigation season. Of the total, 8 ships made 12 voyages within the Baltic. Four of these ships made six voyages to Stockholm; four others made three voyages to Riga, two to Lübeck, and one to Revel'. Twenty-two ships were reported as traveling beyond the Sound. (The Sound tolls registered for that year report thirteen St. Petersburg ships and seven Riga ships passing through westward. The discrepancy of two ships cannot be explained at this point, although an examination of the original Sound accounts might explain it

Table 6.13, cont.   Cargo Shipped to Amsterdam from Russian Ports (in Tons) 1717–96

Year	Cargo from Baltic Ports	Cargo from White Sea Ports	Total Cargo from Russian Ports
1757	38,706	23,306	62,012
1758	44,312	12,608	56,920
1759	62,342	11,202	73,544
1760	54,586	9,430	64,016
1761	59,478	13,686	73,164
1762	64,972	9,590	74,562
1763	61,236	13,376	74,612
1764	65,660	18,596	84,256
1765	61,722	10,466	72,188
1766	73,870	15,428	89,298
1767	52,560	14,314	66,874
1768	67,636	22,242	89,878
1769	80,492	19,598	100,090
1770	64,252	15,752	80,004
1771	44,328	24,192	68,520
1772	76,782	23,974	100,756
1773	72,412	21,828	94,240
1774	85,316	27,014	112,330
1775		24,894	
1776	64,082	17,726	81,808
1777	70,822	14,516	85,338
1778	72,778	24,146	96,924
1779	61,934	9,864	71,798
1780	67,798	14,618	82,416
1781	20,480	14,388	34,868
1782	45,318	12,580	57,898
1783	68,020	15,300	83,320
1784	72,298	14,492	86,790
1785	65,678	10,584	76,262
1786	62,718	12,266	74,984
1787	64,504	16,422	80,926
1788	62,542	16,272	78,814
1789	72,274	16,960	89,234
1790	74,762	12,854	87,616
1791	66,258	8,718	74,976
1792	66,886	13,178	80,064
1793	37,422	6,214	43,636
1794	60,472	15,148	75,620
1795	8,336	4,206	12,542
1796	47,008	5,474	52,482

easily.) Their destinations, involving twenty-four voyages, were reported as follows: to Bordeaux, eight; to Amsterdam, three; two to St. Malo, Nantes, Bilbao, Cadiz, and Port L'Orient (is this a euphemism for the Mediterranean?); and one each to Ostende, Coruna, and Ferrol.

This list of Russian registered ships engaged in the export trade from St. Petersburg sheds additional light on unresolved issues of Russian shipping. It confirms the data of the Sound tolls on the limited participation of Russian ships in the long-distance trade. There was no particular body of Russian shipping engaged exclusively in the import trade. The list also points to the significant share of Russian ships engaged in the intra-Baltic trade out of the total of Russian ships engaged in noncoastal trade, and strengthens the assertion that Russian registered ves-sels were engaged primarily in the coastal trade between Russian ports.

A summary of these findings about Russian shipping points to the following conclusions: first, Russian shipbuilding suffered from poor workmanship and a scarcity of appropriate raw materials, and was relatively expensive. Although there is evidence of ship construction for export even in Arkhangel'sk, it is also a fact that the St. Petersburg yard for private shipbuilding was continuously starved for orders. This alone suggests that Russian-built merchantmen were of poor quality and short service-life.

Second, the most serious shortcoming of Russian shipping was the shortage of skills. Training facilities for the Russian merchant marine were absent. The Russian navy had trained personnel, and at least legally private shippers were able to request the navy

Table 6.14   Ships from Russia to Amsterdam and the British Ports

Year	Number of Ships		Total Tonnage		Average Tons p. Ship	
	To Amsterdam	To British Ports	Amsterdam	Britain	Amsterdam	Britain
1787	231	846	57,896	153,861	250.6	181.9
1788	211	941	52,200	202,477	247.4	273.25
1789	242	613	60,014	149,642	248.0	244.1
1790	262	803	59,776	173,602	228.2	216.2
1791	216	841	55,410	195,741	256.5	232.75
1792	221	927	56,914	222,148	257.5	239.6
1793	188	843	27,548	200,915	146.5	238.3
1794	235	814	52,734	177,072	224.4	217.5
1795	51	792	5,534	174,387	108.5	220.2
1796	259	1,197	32,192	254,687	124.3	212.4
1797	182	691	30,990	161,034	170.3	233.0
1798	111	914	15,276	198,414	137.6	217.1

Sources: Marshall, *Digest*, pp. 222–23; Knoppers, "Dutch Trade."

to release trained servicemen for private employment, but in practice the bureaucratic procedures were difficult and cumbersome. The procedures required a guarantee that the Russian sailors would not jump ship in foreign ports, which in turn involved high risks and potential expense. The result was that there is no mention in the literature of Russian merchantmen ever actually employing naval personnel. The 1780 list mentioned above is revealing on the subject of skills possessed by Russian nationals, for it includes only three Russian captains commanding ships on voyages within the Baltic; the rest were of non-Russian origin.

Third, the costs of Russian shipping, including the costs of shipbuilding, operating the ships, and providing ancillary services, were higher than competitors' costs in long-distance trade. It is total costs that matter, not the cost of any one of these components, in the investment decision to employ Russian ships in long-distance trade. In addition, the quality of service offered by Russian shippers was inferior to that offered by foreign shippers at market prices.

Four, the incentives offered by the Russian government to Russian-registered ships in the form of lower customs duties were insufficient to overcome the cost differential between Russian and foreign shipping in long-distance trade.

Five, the limited participation of Russian shipping in long-distance trade was with areas from which a return cargo was certain. This helps to explain the frequency of Russian voyages to France, Portugal, and Spain, whence the likelihood of a consignment of wines was very likely and, at worst, a load of Bay-salt absolutely certain. Those destinations provided less fierce competition, as from the Dutch, and avoided the discrimination inherent in the British Navigation Laws. Only with a two-way assured cargo was it possible for Russian ships to engage in long-distance trade, while many of their competitors often did it with only one-way cargo.

Six, these considerations forced Russian shipping to remain primarily in the coastal trade, or at best in the intra-Baltic trade. Ordinarily, the Russians ventured out into the long-distance trade only at times of very high demand for shipping services, such as during European famines or periods when European countries were stockpiling "strategic" Russian goods.

Seven, to the extent that shipbuilding represented a substantial investment requiring a number of years of service to recoup, investors had to have access to capital and a certainty of remaining in business for a time sufficient to realize a profit on their investments. Within the Russian trading community, those who enjoyed the means to own ships were primarily merchants of foreign origin or citizenship residing in Russia. Russian legislation, especially between 1782 and 1797, favored either Russian nationals or Russian citizens with lower taxation and special tariff inducements. As a consequence, many, even perhaps most, of the ships owned by resident merchants of foreign origin and commanded by foreign captains were registered in the names of Russian partners. By doing so the real ship owners were trying to avoid discriminatory taxation and to stay in business. Storch even maintained that in its attempt to develop Russian shipping on the Black Sea, the Russian government was ready to register as Russian ships "those which have not seen Russia heretofore."[21] After 1797, when the special incentives were abolished, the number of Russian registered ships decreased, which indicated either that foreign registered ships were more efficient or that, without the special incentives, the previously precarious position of Russian-registered ships deteriorated.

In this short and cursory review I have not dealt with the obvious distinction between Russian shipping and shipping by Russian nationals, a favorite pastime of some Soviet historians.[22] Those historians are full of wrath over the practice of the foreign resident merchants' use of Russians as fictitious own-

Table 6.15 Russian Ships Passing Westward Through the Sound (by Home Port), 1725–85

Year	St. Petersburg	Riga	Other	Total	Year	St. Petersburg	Riga	Other	Total	Year	St. Petersburg	Riga	Other	Total
1725	5	7	—	12	1749	6	8	—	14	1773	9	5	4	18
26	1	2	—	3	1750	2	6	—	8	74	8	5	2	15
27	—	2	—	2	51	3	7	1	11	1775	6	3	—	9
28	2	2	—	4	52	4	7	2	13	76	6	12	2	20
29	8	5	2	15	53	5	4	5	14	77	8	15	—	23
1730	10	8	—	18	54	6	3	2	11	78	10	15	1	26
31	8	7	—	15	1755	5	2	3	10	79	18	14	—	32
32	8	10	1	19	56	3	2	1	6	1780	13	7	—	20
33	3	7	2	12	57	3	1	—	4	81	48	26	3	77
34	—	6	2	8	58	2	2	—	4	82	54	29	5	88
1735	1	4	—	5	59	3	—	—	3	83	32	23	4	59
36	4	5	—	9	1760	1	1	2	4	84				87
37	3	3	1	7	61	3	4	—	7	1785				79
38	2	10	4	16	62	4	—	—	4					
39	2	9	1	12	63	10	2	—	12					
1740	2	7	1	10	64	9	1	—	10					
41	2	6	1	9	1765	8	2	—	10					
42	—	—	—	—	66	6	2	2	10					
43	—	—	1	1	67	7	4	5	16					
44	3	9	—	12	68	3	4	3	10					
1745	1	5	—	6	69	6	6	3	15					
46	3	7	—	10	1770	10	5	4	19					
47	6	5	2	13	71	8	2	3	13					
48	6	3	1	10	72	11	6	7	24					

ers. One can understand their moral indignation and still doubt its utility in explaining the conditions of Russian shipping. Whether Russian foreign trade was harmed by this diminution of government revenue is an issue that could be solved by empirical evidence that the modern economic nationalists among the Russian historians still have to produce. Were this evidence accompanied by economic analysis proving that the absence of foreigners among the owners of Russian-registered ships would have provided more employment and higher incomes for the Russian people, the historians would have made a contribution rather than merely revealing their ideological biases.

7
BANKING AND CREDIT

Some of the major problems in evaluating the economic role of banks and credit institutions in eighteenth-century Russia are semantic or definitional. Heretofore historians have loosely discussed "credit and banking" in a context in which the chief characteristics of the institutions described as banks were the absence of two of the utmost important functions of any banking system, the collection of savings and the creation of liabilities. For most of the period we are examining, those institutions distributed currency among various groups of the Russian population and acted on behalf of the government in increasing the money supply and redistributing income. On these grounds one might seriously question their designation as "banks."

The other problem involves the definition of a "loan" or "credit." In eighteenth-century Russia the boundary between a loan, a subsidy, and an outright grant was blurred. This lack of a clear distinction, however, is itself significant for an understanding of the Russian economy at the time.

The distinction between loans and grants or subsidies is important within a system in which the free market prevails, for loans made to firms will flow into areas in which the loans will yield the highest returns. Loans express the allocative function of the market with respect to investment funds among firms that anticipate the highest market profits. It is easy to argue that under the system prevailing in Russian industry until 1775, in which the government licensed industrial enterprises, it was governmental preference and not market expectations that established eligibility for loans. Government licenses were often coupled with exclusive monopoly rights, and under those circumstances the economic distinction between a loan and a grant is not of major significance. The awarding of a loan would not necessarily identify the borrower as being more efficient, nor would the refusal of a loan be sufficient evidence of a firm's inefficiency, because under a monopoly-ridden system loans do not perform the disciplining function

that they tend to perform under a free-market system.

The economic significance of the difference between loans and grants for the commercial and industrial sectors of the economy in the eighteenth century was not great because of the limited volume of such "loans," which hardly interfered with the allocation of resources between economic sectors or with the income distribution among various social groups. In addition, any loan granted by a government agency or a bank-like institution contained an element of subsidy because of the below-market-rate interest charge. The difference between a loan and a grant was reduced to the difference in the level of the subsidy involved, a quantitative rather than a qualitative difference.

The lack of distinction between a modern concept of a loan and a grant in the matter of "loans" made in eighteenth-century Russia by "banking" institutions was even more prevalent for funds put into the hands (or pockets) of the serf-owning nobility. Officially the nobility mortgaged their serfs, but in fact the "loans" turned into revolving accounts and were rarely repaid during the century. In view of the lack of information on how the funds were used by the borrowers, most historians assume that the funds ought to be considered as grants rather than loans. If it were known that the loans were used for farm improvements, perhaps historians would justify the grants on grounds of increased productivity, investment, economic progress, or many of the other justifications for which intellectuals, regardless of ideological persuasion, for the past century have deigned to forgive a ruling elite for being what it actually was. The idea that a ruling elite somehow has to maintain a balance between what it takes from the rest of society and what it returns to society reflects an ideal state that has yet to be found in any political reality. The historians' righteous condemnation of the Russian nobility of the eighteenth century, which fills pages and volumes, has a hollow sound when applied to a period in which that particular

311

social group's characteristic was consumption and not investment.

When most of the textbook histories refer to institutional credits, they are describing at best a mixture of credits, subsidies, and grants. Most of the real credits were provided by individuals on terms determined by the general scarcity of capital and dependent on the risks involved in such transactions. The idea of institutionally supplied credits originated in the atmosphere of high interest rates and was reinforced by the clumsiness of the judicial system in protecting lenders against certain if not all categories of borrowers. For purposes of economic analysis, the limitations of the volume of institutional lending are of greater importance than the modern legal niceties that differentiate between loans, subsidies, and grants.

Economic analysis requires exploring the relationship of the various "credit institutions" and the government's mechanisms and policies for controlling the money supply. Most Russian historians have ignored the distinction between an expansion of the money supply through use of the mint or printing press and through extension of credit by various credit institutions. Banks create money on the basis of their deposits and a reserve ratio. Russia had no private banks; until 1775 the credit institutions did not accept deposits, and consequently lending by credit institutions depended on the size of the capital the government endowed them with. Although the government did not distinguish between the scarcity of savings and the scarcity of money, the lending operations of the various "credit institutions" involved an injection of currency into circulation as a means of payment by the government for goods and services with newly minted or printed currency. This government policy simultaneously made new currency directly available and "lent" it through the "credit institutions." This simultaneity, in preference to a choice of alternating the two measures, increased the fluctuations in the growth rate of the money supply. Thus the activity of the government-sponsored credit institutions was closely related to changes in the money supply. Henceforth I shall concentrate on the economic, social, and institutional effects of these institutions' activities.

The government as a collector of tax revenues served as a source of credit long before any formal governmental lending institutions were established. This was true for most European countries and must have been true also for Russia, at least to the extent that the local tax-collecting authorities exerted some discretion in sending the taxes to the capital. The money almost certainly was not kept idle while in the safekeeping of the local tax collectors. In addition, government authorities receiving their budget alloca-

tions exerted some discretion in paying their debts or making advance payments to their suppliers. Although there is no direct evidence on such practices, the first legalization of the lending of "idle" balances dates to decrees of 1729 and 1733 and indicates a tendency on the part of the government to capture profits that previously had been reaped by members of the bureaucracy. The 1733 decree grants permission to the mint (*Monetnaia kontora*) to extend loans of copper money against the security of precious metals. Such loans were not to exceed 75 percent of the assessed value of the gold and silver and were granted for a year at 8 percent interest. Such loans could be extended to a maximum term of three years.[1] Very soon this arrangement was extended to the other offices of the central bureaucracy, including the Office of the Army Intendant (*Glavnyi komissariat*), the Admiralty College, the Chief Chancellery of Artillery and Fortifications, the Central Post Office (*Glavnyi Pochtampt*), and the College of Foreign Affairs (*Inostrannaia kollegiia*).

This legal type of lending operation by government offices took place over a period of twenty years. The beneficiaries were mostly high governmental officials and the volume of loans was rather limited. Incomplete data identify a total of 163,000 rubles of "bad" loans (28,512 rubles at the mint, 68,000 rubles at the Office of the Army Intendant, 12,000 rubles by the Admiralty College, and 83,000 rubles by the College of Foreign Affairs and the Central Post Office), but the total could not have been much larger given the problems of access to such loans.[2] The limited volume of such loans can be explained in part by the high costs of the wars in the 1730s and by the government's general deflationary policy in the 1740s. (One of the deflationary measures was to increase the copper content of the copper ruble.) During this period relatively little copper money was minted and attempts were made to withdraw the low-value copper coins from circulation, so we may conclude that the government was not eager to increase the money supply by lavish grants.

The 1733 regulations also stipulated that real estate could not be accepted as security for loans. Although the government was correct in refusing to accept real estate as collateral in view of the legal uncertainties of property rights and because of the lack of administrative machinery to utilize estates in case of default, this provision excluded most of the nobility whose wealth consisted of estates rather than precious metals.

This policy underwent a radical change during the early 1750s. The moving spirit behind most of the economic reforms of the 1750s was count Petr Ivanovich Shuvalov, one of the leading statesmen of the Elizabethan period. Under his guidance the alcohol supply was monopolized by the gentry, a state

Loan Bank was established in 1754, internal tolls were abolished, and the 1757 tariff was introduced. The first state-owned "bank" consisted of two loan offices whose functions were accurately described by their titles as the "Bank for the Nobility" and the "Bank for the Improvement of Commerce at the Port of St. Petersburg." This institutional distinction in the matter of the beneficiaries of the activities of the "Bank" survived through the rest of the century with minimal exceptions. It described not only two branches of the economy, but also two distinct social groups and the relationship of the government's economic and social policy with respect to those groups.

Shuvalov advanced another experiment in the 1750s that illustrates the use of credit-like institutions for the increase of the money supply. The government justified its concern about credit because of high interest rates or, to use the parlance of the times, "usury." During the early 1750s the government decreed a legal ceiling of 6 percent for interest rates. The government disliked high interest rates because it was convinced that they increased the costs of commerce, created difficulties for the landed nobility, who were net borrowers, and also affected the government's budget by raising the prices of the goods it bought. The government frequently promulgated anti-usury decrees, whose impact seems to have been minimal. Consequently the sole remaining solution was to compete with the usurers by providing funds at low interest rates.

This was the reasoning behind two governmental institutions which during a relatively short period helped to increase the money supply in Russia. One was the Bank Comptoir for the Circulation of Copper Money within Russia (referred to in the literature as "The Copper Bank"), the other the Bank of the Artillery and Engineering Corps. Within a period of less than five years (1758–62), according to incomplete data, they loaned, or rather distributed, at least 3,231,069 rubles. The total was certainly more, for data on the activities of the Artillery Bank are lacking. They extended loans at 4 percent yearly interest to a rather small group of high officeholders and merchants or industrialists associated with them in various business ventures.

Except for the lack of randomness in the distribution of the "borrowers," it would have been difficult to design a quicker way of putting this addition to the money supply into circulation. Giving money to the members of the Russian aristocracy assured that it would neither be saved nor hoarded, but spent in the shortest possible time. The merchant-beneficiaries of this credit were certain to put this additional purchasing power into circulation by paying their suppliers. Therefore, regardless of the effect on income distribution and capital formation, the choice of the beneficiaries was correct from the point of view of putting such currency increments into circulation and thereby stimulating domestic and foreign commerce.

If the Bank for the Circulation of Copper Money was an interesting way to increase the volume of currency in circulation derived from the minting of copper money, the feat of the Bank of the Artillery and Engineer Corps exceeded it in ingenuity. It smelted and converted into currency old copper cannons discarded from the arsenals. The fact that P. I. Shuvalov was not only the financial wizard behind the scheme but also the inventor of new artillery pieces and the head of Russian arms supply (General-Feldzekhmeister) helped to insure that the operation had quite visible benefits to the originator of the scheme. When the "banks" were closed in 1763 with little hope of recouping either the principal or the interest, contemporaries were left with the impression of a large scale handout with no visible gains for the government, of an ingenious way to increase the money supply in the tradition of using the mint to offer private "loans." Modern economists concerned about balancing budgets might think it folly to increase the money supply by four million rubles at a time when the yearly deficit on account of the war was at least another four million. Contemporary public opinion, however, was much more charitable and considered it more of an extravagance than an outrage or criminal act.

Although the government's credit policies were inextricably related to its policies on the money supply, its credit policies toward the nobility cannot be taken out of the context of the economic behavior of this class and the political pressures it exerted on the government. When the Bank for the Nobility was organized in 1754, the prevailing assumption was that mobilization of savings was impossible, or at least unlikely, and therefore it would have to operate with capital provided by the government. The Bank for the Nobility started with a capital of 750,000 rubles to be lent in sums of 500 to 10,000 rubles against the security of serf-ownership. It was characteristic that neither land nor income per estate were chosen as criteria for loans. The number of serfs served as the unit approximating or capsulizing other estate indicators. The setting of the assessed value per serf by the bank authorities represented a combination of a liberalized attitude toward the borrowers with a recognition of inflationary pressures in the economy. The price per male serf was set in 1754 at 10 rubles (a sum below the prevailing market price); in 1766 it was raised to 20 rubles, in 1786 to 40 rubles, and in 1801 to 60 rubles.

The original capital was almost exhausted within the first year. The St. Petersburg branch office of the Bank for the Nobility began with a capital of 271,000 rubles. Of that, 228,000 were distributed in the first year, 1754, and during the subsequent three years the loans averaged 57,000 rubles per year. The bank's lending activity slacked subsequently, especially since the terms of repayment of the loans was extended to three years and subsequently to eight years.

Political pressure brought to bear by the nobility forced the government to increase the capital of the bank and thereby to make further loans to a broader group of the Russian nobility. Moreover, the nobility from the Baltic provinces were made eligible for loans, and later serf-owners from Belorussia and the Ukraine were added. During the reign of Peter III and the early years of Catherine II's reign the government was vulnerable to pressures from the nobility. During the early 1770s the government found it easier to meet the demands of the nobility by increasing the money supply through the printing of assignats (paper money). As a result, by 1775 the loans extended to the nobility reached the sum of 4.3 million rubles.

It was during this period that the history of Russian banking began. Symbolically, a new era began in 1770, the year when the government granted permission to the Bank for the Nobility to accept deposits from private individuals.[3] The only previous depositor had been an institution, the State Orphanage (*Vospitatel'nyi dom*). In spite of initial slow growth, there was the danger that the bank would be unable to honor the claims of private depositors because of the lack of reserves. To take care of that problem, the government in 1775 guaranteed deposits. It also instructed the bank not to keep the private deposits separate from the general pool and to lend them to the most trustworthy borrowers.

In 1772 competing institutions were granted the right to accept deposits and to extend loans against the security of landed estates and urban real estate. These institutions, which ultimately became very successful as lending institutions, were the Orphanages (*Vospitatel'nye doma*) in St. Petersburg and Moscow. They developed three parallel institutions that handled credit operations. One was a Loan Fund (*Ssudnaia kazna*), a euphemism for a pawn shop, which lent up to 1,000 rubles against precious metals and jewelry for a year at 6 percent interest. The second was the Widow's Fund (*Vdov'ia kazna*), which sold annuities and life insurance policies. The third, and most important, was the Guarding Fund (*Sokhrannaia kazna*), which accepted time deposits and made loans from those deposits and the Orphanages' free funds. Their rules of lending were much stricter than those of the Bank for the Nobility, especially on the matter of the ratio of liabilities to assets.

These sounder business practices seem to have instilled a greater confidence among savers, and the deposits of the Guarding Funds increased. In 1773 the Moscow Guarding Fund had less than 0.8 million rubles in deposits, in 1783 already 3.2 million rubles, and in 1793 8.7 million, or 0.1 million more than the combined deposits of the Moscow and St. Petersburg funds combined in 1787. By 1803 the deposits in Moscow reached 15.5 million rubles. If we discount for inflation, there was still a considerable growth of deposits. The outstanding loans exceeded the sum of private deposits. The turnover of loans exceeded that in the Bank for the Nobility.[4]

To the extent that loans were made against the collateral of landed estates and depended on the number of serfs, which contemporaries considered the common denominator, one can sum up the lending activity of the St. Petersburg and Moscow Guarding Funds in terms of that common denominator. Thus, according to the reports for the year 1800, the St. Petersburg Fund extended loans against 158,000 male serfs and 191 urban stone buildings, and the Moscow Fund held mortgages on estates with 196,000 male serfs and 207 stone buildings.[5]

The growth of deposits in the Guarding Funds and the Loan Bank can be explained primarily by the fact that, as the only legal savings institutions in Russia, they attracted savings from a population that preferred security combined with some income to high risk and high return from private lending. Moreover, the creeping inflation of the early 1780s induced the depositing of previously hoarded savings in the newly established savings institutions. When the pace of inflation accelerated during the 1790s, the growth rate of savings deposits must have declined and the demand for loans increased.

The developments during the period 1786–1800 in the area of "credit" arrangements must be examined against this background. In 1786 the conversion of paper rubles (assignats) into silver was suspended by the government, an action which contributed to the further decline of the ruble in terms of silver and foreign exchange. Although this made Russian goods cheaper and more attractive to foreigners and thus stimulated an increase of Russian exports from which the commercial agricultural producers, including the nobility, benefitted, the simultaneous price rises in Western Europe tended to diminish some of the advantages of the Russians, who had to pay higher prices for imported Western goods. In addition, domestic prices increased. This provided an opportunity for the landed gentry to repay old debts with cheap money and to incur new debts that could be repaid with even cheaper money in the future. As the inflation psychology took hold of an increasing number of asset-holders, the flight from money into goods, land, serfs, urban real estate, and even consumption goods, became the behavioral norm.

It was not ordinary or extraordinary greed, but the quickening of the pace of exchange brought about by the inflationary situation of the 1790s that influenced the rise in prices, rent payments, and subsequently wages. It also determined an increasing clamor for loans, handouts, and subsidies by those groups in a position to make demands on the government. Thus it is not surprising that, following the suspension of specie payments by the government, a new set of regulations were promulgated which very substantially increased the lending power of the Bank for the Nobility, which as the result of a reorganization was renamed the State Lending Bank. The capital of the bank was increased by government subsidies. Its lending capacity was augmented by about 8 million rubles of deposits, half of which were made by private individuals. Although the plan of reorganization promised to raise the bank's capital by 17.5 million rubles from subsidies alone, the size of government deficits and war expenditures prevented such a massive subsidy.

The accession to the throne by Paul I coupled with the installation of a new group of high government officials, as well as a necessity to win support among the gentry for the new regime, prompted the new government to carry out in a sweeping style what the Catherinian government had balked at doing, contributing a major subsidy "to wipe out the debts owed by the nobility." During the years 1798 and 1799 a newly established institution, the Auxiliary Bank for the Nobility, lent over 47 million rubles in 5 percent bank notes which were negotiable and redeemable in assignats by the nobles' creditors. The loans were repayable in 25 years; during the first 5 years only interest payments (6 percent) had to be made, and repayment of the principal was to start in the sixth year.

The sweeping new measure permitted the repayment of 11.8 million rubles of debts owed to the existing banking institutions and the rest supposedly to private creditors. It also contributed to an increase in the assignats in circulation in the amount of 52.4 million rubles. As soon as the old debts to the banks were repaid, new applications for loans were filed and new loans were obtained. The indebtedness of the nobility probably did not decrease. The measure resulted in a rolling over of debts by converting eight-year debt into twenty-five-year debt.

Table 7.1 presents some of the results of the operations of the Auxiliary Bank for the Nobility in terms of the number of mortgaged serfs pledged against the loans obtained. Similar data on the number of serfs newly mortgaged to the State Loan Bank are not available. The number of serfs known to have been mortgaged in credit institutions was 708,000 for the Auxiliary Bank and 354,000 for the Guarding Funds

of the St. Petersburg and Moscow Orphanages. The incomplete figure for the end of the century is 1,062,000 male serfs out of the total number of 9,787,800 private serfs listed in the fifth census (*reviziia*) of 1795, or a minimum of 10.6 percent.

The eighteenth century initiated a development which became more prevalent in the nineteenth century, the borrowing of money by the mortgaging of estates. Although a number of Russian historians have used the numbers of mortgaged serfs as an index of the crisis of either the institution of serfdom or of Russian agriculture, such an interpretation is presumptuous and unwarranted. The same historians who consider the loans as grants use the meaningless figures (meaningless if a grant was involved rather than a loan) as crisis indicators. Even if we assume that the nobility was mortgaging estates as collateral for loans (rather than getting grants), and that this occurred during the inflationary period of the last decades of the eighteenth century, this would signify a greater sensitivity to market conditions than is usually granted the Russian nobility. One must look further afield than the credits, grants, or subsidies to the nobility to find evidence of crisis.

A somewhat different pattern than the one discussed above emerges from the analysis of the activity affecting the commercial and industrial groups. In the case of the nobility, there was a considerable amount of discrimination exercised with regard to the various groups included in this social category, and the distinction between the aristocracy and lower gentry was significant in terms of access to the government's credit institutions, regardless of the collateral that could be provided. In a similar manner there was a fundamental difference in the access to credit of two groups of merchants and industrialists.

The distinction between the two groups was based on practical considerations: one group was involved in business relationships with the government, the other operated exclusively in the private sector of the economy. In the eighteenth century, under conditions of capital scarcity, the Russian government acted toward the businessmen involved in government contracts exactly in the same manner in which a foreign exporter behaved toward his Russian supplier, or the wholesaler toward the retailer—it provided them with credits in its own self-interest.

As a matter of routine business practice, the government provided advance payments or credits to its suppliers, to those who supplied the army with cloth, armaments, and food, to those who delivered food to the cities and salt and alcohol to the state monopolies. They were "normal" short-term loans, usually for a term not exceeding one year. Historians have not classified such loans as "credits," for they were extended under the routine arrangements governing

Table 7.1   Male Population of Mortgaged Estates in the "Auxiliary Bank for the Nobility" in 1800, by Gubernii

Gubernii	No. of "Male Souls"	Gubernii	No. of "Male Souls"
1st class[a]		*3d class*	
Voronezh	39,864	Belorussia	43,658
Kaluga	36,691	Kiev	35,606
Nizhnii Novgorod	35,824	Lithuania	26,046
Tambov	31,542	Malorussia	25,671
Saratov	31,046	Pskov	22,396
Simbirsk	29,654	Minsk	20,480
Kursk	28,248	Slobodo-Ukraine	20,139
Riazan'	26,767	Novorossiia	11,087
Orel	25,530	Volynia	7,883
Tula	23,734	St. Petersburg	7,284
Vladimir	22,905	Podol'e	4,041
Kostroma	20,454	Orenburg	3,085
Iaroslavl'	16,739	Vologda	2,845
Kazan'	6,426	Total	230,221
Viatka	420		
Total	375,844	*4th class*	
		Perm'	26,559
2d class		Novgorod	6,396
Smolensk	28,994	Total	32,955
Tver'	24,454		
Moscow	13,957	Grand total	708,050
Astrakhan'	525		
Total	67,930		

Source: Borovoi, *Kredit*, p. 77.

[a]1st class: lending rate per serf—75 rubles.
2d class: lending rate per serf—65 rubles.
3d class: lending rate per serf—50 rubles.
4th class: lending rate per serf—40 rubles.

state contracts. They are classified as "credits" in the historical literature, however, whenever such loans were granted by special institutions, such as the Copper Bank. Among the figures involved in government contracts who also benefited from loans or grants by the Copper Bank were the English merchant Gomme, the tax-farmer Shemiaka, the merchants and industrialists Batashev, Bogdanov, Leventsov, Luginin, and Rodionov (see table 7.2).

Although there is no doubt that the merchants who did business with the government received credits, the number of those who appear in the records of the state lending institutions represent merely the tip of the iceberg. It is also likely that the merchants, and perhaps even some of the merchant-industrialists, who had no dealings with the government found it difficult to obtain loans from government institutions. When the capital of the bank to support commerce was exhausted, no new capital was forthcoming, for the merchants lacked the nobility's political power and could not force the government to assure them continuous support. This lack of political power, more than anything else, explains the short-lived and abortive experience of governmental institutionalized credits for commerce, in contrast with the ongoing support for the nobility. It is also not surprising that

the recipients of the small amount of support available to the commercial sector were selected, as was the case with the nobility. In eighteenth-century Russia members of the same estate were not guaranteed equal treatment.

In one respect the establishment of the Bank for Commerce in St. Petersburg Port in 1754 was a break with age-old traditions of Russian domestic policy. That was probably the first time that the government acknowledged not only the need of Russian merchants for credits, but also admitted that the need was legitimate by its own merits, not only because of reasons of state. This was a new tone, markedly different from the attitude that the merchant class was a state servitor that could be drafted into state service, forcibly resettled, and heavily taxed, the old Muscovite attitude that totally ignored the welfare of the individual merchant and considered his accumulated capital a legitimate prey when government revenue had to be increased. Although the capital of the Bank for Commerce was established at only a half-million rubles, and only a fifth of a million rubles were made immediately available, the symbolic value of the gesture was important.

It became clear that the Russian government was unwilling to extend major credits and was also igno-

Table 7.2   Debtors of the Copper Bank and Their Total Indebtedness to the Government (in Rubles)

Nobles, Merchants, Factory Owners & Others	Name	Debt in 1763	Debt in 1762 or Earlier	Assets (Male Serfs or Annual Salary)
Field marshall	P. I. Shuvalov	663,738	650,671	2,737
Chancellor	M. I. Vorontsov	232,863	231,831	
Kamerherr count	Iaguzhinskii	231,070	222,688	6,798
General procurator	A. I. Glebov	204,667	200,000	1,695
General in chief	R. I. Vorontsov	200,213	197,267	2,783
Princess	N. Golitsyn	164,233	160,641	3,808
General lieutenant	Chernyshev	154,542	148,620	2,275
General lieutenant Prince	P. I. Repnin	135,658	122,102	5,431
Kamerherr count	A. Stroganov	125,522	110,000	15,000
General in chief	S. K. Naryshkin	106,264	100,000	7,130
Principality of Estonia		51,803	50,000	
Second major	Gur'ev	47,864		
Oberhofmarshall	K. E. Sievers	45,350	44,256	400
Countess	M. Stroganov	41,153	40,000	6,000
General field marshall	A. B. Buturlin	20,361	20,080	1,540
Prince	P. Khovanskii	19,676	16,750	
Count	N. Apraksin	16,507	14,390	1,819
State councillor prince	I. V. Odoevskii	10,239	10,000	722
State councillor	D. Volkov	10,089	10,000	
General in chief	I. S. Gendrikov	6,540	5,734	
State councillor	Iushkov	5,657	5,000	
Second major	P. Pozharskii	7,055	7,000	
Court councillor	M. Verevkin	4,000	4,000	salary 117 rubles per year
Total		2,505,064		
English merchant	Arnold Gomme	345,245	300,000	
Ober-inspector of customs	Shemiakin	339,390	308,870	
Plant owner	Turchaninov	129,354		
Holstein commerce councillor	H. Gette	102,596	100,000	
St. Petersburg merchant	I. Shchukin	74,254	62,500	
Former Persian trading company		62,785		
St. Petersburg merchant	I. Diakonov	57,489	50,000	
Nezhin burgher	D. Murganov	47,161	43,532	
Opera conductor	Locatelli	30,000		
Tula merchant	L. Luginin	30,000		600
Plant owner	I. Tverdyshev	25,000		1,256
Moscow merchant	I. Batashov	20,000		
Tula merchant	V. Liventsov	16,000		
Kamerdiner	A. Sakharov	5,698	5,500	
Court singer	I. Pavlov	1,508	1,198	100 rubles salary
Total above persons		1,286,480		
Thirty other persons		60,625		
Total debts in copper bank		3,103,123	2,911,501	
Total state ironworks		749,046		
Total debts		3,852,169		

rant of the scope of the real needs of commerce when it prescribed a repayment term of six months for its loans. The loans were granted against the security of warehouse receipts for merchandise deposited in the port of St. Petersburg. Apparently the government had in mind the seasonal factors of St. Petersburg navigation and trade and the fact that capital was "frozen" in inventories, which therefore enabled foreign exporters to force down the price of the

Russian goods. The government obviously missed the complex nature of Russian foreign trade, the fact that seasonal factors were but a minute portion of the huge costs of the slow process of collection and transportation of goods from their source to the ports. The government did not understand that short-term loans could do little to ameliorate the general capital shortage.

The immediate reaction of the St. Petersburg merchants was a curious one, to say the least: they refused to apply for the loans. It was only when the government decided to extend the term of the loans to one year that loans were requested. The St. Petersburg Bank, with its very limited capital and suffering from the insolvency of some clients, was unable to satisfy the needs and aspirations of the merchants. This was especially true because it did not provide any loans against promissory notes. The discounting of promissory notes was considered by the merchants a matter of higher urgency than the granting of loans against commodity inventories. This became clear when the Commerce College established a bank in Astrakhan' in 1764 to facilitate trade with the East. The local merchants insisted upon the inclusion of a clause to have at least a minimal sum for the discounting of bills and promissory notes. Both banks, the St. Petersburg and the Astrakhan', operated on a very low level. This enabled the government to liquidate the St. Petersburg bank in 1782 and to transfer its assets to the Bank for the Nobility.

The idea of credit for the commercial classes received a new lease on life only in 1797, when the Bank of Assignats (a bank for the emission of paper currency) established offices for bill discounting. Only at that point could one begin to speak about an institution that effectively, rather than rhetorically, could aid the interests of the commercial classes in Russia.

8
THE FISCAL SYSTEM

Both the sources for and the studies of the Russian fiscal system of the eighteenth century are glaringly incomplete, particularly for the first half of the century. Apart from the path-breaking study of P. N. Miliukov using the 1724 state budget as a vehicle to gain insight into the fiscal system, the revenues and the expenditures of the Russian state, there is only the more recent study by S. M. Troitskii, which tried to piece together the major revenue and expenditure estimates for another few years.

For the second half of the century, and especially for the reign of Catherine II (1762–96), the data are much more plentiful. This pattern can be explained not so much by the survival of documentary evidence as by the fact that the drawing up of a comprehensive future state budget, a document of projected state revenues and expenditures, was initiated by Peter the Great during the last years of his reign but not continued under his heirs. The documentary evidence for the reconstruction of "historical" state budgets is so widely scattered in local and central archives of the different institutions empowered to raise and spend revenue that up to the present time reconstructing and amalgamating the data has been impossible. A major component of the state military expenses probably could be estimated, but even this has not been done. Until the time of Peter III the expenses of the court were not separated from the expenses of the state; the salaries of the lower echelons of the bureaucracy were seldom paid by the state, but by the sundry petitioners. Consequently it is almost impossible to compare the budget data that can be found for the early period with the budgets of the later period.

Only by constructing estimates from "norms" of taxation (stated rates of taxation of various groups or activities) and by using scattered data on actual payments and revenues can we approximate a continuous series of Russian state budgets. Such estimates should include the following six components: the poll tax estimates, corrected for the changes for particular years[1]; the gross and net revenues from the alcohol and salt taxes[2]; the revenues from sales of state-monopolized commodities in foreign trade; the revenues from customs duties, both in rubles and in foreign currency; the revenues from the 10 percent tax on iron production and the income from copper sales; the revenue from the operation of the mint.

The estimated data contain a substantial margin of error, which probably under "normal" conditions does not exceed 15 percent.

After 1724 the sources of revenue in the Russian state budget remained stable over long periods. Its size should be easily predictable. The budget was devised to create a regular source of revenue for maintaining the armed forces by means of a poll tax. Both the tax assessment and the estimated population base were changed at infrequent intervals. During the eighteenth century there were only five counts (*reviziia*) of the taxable population. The extraordinary funds required in wartime were secured by special taxes, by reminting the currency, or by printing paper money (later in the century). Foreign borrowing was a measure taken only late in the century and primarily to cover military expenses abroad.

The two major components of expenditure, the armed forces and the state administrative bureaucracy, were subject to prediction. Nevertheless, the attempt to estimate and control expenditures to the level afforded by revenues seems to have been considered useless, too complex, or too restrictive for an absolutist government. In practice, budgetary decisions were divided up among various departments of the government, each operating separately. Coordination was done by the central office of the Senate, the Governing Supreme Council, or the General Procurator of the Senate. Responsible for budget decisions and jealous of delegating their authority, these bodies were inefficient in debating the minutiae of state expenditures and lost control over long-range financial planning.

The direct poll tax on serfs was the most important source of revenue. The poll tax was levied on all male peasants registered in the taxable population census and on all urban inhabitants except the gentry, clergy, and tax-exempt officials. The poll tax was equal for all peasants regardless of ownership, whether state, private, or church, unlike the manner in which taxes had been levied in the Muscovite period of Russian history. The poll tax was supplemented for the state peasants, and later for the church peasants after the secularization of the church estates in 1762, by a per capita rent (*obrok*, originally 1.50 rubles, later 2 rubles) payable to the treasury. The poll tax was changed infrequently, except during years of natural calamities or other hardship when the rates were temporarily reduced. Some reductions, as in 1726, 1728, 1730, 1740, and 1742, coincided with the assumption of the throne by a new ruler, and were certainly means of ingratiating the new autocrat with both the peasants and the gentry. The poll tax paid by urban inhabitants was originally set on a per capita basis, and only during the second half of the century was it converted into a tax according to broad categories of estimated or reported income.

The idea behind the poll tax presumably was a calculation of the cost of maintaining each member of the armed forces. Including the costs of maintaining the higher ranks of the regiments, the maintenance of an infantry soldier required the tax from 35.5 "souls" or 26.27 rubles, and of a cavalry soldier 50.25 "souls" or 37.185 rubles. This was the logic behind the poll tax at the time when Peter the Great designed the quarters for his army following the conclusion of the Northern War with the assumption that the regiments would be maintained by the taxable population in the proximity of their quarters, while the tax would be collected by the military units themselves. At the outset the tax was collected by the military directly, or by a relatively small collection apparatus under the control of the army, but after a few years, with the relocation of the army, the poll-tax collection was turned over to the district administration (*voevody*) and the responsibility for the primary tax collection was placed with the serf-owners for private serfs and with the administration of the state and church estates for their respective groups of serfs.

The growth of the poll-tax revenues can be explained by the secular growth of the taxable population and by an increase of the per capita rates. Until the 1760s it was exclusively population growth that was responsible for the increase. Subsequently both sources were important, and taxable population was augmented by the territorial expansion of the Russian Empire.

Among the indirect taxes, the most significant were the tax components of the government monopolies of alcoholic beverages and salt. There were also state monopolies of various goods in foreign trade during various periods, but they played a minor role as a source of revenue and their monopoly revenue could not always be classified as a tax. In the cases of both alcohol and salt the government used either tax farming or a state monopoly of distribution as the means to derive revenue. The tax component was defined as the difference between the sales price and the supply price, or the "true" price, as the costs of production and distribution were described. The costs of production of both commodities were rising, and the tax component, in spite of the rise in the sales price, declined secularly.

The production costs of salt increased secularly during the second half of the century because of rising costs of fuel and labor (both in the process of production and in transportation from the producing regions to the population centers) and reached a point during the 1790s when the salt monopoly became a deficit-ridden operation for the state. In 1754 the government granted the gentry a monopoly on delivering alcohol for sale, and thereby excluded the merchants who had occupied a significant place in the distillery industry. The exercise of the gentry monopoly, coupled with the prevalence of members of the aristocracy and courtiers among the suppliers, tended to increase the production costs of alcohol, in addition to raising the price of grain.

The government monopoly in some areas of foreign trade and in the customs duties had a similar effect. The monopolies represented a continuation of seventeenth century policies designed to maximize state revenue that were gradually abolished by Peter the Great's successors. Given Russia's role as a price-taker in the world market, it is difficult to imagine how a state trade monopoly could reap special advantages, except for the substitution of state trading for private trade, for the convenience of obtaining foreign exchange directly for the treasury. When the government or its agencies were the sole purchasers of designated export commodities, it was possible to keep prices below their market level within the country while exporting all of the highest quality of such goods abroad.

Although the share of the state monopolies in foreign trade never exceeded the approximately 10 percent that it reached under Peter the Great, their significance as a source of foreign exchange and in facilitating government purchases abroad was apparently considerable. As a tool of foreign policy, as in the case of grain shipments to Sweden, state monopolies also had a significant role. As a source of revenue, however, they became negligible.

Of greater significance was the indirect tax embodied in the customs duties. (On other aspects of the tariff policies, see chapter 4 on foreign trade.) Apart from their role in some areas as protection of domestic industry and apart from the government's insistence that they be paid in foreign currency, the customs duties had a clear fiscal purpose. That purpose was revealed especially in 1753 when the internal tolls were replaced by a flat increase in the rate of customs duties on imports. The customs duties were a tax on the Russian consumers of foreign goods. In addition, they raised the prices for domestically produced goods that were close substitutes for imports.

The government derived substantial revenue by reminting old silver coins and through the emission of new silver or copper coins. Unquestionably some of the operations of the mint, especially during the time of Peter the Great, taxed away a part of the wealth in the hands of holders of currency.

The tendency of indirect taxes to grow relative to direct taxes was a result of deliberate governmental policy. Apart from the emergencies of war that required substantial increases in state revenue, the increase in the size of the armed forces under peacetime conditions put considerable stress on the state budget. The number of taxpayers was fixed in intercensal periods and increases in the poll tax were considered fiscally unwieldy and politically dangerous. (The poll tax of course was not only burdensome to the serfs, but competed with the various dues the serfs paid their lords, so that increases in the poll tax thereby adversely affected the serf-owners' interests as well.) On the other hand, the decision-makers discovered that increases in the price of such commodities as salt and alcohol increased tax revenues. It is therefore understandable why the choice of increasing indirect taxes was made. Again the example of the 1750s, when the prices of salt and alcohol were raised and internal tolls were replaced by the increase in customs duties, is very instructive. The substantial increases of the indirect taxes were sometimes accompanied by temporary decreases of the poll tax to demonstrate the government's intention to keep the total tax increase within bounds and to show the compensating effect for the majority of taxpayers. However, the long-run effect was not only one of increasing the total burden of taxation, but also to increase the share of indirect taxes in the total taxes collected.

The Problem of Budget Deficit Financing

The need for budget deficit financing arose either as a result of protracted, continuous debts unpaid by taxpayers, or as a result of increasing expenditures not covered by revenues. On the first cause, a vast literature on arrears payments (*nedoimki*) exists. It is based in part on current budget reports and in part on the campaigns to collect the arrears or to cancel the old debts. Some historians have tried to present the arrears as evidence of an unbearable tax burden, but the data in my possession indicate a rather small percentage of arrears in the total collected revenue. Except for years of famine and other natural calamities, arrears amounted to 4 to 5 percent annually. The problem of arrears in tax payments thus appears to be more of an indicator of either the impact of calamitous events that affected the entire country or a number of extended regions, or of the impact of increased taxation associated with extraordinary expenses such as wars, rather than an indicator of a secular trend of impoverishment of the Russian serf population.

The arrears cannot be considered the main source of budget deficits. The chief culprit was war expenditures. There was no institutionalized public debt, nor were there any banks to speak of. Long-term borrowing from abroad did not start before the 1770s. Therefore one has to resolve the problem of the Russian budget deficit in the sense of detecting the appropriate means by which the budget was balanced in both the short and the long run.

One of the most likely means of covering the budget deficit, defined as the difference between the current expenditures and current revenue, or the current expenditures and past revenue (assuming a reasonable time lag), was through the operation of the mint, and later by the use of the printing press, in the case of paper money.

For the period until the late 1760s, reminting operations and the depreciation of the currency were the chief means of financing the deficit. (Later this was replaced by the transfer of bank notes of the assignat fund to the state treasury. Both replaced the standard Muscovite practice of covering shortfalls by defaulting on payment of state bills.) In calculating eighteenth-century Russian taxation one must include the government's net income from reminting operations and also the net income from the printing of the paper notes that were put into circulation by the government, which used the newly created money to pay for the goods and services it was purchasing.

A cursory inspection of the adjusted data of the state budget deficit and the pattern of the printing of the assignats (not even of the stock of assignats in actual circulation) would indicate the close association between the two indicators. The leading indicator is the budget deficit followed by a lag of approximately two years in the issue of assignats. Apart from the areas in which the government usually supported its suppliers with the loans and advances discussed in chapter 7, there were areas in which the government was slow in paying its bills. Thus the appearance of such a lag should be of no surprise. Moreover, the evidence of a budget deficit did not become available to high governmental officials as a matter of routine, except in emergencies. Therefore, expecting simultaneity of both the realization of a deficit and the remedial action would be presumptuous.

There were three inflationary periods in Russia during the eighteenth century: the Petrine period, the period of the Seven Years' War, and the latter part of the reign of Catherine II.

The major source of the inflationary pressure in each case was the government's policy of increasing the money stock to finance military expenditures. It is difficult to measure the precise effect of the governmental monetary policies in the absence of estimates of the stock of money, the size of the budget deficit, the cost of the wars, and also in the absence of suitable price data for the Petrine period.

In comparison with the other two periods, the Petrine era presents a rather straightforward case. Recognizing that the existing stock of silver currency was inadequate, the government embarked upon a policy of recoinage as early as the beginning of the Northern War and minted coins with a lesser silver content. This policy, whose general dimensions are known, led in 1718 to a huge issue of new silver coins whose silver content was further diminished. The trend of grain prices, exacerbated by famines, was upward and prevailed over the effects of a declining population and demand for consumer goods.

The inflationary pressure of the Petrine period subsequently lost much of its force, but was still present during the 1730s and 1740s. It was fed by the costs of the war against the Crimea in the 1730s and against Sweden at the beginning of the 1740s. Another phase of inflationary pressures started in the 1750s in conjunction with the Seven Years' War. The anti-inflationary policies of the 1740s, curtailing the money supply, had to be discontinued. Moreover, taxation intensified, and copper coins were minted at the rate of 16 rubles per pood of copper after the mint price of 8 rubles per pood of copper was discontinued in 1755.[3]

The emission of the Elizabethan period was insufficient to cover the deficit. Later, Peter III ordered the coinage of 32 rubles of coins per pood of copper and minted 2,337,075 rubles' worth of such money. This was stopped by Catherine II, who returned to a 16 ruble per pood standard.

The coinage of copper money during Catherine II's reign was not the chief cause of inflation. The total coinage of copper money during her reign amounted to 65 million rubles' worth. At 16 rubles per pood of copper, a total of 4,250,000 poods (or 153,000,000 pounds) of copper were utilized for this purpose. The

government did not try to maximize its income from the coinage of copper money, even during the years when it could have done so legitimately because of a rise in the market price of copper. It is difficult to assess whether the government was restrained by the historical experience of the seventeenth-century experiment with copper money (the famous Copper Uprising of 1663) or by the ease with which the population was able to discern the change of copper content of coinage. This revenue became marginal for the government at the time when it began to use paper money as a major way to cover deficit financing.

The Alcohol Tax

The alcohol tax in the eighteenth century produced the largest revenue among the excises. Although its value as a source of revenue was already known in the previous century, during the first half of the eighteenth century its level exhibited hardly any growth. To a large extent the almost stationary level of revenue from alcohol sales was due to the problems of organization involved in enforcing and collecting the tax.

The sale of alcohol as a government monopoly was inherited from the seventeenth century, along with an apparatus that was inadequate to enforce and maintain this monopoly. The supply of alcoholic beverages, primarily grain alcohol (khlebnoe vino) was resolved by a system of awarding contracts to private individuals, members of the gentry and merchants, who supplied specified volumes of liquor to the various government alehouses (piteinye doma), located mostly in cities and towns. However, control over the sales remained in disarray. Although they were officially under the control of the Revenues College, there was no uniform mode of control over sales. In many places the administration of the alcohol monopoly was turned over to the local merchants, members of the corporate urban estate, or during the later years of Peter and his followers to the existing municipal bodies (the magistrat or ratusha). This system placed an additional service burden and responsibility upon the local merchants, who resented it, but it did not assure an efficient administration of sales or a maximization of revenues. In cases where local municipal bodies could not be relied upon to administer sales, retailing was farmed out to local merchants, either to individuals or partnerships.

The prices for alcoholic beverages varied from place to place and from period to period, apparently depending on the local grain-supply conditions and prices. In the 1740s the wholesale price of a pail of ordinary alcohol was on average about 1.30 rubles.

This determination fails to separate the tax from the costs of producing and handling the alcohol.

The discoverer of the real revenue potential of the alcohol tax and the godfather of its rise was P. I. Shuvalov, the architect of fiscal and commercial policies during the reign of Elizabeth (1742–62). It was he who suggested in the late 1740s the introduction of a higher and uniform pan-Russian price for alcohol. The uniformity of the price was a device which would facilitate the estimation and collection of the gross revenue. The price for alcohol was raised to 1.885 rubles per pail in 1750 and then to 2.235 rubles in 1756 to help finance Russia's participation in the Seven Years' War. It was also at the time of Shuvalov's influence on economic policies, in 1753, that the supply of alcohol to the government was made a monopoly of the gentry. All the merchants' distilleries were closed down except in those parts of Siberia where there were no gentry landowners capable of supplying their own alcohol production.

Although Shuvalov demonstrated the government's ability to expand tax revenue from alcohol sales by raising the price and the tax, he did not, however, reform the system of alcohol retailing itself. His legacy as a guide for government policies has survived in Russia down to the present day. A reform of the system of alcohol retailing was introduced in 1766 in conjunction with another rise in the price of alcohol, to 2.54 rubles per pail. It entailed the introduction of a tax-farming arrangement in which the government assumed the responsibility of supplying the alcohol and tax farmers (usually a partnership of prominent and wealthy merchants) assumed the rights and responsibility of administering the alehouses and selling the stipulated volume of alcohol. The margin between the wholesale price and the retail price (both decreed by the government), together with the proceeds from the sales of other alcoholic beverages such as vodka, wine, and beer, made up the legal profits of the tax farmers for the stipulated term (usually four years) of the contract.

A few crucial developments prevented the alcohol tax from repeating the experience of the gabelle, which by the end of the century was converted from an excise tax to a consumer subsidy. First, the government did not feel the same constraints against increasing the price of alcohol as it did against raising the price of salt, and thus between 1750 and 1794 the price per pail of alcohol increased from 1.885 rubles to 4 rubles. Second, technological improvements in distilling significantly reduced the volume of grain required to produce a unit of alcoholic beverage. With costs rising below the rate of inflation the government, by increasing the sales price, managed to prevent its real revenues from alcohol from declining.

Table 8.1   Prices for Alcohol Deliveries (Kopeks p. Pail)

Year	St. Petersburg Province	Moscow Province
1756–65	67	52
1768	103	90
1771–75	92	85
1775–79	n.a.	87
1779–83	92	85

Source: Chechulin, *Ocherki*, pp. 166–67.

The system that was first introduced in 1766 and that was fully developed by 1781 strengthened the effectiveness of the government monopoly and its ability to collect the tax.[4] Some areas of the Russian Empire were exempt from the alcohol sales monopoly. Referred to as "the districts of free alcohol sales," they included the Baltic provinces, the so-called *Ostzeiskie gubernii* (Lifland, Estland, and Vyborg), the territory of *Malorossiia* (Kiev and Khar'kov), and the territory of Eastern Belorussia acquired after the first partition of Poland in 1771. In the territory where the government sales monopoly existed, St. Petersburg was in a position to influence the supply price of alcohol, both as a monopoly buyer and as a producer of alcohol in its own distilleries. The importance of the government's role in controlling the supply price of alcohol ought not to be exaggerated, first, because of the relationship of the government to the members of the aristocracy and the highest officeholders, themselves among the top contractors for alcohol deliveries; and, second, because prices of alcohol delivery contracts varied from province to province and from period to period, following regional grain prices. Table 8.1 presents the prices quoted by N. D. Chechulin for St. Petersburg and Moscow alcohol deliveries.

Another aspect of government control of the supply was its ability to counteract, to some extent at least, the illegal production of alcohol and the possible supply of that alcohol into the legal retail-sales outlets. Illegally produced alcohol competed with the government monopoly and thereby reduced government revenues, so any improvement in the effectiveness of the state monopoly had the effect of maximizing tax revenues.

The data in table 8.2 on the net revenue from the alcohol tax are incomplete and suffer from some imprecision, but are internally consistent and thereby usable.

Although there is little doubt that fiscal considerations, governmental attempts to increase net revenue, played the decisive role in raising the sales price of alcoholic beverages, two other factors also influenced the timing and the extent of price changes. One factor was the cost of obtaining alcohol, which was related to the price of grain. The other factor was

Table 8.2   Estimates of Alcohol Tax Revenues

Year	Net Tax Revenue (in Rubles)	Year	Net Tax Revenue (in 1,000 Rubles)	Year	Net Tax Revenue (in 1,000 Rubles)
1724	850,105	1763	4,376	1789	9,613
1727	916,384	1764	4,016	1790	9,419
1732	915,959	1765	4,199	1791	8,608
1733	945,289	1766	4,339	1792	8,598
1734	909,035	1767	5,085	1793	8,713
1735	820,585	1768	5,081	1794	9,110
1736	715,236	1769	5,081	1795	17,512
1737	887,103	1770	5,923	1796	15,000
1738	910,103	1771	6,644		
1744	992,150	1772	6,641		
1747	1,141,376	1773	6,646		
1748	1,062,024	1774	6,641		
1749	1,263,529	1775	6,887		
1750	1,634,798	1776	6,921		
1751	2,273,466	1777	6,982		
1752	2,362,140	1778	9,419		
1753	2,305,185	1779	9,358		
1754	2,249,491	1780	9,419		
1755	2,662,909	1781	9,419		
1756	2,574,329	1782	9,435		
1757	2,551,890	1783	9,435		
1758	2,731,675	1784	9,517		
1759	3,132,676	1785	9,228		
1760	3,298,379	1786	9,051		
1761	3,329,000	1787	9,228		
1762	3,450,043	1788	9,613		

Sources: Troitskii, *Finansovaia politika;* Chechulin, *Ocherki.*

Table 8.3   Government Expenditures of the Alcohol Monopoly (in 1,000 Rubles)

Year	Government Expenditures	Year	Government Expenditures
1763	932	1783	3,350
1765	1,000	1792	6,943
1766	1,001	1793	6,933
1768	1,416	1794	6,908
1770	1,988	1795	6,611
1772	1,252	1796	7,000
1773	1,252		

Source: Chechulin, *Ocherki*, pp. 171–72, 174.

the general rise in the price level. Keeping the cost of grain low was necessary to maximize the net revenue obtained from the government alcohol monopoly. The rise in the price level may have been used as a justification to bring the price of alcohol into line with the prices for other goods and services in the economy.

The evidence about the role of costs as a possible factor in raising the price of alcohol comes primarily from the 1780s and 1790s, the period of a general price rise. The data on the cost of alcohol to the state presented in table 8.3 have survived for only thirteen of the years between 1763 and 1796 and dramatically portray the price jumps in those two decades.

Although there may be exceptions, separating the two factors is usually quite impossible. This seems to leave most of the price increases to be explained by fiscal considerations. Such considerations were clear for the price increases of both 1750 and 1756. The price rises of 1764 and 1769, although of the same origin, perhaps could be explained by the devaluation of money in 1764 and the price rises of the late 1760s. However, the fiscal needs of the Russo-Ottoman war which started in 1768 were also patent.

When one combines the data on net revenue with the government's expenditures made to obtain the alcohol supply, the result is an order of magnitude approximating the population's expenditures for alcoholic beverages. It approximates rather than reports because many, if not most, transactions were in retail trade, and the retail margin is not included in the available figures. It is possible to estimate, in addition to the series presented in table 8.2 on net revenue from the alcohol tax, another series on gross government income from alcohol sales. Such estimates, presented in table 8.4, were made by Chechulin, and until other documentary evidence becomes available, they represent as good an approximation as it is possible to construct.

The Gabelle in Russia

Salt was one of the earliest commodities to enter interregional trade, at the dawn of history, and the

Table 8.4   Gross Government Income from the Alcohol Sales, 1763–96 (in 1,000 Rubles)

Year	Gross Government Income	Year	Gross Government Income
1763	4,694	1780	12,419
1764	5,199	1781	12,519
1765	5,263	1782	12,635
1766	5,340	1783	12,785
1767	6,291	1784	12,798
1768	6,491	1785	12,901
1769	6,491	1786	13,278
1770	7,911	1787	13,963
1771	7,893	1788	14,119
1772	7,893	1789	14,713
1773	7,893	1790	15,019
1774	8,093	1791	14,808
1775	8,670	1792	15,541
1776	8,820	1793	15,646
1777	9,082	1794	16,018
1778	12,219	1795	24,123
1779	12,319	1796	22,090

Source: Chechulin, *Ocherki.*

Table 8.5   The Gabelle as Percentage of the State's Net Revenues

Year	% of Net Revenue
1724	7.7
1749	8.1
1751	10.6
1758	14.5
1763	10.6
1769	7.9
1773	6.2
1781	3.9
1787	2.8

Note: For 1724, 1749, 1751, 1758, and 1769, see Troitskii, *Finansovaia politika*, pp. 214, 219. The years 1763, 1773, 1781, and 1787 are calculated from Chechulin, *Ocherki*, pp. 199–200, 256–57.

gabelle, or salt tax, was one of the oldest forms of taxation. By the eighteenth century the gabelle was still in existence in the majority of the European countries. It was used in Russia even in view of the relative success of the poll tax.

The share of the gabelle in the net revenues of the Russian state budget changed over the course of the century. It was relatively high at the beginning, increased toward the middle, and declined sharply toward the end. A few hypotheses can be offered to explain this pattern. An indirect tax on a product of universal use, the gabelle was highly visible to taxpayers, who were mindful of the high proportion of the tax relative to the cost of the product. This sensitivity made the government cautious about popular reaction and increases were decreed only at times of severe budgetary difficulties. The increases in the rate of the gabelle during the Elizabethan period, although made reluctantly and largely under the pressure of war expenditures, were extremely unpopular, and Catherine II increased her popularity by decreasing the tax. Moreover, she never dared to increase the rate of the gabelle, even at times when the rising costs of production and distribution finally resulted in a loss of revenue, beginning in 1791. In real terms the gabelle never again reached the level of the 1750s, although the consumption of salt was increasing on a per capita basis as well as on account of the growing population. In terms of the share of the total government revenues, the gabelle declined from 1763 on. Table 8.5 illustrates for selected years the share of the gabelle in the total government income.

Except for a short period from 1728 to 1731, when the sale of salt to the population was not controlled by the government and the tax was relatively small (5 kopeks per pound), the gabelle was coupled with a state monopoly of salt sales. The data on the total sales, in both physical units and in money terms, unmistakenly indicate that the salt monopoly combined with the gabelle were important factors retarding the growth of salt production in Russia. Each increase in the rate of the gabelle resulted in a temporary decline in the sales of salt.

The history of the salt tax is of special interest because it reflects the governmental and general social attitudes to two institutions, government monopolies and indirect taxation. The salt tax accompanied by a government monopoly in wholesale trade covered ninety-one years of the eighteenth century (1701–5 and 1728–31 were excluded). As an indirect tax, it was similar to the foreign trade customs in the sense that no social group in the population was exempt from it. (The gentry were virtually exempt from the alcohol tax because they could distill alcohol for home consumption without paying taxes.)

The salt tax was deeply resented by all strata of the population. Attempts to circumvent or to avoid the payment of the tax were punishable. During the period between 1750 and September 28, 1762, 2,489 persons were found guilty of crimes against the salt tax regulations. Of the total, 511 were punished by fines and property confiscation, 15 were exiled, 79 were sent to the army, and the rest received corporal punishment. Of these, 837 were flogged by the knout, 270 by the whip, and 731 by the lash. The territorial distribution of the crimes points to the areas of salt production, which indicates that attempts were made to smuggle salt out of those regions and thus to "compete" with the government.[5]

For the serfs the tax was an additional payment which could not be avoided because it was attached to a basic necessity. It was especially burdensome because it had to be paid in cash and at various times amounted to a sum ranging from 15 to 45 percent of the per capita poll tax. The real test of the tax incidence of salt is a comparison between the tax per pood of salt and the farm price of the same unit of grain. At its highest levels, in the late 1750s, the tax incidence of a pood of salt was about four times the farm-gate price of a pood of rye.

For the merchants, the salt tax was certainly a smaller share of their taxation, but the government monopoly in salt wholesaling and the stipulated profit margin for retail trade in salt (2 kopeks per pound), as well as the competition of the state retail outlets, deprived the merchants of trade opportunities. Thus they had little love for the salt tax as an institution. The landowning gentry resented the payment of taxes both as a matter of principle and as an excessive expense in their farming and household activities. The only groups that received salt at lower tax rates, and for a time were tax exempt, were those employed in the fisheries in the lower Volga River basin and the Cossacks on the Don and Iaik (Ural) rivers. Although the attitude toward the salt tax was unambiguously negative on the part of the population, the attitude of the government was much more complex.

The introduction of the state monopoly of the wholesale trade in salt in 1705 was exclusively a fiscal measure which imposed a 100 percent tax on the sale of salt in the various Russian markets. The methods used in introducing it tell us that it was an emergency measure: the existing inventories of salt in the trade channels were seized, the salt producers were invited to submit bids to deliver salt to the state offices, and double the wholesale price was charged in the various cities and regions. Once introduced in 1705, it survived unchanged until 1727, when free trade in salt was decreed. That was revoked in 1731 and the monopoly was restored. The mechanical method of introducing the tax had the predictable impact of increasing the price differential for retail sales among the various regions and inevitably invited "corrections" by illicit trading.

During the reign of Elizabeth the transgressions against the law and even popular discontent did not appear to the government to be sufficient reasons for becoming overly concerned with the problem of reforming the tax, probably because the relative sense of stability of Elizabeth's rule in comparison with that of her predecessors conveyed the illusion that real problems were few. The demand for revenue as a result of the war with Sweden, and later the Seven Years' War, compelled review of the existing tax structure. The debate conspicuously involved the salt tax. The range of proposed alterations included such extreme positions as the introduction of free trade in salt on the one hand and the substitution of an expanded gabelle for the existing poll tax on the

other. This range of opinions warrants an examination of the different arguments in the debate, which took place primarily in the Senate, but also involved the officials of the Salt Authority (*Solianaia kontora*).

In its memorandum to the Salt Authority dated December 7, 1744, the Senate inquired about the possibility of abolishing the state monopoly by permitting the free production and sale of lake salt, which was presumably cheaper than brine salt because it did not use fuel. (A concern for the conservation of forests was typical for Elizabeth's reign and was a factor in the policy for locating ironworks.) The Senate also wanted to know which tax rate, under the circumstances, would maximize government revenue. The Salt Authority's answer of May 21, 1745, analyzed the free-trade experience of 1727–31 and stressed that revenue had declined in that period. It suggested a uniform tax of 12 kopeks per pood (the rate in 1727–31 was only 5 kopeks per pood), which the Authority averred would prevent a revenue decrease.

The Senate thought that even this proposed level of tax might be insufficient to prevent a revenue decrease, which, it was assumed, would accompany the abolition of the state monopoly arrangement. The Senate also assumed that the extent of possible evasion under free trade had been underestimated in the Salt Authority's report, and it decided not to abolish the state monopoly. Instead, it accepted a proposal by P. I. Shuvalov of a uniform sales price for salt of 30 or 35 kopeks per pood, instead of the existing average retail price of 21.2 kopeks (based on 1742 data). The additional revenue was to be added to the Empress's purse and for general purposes. The Empress rejected the Senate's proposal, thus postponing its acceptance until 1749, when the proposal included a provision that part of the revenue should be used to decrease the poll tax.

One of Shuvalov's basic assumptions was that the scarcity of government-supplied salt led to high prices paid by the population for salt that was sold illegally. It is now difficult to establish whether that was in fact the case. Shuvalov based his assumption on the decline of salt sales in the years 1744, 1745, and perhaps 1748, which he clearly attributed to supply difficulties for the brine salt coming from the Perm'-Solikamsk region. One might counter his argument by positing that the 1744–45 declines were directly correlated with governmental deflationary policies which may have affected the purchasing power of the serf population. Whatever the actual situation was, Shuvalov assumed a high demand for salt and therefore felt that a rise in price would not decrease the volume of purchases of this commodity. In modern parlance, he assumed a zero elasticity of demand with respect to price.

This line of reasoning led Shuvalov to expand further on the same theme in a memorandum to the Senate dated September 7, 1752, one part of which, on the abolition of internal tolls, is well known. The other part is equally interesting because it touches on the relationship between the poll tax and the salt tax and reflects the role which Shuvalov envisaged for the gabelle in the Russian system of taxation.[6] Shuvalov's argument ran as follows: (1) The basic resource ("power" in Shuvalov's parlance) of the empire is the poll-tax-paying population, which provides the following vital services: (a) manpower for the army; (b) the material means for the maintenance of the army and military installations as well as ordnance; (c) maintenance for the government apparatus, for the nobility, clergy, and all serf-owning institutions; (d) increases in the state income through its work in mines, manufactories, and factories; (e) tilling and harvesting of the fertile land, gathering its produce, providing the bulk of the commerce of the state and performing all kinds of work over and above the ones mentioned; (f) transporting all the goods by land and water for commerce, the government administration, and the military. Thus everybody is supplied with his needs in this enormous state by the services of those who pay the poll tax. (2) The well-being of this basic resource ("power") ought to be the center of attention for government policy and anything that would lead to its diminution ("weakening") ought to be avoided. (3) The salt tax is preferable to the poll tax for the following reasons: (a) it is a tax paid by the whole population and not by specific groups, as in the case of the poll tax; (b) it is less expensive to collect and does not involve any procedures of postponement of payments; (c) no punitive measures have to be resorted to in collecting the salt tax, such as property confiscation and jail sentences, which impose additional hardships on delinquent poll-tax payers and deprive them and the state of useful labor; (d) since the salt tax is not payable on specified dates, as is the poll tax, the taxpayers can avoid the losses incurred in selling their livestock and grain during inappropriate times when they receive low prices, which they do when the poll tax is due. (4) Although an expanded salt tax, which could become a substitute for both the present salt taxes and poll taxes, would not directly decrease the amount of total taxation, it would constitute a substantial saving of real expenditures over and above the nominal taxes and assure a "peaceful life in abundance [affluence]."

Stripping the Shuvalov memorandum of its rhetoric and distilling its rational nucleus, one can discern his observations about the nature of direct and indirect taxation. First, the real costs of direct taxes to the Russian taxpayer exceed the nominal costs by a

Table 8.6	Sales of Salt for Selected Years (in Pounds)
Year	Amount of Salt
1749	7,196,372
1750	6,162,887
1751	6,380,994
1752	6,654,439
1753	7,032,991
1754	6,822,488
1755	7,059,157
1756	7,512,314
1757	5,683,817
1758	6,281,494
1759	6,434,491
1760	6,423,375
1761	6,775,202
1762	6,574,512
1763	7,280,555

substantial margin. Second, the costs to the state of collecting the direct taxes are not negligible. Third, instituting a transfer from direct to indirect taxation would be better for both payees and the recipient.

There is no need to point out the weaknesses in Shuvalov's arguments, to try to predict the behavior of the taxpayers who would have had to pay an increased gabelle, or to estimate the costs of enforcing such a law, for much of his reasoning was based on the assumption of an existing excess demand for salt. As far as is known, Shuvalov never followed up on his initial proposal by producing a detailed program, and the Senate never acted on the proposal.

At least two of the Shuvalov memorandum assumptions were used subsequently, however, in the decree of September 12, 1756, when the price of salt was raised to 50 kopeks per pood. The explicit argument employed was that about a universal tax, which was the reason given for using the salt tax as a vehicle to increase revenue rather than to increase the poll tax. The implicit argument was that of the demand elasticity for salt with respect to price. The net result was an increase in the share of indirect taxes in the total taxation that was not exceeded again until the second half of the nineteenth century.

The data in table 8.6 reflect the resistance of consumers to the increases in 1750 and 1757 in the price of salt. The table also reflects the immediate response in 1763 to the decree of July 5, 1762, when the price of salt was lowered from 50 to 40 kopeks per pood.[7] The fact that Catherine II lowered the salt tax to win popular support is a good indicator of the people's attitude to the previous increases. The decrease in 1775 of the price of salt from 40 to 35 kopeks bears witness to the government's perception of popular attitudes.[8]

Two conclusions seem to follow from an appreciation of the constraints on the Catherinian salt policy. First, the gabelle came to be viewed as a minor source of government revenue. Second, in view of the rising production and transportation costs discussed in chapter 2, the production quota systems of the various producing regions were adjusted to minimize the overall delivery price of the salt supply with a hope of forestalling a constant decrease in the net revenue from the gabelle.

The first conclusion represents a sharp break with previous experience and policies. In part, at least, it could be explained by the government's realization that, of the three major indirect taxes (the tariff and taxes on alcohol and salt—see table 8.7), salt in fact was the least promising for its growth possibility. The government came to reject as erroneous Shuvalov's assumption that there was an excess demand for salt. The relegation of the salt tax to a minor position as a revenue source was facilitated by the government's ability to introduce paper money to help resolve the Catherinian budget deficits.

The second conclusion, the attempt to prevent a decline in the net revenue from the gabelle, resulted in a much more careful designation of supplies to various regions of the country with increased attention to production and transportation costs. The Salt Code of 1781 was introduced as a general policy guide on the organization of supply to various regions based on consumption requirements determined by the provincial authorities. Moreover, a policy was established that a constant two-year reserve should be maintained in designated regional warehouses.[9]

The increased cost-consciousness of the Russian government was reflected during the reign of Catherine II in the relative increase of the share of salt produced in the regions of Perm', Astrakhan', and, toward the end of the century, of Iletsk and the Crimea. For Perm' and Astrakhan' this was a relative restoration of the shares prevailing at the beginning of the century, prior to the upsetting effect that the bringing into production of Elton Lake salt had during the 1750s and 1760s. The reactivation of salt production in the central and western regions of Russia (Balabkua and Staraia Rusa) occurred when the rising production costs in other regions made it profitable, from the government's point of view, by yielding a net revenue comparable to that of the other regions.

Mounting inflation and the rising costs of production and transportation of salt, which followed the rise of the general price level, could not be overcome by the cost-saving manipulations of the delivery quotas. In 1791, in an attempt to avoid subsidizing the retail price of salt, its price was increased from 35 to 40 kopeks. All that did was to avoid a large subsidy. Given the 40-kopek ceiling on the retail price, the subsidy became unavoidable three years

later. That put an end to an effective gabelle in the eighteenth century. We shall probably never know what policy considerations prevented an abolition of the gabelle in 1791.

Perhaps the most important question the material on the gabelle should be capable of answering is whether the salt tax constituted a real burden on the incomes of the Russian population, and, if it was, how that burden was distributed. Assuming that consumption amounted to a pood per "soul," one could calculate the ratio of the tax incidence per pood of salt to the poll tax per "soul" to get a relative measure of the tax. There can be no doubt that after 1750 the salt tax acquired a discriminatory feature, for the introduction of a uniform retail price for all of Russia discriminated against consumers located near the sources of supply. The inhabitants of eastern and northern Russia were discriminated against in favor of those living in western and central Russia. It is not clear whether the Senate, introducing a uniform price in 1750, had any special reasons for redistributing income among the various regions.

The gabelle in Russia was an example of an indirect tax of varying impact on the salt consumers and their incomes. It depressed the level of salt production and consumption. It affected the regional distribution of salt production, and it had some impact on the regional distribution of incomes.

This concludes my discussion of indirect taxation in eighteenth-century Russia. Table 8.7 presents the data on the net tax revenue gained from the taxes on alcohol and salt and the customs duties. The data reveal that the tax on alcohol usually raised the most money, but it was sometimes closely rivalled by customs duties. The gabelle was a strong third strand in the revenue fabric until the reign of Catherine II, when it gradually weakened to the point that the government was subsidizing salt consumption to the sum of more than a million rubles per year.

The Soul Tax

The mainstay of the direct taxation system introduced by Peter the Great was the poll tax, the "soul tax" (*podushnaia podat'*), a tax levied on the taxable male population, from the youngest male babe to the oldest male geriatric. It succeeded the original Muscovite land tax and then the household tax that had prevailed between 1678 and 1721. The bulk of the taxpaying population, the agricultural serfs, actually paid the tax by households rather than by the individual taxpayer, for the very young and the very old, as well as the disabled, had no income. Very often within the estate or within the village commune the tax burden was actually distributed among the households on what amounted to an ability-to-pay basis.

Table 8.7   Reported Net Tax Revenue from Selected Indirect Taxes (in 1,000 Rubles), 1724–96

Year	Alcohol	Gabelle	Customs	Total	Year	Alcohol	Gabelle	Customs	Total
1724	850.1	607.0	849.6	2,306.7	1761	3,329.0	2,182.4	2,669.1	8,180.6
1725		550.1			1762	3,450.9	1,795.8	2,881.2	8,127.0
1726		584.9			1763	4,376.0	1,542.2	3,072.7	8,990.9
1727	916.4	510.9			1764	4,016.0	1,548.2	2,969.2	8,533.4
1728		218.9			1765	4,198.0	1,695.1	3,126.7	10,019.9
1729		213.8			1766	4,339.0	1,677.9	2,875.7	8,892.6
1730		215.8			1767	5,081.0	1,698.0	2,663.9	9,442.9
1731		303.4			1768	5,081.0	1,700.0	2,823.5	9,604.5
1732	916.0	612.5			1769	5,081.0	1,439.0	3,206.1	9,726.1
1733	945.3	661.4			1770	5,923.0	1,900.0	3,191.0	11,014.0
1734	909.0	678.3			1771	6,641.0	1,905.0	3,268.2	11,814.2
1735	820.6	697.5			1772	6,641.0	1,570.0	3,227.0	11,438.0
1736	715.2	711.7			1773	6,641.0	1,586.0	3,614.4	11,841.4
1737	887.1	764.6			1774	6,641.0		3,539.8	
1738	910.7	783.6			1775	6,920.0		3,290.7	
1739		837.8			1776	6,920.0	995.0	3,214.8	11,130.0
1740		821.3			1777	6,982.0	1,115.0	3,229.9	11,327.0
1741		840.7			1778	9,419.0		2,976.5	
1742		804.4	955.3		1779	9,419.0		3,128.3	
1743		816.4	1,060.8		1780	9,419.0		4,078.7	
1744	992.2	706.1	1,001.7	2,700.0	1781	9,419.0	1,115.0	4,384.9	14,919.0
1745		777.7	1,031.8		1782	9,435.0	996.0	4,535.7	14,967.0
1746		813.3	1,055.8		1783	9,517.0	1,115.0	4,963.4	15,595.0
1747	1,141.4	792.7	950.6	2,884.7	1784	9,228.0	1,271.0	5,375.0	15,874.0
1748	1,062.0	753.5	886.6	2,702.1	1785	9,051.0	1,267.0	5,285.0	15,603.0
1749	1,263.5	801.3	1,052.5	3,117.3	1786	9,228.0	1,271.0	4,832.0	15,331.0
1750	1,634.8	1,223.0	1,227.7	4,085.5	1787	9.613.0	1,267.0	5,468.0	16,348.0
1751	2,273.5	1,216.2	1,230.1	4,719.8	1788	9.419.0	1,010.0	5,187.0	15,616.0
1752	2,362.1	1,297.0	1,427.6	5,086.7	1789	9,613.0	1,021.0	5,487.0	16,121.0
1753	2,305.2	1,392.2	1,460.4	5,157.8	1790	9,419.0	758.0	6,957.0	17,134.0
1754	2,249.5	1,318.3	2,134.5	5,702.3	1791	8,608.0	−13.0	6,525.0	15,120.0
1755	2,662.9	1,370.5	2,412.8	6,446.2	1792	8,598.0	−59.0	7,228.0	15,767.0
1756	2,574.3	1,405.0	2,320.9	6,300.2	1793	8,713.0	−21.0	5,017.0	13,709.0
1757	2,551.9	1,887.1	2,516.9	6,955.9	1794	9,110.0	−840.0	5,294.0	13,564.0
1758	2,731.7	2,177.2	2,559.8	7,468.7	1795	17,512.0	−1,175.0	5,409.0	21,746.0
1759	3,132.7	2,012.9	2,654.6	7,800.2	1796	15,000.0		6,470.0	
1760	3,298.4	2,065.2	2,625.0	7,988.6					

Nevertheless, the poll tax clearly was neither a land tax nor an income tax. The poll tax symbolized the right of the government to tax the entire population that was decreed to be taxpaying, and also the property of the landowning, serf-owning classes, whose members were responsible for the collection of the tax from their serfs.

The poll tax constituted a new principle of taxation. The male soul was a new taxable unit which replaced the previous unit, the household (*dvor*). The government changed its method of taxation because the populace had discovered that it could escape taxation partially by combining households, a development which gave birth to the extended family. What was the effect of this shift on the burden of taxation? All that is known from direct evidence is the manner in which the tax was allegedly introduced. The story— or the legend, which perhaps reflects part of reality— is that a calculation of the costs of maintaining the armed forces at the level of the 1720 military regula-

tions came to about four million rubles. The first results of the population count, begun in 1719, suggested a population of five million male taxpayers. Therefore, the poll tax was purportedly set at 80 kopeks per male taxpayer.

Another version, based on instructions given to General Chernyshev, is that the poll tax was determined by approximating the costs of maintaining the infantry and cavalry soldiers and then distributing the tax according to the costs of a desired number of soldiers.[10] It is possible that the decision to introduce the specific poll-tax sum could be explained in such simplistic terms, although it is doubtful whether the decision itself was arrived at as a result of a purely arithmetic formula. It is more plausible to assume that the previous system of taxation was found wanting, either in its production of expected revenue or because of some effects that disturbed the government. One of the fundamental questions, therefore, is to discern the sources and scope of earlier taxation and whether the burden was increased by the introduction of the soul tax. Moreover, economic historians want to know if the revenue under the new system exceeded that produced by the previous one, and by how much.

One of the axioms of the Russian historiography of the fiscal system has been the assumption that the introduction of the poll tax led to an increase in the burden on the Russian serfs. Moreover, it led to an increase not only in the efficiency of tax collection but in state revenue.

This assumption has hardly ever been challenged. No one has reexamined the evidence or the logic for a government's decision, after a war of twenty years' duration, to tax the population even more than it had during wartime. The next few pages are devoted to a reexamination of the traditional view.

Unquestionably the volume of taxation, in money, in kind, and in services rendered, increased greatly during the period of the Northern War. The costs of armaments, of food and fodder, of equipment and clothing for the armed forces rose almost continuously throughout the war. According to the works of Miliukov, Klochkov, and Troitskii, the taxable population during the Northern War may have declined while the taxes were rising, a factor that by itself increased the burden on the survivors.

The direct taxation of the agricultural serf population expanded during the war by an increase in the regular taxes, the invention of new extraordinary taxes, the expansion of the tax base among population groups that previously had been exempt from some taxes, and, last but not least, by the levying of taxes on nonexisting tax units that had to be paid by existing taxpayers. The use of the household (dvor) as the basic taxpaying unit in the first two decades of the century makes comparison over time very difficult, even when the tax rates or the revenues brought in were recorded and preserved.

The rapid rate of inflation in the Petrine period also makes comparisons hazardous. The Russian mint was quite active during Peter's reign. The available data on the recoinage of silver money and the minting of copper money are presented in table 8.8. The real value of the ruble decreased about 50 percent during the first decade of the century, and by another 20 percent during the second decade. This must be kept in mind when comparisons involving longer time periods are made.

Because of these difficulties, no attempt will be made to estimate the burden of taxation at the height of the Northern War, during the years 1705–15, except to indicate that this was not only the period when money taxes kept increasing, but also the time when taxes in kind reached their apex. Everything that could be taxed was prey for Peter's "projectors,"

Table 8.8   Recoinage of Silver Money

Year	Total Minted (in Rubles)	Yearly Average (in Rubles)
1699–1710	19,161,155	1,596,763
1711–17	4,240,491	605,784
1718–24	4,921,172	703,025
	Minting of Copper Money	
1704–17	3,346,538	
1718–24	1,007,604	

Source: Miliukov, *Gosudarstvennoe khoziaistvo*, 2d ed., pp. 149–52, 361–93.

or financial wizards, and the resources of the country were strained in pursuit of the war effort.

The devaluation of the ruble in 1718 was the last major single operation designed to fill the emptying coffers of the treasury. From that point on, the burden of real taxation appears to have ceased its upward climb as the actual revenue receipts tended to decline and the tax arrears increased.

At least fragmentary data on the variety and volume of direct taxes are available for 1719–23, and they permit speculation about the reasons for and the effects of the introduction of the new system of taxation.[11] One of the effects of the rising level of taxation had been a decrease in the number of households. This consequence would have been expected to occur even under conditions of a growing population. The simple postponement of departure from the household by the younger generation would have produced this effect. (The reader should recall the impact of the window tax in England, the impact of taxing closets as "rooms" in British North America, and similar taxes in other countries.) This was particularly easy to achieve since the serfs and landowners were not interested in collecting government revenue, but in raising rents, something that could be achieved regardless of the nominal number of households by requiring rents from the *tiaglo*, a rent-paying unit consisting of a labor rendering unit, or from the *venets*, a husband and wife.

The government tried to counteract the decline in the official number of households in a variety of ways. One of them was to levy the taxes upon the highest number of households ever recorded in particular administrative regions. As a result, regardless of the population count of 1710 in areas such as the Moscow province, for example, the number of households taxed was that recorded in the census of 1678. The rates were adjusted accordingly to cause a balance between the regular tax and the extraordinary taxes in an overall attempt to maximize revenue. Some of the puzzling differences in the tax rates between various provinces shown in table 8.9 would disappear if the differences between the actual and the decreed numbers of taxpayers were taken into

Table 8.9   Tax Payments by Serfs per Household (dvor) by Gubernii, 1723 (in Rubles)

Guberniia	Court Serfs	State Serfs	Ecclesiastical Serfs	Private Serfs
Arkhangel'sk	3.45	3.45	3.47	3.25
Astrakhan'	5.51	n.a.	5.26	2.60
Voronezh	2.45	n.a.	2.90	2.58
Kazan'	2.98	n.a.	3.93	2.65
Moscow	3.88	n.a.	3.37	2.67
Nizhnii-Novgorod	5.45	n.a.	4.10	2.69
St. Petersburg	5.45	n.a.	2.43	2.43
Smolensk	2.65	n.a.	3.24	2.60
Siberia	5.88	5.88	5.88	5.88

Source: Troitskii, *Finansovaia politika*, p. 122.

account. The low tax rates of Moscow and St. Petersburg provinces on privately owned and ecclesiastical serfs are a good example. The lower nominal rates of St. Petersburg province yielded the same revenue per actual household as in Moscow province (we must bear in mind that the estimated number of households was 1.6 times greater than the actual number in St. Petersburg province while in Moscow it was greater by only one-third). According to the data cited by Anisimov, the average revenue for the years 1719–23 from the direct household taxation was 3,436,227 rubles per year. This total was the sum of 1,519,897 rubles raised in direct ordinary taxes (*okladnye sbory*) and 1,916,330 from extraordinary taxes. The latter fluctuated from 1,623,228 rubles in 1723 to 2,194,140 rubles in 1721, the year of the Persian campaign. The tendency of the extraordinary taxes was to decline over the years.[12]

P. N. Miliukov, the chief proponent of the view that taxes rose as a result of the poll tax, maintained that direct taxes were increased by the introduction of the poll tax from 1,778,533 rubles to 4,614,638 rubles, an increase of 2,836,105 rubles, or 61 percent.[13] The data cited by Anisimov suggest that Miliukov's figures were greatly exaggerated and based on erroneous evidence.

One must, however, explain the difference between the 1721 revenue of 3,669,000 rubles and the poll tax income of 4,586,000 rubles (at 80 kopeks per male soul) or 4,234,000 rubles (at 74 kopeks per male soul). The increase in taxes requiring explanation is somewhere between 600,000 and 900,000 rubles, rather than Miliukov's 2,800,000. Any further inquiry would have to be pursued along two lines. First, whether the above-mentioned direct cash taxes in fact exhausted the total of ordinary and extraordinary payments. Second, whether the number of taxpayers included either as groups or as individuals in the population count (the *reviziia*) exceeded the previous number of taxpayers. It is well known that one of the objectives of the *reviziia* was to enserf previously free people to new masters and to make taxpayers out of

previously tax-exempt people; thus it is highly likely that a certain number of new taxpayers were created. If corrections of the above two indicators can account for the gap between the tax reports of the Golitsyn Committee, as reported by Anisimov, and the poll tax introduced by Peter, the conclusion must be that the poll tax did not increase the taxation burden.

Regrettably, the documentary evidence for answering the first question is not available. Although an estimate of the value of services and in-kind payments made in lieu of direct taxes for the pre-poll-tax period is lacking, some evidence is available about the direct and indirect money payments made under the household tax and poll tax rubrics. Using the data on the household tax by different categories and regions (see table 8.9) and household-size estimates, one can reach the following tentative conclusions: (1) the poll tax constituted a reduction in the per capita burden for the state, court, and ecclesiastical serfs in comparison with the cash part of the household tax; (2) for some of the major provinces, notably for Moscow, the poll tax was slightly lower even for private serfs, although for some provinces the poll tax on private serfs exceeded the per capita value of the monetary share of the household tax; (3) for the total rural enserfed population, the poll tax constituted a reduction of the tax in money compared with the household tax, although this reduction may have been arrived at by simultaneously increasing the burden of the private serfs in some regions and decreasing it for the state-owned serfs; (4) if any positive value should be attached to services rendered and payments in kind made in lieu of direct taxes, the total tax burden of the pre-poll-tax period exceeded the poll tax burden of the same taxpayers; and (5) most of the increase in the budgetary revenue originated from the increase of the number of taxpayers rather than from an increase in the burden on those taxpayers who had paid taxes previously.

If we substitute in Miliukov's state budget estimates the known sums of the actual direct taxes, the

Table 8.10   Estimates of State Budget Revenues by Major Categories, 1720–24 (in Rubles)

	1720	1721	1722	1723	1724
Salt tax	659,541	735,184	713,375	696,671	
Customs, alcohol, and other indirect taxes	3,249,924	3,303,083	2,924,003	2,838,530	
Direct ordinary (*okladnye*)	1,519,897	1,519,897	1,519,897	1,519,897	
Direct extraordinary (*zaprosnye*)	1,917,601	2,194,140	1,930,553	1,623,228	
Total current-year account	7,346,963	7,752,304	7,087,828	6,678,396	
Arrears account	808,433	739,400	966,480	1,147,396	
On future accounts	124,339	37,858	1,220	90,044	
Total above	8,279,735	8,529,562	8,055,528	7,915,766	8,172,433

Sources: Miliukov, *Gosudarstvennoe khoziaistvo* 2d ed., pp. 487–90, and Anisimov, "Materialy," p. 352.

estimates of the yearly state budget for the years 1720–24 presented in table 8.10 can be obtained.

Table 8.10 permits only a very iconoclastic conclusion: the introduction of the poll tax reduced the tax burden on the Russian peasantry from the high level of the taxation in money and in kind that was reached during the Northern War. The impression that the poll tax was harsh was created, and it persisted both in folklore and in the historical memory of the people because the introduction of the tax coincided with years of famine and privation, when the state requisitioned grain at confiscatory prices and when the military, rather than the landowners, collected the tax in money. The high price of grain, the consequence of poor grain harvests that forced many peasants to buy rather than to sell grain, combined with the export of specie to pay the 2-million-ruble debt to Sweden (the settlement for Swedish claims in Lifland and Estland in accord with the 1721 Nystadt peace treaty), created a temporary decline of the money supply and caused difficulties in collecting the taxes.

The conclusion is inescapable: the circumstances of the introduction of the poll tax created a lasting impression in the collective memory of the serfs. This did not permit separating the economic effects of the new mode of taxation from the calamities that accompanied its introduction. It is the task of students of economic history to disentangle the causes and the effects of taxation from the effects of other calamities.

Additional support for the hypothesis that the poll tax instituted by Peter the Great in 1724 did not constitute an increase in government taxation, but in fact was a decrease from the Northern War level, is provided by data pertaining to taxation levied on serfs living on monastery lands.[14] These data, presented in table 8.11, indicate that the rise in government taxation started in 1701 and was doubled between then and 1708–10. It kept rising in nominal terms until 1719. The tax burden per serf household began to decline in 1720. The imposition of the poll tax (assuming an average household size of four male

taxpayers) resulted in a lower burden than the tax rate of the preceding four years and, in nominal terms, was a return to the level of 1704–10. In real terms, taking into consideration the decrease in the value of money during the first quarter of the century and the subsequent rise in grain prices during the second and third decades, except for a few selected years, taxes did not exceed the level achieved during 1708–10.[15]

The *podushnaia podat'* constituted only a portion of what contemporary statesmen and Russian historians have labeled as government revenue from the poll tax. One of the sources of the mislabeling or even confusion stemmed from the fact that government accounting, budgetary planning, and reporting, on the three occasions when it was engaged in, failed to distinguish between the tax element paid by the various categories of state-owned serfs and the rent element (*obrok*) paid by those serfs to the state treasury. The tax element for private and state-owned serfs remained unchanged from 1725 to 1761, but the rent element for the latter was raised in that year to follow the rise in rent payments by private serfs. Successive increases of the rent component paid by state-owned serfs were introduced in 1769, 1783, and 1794. They followed a steep stepwise pattern upward which is illustrated in table 8.12 on the norms of the poll tax. They provided the largest additions to state revenue from direct taxation.

Any discussion of the poll tax on serfs should deal with the dual role of the government. On the one hand, the government was a fiscal authority taxing the total serf population. On the other hand, it was a major serf-owner and collected rents from its human property, the serfs, and used the proceeds for state purposes.

Tables 8.13 and 8.14 separate the government's two roles as tax collector and serf-owner. Employing the data on the taxable serf population and the obligatory norms of the poll tax, the tables show the approximate distribution of the direct tax revenue derived

Table 8.11   Government Taxes Levied Upon the Serfs of Monasteries, 1701–23 (in Kopeks per Household)

Year	Money Value of Taxes in Kind	Money Taxes		Total	3-Year Moving Averages	3-Year Averages
		Total	Of Which, Extraordinary			
1701	101	48.75	1.25	149.75		
02	251	56.5		307.5	210.91	
03	108.5	67	10.5	175.5	260.58	244.58
04	227	71.75		298.75	262.25	
1705	200	112.5	35	312.5	274.08	
06	101	110		211	262.17	261.53
07	125	138	10	263	248.33	
08	149	122		271	259	
09	115	128		243	285	298.33
1710	212	129		341	351	
11	200	269	93	469	451.58	
12	240	304.75	90	544.75	521.5	484.69
13	248	302.75	48.5	550.75	481	
14	54	293.5	36.25	347.5	471.33	
1715	180	335.75	72	515.75	482.5	492.22
16	173	414.25	10	587.25	522.83	
17	93	375.5		468.5	507.83	
18	123	347.75	8	470.75	523.58	520.53
19	259	372.5	19.125	631.5	530.17	
1720	156.5	331.75		488.25	536.04	
21	137	351.375		488.375	484.46	
22	128	348.75		476.75	448.29	
23	52	327.75		379.75		

Source: Bulygin, *Monastyraskie krest'iane*, pp. 155–57.

Table 8.12   Norms of the Poll-Tax Per Male Soul for the Russian Districts (in Kopeks)

	Private	Court	Ecclesiastic	State[a]	State[b]	Merchants	Burghers
1724	74	74	74	114	114	120	120
1725	70	70	70	110	110	120	120
1761	70	70	70	170	110	120	120
1762	70	70	220	170	110	120	120
1765	70	70	220	170	170	120	120
1769	70	270	270	270	170	200	200
1775	70	270	270	270	170	1%	120
1783	70	370	370	370	370	1%	120
1794	100	400	400	400	400	1%	120

Source: Chechulin, *Ocherki*, pp. 122–23.

Note: For the court, ecclesiastic, and state serfs for the period 1761–83, the difference between 70 kopeks and the actual tax norm is accounted for by the size of the money rent.

[a]This category of state serfs denotes the former *chernososhnye* ("taxpaying"), mostly concentrated in the northern provinces.
[b]This category refers to the previously free settlers known as *odnodvortsy* ("single householders"), mostly concentrated in the southern and southeastern regions.

from the poll tax and that derived from rent collections.

For a government-owned serf there was probably little significant distinction between the tax and rent components. What mattered was the total burden of household payments to the owner, the state. For comparing the burden of payments of the state-owned serfs with the money rents, labor services (*barshchina*), and tax payments of the privately owned serfs, however, and for analyzing fiscal policies as well as fiscal burdens, the distinction appears to be a valid one.

I made the comparison, which, to simplify the procedure, was made for the serf population only in the territory of the first population census (*reviziia*), within which the tax norms were uniform, as distinct from the taxes paid in territories acquired later. This comparison yields very interesting results on the roles of the state as tax collector and rent collector. While the tax revenue from the poll tax proper increased during the years 1726–96 from about 4,000,000 to 10,400,000 rubles, the volume of money rent collected by the state from its own serfs increased from about 700,000 to over 14,000,000 rubles

Table 8.13   The State as a Tax Collector from Serfs (in Rubles)

Year	Court Serfs	Church Serfs	State Serfs	Church + State Serfs	Private Serfs	Total
1726	356,639	554,259	859,576	1,216,215	2,235,160	4,005,634
1744	300,498	628,930	1,111,991	1,412,489	2,646,768	4,688,187
1764	345,315	718,851	1,420,710	2,484,876	3,081,119	5,565,995
1784	421,018	831,358	1,913,413	3,165,789	3,573,494	6,739,283
1794	601,454	1,187,654	2,733,447	4,522,555	5,104,991	9,627,546
1796	494,262	1,304,794	2,953,039	4,752,095	5,617,256	10,369,351

Table 8.14   The State as a Serfowner: Volume of Obrok (Money Rent) Collected (in Rubles)

Year	Court Serfs	Church Serfs	State Serfs	Total	No. of Serfs
1726	203,793	—	491,186	694,979	1,137,449
1744	171,713	—	635,424	807,137	2,017,842
1764	641,299	1,540,395			3,549,882
1769	986,614	2,053,860			3,549,822
1784	1,804,362	3,562,962	8,200,341	13,567,665	4,522,555
1794	1,804,362	3,562,962	8,200,341	13,567,665	4,522,555
1796	1,482,786	3,914,382	8,859,117	14,256,285	4,752,095

money rents is obvious. Another central feature here is the use of the state's rent income within the fiscal framework. Faced with the opposition of the private serf-owners to an increase of the poll tax on their serfs, encountering the desires of the private serf-owners to divide the secularized ecclesiastical estates among private noblemen, and, most important, understanding the need for a buildup of a more efficient and dependent bureaucracy, the state decided to use the rent income from its own serfs as a means to augment the state treasury.

The ability of the state to raise the rents from its serfs compensated not only for the rising expenditures of the imperial court, but went a long way toward defraying the costs of the government bureaucracy. This was a major contribution toward making the government less dependent upon the serf-owning class. Beginning with the 1760s, the combined revenues of the poll tax and rent payments by the state-owned serfs began to exceed the revenues from the poll tax levied on the private serfs. Already in the 1780s the rents from the state serfs were twice as large as the revenues provided by the poll tax proper.

When encountering the data on the poll tax for the eighteenth century, one must be aware of the fact that the reported data consisted of two distinct components which for political rather than economic purposes were lumped together in the government accounts.

Regional Tax Burdens

Study of the development of and changes in the taxation patterns for the population of particular regions is difficult without access to Soviet archives. The only available summary data representing the volume of taxation on a particular district pertain to Livland, an area in which the entire Russian system of taxation was imposed during the 1780s. Such data are not typical for the Russian provinces, and they include three additional "distorting" factors. One is the presence of the port of Riga with its very substantial incomes from customs duties. The second factor is the presence of a tax in kind, mostly in grain, which was entered into the tax revenues not according to current market prices but according to fixed rates in the local currency, the Albertustaler. The third distortion in the original accounts is the entering of Albertustalers in nominal exchange rates, not in terms of their actual exchange rate for Russian rubles. I have corrected the last distortion by using an index of market exchange rates of the Albertustaler in terms of rubles.

For these reasons the series presented in table 8.15 represents an order of magnitude that is only partially adjusted to the current value of tax revenues and understates the burden of taxation. The series includes both the direct taxes on the agricultural population paid in kind, the various direct and indirect taxes paid in money, and the revenues desired from state property.

The most interesting feature of the series is the sheer size of the tax burden on a province which had, relative to other Russian provinces, a small population. Livland's capacity to bear the considerable burden was a manifestation of its relative affluence based on relatively higher agricultural productivity and incomes derived from international trade. Livland not only provided the Russian government with a steady source of revenue, but, thanks to its payment in silver currency, it supplied the Russian mint with the silver needed to support the Russian money

Table 8.15   Taxation of the Lifland Province

Year	In Rubles	In Albertus-talers	Including Land Tax (in Albertus-talers)	Albertus-talers in Ruble Equivalents	Total Current in Rubles	Tax Arrears
1730	18,179	369,165	92,462	372,857	391,036	29,749
1731	15,615	301,100	93,285	313,144	328,759	29,977
1732	21,546	297,837	103,261	318,686	340,232	34,249
1733	18,538	325,579	120,804	348,370	366,908	79,641
1734	16,752	321,617	126,111	344,130	360,882	63,469
1735	27,596	380,407	126,428	407,035	434,631	124,053
1736	24,231	373,500	126,526	388,440	412,671	100,298
1737	17,293	399,352	125,806	403,345	420,638	89,529
1738	22,535	396,936	132,838	412,813	435,348	60,403
1739	18,189	400,234	133,160	434,670	452,859	49,664
1740	22,999	392,958	132,131	424,395	447,394	159,477
1741	24,525	462,305	134,963	494,666	519,191	42,149
1742	23,852	422,704	135,066	456,520	480,372	170,672
1743	24,491	380,963	135,066	426,678	451,169	89,821
1744	29,430	349,726		381,201	410,631	100,165
1745	36,251	387,643		434,160	470,411	195,189
1746	36,701	384,780		434,801	471,502	165,774
1747	38,897	386,367		432,731	471,628	59,675
1748	29,078	340,057		387,665	416,743	55,599
1749	27,754	371,377		430,797	458,551	73,491
1750	22,999	366,011		420,913	443,912	79,899
1751	28,012	379,725		429,089	457,101	28,269
1752	29,669	409,123		458,218	487,887	36,964
1753	36,048	387,305		418,289	454,337	94,409
1754	60,130	456,413		483,798	543,928	62,234
1755	45,473	366,339		388,319	433,792	69,048
1756	57,796	431,369		470,192	527,988	162,147
1757	44,597	388,154		450,259	494,856	190,772
1758	50,710	390,187		456,519	507,229	50,538
1759	60,587	419,096	104,953	494,533	555,120	45,651
1760	43,813	375,167		450,200	494,013	19,905
1761	27,756	414,819		510,227	537,983	64,311
1762	34,665	549,418		670,290	704,955	50,351
1763	85,132	494,790		559,113	644,245	95,835
1764	30,612	489,810		568,180	598,792	107,440
1765	82,942	433,259		489,583	572,525	162,961
1766	61,929	441,347		507,549	569,478	149,121
1767	66,319	470,734		560,173	626,492	194,999
1768	83,778	455,978		547,174	630,952	28,678
1769	71,639	578,688		700,212	771,851	48,961
1770	67,213	565,182		717,781	784,994	35,960
1771	68,512	583,546		746,939	815,451	122,647
1772	104,930	710,132		880,564	985,494	61,011
1773	109,105	690,427		876,842	985,947	51,153
1774	86,960	671,294	125,083	865,969	952,929	95,597
1775	71,100	702,707	122,313	836,924	908,024	77,192
1776	67,321	502,963	121,543	599,029	666,350	125,936
1777	74,578	540,471	118,498	647,484	722,062	84,318
1778	65,398	564,075	118,528	683,659	749,057	125,701
1779	59,542	555,693	118,011	685,725	745,267	88,703
1780	66,243	652,334	118,529	927,619	993,862	113,659

Source: Zutis, *Politika*, pp. 212–13.

market. That in turn created for the government a secondary source of income from the minting operations.

The data on tax arrears in table 8.15 provide an incidental source of information about the ups and downs of the economy of Livland. Tax arrears could be calculated only in terms of the permanent and stable (within discreet intervals) revenues, such as the land taxes. (The poll tax was introduced in Livland only in 1783.) They have nothing to do with customs duties. Consequently the data for the years of greatly increased tax arrears tend to indicate the existence of natural calamities, wars, and other events that introduced major disturbances in the economic activities of the province.

Governmental Expenditures

The justification of the various fiscal policies of the Russian government during the eighteenth century has to be sought among the demands made for expenditures. The key to the growth of budget income is in the changes of the major categories of government expenses. This is not tantamount to assuming that there were no constraints operating on the expenditure side of the budget ledger to rein in expenditures to the predicted size of expected state revenues. The awareness of such constraints appears repeatedly in the minutes of the Senate's budget debates and in the deliberations of the various committees appointed to deal with fiscal matters. Regardless, from the beginning of the 1770s the government grew accustomed to the idea of mounting budget deficits. This change of attitude clearly weakened the constraint of actual revenue on government expenditures.

The following have to be singled out among the particular items of the budget expenditures which either permanently occupied a prominent position in the total, or were growing significantly during the second half of the eighteenth century: military expenditures; costs of maintaining the imperial court; costs of tax collection; costs of central and provincial administration. The pattern of each of these categories must be examined separately under the assumption that the pattern of each was determined by causes independent of the others. Then I shall attempt to generalize and explain their interdependence and relationship.

The data in table 8.16 for the reign of Catherine II clearly indicate that military expenditures, regardless of whether the country was at war or at peace, seldom constituted less than half the net budget. The situation had been the same during the reigns of Peter I and Elizabeth. Fragmentary data for other years of the century corroborate that generalization. Whether these expenditures are measured as a percentage of gross budget expenditures, or as a percentage of the actual net budget revenue, the result is the same, except that the latter measure more vividly compares the actual military outlays with the actual current income of the government.

At this point I am not concerned with the political justification of Russian military policies or with the efficiency with which the country used vast resources to achieve military objectives, and need only point out that the military-political successes during the eighteenth century resulted not only from the relative weakness of its neighbors, or from skillful Russian diplomacy, but also from a capacity and ability to carry continuously a fiscal burden that was of considerable magnitude for the population and economy of Russia.

The annual state subsidy for the maintenance of the emperor's (or empress's) palace court appeared on the expenditure side of the state budget ledger. After Peter the Great basically separated the government treasury from the palace court treasury and established a civil list of state payments to members of the imperial family, the principle—if not the practice—of stipulated, budgeted expenditures for the court was implied. Consistent with the practice of budgetary procedures of the times, such expenditures not only had to be authorized, but also the source (meaning the specific tax revenue) specified and arranged. For a while the court expenditures were assigned from the gabelle income.

The court maintenance allowance was by no means the only source of income for the tsar and his family. Lands, forests, mines, and other properties which belonged to the tsar's family and were under the supervision of the so-called "Cabinet" constituted the private property of the ruler. They were distinguished from the court (or public) property of land and humans as another group of crown assets, which were administered by the state. Until 1797 the court estates were called *dvortsovye* ("court estates") and after 1797 *udel'nye* ("appanage estates"), indicating the historical origin of the sovereign lands. For example, the Altai gold and silver mines made the emperor or empress for half a century the largest silver producer in Russia, and made him or her (or the Cabinet) the seller of silver to his (or her) own government. As the formal owner of the court estates, the emperor or empress was responsible for the payment of the tax of the court serfs into the government treasury.

The growth of court expenditures was not only a result of a shift from relative thriftiness to love of luxury by the ruler, but also of a number of tendencies prevalent in Russia, not all of which were directly related to the monarch's taste for luxury. Peter the Great is usually described as a man of austere military tastes, perhaps a consumer of excessive amounts of alcohol, who enjoyed martial splendor and shows. Although Anna and Elizabeth were famous for their insatiable taste for jewels, their courts hardly matched the splendor of Versailles or Schönbrünn and did not possess the permanent residence that made the court a central cultural institution. The Elizabethan court was often compared to a pack of gypsies on the move. It was only under Catherine II

Table 8.16 Military Budget Expenditures, 1762–96 (in 1,000 Rubles)

Year	Army	Navy	Special War Appropriation	Total Military	% of Gross Expenditures	% of Net Revenues
1762	9,219	1,200		10,419	63.15	
1763	7,920	1,200		9,120	52.92	62.75
1764	8,723	1,230		9,953	46.12	56.09
1765	9,676	1,508		11,184	49.44	58.77
1766	9,806	1,309		11,115	46.14	55.17
1767	9,828	1,263		11,091	47.60	52.22
1768	10,013	1,313	1,300	12,626	50.61	60.53
1769	10,000	1,400	1,800	13,200	49.48	65.16
1770	9,904	1,445	7,600	18,949	54.11	76.69
1771	10,282	2,578	9,000	21,860	56.62	82.82
1772	10,508	1,378	7,700	19,586	49.85	76.12
1773	10,812	1,433	7,355	19,600	50.27	76.40
1774						
1780	n.a.	n.a.	n.a.	n.a.		
1781	10,600	3,250		13,850	33.81	48.18
1782	10,800	3,270		14,070	34.39	44.49
1783	13,720	3,820		17,540	36.40	55.54
1784	14,320	3,930		18,250	36.65	45.04
1785	16,400	4,130		20,530	36.36	51.22
1786	19,110	8,640		27,750	44.28	67.25
1787	21,060	4,640	5,000	30,700	46.00	68.66
1788	18,690	4,350	16,000	39,040	51.29	89.41
1789	20,170	5,310	16,000	41,480	52.38	93.57
1790	21,620	5,470	16,000	43,090	52.10	94.28
1791	24,590	5,470	15,000	45,060	53.09	101.47
1792	23,100	6,200		29,300	40.55	67.94
1793	23,300	5,430		28,730	37.59	69.51
1794	21,600	5,670		27,270	37.71	63.87
1795	22,200	7,000		29,200	36.89	52.98
1796	21,000	6,680		27,680	35.41	49.96

that the construction of splendid court palaces was undertaken or finished. Moreover, at that time the court asserted its role not only in the government structure but assumed the qualities which other courts in Europe were playing at the time of "enlightened absolutism." The growth of expenditures can be explained in part at least by the numerical growth of the reigning elite, by the growth of the various formal occasions at which the top bureaucrats, and also members of the aristocracy and gentry, had to conduct business and participate in ceremonial affairs. It was also a manifestation of the rising international prestige of Russia and its relations with foreign countries. The growth of expenditures increased with the spread of tastes for sophisticated Western-type consumption and life-style. Last but not least, expenditures increased as a result of price inflation.

The only constraint on court expenditures had to come, given the existing governmental structure, exclusively from the monarch. It seems unlikely that members of the governing bodies resisted the demand by the monarch for additional funds. At least there is no evidence of such resistance. Perhaps self-restraint was occasionally displayed when the monarch was confronted with the fiscal plight of the

government. For example, there is a hint (rather than a confirmed report) that Elizabeth, when confronted with a budget deficit, turned over to the government certain sums from her "Cabinet" revenues.

One might speculate that one of the reasons why Catherine II exercised little self-restraint in the matter of appropriations for her court was a consequence of the fact that the income from taxing the court serfs, augmented during her reign by the increases in rent, compensated for a share of the court expenditures. By demanding greater expenditures for the court, she simply discounted what she considered a mere transfer, thereby diminishing in her eyes the state's subsidy of the court. The incomes from the court serfs (including both the poll tax and rent payments) increased from over 1,000,000 rubles in 1762 to 2,200,000 rubles in 1784 and 2,400,000 rubles in 1794. The expenditures for the court rose from 1,750,000 rubles in 1762 to 5,900,000 rubles in 1784 and 6,800,000 rubles in 1794.

One of the most important and interesting items of the budget's expenditure account is the one that could be labeled as the cost of collection. This item does not reflect what would be considered the costs of tax collection in the modern sense of the term. For example, it does not include the costs of most of the

Table 8.17   Comparison of the Taxes on Alcohol and Salt as Revenue Generators

	Gross Receipts		Net Income		Cost to the Government			Cost as % of Gross Receipts
	Alcohol Tax	Gabelle	Alcohol Tax	Gabelle	Alcohol	Gabelle	Total	
1763–65	15,487	8,288	12,590	4,787	2,897	3,501	6,398	26.9
1771–73	23,679	10,370	19,923	5,061	3,756	5,309	9,065	26.6
1781–83	37,939	11,700	28,371	3,226	9,568	8,474	18,042	36.3
1791–93	45,995	16,244	25,919	−93	20,076	16,337	36,413	58.5

administrative expenditures directly related to tax collection. It represents primarily the difference between the gross receipts and the net revenue from certain government operations or government monopolies. The two most obvious for the eighteenth century are the alcohol monopoly and the gabelle. Two other, less obvious and less significant, examples are the operations of state-owned iron or copper works and the customs duties. For nineteenth-century Russia, an important item would be the government-owned railroads, the revenues and expenditures of which were included in the state budget.

To illustrate the secular growth of "collection costs," the differences between the gross and net revenues, the costs of the government, of the alcohol tax and the gabelle are presented in table 8.17 for selected years during the second half of the eighteenth century. The table indicates that there was a rising trend in government expenditures in operating the alcohol and salt monopolies that began some time in the middle of the 1770s. (The data for 1776 and 1778 are similar to those of the early 1780s, which would support a hypothesis that the upward trend in the government's costs began a few years earlier in the decade.)

This rising trend unquestionably was strongly influenced by the official decision to keep the price of salt constant during a period of generally rising prices and costs. That it was done for political, rather than economic, reasons, is beside the point. On the other hand, the largest effect on the growth of costs in operating the alcohol monopoly was exercised by the rising prices of grain, the major cost of distilling. Those costs more than doubled between the early 1760s and the 1790s. The rise in grain prices during this period in Russia, excluding the price fluctuations due to the size of the harvest, was a part of the rise in the general price level at the end of the century, which affected not only Russia, but also all of the rest of Europe. Although the beneficiaries of the price increases in grain were primarily the large landowners, who supplied the government with either distilled alcohol or with grain for the state-owned distilleries, this could hardly be described as favoritism in view of the continuous and general rise in market prices.

The growing share of government expenditures incurred while operating its revenue-generating monopolies contributed to the widening of the gap between the gross receipts and the net government incomes of the state budget. This made it more difficult, and more expensive in the economic sense (although the government did not charge itself any interest), for the government to increase its net revenue. The data purporting to reflect the government costs are not very precise but appear to be within a range close to the order of magnitude indicated by the available evidence for its most important components.

One of the least explored subjects, and also one for which the data are the least precise, is the budgetary expenditure for administration. The data are imprecise because the documentation of the period did not register this category of expenses separately from the expenses for ear-marked purposes or institutions. The fascinating history of the formation and changes in the structure of the Russian bureaucracy during the eighteenth century does not provide any direct clues that might assist in estimating the costs of the civil service in Russia. Although recent studies of the Russian bureaucratic apparatus are increasingly using quantitative data available in archival sources, their chief emphasis at this point has been primarily on the social composition, the educational endowment, the service patterns, and the mobility of particular groups within the bureaucracy.[16]

A serious obstacle to studying the costs of civil administration in Russia lies in the fact that, after the death of Peter the Great, the provincial and lower-level civil servants did not receive salaries, but had to obtain their livelihood from the clients whom they were supposed to serve. The system combined elements of voluntary payments for services rendered with elements of requested demands by the civil servant from his clientele. The payment depended upon the expected return to the client from the service. This restored elements of legalized bribery that had at least formally been abolished in the *Sudebnik* of 1497. Such an arrangement prevailed in all the local governmental institutions in Russia during the 1730s to the 1760s.

The available data do not reflect the actual costs to the public of administrative service, except for the central institutions in which salaries were maintained. It was only after Catherine II reinstituted the system of a salaried bureaucracy during the years 1763–64 that data can be found on the budgetary expenses for administration. The documentary evidence for expenditures on administration can be found in the multitude of government decrees which set up the number of offices and the salary levels for the various government institutions. This is a very valuable and interesting source, except for the fact that it was normative in nature and provides no clue to the degree to which the various offices were actually filled, whether the prescribed categories were actually followed, and whether the stipulated salaries were paid. This is a bureaucratic system about which full knowledge is lacking.

The most practical method of estimating administrative costs is to treat them as a residual from the total expenses after deducting as many of the other expenditures as can be identified and verified. The classical work by Chechulin is helpful for the period 1781–96. There is an obvious error in his data for the years 1763–73. The lack of data for construction, communications, and other expenditures makes the estimates very tenuous indeed.

The data of the early 1760s show an extremely low level of expenditures on government administration, although there can be no doubt that the population bore the unrecorded burden of its maintenance outside the fiscal system. Expenditures rose rapidly with the institutions of salaries for the lower level of civil servants in the 1760s, and they continue a steep rise during the 1770s. The introduction of the *guberniia* reform in 1775 resulted in both a growth of the provincial bureaucracy and its costs and raised the floor of administrative expenses to a high level.

Currency Debasement

One of the means by which the government was able to deal with its deficits was by minting new currency and then by printing paper money. The mint derived revenue from minting silver and copper coins. The revenue from the minting of silver coins was based on the receipts of foreign silver coins from customs duties paid by foreigners at a fixed price below the market price and from the profits gained by reminting older Russian coins with a higher silver content, coins which the government obtained from its tax receipts and from decrees announcing the reminting of certain coins.

One might question the effectiveness of recalling higher-value coins in exchange at par for lower-value ones, but the possibility of such operations in eighteenth-century Russia with its diversity and localization of markets, and also the tenuous relation of

Table 8.18   Profit from Minting of Silver Coins (in Rubles)

Year	Revenue	Year	Revenue
1724	137,210	1734	285,056
1725	215,974	1735	252,468
1726	144,915	1736	131,979
1731	279,399	1737	288,234
1732	168,207	1738	440,415
1733	154,491	1739	278,799

Source: Troitskii, *Finansovaia politika*, pp. 200, 204.

many taxpayers to the money market, is plausible. There was a massive recoinage of silver coins during the reign of Peter the Great, and even during the post-Petrine period the reminting of silver coins yielded a substantial profit. The profits listed in table 8.18 from the reminting of silver coins are illustrative.

The coinage of silver, according to government calculations presented in table 8.19, provided only a relatively small revenue. For the period 1731–39 the revenue of 2,279,048 rubles was derived from minting 18,814,991 rubles, or a profit of less than 13.8 percent. This was acceptable as a source of revenue, but certainly did not resolve the problem of mounting government deficits.

As a deficit-financing operation, the coinage of copper coins was much more effective than the coinage of silver. There were no spectacular changes in policies or even in the volume of copper coinage. The period shows the notorious need of the government for deficit-financing and emphasizes the impact upon the government itself of such policies as copper coinage and printing paper money. Let us ignore for the moment the impact on the general price level of increasing the money stock (see chapter 7 on prices), and look at table 8.20, which illustrates the effect of increasing copper prices in terms of silver and of the declining value of copper money following the issuance of assignats (paper money) on the policies of deficit financing. Table 8.21 indicates that the declining value of the paper ruble, which determined the value of copper money by the end of the 1780s and certainly during the 1790s, reduced and nullified the government's profits from the coinage of copper money. That forced the government to rely on the printing press rather than on the minting stamp for deficit financing.

Eighteenth-Century Budgets

State budget data for most of the eighteenth century are scarce. Moreover, for most of the period no budget planning occurred. Consequently it is difficult to describe the budget policy with a degree of certainty that would satisfy present conventions of analysis. General conclusions can be drawn only on the basis of the budgets of the last third of the century

Table 8.19   Silver Coinage, 1699–1800

Years	In Current Rubles	In 1718 Rubles	In Weight of Silver (Poods)	Yearly Average of Silver Weight
1699–1710	19,161,155	22,995,060	29,107.6	2,425.6
1711–17	4,240,491	5,088,957	6,441.7	920.2
1718–24	4,921,172	4,921,172	6,229.3	889.9
1699–1724	28,322,818	33,005,189	41,778.6	1,606.9
1725–29	5,157,670	5,157,670	6,529.6	1,305.8
1730–40	20,094,975	20,094,975	25,433.3	2,384.3
1740–41	1,111,387	1,111,387	1,406.9	1,406.9
1742–60	32,317,799	32,317,799	40,911.6	2,272.9
1761	643,000	643,000	814.0	814.0
1762–71	24,359,676	21,141,032	26,761.6	2,676.2
1772–81	21,421,128	18,590,755	23,533.4	2,353.3
1782–91	17,237,763	14,960,137	18,937.5	1,893.8
1792–96	7,924,046	6,877,042	8,705.4	870.5
1762–96	70,942,614	61,568,966	77,937.9	2,226.8
1797–1800	10,018,471	8,694,730	11,006.3	2,751.6
Total		162,593,716	205,817.8	
Yearly Average		1,594,056	2,017.8	2,017.8

Table 8.20   The Issue of Copper Coins in Rubles, 1763–1800

Year	New Issue of Copper Coins	Silver Cost of Copper	Nominal Profit	New Issue in Silver	Profit in Silver Rubles
1763	1,854,386	886,628	967,758	1,854,386	967,758
1764	1,719,267	822,025	897,242	1,719,267	897,242
1765	2,089,758	999,165	1,090,593	2,089,758	1,090,593
1766	1,383,320	661,400	721,920	1,383,320	721,920
1767	1,900,756	908,806	991,950	1,900,756	991,950
1768	1,471,653	703,636	768,017	1,471,653	768,017
1769	2,020,517	1,035,515	985,002	2,000,312	964,797
1770	2,565,411	1,315,347	1,250,064	2,539,757	1,224,410
1771	2,917,275	1,495,103	1,422,172	2,858,930	1,363,827
1772	2,370,101	1,214,677	1,155,424	2,298,998	1,084,321
1773	2,008,718	1,029,468	979,250	1,968,544	939,076
1774	739,772	379,133	360,639	739,772	379,133
1775	1,557,224	963,534	593,690	1,541,652	578,118
1776	1,669,499	1,033,002	636,497	1,652,804	619,802
1777	1,903,359	1,189,599	713,760	1,884,325	694,726
1778	2,382,907	1,489,317	893,590	2,359,078	869,761
1779	1,988,044	1,242,528	745,516	1,968,164	725,636
1780	2,550,352	1,593,970	956,382	2,524,848	930,878
1781	2,176,932	1,360,582	816,350	2,155,162	794,581
1782	2,169,454	1,355,809	813,545	2,147,759	791,850
1783	1,660,114	1,037,571	622,543	1,643,513	605,942
1784	2,033,867	1,271,167	762,700	1,993,190	722,023
1785	2,432,335	1,489,805	942,530	2,383,688	893,883
1786	1,713,814	1,049,711	664,103	1,679,538	629,827
1787	1,099,950	673,719	426,231	1,066,951	393,232
1788	2,624,742	1,607,654	1,017,088	2,430,511	822,857
1789	1,543,695	945,513	598,182	1,416,340	470,827
1790	2,322,386	1,422,461	899,925	2,020,476	598,015
1791	1,394,366	854,049	540,317	1,134,038	279,989
1792	1,508,825	924,155	584,670	1,196,951	272,796
1793	1,341,480	821,656	519,824	992,695	171,039
1794	1,259,070	771,180	487,890	893,940	122,760
1795	1,046,468	739,068	307,400	716,831	−22,237
1796	352,613	249,033	103,580	248,592	−441
1797	2,071,133	1,462,738	608,395	1,643,030	180,292
1798	1,538,737	1,086,733	452,004	1,123,278	36,545
1799	1,550,768	1,095,230	455,538	1,046,768	−48,462
1800	1,865,572	1,603,226	262,346	1,218,778	−384,448

Table 8.21   Budget Incomes, 1763–96 (in 1,000 Rubles)

| | Budget Income Total | | |
Year	Gross Revenue	Costs and Collection Expenditures	Net Revenue
1763	18,555	4,020	14,535
1764	21,895	4,150	17,745
1765	23,050	4,020	19,030
1766	23,523	3,377	20,146
1767	25,245	4,005	21,240
1768	25,405	4,545	20,860
1769	24,717	4,460	20,257
1770	29,719	5,010	24,709
1771	30,804	4,409	26,395
1772	29,974	4,244	25,730
1773	30,693	5,040	25,653
1774	31,152	5,500	25,652
1775	31,835	6,000	25,835
1776	32,089	5,900	26,189
1777	32,586	6,400	26,186
1778	36,120	8,000	28,120
1779	36,882	8,500	28,382
1780	36,442	9,000	27,442
1781	40,166	11,241	28,925
1782	40,880	9,261	31,619
1783	42,824	11,241	31,583
1784	51,114	10,590	40,524
1785	49,725	9,643	40,082
1786	51,380	10,119	41,261
1787	54,922	10,206	44,716
1788	54,056	10,390	43,666
1789	55,278	10,950	44,328
1790	58,935	13,231	45,704
1791	59,406	15,000	44,406
1792	58,738	15,613	43,125
1793	57,937	16,607	41,330
1794	59,293	16,595	42,698
1795	71,961	16,846	55,115
1796	73,112	17,706	55,406

Table 8.22   Budget Incomes, 1763–96 (in 1,000 Rubles)

| | | Chancellery Tax | | |
Year	Poll Taxes	Gross Revenue	Collection and Other Expenditures	Net Revenue
1763	5,667	900	300	600
1764	9,119	1,005	330	675
1765	9,376	1,490	500	990
1766	9,580	1,600	500	1,100
1767	9,770	1,950	650	1,300
1768	9,712	2,218	750	1,468
1769	9,375	1,920	650	1,270
1770	12,163	2,050	700	1,350
1771	12,238	3,268	132	3,136
1772	12,219	3,226	76	3,150
1773	12,180	3,614	616	2,998
1774	12,220	3,539		
1775	12,275	3,290		
1776	12,325	3,124	222	2,902
1777	12,375	3,229	518	2,711
1778	12,625	2,976		
1779	12,885	3,128		
1780	13,045	4,078		
1781	13,419	4,384	1,252	3,132
1782	13,525	4,544	457	4,087
1783	13,310	6,017	600	5,417
1784	21,691	5,375	626	4,749
1785	20,184	4,200	1,400	2,800
1786	20,261	4,500	1,500	3,000
1787	22,366	5,100	1,700	3,400
1788	22,767	5,550	1,800	3,750
1789	22,789	6,000	2,000	4,000
1790	22,702	6,750	2,200	4,550
1791	22,749	6,676	2,200	4,476
1792	22,745	6,700	2,200	4,500
1793	23,164	6,350	2,100	4,250
1794	23,392	7,300	2,400	4,900
1795	26,021	8,500	2,800	5,700
1796	24,721	13,830	4,470	9,360

about the extent to which the government was capable of collecting taxes and controlling its own expenditures. The budget incomes for the Catherinian period are presented in tables 8.7 and 8.21–26.

Early budget policies may be characterized as "pay as you go" attempts to meet permanent commitments and somehow to pay for extraordinary expenditures. This left the government in no position to build up a "war chest." Moreover, there was no institutional framework for public borrowing inside of Russia. Consequently extraordinary war expenditures were the most fiscally destabilizing factor for budgetary policy.

There was an institutionalized factor which limited the revenue side of the state budget: the poll taxes could be increased primarily as a result of a new census of taxpayers, and only five were conducted during the century. This explains much of the stepwise nature of government revenue increases, most of which were directly related in time to the censuses.

Another constraint upon the government's ability to raise revenues in the short run was created by the limited purchasing power of the bulk of the taxpayers, the serfs. The years when the serfs were relatively prosperous, a function often of the size of the harvest and of agricultural prices, did not necessarily coincide with the years of the government's increase in demand for revenue.

All the available evidence points to the leading role of government expenditures in budget formation. They were followed, with a time lag, by government revenues.

The rate of increase of government budget expenditures varied. The highest increases were in 1770, 31.3 percent; 1764, 25.5 percent; and 1783, 17.8 percent. The highest rates of growth for government revenues were 21.4 percent in 1795, 20.2 percent in 1770, and 20.0 percent in 1786.

In the last third of the century, aside from war expenditures, government-induced inflation became a major propellant of budget expenditures in current

Table 8.23   Budget Incomes, 1763–96 (in 1,000 Rubles)

| | Alcohol Tax | | |
Year	Gross Revenue	Production, Distribution, and Collection Costs	Net Revenue
1763	5,308	932	4,376
1764	4,980	964	4,016
1765	5,199	1,001	4,198
1766	5,340	1,001	4,339
1767	6,291	1,210	5,081
1768	6,497	1,416	5,081
1769	6,497	1,416	5,081
1770	7,911	1,988	5,923
1771	7,893	1,252	6,641
1772	7,893	1,252	6,641
1773	7,893	1,252	6,641
1774	8,093	1,452	6,641
1775	8,670	1,750	6,920
1776	8,820	1,900	6,920
1777	9,082	2,100	6,982
1778	12,219	2,800	9,419
1779	12,319	2,900	9,419
1780	12,419	3,000	9,419
1781	12,519	3,100	9,419
1782	12,635	3,200	9,435
1783	12,867	3,350	9,517
1784	12,798	3,570	9,228
1785	12,901	3,850	9,051
1786	13,278	4,050	9,228
1787	13,963	4,350	9,613
1788	14,119	4,700	9,419
1789	14,713	5,100	9,613
1790	15,019	5,600	9,419
1791	14,808	6,200	8,608
1792	15,541	6,943	8,598
1793	15,646	6,933	8,713
1794	16,018	6,908	9,110
1795	24,376	6,611	17,765
1796	22,000	7,000	15,000

Table 8.24   Budget Incomes, 1763–96 (in 1,000 Rubles)

| | Salt Tax | | |
Year	Gross Revenue	Production, Distribution, and Collection Costs	Net Revenue
1763	2,608	1,098	1,510
1764	2,820	1,244	1,576
1765	2,860	1,255	1,605
1766	3,028	1,303	1,725
1767	2,953	1,255	1,698
1768	2,955	1,255	1,700
1769	2,519	1,080	1,439
1770	3,295	1,395	1,900
1771	3,630	1,725	1,905
1772	3,284	1,714	1,570
1773	3,456	1,870	1,586
1774	3,400		
1775	3,400		
1776	3,400	2,405	995
1777	3,400	2,285	1,115
1778	3,500		
1779	3,600		
1780	3,700		
1781	3,800	2,685	1,115
1782	3,900	2,904	996
1783	4,000	2,886	1,114
1784	4,100	2,829	1,271
1785	4,200	2,933	1,267
1786	4,300	3,029	1,271
1787	4,400	3,133	1,267
1788	4,500	3,490	1,010
1789	4,451	3,430	1,021
1790	4,798	4,040	758
1791	5,000		
1792	5,470		
1793	5,774		
1794	5,287		
1795	5,435		
1796	5,236		

prices. The growth of expenditures from 1762 to 1791 (when they reached their highest level in current prices) was 414 percent, from 16,500,000 rubles to 84,870,000 rubles. In 1762 prices, the growth was from 16,500,000 to 55,600,000 rubles, or 237 percent. The non-military budget expenditures are presented in table 8.27. (Military budget expenditures are in table 8.16.) Thus price increases motivated a major part of the growth in government expenditures. The 1762 budget was balanced, but the 1791 one had a deficit of 25,460,000 rubles (see table 8.28), which was covered by the printing of paper money that tended to increase inflationary pressures further.

While budgetary expenditures were rising, the central government authorities were faced with the need to reallocate revenue among alternative uses. The reallocations were necessitated by the growth of the provincial bureaucracy and the practice of retaining parts of revenue collections for local use. The administrative reforms reinstituting budgetary pay-

ments for public officials and regulating the operations of local authorities have been considered beneficial for the governance of Russia, but they did strengthen the role of the bureaucracy. They also made budgetary allocations less flexible for policymakers by reducing the residual over which they exercised control.

A similar tendency became apparent on the revenue side of the budget. As noted above, there was a slow but steady increase of collection expenditures and in the government's costs of operating its monopolies. Part of the reason for this trend can be found in the growth of the bureaucracy and in the secular inflationary tendencies. The latter affected the costs of operating the monopolies, with a lag in the price increases of the monopoly commodities. The result of the observed tendency was a decline in the share of the net budget revenue relative to the gross revenue, as noted above in table 8.17.

A final issue in the features of Russian budgetary

Table 8.25 Budget Incomes, 1763–96 (in 1,000 Rubles)

	Customs Duties		
Year	Gross	Collection and Other Costs	Net Receipts
1763	3,072	1,075	1,997
1764	2,969	1,012	1,957
1765	3,125	672	2,453
1766	2,875	73	2,802
1767	3,080	290	2,790
1768	2,823	525	2,298
1769	3,206	714	2,492
1770	3,190	330	2,860
1771	3,268	550	2,718
1772	3,226		
1773	3,614		
1774	3,539		
1775	3,290		
1776	3,214	650	2,564
1777	3,229	600	2,629
1778	2,977		
1779	3,128		
1780	4,078		
1781	4,384	600	3,784
1782	4,536	900	3,636
1783	4,963	1,000	3,963
1784	5,375	1,000	4,375
1785	5,285	460	4,825
1786	4,832	540	4,292
1787	5,469	23	5,446
1788	5,188	600	4,588
1789	5,488	620	4,868
1790	6,958	391	6,567
1791	6,525	800	5,725
1792	7,229		
1793	5,017		
1794	5,294		
1795	5,424		
1796	6,471		
1797	6,091		

Table 8.26 Budget Incomes, 1763–96 (in 1,000 Rubles)

	Mining Revenue		
Year	Gross Revenue	Production, Distribution, and Collection Costs	Net Revenue
1763			1,000
1764			1,000
1765			1,000
1766			1,000
1767			1,200
1768			1,200
1769			1,200
1770			1,200
1771	2,175	750	1,425
1772	1,750	600	1,150
1773	1,850	600	1,250
1774	2,100	700	1,400
1775	2,300		
1776	2,500		
1777	2,700		
1778	3,000		
1779	3,150		
1780	3,400		
1781	3,650	2,460	1,190
1782	3,900	2,215	1,685
1783	4,050	2,170	1,880
1784	4,050	1,960	2,090
1785	2,955	1,000	1,955
1786	3,025	1,000	2,025
1787	3,025	1,000	2,025
1788	2,058	800	1,258
1789	2,071	800	1,271
1790	2,708	1,000	1,708
1791	2,161	800	1,361
1792	1,854	800	1,054
1793	1,986	800	1,186
1794	2,002	1,000	1,002
1795	2,220	1,000	1,220
1796	2,325	1,000	1,325

policies involves the use of direct versus indirect taxation. For most of the period a higher share of the total government budget revenue came from direct taxes than from indirect taxes. The share of direct taxes varied from about 52 percent to over 64 percent, but one cannot assume that the government deliberately opted for more stable sources of revenue represented by direct taxation over the more volatile, fluctuating revenues provided by indirect taxes. Declarative policy statements on the issue may still be buried in the archives, and the budgetary data themselves do not provide an unequivocal answer. For most years the excess of direct over indirect tax revenues were a result of rent payments by state peasants rather than of tax payments proper, as discussed above. In addition, the fragmentary data for the 1750s clearly reflect the policy-makers' (such as Shuvalov's) preference for indirect taxes at times of rising government expenditures.

It appears as though the Russian policy-makers of the eighteenth century were not committed to any particular "fiscal philosophy." They did not necessarily tie their hopes to a steady rise of the taxpayers' incomes, a dream that would have been often contradicted by the reality. On the other hand, they were aware of the institutional, and perhaps political, consequences of relying exclusively on a system of direct taxation. In a situation in which the landowners were exempt from taxation and a land-use tax or income tax was impossible to administer, policymakers relied on a system combining direct and indirect taxes in nearly equal portions. As a second-best solution, it helped the government to muddle through the changes in the fortunes of its taxpayers.

The Tax Burden

The tax burden on the Russian population, on the taxpaying estates in particular, is a subject shrouded in mystery. This state of affairs can be explained in

Table 8.27   Nonmilitary Budget Expenditures, 1762–96 (in 1,000 Rubles)

Year	Administration[a]	Church	Schools Charitable Institutions
1762	—	—	—
1763	—	—	—
1764	5,055	374	—
1765	5,020	—	—
1766	7,000	—	—
1767	5,657	—	—
1768	4,992	—	—
1769	5,019	—	—
1770	7,814	—	—
1771	9,244	—	—
1772	12,494	—	—
1773	11,314	—	—
1774–80	—	—	—
1781	18,480	470	540
1782	17,680	540	540
1783	19,980	620	560
1784	20,580	680	580
1785	20,690	760	620
1786	21,200	760	630
1787	21,950	820	690
1788	20,720	690	690
1789	21,940	690	700
1790	24,000	710	910
1791	25,920	710	920
1792	27,040	710	920
1793	28,610	740	960
1794	28,130	780	1,000
1795	28,780	810	1,110
1796	30,230	820	1,340

part by the absence of systematic budget data for six decades of the century, and in part by the difficulties of utilizing the available data.

The general pattern of the tax burden can be reconstructed. I adjusted the budget income data by deducting the government's costs of production and distribution of alcohol and salt, the two major commodities on which state monopolies realized substantial revenues. My next working assumption was that the ratio of taxpayers to the total population of Russia was more or less stable, as shown in V. M. Kabuzan's calculations presented in table 8.29. Therefore the tax burden can be estimated by using a reasonably good set of population data to calculate the per capita tax burden.

The per capita estimates of the total money taxes were distributed by the major known components, such as the poll tax and chancellery taxes, and some of the indirect taxes, particularly the alcohol and salt taxes and the customs revenues, for which continuous series could be utilized. The results are presented in table 8.30.

Any long-term series of data in current prices or monetary units requires an adjustment for changes in the value of the unit. An index of the value of the

ruble in terms of silver was used to deflate the series, the results of which are presented in table 8.31. The results may not be highly accurate, but they tend to bear out some of the conclusions and interpretations provided in the earlier discussion of the tax components.

The emerging pattern can be summarized as follows:

1. The Petrine level of taxation was relatively high, and the introduction of the poll tax increased the money component of the tax.

2. A significant decrease in the level of taxation occurred during the reigns of Peter's successors, Anna and Elizabeth.

3. The increases in the level of taxation occurred at times of war, either in the form of indirect taxation (during the Seven Years' War and the Russo-Turkish wars during the reign of Catherine II) or through direct taxation.

4. The increased and sustained level of taxation preceding the Pugachëv uprising was perhaps a contributing factor explaining the uprising.

5. During the 1780s and 1790s there was a tendency to increase the tax burden, a tendency which ultimately was thwarted by the race between the tax

Table 8.27, cont. Nonmilitary Budget Expenditures, 1762–96 (in 1,000 Rubles)

Year	Roads, Buildings, Post Office	Colonization and Other Expenses	Total	Empress's Court	Interest on Loans	Total Expenditures
1762	—	—	4,228	1,753	—	16,500
1763	—	—	6,463	1,648	—	17,235
1764	—	—	9,205	2,420	—	21,580
1765	—	—	9,040	2,400	—	22,620
1766	—	—	10,377	2,600	—	24,090
1767	—	—	9,662	2,550	—	23,300
1768	—	—	9,537	2,790	—	24,950
1769	—	—	9,479	3,000	125	26,680
1770	—	—	12,824	3,250	140	35,020
1771	—	—	13,653	3,100	180	38,610
1772	—	—	16,738	2,960	—	39,290
1773	—	—	16,354	2,960	300	38,910
1774–80	—	—	n.a.	n.a.	n.a.	n.a.
1781	1,950	360	21,800	4,650	660	40,960
1782	2,190	390	21,340	4,716	790	40,910
1783	2,350	420	23,930	5,930	790	48,190
1784	2,600	440	24,880	5,870	790	49,790
1785	2,670	440	25,180	6,770	3,980	56,460
1786	2,790	470	25,850	6,630	2,440	62,670
1787	2,680	470	26,610	5,950	3,480	66,740
1788	3,110	470	25,680	7,260	4,140	76,120
1789	3,200	440	26,970	7,210	3,914	79,190
1790	3,400	440	29,460	6,400	3,750	82,700
1791	3,630	430	31,610	6,390	1,810	84,870
1792	3,680	430	32,780	6,400	3,770	72,250
1793	3,590	420	34,320	6,210	7,160	76,420
1794	4,110	430	34,450	6,800	3,790	72,310
1795	4,020	440	35,160	10,640	4,150	79,150
1796	4,700	440	37,530	8,760	4,190	78,160

aInclusive of costs of tax collection, and of production and distribution of state-monopoly products.

collector and the paper-money printer. Inflationary pressures tended to restore the earlier levels of taxation in real terms.

6. If one uses the existing classification of money taxes, including the rent payments of the government-owned serfs, the increase of the tax burden on the taxpaying population toward the end of the eighteenth century, in comparison with the first years of the century, was on the order of a maximum of 80 percent. Adjusting for the rent payments, the burden increase would be reduced to less than 50 percent.

7. The tax burden, calculated as a share of the per capita income of the taxpayers, did not exceed 12 to 15 percent of their income.

This is not to suggest that the fiscal demands of the government were easy for the taxpayers to bear. For the majority of the population, the fiscal demands came on top of claims to their labor, land, and other resources. Given the relatively low level of commercial agriculture and the slim margin above subsistence, the tax burden was very great indeed. However, the eighteenth-century Russian fiscal policies have to be absolved of the blame inherent in the charge that the tax burden was the prime mover

keeping the taxpayers at the subsistence level or even pushing them below that level.

The Army Draft as a Tax

The Council considered the volume of the various taxes which peasants pay in the Russian Empire. All are subject to the poll tax of 70 kopeks per soul. The state peasants, except for those in some border *gubernii*, have been subjected to a 3.00 ruble money rent [*obrok*]. The serfs owned by private land owners [*pomeshchiki*] pay the same, or even somewhat higher rent to their owners. Every year one recruit per five hundred souls is mobilized. In 1787, 1788, and in the present year, 1789, five recruits have been mobilized per five hundred souls. Based upon the experience of the most recent years, it would appear that every male peasant, not excluding the aged or youngsters, pays from 8.00 to 10.00 rubles.[17]

The above calculation, which attaches a money value to the military recruits, reflects an interesting view of the obligatory military service as either a substitute for a mercenary force or a burden on the

Table 8.28   State Budget of Russia, 1762–96 (in 1,000 Rubles)

Year	Gross Revenue	Total	Total Expenditures	Total	Budget Deficit (−) or Surplus (+) Yearly	Total	Cumulative
1762	n.a.		16,500				
1763	18,555		17,235		+1,320		
1764	21,895		21,580		+315		+1,635
1765	23,050		22,620		+430		+2,065
1766	23,523		24,090		−567		+1,498
1767	25,245		23,300		+1,945		+3,443
1768	25,405		24,950		+455		+3,898
1769	24,717		26,680		−1,963		+1,935
1770	29,719		35,020		−5,301		−3,366
1771	30,804		38,610		−7,806		−11,172
1772	29,974		39,290		−9,316		−20,488
1773	30,693		38,910		−8,217		−28,705
1774	31,152						
1775	31,835						
1776	32,089						
1777	36,586	241,106		215,000		+26,106	
1778	36,120						
1779	36,882						
1780	36,442						−2,599
1781	40,166		40,960		−794		−3,393
1782	40,880		40,910		−30		−3,423
1783	42,824		48,190		−5,366		−8,789
1784	51,114		49,790		+1,324		−7,465
1785	49,725		56,460		−6,735		−14,200
1786	51,380		62,670		−11,290		−25,490
1787	54,922		66,740		−11,818		−37,308
1788	54,056		76,120		−22,064		−59,372
1789	55,278		79,190		−23,912		−83,284
1790	58,935		82,700		−23,765		−107,049
1791	59,406		84,870		−25,464		−132,513
1792	58,738		72,250		−13,513		−146,026
1793	57,937		76,420		−18,483		−164,509
1794	59,293		72,310		−13,017		−177,526
1795	71,961		79,150		−7,189		−184,715
1796	73,112		78,160		−5,048		−189,763

Table 8.29   Taxable and Nontaxable Male Population of Russia

Year	Taxable	Nontaxable	Total Population	% Taxable Population
1719	7,126,135	444,241	7,570,376	94.13
1744	8,481,213	451,938	8,933,151	94.94
1762[a]	10,906,144	(293,851)	11,199,995	97.37
1782	13,013,980	672,711	13,686,691	95.08
1795	17,182,775	1,075,273	18,258,048	94.11

Source: Kabuzan, *Izmeneniia*.

[a]The decline of the nontaxable population between 1744 and 1762 was due to a change in procedures; there was not a real decline in that population.

taxpayers. In a society where human beings were subject to purchase and sale, and were the object of private or state property, such a view was at least understandable and consistent with the basic concepts of state and society. A 1789 source suggested that a money substitute of 500 rubles per recruit from merchants would be a reasonable tax, which seems to have assumed that the market price per recruit was in the vicinity of that sum.[18] Since recruits could be bought by the subjects of the draft and delivered in their stead, and since expenditures had to be incurred in the equipment and delivery of draftees even when they were chosen from among the taxpayers, a calculation of the draft as a form of taxation was justified conceptually.

It is possible to estimate some of this burden in money terms to the extent that the government was withdrawing resources from society and imposing a

Table 8.30   Per Capita Money Taxes (in Rubles)

Year	Total	Direct Taxes[a]	Indirect Taxes[b]	Including Alcohol	Including Salt	Including Customs	Index 1725=100
1724	1.061	.589	.347	.121	.82	.144	84.9
1725	1.25						100.0
1734	1.10						88.0
1749	1.02	.561	.325	.132	.083	.110	81.6
1751	1.16	.549	.482	.232	.124	.126	92.8
1758	1.42	.515	.708	.259	.206	.243	113.6
1765	1.832	.957	.795	.370	.149	.275	146.6
1769	1.879	.955	.823	.430	.122	.271	150.3
1770	2.205	1.19	.922	.496	.159	.267	176.4
1771	2.290	1.285	.979	.550	.158	.271	183.2
1772	2.21	1.271	.941	.547	.129	.265	176.8
1773	2.131	1.221	.915	.513	.123	.279	170.5
1777	2.383	1.155	.838	.517	.082	.239	190.6
1782	2.45	1.272	1.054	.664	.070	.319	196.0
1783	2.56	1.352	1.091	.666	.078	.347	204.8
1785	2.967	1.684	1.078	.625	.088	.365	237.4
1787	3.236	1.874	1.115	.656	.086	.373	258.9
1789	3.149	1.939	1.086	.648	.069	.370	251.9
1792	3.06	1.974	1.042	.568	−.004	.478	244.8
1795	3.14	1.845	1.289	.936	.063	.290	251.2

[a]The category of direct taxes includes (apart from the poll tax) the chancellery taxes.
[b]The indirect taxes include only the alcohol, salt taxes and the custom revenues. A full measure of indirect taxes would include the residual of total minus the direct taxes.

Table 8.31   Per Capita Taxes, Deflated by Price Index

Year	Total	Direct Taxes	Indirect Taxes	Index 1725=100
1724	1.06	.589	.347	84.8
1725	1.25			100.0
1734	1.03			82.4
1749	.88	.484	.280	70.4
1751	1.03	.486	.427	82.4
1758	1.21	.444	.605	96.8
1765	1.621	.847	.704	129.6
1769	1.553	.789	.680	124.2
1770	1.736	.937	.726	138.9
1771	1.789	1.004	.765	143.1
1772	1.78	1.025	.759	142.4
1773	1.678	.961	.720	134.2
1777	1.988	.964	.699	159.0
1782	1.81	.944	.782	144.8
1783	1.901	1.004	.810	152.1
1785	2.231	1.266	.811	178.5
1787	2.338	1.354	.806	187.0
1789	1.845	1.136	.636	147.6
1792	1.60	1.031	.544	128.0
1795	1.73	1.018	.711	138.4

financial burden on some categories of taxpayers in the form of a draft into the armed forces.

The easiest procedure is to estimate for each period the size of the draft in fractions of a man per taxpayer. The market value of young male serfs could be used as an approximation of the value of a draftee. The total value of the draftees apportioned among the taxpayers would provide an estimate of the magnitude of the tax burden of the military draft.

There is more to this approach than a procedure of estimating a tax by using the market value of human beings (serfs). To be consistent, one also should calculate the burden of the military draft upon the Russian nobility, at least until the year 1762, when military service became optional rather than obligatory. In this case the estimating process is more complex. In the absence of a market price for nobles, one should calculate the income foregone as a result of the service minus payments received for military service. Although a redistribution of income within

Table 8.32   Estimated Cost of the Military Draft of Serfs by Decade

Years	Military Draft	Price per Draftee (in Rubles)	Total Costs
1730–39	284,211	35	9,947,385
1740–49	199,017	45	8,955,765
1750–59	232,234	55	12,772,870
1760–69	119,703	100	11,970,300
1770–79	298,288	175	52,200,400
1768–89	449,785	320	143,931,200
1790–99	388,002	400	155,200,800

Source: Data on the military draft from Beskrovnyi, *Russkaia armiia*, pp. 23–29, 33–38, 294–99.

the nobility may have occurred as a result of the military service obligation, as well as a redistribution of income over the life-cycle of the nobles, except for periods of protracted wars, some might question the existence of a "burden" on the nobility as a collective.

The army draft of serfs initially was perceived by the serf-owning nobility as a tax on the nobility and its property. It became obvious from the very beginning, however, that the burden of the draft was shifted from the serf-owners to the serfs themselves. The village commune was burdened with the task of assigning the draftee, and its members were taxed either to buy an army recruit substitute or for the recruit's clothing, food, transportation, and the costs of guarding his delivery to the army. In cases where a number of smaller serf estates were responsible in common for the delivery of a recruit, the costs were shared by the owners but borne by their serfs.

Although suggesting that inclusion of the military draft in the burden of the taxpaying social groups does not violate any conceptual principles of dealing with a serf-based economy and polity, the following crude calculations must be treated as an attempt to broaden the concept of taxation and to estimate the additional burden on the income of the taxpaying population.

The following exercise assumes for the period 1730–99 a market price per draftee based either on directly available evidence or on the ratio of known market prices for recruits to the prevailing average price per census-male-serf. In table 8.32 the known number of army draftees per decade was multiplied by the assumed price per draftee for each decade to arrive at the estimated total cost of the military draft of serfs by decade.

If we divide the assumed value of the draftees by the number of taxpayers listed in the census, a per taxpayer estimate of the average yearly cost of the military draft is arrived at in table 8.33.

In nominal terms the burden of the draft increased dramatically, particularly during the second half of the century. In real terms, however, the rise was much less spectacular. Assuming that the taxpayers, primarily agricultural serfs, had to give up a quantity

Table 8.33   Tax of the Military Draft per Male Taxpayer per Year (in Kopeks)

Decades	Tax per Year
1730s	16.7
1740s	11.1
1750s	15.8
1760s	12.5
1770s	51.0
1780s	111.0
1790–95	115.0
1796–99	96.0

Table 8.34   The Military Draft Tax in Units of Rye (Poods per Male Taxpayer)

Decades	Quantity
1730s	2.1
1740s	1.3
1750s	1.6
1760s	.8
1770s	2.4
1780s	3.1
1790–95	2.6
1796–99	1.9

of their staple product to acquire cash, I have used as a proxy for a price index the prices of rye from the Strumilin series.[19] Table 8.34 presents the per capita tax burden of the military draft on male taxpayers in units of rye.

For purposes of historical accuracy and relevance, one must glance at the distribution of the burden by decade. The draft was related to the Russian Empire's wars, and years of major military effort require closer scrutiny. The results are quite instructive when they are compared with the average data per decade. For example, the actual yearly burden during the years 1736–39 turns out to be 24.1 kopeks per taxpayer instead of the 16.1 kopek per decade average. The burden of the 1750s was concentrated in the years 1755–59, and the annual tax was 31.6 kopeks, rather than the decade average of 15.8 kopeks. The relatively light burden calculated for the 1760s of 12.5 kopeks per taxpayer was 42.7 kopeks per year for 1767–69. If one adds that this burden was immediately followed by a tax for the years 1770–73 of 109 kopeks for each of the four years, is it surprising that the serfs were ready for the Pugachëv rebellion of 1774? During the years 1787–89 the military draft imposed an average burden of 228 kopeks per year on each taxpayer.

The real hardship caused by the costs of the military draft varied because of the facts that the Russian serf population had at its disposal no substantial cash reserves, that the taxes had to be paid primarily from current incomes, and that the taxpayers lived in a world of famines and fluctuating grain prices. Those costs constituted, however, an important aspect of the existing reality. Although the above exercise is largely illustrative, it is by no means hypothetical.

9
THE POLITICAL ORDER

The Civil Administration

The Russian autocracy of the eighteenth century relied upon a specialized group of civil servants to communicate its decisions to the population, to execute and to enforce the policies enunciated by the supreme decision-makers. The administrative apparatus represented to some extent a transformed version of the old, inherited administrative apparatus which was adjusted to the demands of an expanded territory and a further centralization of governmental authority.

A number of tendencies reflecting change can be observed. Earlier in the century there was a tendency toward militarization of the apparatus as manifested in the use of the military in extraordinary administrative tasks and interference by special, "trusted" officials with special assignments to control the working of the administration at various levels. This interference from above, the disregard of the existing hierarchical system, was a clear legacy of the Petrine period, when the central administration attempted to become informed about and to introduce changes in various areas of fiscal, judicial, and administrative policies. On the other hand, there was a tendency which perhaps began in the 1750s toward a bureaucratization of the administrative apparatus and a routinization of its functions.

The latter tendency was related to the professionalization of the civil administrators and the solidification of a few strata of administrators and administrative personnel, or people who viewed their careers and employment as a distinct pattern of service. This was the formation of strata of *chinovniki*, people holding a distinct rank in the civil bureaucracy who expected advancement in salary and status in recognition of their merit and contribution to the state. Some of the *chinovnik* officeholders hoped to obtain opportunities to promote their heirs in the same area of service. The increasing consciousness by the civilian officeholders of their social role, the systematization of the hierarchical service structure, the promotion from one level to another, as well as the routinization of the tasks of particular offices and officeholders, all contributed to what may be termed bureaucratization.

This type of bureaucratization was an ongoing process during the eighteenth century while recruitment into the civil bureaucracy permitted the entrance of diverse social elements, before it was rigidly divided into a few distinct subgroups. During the eighteenth century there were no fixed formal educational prerequisites or specific social and income requirements for recruitment into the bureaucracy, and thus the process was relatively dynamic. Detecting and describing the dynamics of the civil administration is difficult because of the dearth of published documentary evidence and specialized studies. One must rely upon the pre-Revolutionary studies of A. D. Gradovskii, Iu. V. Got'e, and M. V. Klochkov for much of the data. Among more recent studies, the work of Marc Raeff on the role of the noble component, and especially the work of the late Soviet historian S. M. Troitskii, are valuable contributions to knowledge of this topic.

The difficulty of studying the dynamics of Russian government is compounded by the fact that exact data are lacking on the size of the central and local administration of the Muscovite state at the end of the seventeenth century. N. F. Demidova estimated the number of clerical employees (*podiachie*) working in the central institutions of the Muscovite state in 1686–87 at 1,935, a figure that does not include those working in the Patriarchal chancelleries, the Apothecary Chancellery, and various chancelleries producing weapons and various luxury items.[1] Regrettably, data are lacking on the precise number of officials directing the chancelleries in which the approximately two thousand clerical employees worked. Their number could be estimated at anywhere from 650 to 900 persons. They provided service in exchange for land allotments, salaries paid in money and in kind, or both.

Table 9.1   Composition of the Civil Administration Employment for the 1720s.

Category and Location	Office Appointees	Fiskaly	Total Appointees	Chancellery Employees	Total	Special Service	Total
Central institutions—St. Petersburg	155	4	159	1,225	1,384	381	1,765
Central institutions—Moscow	46	7	53	367	420	93	513
Total—central institutions	201	11	212	1,592	1,804	474	2,278
local institutions	988	222	1,210	2,093	3,303	1,843	5,146
Total	1,189	233	1,422	3,685	5,107	2,317	7,424

Source: Kirilov, *Sostoianie.*

The eighteenth century witnessed a reform of the central governmental apparatus. It was reorganized and streamlined in conformity with Peter's introduction of the Table of Ranks. The obligatory service of the nobility, which at the end of the seventeenth century had occasionally been honored in the breach, was made compulsory. Money salaries for the civilian administration by and large were substituted for the various forms of remuneration which had existed earlier.

The reorganized civilian administration consisted of three functional groups. One included appointed officials in both the central and local provincial institutions. The second group consisted of the "chancellery" employees, mostly clerical, called in Russian *prikaznye.* The third group included couriers and supporting military and service personnel, who performed various functions for the administrative offices. During the Petrine period and for a short while after Peter's death there was yet a fourth group of officials designated to control and report on the activities of the other officeholders and administrative personnel, who were called *fiskaly* because they presumably represented the fiscal interests of the state. Table 9.1 presents estimates of the size of the civilian administration in the last years of Peter's reign and the early years of his heirs' reigns.

Unfortunately, data on the composition of the civil administration in later periods cannot be organized in the same categories as those in table 9.1 for the 1720s. This makes comparisons very difficult. In a sense the 1720s data (e.g., the 2,278 central institutional employees) are difficult to compare with the estimate of the 1680s (e.g., the 2,650–2,900 employees who worked in the Moscow chancelleries) because the definitions may have changed. Another, presumably independent, source estimated that in 1726 the provincial chancellery employees totaled 123 secretaries and 2,905 lower clerical workers.[2] This differs only by about 1.7 percent from the figure 3,081 in table 9.1

(the total provincial office and chancellery employees minus the *fiskaly*), but is still the result of summing different categories of employees. Consequently one must treat the problems of the civil administration not as a continuum but as a subject that can be discussed for periods in which descriptive or quantitative data are available.

Legislative acts of the period following Peter's death make it clear that serious attempts were made by successive governments to reduce the size of the civilian administration and its drain on the state budget. The attempts were marked by a return to the pre-Petrine practice of having petitioners pay the lower officeholders and the clerical staff directly for the services they were performing. The historian Iu. V. Got'e showed that this system lowered state budget expenditures for local administrators to the sum of only 198,351 rubles.[3]

By the middle of the eighteenth century the time was ripe for a change, at least for a return to the Petrine principle that the civil bureaucracy should be paid from the budget.[4] A large body of documents on this change was the chief source for S. M. Troitskii's excellent study of the government apparatus in the period around 1755, in which he categorized the bureaucrats according to the hierarchical stratification established by the Table of Ranks. All the lower-level employees outside the Table of Ranks he put into a separate category.[5] Officials classified in the Table of Ranks were divided into three groups. One included the official ranks 1 to 5; the second, ranks 6 to 8; the third, ranks 9 through 14. This distribution thus distinguished between the highest officials of the central government administration and court officers (group 1) and officeholders of the central as well as the provincial administration who were lower in rank (group 2). The third group was far less homogeneous than the two "higher" groups, for it included officeholders as well as clerical personnel of both the central and provincial administration.

Table 9.2   Distribution of the Members of the Civilian Bureaucracy, 1755

	I	II	III	IV	Known Total
Central government institutions	73	180	648	No data	901
Local offices of central government	4	30	111	No data	145
Local administration	37	317	393	3,328	4,075
Total, government administration	114	527	1,152	3,328	5,121
Court	31	35	192	No data	258
Total, government and court	145	562	1,344	3,328	5,379

Source: Troitskii, *Absoliutizm*, p. 179.

Although the Troitskii classification is modeled upon a rigid hierarchical structure and uses data for only one point in time and thus is unable to convey the full extent of upward mobility either over the lifetime of the officeholders and clerks or from one social category into another, it is useful as a cross-section of the composition of civilian administration. It contributes to our knowledge about social stratification, educational background, and economic resources of at least the upper ranks of the administrative apparatus. The data for the three groups corresponding to the Table of Ranks which Troitskii assembled (see table 9.2) cover 2,051 state bureaucrats or court officeholders and, although not complete, represent the majority of those employed in this capacity and could, therefore, be considered as representative of those groups. Those employed in the fourth category, those outside the Table of Ranks, are insufficiently represented in the Troitskii data. They may not be representative, in spite of their number (3,328), primarily because they are all concentrated in the offices of provincial administration. The distribution of the data base of Troitskii's work is sufficient for analyzing the upper three categories.

Troitskii assumed, on the basis of a 1740 sample, that there were 3.5 chancellery employees (his category IV) for each officeholder in the first three categories. This estimate appears to be on the high side, and a proportion of 2.5 for the central government offices, their local provincial branches, and the palace court might be more accurate. This would yield a total central government and court apparatus (local administration is excluded) of 7,360 persons. This estimate for 1755 does not differ much from other data available for the later date of 1763. For 1763 an available estimate of employees in the civilian administration, which excludes the military and police detachments at the permanent disposal of the civilian administration as well as the employees of the Holy Synod, gives the number of 6,740.[6]

A major expansion of the government's total administrative apparatus occurred during the reign of Catherine II. The expansion was the result of a number of factors, of which the following were the most significant: (1) the reform of provincial and local administration which began in 1775; (2) the extension of the boundaries of the Russian Empire during the 1770s and 1790s; (3) the pressure by the nobility for additional sources of income, of which one was governmental salaries. According to one estimate, toward the end of Catherine II's reign, the total number of officials and chancellery personnel outside the central governmental institutions had grown to 23,460.[7] This growth of the administrative apparatus at the provincial and county level was not accompanied by a proportionate expansion of central governmental offices, which grew at a much slower pace. This tendency made the hierarchical pyramid of the civilian administration flatter than it had been previously and in turn had a number of social consequences.

The social composition of the civilian administrative officeholders and employees must be viewed in the context of two tendencies: a tendency on the part of the nobility to dominate the governmental administration, and the tendency by the government to bureaucratize the administration. The tendencies were not necessarily mutually exclusive or necessarily adverse to one another, but each proceeded separately along its own course and at its own speed. Although the Petrine period witnessed a considerable progress of both tendencies, the government's financial difficulties and the reaction of the nobility against the harshness of the Petrine service obligations retarded both processes. The fact that a large number of local administrators and their office personnel had their government salaries discontinued and had to "live off the land" or charge petitioners direct fees for their services clearly worked as a deterrent to both bureaucratization and a further influx of nobility into the ranks of the civilian administration. In view of those facts, the participation of the nobility at various levels of governmental service is of interest.

Troitskii's study provides data (presented in table 9.3) for an examination of the problem. Although nobles constituted only 21.6 percent of the total personnel in Troitskii's data, their participation in the first three categories, which corresponded to the Table of Ranks, was 49.8 percent.

The relatively high proportion of nobles in the highest two categories of officials is not surprising. It basically confirms the conventional view that in the

Table 9.3   Participation of Nobility at Various Levels of the Civilian Administration, 1755

Category	Total	Nobles	Non-Nobles	Among Non-Noble children of				For-eigners	Personal Nobles
				Government Officers	Razno-chintsy	Sol-diers	Clergy		
I	145	127	18	2	6	—	3	3	1
II	562	432	130	19	64	5	5	23	10
III	1,344	463	881	236	395	12	36	126	50
IV	3,328	138	3,190	2,354	86	275	234	4	21
Total	5,379	1,160	4,219	2,611	551	292	278	156	82

Source: Troitskii, *Absoliutizm*, p. 21.

Table 9.4   Serf Ownership by Members of the Administrative Apparatus

Category	Total	Without Serfs	Serf-Owners	No. of Male Serfs	Serfs per Owner
I	125	15	110	157,213	1,429.2
II	544	74	470	93,075	198.0
III	1,321	528	793	38,130	48.1
IV	3,328	2,709	619	7,011	11.3
Total	5,318	3,326	1,992	295,429	148.3

Source: Troitskii, *Absoliutizm*.

eighteenth century the Russian Empire and its government were dominated by noblemen or aristocrats. More surprising, perhaps, is the relatively high percentage of non-nobles within the third category. The relationship between nobles and non-nobles in the third category of officials, still included in the Table of Ranks, perhaps can be explained by two factors. Non-noble bureaucrats promoted from the ranks of the chancellery employees owed their promotion to performance, education, sponsorship and protection by highly-placed officials, and sometimes, especially in the provinces, by a lack of competition from the nobility who either were not sufficiently numerous to fill the positions in a given province or country or felt that the prestige offered by such posts was incommensurate with their deserts. On the other hand, members of the nobility who decided upon a service career often had a strong preference for the military, a preference which led, through service in the guard regiments stationed in the capital, to "interesting" experience for the young and promised more rapid advancement, more remunerative salaries, and more varied opportunities. Thus the penetration of the nobility into the civil administration, which almost unquestionably had been a preserve of slaves in the Middle Ages, was a slow process. The eighteenth century did witness the beginning of the formation of "dynasties" of noble civilian administrators, which suggests that successful parents perceived that there were advantages for their children to follow in their footsteps. The data also suggest that such patterns were more likely for nobles who possessed no serfs at all, or very few serfs, rather than for families well endowed with serf-holdings.

The relationship between the status of the nobility and serf ownership by nobles serving in the civilian administration is partially revealed by the data on the size of their serf-holdings. Such data also reflect some of the differences between the various strata of the nobility and the levels of those strata in the bureaucratic hierarchy. Although the data in table 9.4 do not distinguish between inherited serf-holdings and those acquired during a tenure of office, they nevertheless suggest that recruitment into and advancement within the bureaucracy was not a random process.

The number of serfs owned by each serf-owning bureaucrat suggests that, except for the relatively small number of serf-owners concentrated in the first category and perhaps mainly in the second category, serf-ownership alone could not constitute the major share of the officials' income. For the vast majority of the officeholders even within the Table of Ranks, the governmental service salary constituted a major portion of their income. To the extent that the salaries of officials in the first two categories were relatively high by comparison with the third category, the salary was important even for those who, on the basis of the number of serfs owned, could be considered independently wealthy. One may assume, except for the small number of individuals who, thanks to their great wealth, served primarily for reasons of status and power, that the rest served for the salaries or opportunities to earn additional income that service provided.

The general problem of official salaries during the eighteenth century is a complicated one. As mentioned earlier, during the reign of Peter the Great the old practice of assigning land and peasants, or payment in kind to supplement a small monetary allowance, for governmental civil service was discontinued. The practice of having the localities, whether districts or cities, "feed" the officials was also discontinued. Although supplementary allowances of grain were maintained for some officeholders and were continued by analogy with the "rations" of military officers, monetization of salaries became the rule. Peter also introduced for many levels of the administrative hierarchy a salary differential between St. Petersburg and Moscow, as well as between the capitals and the provincial cities. Presumably he had both incentives and a built-in cost-of-living differential in mind.

Peter vacillated on the subject of a military-civilian salary differential. He seems to have started with a notion of uniformity, but was forced by budgetary constraints to award the military a higher level of pay than a like-ranking civilian counterpart. The Petrine reforms raised the costs of the civilian bureaucracy within the government budget, which by the end of his reign reached a substantial sum.[8]

The immediate post-Petrine period witnessed a change in the mode of payments and maintenance of whole layers of the bureaucracy. There was a return to the pre-Petrine mode for large numbers of local officials and chancellery employees. They were required to obtain their livelihood from direct payments by clients, petitioners, and members of the general public. Prince Aleksandr Menshikov, the architect of this reversal, spoke in favor of this system with an efficiency argument: "The chancellery employees in the cities, according to my conviction, ought not to be paid. They ought to charge the previous fees for their services, which will be sufficient for their livelihood. Cases will be processed better and without delay when each works to earn fees."[9] A part of the burden of maintaining the civilian administration was shifted from the government budget to that part of the population which needed to deal with the government offices. Although unquestionably there was a redistributive effect, it is difficult to establish whether the new system, introduced as an economy measure, actually increased the real burden on the taxpayers. Although the official tax burden inherent in the budget rose less sharply, it is possible that the government increased the size of the civilian bureaucracy, because the increase was not reflected in direct budget expenditures.

Governmental decision-makers became dissatisfied with the state of provincial administration, and various projects for administrative reforms began to

circulate within the upper levels of the government during the 1750s. Particularly noteworthy were the projects of P. I. Shuvalov and Ia. P. Shakhovskoi.[10] Shakhovskoi envisaged the reinstatement of the Petrine system of centralized payment of local officials and estimated the rise in cost of local administration to the state budget would be from 198,351 rubles to 1,134,370 rubles, based on the existing number of local officials and employees and salary changes proposed for them.

In 1763 Catherine II approved a new list of offices and the size of the civilian administration and its salaries.[11] Although the different governmental offices had various proportions of officials and chancellery personnel and average salaries for different offices are not very meaningful, nevertheless some comparisons are instructive. For example, the average salary for the central governmental offices in St. Petersburg was about 328 rubles a year, while in Moscow it was about 253 rubles per year. The average salary for local administrative officials in 1763 was approximately 112 rubles.

There was not only an increase in the size of the civilian administration from Peter I to Catherine II, but the nominal level of salaries also increased. Although it is difficult to find exactly matching categories, the examples in table 9.5 illustrate the range of changes in the salary levels. Given the low price of grain during most of the Petrine period, the data in the table suggest an increase in salaries. However, the decline in the purchasing power of the ruble during this period reduces the size of the increase in real terms. Troitskii, using global figures for "costs of administration" that he estimated at 2,150,000 rubles in 1725 and 5,660,000 rubles in 1767, argued that this item rose as a share of the total government expenditures for the respective years only from 21.2 to 24.3 percent. By comparison with the expenditures on the imperial court, which rose from 4.4 percent under the austere Peter (450,000 rubles in 1725) to 10.9 percent of total expenditures under the splendor-loving Catherine (2,218,000 rubles in 1767), the increase in "administrative expenses" was rather "modest."[12]

The subsequent numerical growth of the civilian bureaucracy during Catherine's reign resulting from the local-government reform of 1775 and territorial acquisitions, as well as from some adjustments in the level of salaries due to inflation, led to an increase of expenditures. The statutory salaries of the provincial, district, and county administrations for the year 1785, including some expenditures for military commands and border guards, added up to 5,524,000 rubles plus 76,000 Albertustalers. The annexation of additional formerly Polish provinces and Kurland raised the statutory salary expenditures for provincial adminis-

Table 9.5   Comparison between Petrine (1715) and Catherinian (1763) Salaries

| Office or function, (rank) | Petrine salaries | | Rank | Catherinian salaries |
	Money (in Rubles)	Grain (in Chet')		Money (in Rubles)
Governor (V)	1,200	600	V	840–1,200
Vice-governor (VI)	600	300	VI	600–1,000
Landrichter	300	150	VII	360
Landrat	120	120	VIII	300
D'iak	120	60	IX	250
Pod'iachii, staryi	60	30	X	200
Pod'iachii, srednii	40	20	XI	150–250

Sources: PSZ 5, no. 2879 (January 27, 1715), and Arndt, *Verordnungen*, pp. 188–96.

tration to 6,473,000 rubles and 212,000 Albertustalers by 1796.[13]

This seemingly large increase in the salary expenditures for officials and chancellery personnel outside of the central governmental institutions is not tantamount to large increases of the salary levels if we accept some of the estimates of the numerical growth of the bureaucracy toward the end of Catherine's reign. The historian M. V. Klochkov estimated the size of this group in 1796 at 23,460 persons. If we divide Klochkov's salary estimate of 6,027,000 rubles by the estimated number of officials and clerical employees, the average salary would be about 256.9 rubles per person.[14] Two phenomena indicate that the salaries of some groups within the civilian administration were not sufficient to motivate a high level of performance. One was the clamor and demand for extra legal payments, gratuities, and gifts (or bribes) by officials and chancellery employees at all levels. The other was the accumulating backlog of cases awaiting processing or decision in all offices. Of course the backlog cannot be entirely attributed to a lack of motivation due to low remuneration: much of it could be blamed on the sloppy procedures and lack of control to which the bureaucrats succumbed. There was, however, no denial of the fact that by the end of Catherine's reign the civil administration was less efficient than it had been before.

It was against this background that the harsh disciplinarian and economy-minded Paul I, reacting against many of the policies and institutional arrangements of his hated mother, Catherine, tried to reduce the size of the bureaucracy, to force it to work harder. He ordered the hiring of temporary personnel to liquidate the large backlog of cases pending in the Senate and other central governmental institutions. He decreased the statutory number of officials on the rolls in provincial administration. The reduction involved primarily offices that were basically honorific but provided the provincial nobility with small additions to their incomes. That policy did not endear the tsar to those who viewed their participation in the civil administration primarily as a convenient aug-

mentation of their incomes rather than as a payment for real services. Paul did not have time to complete his intended reduction of the size of the local bureaucracy. He also imposed a tax on the nobility, who were forced to contribute to the maintenance of the local administrative apparatus. This measure was a departure from the principle which had prevailed during the eighteenth century that the nobility should be exempt from direct taxation. According to rough estimates, Paul's 1797 reforms of provincial administration would have reduced the central budget expenditures by a few million rubles, and he would have made the nobility contribute 1.7 million rubles in new taxes.[15]

Paul's attempts to reform the administration, especially those elements that might have affected the interests of the nobility, were short-lived. They underscored the need for reform, which in fact occurred during the reign of his heir Alexander I but is chronologically outside my period.

This short and perhaps inconclusive discussion of the officials' salaries and their background in terms of noble status and serf-holdings is insufficient to explain other features of the recruitment into and promotion within the government apparatus. For eighteenth-century Russia the officials' educational background is of some importance and considerable interest.

There are no comprehensive published data on the educational level of the Russian bureaucracy. The Troitskii data of 1755 provide some information for that relatively early date. Later in the century the share of officials with formal education was higher, if only for the reason that formal higher schooling became available only at that time. For example, Moscow University first opened its doors in 1755, the year of the Troitskii survey data. By 1755 there were three main institutional sources of formal education. One was the various military academies, such as the Corps of Cadets and Naval Academy. The second was the church academies. The third form of formal education was the schooling provided by the major central government departments for those among the

Table 9.6   Formal Education of the Civilian Officeholders, 1755

Service Category	Total Officeholders	Type of Education				% of Total Officeholders
		Civilian	Military	Church	Total	
I	145	19	18	2	39	26.9
II	562	21	71	1	93	16.6
III	1,344	146	95	23	264	19.6
Total	2,051	186	184	26	396	19.3

Source: Troitskii, *Absoliutizm*, pp. 276–77.

young men who were assigned to work and study on the job there. The third category did not provide broad education, but was a system of on-the-job training which, for example, for students assigned to the College of Foreign Affairs, consisted primarily of the study of foreign languages. In comparison with the education provided by the military and church academies, the third category might be labeled as civilian-administrative training.

Troitskii's data presented in table 9.6 on educational background are only for officials, not for the lower-level, extra-Table-of-Ranks chancellery personnel. The data suggest both the educational backwardness of the Russian ruling and administrative government elite and the limited impact of the Petrine reforms even a generation or two after their enactment. They also illustrate the impact of Peter's legacy, with its emphasis on military-technical training even among members of the civilian bureaucracy, many of whom transferred from the military or officer corps. However, the important feature of the data is that the percentage of children of officeholders who had attended schools was higher than the school attendance of the parents. Although there is no evidence that formal education became a prerequisite of administrative service or office, the growth of school attendance by the children of government officials suggests that more rapid promotion was expected by those who possessed formal education.

Troitskii's discussion of the 1755 data shows that prior to that date education was hardly the most powerful means of advancement within the civilian administration. The career patterns of 1,958 officeholders are quite diverse. Of this number, 719 or 36.7 percent began their service in the military, in the regular army (515) and in the guards regiments (204). Of those who started their career in the civilian branch of the government, the vast majority, or 609 out of 684, began at the lowest level of chancellery clerkships, as copyists; only 75 of the 684 started out at a higher level of the service pyramid. This might explain why, given the relatively long periods between promotions from one level to the next, it took the majority of officeholders such a long time to move up to the higher categories. The advanced age of

many who served as petty officials is a pattern contrasting with the rapid, brilliant careers of some individuals. Simple seniority was the rule for advancement. Education appears to have played a very secondary role during this period. It is likely that, when formal education became more widespread among members of the nobility and sons of officials, it began to serve as a sign of distinction, a means of differentiating between the officials and the lower-level chancellery personnel.

To what extent did civilian government service employees during the eighteenth century become a hereditary social group? Did the civilian administrators already at that time become the proverbial *chinovniki* immortalized in Russian folklore and literature?

The first question can be answered only in the sense that the available documents suggest the beginning of such a process. Answering the second question is difficult because for the end of the century, the reigns of Catherine and Paul, the detailed descriptions which exist for the nineteenth century are lacking. Even the data and descriptions for the local bureaucracy that are available for Perm' province during Paul's reign are insufficient to ascertain whether the *chinovnik* mentality was already formed by that time.

Documents on the Perm' provincial government partially reveal the effects of Paul's attempt to reconstruct the government bureaucracy.[16] Paul's idea of streamlining and routinizing the provincial bureaucracy included the notion that all provinces should consist of a uniform number of counties (twelve per province). Therefore county boundaries had to be redrawn to redistribute the population evenly. The abolition of excess counties led to the abolition of county governments or city governments in cities which had served as county seats. The Perm' government documentation suggests that the job of redrawing county lines, as well as the decision about the abolition of city status for particular cities involved, was left to the local governors, subject to the approval of the Senate.

As a result of the reconstruction of the Perm' provincial government apparatus in 1797 the number of government officeholders in the province was reduced from 298 to 210, a greater reduction than the decrease in the number of counties from fifteen to twelve would have warranted. A number of offices were abolished throughout the provinces, such as the Court of Arbitration (*Somestnyi sud*), the Chief Land Court, lower-court executive offices (*Nizhniaia rasprava*), the office of the county overseer (*striapchii*), and others. That was how the number of office-holders was reduced by 30 percent, rather than just the 20 percent called for by the reduction in the number of counties.

The governor had to make a number of decisions about who was to be retained and who was to be dismissed from active service. The documents on those personnel decisions provide a valuable source on the profile of provincial and county administration in Perm' province. Assuming that the governor did not engage in any blatant discrimination against particular categories of his administrative apparatus and that age must be ruled out on the basis of the evidence as the most likely discriminative factor, one may divide the 88 bureaucrats removed from service into the following categories: retiring, 9; removed without prejudice, 47; and removed for reasons of their past behavior, 32. Of the last category, 10 were officials (judges, secretaries, or heads of county offices) facing court proceedings or investigations. Another 7 were dismissed for alcoholism, 3 for accepting bribes (all were secretaries), 4 for inability to perform their duties, and 8 for just being "average."

Perm' was a province with relatively fewer nobles than other provinces, and thus a larger percentage of the officials, especially the minor ones, were probably recruited from nongentry groups. This may have been one of the reasons why the advancement of Perm' officials up the hierarchical ladder was relatively slow and the reason why there were so many officials with such a long service record. As in other provinces, the officials with few years of experience in civil administration were the ones who transferred from the military. Apparently after the transfer advancement was also slow for them. The Perm' data do not permit judging whether kinship or any other relations between officials was instrumental for advancement in the provincial civil bureaucracy as that can be sometimes ascertained for gentry families in other provinces.

Another characteristic of the civil administration in Perm' province was the rather advanced age of the bureaucrats, if that can be judged by their length of service. When categorized by length of service, 161 officials (excluding the medical personnel) can be represented by the groups presented in table 9.7.

Service started between the ages of 15 and 20. If we add that to the range of service for each category, an approximate age distribution of the Perm' provincial

Table 9.7   Perm' Officials According to Length of Service in 1797

Up to 10 years of service	8
10–19	46
20–29	51
30–39	37
40–49	17
50 years and above	2
Total	161

Table 9.8   Perm' Officials by Rank and Range of Service Length in 1797

Rank	No.	Range of Years in Service
V	1	32
VI	9	28–45
VII	19	22–45
VIII	14	20–46
IX	49	15–56
X	5	29–34
XII	27	12–36
XIII-XIV	69	15–45

Source: Kapustin, *Sto let nazad*, p. 113.

bureaucracy can be obtained. (The resulting figures are the lower bound, for some individuals began civil service after they had devoted some time already to military service.) This age distribution is probably typical of the provincial bureaucracy elsewhere. That upward mobility was slow can be ascertained from the distribution of the officials by the rank and length of service represented in table 9.8.

The range of the length of service, especially for the lower categories in the Table of Ranks (ranks XII–XIV), indicates a slow rate of advancement. The slow career progress probably can be explained by the combination of non-noble social background and the low level of education. Eight officials who retired had an average length of service of 38.25 years, a fact which suggests that for those who remained in service the road to advancement was a rocky one.

The Perm' data also reveal that half of the enumerated civil servants were earning very meager incomes, if they had to rely exclusively on their salaries. The salary of the lowest category of civil servants was not much higher than the total income of a serf household at the time and was comparable to what poor parish clergy were earning. Although the occupation of any particular rank was to some extent age-graded, and one does not expect beginners to have high salaries, the data in table 9.8 show that even those occupying the bottom ranks, XIII and XIV, were often mature adults who probably had families to support. The year 1797 was one of inflationary pressures in the economy, and the purchasing power of officials' salaries was declining. Expectation of a high level of efficiency and productivity from the lower ranks of provincial officialdom was a dream to which few experienced administrators subscribed.

The Knout and Its Use

Regardless of which label is attached to the Russian political regime during the eighteenth century, be it autocracy, absolute monarchy, or any other, clearly it was a regime under which a few governed the many, a regime that ruled a highly stratified society in which freedom was a privilege for a small minority and serfdom the condition of the vast majority of the population. How was the government capable of exercising its power over such a huge subjugated population on such a vast territory?

The chief element in the maintenance of the regime was the tacit agreement by the majority of the population, which considered the rulers and their government as legitimate in their exercise of power. Whether that legitimacy was derived from a "social contract" historically explained and involving some form of consent of the governed, or from an acknowledgment of the ruler's divine origin, is of lesser importance than the fact that its legitimacy was recognized by the majority of those who carried the burden of the existing political and social order. The regime also enjoyed the active support of the privileged stratum or social class, the nobility, which served the government in the exercise of its power. Support by the church helped to inculcate the ideas of both legitimacy and subordination into the consciousness of the populace and to counteract ideas of opposition and dissent.

It is also important to keep in mind the fact that the state had at its disposal a refined apparatus of political control, both a specialized political police as well as an army which could and did use power and performed police functions against potential and actual opponents of the regime and against those who by their words or deeds challenged the existing political elite and state institutions. Firearms made mass movements and rebellious outbreaks by the oppressed classes less threatening than such movements had been during earlier centuries. Although there was no legal prohibition against the possession of firearms by serfs or townsmen, the relatively high cost of the firearms and the degree of government control over their production (and also the production of gunpowder) made their possession by the lower classes very unlikely.

Every encounter between rebellious serfs and armed gentry or army detachments had a predictable outcome because of the difference in the arms of both sides. Clubs, pitchforks, and pikes in the hands of the rebels were no match for the government forces' firearms. This helps to explain why the only effective military components of the rebellions led by Razin, Bulavin, and Pugachëv were mutinous cossacks, who as trained military auxiliaries possessed and used firearms. In those civil disorders the military effectiveness of the much more numerous serfs and townsmen was virtually nil.

Another important consideration must be borne in mind. Army recruits were serfs who did not return to their villages in the instances when they survived, completed their service, and were retired from the armed forces. They were granted personal freedom and resettled in towns or in distant regions, but rarely returned to the places in which they had roots. This policy denied to the serf population any elements possessing military training and decreased the likelihood of serious military threat from the serfs. Paradoxically, the contrast between the well-armed government forces and the virtually unarmed peasant rebels may have contributed to the ferocity of the spontaneous, elemental serf outbreaks that occurred.

There were four institutions that performed police functions. One was the political police; the second, the urban police force; the third, army detachments permanently assigned to assist the central and provincial institutions of civilian administration; and the fourth, a means of last resort used in "emergency situations," the regular armed forces.

The secret political police was an institution whose function was to anticipate intentions and to combat activities opposed to the government regardless of the social groups where such opposition might originate. It had a number of antecedents in earlier periods of Russian history. The institutional form in which it existed in the eighteenth century started to function in 1692 as the *Preobrazhenskii prikaz*, later renamed the Secret Chancellery (*Tainaia kantselariia*) in Moscow, with a branch, the Secret Office (*Tainaia kontora*), in St. Petersburg. It was abolished by Peter III, with dire consequences for that ruler, and almost immediately reestablished, under the name of the Secret Expedition of the Senate, by Catherine II upon her ascension to the throne.[17]

The dreaded secret-police apparatus was relatively small. The precise number of its regular officeholders is unknown, although there are data on its case load (table 9.9) that convey some idea of how much business it had. The power of the secret police was derived not only from the fact that it was a direct arm of the ruler, that the autocrat himself in the person of Peter the Great took a personal interest, and participated on occasions, in the work of the *Preobrazhenskii prikaz*. The power of the secret police was enhanced by the knowledge that its head was one of the most trusted servants of the ruler with the privilege of constant and immediate access to him. The enormous power of the secret police was based on its special

Table 9.9   Caseload of the Preobrazhenskii Prikaz

Year	Cases	Year	Cases	Year	Cases
1692	1	1706	100	1718	91
93	1	07	83	19	93
94	2	08	94	20	136
95	4	09	78	21	147
96	11	10	58	22	229
97	14	11	68	23	316
98	24	12	72	24	448
99	9	13	75	25	534
1700	92	14	47	26	691
01		15	61	27	593
02	99	16	53	28	562
03	125	17	56	29	260
04	184			1730	49
05	183			Total 1692–1730	5,743

Note: During 1741–1748, when the archives of the *Probazhenskii Prikaz* were put in order, 15,251 files turned up, of which 8,729 were categorized as important and secret. Another 566 files were summoned from the Kremlin and those also had to be preserved (Novombergskii, *Slovo i delo*, 2: 110).

status: it was not liable to any interference by any other government office. Its autonomy, its power to interfere with other offices and to avoid the official bureaucratic hierarchy while being immune from any obligations to the highest civilian, military, and judicial offices of the land provided the secret police with extraordinary power not matched by any other institutionalized office.

On May 4, 1732, the head of the Secret Chancellery, General Andrei Ivanovich Ushakov, circulated an instruction to his clerical staff which, according to an order of Empress Anna, prohibited them from revealing any information pertaining to priests' cases should the Holy Synod request it. The empress's order was also made known to the Holy Synod, but, as a matter of precaution, General Ushakov informed his clerical staff about it. The document bears the signatures of all the staff members who acknowledged either reading or listening to the instruction.[18]

A second document conveying information about the clerical staff of the Secret Chancellery pertains to salary increases for some members of the staff and lists the present and future annual salaries of the clerical staff. The newly increased salaries ranged from 30 rubles for copyists to 500 rubles for the secretary of the St. Petersburg branch; the average was over a hundred rubles per year for all the employees (table 9.10). This was probably more than any other government office with a similar employee structure paid. Of course this was not an "ordinary" governmental office, and its "clerical" employees performed tasks of a nonclerical nature in matters of the highest importance to the state. For example, documents of this period abound with data on inspection tours, the escorting of high dignitaries to their places of exile, and other such matters; most of these tasks were performed by "lowly clerks" of the Secret Chancellery.

Nevertheless, a fundamental question remains: how could an office employing twenty-seven clerks, two executioners, a physician, and a watchman (see table 9.11) perform the functions of the secret police? The answer is not difficult to ascertain. This office had at its disposal other governmental offices and the army. For example, Prince Iakov Shakhovskoi, at the time employed in the Holy Synod and not in the Secret Chancellery, vividly described in his memoirs how he was "mobilized" to arrange the exile from St. Petersburg of Münnich, Ostermann, Mengden, and others in 1742. The entire operation, in which he had at his disposal a goodly number of officers and soldiers, was typical of the manner in which the secret police operated. As evident in the Shakhovskoi and other operations, it was the army that provided most of the manpower, the facilities, and the communications for the Secret Chancellery. The availability of the army made the setting up of a huge, separate secret-police apparatus unnecessary. Consequently the government was able to save what might have been the enormous costs of such an apparatus because it used an existing, relatively efficient, apparatus of force.

A comparison of the documents summarized in tables 9.10 and 9.11 reveals the divergent patterns of the growth of the Moscow and St. Petersburg secret-police chancelleries. The relatively greater growth of the St. Petersburg office can be clearly attributed to the continuing shift of central government offices and operations from Moscow to St. Petersburg. Although the court was still moving between both capitals during the reign of Elizabeth (to which the 1752 document pertains), most of the central governmental operations were already concentrated on the Neva.

Indicative of the importance of the St. Petersburg office was not only the numerical growth of its staff,

Table 9.10   Officials of the Moscow Secret Chancellery and the St. Petersburg Secret Office and Their Yearly Salaries, 1752.

Moscow Secret Chancellery Official Position	Individual	Salary (in Rubles)	
		Previous	Increase
Secretary	Mikhailo Krushchov	400	
Notary	Nikita Iaroi	130	
Actuary	Mikhailo Poplavskoi	130	
Registrar	Vasilii Prokof'ev	130	10
Clerks	Fedor Afanas'ev	100	30
	Petr Vasil'ev	70	
	Alexander Martynov	50	10
	Mikhailo Cheredin	45	5
	Alexander Baranov	40	5
	Ivan Iaroi	30	10
Copyists	Alexei Kononov	20	15
	Vasilii Il'in	20	15
	Vasilii Mikhailov	20	10
	Sergei Federov	20	20
	Osip Ivanov	20	10
Watchman	Grigorii Firosov	18	
Executioner	Mikhailo Mikhailov	12	
Total	17	1,255	140

Table 9.10(2)

St. Petersburg Secret Office Official Position	Individual	Salary (in Rubles)	
		Previous	Increase
Secretary	Ivan Nabokov	500	
Physician	Khristofor Genner	250 and housing	
Archivist	Stepan Sheshkovskii	180	20
Actuary	Alexei Emelianov	200	
Registrar	Matvei Zotov	200	
Junior Clerks	Ivan Sokolov	70	
	Piotr Ivanov	70	
	Ilia Emelianov	60	
	Andrei Nabokov	60	
	Ulian Stepanov	55	5
	Ivan Kononov	55	5
	Artemii Shmagin	45	15
Copyist	Fedor Tumannoi	45	5
Executioner	Matvei Krylov	15	
Total	14	1,805	50

Source: Novombergskii, *Slovo i delo*, 2: 176–77.

but also its employment of a foreign physician. This was probably because the St. Petersburg office dealt with a different clientele than did the Moscow one and thus required the services of a physician either during torture or for post-torture treatment.

The documents suggest some interesting features about the functioning of the institution. The 1752 document lists two Iarois, two Emelianovs, two Nabokovs, and several Kononovs among the employees. The patronymics of those individuals are not given and thus their kinship cannot be established with any degree of certainty, but nevertheless it seems plausible that, although service in the secret chancellery was not hereditary, close relatives were preferred by the employers for security reasons.

Personnel turnover was not rapid. Four of the eleven officials mentioned in the 1752 document had been cited as employed twenty years earlier in the 1732 document. In the same context one might note Stepan Sheshkovskii, identified as the archivist, an individual who rose in the ranks to become under Catherine II the ferocious, hated, and feared head of the Secret Expedition of the Senate.

The small number of personnel attached to the secret police cannot be explained solely by the assistance rendered by other institutions. One might argue that the numerical size of the institution's apparatus was inversely correlated with the fear that the institution instilled. How can the extraordinary fear by all Russians of the secret political police be explained? To a very large extent that fear was based on the historical record of the institution, on its involvement in the suppression and punishment of the participants in the Moscow musketeers' rebellion and the Astrakhan' uprising early in Peter's reign. In those cases the *Preobrazhenskii prikaz* acted as a tribunal rather than as an investigative institution. Punishment was not meted out according to the degree of participation in the disorder, but according to the participants' social or service position. That clearly created the impression that the populace of the Russian Empire was dealing with an institution that established arbitrary rules, that both guilt and suspicion of guilt by association was sufficient to condemn an accused, who had no recourse to appeal.

Fear was nourished also by the realization that birth, family connection, social position, and rank in service were insufficient to shield anyone from the secret police. This was unlike the case with judicial institutions where those qualities, or bribes, could make a real difference in the outcome of a court process. Although the treatment of a serf by the administrative and judicial authorities differed little from treatment by the secret police, for members of the privileged groups an encounter with the secret police provided a taste of what it meant to be an ordinary criminal and to be treated as such. In fact, fear of the secret police by members of the nobility and clergy was relatively greater than among the serfs, and the historical and literary documents expressing this fear issue from members of the privileged classes.

One could also argue that the fear of the police was intensified by the knowledge that two of the basic judicial procedural precepts, often employed by the courts when dealing with the serfs and burghers, were employed indiscriminately by the secret police. One was the principle that an acknowledgment of guilt, a self-accusation, was necessary, and in most cases sufficient, to sentence an individual accused of a real or alleged crime. The second was that torture had to be used almost as a mandatory procedure in obtaining the accused's deposition, even in instances where he was willing to provide the required deposition without the use of torture. The Russians learned from experience that, given the arbitrariness of the secret police and the lack of control over the police by other governmental institutions, any brush with them would have injurious consequences for that individual and his acquaintances.[19] The Russians also learned that the relationship between the crime, guilt, and punishment was often very tenuous. In addition, the location of the Secret Chancellery in the St. Petersburg Peter-Paul fortress with its sinister prisons and torture chambers in the Trubetskoi Bastion and the Alekseev Ravelin of the fortress contrib-

uted to the other elements in creating an extraordinary fear of the secret police.

Other elements contributed to the success of the tsarist secret police. One was the large body of informers actively encouraged and rewarded by the government. Another was an efficient filing system that enabled the police to keep and retrieve records on suspected individuals. Operating within an atmosphere of fear and a general belief in the omnipotence of this institution of investigation and repression, a small staff was quite effective in performing its primary functions.

Any indication that there was a political aspect to a crime, any mention of the magic formula *gosudarevo slovo i delo* (the sovereign's word and deed) required a report by any level of the administration to the political police. Local authorities were forbidden to interrogate political suspects, and until very late in the century they were required to send an accused or a witness to the police offices in Moscow, and St. Petersburg. Only at the end of the century were district and provincial administrations asked to conduct preliminary investigations to determine whether a semblance of a political crime existed before sending a suspect to the offices of the political police. The local authorities who conducted such preliminary interrogations, fearing the police, hesitated to recommend a dismissal of charges. Even when the fateful

Table 9.11   Personnel of the *Preobrazhenskaia Kantselariia*, 1727

Moscow Preobrazhenskaia Kantselariia Head:
Prince Ivan Federovich Romodanovskii
Employees

Prikaznye po shtatu

Commissar	1
Secretary	1
Clerks	6
Copyists	20

Lower-level servitors

Watchmen	2
Executioners	2
Total	32

St. Petersburg Preobrazhenskaia Kantselariia head:
Ivan Federovich Romodanovskii

Prikaznye po shtatu

Secretary	1
Clerks	2
Copyists	5
Watchmen	
Executioner	1
Total	10

Source: Kirilov, *Sostoianie*, p. 113.

Table 9.12 Punishments of 506 Accused Individuals in the Preobrazhenskii Prikaz

Sentence	No.	Comment
Death	48	
Knouting	127	
Cudgeling	30	
Whipping	21	
Flogging	7	
Banishment	273	Prior to banishment knouted and tongue cut off—39
and forced labor for life	60	
and forced labor for a term	15	Before banishment knouted and branded—89
and settlement in Siberia	144	Before banishment knouted—86
to a monastery	51	Before banishment cudgeled—4
to a spinning mill	3	Before banishment whipped—3

Source: Golikova, *Politicheskie protsessy*, pp. 48, 319.

words were spoken in a state of intoxication (which occurred surprisingly often), local officials recommended a dismissal only if accompanied by a severe punishment and in clear absence of any knowledge of things "political."

The interrogation and investigation procedures, as well as the ranking of punishments by the secret police, suggest that the accused were classified into two basic categories. Those accused of intended or actual participation in rebellious acts, and those who were presumed to have knowledge of them, belonged to one category. To the second category belonged those who exhibited a lack of deference to the authorities, primarily in conversations with third persons. In more modern terms, the latter might be labeled as spreading antigovernment propaganda, of sorts.

Punishments reflected the described differentiation. Incomplete data for the years 1697–1708 presented in table 9.12 illustrate the range of punishments meted out by the *Preobrazhenskii prikaz*. The data are incomplete, for they do not include the more than one thousand musketeers executed in the aftermath of their rebellion in Moscow, the 45 deaths that occurred during the interrogation of the Astrakhan' rebellion, and the 320 death sentences handed out as a result of the interrogation. Moreover, an undetermined additional number of cases have not survived in the archives. Be that as it may, table 9.12 reveals that capital and corporal punishment, mutilation, and/or exile and forced labor were generously meted out to political criminals opposed to the regime of Peter the Great.

The urban police was another institution that performed police functions and helped preserve law and order in areas of high population density. The police first began to function in St. Petersburg and Moscow during the later years of Peter's reign and only gradually expanded to serve other major cities. The

police combatted crime, regulated traffic on market days, and enforced observance of the sanitation codes. The urban police did not compare with the secret police, but its presence as a visible arm of the government had its effect. At the outset St. Petersburg and Moscow only had about 750 policemen, but their number grew during the century.

The army detachments at the disposal of both central and provincial administrations represented a much more tangible force. They protected public buildings and property and guarded penal labor and the transportation of government funds. Those army detachments were also the force which the bureaucracy used to support its routine procedures and in emergencies when antigovernment or antisocial acts had to be met with force. According to the 1763 governmental table of organization, the total military personnel attached to the civil administration numbered 8,986 men. This number was increased when the 1775 administrative reform added new units of provincial and local administration.

Those military detachments were often insufficient to deal with riots that erupted on a larger scale. Whether they were riots by serfs attached to the Olonets ironworks in the 1740s, similar riots in Izhevsk in the 1760s, or peasant-serf riots against estates in larger regions, the regular army was called in to deal with the situation. The army dispatched detachments from adjacent garrisons and conducted operations in a military fashion with small firearms and even artillery pieces. After such riots and the punishment of ringleaders, army detachments were stationed in the rebellious villages for some time. Their sheer presence was deemed a severe punishment, one that might ruin such villages' economy.

The use of military detachments against serf riots became more frequent after the peasant rebellion led by Pugachëv. The rebellion frightened the government, which considered that stern, repressive measures were the most effective means to prevent another peasant war.

No matter how large or efficient the combined police forces were, no matter how oppressive their presence may have been, one of the salient features working to maintain the regime was the cooperation of the oppressed themselves. Most of the actual policing of the countryside was done by the serfs, either on instructions of the estate owners and managers, or in the case of the state peasants, in response to orders from the local authorities or the peasant commune. The serfs provided guard duty directed against theft, arson, and robbery. They were obliged to report, and in most cases did report, the arrival of outsiders in the villages and often apprehended such strangers. The serfs participated actively in the search for and apprehension of fugitives from justice, army deserters, and fugitive serfs. The serfs also executed the orders of the local authorities whenever punishments were meted out. In most cases, serfs, not the masters, carried out the corporal punishments inflicted upon their brethren. One must keep this behavior in mind to understand why, given the acknowledgment of the legitimacy of the existing social and political order, acquiescence with its value system and its consequences was the rule and a rebellious attitude the exception to the rule. This, perhaps more than the oppressive governmental police measures, explains much of the social and political stability one encounters in eighteenth-century Russia.

The knout was there, but more important was the belief that those who had it also had the right to wield it.

CONCLUSION
Richard Hellie

Arcadius Kahan studied the eighteenth-century Russian economy from the point of view of a historian and an economist. As a historian, he knew that antecedents should be sought, contemporary relationships established, and consequences posited. As an economist, he studied the eighteenth-century Russian economy by raising the issues and employing the tools of neo-classical economics: opportunity costs, land-labor ratios, supply and demand factors, social costs, skill acquisition, efficiency, income distribution, capital formation, the state budget, a concern for entrepreneurship, marginal productivity, supply and demand elasticities, cost-benefit analysis, analysis of the money supply. This had not been attempted on so thorough a scale before, and is unlikely to be replicated in the foreseeable future.

The eighteenth-century Russian economy was shaped by its past, by its geography and climate, by the location of its resources, by the nature of its population, and by the domestic political world and the international milieu. All of those elements contributed to the development of the economy, and all of them also retarded it. The central elements of the economy were agriculture, mining and manufacturing, transportation, and domestic and international exchange. All of them were closely interrelated with one another, and all attempts to make dramatic leaps in any one sector of the economy were rapidly hindered by bottlenecks and shortages of materials and labor in another. Eighteenth-century Russians were the first of their kind who believed that men could rationally will a change of given conditions, but there is some question whether the efforts of the great shakers and mobilizers had much long-term impact, whether their interference in what might have been the natural evolution of the economy had much impact other than to make the Russian people suffer unnecessarily.

The eighteenth century was a period of dramatic change for Russia. Between 1701 and 1800 the borders of the Russian Empire expanded to the Baltic and the Black seas with the incorporation of Ingria, Estonia, Livonia, much of Poland, New Russia, and the Crimea, and it becomes necessary in discussing "Russian" economic history in this era to distinguish the old Slavic heartland from the newly annexed areas. Population often grew at the rate of 1 percent a year, the total population increased 2.4 times, and the planted area increased 2.5 times. Although agricultural technology did not improve, the move southward into the Ukrainian chernozëm increased yields. Industries were created that had not existed previously, and the output of nearly all industries increased dramatically. Domestic markets expanded enormously, and between the early 1740s and the middle 1790s alone exports grew 6.4 times and imports increased 5.3 times. The Petrine service-state revolution revitalized the government and gave it a new sense of purpose whose influence was felt throughout society. In the wider world, Russia was still on the European periphery in 1701, but by 1800 the Russian army was one of the most powerful in Europe, the Russian gentry often spoke French, and the Russian economy was well integrated into the European economy. Yet in spite of the marked changes between 1701 and 1800, the observed developments were continuous with the Russian past and gradually incremental within the eighteenth century itself.

Production costs in Russia were higher than in Western Europe, for example, because the climate was continental, the population density was low, urban concentrations were few and far between, levels of investment in human capital were low, mining sites were remote from population centers, transportation services were primitive, raw materials for manufactured goods were generally dear, and labor was often in short supply. Agricultural productivity was low because the nonblacksoil lands were poor, the precipitation in those podzol-soil regions was excessive, the yield ratio (output:seed) was low, and serfdom tended to keep agricultural labor in those areas rather than to allow it to move freely to locales such as the chernozëm region where yields were higher. In spite of serfdom, however, there was considerable geographic mobility, and supplies of hired and contracted labor increased, both among serfs and nonserfs. Moreover, as the severity of the serf regime moved towards, and then past, its peak in 1797, the number of private, seignorial serfs grew much more slowly than did the number of serfs belonging to the state.

The structure of industry varied from branch to branch. The general tendency of the industrialization process was for large-scale production based in manufactories to drive out cottage and small-scale industry. There were exceptions, such as the leather, flour-milling, and seed-crushing industries, but they were few. Further, cottage industries and other rural and urban specialized producers grew at the expense of home production as more people were drawn further into the market. The growth of intravillage, intervillage, and interregional trade, the rise in the number of peddlers, bazaars, and fairs, was one of the major stories of the eighteenth century, and the expansion of market areas and their integration were nothing short of extraordinary. By the end of the century, interregional price differentials for grains declined and there were mega-market regions for a few commodities. All of this was facilitated by declining transportation costs.

Native Russian industries were nearly always backward by world standards, rarely were they in the forefront technologically. In the second half of the eighteenth century the domestic iron industry may have been an exception, but it was a rare one. Whether the Russians were naturally less inventive than other peoples cannot be measured, but it is a fact that they had great difficulty in translating ideas into working, productive technology. This failure of entrepreneurship had many causes, ranging from a shortage of capital (which was not itself critical), because of the non-existent and then only primitive banking system, to the lack of a long-term time horizon, because entrepreneurs (some of whom were of serf origin) often were fundamentally interested in climbing the ladder of social prestige into the gentry rather than in remaining as "socially inferior" merchants or manufacturers. Be that as it may, by the end of the eighteenth century Russia had developed most of the industries known to the rest of the civilized world, and the output of most industries increased manyfold during the century under review in this monograph.

Historians of Russia often attribute great significance to governmental activity. Unquestionably such activity was important in many spheres. Russia was one of the most effective police states of its time. Violations of the centrally directed consensus, active dissent, and many other forms of deviance were forbidden, always crushed by resort to the knout, exile, forced labor, or capital punishment if the reigning political authorities found the activities sufficiently objectionable. Travel abroad without official permission was almost impossible, and internal mobility was more effectively channelled in directions the government desired than it was in any other European state.

The government also played a significant role in the economy. Its primary role was that of granter of monopolies, licenses, and subsidies, the setter of often moderate protectionist tariffs, a collector of taxes, builder of canals, a major purchaser (and allocator) of labor services and goods. It was able thereby to direct the movement of labor and the manufacturing of goods, particularly goods that it desired. Most of this was done in the "free market." Throughout the century the government itself owned and operated only a relatively few mines, primarily in nonferrous metals, or industries, such as shipbuilding under the Admiralty and the manufacture of small firearms and gunpowder. The government began to discover after the death of Peter the Great that operating establishments ranging from copper mines to silk manufactories was not one of the things it did best, and often turned them over to private entrepreneurs, whom it encouraged in sundry ways. Paradoxically, perhaps, the greater productivity of freely hired labor was also discovered, but no steps were taken to emancipate the serfs. By the reign of Catherine the Great, most state trading monopolies and monopoly grants to individuals ended, but the gentry monopoly of peasant labor was strengthened. The government, i.e., the broad mass of the taxpayers, thus shouldered the start-up costs of industries that otherwise might have appeared only later and under different conditions. Nevertheless, the government throughout the century played a major role because it was a monopsonist in some industries, such as armaments, precious metals, and wool cloth (for a considerable length of time), and the major customer of the other nonferrous and ferrous metal industries, and also the paper, brick, and forest-products industries. Only in industries such as nonwool textiles, glass, leather, and flour-milling did the government play a minor part. The government's activity in the distilling and salt industries was atypical because it was interested not in alcohol or salt, but in the revenues that taxing them produced, and thus carefully regulated the industries to monitor its hoped-for revenue flow. Most disconcertingly, the revenue flow from the gabelle turned to subsidy.

As a tax collector, the government had a major impact on every subject as it took in 12 to 15 percent of personal income. The major burden was the "soul tax," paid by all peasants and most townsmen. The soul tax did not increase the tax burden when it was introduced, was not so burdensome as to cause incremental arrears, and declined secularly as a percentage of revenue as the government moved toward reliance on indirect taxes, plus rent from the state's own serfs. As the share of indirect taxes (especially customs duties and "profits" on government monopolies and reminting operations) increased, the role of the fiscal system in redistributing national income from the primary producers to the gentry and other members of the elite diminished. (In modern parlance, the excise taxes on alcohol and salt were both "regressive.") Government deficits were paid for by debasing the currency, inflation, which benefited the peasantry while the primary producers paid their taxes, and rent in cash. In the second half of the century, however, the gentry began to convert cash rent-payments into compulsory labor requirements (and the serfs looked even more like slaves to impartial observers) and learned to borrow money. Those practices, combined with the gentry's liberation from compulsory governmental service in 1762, produced what is sometimes called "the era of gentry ascendancy."

War was of major importance in the eighteenth-century Russian economy. Few battles were fought on Russian soil throughout most of that period, and thus primary destruction was minimal. The Russian military forces attained an international reputation between the end of the Northern War and the beginning of the Crimean War that was not achieved again until the reign of Brezhnev. That military machine drafted hundreds of thousands of men from what might have been productive lives into the consumption-oriented military. Enormous sums—over half the state budget—were collected for the upkeep of that machine, sums that otherwise might have been spent and invested in the private sector. Another major cost imposed by wars was the temporary disruption of long-term secular developments, which often had to be resumed at something approaching initial start-up costs. The wool industry was founded to clothe the army, and significant resources were invested in munitions. Technological spin-offs and transfers from the military to the private sector apparently were few, but skills acquired in war industries were transferred to civilian industries. Military service was essentially for life, and those rare soldiers who were discharged almost never returned home to leaven the rural loaf. Some entrepreneurs moved from the military to the civilian sector, but they were few. In general, the military sector consumed enormous resources and returned little other than inflation, currency debasement, and untold human misery, plus national aggrandizement, prestige, and independence. Whether those who paid for the military machine would have preferred some other system is unknown, although it is doubtful that the "average Russian" would have willingly exchanged his situation for that of a tribute-payer to Sweden or of a Tatar slave.

Russia has never been isolated from the outside world, if only because of military realities. In consequence, Russia has been importing specialists (most of them with an initial military orientation) for centuries. This manpower flow greatly increased in the eighteenth century. In addition to that, however, there has always been a cultural reality and a commercial reality. The Russian upper classes were positively seduced by the material trappings of Western culture, and their striving for those commodities was one of the primary motivating factors of economic development in the eighteenth century. The creation of import-substitution industries was one of the major concerns of tariff policy, and also one of the major developments in the economy. In addition to luxury consumer items and other "colonial goods," Russians imported silver for specie, some military hardware, textiles, dyes, nails, needles, lead, tin, sulphur, alum, and herring over its western borders, and horses, sheep, silks, cotton goods, and tea across its oriental frontiers. The commercial reality was such that foreign, and especially Western European, demand for Russian commodities such as hemp, flax, linseed oil, linen, grain, naval stores and other forest products, furs, hides, leather, tallow, butter, and iron increased significantly in the eighteenth century. The composition of the demand for those commodities was always changing, and sometimes played a major role in domestic Russian decision-making, whether it was to make and export iron or to grow flax and export narrow linens. Russian foreign-trade growth was also encouraged by the gradual decrease of the customs revenue as a percentage of the total trade turnover. Finally, as Russia became more integrated into the European economy, pan-European inflation had increasingly negative consequences for that country.

The Russians lacked the wherewithal and know-how (loans, insurance, brokerage, cost-effective ship construction, general mercantile expertise) to engage in international trade, with the consequence that nearly all transactions were conducted on Russian soil, either by foreign merchants or their Russian factors. Rarely did Russian merchants venture abroad, and shipping (except coastal) was seldom done in Russian bottoms. Russian sellers and consumers were able to sell abroad for less and pay less for imported commodities because the intervening transactions costs were lower than they would have been had such functions been performed by high-cost

Russian nationals. This may have contributed to the fact that Russia nearly always had a favorable balance of trade.

The impetuses to economic development in eighteenth-century Russia were many. They can be listed, but not necessarily rank-ordered. Perhaps the major one was the outside world, which compelled industrialization if the country was to survive military attack. The outside world also offered alternative models, ideas, technicians, entrepreneurs, and markets. Such outside stimuli were responded to by both governmental officials and private individuals. Those outside stimuli almost certainly had a combined catalytic and multiplier effect propelling the thousands of gentry living off rents and millions of serfs into the market as producers and consumers. It was those millions of decisions which caused most of Russia's economic change. They were facilitated by the tens of thousands of Russians who improved their skills and learned how to produce goods and trade them themselves at lower cost in a potentially bountiful, although high-cost, environment.

NOTES

Chapter One

1. For convenience, the dates of the *revizii* are stated as 1719, 1744, 1762, 1782, and 1795, although the actual counts took more than a single year to complete.

2. Among the historical demographers, the names of Krafft, Herman, Koeppen, Semevskii, and Kabuzan are the most prominent, and any corrections in the official population data that might be introduced in this work are attributable to their reporting. Whatever margin of error exists in the population estimates is not assumed to have had any systematic, consistent bias; the size of the errors would not affect conclusions based on the existing data.

3. The existing data about the hearth-count (household census) of 1710 and the fragmentary data from the subsequent *landrat* population count of 1715-17 are not comparable with the censuses, and a special study is required to compare the data of the 1710 hearth-count with the first census. Such a study could be made only by comparing the primary data and the extant archival sources.

4. We lack estimates for the sex distribution of the population for the various periods.

5. The reader should not be under the illusion that the correlation of the rates of population growth with the occurrence of external events can explain the total picture of the fluctuating rates. It is clear, however, that at least part of the changes were brought about by factors which can be identified, although their effect cannot always be measured.

6. According to Kabuzan, the estimated strength of the Russian armed forces was: in 1724, 219,000; 1744, 170,000; 1762, 418,000; 1782, 518,000; 1795, 450,000 (*Narodonaselenie*, p. 16).

7. For the numbers of draftees in Russia, see table 1.2.

8. The mortality rate during the years 1826-40 (excluding war losses) was 42 per thousand; for 1841-52, it was 37 per thousand (Beskrovnyi, *Russkaia armiia*). In addition, data are available for deaths from diseases in the Russian army in 1802.

9. Zhurovskii, *Statisticheskoe obozrenie*, p. 106.

10. PSZ 25: 721-27, no. 19,036.

11. *Tabeli k Otchetu Ministra vnutrennykh del za 1803 god* (1804).

12. German, *Statisticheskie issledovaniia*, vol. 1.

13. PSZ 15: 481, no. 13,406.

14. Beskrovnyi, p. 300.

15. The underlying figures can be found in table 1.6.

16. The above estimate cannot pretend to be very accurate. A margin of error of 20 percent would be cheerfully accepted.

17. The available evidence suggests that the peasants considered army service as a departure with no return. The price for recruits exceeded that for serfs, an approximation of the price of human life compared with the price of lifelong human labor.

18. During most of the century England had considerable numbers of foreign recruits, as did France.

19. This was true except for the decade of the 1780s, which clearly registered the decrease in the rate of population growth.

20. The years accounted for were 1704, 1709, 1716, 1729, 1732-36, 1739, 1757, 1767, 1774, 1780, 1781, 1785, and 1788. See Kahan, "Natural Calamities," pp. 353-77.

21. The population data are from Kabuzan. The number of years of natural calamities are from Kahan, p. 363.

22. *Population Change between 1719 and 1744 in Selected Districts (Males Only)*

District	1719	1744	Change
Moscow	385,148	388,867	+ 3,719
Vladimir	449,383	380,321	−69,062
Iaroslavl'	333,994	313,615	−20,379
Nizhnii Novgorod	296,267	291,985	− 4,282
Total	1,464,792	1,374,788	−90,004

Source: Kabuzan, p. 159.

23. *Population Change between 1744 and 1762 in Kursk and Orel Districts (Males Only)*

District	1744	1762	% Change
Kursk	386,525	418,104	8.17
Orel	355,265	374,990	5.55
Total, Central Agricultural	1,789,495	2,095,453	17.10

Source: Kabuzan, pp. 158-59.

24. The population growth of Khar'kov during the years 1763-82 of 11.33 percent (from 337,360 to 375,573) contrasts with the growth of 68.67 percent for the period 1744-62 and 31.76 percent growth for the subsequent period of 1782-95.

25. The population of Riazan' district grew by 4.07 percent, Orel district by 3.79 percent, and the Central Industrial region by 3.36 percent, according to the Kabuzan data. A map of the various regions of Russia can be found on p. 393 of Jerome Blum's *Lord and Peasant in Russia* (Princeton: Princeton University Press, 1961).

26. According to V. M. Kabuzan (p. 165), the yearly growth rate of the population in the territory of the first population census during the period 1719-44 was .66 percent. However, three severe famines occurred during the years 1704-16, prior to the census. There is strong evidence to support an assumption that during the Petrine period the population increased at an even lower rate than during the period between the first and second censuses. As a result, the rate of population growth for the first half of the eighteenth century was probably even less than the one quoted here.

27. Kula, *Teoria ekonomiczna ustroju*.

28. By the end of the century, there were quarantine offices in the following localities: Isakovets, Mogilev, Dubossary, Odessa, Evpadokiia, Sevastopol, Taganrog, Kizlar, Sedistov, Kafa, and Seskarsk. In addition, there were quarantine roadblocks (*zastavy*)

supplied with medical personnel in the following localities: Kerch, Ekaterinodar, Gliniany, Mozdok, Guriev, and four places described as Georgian (*gruzinskie*). See *Tabeli k otchetu...1803* (1804), Table N. For an excellent account of the plague of 1771-72, see the recent book by J. Alexander.

29. Krafft, *Mémoires*.

30. See Becker, *Treatise*.

31. This evidence easily can be found in the works by the historians Semevskii, Indova, and Milov.

32. One is still uncertain, however, as to the magnitude of the differences in the rate of population increase, independent of migration movements. Two alternative estimates will be used to demonstrate the significance of the lack of this information for estimating the migration movement in Russia during the eighteenth century.

33. The areas of colonization included the Voronezh district, the areas of Novorossiia, Lower Volga, the Urals, and Siberia.

34. Kabuzan, p. 165.

35. Fal'k, *Zapiski*, pp. 384, 398, as quoted in M. M. Gromyko, *Zapadnaia Sibir'*, pp. 22-23.

36. Both the distinction and verification of the historical accuracy of the various labels may be very important for students of Russian political thought and foreign policy. I hope that colleagues in other fields of inquiry in Russian history will forgive my cavalier treatment of definitions which are very meaningful to their areas of study.

37. Those policies were increasingly successful in preventing the annual inroads by the Tatars and other nomadic hordes in the southeast (Hellie, *Enserfment*).

38. The Russians were also known for their reluctance to allow prisoners of war to leave the country, especially after a protracted war and a long stay by the prisoners in Russia. While the Muscovites occasionally had made concerted efforts to return military captives, such as in the years following the Smolensk War (1632-34), it was only after the mid-eighteenth century that the Russians felt obliged to conform to this long-established Western European convention.

39. Mirabeau's famous dictum defining Prussia as not a territory inhabited by a population and possessing a military establishment, but as a military establishment that conquered a territory with a population, perhaps ought to be modified to: a military establishment that conquered a territory and created a population through a policy of colonization.

40. Catherine II expressed her views on the problems of population on numerous occasions. Prior to her ascension to the throne, she even questioned the wisdom of converting Muslims to Christianity, "since a system of polygamy produces more children per family." She wrote: "We need population....I doubt whether, in order to achieve it, we ought to force our non-Christian subjects to convert to our faith—polygamy is even more useful for the augmentation of the population" (*Sbornik RIO* 3 [1878]: 85). Such a tune has not been heard lately in the Soviet Union, where the rate of population growth among the Muslim peoples is causing some concern among the rulers in the Moscow Kremlin.

41. A statement about the population problem to the Legislative Assembly in 1767 conveys Catherine's convictions on where the blame belongs. "Russia not only does not have enough inhabitants, but has enormous stretches of land that are neither inhabited nor tilled. It seems as though we have been unable to find means to encourage the multiplication of the population of our state..." (*Nakaz Komissii o sochinenii proekta novogo Ulozheniia*, pars. 265, 279).

42. Catherine created a Chancellery for the Guardianship of Foreigners (*Kantselariia opekunstva inostrannykh*). It had the status of a college (a separate ministry) reporting directly to the empress with a yearly budget of 200,000 rubles.

43. Manifesto of July 22, 1763 (PSZ 16: 212-13, no. 11,879).

44. Oddly enough, settlers were permitted to convert Muslim subjects of Russia's neighboring states and even to enserf them. Here the manifesto simply legalized for them an age-long privilege enjoyed by Russian nationals.

45. Those who would volunteer for army service were to receive 30 rubles above their normal pay.

46. The stigma of "headhunters," "slave recruiters," and the like was reflected in the attitudes toward them and their activities. Such attitudes are reflected in European folklore.

47. Pisarevskii, *Iz istorii inostrannoi kolonizatsii*.

48. German, *Statisticheskie*, p. 169.

49. Ibid., p. 177.

50. The famous "Potëmkin villages," which became the Russian metaphor for a hoax or deception created by a facade, entered Russian folklore during Catherine's travels through southern Russia.

51. The rest either escaped, died, or enlisted in the army. See Pisarevskii, p. 289, and *Zhurnal Ministerstva gosudarstvennykh imushchestv*, August 1854.

52. The difficulties that Jewish agricultural colonization experienced in this region in the early nineteenth century were a repetition of this earlier experience, which did not, however, teach the bureaucrats anything about colonization failures.

53. Those reading about this experience, and also those aware of Stalin's deportation of the Crimean Tatars, should be aware of the centuries-long relation between the Russians and the Crimean Tatars: For centuries the Crimean Tatars kidnapped Russians and sold them into the slave markets of the world. Catherine was aware of this, and did not forgive them (Alan Fisher, "Muscovy and the Black Sea Trade," *Canadian-American Slavic Studies* 1972, no. 4: 575-99).

54. For an interesting discussion of the attitudes and policies toward the Old Believers in the Urals and Siberian regions, see the work of N. N. Pokrovskii, *Antifeodal'nyi protest*.

55. The government conducted a policy of viewing the clergy as a hereditary estate, but could not employ all male members of this estate as active clergymen. The prohibition against serfs' entering monasteries also limited the overall number of the clergy.

56. Some members of the nobility also resided temporarily or permanently in the urban areas. Most of the assets of the nobility, its economic base, however, consisted of landed estates and that justifies classifying its members as primarily a rural group. Data on the noble population were kept in the special *Geroldmeisterskaia kontora*, where the documents of the nobility and current registers were maintained. Apparently the surviving documents in those archives have been in a state that has defied attempts by historians to quantify them.

57. Kahan, "Costs of Westernization," pp. 42-43. The article discusses some of the economic problems of the Russian nobility and raises the issue of income differentiation within that estate.

58. Storch, *Supplementband*.

59. Kabuzan, *Izmeneniia*, p. 118.

60. The size of the St. Petersburg garrison alone was about 40,000. The garrisons in the Baltic provinces and in Astrakhan' were also very substantial. Naval personnel were stationed in the ports. A large number of the retired military personnel settled in the cities and lost their attachment to the land.

61. According to Kopanev, there were 26,104 domestics registered in St. Petersburg alone in 1801 (*Naselenie Peterburga*, p. 25).

62. Kopanev noted 35,002 *raznochintsy* in St. Petersburg alone (ibid.).

63. Moscow in 1770 had 10,724 male souls attached to its manufactories. This would account for over one-quarter of the estimated total of factory workers. That figure does not include the larger number of hired workers in the Moscow textile manufactories. There were 50,454 serfs in St. Petersburg in 1801.

64. Ryndziunskii, *Gorodskoe grazhdanstvo*, pp. 98-103.

65. Ibid.

66. The data in this section for the fifth *reviziia* are from Kabuzan and Troitskii, "Izmeneniia v chislennosti," pp. 162-65.

67. The earliest estimate of privately owned houses (*obyvatel'skie dvory*) in St. Petersburg probably did not include the mansions of the aristocracy. The estimate, made for taxation purposes, evaluated the taxable housing stock at 70,597,575 rubles (PSZ 28: 28-29, no. 21,131).

68. Krafft, "Mémoires sur les listes."

69. Sankt Petersburgskii eparkhial'nyi istoriko-statisticheskii komitet, *Istoriko-statisticheskie svedeniia*, 2: 282.

70. Georgi, *Versuch*, p. 134, corrected according to *Ocherki istorii Leningrada*, 1: 103.

Krafft estimates in his first essay, published in 1782, that the average population for the three earlier periods was: 1764-70, 158,782; 1771-75, 158,565; 1776-80, 174,774. The average population for the years 1764-80 was 164,052, a figure he divided between roughly 143,800 Russians and 20,500 foreigners.

71. Arkhimandrit Makarii, "Materialy dlia geografii," pp. 634-59. For the strange sex-distribution demography of Muscovite slavery, see Hellie, *Slavery*, pp. 442-57.

72. Kabuzan calculated the actual figures for the population at 296,267 for 1719 and 291,985 for 1744 (p. 159).

73. The pioneering effort in the study of the Russian family and household belonged to Frederic Le Play, who studied different types of Russian families and households during 1844 and 1853 and reported his results in vol. 2, chaps 1-5, of his classic *Les Ouvriers Européens*.

74. See the following works: Tikhonov, *Pomeshchichie krest'iane*; Sivkov, *Materialy*; Aleferenko, *Krest'ianskoe dvizhenie*; Semevskii, *Krest'iane*; Shchepetov, *Krepostnoe pravo*; Rubinshtein, *Sel'skoe khoziaistvo*; German, "Sur L'exploitation."

75. The population censuses and the general land cadastre of the eighteenth century contain all the pertinent data for even a larger population. Although the numbers of male souls were published for various regions, the numbers of households as a rule were not extracted from the primary documents; they are available only for small samples of particular estates.

76. For the period of the 1730s and 1740s, the differentials between the number of males per household by regions is supplemented by the intraregional differentials which are attributed to endowment in land, horses, and livestock in the work by P. K. Aleferenko (*Krest'ianskoe dvizhenie*, pp. 35, 64-68, 70, 83-84).

77. Unfortunately the differential between the two categories was submerged in the eighteenth-century data. When the legal and social differences were done away with, both strata merged into one class of serfs, and the continuity of the data was lost.

78. The data on the Sheremet'ev estates provide an average of 3.51 males per household, with extremes of 2.40 for Kostroma *guberniia* and 7.03 for Khar'kov *guberniia*. The lower average size of the Sheremet'ev serf households in comparison with Vodarskii's calculated size may be due to the high percentage of "industrial" villages" in Sheremet'ev's estates, such as Ivanovo, Pavlovo, and Vorsma (Vodarskii, "Krest'iane" and Shchepetov, *Krepostnoe pravo*, pp. 286-87, 248-53).

79. Vodarskii calculated that the average sizes of households in the late seventeenth century in Vologda and Ustiug *uezdy* were 3.44 males and 3.56 females, respectively ("Krest'iane.") See also Kolesnikov, *Severnaia Rus'*, 2: 135-49.

80. The limitations of such options are well illustrated in the works by V. A. Fedorov (*"Zemlevladenie" and Pomeshchichie krest'iane*).

81. Among the recently published studies on this subject one could mention those by Vdovina ("Zemel'nye peredely") and V. A. Aleksandrov, ("Sel'skaia obshchina i votchina" and *Sel'skaia obshchina v Rossii*).

82. The evidence is derived from an examination of household size for a large number of *uezdy*; the Vodarskii data, the data on confiscated estates, and some data from the 1710 and 1717 population counts were used. See Vodarskii, "Krest'iane," Kolesnikov, *Severnaia Rus'*, and Sivkov, *Materialy*. In addition, Tikhonov's data vividly show the dramatic increase in household size which coincided with the rise in household taxation in Peter's reign.

83. Some of the original population census lists were published in the multivolume work *Materialy dlia istorii moskovskogo kupechestva*.

84. One can clearly identify the Evreinov family with reported households of 12 and 11 male members, or the Demidov and Zinov'ev families with 10 and 8 members, respectively, which had chosen to maintain a common household for tax purposes but actually, in terms of residence, represented each at least two multigenerational households. The difference between tax households, as represented by the census, and residence households can be studied in the third census for others than *Gostinaia sotnia* households.

85. K. F. Herman, "Tablitsy po vsem kazennym zavodam," tables A-D, I, i.

Chapter Two

1. Rubinshtein, *Sel'skoe khoziaistvo*, p. 232.

2. Kabuzan, *Narodonaselenie*, p. 165.

3. This is a fragment of an extensive manuscript completed by Levshin in Tula in 1803 under the title *Topograficheskoe opisanie tul'skoi gubernii* and published a century and a half later in *Istoricheskii arkhiv* (1957, no. 1), pp. 253-54.

4. Indova, "Urozhai," pp. 144-55.

5. The study of agricultural markets in eighteenth-century Russia has made a giant step forward thanks to the publication of the work by the outstanding Soviet historians I. D. Koval'chenko and L. V. Milov, who compiled local price data for rye and oats for the middle of the eighteenth and the beginning of the nineteenth centuries (*Vserossiiskii agrarnyi rynok*).

6. Ibid., p. 125.

7. Zhuravskii, *Statisticheskoe obozrenie raskhodov*, pp. 20-23.

8. Ibid., p. 21.

9. PSZ 7: 512, no. 4787.

10. On the increase of the poll tax, see the decree of June 23, 1794, in PSZ 23: 529-31, no. 17,222. Originally in 1789 the grain tax was levied in Kiev, Chernigov, Novgorod Seversk, Kursk, Tambov, Voronezh, and Khar'kov. The following districts were added in 1794: Orël, Kazan', Riazan', Penza, Saratov, Simbirsk, Ufa, Nizhnii-Novgorod, Viatka, Tobol'sk, Tula, Kaluga, Smolensk, Ekaterinoslav, and Mogilev. In the following year the districts of Kostroma, Iaroslavl', and Novgorod were included in the grain tax. That made it nearly universal throughout most of Russia. See decrees of July 23, 1794, and September 26, 1795.

11. PSZ 24, 681, no. 18,278.

12. PSZ 8: 526, no. 5819.

13. Pavlenko, *Istoriia metallurgii*, pp. 441, 482-85.

14. Ibid., pp. 444-55.

15. Ibid., p. 450.

16. The data were obtained from Rubinshtein, *Sel'skoe khoziaistvo*, pp. 442-53.

17. The approximate balance between planting-areas of winter and spring grains is obscured in Russian statistics by the reported use of seeds. Wherever there is a direct reference to the planted area in actual size, the balance emerges. On the balance between winter and spring grains in Samara and Saratov *uezdy* of Simbirsk *guberniia*, see Gritsenko, *Udel'nye krest'iane*, pp. 158, 182-83.

18. Kabuzan, "Izmeneniia chislennosti."

19. For a set of similar calculations for the seventeenth century, see Richard Hellie, "The Stratification of Muscovite Society: The Townsmen," *Russian History* 5, pt. 2 (1978): 120. For a very different set of eighteenth-century estimates, which are also based upon shaky evidence, see Gilbert Rozman's *Urban Networks*.

20. Storch, *Supplementband*, pp. 34, 38.

21. Isaev, *Rol' tekstil'noi promyshlennosti*, p. 53.

22. Descriptive material on the participation of serfs in the construction trades can be found in A. N. Radishchev's "Opisanie moego vladeniia," in his *Polnoe sobranie sochinenii*, 1: 171-77.

23. Tatishchev, "Ekonomicheskie zapiski," pp. 12-23.

24. For an example of the incentives offered to serfs, see Indova, "Instruktsii Shcherbatova prikazchikam," pp. 465-66.

25. Semevskii, "Pozhalovanie naselennykh imenii."

26. For a discussion of the borrowings by the institution of serfdom from the institution of slavery, see Hellie, *Slavery*, p. 769.

27. For the derivation of the estimates, see Kahan, "Costs," pp. 42-43.

28. Ibid., pp. 63-65.

29. Ustiugov, "Instruktsiia prikazchiku," p. 167.

30. Indova, "Instruktsiia Shcherbatova prikazchikam," p. 435.

31. PSZ 11: 123-27, no. 8619.

32. Rezorenova, "Beglye krest'iane," p. 28.

33. On the origins of collective responsibility, see Horace W. Dewey and Ann M. Kleimola, "From Kinship Group to Every Man His Brother's Keeper: Collective Responsibility in Pre-Petrine Russia," *Jahrbücher für Geschichte Osteuropas* 30 (1982): 321-35.

34. See the instruction of the landowner Ivan Alekseevich Meshcherinov to his slave Grigorii Stepanov on the search for fugitive serfs and their return in 1688. This vividly described case is to be found in Mikhail Semevskii's collection of "Istoricheskie i iuridicheskie akty," pp. 80-82. Private initiative in the search for fugitive serfs was part of serfdom's heritage from slavery (Hellie, *Slavery*, pp. 567-73).

35. See the decree of May 13, 1754 in PSZ 14: 75-85, no. 10,233.

36. PSZ 22: 974-1008, no. 16,603.

37. Got'e, "Iz istorii peredvizheniia naseleniia," pp. 8-11.

38. Polonska-Vasilenko, *Zaporozhzhia*, p. 101.

39. Snezhnevskii, "K istorii pobegov"; Gatsitskii, *Nizhegorodskoi sbornik*, p. 584.

40. Solov'ev, *Istoriia Rossii*, 12: 15-16.

41. Vodarskii, *Naselenie Rossii*, p. 53.

Chapter Three

1. Here the term "government" includes both the state and the person of the ruler. Most of the silver mines during the eighteenth century belonged to the sovereign and were administered for him or her by the Cabinet, the highest administrative executive body.

The attempt by the iron and copper producer Akinfii Demidov to exploit his silver mines in the Altai region of Western Siberia was very short-lived. In spite of his privileged position at the court and his role as the leading metal producer, the silver mines were confiscated from him without indemnity payments or compensation for substantial past direct investment. There is a case in which the state tolerated for a while the existence of a private silver smelter, at Vozdvizhenskii, owned by the merchant Serebriakov, near and under the control of the state mining works in Nerchinsk.

2. The net profits, estimated by the government administration of the Altai mining region (including the copper mining operations) constituted 297,963 rubles yearly for the period 1747-65, and 1,458,942 rubles annually for the years 1766-76. By the year 1799 the reported profits had declined to 597,664 rubles. Although the concept of "net profits" does not exclude interest returns on capital, the reported sums were still very impressive indeed (Karpenko, *Gornaia promyshlennost'*, p. 197).

3. The experience of gold mining in the Olonetsk region is a good example. The attempts to create an economically profitable gold-producing region were given up only after a long period of costly trials (Danilevskii, *Russkoe zoloto*).

4. The tariff of 1667 established that most customs payments for foreign imports had to be paid in Joachimstalers ("efimki") at a lower than market-rate of exchange. The Joachimstalers were easily reminted (stamped) into Russian currency.

5. The coinage during the years 1699-1710 constituted 1,596,763 rubles annually vs. a yearly coinage of 348,387 rubles during the earlier years of 1690-98. Since the value of the rubles was changed in 1698-99, the difference can be presented as a coinage of 2,426 poods of silver per year during the latter period vs. 756 poods of silver during the earlier period.

6. See table 3.7 for estimates of silver production by various regions of Russia.

7. Only in 1764 was the gold:silver parity ratio established at 1:15 (Kaufman, *Serebrianyi rubl'*, pp. 147-48, 157-59, 165-66).

8. Changes in the official prices for silver can be followed in the published sources. According to a decree of May 12, 1711 (PSZ 4: 691, no. 2371), the government paid for a pound of pre-1698 Russian coins or Joachimstalers the sum of 12 rubles, and 13 rubles for a pound of pure silver, or 13.54 kopeks per zolotnik (a ninety-sixth of a pound). A decree of July 29, 1723 (PSZ 7: 97-98, no. 4278), allowed the government mint to accept silver for recoinage at the rate of 19.205 rubles per pound or 20.005 kopeks per zolotnik and gold at 260 kopeks per zolotnik. A decree of March 23, 1731 (PSZ 8: 404, no. 5726) established the rate for a zolotnik of silver at 18 kopeks, but Kaufmann claimed that the mint was allowed to pay in 1732 even 19.5 kopeks per zolotnik (p. 153). A decree of June 8, 1741, established the price of silver at 19 kopeks per zolotnik (PSZ 11: 439, 12: 417-18, 13: 276-77, nos. 8395, 9187, 9751).

9. Miliukov claimed that during the years 1701-9 about 6,342,680 old rubles were recoined (*Gosudarstvennoe khoziaistvo*, p. 203).

10. Miliukov mentioned that 9,076,117 rubles were reminted out of the old 6,342,680 rubles, which provided a handsome profit for the state (ibid.).

11. The relative demand for copper vs. silver coins was often determined not so much by the demand for coins of different denominations, but by the relative size of the government revenue from coinage of copper or silver. During the Petrine period (1704-24), 4,354,000 rubles of copper money were minted. Under his successors (1725-61), 22,046,000 rubles and during Catherine II's reign (1762-96) 79,965,039 rubles of copper money were minted.

12. The issuance of paper money (assignats) in Russia is an interesting economic and historical phenomenon. It was started on the assumption that their limited circulation would not exert any inflationary pressures in the economy, unlike additional issues of silver and copper money. In this sense, at least in the minds of the decision-makers, paper money was not a substitute for silver because of the actual silver scarcity.

13. Comparing the total silver used for coinage and silver output data for selected years, one can get a rough relationship between the two magnitudes.

14. The regulations for the *katorzhniki* in Nerchinsk, in effect until 1763, envisaged a yearly per capita assignment of 18.8575 rubles. Out of this sum only 6 kopeks were paid in cash. The bulk of the sum defrayed the costs of guards for them, food, clothing, and hospital care (which was almost nonexistent). Clothing and footwear were distributed every two years; the bulk of the food consisted of a monthly ration of 1 pood and 32.5 pounds of rye flour.

15. Danilevskii, *Russkoe zoloto*, p. 315.

16. A very interesting way of providing incentives for the higher mining personnel of the Altai mines and smelters is presented in a

Senate decree of May 2, 1761. According to the decree, a hierarchy of mining officials was instituted that was parallel to and given the same privileges as the hierarchies for military and civil-service ranks (Karpenko, *Gornaia promyshlennost'*, p. 92).

17. The conversion of state-owned serfs' labor-input obligations into full-year worker equivalents was made according to a ratio established in decrees of Paul I (November 9, 1800) and Alexander I (March 15, 1807), which substituted the services of 1,000 serfs with the annual employment of 58 permanent workers.

18. Karpenko explains a case of the transportation of 2,474,569 poods of ore during 1783 in the Altai mines using hired labor at the cost of 157,891 rubles in which the alternative costs of using serf labor would have been 209,543 rubles (including 61,989 rubles compensation for travel)(*Gornaia promyshlennost'*, p. 80).

19. Ibid., p. 78.

20. The thesis that the labor supply was *the* limiting factor in the production of precious metals was advanced in a very interesting essay by the Soviet historian Savel'ev. He supported his claim by using coefficients of silver content of the ore mined and a number of other indicators. Unfortunately his labor productivity data are so weak that the main thesis cannot be proved by the available data.

21. *Materialy dlia istorii russkogo flota* 3 (1866): 153. In 1713 the number employed by the Admiralty reached 9,370 persons (ibid., pp. 158-59). For the 1716 estimate, see Semenova, *Rabochie Peterburga*.

22. A decree of March 31, 1721, abolished the personal service obligation to work on the construction of St. Petersburg and substituted for it a money tax (Luppov, *Istoriia stroitel'stva Peterburga*, pp. 83-84).

23. The figures for the Admiralty and navy personnel who were mobilized for this purpose were 5,676 for the Dnepr and 4,638 for the Don wharves (*Materialy po istorii russkogo flota* 8 [1886]: 359, 502, 546-47).

24. A decree of October 31, 1715 (PSZ 5: 179, no. 2943).

25. Pazhitnov, *Ocherki istorii tekstil'noi promyshlennosti*, p. 162. Following Tugan-Baranovskii's *Russkaia fabrika*, Pazhitnov reported the renewed attempt by Elizabeth to outlaw the production of narrow linen. He attributed the decree's lack of success to the fact that the larger looms needed to weave broad linen cloth did not fit into the peasants' huts, involved larger investment outlays, and were too difficult for women to operate.

26. Ibid., p. 26.

27. Ibid., pp. 170, 172.

28. Strumilin modified the 1799 official figure of a total labor force of 29,303 distributed between 10,208 serfs and 19,095 hired workers and assumed the number of hired workers to be 23,000. This raises the total employed to 33,208, of whom 10,208 were serfs either owned by the manufacturers or attached to the enterprises (*Ocherki*, p. 358).

29. Ibid., p. 79.

30. It appears that the tariff rates for silk products were increased substantially by the tariff of 1757 and the subsequent ones. Raw silk imports were not burdened by customs duties. An examination of the imports of 1790-93 and 1793-95 and the customs duties paid reveals that the rates were effectively higher for such items of mass consumption as silk scarves than for brocades, velvets, and similar luxury products for elite consumption. Items consumed by the upper-income groups were taxed at about 10 percent ad valorem. Regardless of the legislators' intentions, the high tariff on silk scarves provided the domestic output with a degree of protection lacking in the case of the higher-value silk goods.

For tariff rates, see V. I. Pokrovskii, *Sbornik svedenii*, pp. 18-19. On the imports of silk wares, see Storch, *Supplementband*, pp. 53-54. See also Lodyzhenskii, *Istoriia russkogo tamozhennogo tarifa*, p. 147.

31. In one case, members of the nobility were partners in a silk manufactory, but apparently only loaned their names for a share in the profits. In 1744 three owners of silk manufactories, A. Miliutin, E. Evreinov, and A. Zatrapeznov, were awarded nobility patents.

32. The total output of silk wares of 1797 was estimated at 3,938,000 rubles. The average yearly imports totalled 620,000 rubles in 1790-93 and over 584,000 rubles in 1800 (Lodyzhenskii, *Istoriia*, p. 147, and von Reden, *Das Kaiserreich Russland*, p. 230). Adjusting for the value of the ruble at the various dates, the domestic production was over 84 percent.

33. The introduction of the gabelle and state monopoly in 1705 (PSZ 4: 279-80, no. 2009) helped to maintain the oligopolistic structure of the industry and strengthened it by direct allocation of government contracts among the major suppliers. In 1724, for example, the direct allocation of production and delivery orders were: the Stroganovs, 3 million poods; the Preobrazhenskii Pyskorskii monastery, 1.2 million poods; other producers in the North Urals region, 200,000 poods; and various salt producers in other regions, 901,181 poods (Troitskii, *Finansovaia politika*, p. 161).

34. Ibid., pp. 161-63.

35. The sharpest decline in the sales of salt took place in 1750 in the areas in which previously Astrakhan' salt was sold at a nominal price of 3.5 kopeks even after the price increase to 17.5 kopeks per pood. Some of the decline can be explained by illicit sales of salt in the Lower Volga region. For the effect of the 1750 price increase on regional salt sales, see Svirshchevskii, "Materialy," p. 193.

36. The cost of producing Perm' salt by the late 1750s was 5 kopeks per pood. The transportation costs to the central salt supply depot in Nizhnii Novgorod was another 5 kopeks per pood. Although the cost of Elton salt at the source was negligible and usually disregarded in the calculations done in terms of the transportation costs to Kamyshyn (4 kopeks per pood) or Saratov (7 kopeks per pood), the cost of Elton salt in Nizhnii Novgorod was about 16 kopeks, or higher than for Perm' salt. The differential between the costs of the two salts in Moscow was about 3.5 to 4 kopeks per pood in favor of Perm' salt.

37. PSZ 22: 1140-63, no. 16,736 and Ministerstvo vnutrennikh del, *Tabeli k otchetu za 1804 god* (1806). The calculations by the Ministry of Internal Affairs for the salt supply of 1803-4 provide not only data on costs in the consumption regions but also the estimates for each region of profits or deficits by sources of supply.

38. Hellie, *Enserfment*, pp. 151-234 and idem, "The Petrine Army: Continuity, Change, and Impact," *Canadian-American Slavic Studies* (Summer 1974): 237-53.

39. Beskrovnyi, *Russkaia armiia*, p. 349.

40. Bakulev and Solomentsev, *Promyshlennost'*, p. 21.

41. Kirilov, *Tsvetushchee sostoianie*, 1: 22.

42. Among the most successful innovations introduced by the officers M. Danilov, M. Zhukov, M. Martynov, I. Meller, and M. Rozhnov was the cannon, the "edinorog," which became known during the Seven Years' War as the "Shuvalov cannon" (*Sovetskaia voennaia entsiklopediia* 3 [1977]: 302). According to Kirilov's data for the early part of the century, the permanent labor force of the St. Petersburg armory in 1714 was 218 workers and the Moscow armory in 1725 had 131 workers (*Tsvetushchee sostoianie*, pp. 21, 89).

43. Beskrovnyi listed the following private gunpowder mills: (1) Meyer, on the Iauza River (near Moscow); (2) Anikeev, on the Iauza; (3) Isbrandt, on the Vora River; (4) Ruchter and Berkuzin, on the Kliaz'ma river; (5) Kondrat'ev, near the Danilov monastery; (6) Selivestrov; (7) Marykeev; (8) Bel'skii; (9) Ivanov; (10) Kadyshev, near Simbirsk (*Russkaia armiia*, p. 96).

44. While the demand increased during the quarter century of uninterrupted wars from about 15,000 poods to about 30,000 poods, some of the private enterprises supplied substantial volumes of gunpowder. Mayer supplied 9,000 poods in 1696; Anikeev, 8,000 poods in 1704; Bel'skii and Ivanov, 12,000 poods in 1704, and Meyer and Ruchter, 30,000 poods in 1710.

In 1712 a gunpowder mill was established in St. Petersburg which by 1714 produced about 2,000 poods, a quantity which rose to 4,000 and then 6,000 poods in a short time. In 1715 the Okhtenskii gunpowder mills were set up with 85 workers whose original output was 600 poods in 1716. By 1726 the mills were completed and greatly increased their output. During the 1730s the Shostenskii gunpowder mills were established near Kazan' and later in the century became the chief producer among the state-owned gunpowder mills.

45. The demand of the field army, according to Peter the Great's specifications in 1724 of 500 charges per cannon and gunpowder for an army reserve of 80,000 men, was estimated at 60,000 poods annually, not including the needs of the navy and fortresses (Beskrovnyi, *Russkaia armiia,* p. 98).

The Okhtinskie gunpowder mills produced 86,407 poods during 1733-58; 14,306 poods in 1769-70; 47,786 poods in 1777-82; 141,883 poods in 1783-91; 83,902 poods in 1792-99, for a total of 273,571 poods in the years 1777-99. The Shostenskii gunpowder mills produced 10-15,000 poods until the 1780s, when they were reconstructed. Then they produced 50,000 poods, which rose to about 60,000 poods in the last year of the century, 1800. The Kazan' state-owned gunpowder mill (established in 1788) started with an output of 5-6,000 poods annually and increased its output by the end of the next decade to 8-10,000 poods yearly.

46. B. I. Kurakin, Russian envoy to the Hague, hired the powder-master Peter Schmitt, who arrived in St. Petersburg in the spring of 1719. Before his death, he revealed his secrets to his wife Helen de Voel. By a combination of high monetary reward (she was hired as a powder-master at a yearly salary of 780 rubles and worked for nearly forty years in that capacity) and economic intelligence obtained by pretended romance (on the part of Ivan Leont'ev, who was charged with finding out the secrets), the Russians were able to learn the new process (A. I. Andreev, *Petr Velikii,* pp. 261-77).

47. Beskrovnyi, *Russkaia armiia,* p. 363.

48. Kafengauz, *Istoriia khoziaistva Demidovykh,* pp. 424-75.

49. The state ironworks in Lipetsk produced the following weights and quantities of guns: 1768, 37,700 poods; 1769, 61,116 poods; 1770-76, repaired 720 field guns; 1779, produced 9,337 poods of guns; 1788-90, produced 1,458 field guns, of which 400 were three-pounders, 222 were six-pounders, 150 were twelve-pounders, 116 were eighteen-pounders, 94 were twenty-four-pounders, 82 were thirty-pounders, and 80 were thirty-six pounders. In addition, during the years 1788-90 168 eighteen-pound *edinorogi* and 146 twenty-four-pound *edinorogi* were produced (Beskrovnyi, *Russkaia armiia,* p. 354).

50. The Soviet historian L. G. Beskrovnyi exhibited a particular eagerness to prove the superiority of Russian products over foreign ones (ibid., pp. 100-102).

51. Zhuravskii, *Statisticheskoe obozrenie,* p. 115.

52. See the law of November 20, 1791 (PSZ 23: 274-77, no. 16,998).

53. The 1762 results are obtained by assuming that *karazeia* cost 23 kopeks per arshin, noncolored cloth 60 kopeks per arshin, and colored cloth 72 kopeks per arshin. It was also assumed that two-thirds of the total cloth was colored. By 1791 the prices rose to 28 kopeks for *karazeia,* 72 kopeks for noncolored cloth, and 84 kopeks for colored cloth, which yield the results for 1791 and 1798.

54. Some of the information on the state of the woolcloth manufactories during the 1790s was derived from a chaotic and confusing article by the Soviet historian I. V. Pevzner ("Sukonnaia promyshlennost'," pp. 223-45). The author describes in the article a report on the wool-cloth manufactories in 1797, but the data are based upon the reports of 83 manufactories and differ in quality and coverage.

55. *Ukazy Petra Velikogo s 1714 po 1725 gg.,* pp. 15, 21.

56. PSZ 10: 799, no. 7831 and 11: 551, no. 8486.

57. All of the information on the technology of papermaking in Russia and much of the information on the paper mills has been drawn from the remarkable book by Zoia Vasil'evna Uchastkina, *Razvitie bumazhnogo proizvodstva v Rossii.*

58. The government was not only a consumer of paper for all kinds of chancellery uses and for printed or written communications, but also was a seller of paper stamped with the government seal required for contracts and petitions, the source of the so-called "stamp tax."

59. The combined output of those firms amounted in 1800 to about 3,160,000 poods of iron out of a total reported output of 6,154,000 poods (Pavlenko, *Istoriia,* p. 463).

60. PSZ 5: 129, no. 2858.

61. PSZ 4: 842-43, no. 2546.

62. A decree of October 9, 1714 (PSZ 5: 126, no. 2848).

63. *Doklady i prigovory,* vols. 1-6.

64. Semenova, *Rabochie Peterburga,* pp. 84-86.

65. Ibid., p. 87.

66. Voronov, "Dokumenty o kirpichnom proizvodstve," pp. 64-66.

67. Ibid., pp. 50-54. Apparently the list of brickworks was incomplete.

68. Voronov, "O rynke rabochei sily," p. 96. The maximum annual capacity per kiln was 300,00–350,000 bricks and 50,000–60,000 for private enterprises.

69. Voronov, "Dokumenty," pp. 112-14.

70. Stolpianskii, *Zhizn' i byt,* pp. 16-23.

71. Ibid., p. 23.

72. Voronov, "Dokumenty," pp. 97-98.

73. Volodarskaia, "Sotsial'nyi sostav," p. 181.

74. Pazhitnov, *Ocherki,* pp. 28-29.

75. Strumilin, *Istoriia,* p. 319.

76. Pazhitnov, *Ocherki,* p. 29.

77. Among the oldest enterprises was the one established by Chamberline and Cozzens in 1753 in Krasnoe Selo near St. Petersburg, which received a ten-year monopoly privilege. In 1763 another manufactory was established by Lehman, who received a loan of 30,000 rubles to build a plant in Schlüsselburg, near St. Petersburg (ibid., pp. 46-48).

78. Ibid., p. 50.

79. Ibid., pp. 48-49.

80. Kafengauz, *Istoriia khoziaistva Demidovykh,* pp. 421-22, 479.

81. Ibid., p. 310.

82. Pavlenko, *Istoriia,* pp. 324-25.

83. The number of foreigners in the upper echelons of the armed forces was substantial throughout the eighteenth century. It tended to decline over time thanks to the training of Russian nationals and to their advancement in the ranks. Early in the century the highest concentration of foreigners was at the level of the "generalitet" (the highest army ranks), but even for the entire office corps the percentage of foreigners was high. M. D. Rabinovich found that in 1720-21, 281, or 12.5 percent, of the officers in his purview (about two-thirds of the entire office corps) were foreigners, which was below the one-third maximum of foreigners envisaged by the military statutes of 1711. Among the staff officers (ranks of majors and colonels), however, the number of foreigners was 62, or 31.1 percent, very close to the prescribed maximum ("Sotsial'noe proiskhozhdenie," pp. 133-71).

84. G. V. Alferova, "Gosudarstvennaia sistema stroitel'stva gorodov i osvoeniia novykh zemel' v XVI—XVII vv. (na primere goroda Kozlova i ego uezda)," *Arkhitekturnoe nasledstvo* 27 (1979): 3-11.

85. PSZ 6: 311-12, no. 3711.

86. PSZ 12: 181-83, no. 9004.

87. The total reported for private iron and copper works was 11,142 of the gentry category, from which I have deducted 1,203 owned by Stroganov (Strumilin, *Istoriia*).

88. Ibid., p. 305.

89. I have arrived at this total by deducting 4,438 serfs owned by the Stroganovs and Golitsyn from the reported total of 33,731.

90. *K voprosu o pervonachal'nom nakoplenii*, p. 479.

91. *Sbornik russkogo istoricheskogo obshchestva* 7 (1871): 94.

92. The reported total for all metallurgy was 54,706, from whom I have excluded 6,421 serfs belonging to the Stroganovs, Golitsyn, and Shakhovskoi.

93. Zaozerskaia, *Rabochaia sila*, pp. 47, 236.

94. Indova, "O rossiiskikh manufakturakh," pp. 316-25.

95. Zaozerskaia, *Rabochaia sila*, pp. 189-90.

96. PSZ 9: 707-12, no. 6858.

97. Ibid.

98. Zaozerskaia, *Rabochaia sila*, pp. 192, 196; Kafengauz, *Khoziaistvo Demidovykh*, p. 366.

99. The secondary sources most complete on this problem are by Strumilin for the iron- and copperworks and by Zaozerskaia for the textile industries.

100. Artamenkov, "Naëmnye rabochie," p. 134.

101. Zaozerskaia, *Rabochaia sila*, p. 218.

102. Ibid., p. 217.

103. Strumilin cited for 1755 the figure of 6,852 males whose status was to be determined "by decree," of whom 2,357 were in state enterprises (*Istoriia*, pp. 302-4). That leaves a total of 4,495 for private enterprises. The Senate decree of December 30, 1755, required them to remain at the iron- and copperworks forever. If we add to them the 1,221 males whom Demidov received under decrees of 1736 and 1746, the total would be 5,716.

104. Ibid., pp. 325, 358.

105. Orlov, "Chelobitnye," pp. 135-52.

106. The point of the work far above statutory wage was made by the *ascripti* (929 souls) of the Sylvinskii and Atkinskii ironworks given by the government to Iaguzhinskii. The complaint about the travel expenses was made by the *ascripti* (8,433 souls) of the Votkinsk and Izhevsk ironworks given to Shuvalov. The travel distance for the latter was up to 300 versts.

107. In this particular case, as in many others, the village commune corrected the inequities involved in the poll tax by dividing up the difference between the census and the actual number of taxpayers according to ability to pay. "Ability to pay" was determined by the actual income of the peasant households. Work obligations in the ironworks were assigned accordingly. It was this sensible arrangement which the ironworks administration disregarded by treating the men as workers subject to management decisions rather than as peasants subject to the decisions of the village commune (Orlov, "Chelobitnye," p. 142).

108. A. A. Aleksandrov, *Izhevskii zavod*, pp. 22-23.

109. Artamenkov, "Naëmnye rabochie," pp. 138, 140, 142. Artamenkov noted that, in his sample of 14,331 hired workers, 60 percent were hired out by the serf-owners and 40 percent had hired themselves out.

110. Ibid., pp. 140-41.

111. The savings in the cost of transporting 40,533 tons of ore were 56,651 rubles: 157,891 rubles were paid to hired labor, vs. an estimated cost of 214,542 rubles had owned serfs been used (Karpenko, *Gornaia promyshlennost'*, p. 80).

112. Artamenkov, "Sotsial'nyi sostav," pp. 154-76.

113. Over one-third of all the hired workers for the Moscow manufactories were recruited from Moscow county (*uezd*), and there was a high correlation between proximity to Moscow and the share in the total of hired workers (ibid., pp. 160-61).

114. There is ample documentary evidence not only for the hiring out of serfs by their owners to industrial enterprises, but for the existence of long-term arrangements between major industrialists, often foreigners, and some major serf-owners in the Moscow region for the supply of manpower for hire to the manufactories (ibid., pp. 116-17).

115. Ibid., pp. 167-68.

116. See the decrees of January 7, 1736 (PSZ 9: 707-12, no. 6858); 1744 (PSZ 12: 181-83, no. 9004), and 1753 (PSZ 13: 828-29, no. 10,095).

117. PSZ 15: 956-57, no. 11,485

118. Artamenkov, "Sotsial'nyi sostav," p. 167.

119. Pavlenko, " 'Nakaz shikhtmasteru'."

120. PSZ 5: 78, 86, nos. 2762, 2778.

121. Kizewetter, "Shkol'nye voprosy," p. 91.

122. The estimates are derived by assuming that only 10 percent of those attending the church schools were enrolled in the seminaries, while 90 percent were receiving an elementary education. The 9,000 students estimated above as having been in elementary educational institutions may be an overestimate. Actual attendance greatly depended on the curriculum in the private boarding schools, for which information was not available.

123. This practice even became institutionalized in the armed forces, where foreign officers of the same rank were paid double the salary of Russians. The sources do not make clear, in the case of the armed forces, whether the *pomest'e* of the Russian nobleman-officer was a contributing factor to his income and thus the foreigner who had no *pomest'e* had to be compensated for that lack, or whether it was simply an incentive bonus. It is also not clear whether the salary differential was carried over from manufacturing to the armed forces, or vice versa. It is also possible that such matters had something to do with the relation of the salary level abroad to the salary level in Russia and calculations of what would make it worthwhile for foreigners to come to Russia for shorter or longer periods of time.

124. PSZ 6: 525-637, no. 3937.

125. PSZ 15: 188-89, no. 10,823.

126. Pavlenko, " 'Nakaz shikhtmasteru'," p. 221.

127. Ibid., p. 229.

128. PSZ 24, 883, no. 17,996.

129. On the frequency of idleness at ironworks, see Kafengauz (*Istoriia khoziaistva Demidovykh*, pp. 196-99). On the attitude of the industrialists, see Pavlenko (" 'Nakaz shikhtmasteru'," pp. 220-21, 229).

130. *Arkhiv istorii truda v Rossii* 5 (1923): 97.

131. Ibid.

132. Ibid., p. 98.

133. PSZ 6: 525-637, no. 3937.

134. V. I. Semevskii, *Krest'iane*, 2: 368-73.

135. PSZ 9: 707-12, nos. 6858 ("Ob otsylke s fabrik masterovykh liudei za durnoe povedenie v dal'nye goroda") and 16: 214-19, no. 11,790.

136. PSZ 21: 22-23, no. 15,115.

137. PSZ 17: 10, no. 12,311.

138. Miliukov's contention that only 22 of the 300 manufactories set up during Peter's reign survived until 1780 is inaccurate, for only about 200 were created, including sawmills, brick factories, and other works. It is also misleading, if one takes into account the high rate of enterprise ownership turnover. The history of mercantile and industrial enterprises of both Russia and other countries bears witness to this process of turnover.

139. PSZ 7: 862-63, no. 5162.

140. PSZ 7: 743-44, no. 5016.

141. PSZ 8: 976-77, no. 6262.

142. Polianskii, "Promyshlennaia politika," p. 98.

143. PSZ 10: 726-28, no. 7756.

144. PSZ 10: 734-39, no. 7766.

145. Polianskii, "Promyshlennaia politika," p. 108.

146. PSZ 8: 507-12, no. 5794.

147. Polianskii, "Promyshlennaia politika," p. 105.

148. Pavlenko, " 'Nakaz shikhtmasteru'."

149. Ibid., p. 106.

150. Kahan, "A Proposed Mercantilist Code."

151. PSZ 11: 79-80, no. 8064.

152. Polianskii, "Promyshlennaia politika," p. 104.

153. PSZ 11: 233-34, no. 8222.

154. Akademiia nauk SSSR. Istoriko-arkhivnyi institut, *Moskovskii sukonnyi dvor,* p. 72.

Chapter Four

1. Abel, *Massenarmut.*

2. Storch, *Historisch-statistisches Gemälde,* 8: 349.

3. For the analysis of price changes in Western Europe, the yearly price series in Sir William Beveridge's *Prices and Wages in England* were used (pp. 674-80). For Russian exports, the data from the port of St. Petersburg and the import data for Great Britain by the Inspector General of Customs (P.R.O., London, BT6/231) were used.

4. Chulkov, *Istoricheskoe opisanie,* 7, bk. 1, table 3.

5. Storch, *Historisch-statistisches Gemälde,* 8: 152.

6. Some lists of exports compiled by the St. Petersburg Customs Office distinguished between private and government sales. The lists record government sales of 44,230 poods in 1776 and 38,239 poods (for 30,591 rubles) in 1777 (P.R.O., London, BT6/231).

7. See the documents on the British-Russian trade negotiations of 1786, especially Fitz-Herbert's memorandum (P.R.O., London, BT 6/232, pp. 242-43).

8. The comparison of the three series also enables us to suggest corrections in the Strumilin series, for what might be errors made in copying old primary sources. With all due respect to that venerable scholar, I would suggest that his data for 1765 and 1772 contain errors of a large magnitude, for the other two independent sources are very much in agreement on the volume of exports from St. Petersburg for the respective years. See table 4.31 on iron exports.

9. P.R.O., London, Cook and Heat Papers.

10. The results of the attempt to use import data for all of Russia during the years 1793-95 have supported my hypothesis (Kahan, "Costs of Westernization," pp. 40-66).

11. Ibid.

12. Schmoller, "Die Russische Kompagnie," 20, nos. 1-2; idem, *Umrisse,* pp. 457-529; Ostroukhov, *Dogovor 1734 g.,* pp. 170-81.

13. For a classic example of "scholarly" ignorance, see Iakovtsevskii, *Kupecheskii kapital.*

14. See *Tables of Ships and Cargoes Frozen in at Cronstadt in 1780, 1786, 1787* (P.R.O., London, BT 6/231).

15. An excellent insight into the operations of this group of English traders can be found in the papers of William Heath and Alexander Cook for the period 1742-57 (P.R.O., London, C104, 141 FJ370).

16. P.R.O., London, FJ370.

17. Letter of Edward Fowell, March 5, 1743 (P.R.O., London, FJ370).

18. Ibid.

19. See P.R.O., London, BT 6/231, no. 35, for 1764-83. Tooke's price series can be found in his *Thoughts and Details* (Appendix to pt. 4: 18-19).

20. P.R.O., London, BT 6/231.

21. Tooke, *Thoughts and Details,* Appendix, p. 23.

22. Schumpeter, *English Overseas Trade Statistics,* "Introduction."

23. Kirchner, "Franco-Russian Economic Relations."

24. *Arkhiv gosudarstvennogo soveta* 2 (1888): 67-68.

25. Our knowledge about the eighteenth century trade between Russia and the old Hansa town of Lübeck has been greatly enriched by the labors of Elisabeth Harder-Gersdorf, who tried to reconstruct the pattern of those trade relationships in her publications ("Seehandel" and "Handelskonjunkturen").

26. One source for the 1738-54 period of the Orenburg trade as portrayed in duty-collection data is the work by the governor of Orenburg, Petr Ivanovich Rychkov (*Topografiia orenburgskoi gubernii*), published in F. N. Mil'kov, *Orenburgskie stepi,* p. 104.

27. Apollova, *Ekonomicheskie sviazi Kazakhstana,* pp. 289, 313-14.

28. Foust, *Muscovite and Mandarin.*

29. Kahan, "Observations on Petrine Foreign Trade," pp. 235-36.

30. "Kniga tarifov," PSZ 45: 2-122.

31. For details, see the section on the iron industry. Hegel said that when a tragic event is repeated in history, the second event is usually not a tragedy but a farce. Such was the case of the daughter who heedlessly tried to ape her great father.

32. Lodyzhenskii, *Istoriia tarifa,* pp. 90-92.

33. Volkov, "Tamozhennaia reforma," p. 136, n. 11.

34. The data on customs revenues are those reported by Storch (*Supplementband,* pp. 3-4).

35. Balance du Commerce de St. Petersbourg. Archives d'Affaires Etrangères Russie, 22.

36. P.R.O., London, BT 6/332.

37. On the trade of Riga in the seventeenth century, see Dunsdorfs, "Der Aussenhandel Rigas"; idem, *Latvijas Vesture;* Soom, *Der baltische Getreidehandel.*

38. Radishchev, "Primechaniia," in *Sochineniia,* p. 89.

39. It will be possible within the next few years to continue this series for the remaining years of the eighteenth century thanks to the effort of Professor Hans Christian Johansen of the University of Odense, who is in charge of a monumental project of tabulating and publishing the totality of the Sound toll data for those years.

40. Ogorodnikov, *Ocherki istorii goroda Arkhangel'ska,* p. 179, n. 32, which refers to the Arkhangel'sk *guberniia* chancellery file no. 1304/1347.

41. Ibid., p. 232.

42. Ibid., p. 243, n. 31.

43. Kozintseva, "Vneshnetorgovyi oborot," pp. 128-30, 135-38.

44. Akademiia nauk SSSR. Institut narodov Azii, *Russko-indiiskie otnosheniia v XVIII v.,* p. 238.

45. Ibid., pp. 263-64.

46. Ibid., pp. 236-47.

47. Kukanova, *Ocherki po istorii russko-iranskikh torgovykh otnoshenii;* Markova, *Rossiia, Zakavkaz'e i mezhdunarodnye otnosheniia.*

48. Agaian, *Rol' Rossii,* p. 133.

49. See Hellie, *Slavery,* chapter 12, for a discussion of the problem of Russian identity in Muscovy.

50. Examples of such preoccupation are the following writings by distinguished Soviet historians: Rubinshtein, "Vneshniaia torgovlia Rossii," and Mironov, "K voprosu o roli russkogo kupechestva."

Chapter Five

1. Bakmeister, *Topograficheskie izvestiia;* Chulkov, "Slovar' uchrezhdennykh iarmarok"; Shchekatov, *Geograficheskii slovar'.*

2. Mironov, *Vnutrennyi rynok.*

3. Among available sources, the earliest one, by Bakmeister, is based upon surveys conducted by the Imperial Academy of Sciences and by the Cadet Corps during the years 1760-67.

4. Mironov, *Vnutrennii rynok,* pp. 62, 161-63.

5. Ibid., p. 160.

6. PSZ 8: 65, no. 5306.

7. PSZ 13: 47-50, no. 9609.

8. Mironov, *Vnutrennii rynok,* pp. 190, 192.

9. Prokhorov, "Vedomosti," p. 73.

10. This view was suggested both by S. G. Strumilin (*Ocherki ekonomicheskoi istorii Rossii*) and N. L. Rubinshtein, in an article which has a number of shortcomings ("Russkaia iarmarka XVIII veka").

11. The study is the otherwise innovative work by I. D. Koval'chenko and L. V. Milov, *Vserossiiskii agrarnyi rynok.*

12. PSZ 7: 141-42, no. 4336.

13. PSZ 3: 989, no. 1718.

14. PSZ 11: 646-48, no. 8608.

15. PSZ 13: 200-202, no. 9715.

16. Klokman, *Ocherki istorii gorodov*, pp. 144-47.

17. Indova, "Rol' dvortsovoi derevni," pp. 191-93.

18. The transformation of status by settlements in northwestern Russia was well documented by Klokman (*Ocherki istorii gorodov*, pp. 120-85). See also Indova, "Rol' dvortsovoi derevni," pp. 193-94.

19. Volkov, "Materialy pervoi revizii," pp. 276-77, 282.

20. Vartanov, "Moskovskoe kupechestvo," p. 282.

21. Ibid., p. 281.

22. See the data for the Gostinaia sotnia in Moscow in *Materialy po istorii moskovskogo kupechestva* (1886).

23. For data on the serfs owned by merchants, see ibid. (1884-88).

Chapter Six

1. Eckhard, *Livland*, pp. 263-5.

2. Meleshko, *Ocherki agrarnoi istorii*, p. 206.

3. PSZ 15: 954-56, no. 11,484.

4. PSZ 16: 125-26, no. 11,719.

5. PSZ 21: 306-8, no. 15,279.

6. Golikova, *Naëmnyi trud*, pp. 23-24.

7. Rodin, *Burlachestvo*, pp. 93-95, 152-54.

8. Ibid., pp. 93-95, 152-54.

9. Ibid., pp. 91-92.

10. Ibid., pp. 80, 82.

11. Ministerstvo finansov, *Obzor meropriiatii*, p. 82.

12. Ibid., p. 68.

13. Ibid., pp. 69-70.

14. PSZ 28: 296-301, no. 21,283 (Report of the Shipbuilding Committee of the Admiralty).

15. Ministerstvo finansov, *Obzor meropriiatii*, pp. 131-33.

16. The use of modern computer techniques enabled Dr. Knoppers to analyze the voluminous archival documents on the "Galjootsgeld," the levy on cargoes entering Amsterdam compiled by the Board of Directors for Muscovite Trade (*Directie van dem Moscovische Handel*) and by the Board of Directors for Baltic Trade and Shipping (*Directie van den Oostersdie Handel en Reederijen*), preserved in the Gemeente Archief, Amsterdam. Dr. Knoppers' dissertation undertook a herculean task, performed it brilliantly, and is essential reading for economic historians interested in both Russian and Dutch trade. He proved that unpublished data are still available in various archival collections and that imaginative interpretation and analysis of available data can provide new insights into the past.

17. Storch, *Supplementband*, pp. 29-31.

18. It is a copy of a report of the Commerce College of December 23, 1774 (Chulkov, *Istoricheskoe opisanie*, vol. 4, bk. 5: 627-33).

19. "Navigation between Great Britain and Russia" (P.R.O., London, BT 6/231, no. 30).

20. Ibid., no. 191.

21. Storch, *Historisch-statistisches Gemälde*, 6: 137-38.

22. Mironov, "K voprosu o roli kupechestva."

Chapter Seven

1. PSZ 9: 6-7, no. 6300.

2. Borovoi, *Kredit i banki Rossii*, pp. 36-37.

3. PSZ 19: 85, no. 13,481.

4. Filimonov, "Kreditnye uchrezhdeniia," p. 269.

5. Borovoi, *Kredit i banki Rossii*, p. 70.

Chapter Eight

1. These are mentioned in Troitskii, *Finansovaia politika* and the data on the tax arrears (*nedoimki*) are available there and in Chechulin, *Ocherki po istorii finansov*.

2. The series can be found in Troitskii, *Finansovaia politika*, and in other sources, such as the nineteenth-century journal *Prodazha pitei*.

3. PSZ 15: 868, no. 12,603.

4. A decree of September 17, 1781, "Ustav o vine" (PSZ 21: 248-71, no. 15,231).

5. Svirshchevskii, "Materialy po istorii oblozheniia soli," p. 210.

6. In this discussion the information supplied by A. Svirshchevskii serves as the source. Unfortunately, I could not obtain a copy of the original document or locate any other sources.

7. PSZ 16: 12, no. 11,597.

8. PSZ 20: 126, no. 14,303.

9. For the text of the 1781 Salt Code and its role in the revision of governmental policy, see LeDonne, "Indirect Taxes," pp. 161-90.

10. PSZ 6: 503-10, no. 3901 of February 5, 1722.

11. Anisimov, "Materialy kommissii Golitsyna," pp. 338-52.

12. Ibid., p. 352.

13. Miliukov, *Gosudarstvennoe khoziaistvo*, p. 480; *SbRIO* 40 (1884): 439-49.

14. Bulygin, *Monastyrskie krest'iane*.

15. Mironov, "Dvizhenie tsen rzhi," pp. 156-63.

16. The best recent work on the eighteenth-century Russian bureaucracy is the one by S. M. Troitskii, *Russkii absoliutizm*.

17. *Arkhiv Gosudarstvennogo soveta* 1 (1869): 471-72.

18. Ibid., p. 470.

19. Strumilin, *Ocherki*, p. 273.

Chapter Nine

1. Demidova, "Biurokratizatsiia gosudarstvennogo apparata," p. 216. For additional information on the Muscovite government, see Peter B. Brown's two-volume University of Chicago doctoral dissertation, "Early Modern Russian Bureaucracy: The Evolution of the Chancellery System from Ivan III to Peter the Great, 1478-1717" (1978).

2. Demidova, "Biurokratizatsiia," p. 207.

3. Got'e, *Istoriia oblastnogo upravleniia*, p. 174.

4. On the proposals by Prince Iakov Petrovich Shakovskoi for administrative reform, see his *Zapiski* and Got'e, *Istoriia*.

5. Troitskii, *Russkii absoliutizm*. Troitskii focused his attention primarily on the role of the nobility in the governmental administration. Detailed study of the lower-level administrative positions of the clerical employees in the chancelleries, occupied mostly by non-nobles, was of marginal interest to him and provided only examples of upward social mobility on the occasions when promotions to the higher levels and into the nobility took place.

6. PSZ 44, pt. 2: 71. The 1763 figure of 6,740 was derived by subtracting the 8,986 members of the military detachments and the 778 employees of the department of police from the total of 16,504 employed.

7. Klochkov, *Ocherki pravitel'stvennoi deiatel'nosti*.

8. The sum of 2,150,000 rubles for 1725 (see Troitskii, *Finansovaia politika*, p. 243) clearly included more than the salaries of officials. It may have included the cost to the government of operating a number of its monopolies and other expenses.

9. Ibid., p. 277.

10. Got'e, *Istoriia oblastnogo upravleniia*, pp. 172-74.

11. *Kniga shtatov* (PSZ 44, pt. 2).

12. Troitskii, *Finansovaia politika*, p. 243.

13. For 1785 and 1796, see PSZ 44, pt. 2: 260-63. Got'e estimated the figure of 6,979,000 rubles for 1796 (*Istoriia oblastnogo upravleniia*, p. 174). Klochkov used data that suggested 1796 expenditures of 6,027,000 rubles (*Ocherki pravitel'stvennoi deiatel'nosti*).

14. Klochkov, *Ocherki pravitel'stvennoi deiatel'nosti*. If we divide his salary estimate of 6,027,000 rubles by the estimated number of officials and clerical employees, the average salary amounts to approximately 256.90 rubles per person.

15. Ibid.

16. Kapustin, "Sto let nazad," pp. 102-13.

17. For unexplained reasons, Soviet historians have been shy about studying and publishing the history of the eighteenth-century secret police. The only work published by a Soviet historian, N. B. Golikova's volume *Politicheskie protsessy pri Petre I* on the *Preobrazhenskii prikaz*, is clearly incomplete and based upon a narrow selection of the surviving documents. A student of Russian history would be well advised to read instead N. I. Novombergskii's compilation of primary sources, *Slovo i delo gosudarevy*.

18. Novombergskii, *Slovo i delo gosudarevy*, vol. 2.

19. The memoirs of E. S. Vinskii described vividly some of the problems of a nobleman's encounter with the procedures of the secret police (*Moe vremia*, pp. 75-98).

BIBLIOGRAPHY

Archives

French National Archives. Archives d'Affaires Etran-
gères. Russie, 22. Balance du Commerce de St.
Petersbourg.
London. Public Record Office. BT 6/231.
Stockholm. Kommerskollegii Arkiv DC 3. Utrike-
shandeln (Serie 3. 1739–1799).

Books and Articles

Abel, Wilhelm. *Massenarmut und Hungerkriesen im
Vorindustriellen Europa (Versuch einer Synopsis)*.
Hamburg and Berlin: Paul Parey, 1974.
Agaian, Ts. P. *Rol' Rossii v istoricheskikh sud'bakh
armianskogo naroda*. Moscow: Nauka, 1978.
Akademiia nauk Kazakhskoi SSR. *Kazakhsko-russkie
otnosheniia v XVI–XVIII vekakh. Sbornik dokumentov i
materialov*. Compiled by F. N. Kireev et al. Alma-
Ata: AN KSSR, 1961.
———. *Kazakhsko-russkie otnosheniia v XVIII–XIX
vekakh (1771–1867 gody). Sbornik dokumentov i materi-
alov*. Compiled by F. N. Kireev et al. Alma-Ata:
Nauka, 1964.
Akademiia nauk SSSR. *Ocherki istorii Leningrada*. Ed-
ited by M. P. Viatkin et al. 4 vols. Moscow and
Leningrad: AN SSSR, 1955.
———. *Problemy istochnikovedeniia*. 11 vols. Moscow:
AN SSSR, 1933–63.
———. Institut ekonomiki. *Voprosy istorii narodnogo
khoziaistva SSSR*. Edited by I. V. Maevskii and F. Ia.
Polianskii. Moscow: AN SSSR, 1957.
———. Institut istorii. *Istoricheskii arkhiv*. 10 vols.
Moscow: AN SSSR, 1936–54.
———. *Istoriia Moskvy*. Edited by S. V. Bakhrushin et
al. 6 vols. Moscow: AN SSSR, 1952–59.
———. *K voprosu o pervonachal'nom nakoplenii v Rossii
(XVII–XVIII vv.). Sbornik statei*. Edited by L. G.
Beskrovnyi, E. I. Zaozerskaia, and A. A. Preo-
brazhenskii. Moscow: AN SSSR, 1958.
———. Institut narodov Azii. *Russko-indiiskie otno-
sheniia v XVIII v. Sbornik dokumentov*. Edited by K.

A. Antonova and N. M. Gol'dberg. Moscow:
Nauka, 1965.
———. Istoriko-arkhivnyi institut. *Moskovskii sukonnyi dvor*. Leningrad: AN SSSR, 1934. [volume 13 of
its *Trudy*, part 5 of the series *Krepostnaia manufaktura
v Rossii*.]
Aleferenko, Pelageia Kuz'minichna. *Krest'ianskoe
dvizhenie i krest'ianskii vopros v Rossii v 30–50kh
godakh XVIII veka*. Moscow: AN SSSR, 1958.
Aleksandrov, A. A. *Izhevskii zavod*. Izhevsk: Udmurt-
skoe knizhnoe izd-vo, 1957.
Aleksandrov, V. A. "Sel'skaia obshchina i votchina v
Rossii (XVII–nachalo XIX v.)." *Istoricheskie zapiski* 89
(1972): 231–94.
———. *Sel'skaia obshchina v Rossii (XVII–nachalo XIX
vv.)*. Moscow: Nauka, 1976.
Alexander, John T. *Bubonic Plague in Early Modern
Russia: Public Health and Urban Disaster*. Baltimore:
Johns Hopkins University Press, 1980.
Andreev, A. I., editor. *Petr Velikii: Sbornik statei*.
Moscow: AN SSSR, 1947.
Anisimov, E. V. "Materialy komissii D. M. Golitsyna
o podati (1717–1730 gg.)." *Istoricheskie zapiski* 91
(1973): 338–52.
———. *Podatnaia reforma Petra I. Vvedenie podushnoi
podati v Rossii 1719–1728 gg*. Leningrad: Nauka,
1982.
Apollova, N. G. *Ekonomicheskie i politicheskie sviazi
Kazakhstana s Rossiei v XVIII–nachale XIX v*. Moscow:
AN SSSR, 1960.
Arkhiv gosudarstvennogo soveta. 5 vols. St. Petersburg:
E. I. V. Kantseliariia, 1869–1904.
Arkhiv istorii truda v Rossii. 10 vols. Petrograd:
Uchenaia komissiia po issledovaniiu istorii truda v
Rossii, 1921–23.
Arndt, C. G. *Ihro Kaiserlichen Majestät Catharina der
Zweiten. Verordnungen zur Verwaltung der Gover-
ments des Russischen Reichs*. St. Petersburg, 1776.
Artamenkov, M. N. "Naëmnye rabochie moskov-
skikh manufaktur v 40–70kh godakh XVIII v."
Istoriia SSSR. 1964, no. 2: 133–43.

———. "Sotsial'nyi sostav naemnykh rabochikh moskovskikh manufaktur v seredine XVIII v." *Uchenye zapiski Leningradskogo gos. pedagogicheskogo instituta im. Gertsena* 278 (1965): 151-76.

Baburin, Dm. *Ocherki po istorii Manufaktur-kollegii.* Moscow: Istoriko-arkhivnyi institut, 1939.

Bakmeister, L. I. *Topograficheskie izvestiia sluzhashchie dlia polnogo opisaniia rossiiskoi imperii.* 4 parts. St. Petersburg: Akademiia nauk, 1771-74.

Bakulev, G. D. and Solomentsev, D. *Promyshlennost' tul'skogo ekonomicheskogo raiona.* Tula: Tul'skoe knizhnoe izd-vo, 1960.

Balagurov, Ia. A. *Formirovanie rabochikh kadrov olonetskikh petrovskikh zavodov (Pervaia polovina XVIII veka).* Petrozavodsk: Gosizdat K-F SSR, 1955.

Bang, N. E. and Korst, K., editors. *Tabeller over skibsfort of varentransport gennen fresund 1661–1783, og gennem Storebalt 1701–1748.* 2 vols. in 4. Copenhagen: Gylendalske boghandel, Nordisk forlag, 1930–53.

Becker, Gary S. *Human Capital.* 2d edition. New York: Columbia University Press, for the National Bureau of Economic Research, 1975.

———. *A Treatise on the Family.* Cambridge: Harvard University Press, 1981.

Beliavskii, M. T. "Shkola i sistema obrazovaniia v Rossii v kontse 18 v." *Vestnik Moskovskogo universiteta. Istoriko-filologicheskaia seriia.* 1959, no. 2: 110-19.

Bernadskii, V. N. "Krepostnicheskoe i kapitalisticheskoe predprinimatel'stvo v tret'ei chetverti XVIII v." In *Voprosy genezisa kapitalizma v Rossii. Sbornik statei.* Edited by V. V. Mavrodin. Leningrad: LGU, 1960. Pp. 110-19.

Beskrovnyi, L. G. *Russkaia armiia i flot v XVIII veke: Ocherki.* Moscow: Voenizdat, 1958.

Boethius, B. and Heckscher, Eli F., eds. *Svensk Handelsstatistik 1637–1737 (Samtida bearbetningar, med understöd av statsmedal och anslag av vetenskapsakademien utgivna av Stockholms Stadsarkiv).* Stockholm: Bokfördags aktiebolaget Thule, 1938.

Borovoi, S. A. *Kredit i banki Rossii: seredina XVII v. – 1861 g.* Moscow: Gosfinizdat, 1958.

Brzheskii, Nikolai. *Gosudarstvennye dolgi Rossii.* St. Petersburg: Tipo-litografiia A. M. Vol'fa, 1884.

Beveridge, Sir William. *Prices and Wages in England from the Twelfth to the Nineteenth Century.* London: Longmans, Green, 1939.

Bulygin, I. A. *Monastyrskie krest'iane v pervoi chetverti XVIII veka.* Moscow: Nauka, 1977.

———. *Polozhenie krest'ian i torvarnoe proizvodstvo v Rossii. Vtoraia polovina XVIII veka. (Po materialam Penzenskoi gubernii.)* Moscow: Nauka, 1966.

Chechulin, N. D. *Ocherki po istorii russkikh finansov v tsarstvovanie Ekateriny II.* St. Petersburg: Senatskaia tipografiia, 1906.

Chulkov, Mikhail D. *Istoricheskoe opisanie rossiiskoi kommertsii pri vsekh portakh i granitsakh ot drevnikh vremen do nyne nastoiashchego i vsekh preimushchestvennykh uzakonenii po inoi gosudaria imperatora Petra Velikago i nyne blagopoluchnoi tsarstvuiushchei gosudaryni imperatritsy Ekateriny Velikoi.* 7 volumes in 21 books. St. Petersburg: Imp. Akademiia Nauk, 1781–88.

———. "Slovar' uchrezhdennykh v Rossii iarmarok i torgov." In *Novyi i polnyi geograficheskii slovar' Rossiiskogo gosudarstva.* Moscow: Tip. Ponamareva, 1788. Part 4.

Danilevskii, V. V. *Russkoe zoloto. Istoriia otkrytiia i dobychi do serediny XIX veka.* Moscow: Gos. nauchno-tekhnich. izd-vo, 1959.

Demidova, N. F. "Biurokratizatsiia gosudarstvennogo apparata absoliutizma v 17–18 vv." In *Absoliutizm v Rossii (XVII–XVIII vv.). Sbornik statei k semidesiatiletiiu so dnia rozhdeniia i sorokapiatiletiiu nauchnoi i pedagogicheskoi deiatel'nosti B. B. Kafengauza.* Moscow: Nauka, 1964. Pp. 206-42.

Doklady i prigorovy sostoiavshchiesia v pravitel'stvuiushchem Senate v tsarstvovanii Petra Velikogo. Edited by N. V. Kachalov. 6 vols. in 5 books. St. Petersburg: Akademiia nauk, 1880–1901.

Dunsdorfs, Edgar. "Der Aussenhandel Rigas im 17. Jarhhundert." In *Baltijas vesturnieku konference. 1st. Riga 1937.* Riga: Latvijas vestures instituta izdevums, 1938. Pp. 457-86.

———. *Latvijas Vesture, 1600–1710.* Uppsala: Daugava, 1962.

Eckard, Julius W. A. von. *Livland in Achtzehnten Jahrhundert.* Leipzig: Brochhaus, 1876.

Fal'k, I. P. [Falck, Johan Peter]. *Zapiski puteshestviia akademika Fal'ka.* [volumes 6 and 7 of *Polnoe sobranie uchenykh puteshestvii po Rossii, izdavaemoe imp. Akademieiu nauk, po predlozheniiu eë prezidenta: S primechaniiami, iz'iasneniiami i dopolneniiami.* St. Petersburg: Akademiia nauk, 1818–25.]

Fedorov, V. A. *Pomeshchich'i krest'iane tsentral'no-promyshlennogo raiona Rossii: kontsa XVII–pervoi poloviny XIX v.* Moscow: MGU, 1974.

———. "Zemlevladenie krepostnykh krest'ian v Rossii." *Vestnik Moskovskogo universiteta. Istoriia.* 1969, no. 1: 47-66.

Filimonov, D. "Kreditnye uchrezhdeniia moskovskogo vospitatel'nogo doma." *Russkii arkhiv.* 1876, no. 3: 265-76.

Firsov, N. "Otrkytie narodnykh uchilishch v permskoi gubernii." *Permskoi sbornik* 1 (Moscow, 1859).

Foust, Clifford M. *Muscovite and Mandarin: Russia's Trade with China and Its Setting, 1727–1805.* Chapel Hill: University of North Carolina Press, 1969.

Friebe, Wilhelm Christian. *Ueber Russlands Handel Landwirtschaftliche Kultur, Industrie und Produkte.* 3

vols. Gotha and St. Petersburg: Gerstenberg und Dittmar, 1796–98.

Gamrekeli, V. N. *Torgovye sviazi Vostochnoi Gruzii s Severnym Kavkazom v XVIII v.* Tbilisi: Metsniereba, 1968.

Gatsitskii, A. S. *Nizhegorodskii sbornik.* 10 vols. Nizhnii Novgorod: Tip. Nizhegorodskogo gubernskogo pravleniia, 1867–90.

Gennin, Vil'gel'm de- [Wilhelm de-Hennin]. *Opisanie ural'skikh i sibirskikh zavodov 1735.* Foreword by M. A. Pavlov. Moscow: Gosizdat, 1937.

Georgi, Johann Gottlieb. *Versuch einer Beschreibung der Russisch Kayserlichen Residenzstadt St. Petersburg und der Merkwurdigkeiten der Gegend.* St. Petersburg: C. W. Müller, 1790.

German, Karl Fedorovich. *See* K. F. Herman.

Golikova, N. B. *Naemnyi trud v gorodakh Povolzhiia v pervoi chetverti XVIII veka.* Moscow: MGU, 1965.

———. *Politicheskie protsessy pri Petre I.* Moscow: MGU, 1957.

Got'e, Iu. V. "Iz istorii peredvizheniia naseleniia v XVIII veke." *Chteniia OIDR* 224 (1908, book 1), section iv, pp. 1-26.

———. *Istoriia oblastnogo upravleniia v Rossii ot Petra I do Ekateriny II.* 2 vols. Moscow: Tipografiia G. Lissnera i D. Sobka and AN SSSR, 1913 and 1941.

Gritsenko, N. P. *Udel'nye krest'iane srednego Povol'zhiia.* Groznyi: Chicheno-Ingushskii gos. ped. institut, 1959. [*Uchenye zapiski* Chicheno-Ingushskogo gos. ped. instituta, no. 11.]

Gromyko, M. M. *Zapadnaia Sibir' v XVIII veke. Russkoe naselenie i zemledel'cheskoe osvoenie.* Novosibirsk: Nauka, 1965.

Harder, E. "Seehandel zwischen Lübeck und Russland im 17/18 Jahrhundert (zweiten Teil)." *Zeitschrift des Vereins für Lübeckische Geschichte und Altertumskunde.* 42 (1962): 5-54.

Harder-Gersdorf, E. "Handelskonjunkturen und Warenbilanzen im Lübeckisch-Russischen Seeverkehr des 18. Jahrhunderts." *Vierteljahrschrift für Sozial und Wirtschaftsgeschichte.* 57 (April 1970): 15-45.

Heckscher, Eli F. *Sveriges Ekonomiska Historia frän Gustav Vasa.* Stockholm: Albert Bonniers Förlag, 1935.

Hellie, Richard. *Enserfment and Military Change in Muscovy.* Chicago: University of Chicago Press, 1971.

———. *Slavery in Russia, 1450–1725.* Chicago: University of Chicago Press, 1982.

Herman, B. F. J. *Statistische Schilderung von Russland in rücksicht auf Bevölkerung, Landesbeschaffenheit, Naturprodukte, Landwirtschaft Bergbau Manufakturen und Handel.* St. Petersburg-Leipzig: C. Tornow, 1790.

———. "Sur L'exploitation des mines de l'Empire de Russie." In *Nova acta* (Academiae scientiarum imperialis Petropolitanae) 11 (1798): 418-33.

Herman, Karl Feodorovich (also German, Hermann). *Statisticheskie issledovaniia otnositel'no Rossiiskoi imperii.* St. Petersburg: Imp. Akademiia nauk, 1819.

———. "Tablitsy po vsem kazennym zavodam i monetnogo dvora pod vedomstvom glavnogo nachalnika ekaterinburgskogo gornogo nachal'stva, 1802 god." *Statisticheskii zhurnal.* St. Petersburg, 1806.

Hermann, Ch. Th. *Calcul Statistiques sur la Mortalité en Russie parmi la population male de religion Grecque depuis 1804 jusqu'au 1814.* St. Petersburg: Académie Imperiale des Sciences, 1832, 1834. [*Mémoires de l'Academie Impériale de Sciences de Sixième Série, Sciences Politiques, Histoire et Philologie, Sciences de Saint-Petersbourg,* vol. 1, pts. 1, 2; vol. 2.]

Iakovtsevskii, V. N. *Kupecheskii kapital v feodal'no-krepostnicheskoi Rossii.* Moscow: AN SSSR, 1953.

Iatsunskii, V. K. *Sotsial'no-ekonomicheskia istoriia Rossii XVIII–XIX vv. Izbrannye trudy.* Moscow: Nauka, 1973.

Indova, E. I. *Dvortsovoe khoziaistvo v Rossii. Pervaia polovina XVIII veka.* Moscow: Nauka, 1964.

———. "Instruktsii kniazia M. N. Shcherbatova prikazchikam ego iaroslavskikh votchin." In *Materialy po istorii sel'skogo khoziaistva i krest'ianstva SSSR* 6 (1965): 432-69.

———. "O rossiiskikh manufakturakh vtoroi poloviny XVIII veka." In *Istoricheskaia geografiia Rossii XII–nachalo XX v.* Edited by A. L. Narochnitskii et al. Moscow: Nauka, 1975. Pp. 248-345.

———. "Rol' dvortsovoi derevni v formirovanii kupechestva." *Istoricheskie zapiski.* 68 (1961): 189-210.

———. "Urozhai v tsentral'noi Rossii za 150 let (vtoraia polovina XVII–XVIII v.)." In *Ezhegodnik po agrarnoi istorii Vostochnoi Evropy za 1965.* Moscow: AN SSSR, 1970. Pp. 141-55.

Isaev, G. S. *Rol' tekstil'noi promyshlennosti v genezise i razvitii kapitalizma v Rossii 1760–1860 gg.* Leningrad: Nauka, 1970.

Istomina, E. G. *Vodnye puti Rossii vo vtoroi polovine XVIII–nachale XIX veka.* Moscow: Nauka, 1982.

Iukht, A. I. "Torgovye sviazi Astrakhani v 20-kh godakh XVIII v." In *Istoricheskaia geografiia Rossii XII–nachalo XX v.* Edited by A. L. Narochnitskii et al. Moscow: Nauka, 1975. Pp. 177-92.

"Iunosti chestnoe zertsalo." In *Khrestomatiia po istorii SSSR.* Moscow: Sotsekgiz, 1963. Pp. 215-16.

Johansen, H. Chr. *Sund Toll Accounts, 1784–89.* Copenhagen, 1975.

Kabuzan, V. M. *Izmeneniia v razmeshchenii naseleniia Rossii v XVIII–pervoi polovine XIX v. (Po materialam revizii.)* Moscow: Nauka, 1971.

382   Bibliography

———. "Krest'ianskaia kolonizatsiia severnogo Prichernomoria (Novorossii) v XVIII–pervoi polovine XIX vv. (1719–1857 gg.)." In *Ezhegodnik po agrarnoi istorii Vostochnoi Evropy za 1964 god*. Kishinev: Kartia Moldoveniaske, l966. Pp. 313-24.

———. *Narodonaselenie Rossii v XVIII–pervoi polovine XIX v. (po materialam revizii)*. Moscow: AN SSSR, 1963.

——— and Troitskii, S. M. "Dvizhenie naseleniia Sibiri v XVIII v." In *Sibir' XVII–XVIII vv*. Edited by T. M. Nazariants. Novosibirsk: AN SSSR, l962. Pp. 139-57. [vol. 1 in series *Sibir' perioda feodalizma*.]

———. "Izmeneniia v chislennosti, udel'nom vese i razmeshchenii dvorianstva v Rossii v 1782–1858 gg." *Istoriia SSSR*. 1971, no. 4: 153-68.

Kafengauz, B. B. *Istoriia khoziaistva Demidovykh v XVIII–XIX vv. Opyt issledovaniia po istorii ural'skoi metallurgii*. Moscow-Leningrad: AN SSSR, 1949.

———. *Ocherki vnutrennego rynka Rossii pervoi poloviny XVIII v. (Po materialam vnutrennikh tamozhen.)* Moscow: AN SSSR, 1958.

Kahan, Arcadius. "The Costs of Westernization in Russia: The Gentry in the Eighteenth Century." *Slavic Review* (March, 1966): 40-66.

———. "Natural Calamities and Their Effect upon the Food Supply in Russia." *Jahrbücher der Geschichte Osteuropas* 16 (1968): 353-77.

———. "Observations on Petrine Foreign Trade." *Canadian-American Slavic Studies* 8, no. 2 (Summer 1974): 222-36.

———. "A Proposed Mercantilist Code in the Russian Iron Industry, 1734–36." *Explorations in Entrepreneurial History*. 2d series. 2, no. 2 (1965): 75-89.

Kaluzhskii krai: dokumenty i materialy. Kaluga: Gosudarstvennyi arkhiv Kaluzhskoi oblasti, 1976.

Kapustin, M. *Sto let nazad. Shtaty i sluzhashchie permskoi gubernii*. Perm, 1897. [Permskaia gubernskaia uchenaia arkhivnaia komissiia. *Trudy*. Fasc. 3.

Karpenko, Z. G. *Gornaia i metallurgicheskaia promyshlennost' zapadnoi Sibiri v 1700–1860 gg*. Novosibirsk: AN SSSR, 1963.

Kaufman, I. I. *Serebianyi rubl' v Rossii, ot ego vozniknoveniia do kontsa XIX veka: opyt issledovaniia*. St. Petersburg: B. M. Vol'f, 1910.

Kent, H. S. K. *War and Trade in Northern Seas. Anglo-Scandinavian Economic Relations in the Mid-Eighteenth Century*. Cambridge: Cambridge University Press, 1973.

Kirchner, Walther. "Relations économiques entre la France et la Russie au XVIIIe siècle (I)." *Revue d'Histoire économique et sociale*. 39 (1961): 158-97.

Kirilov, I. *Tsvetushchee sostoianie vserossiiskogo gosudarstva v kakovoe nachal i privel i ostavil neizrechennymi trudami Petr Velikii. Sobrano trudami statskogo sovetnika G. Ivan Kirilova, iz podlineishikh senatskikh arkhivov v fevrale mesiatse 1727 goda*. Moscow: Universitetskaia tipografiia, 1831. [Republished: Moscow: Nauka, 1977.]

Kizewetter, A. A. "Shkol'nye voprosy nashego vremeni v dokumentakh XVIII st." In his *Istoricheskie ocherki*. Moscow: A. A. Levenson, 1912. Pp. 91-118.

Klochkov, M. V. *Ocherki pravitel'stvennoi deiatel'nosti vremeni Pavla I*. Petrograd: Senatskaia tipografiia, 1916.

Klokman, Iu. R. *Ocherki sotsial'no-ekonomicheskoi istorii gorodov severo-zapadnoi Rossii v seredine XVIII v*. Moscow: AN SSSR, 1960.

———. *Sotsial'no-ekonomicheskaia istoriia russkogo goroda. Vtoraia polovina XVIII veka*. Moscow: Nauka, 1967.

Knoppers, Jake V. T. "Dutch Trade with Russia from the Time of Peter I to Alexander I. A Quantitative Study in Eighteenth-Century Shipping." Montreal: McGill University doctoral dissertation, 1975.

Kolesnikov, P. A. *Severnaia Rus'*. 2 vols. Vologda: Vologodskii gos. ped. institut, 1973.

Kopanev, A. I. *Naselenie Peterburga v pervoi polovine XIX veka*. Moscow-Leningrad: AN SSSR, 1957.

Koval'chenko, I. D. and Milov, L. V. *Vserossiiskii agrarnyi rynok XVIII–nachala XIX veka. Opyt kolichestvennogo analiza*. Moscow: Nauka, 1974.

Kozintseva, R. I. "Vneshnetorgovyi oborot arkhangelogorodskoi iarmarki i eë rol' v razvitii vserossiiskogo rynka." In *Issledovaniia po istorii feodal'no-krepostnicheskoi Rossii*. Edited by S. N. Valk, K. N. Serbina, and A. L. Fraiman. Moscow-Leningrad: Nauka, 1964. Pp. 116-63.

———. "Uchastie kazny vo vneshnei torgovle Rossii v pervoi chetverti XVIII v." *Istoricheskie zapiski*. 91 (1973): 267-337.

Kozlovskii, P. G. *Magnatskoe khoziaistvo Belorussii vo vtoroi polovine XVIII v. (tsentral'naia i zapadnaia zony)*. Minsk: Nauka i tekhnika, 1974.

Krafft, W. L. *Mémoires sur les listes des marriages et des naissances et des morts à St. Petersbourg*. [*Nova Acta Academiae Imperiale Scientia*, 1798.]

Kukanova, N. G. *Ocherki po istorii russko-iranskikh torgovykh otnoshenii v XVII–pervoi polovine XIX veka: po materialam russkikh arkhivov*. Saransk: Mordovskoe knizhnoe izd-vo, 1977.

Kula, Witold. *Teoria ekonomiczna ustroju feudalnego: proba modelu*. Warsaw: Panstwowe wydawnictwo naukowe, 1962.

Lappo-Danilevskii, N. S. *Russkie promyshlennye i torgovye kompanii v pervoi polovine XVIII stoletiia*. St. Petersburg: V. S. Balashev, 1899.

LeDonne, John P. "Indirect Taxes in Catherine's Russia: The Salt Code of 1781." *Jahrbücher für Geschichte Osteuropas*. 23 (1975): 161-90.

Le Play, Pierre Guillaume Frédéric. *Les Ouvriers Européens*. 6 vols. Paris: Dentu, 1877–79

Levshin, Vasilii. "Topograficheskoe opisanie tul'skoi gubernii." *Istoricheskii arkhiv*. 1957, no. 1: 253-54.

Liubomirov, P. G. "Iz istorii lesopil'nogo proizvodstva v Rossii v XVII–XVIII i nachale XIX vv." *Istoricheskie zapiski* 10 (1941): 222-49.

Lodyzhenskii, K. N. *Istoriia russkogo tamozhennogo tarifa: Issledovanie*. St. Petersburg: Tip. V. S. Balasheva, 1886.

Luppov, S. P. *Istoriia stroitel'stva Peterburga v pervoi chetverti XVIII veka*. Moscow: AN SSSR, 1957.

Makarii, Arkhimandrit. "Materialy dlia geografii i statistiki Nizhegorodskoi gubernii." In Russkoe geograficheskoe obshchestvo. Statisticheskoe otdelenie. *Sbornik statisticheskikh svedenii* 3 (1858): 634-59.

Markova, O. P. *Rossiia, Zakavkaz'e, i mezhdunarodnye otnosheniia v XVIII veke*. Moscow: Nauka, 1966.

Marshall, J. *Digest of All the Accounts Relating to the Population, Productions, Revenues, Financial Operations, Manufactures, Shipping, Colonies, etc., of the United Kingdom of Great Britain and Ireland*. London: J. Haddon, 1833.

Materialy dlia istorii moskovskogo kupechestva. 9 vols. Moscow: Tipo-Litografiia I. N. Kushnereva, 1886–1909.

Materialy dlia istorii russkogo flota. Edited by S. Elagin, O. Veseloi, and S. Ogorodnikov. 17 vols. St. Petersburg: Tip. Morskogo ministerstva, 1865–1904.

"Materialy dlia statistiki Saratovskoi gubernii." *Statisticheskii zhurnal* 1, part 1 (1806): 96-157.

Meleshko, V. I. *Ocherki agrarnoi istorii Vostochnoi Belorussii: vtoraia polovina XVII–XVIII vv*. Minsk: Nauka i Tekhnika, 1975.

Meshalin, I. V., ed. *Tekstil'naia promyshlennost' Moskovskoi gubernii v XVIII i nachale XIX v*. Moscow-Leningrad: AN SSSR, 1950. [vol. 2 of *Materialy po istorii krest'ianskoi promyshlennosti*.]

Mikhaleva, G. A. *Torgovye i posol'skie sviazi Rossii so sredneaziatskimi khanstvami cherez Orenburg (vtoraia polovina XVIII–pervaia polovina XIX v.)*. Tashkent: Fan, 1982.

Miliukov, P. N. *Gosudarstvennoe khoziaistvo Rossii v pervoi chetverti XVIII stoletiia i reforma Petra Velikogo*. St. Petersburg: Tip. V. S. Balasheva, 1892. [2d ed., 1905.]

Milov, L. V. *Issledovanie ob "ekonomicheskikh primechaniiakh" k general'nomu mezhevaniiu. (K istorii russkogo krest'ianstva i sel'skogo khozaiastva vtoroi poloviny XVIII v.)*. Moscow: MGU, 1965.

Ministerstvo finansov. *Istoricheskii obzor pravitel'stvennykh meropriiatii dlia razvitiia russkogo torgovogo morekhodstva*. St. Petersburg: V. Kirshbaum, 1895.

Ministerstvo narodnogo prosveshcheniia. *Sbornik materialov dlia istorii prosveshcheniia v Rossii*. Volumes 1 and 4. St. Petersburg, 1893 and 1902.

Ministerstvo vnutrennikh del. *Tabeli k otchetu ministra vnutrennikh del za 1803 god*. St. Petersburg, 1804.

———. *Tabeli k otchetu ministra vnutrennykh del za 1804 god*. St. Petersburg, 1806.

Mironov, B. N. "Dvizhenie tsen rzhi v Rossii v XVIII v." In *Ezhegodnik po agrarnoi istorii Vostochnoi Evropy za 1965 god*. Moscow: Nauka, 1970. Pp. 156-63.

———. "Eksport russkogo khleba vo vtoroi polovine XVIII– nachale XIX v." *Istoricheskie zapiski* 93 (1979): 149-88.

———. "K voprosu o roli russkogo kupechestva vo vneshnei torgovle Peterburga i Arkhangel'ska vo vtoroi polovine XVIII–nachale XIX veka." *Istoriia SSSR* 1973, no. 6: 129-39.

———. *Vnutrennii rynok Rossii vo vtoroi polovine XVIII–pervoi polovine XIX v*. Leningrad: Nauka, 1981.

Nakaz komissii o sochinenii proekta novogo ulozheniia. Edited by Nikolai D. Chechulin. St. Petersburg: Akademiia nauk, 1907. [*Pamiatniki russkogo zakonodatel'stva 1649–1832 gg.*, vol. 2.]

Novombergskii, N. N. *Slovo i delo gosudarevy (Materialy)*. 2 vols. Tomsk, 1908–9.

Novosel'skii, S. A. "Smertnost' i prodolzhitel'nost' zhizni v Rossii." *Obshchestvennyi vrach* 1916, no. 3.

Ogorodnikov, S. F. *Ocherki istorii goroda Arkhangel'ska v torgovo-promyshlennom otnoshenii*. St. Petersburg: Tip. Morskogo ministerstva, 1890.

Oreshkova, S. F. *Russko-turetskie otnosheniia v nachale XVIII v*. Moscow: Nauka, 1971.

Orlov, A. S. "Chelobitnye ural'skogo gornozavodskogo naseleniia v komissii A. A. Viazemskogo (1763–64 gg.)." *Ural'skii arkheograficheskii ezhegodnik za 1971 god*. Sverdlovsk: Ural'skii gosud. universitet, 1974. Pp. 135-52.

Ostroukhov, P. A. *Anglo-russkii torgovyi dogovor 1734 g. Ocherk po istorii russkoi torgovoi politiki (na osnovanii arkhivnykh istochnikov)*. St. Petersburg: Izd-vo St. P. Politekhnicheskogo Instituta, 1914.

Pavlenko, N. I. *Istoriia metallurgii v Rossii XVIII veka. Zavody i zavodovladel'tsy*. Moscow: AN SSSR, 1962.

———. "'Nakaz shikhtmasteru' V. N. Tatishchevu." *Istoricheskii arkhiv* 6 (1951): 199-244.

———. *Razvitie metallurgicheskoi promyshlennosti Rossii v pervoi polovine XVIII veka. Promyshlennaia politika i upravlenie*. Moscow: AN SSSR, 1953.

———, editor. *Rossiia v period reform Petra I*. Moscow: Nauka, 1973.

Pazhitnov, K. A. *Ocherki istorii tekstil'noi promyshlennosti dorevoliutsionnoi Rossii. Khlopchatobumazhnaia, l'no-pen'kovaia i shelkovaia promyshlennost'*. Moscow: AN SSSR, 1958.

Pevzner, I. V. "Polozhenie rabotnykh liudei i klassovaia bor'ba na sukonnykh manufakturakh vo vtoroi polovine XVIII v." In *Promyshlennost' i torgovlia v Rossii XVII–XVIII vv. Sbornik statei.* Edited by I. A. Bulygin et al. Moscow: Nauka, 1983. Pp. 118-37.

———. "Sukonnaia promyshlennost' Rossii na rubezhe XVIII i XIX vv. i ekonomicheskaia politika pravitel'stva." *Istoricheskie zapiski* 102 (1978): 223-45.

Pisarevskii, Grigorii. *Iz istorii inostrannoi kolonizatsii v Rossii v XVIII v. (Po neizdannym arkhivnym dokumentam).* Moscow: Moskovskii arkheologicheskii institut, 1908. [*Zapiski moskovskogo arkheologicheskogo instituta,* vol. 5.]

Platonov, S. F. and Nikolaev, A. S. *Opisanie del arkhiva Ministerstva narodnogo prosveshcheniia.* Petrograd: Tipografiia K. N. Gubinskogo, 1917.

Pokrovskii, M. V. *Russko-adygeiskie torgovye sviazi.* Maikop: Adygeiskoe knizhnoe izd-vo, 1957.

Pokrovskii, N. N. *Antifeodal'nyi protest uralo-sibirskikh krest'ian-staroobriadtsev v XVIII v.* Novosibirsk: Nauka, 1974.

Pokrovskii, V. I., editor. *Sbornik svedenii po istorii i statistike vneshnei torgovli Rossii.* St. Petersburg: M. P. Frolov, 1902.

Polianskii, F. Ia. *Gorodskoe remeslo i manufaktura v Rossii XVIII v.* Moscow: MGU, 1960.

———. "Promyshlennaia politika russkogo absoliutizma vo vtoroi chetverti 18 v. (1725–1740 gg.)" In *Voprosy istorii narodnogo khoziaistva SSSR.* Moscow: AN SSSR, 1957. Pp. 85-137.

Polnoe sobranie zakonov Rossiiskoi imperii. 45 volumes. St. Petersburg: 2-e otd. E. I. V. Kantseliarii, 1830. Cited as PSZ.

Polonska-Vasilenko, N. *Zaporozhzhia XVIII stolittia ta ioho spadshchina.* 2 vols. Munich: Dniprova khvylia, 1965–67.

Ponomarev, A. M. "Torskii i Bakhmutskii solianye zavody v XVIII v." In *Promyshlennost' i torgovlia v Rossii XVII–XVIII vv.* Edited by I. A. Bulygin et al. Moscow: Nauka, 1983. Pp. 153-67.

Poschman, Anton von. *Opisanie Arkhangel'skoi gubernii 1802 g.* 2 volumes in 1. Arkhangel'sk: Gubernskaia tipografiia, 1873.

Price, Jacob M. *The Tobacco Adventure to Russia. Enterprise, Politics, and Diplomacy in the Quest for a Northern Market for English Colonial Tobacco, 1676–1722.* Philadelphia: American Philosophical Society, 1961. [*Transactions* of the APS, New Series—volume 51, part 1.]

Prokhorov, M. F. "'Vedomosti' k mezhevym atlasam kak istochnik po istorii promyshlennosti i torgovli v gorodakh Podmoskov'ia v seredine 80-kh godov XVIII v." In *Russkii gorod* 4 (1981): 66-75.

Pushkin, A. S. "Kapitanskaia dochka." *Polnoe sobranie sochinenii.* Leningrad: AN SSSR, 1948. 8: 277-384.

Rabinovich, M. D. "Sotsial'noe proiskhozhdenie i imushchestvennoe polozhenie ofitserov regularnoi russkoi armii v kontse Severnoi voiny." In *Rossiia v period reform Petra I.* Edited by N. I. Pavlenko. Moscow: AN SSSR, 1973. Pp. 133-71.

Radishchev, A. N. *Polnoe sobranie sochinenii.* 3 vols. Moscow-Leningrad: AN SSSR, 1938–41. Another edition, 1952.

Reden, F. W., von. *Das Kaiserreich Russland. Statistisch- geschichtliche Darstellung seiner kulturverhältnisse, namentlich in landwirtschaftlichen, gewerblicher und kommerzieller Beziehung.* Berlin: E. S. Mittler, 1843.

Rezorenova, N. V. "Beglye krest'iane v gorodakh srednego Povolzhiia v pervoi chetverti XVIII v." *Vestnik moskovskogo universiteta. Seriia istorii.* 1979, no. 4: 28-41.

Riazanskaia uchenaia arkhivnaia komissiia. *Trudy.* 5, nos. 1-2 (1890) and 14, no. 1 (1899).

Rodin, F. N. *Burlachestvo v Rossii: istoriko-sotsiologicheskii ocherk.* Moscow: Mysl', 1975.

Rozhdestvenskii, S. V. *Ocherki po istorii sistem narodnogo prosveshcheniia v Rossii v 18–19 vv.* St. Petersburg, 1912.

Rozman, Gilbert. *Urban Networks in Russia, 1750–1800, and Pre-Modern Periodization.* Princeton: Princeton University Press, 1976.

Rubinshtein, N. L. "Russkaia iarmarka XVIII veka." *Uchenye zapiski Moskovskogo pedagogicheskogo instituta* 1 (1939): 5-28.

———. *Sel'skoe khoziaistvo Rossii vo vtoroi polovine XVIII v. Istoriko-ekonomicheskii ocherk.* Moscow: Gospolitizdat, 1957.

———. "Vneshniaia torgovlia Rossii i russkoe kupechestvo vo vtoroi polovine XVIII v." *Istoricheskie zapiski* 54 (1955): 343-61.

Russkoe geograficheskoe obshchestvo. *Sbornik statisticheskikh svedenii.* St. Petersburg, 1858. Vol. 3.

Rychkov, P. I. "Topografiia orenburgskoi gubernii." In *Orenburgskie stepi v trudakh P. I. Rychkova, E. A. Eversmana, S. S. Neustroeva.* Edited by F. N. Mil'kov. Moscow: Geografgiz, 1949.

Ryndziunskii, P. G. *Gorodskoe grazhdanstvo doreformennoi Rossii.* Moscow: AN SSSR, 1958.

Sakharov, A. N. and Troitskii, S. M. *Zhyvye golosa istorii.* Moscow: "Molodaia gvardiia," 1971.

Sankt Peterburgskii eparkhial'nyi istoriko-staticheskii komitet. *Istoriko-staticheskie svedeniia S. Peterburgskoi eparkhii.* Edited by Paul, Bishop of Ladoga et al. 10 volumes. St. Petersburg: Pechatnia V. Golovina, 1869–85.

Sbornik imperatorskogo russkogo istoricheskogo obshchestva. 148 vols. St. Petersburg: A. Transhel', 1867–1916. Cited as SbRIO.

Schmoller, Gustav. "Die russische Kompagnie in Berlin, 1724–1738." *Zeitschrift für preussische Ges-*

chichte und Landeskunde 20, nos. 1-2 (1883). [Reprinted in *Umrisse und Untersuchungen zur Verfassungs-Verwal-tungs-und Wirtschaftsgeschichte besonders des preussichen Staates in 17 und 18 Jahrhundert.* Leipzig, 1898.]

Schumpeter, Elisabeth. *English Overseas Trade Statistics 1697–1808.* Oxford: Clarendon Press, 1960.

Scrivenor, Harry. *A Comprehensive History of the Iron Trade throughout the World.* London: Smith, Elder and Company, 1841.

Semenov, A. *Izuchenie istoricheskikh svedenii o rossiiskoi vneshnei torgovle i promyshlennosti s poloviny 17-go stoletiia po 1858 god.* St. Petersburg, 1859. Vol. 3.

Semenova, L. N. "Obuchenie masterovykh v Peterburge v pervoi treti XVIII v." In *Promyshlennost' i torgovlia v Rossii XVII–XVIII vv. Sbornik statei.* Edited by I. A. Bulygin et al. Moscow: Nauka, 1983. Pp. 82-100.

———. *Ocherki istorii byta i kul'turnoi zhizni Rossii. Pervaia polovina XVIII v.* Leningrad: Nauka, 1982.

———. *Rabochie Peterburga v pervoi polovine XVIII veka.* Leningrad: Nauka, 1974.

———. *Russko-valashskie otnosheniia v kontse XVII–nachale XVIII v.* Moscow: Nauka, 1969.

Semevskii, Mikhail, editor. "Istoricheskie i iuridicheskie akty XVII i XVIII stoletii." *Chteniia OIDR* 1869, book 4, part v: 1-88.

Semevskii, V. I. *Krest'iane v tsarstvovanie imperatritsy Ekateriny II.* 2 vols. St. Petersburg: Tip. M. M. Stasiulevich, 1881.

———. "Pozhalovanie naselennykh imenii pri Imperatore Pavle." *Russkaia mysl'* 1882, no. 12.

———. *Pozhalovanie naselennykh imenii v tsarstvovanii Ekateriny II: ocherk iz istorii chastnoi zemel'noi sobstvennosti v Rossii.* St. Petersburg: N. N. Kushenev, 1906.

Senat. *Senatskii arkhiv.* 15 vols. St. Petersburg: Senatskaia tipografiia, 1888–1913.

Shchekatov, Afanasii. *Geograficheskii slovar' rossiiskogo gosudarstva.* 7 vols. Moscow, 1801–1809.

Shchepetov, K. N. *Krepostnoe pravo v votchinakh Sheremet'evykh. (1708–1885).* Moscow: Izd-vo Dvortsa-Muzeia, 1947.

Sivkov, K. V., editor. *Materialy k istorii krest'ianskogo i pomeshchich'ego khoziaistva pervoi chetverti XVIII v.* Moscow: AN SSSR, 1951.

Snezhnevskii, V. I. "K istorii pobegov krepostnykh v poslednei chetverti XVIII i v XIX stoletiiakh." In *Nizhegorodskii sbornik.* Edited by A. S. Gatsitskii. 10 (1890): 517-95.

Soikelli, Kaarle. *Wiipurin Kaupungen Tuonti ja Vienti.* Wiipuri, 1917.

Solov'ev, S. M. *Istoriia Rossii s drevneishikh vremen.* Edited by L. V. Cherepnin. 29 volumes in 15 books. Moscow: Sotsekgiz, 1959–66.

Soom, Arnold. *Der baltische Getreidehandel im 17 Jahrhundert.* Stockholm: Almquist & Wicksell, 1961.

Sovetskaia voennaia entsiklopediia. Edited by A. A. Grechko et al. 8 volumes. Moscow: Voenizdat, 1976–80.

Spiridonova, E. V. *Ekonomicheskaia politika i ekonomicheskie vzgliady Petra I.* Moscow: Gosizdat, 1952.

Stashevskii, E. D. *Istoriia dokapitalisticheskoi renty na pravoberezhnoi Ukraine v XVIII–pervoi polovine XIX v.* Moscow: Nauka, 1968.

Stolpianskii, P. N. *Zhizn' i byt peterburgskoi fabriki za 210 let eë sushchestvovaniia (1704–1914).* Leningrad: Izd-vo Leningradskogo gubernskogo soveta professional'nykh soiuzov, 1925.

Storch, Heinrich Friedrich von. *Historisch-statistisches Gemälde des russischen Reichs am Ende des achtzehnten Jahrhunderts.* Riga: J. F. Hartknoch, 1805.

———. *Supplementband zum fünften, sechsten und siebenten Theil des historisch-statistischen Gemäldes des russischen Reichs.* Leipzig: J. F. Hartknoch, 1803.

Strumilin, S. G. *Istoriia chernoi metallurgii v SSSR.* Moscow: Nauka, 1967.

———. *Ocherki ekonomicheskoi istorii Rossii i SSSR.* Moscow: Nauka, 1966.

Svirshchevskii, A. R. "Materialy po istorii oblozheniia soli v Rossii." *Iuridicheskie zapiski* [of the Demidovskii Iuridicheskii Litsei in Iaroslavl'] 1 (1908).

Sweden. Statistika Centralbyran. *Historisk Statistik for Sverige.* Del. 3 Utrikeshandel 1732–1970. Stockholm: Statistika Centralbyran, 1972.

Syromiatnikov, B. I. *"Reguliarnoe" gosudarstvo Petra Pervogo i ego ideologiia.* Moscow-Leningrad: AN SSSR, 1943.

Tarasov, Iu. M. *Russkaia krest'ianskaia kolonizatsiia iuzhnogo Urala. Vtoraia polovina XVIII–pervaia polovina XIX v.* Moscow: Nauka, 1984.

Tatishchev, V. N. "Kratkie ekonomicheskie do derevni sleduiushchie zapiski sostavlennye Vasiliem Nikitichem Tatishchevym 1742 goda." Edited by N. N. Serebriakov. *Vremennik* 12, part 3 (1852): 12-32.

Tikhonov, Iu. A. *Pomeshchichie krest'iane v Rossii: Feodal'naia renta v XVII–nachale XVIII veka.* Moscow: Nauka, 1974.

Tomsinskii, S. G., editor. *Sotsial'nyi sostav rabochikh pervoi poloviny XVIII veka.* Leningrad: Akademiia nauk SSSR, 1934. [*Trudy Istoriko-arkheograficheskogo instituta,* vol. 11, *Krepostnaia manufaktura v Rossii,* part 4.]

Tooke, Thomas. *Thoughts and Details on the High and Low Prices of the Thirty Years from 1793 to 1822.* 2d ed. London: G. Murray, 1824.

———. *View of the Russian Empire during the Reign of Catherine the Second and to the Close of the 18th Century.* 2d ed. London: A. Strahan, 1800.

Troitskii, S. M. *Finansovaia politika russkogo absoliu-tizma v XVIII veke.* Moscow: Nauka, 1966.

———. *Rossiia v XVIII veke. Sbornik statei i publikatsii.* Moscow: Nauka, 1982.

———. *Russkii absoliutizm i dvorianstvo v XVIII v. Formirovanie biurokratii.* Moscow: Nauka, 1976.

———. "Zapiska senatora N. E. Murav'ëva o razvitii kommertsii i putei soobshcheniia v Rossii (60-e gody XVIII v.)." In *Istoricheskaia geografiia Rossii XII–nachalo XX v.* Edited by A. L. Narochnitskii et al. Moscow: Nauka, 1975. Pp. 234-47.

Tsvetkov, M. A. *Izmenenie lesistosti evropeiskoi Rossii s kontsa XVII stoletiia po 1914 god.* Moscow: AN SSSR, 1957.

Tugan-Baranovskii, M. I. *Russkaia fabrika v proshlom i nastoiashchem: istoriko-ekonomicheskoe issledovanie.* St. Petersburg: O. N. Popov, 1900.

Uchastkina, Zoia Vasil'evna. *Razvitie bumazhnogo proizvodstva v Rossii.* Moscow: Lesnaia promyshlen-nost', 1972.

Ukazy Petra Velikogo s 1714 po 1725 gg. St. Petersburg: Imp. Akademiia nauk, 1739.

Urlanis, B. Ts. *Voiny i narodonaselenie Evropy. Liudskie poteri vooruzhennykh sil evropeiskikh stran v voinakh XVII–XX vekov. Istoriko-staticheskoe issledovanie.* Moscow: Sotsekgiz, 1960.

Ustiugov, N. V. "Instruktsiia votchinnomu prikaz-chiku pervoi chetverti XVIII v." *Istoricheskii arkhiv* 4 (1949): 150-83.

Vartanov, G. L. "Moskovskoe i inogorodnoe kupe-chestvo vo vtoroi polovine XVIII v." *Uzhenye zapiski leningradskogo pedagogicheskogo instituta im. Gertsena* 278 (1965): 272-90.

Vdovina, L. N. "Zemel'nye peredely v krest'ianskoi obshchine v 20–50kh godakh XVIII veka (po materialam monastyrskikh votchin)." *Istoriia SSSR* 1973, no. 4: 140-54.

Vinskii, G. S. *Moe vremia. Zapiski E. S. Vinskogo.* St. Petersburg: Ogni, 1914.

Vodarskii, Ia. E. "Chislennost' naseleniia i koli-chestvo pomestno-votchinnykh zemel' v XVII v. (po pistsovym i perepisnym knigam)." *Ezhegodnik po agrarnoi istorii vostochnoi Evropy za1964 god.* Kishinev: Kartia Moldoveniaske, 1966. Pp. 217-30.

———. "Krest'iane i sel'skie bobyli v Rossii v kontse XVII v." *Ezhegodnik po agrarnoi istorii vostochnoi Evropy za 1968 god.* Leningrad: Nauka, 1972. Pp. 65-71.

———. *Naselenie Rossii v kontse XVII–nachale XVIII veka: chislennost', soslovno-klassovyi sostav, razmesh-chenie.* Moscow: Nauka, 1977.

Volkov, M. Ia. "Materialy pervoi revizii kak istochnik po istorii torgovli i promyshlennosti Rossii pervoi chetverti 18 v." *Problemy istochnikovedeniia* 11 (1963): 266-306.

———. "Tamozhennaia reforma 1753–1757 gg." *Istoricheskie zapiski* 71 (1962): 134-57.

Volkov, S. I. *Krest'iane dvortsovykh vladenii podmos-kov'ia v seredine XVIII v. (30–70-e gody.)* Moscow: AN SSSR, 1959.

Volodarskaia, Ch. G. "Naëmnyi trud na shelkovykh possessiiakh v 60-kh godakh XVIII v." In *Voprosy genezisa kapitalizma v Rossii.* Edited by V. V. Mavrodin. Leningrad: LGU, 1960. Pp. 120-34.

———. "Sotsial'nyi sostav rabotnykh liudei na stekolnykh possessiiakh v seredine XVIII v." *Nauchnye zapiski gos. pedagogicheskogo instituta im. Gertsena* 278 (1978): 177-205.

Voronov, N. V. "Dokumenty o kirpichnom proiz-vodstve XVII– XVIII vv." In *Materialy po istorii SSSR.* Edited by A. A. Novosel'skii, B. B. Kafengauz, and L. N. Pushkarev. 5 (l957): 5-114.

———. "O rynke rabochei sily v Rossii v XVIII veke (po materialam kirpichnoi promyshlennosti)." *Voprosy istorii* 1955, no. 3: 90-99.

Zaozerskaia, E. I. *Manufaktura pri Petre I.* Moscow-Leningrad: AN SSSR, 1947.

———. *Rabochaia sila i klassovaia bor'ba na tekstil'nykh manufakturakh v 20–60 gg. XVIII v.* Moscow: AN SSSR, 1960.

———. *Razvitie legkoi promyshlennosti v Moskve v pervoi chetverti XVIII v.* Moscow: AN SSSR, 1953.

Zhuravskii, D. I. *Statisticheskoe obozrenie raskhodov na voennye potrebnosti s 1711 po 1825 god.* St. Petersburg, 1859.

Zhurnal Ministerstva gosudarstvennykh imushchestv. Au-gust, 1854.

Zutis, Ianis Ia. *Politika tsarizma v Pribaltike v pervoi polovine XVIII v.* Moscow: Sotsekgiz, 1937.

INDEX

The purpose of this index is to make the volume of greater utility to readers interested in specific topics, particularly in light of the general dearth of publications on eighteenth-century Russia. Therefore all names, places, commodities, and economic concepts mentioned in the text have been indexed. The tables have also been indexed by title for the benefit of those desiring access to quantitative material. The place names (e.g., Moscow, Kiev) may signify a city, province, guberniia, bishopric, or region.